1 MONTH OF
FREE
READING

at

www.ForgottenBooks.com

By purchasing this book you are eligible for one month membership to ForgottenBooks.com, giving you unlimited access to our entire collection of over 1,000,000 titles via our web site and mobile apps.

To claim your free month visit: www.forgottenbooks.com/free85815

ISBN 978-0-484-58424-1
PIBN 10085815

Forgotten Books is a registered trademark of FB &c Ltd.
Copyright © 2018 FB &c Ltd.
FB &c Ltd, Dalton House, 60 Windsor Avenue, London, SW19 2RR.
Company number 08720141. Registered in England and Wales.

For support please visit www.forgottenbooks.com

BURT FRANKLIN: RESEARCH AND SOURCE WORKS SERIES # 133

(AMERICAN CLASSICS IN HISTORY AND SOCIAL SCIENCE #16)

MISCELLANEOUS

WORKS

VOL 2

MISCELLANEOUS

WORKS

OF

HENRY C. CAREY, LL. D.,

harles

AUTHOR OF "PRINCIPLES OF SOCIAL SCIENCE," ETC. ETC.

VOL 2

BURT FRANKLIN: RESEARCH AND SOURCE WORKS SERIES # 133

(AMERICAN CLASSICS IN HISTORY AND SOCIAL SCIENCE #16)

BURT FRANKLIN
NEW YORK

Published By
BURT FRANKLIN
235 East 44th St.
New York, N.Y. 10017

HC
105
C 2.

ORIGINALLY PUBLISHED
PHILADELPHIA: 1883

Printed in U.S.A.

THE CURRENCY QUESTION.

Dear Sir:—

Side by side with the question of protection, and equal with it in its importance, stands that of the Currency, to which I propose now to ask your attention.

Had it been possible, on the 4th of March, 1861, to take a bird's-eye view of the whole Union, the phenomena presenting themselves for examination would have been as follows :—

Millions of men and women would have been seen who were wholly or partially unemployed, because of inability to find persons able and willing to pay for service.

Hundreds of thousands of workmen, farmers, and shopkeepers would have been seen holding articles of various kinds for which no purchasers could be found.

Tens of thousands of country traders would have been seen poring over their books seeking, but vainly seeking, to discover in what direction they might look for obtaining the means with which to discharge their city debts.

Thousands of city traders would have been seen endeavoring to discover how they might obtain the means with which to pay their notes.

Thousands of mills, factories, furnaces, and workshops large and small, would have been seen standing idle while surrounded by persons who desired to be employed ; and

Tens of thousands of bank, factory, and railroad proprietors would have been seen despairing of obtaining dividends by means of which they might be enabled to go to market.

High above all these would have been seen a National Treasury wholly empty, and to all appearance little likely ever again to be filled.

Why was all this? The laborer needing food, and the farmer clothing, why did they not exchange? Because of the absence of power on the part of the former to give to the latter anything with which he could purchase either hats or coats.

The village shopkeeper desired to pay his city debts. Why did he not? because the neighboring mill was standing idle while men and women, indebted to him, were wholly unemployed.

The city trader could not meet his notes, because his village correspondents could not comply with their engagements. The doctor could not collect his bills. The landlord could not collect his rents; and all, from laborer to landlord, found themselves compelled to refrain from the purchase of those commodities to whose consumption the National Treasury had been used to look for the supplies upon which it thus far had depended.

With all, the difficulty resulted from the one great fact already indicated in regard to the laborer. If *he* could have found any one willing to give him something that the farmer would accept from him in exchange for food—that the farmer could then pass to his neighbor shopkeeper in exchange for cloth—that that neighbor could then pass to the city trader in satisfaction of his debt—and that this latter could then pass to the bank, to his counsel, his physician, or his landlord—the *societary circulation* would at once have been re-established and the public health restored.

That one thing, however, was scarcely anywhere to be found. Its generic name was *money*, but the various species were known as gold, silver, copper, and circulating notes. Some few persons possessed them in larger or smaller quantities; but, the total amount being very small when compared with that which was required, their owners would not part with the use of them except on terms so onerous as to be ruinous to the borrowers. As a consequence of this, the city trader paid ten, twelve, and fifteen per cent. per annum for the use of what he needed, charging twice that, to the village shopkeeper, in the prices of his goods. The latter, of course, found it necessary to do the same by his neighbors, charging nearly cent. per cent.; and thus was the whole burthen resulting from deficiency in the supply of a medium of exchange thrown upon the class which least could bear it, the working people of the country—farmers, mechanics, and laborers. As a consequence of this they shrunk in their proportions as the societary circulation became more and more impeded, while with those who held in their hands the regulation of the money supply the effect exhibited itself in the erection of those great palaces which now stand almost side by side with tenement houses whose occupants, men, women, and children, count by hundreds. The rich thus grew richer as the poor grew poorer.

Why was all this? Why did they not use the gold of which California had already sent us so many hundreds of millions? Because we had most carefully followed in the train of British free trade teachers who had assured our people that the safe, true, and certain road towards wealth and power was to be found in the direction of sending wheat, flour, corn, pork, and wool to England in their rudest form, and then buying them back again, at quadruple prices, paying the difference in the products of Californian mines! Because we had in this manner, for a long period of years, been selling whole skins for sixpence and buying back tails for a shilling! Because we had thus compelled our people to remain idle while consuming food and clothing, the gold meanwhile being sent to purchase other food and clothing for the workmen of London and Paris, Lyons, Manchester, and Birmingham!

Why, however, when circulating notes could so easily be made, did not the banks supply them, when all around them would so gladly have allowed interest for their use? Because those notes were redeemable in a commodity of which, although California gave us much, we could no longer retain even the slightest portion, the quantity required abroad for payment of heavy interest, and for the purchase of foreign food in the forms of cloth and iron, having now become fully equal to the annual supply, and being at times even in excess of it. That demand, too, was liable at any moment to be increased by the sale in our markets of certificates of debt then held abroad to the extent of hundreds of millions, the proceeds being claimed in gold, and thus causing ruin to the banks. To be out of debt is to be out of danger, but to be in debt abroad to the extent of hundreds of millions is to be always in danger of both public and private bankruptcy. *The control of our whole domestic commerce was therefore entirely in the hands of foreigners who were from hour to hour becoming richer by means of compelling us to remain so dependent upon them that they could always fix the prices at which they would buy the skins, and those at which they would be willing to sell the tails.* As a necessary consequence of this, the nation was not only paralyzed, but in danger of almost immediate death.

Such having been the state of things on the day of Mr. Lincoln's inauguration, let us now look at the remedy that was then required. Let us, for a moment, suppose the existence of an individual with wealth so great that all who knew him might have entire confidence in the performance of what he promised. Let us then suppose that he should have said to the laborers of the country, "Go into the mills, and I will see that your wages are paid;" to the millers, "Employ these people, and I will see that your cloth is sold;" to the farmers, "Give your food to the laborer and your wool to the millers, and I will see that your bills are at once discharged;" to the shopkeepers, "Give your coffee and your sugar to the farmer, and I will see that payment shall forthwith be made;" to the city traders, "Fill the orders of the village shopkeeper and send your bills to me for payment;" to the landlords, "Lease your houses and look to me for the rents;" to all, "I have opened a *clearing house* for the whole country, and have done so with a view to enable every man to find on the instant a cash demand for his labor and its products, and my whole fortune has been pledged for the performance of my engagements;" and then let us examine into the effects. At once the societary circulation would have been restored. Labor would have come into demand, thus doubling at once the productive power of the country. Food would have been demanded, and the farmer would have been enabled to improve his machinery of cultivation. Cloth would have been sold, and the spinner would have added to the number of his spindles. Coal and iron would have found increased demand, and mines and furnaces would have grown in numbers and in size. Houses becoming more productive, new ones would have been built. The *paralysis* would have passed away, life, activity, and energy having taken its place, all these wonderful effects having resulted from the simple pledge of the one sufficient man that he would see the contracts carried out. He had pledged his credit and nothing more.

What is here supposed to have been done is almost precisely what *has* been done by Mr. Lincoln and his Administration, the only difference being, that while in the one case the farmers and laborers had been required to report themselves to the single individual or his agents, the Government has, by the actual purchase of labor and its products, and the grant of its pledges in a variety of shapes and forms, enabled each and every man in the country to arrange his business in the manner that to himself has seemed most advantageous. To the laborer it has said, We need your services, and in return will give you that which will enable your family to purchase food and clothing. To the farmer it has said, We need food, and will give you that by means of which you can pay the shopkeeper. To the manufacturer it has said, We need cloth, and will give you that which will enable you to settle with the workman and the farmer. To the naval constructor it has said, We need your ships, and will give you that which will enable you to purchase timber, iron, and engines. In this manner it is that domestic commerce has been stimulated into life, the result exhibiting itself in the facts, that while we have in the last three years increased to an extent never known before the number of our houses and ships, our mills, mines, and furnaces, our supplies of food, cloth, and iron; and while we have diversified our industry to an extent that is absolutely marvellous; we have been enabled to lend, or pay, to the Government thousands of millions of dollars, where before, under the system which made us wholly dependent on the mercy of the "most wealthy capitalists" of England, we found it difficult to furnish even tens of millions. The whole history of the world presents no case of a financial success so perfect.

In the physical body health is always the accompaniment of rapid circulation, disease that of a languid one. Now, for the first time since the settlement of these colonies, have we had experience of the first. Every man who has desired to work, has found a purchaser for his labor. Every man who has had labor's products to sell, has found a ready market. Every man who has had a house to rent, has found a tenant. And why? Because the Government had done for the whole nation what Companies do for localities when they give them railroads in place of wagon roads. It had so facilitated exchange between consumers and producers, that both parties had been enabled to pay on the instant for all they had had need to purchase.

Important, however, as is all this, it is but a part of the great work that has been accomplished. With every stage of progress there has been a diminution in the general rate of interest, with constant tendency towards equality in the rate paid by the farmers of the East and the West, by the owner of the little workshop and by him who owns the gigantic mill. For the first time in our history the real workingmen—the laborer, the mechanic, and the little village shopkeeper—have been enabled to command the use of the machinery of circulation at a moderate rate of interest. For the first time have nearly all been enabled to make their purchases cash in hand, and to select from among all the dealers those who would supply them cheapest. For the first time has this class known anything approaching to real independence; and therefore has it been that, notwithstanding the demands of the war, capital has so rapidly accumulated. The gain to the working people of the Union thus effected, has been more than the whole money cost of the war, and therefore has it been that all have been able to pay taxes, while so many have been enabled to purchase the securities offered by the Government.

Further than all this, we have for the first time acquired something approaching to a *national independence*. In all time past, the price of money having been wholly dependent on the price in England, the most important intelligence from beyond the Atlantic was that which was to be found in the price of British securities on the Exchange of London. With each arrival, therefore, we were, to our great enlightenment, and that too by means of flaming capitals, informed that Consols had risen or had fallen, our railroad shares then going up or down because the Bank of England had seen fit to purchase a few Exchequer bills, or had found it necessary to part with some of those it previously had held. In all this there has been a change so complete that the price of British Consols has ceased entirely to enter into American calculations. The stride, in this respect alone, that has been made in the direction of independence, is worth to the country more than the whole money cost of the great war in which we are now engaged.

The time had come to make it, the course of Britain having recently been in a direction that limits the circulation and insures a rise in the rate of interest. The Bank of England is limited to £14,000,000 as the amount of notes that may be issued in excess of the gold actually in its vaults. All other banks being limited to the amount that existed on a certain day in 1844, and some of them having since that time gone out of existence, the result exhibits itself in the fact that the total machinery of circulation supplied by the banks is less now than it was twenty years since. As a consequence of this, and in despite of the extraordinary influx of gold from California and Australia, the rate of interest charged for the use of such machinery has been for some years past higher than that paid in any of our Atlantic cities, the fluctuations in regard to paper of the highest character having been between six and ten per cent. By the last accounts it had fallen to $5\frac{1}{2}$, and that is now, as English journalists advise us, as much to be regarded as the normal price of money as was 4 per cent. before the discovery of California mines. The danger of dependence upon the British money market, always great, has now been much increased; and it must become greater with every year, so long as British banking operations shall continue to be governed by that wonderfully absurd system for which the British people stand to-day indebted to the financial ignorance of Sir Robert Peel.

Great and obvious as have been the benefits derived by the country from the system inaugurated under the administration of Mr. Lincoln, they are, as we are assured, counterbalanced by their tendency to produce inflation, and thus to increase the price of gold. How little truth there is in this, I propose to show in another letter, and meanwhile remain, my dear sir,

Very truly and respectfully yours,

HENRY C. CAREY.

Hon. SCHUYLER COLFAX.

PHILADELPHIA, Feb. 13, 1865.

THE CURRENCY QUESTION.

LETTER SECOND.

DEAR SIR:—

That the currency has been, and is, inflated, is beyond a question. Whence, however, has come the inflation? What has caused the existence of disease? Such are the questions to which an answer must be obtained before we undertake to prescribe the remedy to be adopted. Failing to do this, we shall certainly kill the patient.

By all the currency doctors, both here and abroad, the cause of financial crises is found in the circulation; and hence it has been that both here and elsewhere the world has been furnished with so many laws in regard to it, none of which would ever have existed had the matter been properly understood. To that question it was that Sir Robert Peel addressed himself when he framed a law that has already twice broken down, and that must continue to break down on each successive recurrence of the state of things it was intended to prevent. The statute-books of nearly all of our States present to view similar laws, all of which have proved as utterly worthless, and some of them almost as injurious, as that British one above referred to.

The circulation needs no regulation, and for the simple reason that the people regulate it for themselves. For proof of this, look, I pray you, to the fact that the Treasury has been for several years past engaged in trying to obtain for small notes a circulation amounting to fifty millions, and yet has not, at this hour, one of even the half of that amount. Why has it not? Because the people need no more than twenty or twenty-five millions. If they did need more, they would gladly take it. When Congress had before it a bill authorizing the emission of that description of currency, it would have been deemed rank heresy to say that no limitation was needed, yet has experience proved that such was certainly the case. Had they omitted all restriction on the "greenbacks," they might perhaps have found, as in the case of the smaller notes, that the people understood better what they needed than did their legislators. That they would have done so, I regard as beyond a question.

It is constantly assumed that it is the banks that determine how many notes shall be in use, and yet the experience of each and every individual in the community proves that exactly the reverse of this is true. That you, my dear sir, may satisfy yourself of this, I pray you to look for a moment to your own constant action in regard to the question now before us. On a given day you receive a quantity of bank-notes, which are *then* in circulation. What do you then do with them? You place them in a bank, and thus put them *out of circulation*. On the following day you perhaps take them from the bank and pay them out, thus putting them *again in circulation*. What control did the bank exercise over these several operations? None whatsoever. It is you, your friends, neighbors, and fellow-citizens generally, that regulate the circulation, and it is just as wise to pass laws limiting its amount as it would be to pass other laws determining the quantity of coal, iron, sugar, or coffee to be provided for their use.

To this it is due that in communities that are really independent the circulation is so very nearly a constant quantity. That of the Bank of England, in the eventful period from 1832 to 1841, averaged £18,000,000, and although it embraced the time of one of the greatest excitements and one of the most fearful reverses ever known in that country, the circulation never went beyond that average to the extent of five per cent., nor fell below it to that of eight per cent. The differences exhibited are less even than might be reasonably looked for by any one familiar with the fact that during several of the years every workingman had been fully employed, while in several others a large portion of the manufacturing population was either idle or but half employed.

Take now the following figures representing, in millions, the circulation of the New York banks, and see how uniform was its amount until the withdrawal in 1857, by the banks, of many millions of *loans that had been based upon deposits*, had almost annihilated the commerce of the country, and thus deprived our people of the power to make use of notes.

1855 . . . 41	1859 . . . 36	1862 . . . 42
1856 . . . 41	1860 . . . 38	1863 . . . 42
1057 . . . 41	1861 . . . 36	1864 . . . 40
1858 . . . 35		

In every case, as here presented, reduction had been a *consequence* of stoppage of the societary circulation, and *not a cause of it.*

We are told, however, of the depreciation of Continental money, French *assignats*, and Confederate notes, and are threatened that we shall here experience the same result; but those who present such views can scarcely properly appreciate the difference between the conditions under which such paper was emitted and those in which we stand. The first was issued by a Confederation that was little better than a rope of sand, and that had no certain power to provide for the ultimate payment of either principal or interest of any debt it might contract. The second were at first receivable only in payment for confiscated property, and were of no value for any other purpose. As the country became more and more "a scene of rude commotion," and as employment for the people passed away, their quantity 'was more and more increased, and they then were made a legal tender, but there existed then no organized government capable of giving protection to either property or life—none capable of making secure provision for any ultimate assumption of payment by the State. The last has been issued by an authority the permanent maintenance of which has been so much doubted that few have held its securities longer than was required for enabling them to pass them off to some one else. They have been received by a community that has been cut off from the outer world, and whose single source of wealth has wholly disappeared. They are now used by one whose numbers are constantly diminishing, and over a surface that is becoming daily more and more circumscribed. When the notes were few in number the Southern people were still rich, and, with the exception of Maryland, the notes circulated in every State south of Mason and Dixon's Line, the Ohio and the Missouri. Now, when they so much abound, the rich have become poor, the poor have become poorer, rich and poor to a great extent have passed out of existence, and the theatre of circulation has become limited to portions of half a dozen

States. No one desires to convert Confederate paper into a permanent security, it being clearly obvious that of security for future payment there can be none. The notes will still at some price help to pay for a negro or a horse, but the bonds will not do so at any price whatsoever.

Contrast here, my dear sir, the circumstances above described with those under which our " greenbacks" have been issued. They have gone out in payment for property purchased of, or services rendered by, persons who have freely sold the one or rendered the other. The authority by which they have been issued is one quite as capable of binding posterity as was the Government of Washington and Adams. They are used by a people whose numbers are constantly growing, and whose productive powers are steadily increasing in the ratio which they bear to population. The man who receives them finds himself surrounded by other men who gladly give him houses and lands at prices little greater than those he would have paid ten years since, and before the great free trade crisis of 1857. In all this the Government co-operates by authorizing him to deposit with its officers, for periods long or short, any amount for which he may not have present use, receiving in return certificates by means of which he can withdraw the amount on giving certain notice; or at his pleasure receive bonds payable in three, four, ten, twenty, or forty years, receiving interest in gold or paper, according to the terms agreed upon; and here we have a security against depreciation the like of which the world had never seen before. It is a *safety valve* such as could not have been provided by any of the authorities to which the world has been indebted for those chapters of financial history which are connected with the Continental paper, the Assignat, or the Confederate notes.

Having thus shown what had been the circumstances under which the "greenbacks" have been offered for acceptance by the world, I propose now to show what is the extent to which they have been issued, and what have been the gold phenomena by which that issue has been attended.

The first batch of notes amounted to $60,000,000, and were issued under laws passed in July and August, 1861. Nearly the whole of these have since been withdrawn and cancelled.

The second emission was under a law of February, and the third under one of July, 1862, giving us at the close of that year a total

Government circulation of little less than $300,000,000. The price of gold as yet had changed but slightly. In June, 1862, it still stood at 104. In July and August it fluctuated between 109 and 119. In October it rose to 124, and for the rest of the year it varied between 130 and 137. Compared with what we since have seen, the advance thus far seems as very trifling; and yet the amount of legal tender notes then existing bore a very much *larger proportion* to the number of persons to whom a currency was to be supplied—to the business that was to be transacted—and to the surface that was to be covered than is at this moment borne by the notes now in circulation. Such being the case, as I propose to show it is, we must certainly look elsewhere for the cause of the present price of gold.

In February, 1863, that price rose to 171. Why was this? Not certainly because of any increase in the "greenback" circulation, the further emission of these having been accompanied by the withdrawal of the original $60,000,000 of treasury notes of which but $3,351,000 remained out in the following June. The amount of circulation must, therefore, have been but little more at this time, when gold was at 171, than it had been in the previous autumn when its price ranged between 115 and 124.

In the following month a further issue to the extent of $150,000,000 was authorized, and, according to the generally received theory, gold should now have risen. Did it so? On the contrary it fell, and in July, although the greenbacks then outstanding amounted to $400,000,000, was as low as 124. As it seems to me, we cannot in this direction find the cause of changes such as these.

In September the greenbacks issued had risen to $415,000,000, and the price of gold to 143. The two, however, could have had no necessary connection with each other, gold being now much *lower* than it had been in the previous February, while the circulation was *higher* by little less than $100,000,000.

By the act of March, 1863, the Secretary had been empowered to issue interest-bearing notes, legal tender for their face, to the extent of $400,000,000. Of this power no use appears to have been made prior to the first of October of that year. In that and the following month there were issued of greenbacks $15,000,000, and of interest-bearing legal tenders $35,000,000; and it is fair to assume a further issue for December of $30,000,000, bringing up the total amount to nearly $500,000,000. What was the effect of this upon gold? Did it carry it up to, or beyond, the price at which it had stood in the previous February? On the contrary, although in the meantime $200,000,000 had been added to the legal tenders issued, it remained 20 per cent. lower, the price on the first of January being only 151. How the opponents of what is called "the paper money system" can reconcile these facts, I do not clearly see.

Since then the price has been nearly as follows :—

January . . . 157	May 192	September . . 220
February . . . 159	June 240	October . . . 220
March 165	July 276	November . . . 230
April 178	August 257	December . . . 220

Throughout the whole of these latter months there had been the most violent fluctuations, but these figures will, I think, suffice to give you, my dear sir, a general idea of the whole movement.

What, in the meantime, had been the course of the Treasury in regard to the issue of legal tender notes? For a reply to this question I must refer you to the following figures exhibiting the state of that portion of the public debt on the first of November last :—

I. Of greenbacks the amount then outstanding was .	$433,000,000
II. Of one year notes	43,000,000
III. Of two year notes	16,000,000
IV. Of two year coupon notes	61,000,000
V. Of three year notes	102,000,000
	$655,000,000

The amount is here shown to have been greater by about one hundred and fifty millions than it had been a year before, but of this how much was there that really remained in circulation? At the present moment, as I am assured, two-thirds of Nos. II., III., and IV. have been absorbed by individuals and institutions, and have ceased to constitute any portion of the circulation. Such, likewise, is the case with a portion of No. V. Admitting, now, the quantity since issued of this last to be equal to the amount of the others so absorbed in the last three months, we obtain, as a deduction from the above *apparent* circulation, the large sum of $80,000,000, and thus reduce the real amount to $575,000,000.

Is this, however, all the deduction needed to be made? By no means! Throughout this period banks have been parting with their gold, and substituting for it United States notes, both demand and interest-bearing, and individuals, to a vast extent, have followed their example. The farmer pays for what he needs in local notes, but he puts aside his "greenbacks." The miner and the mechanic—the laborer and the village shopkeeper—the soldier and the sailor—the immigrant who is seeking to invest his little capital, and the sempstress who is trying to accumulate the means with which to purchase a sewing-machine—all of these have become hoarders of "greenbacks," which have thus been withdrawn from circulation, and have, for the time being, no more influence upon either the gold or produce markets than they would have had they been altogether blotted out of existence. Adding now together all these quantities, we shall, as I think, readily obtain the sum of $75,000,000, and thus reduce the actual Treasury circulation to the precise point at which it stood at the close of 1863, when the price of gold was 151.

There is, however, another portion of the circulation which now demands attention. At the date of which I have spoken there were in existence 631 national banks, with an authorized capital of $428,000,000, to which there had been *issued* notes amounting to $72,000,000. To what extent those notes had then been *circulated* we cannot tell, but we know, from the Report of the Commissioner of the Currency, that on the first Monday of the previous October their actual circulation amounted to only $45,260,000, to meet which, and to provide for payment of their depositors, they held, in "specie and other lawful money," $44,801,000. Of the first, the quantity held is likely to have been very small indeed, but admitting it to have been even as much as $10,000,000, and that another sum of equal amount had been in the form of interest-bearing legal tenders, the quantity of "greenbacks" held by them must have been $25,000,000. This would reduce their *apparent* addition to the quantity of "paper money" to but $20,000,000; but when we take into view the fact that in the year embraced in the Report 168 State banks had become national institutions, and that, to the extent of their issues, the new notes had been mere substitutes for those previously in existence, we see that the *real* addition thus made to the circulation had been a quantity too small to be worthy of any serious attention.

At the date of the battle of Gettysburg, say July 3, 1863, the legal tender circulation was, as has been shown, $400,000,000, with gold at 124. With a present circulation of only $500,000,000, gold is above 200 ; and yet, as I propose now to show, its amount is *very far less*, in proportion to the space over which it is circulated, to the population to be supplied, and to the work to be done, than it was at the date to which I have referred.

At that time we had secure possession of scarcely any portion of the country south of Mason and Dixon's Line, the Ohio and the Missouri. We did, it is true, still hold Washington, but a rebel army was then in Maryland. South of that, in the Atlantic States, we held Fortress Monroe, Norfolk, Newbern, Hilton Head and its immediate neighborhood. Kentucky was then exceedingly disturbed, while Tennessee was mainly occupied by rebel armies. Missouri was, in almost its whole extent, a "debateable land," while rebel forces occupied nearly the whole of Arkansas and by far the larger portion of Louisiana. On the Mississippi we held Memphis at the north and New Orleans at the South. Throughout the border and Southern States, therefore, there was little work being done, and little use for circulation of any description whatsoever; and of what was used nearly the whole consisted of Confederate notes.

To-day, the Federal circulation is needed throughout Maryland, the larger portion of old Virginia, Kentucky, Tennessee, Missouri, Arkansas, much of Mississippi and Louisiana, parts of Georgia, Alabama, and North Carolina, and throughout the whole region bordering on the Mississippi. It is needed, too, by every emigrant to Minnesota, Nebraska, Colorado, and Nevada; and thus, while we have, in the last eighteen months, added largely to the population to be supplied, we have almost doubled the territory within which that population may be found.

Simultaneously with all this we have added little less than one-half to the productive powers of our people, and to the transactions for facilitating which a general medium of circulation is required.

Having studied these things you will, my dear sir, as I think, be disposed to agree with me in the conclusions at which I have arrived, as follows :—

That the circulation bears now a much smaller proportion to the need for it than it did at the time when gold stood at 124.

That to this is to be attributed that the " greenback" is frequently so scarce as to interfere, and that seriously, with the operations of the Government; and

That, if we desire to find the cause of the present high price of gold, it is in quite another direction we must look for it.

What that direction is I propose to show in another letter, and meanwhile remain,

Yours, very truly,

HENRY C. CAREY.

Hon. SCHUYLER COLFAX.

PHILADELPHIA, February 13, 1865.

THE CURRENCY QUESTION.

DEAR SIR :—

The power of a bank to make loans is derived from the use of its capital; from its power to furnish circulation; and from its further power to apply to the purchase of securities the moneys standing to the credit of those with whom it deals, and known by the name of *deposits*.

That it is not to the use of the first we are indebted for the inflation now complained of is very certain. That variations in the second have been only those consequent upon changes otherwise produced has been already shown. There remains, then, only the third, and to that it is that I now propose to call your attention, first, however, asking you to accompany me for a moment in an examination of the effect which necessarily results from the loan by banks of moneys for which they themselves are indebted to others, and which they may, at any moment, be called upon to refund.

Let us suppose you, yourself, to have received on any given day notes, or specie, amounting to ten, fifteen, twenty, or fifty thousand dollars, and that while waiting to re-invest them you have placed them in your safe. Going now on change, you find that sum to be there represented by *yourself alone*.

Let us next suppose that instead of so placing them you had had them put to your credit in a neighboring bank, and that the bank had forthwith lent them to a dealer in money, or in stocks. Going on change under these circumstances you find your money *twice represented;* first by yourself who have it, as you suppose, in the bank; and next, by the man who had borrowed it and had had it put to *his* credit precisely as it had previously been placed to *yours.* Here is a very simple operation by means of which the amount of deposits has been doubled *by the action of the bank itself;* and here it is that we find the cause of all the inflation of which we so often have had reason to complain, and to which, as I propose to show, we chiefly owe the numerous and extraordinary changes in the price of gold.

By the last report of the Superintendent of the New York banks the amount for which they then stood indebted to individuals, called depositors, was nearly $250,000,000. The owners of this vast sum might be seen passing up and down Wall Street, as fully ready to purchase stocks or notes as they could have been had it been in their private safes. Side by side with them, however, might be seen other individuals to whom *that same amount* had been lent, and who were equally ready to bid for any securities that might be offered. The $250,000,000 of *capital* had thus become $500,000,000 of *currency*, so to remain until the owners might claim to be repaid. The bank then making the same demand upon its debtors the $500,000,000 of currency would forthwith shrink into its original dimensions, and become once again but $250,000,000.

No such general demand would, of course, ever be made, and that none such has been needed for producing the crises of the past, or the gold excitements of the present, will be seen on an examination of the following figures, presenting, in millions, the movements of the New York banks before and after the great crisis of 1857 :—

	June '56.	Sept. '56.	June '57.	Sept. '57.	Dec. '57.
Capital . . .	92	96	104	107	107
Circulation . .	31	34	32	27	24

Leaving the circulation now wholly unprovided for, we will take the amount of the so-called deposits, and set against these latter the whole amount of specie with a view to ascertain what had been the amount of currency created by *the ballooning system* :—

	June '56.	Sept. '56.	June '57.	Sept. '57.	Dec. '57.
Deposits . .	103	104	109	85	83
Specie . . .	14	15	14	14	29
Lent out . .	89	89	95	71	54

In the first two of these periods 89 millions of real capital had become 178 of currency. In the third *that* currency had risen to 190. In the last it had, by the simple process of calling in loans, been carried down to 108.

The facts here exhibited in regard to the circulation are—

First, that up to the moment just preceding the explosion there had not only been no increase, but an actual reduction in its amount; second, that that reduction had been *consequent* upon a closing of workshops and suspension of business otherwise produced; and third, that, notwithstanding the almost entire suspension of business, the apparent reduction was but $8,000,000. That the real one must have been very far less than this will be obvious to all who know how large is the amount of notes of other banks remaining unexchanged, and for the time being out of circulation, at a time of financial ease, compared with that which is so retained in a period of crisis as severe as that now under examination.

Those exhibited in regard to the process of *duplication* to which your attention has been called, are as follows :—

First. The very small increase that had been required for producing the largest excitement throughout the country at large. The total amount from June, 1856, to June, 1857, was, as here is shown, but six millions; and yet there had been thus produced an inflation of the value of property throughout the country to the extent of many hundreds of millions :

Second. The very small reduction required for precipitating a whole community into a state of absolute and entire ruin, such as existed at the date of the last returns here given. The whole reduction had been but forty-one millions, and yet the changes in the value of property thereby produced counted certainly by thousands of millions.

What caused the rise? The use *by* banks of the property of others. What caused the fall? The demand *of* the banks for payment by their debtors. Who suffered? Every man who was in debt. Who profited? Every one who had the command of money. The rich were thus made richer and the poor made poorer by means of an inflation caused by the action of those very bank managers who, in all times past, had largely profited of such changes.

With all this, as has been shown, the circulation had nothing whatsoever to do, nor could it have, for the reason that *that* portion of the currency is governed by the people themselves, and not in any manner controlled by bank directors. Nevertheless, all our laws are framed as if the circulation were really the portion which needed regulation.

Following out the view thus presented I give you now, in

the following figures, the movement of the same institutions in the past four years:—

	June '61.	June '62.	Dec. '62.	June '63.	Sept. '63.	Mar. '64.	June '64.	Sept '64.
Capital	110	109	109	108	109	109	108	107
Circulation	26	39	39	32	33	31	32	33

In the first of these periods the circulation was small because our people were almost wholly unemployed. This was a *consequence* of error elsewhere, and not itself a cause of error.

Deposits and bank balances	139	206	258	272	288	354	298	297
Specie and bank balances	60	55	65	63	53	46	43	40
Lent out	79	151	193	209	235	308	255	257

The duplication of these vast sums, consequent upon the very simple process of placing money to the credit of A, as a depositor of his own property, and to that of B as a borrower of the same money, gives the following very remarkable figures:—

	158	302	386	418	470	616	510	514
Price of gold at same dates	par	103 to 109	131 to 133	147	128 to 142	161 to 165	195 to 245	255 to 191

The seventh column gives the precise period of the agitation caused by the passage of *the gold bill;* and from that to the eighth we have in the price of gold the effect of the extreme depression of the public mind of July and August last. It is by no means to be assumed that the gold variations have been altogether caused by the inflation above exhibited; but, that they have to nearly their whole extent been so, the figures above most clearly prove. Were bank loans reduced to the point at which they stood three years since, gold would be now as cheap as it was then.

The *addition* to the currency that had thus been made by the banks of the single State of New York, in comparing March, '64, with June, '61, appears to have been precisely $229,000,000. In all such movements the rest of the country, although at a long distance, follows suit to New York city. Three years since, when gold was still at par, the debts, called deposits, of the Pennsylvania banks, stood at $25,000,000. A year since, with gold at 165, they had already doubled; and since that time the movement in the direction of expansion has been at a greatly accelerated pace. In the last twelve months the deposit line of the Philadelphia banks alone has increased $14,500,000, most of their gold meanwhile having been converted into interest-bearing legal tender notes. As a consequence of all this, the interest-bearing securities held by them are little less than quadruple the amount of their capital. The inflation of this city alone is greater than was that of New York city prior to the great crisis of 1857.

The *addition* thus made to the currency of Pennsylvania can scarcely be estimated at less than $40,000,000. Allowing now for all the rest of the loyal States only twice that sum, we obtain $120,000,000, which, added to that of New York, gives us a total of $349,000,000.

Of what does this addition consist? Of precisely the same material that is used for inflating all other balloons—gas, *and nothing else*. The slightest pinhole causes it to disappear, and therefore is it that we meet with changes in the dimensions of the machine violent as are those here exhibited in figures representing, in millions, the loans, throughout the past year, of New York city banks :—

January	.	.	174 to 162	July . . .		198 to 185
February	.	.	163 to 174	August . .		185 to 188
March	.	.	182 to 199	September . .		189 to 185
April .	.	.	203 to 194	October . .		185 to 186
May	.	.	198 to 195	November . .		187 to 192
June	.	.	196 to 197	December . .		196 to 204

At one moment, as we see, gas is injected, and prices of gold, stocks, and commodities generally throughout the country, rise— and then the initiated sell. At another, it is compelled to escape, prices then falling, to the great advantage of those who had so lately sold. Such is the movement that is allowed to remain unregulated, the aid of Congress being meanwhile invoked in favor of establishing control over a circulation already regulated by means of that "higher law" which subjects to the popular will that portion of the financial movement.

Most widely different from all this is the action of that portion of the currency furnished by the Treasury, and known by the popular name of "greenbacks." In the one case, the addition represents nothing but *the will* of certain persons whose interests are to be promoted by expansion, to be followed, on the succeeding day probably, by contraction. In the other, it represents property delivered or service rendered to the Government. In the one, it is local, and the effect upon prices is great in proportion to the limitation of the space. In the other, it is paid out to the soldier, wherever found, whether in the hospitals of New England, the camps of the Centre, or the armies of the South and Southwest. It goes into the pocket of each individual, there to remain until he can find an opportunity to send it home, or in some other manner to use it for his private benefit. It goes into the pockets of farmers, miners, mechanics, laborers, sailors, traders large and small, enabling each and every one to buy for cash, and cheaply, what before he could obtain only at the single shop at which he could have credit. It helps to build ships on the Atlantic and the Pacific, on the lakes, and on the Mississippi; and it pays the men who sail or work those ships. It enters into every home of the Union, and into every old stocking by help of which the sewing-woman is preparing for the purchase of a machine, or the laborer for that of a house. The field of its operation is coextensive with the Union, and its power to affect injuriously the prices of gold, labor, or commodities generally, is in the *inverse ratio* of the extent of that field. Nevertheless, to prevent the possibility of injury from that source, the Treasury has created an acceptable investment, coextensive with the "greenbacks" in amount, by means of which every holder is enabled to convert into an interest-bearing security whatsoever surplus may be in his hands. Having thus provided a perfect *escape-valve*, neither the captain nor the crew need fear explosion.

The banker, on the contrary, desires that there may be no valve whatsoever but that which he himself controls. When it suits him, he injects the gas, and continues so to do until he has arrived as near as he dares to go to the point at which explosion may be looked for. Next he withdraws the gas with equal rapidity, and thus produces crises like that of 1857, the following brief account of which, taken from Gibbons's *Banks of New York*, may now, my dear sir, have some interest for you :—

"The most sagacious of our city bank officers saw no indications of an unusual storm in the commercial skies. When the loans reached the unprecedented height of one hundred and twenty-two millions of dollars, on the eighth of August, they pointed to the annual reduction of ten or twelve millions in the autumn months, as one of the regular ebbs to which the market is subject; but they had no foresight of extraordinary pressure, and no dreams of panic. Credit was extended, but 'the country never was so rich.'

"The banks began to contract their loans about the eighth of August. Securities immediately fell in price at the Stock Board. The failure of a heavy produce house was explained by the depression of that particular interest in the market. A report of dishonest jobbing, and of the misuse of funds in a leading railway company, caused partial excitement, without seriously disturbing confidence in mercantile credit.

"On the twenty-fourth of August, the suspension of the Ohio Life Insurance and Trust Company was announced. It struck on the public mind like a cannon shot. An intense excitement was manifested in all financial circles, in which bank officers participated with unusual sensitiveness and want of self-possession. Flying rumors were exaggerated at every corner. The holders of stock and of commercial paper hurried to the broker, and were eager to make what a week before they would have shunned as a ruinous sacrifice.

"Several stock and money dealers failed, and the daily meetings of the Board of Brokers were characterized by intense excitement.

"Every individual misfortune was announced on the news bulletins in large letters, and attracted a curious crowd, which was constantly fed from the passing throng.

"The Clearing House report for the twenty-ninth of August—the first after the suspension of the Ohio Life Insurance and Trust Company—showed a reduction of four millions of dollars in the bank loans during the previous week.

"The most substantial securities of the market fell rapidly in price at public sale.

"The safety of bank-notes in circulation was suspected or denied. The publishers of counterfeit detectors spread alarm among the shopkeepers and laborers, by selling handbills with lists of broken banks, which were cried about the streets by boys, at 'a penny a-piece.'

"One of the Associated Banks fell into default at the end of August, and a fraud of seventy thousand dollars by the paying teller roused suspicion of similar misconduct in other institutions.

"The regular discount of bills by the banks had mostly been suspended, and the street rates for money, even on unquestionable securities, rose to three, four, and five per cent. a month. On the ordinary securities of merchants, such as promissory notes and bills of exchange, money was not to be had at any rate. House after house of high commercial repute succumbed to the panic, and several heavy banking firms were added to the list of failures.

"The settlements of the Clearing House were watched with the expectation of new defaults; and their successful accomplishment, each day, was a subject of mutual congratulation among bank officers.

"The statement of the city banks for the week ending September 5th showed a further reduction in the loans of more than four millions of dollars.

"Commercial embarrassments and suspension became the chief staple of news in all the papers of town and country. The purchase and transportation of produce almost entirely ceased.

"From this period, there was nothing wanting to aggravate the common distress for money. The failure of the Bank of Pennsylvania, in Philadelphia, was followed by that of the other banks of that city, and by those of Baltimore, and of the Southern Atlantic States generally. Commercial business was everywhere suspended. The avalanche of discredit swept down merchants, bankers, moneyed corporations, and manufacturing companies, without distinction. Old houses, of accumulated capital, which had withstood the violence of all former panics, were prostrated in a day, and when they believed themselves to be perfectly safe against misfortune.

"The bank suspension of New York and New England, in the middle of October, was the climax of this commercial hurricane.

"Such is the outline of the most extraordinary, violent, and destructive financial panic ever experienced in this country. What caused it? To what source or sources can it be traced? Where lies the responsibility of it? What lessons does it teach? What preventives are indicated against the recurrence of similar disaster? These are questions which agitate the public mind, and which ought to be answered, if possible, for our instruction and future guidance."

Seeking an answer to these questions, the author furnishes a full statement of the movement, its result being that of showing, as he says, "beyond cavil, that *the banks*, not the depositors, *took the lead in forcing liquidation*. In the twenty days prior to the 26th of September," as he adds, "the deposits fell off but $341,746, while the resources of the banks were increased $6,694,179."

The men who had taken "the lead" in measures which had prepared for the explosion proved now to be those most active in "forcing liquidation," and thus enabling themselves to purchase, at low prices, stocks, bonds, and real estate which they had sold at high ones. Aided by the large fortunes thus acquired men of the same stamp are this day exercising a power thrice greater than was then exhibited, the tendency of all their measures being in the direction of making the poor poorer and the rich richer than ever before; those of the Treasury, meanwhile, looking in a precisely opposite direction, and tending to lower the rate of interest, while increasing the power over his own actions exercised by the laborer, the miner, the mechanic, and the farmer.

The "greenback" has fallen on the country as the dew falls, bringing with it good to all and doing injury to none. The gas-formed currency, on the contrary, is in the financial world what the water-spout is in the natural one. Whirled about by the wind, and wholly uncertain in its movements, none can predict of this latter when or where its effects will most be felt, and all around are therefore kept in a state of fever closely resembling that which distinguishes the financial action of the present hour. The deluge comes at·last, destroying both property and life, and making a desert where all before had been happiness and peace.

It is to restrictions upon the formation of the dew that we are now invited, leaving wholly unchecked the action of those who profit of the desolation caused by the water-spout. What are the results that seem to me likely to be obtained as a consequence of acceptance of the invitation, I propose to show in another letter, and meanwhile remain, my dear sir,

Yours, very truly,

HENRY C. CAREY.

Hon. SCHUYLER COLFAX.

PHILADELPHIA, Feb. 15, 1865.

THE CURRENCY QUESTION.

LETTER FOURTH.

DEAR SIR :—

The lugubrious predictions of the London *Times* have, thus far, not been verified. The war is now, to all appearance, coming rapidly to a close, and not only are we not yet ruined, but there prevails throughout the country a prosperity such as, until recently, had never before been known. To what causes may this properly be attributed? How has it been possible that a community should have furnished so many hundreds of thousands of men, and so many thousands of millions of the material of war, without becoming even poorer than before? Let us see.

The act of secession *by* the South was an act of emancipation *for* the North. Up to that date, the latter had been mere colonies, governed by those "wealthy British capitalists" whose mode of action is so well described in the Parliamentary Report, an extract from which has already more than once been given, but here repeated because of its powerful bearing on the question now before us :—

"The laboring classes generally, in the manufacturing districts of this country, and especially in the iron and coal districts, are very little aware of the extent to which they are often indebted for their being employed at all to the immense *losses* which their employers voluntarily incur, in bad times, in order *to destroy foreign competition, and to gain and keep possession of foreign markets.* Authentic instances are well known of employers having in such times carried on their works at a loss amounting in the aggregate to three or four hundred thousand pounds in the course of three or four years. If the efforts of those who encourage the combinations to restrict the amount of labor and to produce strikes were to be successful for any length of time, the great accumulations of capital could no longer be made *which enable a few of the most wealthy capitalists to overwhelm all foreign competition in times of great depression,* and thus to clear the way for the *whole trade* to step in when prices revive, and to carry on a great business before *foreign* capital can again accumulate to such an extent as to be able to establish a competition in prices with any chance of success. *The large capitals of this country are the great instruments of warfare against the competing capital of foreign countries*, and are *the most essential* instruments now remaining by which our manufacturing supremacy can be maintained; the other elements—cheap labor, abundance of raw material, means of communication, and skilled labor—being rapidly in process of being equalized."

Profiting of its liberty, the North at once determined on the adoption of measures of protection to the farmer in his efforts for bringing the consumer of his products to take his place in the immediate neighborhood of the place of production, and thus to relieve him from the oppressive tax of transportation imposed upon him by the system above so well described. The effect of this now exhibits itself in the facts—

That the development of our mineral resources has been great beyond all former example:

That diversification in the pursuits of our people now exhibits itself in the naturalization of many of the minor branches of industry in regard to which we had before been wholly dependent upon Europe:

That the demand for labor has been so great as to cause large increase of wages:

That the high price of labor has caused great increase of immigration:

That demand for the farmer's products has so largely increased as to have almost altogether freed him from dependence on the uncertain markets of Europe:

That the internal commerce has so largely grown as to have doubled in its money value the many hundreds of millions of railroad stock:

That the prosperity of existing railroads has caused large increase in the number and the extent of roads:

That here, for the first time in the history of the world, has been exhibited a community in which every man who had labor to sell could sell it if he would, while every man who had coal, iron, food, or cloth to sell could find at once a person able and willing to buy and pay for it:

That, for the first time, too, in the history of the world, there has been presented a community in which nearly all business was done for cash, and in which debt had scarcely an existence:

That, as a necessary consequence of this, there has been a large and general diminution of the rate of interest :

That farmers, laborers, miners, and traders have therefore become more independent of the capitalist, while the country at large has become more independent of the "wealthy capitalists" of Europe:

That, so great have been the economies of labor and its products, resulting from great rapidity of the societary circulation, that, while building more houses and mills, constructing more roads, erecting more machinery, and living better than ever before, our people have been enabled to contribute, in the form of taxes and loans, no less a sum than three thousand millions of dollars to the support of government.

These are wonderful results, and for them we have been largely, yet not wholly, indebted to the re-adoption of the protective system. That alone was capable of doing much, but we should have failed in the prosecution of the war had not the Treasury, by the establishment of a general medium of circulation, given us what has proved to be a great *clearing house*, to which were brought labor and all of labor's products to be exchanged. Increased rapidity of circulation was a necessary consequence of this, and to that increase the greatly improved health of the societary body has been wholly due.

Such having been the results of the two great measures by which the first period of Mr. Lincoln's administration had been distinguished, it might have been believed that neither one of them would be abandoned without at least a full and fair inquiry into the probable consequences of any changes that might be suggested. Those who might have so thought could scarcely, however, have reflected upon the general character of our legislation. "No people," as it has been said, "so soon forget yesterday." None take so little thought of to-morrow. No one looks back to study the cause of the good or evil that exists, and it is as a consequence of this that we have so constantly relapsed into British free trade almost at the first moment that protection had brought about a cure of the evils of which it had been the cause. Hitherto, since 1861, our course has been onward, and in the direction that above is indicated. Now, as I propose to show, we are steadily retracing our steps; and if the forward movement has led us to our present prosperous state, it can scarcely well be doubted that the backward one will lead us once again to that calamitous one from which we so recently have emerged.

The most serious move in the retrograde direction is that one we find in the determination to prohibit the further issue of that circulation to which we have been so much indebted. Why is it made? Because journalists fancy that it is to "paper money" they must attribute the, to them, great fact that paper is so high! Because men who depend on fixed incomes fancy that they should live better were the gold standard once again adopted! Because every free-trader in the land charges the high price of gold to the use of "greenbacks," and sees therein the causes why he cannot, with profit to himself, fill our markets with British cloth and British iron!

What is the present effect of the hesitation of the Treasury to use the power that yet remains at its command? It is paralyzing the societary movement, to the great loss of both the people and the Government. Labor is less in demand. Cloth, iron, and a thousand other commodities move more slowly. Why all these things? Because the Treasury does not fulfil its contracts. The unpaid requisitions amount to $125,000,000, and the Treasury is empty. The contractor who obtains a certificate sells it at heavy loss; while many, as I am told, find difficulties interposed in the way of obtaining certificates, most of which have their origin in the indisposition to *acknowledge* debt when there exist no means with which to *pay* it. How it is with the men who are now serving in the field was well shown, a few days since, by Senator Wilson, when he told his brother Senators that "they needed more money than they could obtain to pay their just debts—what they had agreed to pay." "Tens of millions of dollars," he continued, " are now due to our armies, many of whose officers have been unpaid for months; the Generals, meanwhile, holding by handfuls resignations tendered by men who find themselves forced to retire, as the only means now left to them of providing for their families."

Turning now to a letter in this day's *Tribune*, I find a statement of the facts of the case, and their effects, to which you may perhaps excuse me for asking your attention. It is as follows:—

"It is useless to deny the fact that men once ardent in the cause are becoming lukewarm in their attachment to a Government which so sadly fails to discharge, in this respect, its self-imposed obligations, and seems so careless of those over whom specially the ægis of its protection should be thrown. No wonder that the soldier should grow weary when he reflects that his arduous hardships, undergone on long marches, in the trenches, on the picket line, scorching then under the rays of a midsummer's sun, and shivering now in the merciless blasts of winter, exposed to all the inclemencies of a variable climate, are·suffered to go so long unrecognized by his Government; no wonder that when every mail brings him the old story of his family's destitution, and when he remembers his inability to aid them, he should grow lukewarm in the cause which years ago he espoused with all the ardor of a man and a patriot. It is in vain that he tries to place country above home—above the wife whom he has solemnly sworn to cherish and protect, the offspring whom Heaven has given him to support, or the aged parents whose infirmities demand his filial consideration; the thought of his domestic responsibilities will absorb all others, and will embitter every hour of his soldier-life.

"Every day resignations are forwarded by officers whom stern necessity has compelled to ask for their discharge from the military service, in order that they may return home to relieve the pressing wants of their families, and shall we say, too, that desertions to the enemy frequently occur whenever men are impelled by the same motives. Officers and men, in making application for leaves and furloughs, are often forced to make the humiliating confession that they desire to go home.to restore order to their households, upon which, during their absence, shame and dishonor have fallen, and the plea of their families' extreme destitution is still more frequent. In the name of humanity, then, let the troops be paid with as little delay as possible; the best interests of the service demand it."

Entirely in keeping with this are statements coming from the West, of the great distress of Government contractors compelled to forced sales of the vouchers in their hands—of the great rise in the general rate of interest—and of the extremely sluggish state of the societary circulation. The Government has made itself responsible for the financial movement of the country, and when it stops payment there is stoppage everywhere.

Why has it stopped? Because those in the control of public journals fail to see that the cause of the high price of paper and of gold *cannot* be found in the circulation! Because the Government itself fails to see that the circulation now furnished bears a smaller proportion to the needs of the people, and to the extent of country requiring to be supplied, than did that which was furnished when gold could be bought at an advance of 10, 12, or 15 per cent.! Because all who write or speak on this subject fail to see that, with the extension of the power of the Union over the Cotton States, there must arise an absolute necessity for furnishing to the people of those States machinery of circulation adequate to the performance of the same work that has so well been done in these

Northern States! So far from diminishing the supply of that machinery, there is a pressing necessity for its increase.

Anxious for a reduction in the price of gold, journalists are almost everywhere calling upon Congress to increase the taxes, to give up *selling* machinery of circulation that costs it nothing, and to take to *buying* such machinery at the market price. Obedient to their orders the treasury *is* buying it, and the price at which it buys is shown in the following extract from an advertisement of the loan that is now on sale :—

" By authority of the Secretary of the Treasury, the undersigned has assumed the general subscription agency for the sale of United States treasury notes bearing seven and three-tenths per cent. interest per annum, known as the SEVEN-THIRTY LOAN. These notes are issued under date of August 15, 1864, and are payable three years from that time, in currency, or are convertible at the option of the holder into U. S. 5-20 SIX PER CENT. GOLD-BEARING BONDS. These bonds are now worth a premium of nine per cent., including gold interest from November, which makes the actual profit on the 7-30 loan, at current rates, including interest, about ten per cent. per annum, besides its *exemption from State and municipal taxation, which adds from one to three per cent. more,* according to the rates levied on other property."

This is certainly a high price to pay for the use of a little money, and the reason why it is so high is that the supply of the commodity needed is diminishing in the proportion borne by it to public and private needs.

We have here, however, only $200,000,000, interest upon which is to be paid in gold three years hence. Six hundred millions more are now asked for, and the demand is, we are told, to be accompanied by a withdrawal of even the existing power to furnish legal tenders bearing interest. As those now existing become more and more withdrawn from circulation, the societary machinery must gradually diminish in its quantity, and that, too, just at the time when the theatre on which it is to be employed is likely to be almost doubled. The necessary consequence of this must be such a rise in the rate of interest as will compel the export of Government bonds, and the rapid increase of dependence on the money markets of Europe—each step backward being thus but the precursor of another and greater one. So long as they shall continue to be sold abroad money will continue to be obtainable ; but when the foreign market shall have become fully glutted it will, as in the period from 1837 to 1842, become unobtainable at any price.

The gold interest now payable requires $60,000,000. Adding these new loans, and making their interest payable in gold, we shall, three years hence, need $108,000,000, most of which is likely to have to go to Europe. Add now to this, first, the $30,000,000 required for payment of interest on the old foreign free trade debt; second, only an equal amount for absentees, temporary and permanent; and we obtain a demand amounting to $168,000,000, that *must* be met before we can purchase a piece of cloth or a ton of iron. Where is all this gold to come from?

Tax the people! is the answer. Give us an income tax of 25 per cent.! Tax sales! Tax manufactures! All this is being done, and so thoroughly that important branches of manufacture are likely to be taxed entirely out of existence. Paying his taxes in paper, and obtaining cash for his products, the ironmaster can scarcely even to-day make head against those " wealthy capitalists" of England who have already placed themselves on such a footing, as regards freight and duty, that it is *they* who, under a gold system, will be protected, and not their American competitors. So, too, with paper, the domestic taxes on which are ten per cent., while foreign paper is likely to be admitted at three. So, too, as I understand, is it with leather. Mr. Sherman tells us that $40,000,000 in gold will be required to purchase paper abroad that if made at home would yield $10,000,000 to the treasury. Add to this $100,000,000 to pay for the iron needed for taking the place of that now made in furnaces that will then be out of blast, and we shall have quite enough to pay to those European nations whose markets are now glutted with food, and who have taken from us, in the past five months, of flour, wheat, and corn, just as much, *and no more*, as would command in gold somewhat less than *two millions of dollars.**

The contributions to the internal revenue made by paper, iron, and leather, appear, under the retrograde system now inaugurated, likely to be very small indeed. How will it be with other manufactures, paying as they must, at a gold value, duties that had been laid when two dollars in paper had been but the equivalent of one

* The precise quantities of these commodities shipped to Belgium, France, and Britain, has been: Of flour, 59,998 barrels; of wheat, 1,305,313 bushels; and of corn, 56,933 bushels.

in gold ? How will it be with the farmer, obliged to look to Europe for a market for his products ? How will it be with the miner and the laborer when rolling-mills are closed and mines have ceased to be worked ? The answer to all these questions will be found in the simple propositions, that the power of accumulation increases almost geometrically as the rapidity of the *societary circulation* increases arithmetically; and that it declines in the same proportion as the circulation becomes more languid. In the few years through which we just have passed it has been increasing rapidly, but, under the change of policy that has been now inaugurated, it is already slowly moving in the opposite direction. Admitting the truth of those propositions, then must it be also admitted that, prompted by an anxious desire once again to handle gold, we are killing the goose that has already laid the many golden eggs so well described in the following paragraph, from this day's *Tribune* :—

"The internal revenue for the month of January just past amounted to the enormous sum of \$31,076,902 89—over a million of dollars a day, including Sunday ! And yet confessedly the machinery for collecting this branch of the nation's income is imperfect and undergoing change. Vast as is that sum of internal revenue, daily and monthly, how light a burden is it to the business of this rich and vigorous nation ! And with what patriotic cheerfulness and acquiescence the people pay this tax to preserve their nation and to maintain democracy."

To' what do we owe these wonderful results of a state of civil war ? To rapidity of the societary circulation, and to nothing else ! To what have we been indebted for that rapidity ? To protection and the "greenbacks" ! What is it that we are now laboring to destroy ? Protection and the Greenback !

Let us continue on in the direction in which we now are moving, and we shall ere long see, not resumption but repudiation; not a contradiction but a confirmation of the predictions of the *Times ;* not a re-establishment of the Union, but a complete and final disruption of it.

What are the means by which these calamities may be avoided, I propose to show in another and final letter, and meanwhile remain, my dear sir,

Yours, very truly,

HENRY C. CAREY.

Hon. SCHUYLER COLFAX.

PHILADELPHIA, February 17, 1865.

THE CURRENCY QUESTION.

DEAR SIR:—

The measures now in preparation, as regards both the customs and internal revenues, tend, as it appears to me, in the direction of stoppage of the societary circulation, of rise in the rate of interest, of increase in the power of men engaged in the creation of financial water-spouts, and of permanent maintenance of a premium on the precious metals. If so, then, if we are ever again to witness here the regular redemption of promises to furnish gold and silver, it must occur as a consequence of the adoption of a course of policy directly the reverse of all that recently has been done, and all that, if we are to credit the public journals, is in the contemplation of those who are charged with the direction of our financial movements.

The existing derangement of the currency is wholly due to the action of those who manage *the windbag system* described in a former letter, and while their operations shall continue to be, as now they are, wholly unrestrained, financial crises must continue to reappear, and the price of gold must continue to be as uncertain as is their course of action. Such being the case, it is of high importance that proper checks be forthwith instituted, and now, for the first time in our history, is it in the power of Congress to let us have them. To that end, let us have a law declaring—

First, that no bank shall hereafter so extend its investments as to hold in any form other than those of gold, silver, U. S. notes, or notes of national banks, more than twice its capital:

Second, that in the case of already existing banks whose investments are outside of the limits above described, any extension thereof beyond the amount at which they stood on the first of the present month shall be followed by instant forfeiture of its charter.

Having thus established a check upon further extension, the

next step should be in the direction of bringing the operations of existing banks within proper limits. To that end, let us have a provision imposing on all investments outside of the limits above described a tax which, when added to that already existing, shall amount for the present year to one per cent. In the second year let it be made 1¼ per cent. on all over 90 per cent. in excess of the actual capital upon which dividends are paid. In the third, 1½ per cent. over 80 per cent.; and in the fourth, 1¾ over 70 per cent. Thenceforth let the tax grow at the rate of a quarter per cent. per annum until, by degrees, all banks shall have so enlarged their capitals, or so reduced their loans, as to free themselves from its further payment.

Holding interest-paying securities 70 per cent. in excess of its capital, a bank would be always in a condition of perfect safety, and could give to its stockholders dividends of at least 8 per cent. Such stock would be preferable to almost any other securities in the market, and there would be no difficulty in so enlarging the foundation as to give to the whole structure the form of a true pyramid, instead of the inverted one which now presents itself to the eye of all observers.

Let us have a law embracing these provisions, and we shall then be fairly on the way towards the establishment of a financial system the most perfect the world has ever seen. Let us have it, and, as you will clearly see, the need for restrictions on the circulation will wholly have passed away. The day, indeed, will then be near at hand when banks will have ceased to be competitors with the Treasury for furnishing circulating notes of any kind, and when the nation may profit to the extent of 50, if not even 60 millions a year of the power to furnish the machinery of circulation.

Simultaneously with the passage of such a law, let the Government determine honestly to pay its debts. The soldier in the field, and the officer who is placing his life in daily hazard, have a right to demand of the Treasury that it shall give them such certificates of its indebtedness as will enable their wives and children to go to the neighboring shop and purchase food and clothing.* The contractor and the shipbuilder have a right to claim that when certificates are issued they shall be in such a form as will enable them to

---

* The amount now due to the army alone is stated by Senator Wilson at the enormous sum of one hundred and thirty-eight millions of dollars.

avoid the further payment of the usurious interest to which they have so long been subjected. Paying promptly, the Government will buy cheaply; and should such payment have the effect of causing the supply of "greenbacks" to be in excess of the demand, the Treasury will thence derive a double benefit: first, in being thus enabled to borrow what it needs at reasonable rates; and second, in having its need for borrowing diminished by reason of the increased stimulus thereby given to that societary circulation upon the rapidity of which it is dependent for both the maintenance and the growth of the Internal Revenue.

The whole South now requires reorganization, and one of the first steps in that direction should be found in furnishing machinery of circulation. As much in need of this stands the whole of that great West for the development of whose wonderful powers we are now exporting in that direction so many hundreds of thousands of our people. If the Government does not supply that machinery, who is there that can or will do so? Look carefully, I pray you, my dear sir, at the vast field that is to be occupied, and at the great work that is to be done, and then wonder with me that the Government should permit its soldiers to perish in the field, while it is debating the terms of a loan to be made to it by men all of whose interests are to be promoted by a diminution of the circulation and an increase of the rate of interest. Let our soldiers be paid, let the credit of the Government be once again re-established, let the rate of interest be kept down, and let the Treasury reassert its independence, and all will yet go well.

Having thus, as paymaster, re-established its credit, let it next place itself in a creditable position as regards those who had been led to see in the Morrill Tariff a pledge of protection against those "wealthy capitalists" whose fortunes count by millions, and who use those millions as "instruments of warfare" by means of which they are enabled to "overwhelm all foreign competition, and to gain and keep possession of foreign markets." Let it restore those great fundamental branches of industry which constitute the pillars of our national temple to the position in which they stood in 1861, increasing the duties on foreign products by just so much as the taxes since imposed on domestic ones, and the result will then exhibit itself in the fact that sugar, tea, coffee, soda ash, and other raw materials of food and manufacture, will twice over make amends for any loss that may be experienced by the revenue because of the substitution of domestic cloth or iron for that now made in foreign furnaces or on foreign looms.

Let these things be done, and we shall then cease to look abroad for purchasers of our bonds. Let this be done, and we shall soon find ourselves on the road towards becoming purchasers of those now held abroad, *every one of which should be redeemed before we ever again place ourselves in a position to be required to furnish gold and silver in payment of our notes.*

To many it might seem that this would be a postponement of resumption to a date so distant that none of them would live to see it. Let, however, all such persons study what was done in this respect in the brief period of the existence of the tariffs of 1828 and 1842; let them next look to what has been done in the past four years; and they will see that all that I have indicated as what is needed to be done, is only what, under a sound and permanent system, *may be done before the lapse of the next decade.*

As a rule, reformers desire to move too rapidly, and therefore fail to attain their objects. They omit to see that when Nature has important purposes to accomplish, she works slowly and with almost invisible machinery, as when she sends the daily morning dew. When she desires merely to destroy a ship or to root up a forest, she sends the tornado or the water-spout. Let us follow her example. We have a great work to accomplish, and we should now profit of the lesson read to the world in that period which followed the close of the great war of the French Revolution, and exhibited a scene of destruction that had never before, in time of peace, been witnessed. Believing it to be one that should be carefully studied, I now invite you, my dear sir, to accompany me in a brief review of the facts in the order of their occurrence.

For twenty years the Bank of England had been injecting gas into the currency, but with the return of peace it became necessary that it should be steadily withdrawn. In the two years from 1815 to 1817, the bank directors had, by means of the very simple operation of calling in its claims on one hand, and reducing its liabilities on the other, reduced the apparent quantity of money at the command of the community to the extent of £12,000,000, or little short of $60,000,000. So far as regarded the operations of society, this had been equivalent to a total annihilation of that large sum, and to that extent a contraction of the standard by which the community was required to measure the value of all other commodities

and things. Had the yardstick been doubled in length, or the
pound in weight, for the benefit of all persons who had contracted
to purchase cloth or corn, the injury inflicted would have been
trivial by comparison with the change that was thus effected. As
compared with the property of the people of Great Britain, that
sum was utterly insignificant, yet did its abstraction cause an arrest
of the circulation almost as complete as would be that produced
in the physical body by stoppage of the supply of food. Farmers
and merchants were everywhere ruined. Of the country banks, no
less than two hundred and forty—being one in four of their whole
number—stopped payment; while one in ten and a half became
actually bankrupt. "Thousands upon thousands," says Mr. Mc-
Culloch, "who had in 1812 considered themselves affluent, found
they were destitute of all real property, and sunk, as if by enchantment, and without any fault of their own, into the abyss of
poverty." Throughout the country, there was, to use the words of
Mr. Francis Horner, "an universality of wretchedness and misery
which had never been equalled, except perhaps by the breaking
up of the Mississippi Scheme in France." *In the midst of all this
ruin, however, the bank, which had supplied the gas, prospered more
than ever, for the destruction of private credit rendered its vaults
and its notes more necessary to the community.*

The groundwork having thus been laid by the bank, Parliament
passed, in 1819, an act providing for the resumption of specie
payments, and thus re-established, as the law of the land, the
standard that had existed in 1797—among the most remarkable
measures of confiscation to be found in the annals of legislation.
For more than twenty years all the transactions of the United
Kingdom had been based upon a currency less in value than that
which had existed in 1796. In the course of that long period,
land had been sold, mortgages given, settlements made, and other
contracts of a permanent nature entered into, to the extent of thousands of millions of pounds, the terms of all of which were now to
be changed for the benefit of the receivers of fixed incomes, and to
the loss of those who had land, labor, or the produce of either, to
sell. As a necessary consequence, land fell exceedingly in price,
and mortgagees everywhere entered into possession. Labor became superabundant, and the laborer suffered for want of food.
Machinery of every kind was thrown out of use, and manufacturers
were ruined. Manufactures, being in excess of the demand, were

forced upon foreign markets, to the ruin of the capitalists and workmen, miners and machinists, of the other countries of the world.

Peace had brought with it widespread ruin, but it everywhere
enriched the money-lender—*his* commodity rising, while land became so cheap that he could purchase at less than half its previous
price. The annuitant and office-holder profited—their dividends
and salaries having become payable in coin, that would purchase
double the quantity of food and clothing for which they had at
first contracted. Farmers and laborers, mechanics and merchants,
were impoverished—their taxes remaining unchanged, while their
labor, and its products, commanded less than half the money for
which they would before have sold.

Bad as is this, it will be *infinitely* worse with us if we shall attempt to follow the example here placed before us. Let us put our
house in order; let us adopt the measures needed for making the
Declaration of Independence something more than a mere word
of small significance; let us do all this slowly and quietly, and we
shall set to the world an example in peace even more remarkable
than that which has been set in the course of the present extraordinary war—returning to the old standard, and without the occurrence of the slightest crisis.

That this may be done, it is needed only that those who direct
our fiscal operations shall recollect that the National Treasury
has now become a partner in, and entitled to the lion's share of,
the profits of every mine, every furnace, every mill, every workshop, and every farm in the land, and that every increase in the
prosperity of such works must be to it a source of double profit:
first, that arising out of the direct contributions of the work itself;
and second, that resulting from the increased consumption of sugar,
tea, coffee, and other commodities consumed by those who mine
the coal, roll the iron, and make the engines and the cloth. The
day for a clear perception of the existence of this harmony of all
real interests may or may not be near at hand. For the promotion
of its arrival, we need to see extended throughout the Union the
same principle of association that has proved to be so effective
throughout the present war. We need to see A GREAT NATIONAL
LEAGUE, embracing men who grow wool, and others who convert
it into cloth; men who make iron, and others who need railroad
bars; men who raise food, and others who combine food and ore
into iron; men who build ships, and others who consume the

sugar and the tea that ships transport; and finally, men who pay taxes, and others who make the laws under which those taxes are collected. In the words of Jackson, we need to be *Americanized*. Whenever the day shall arrive when we shall have so become, then, and not till then, shall we have placed ourselves in a position successfully to contend for the control of the commerce of the world, and thus to

OUTDO ENGLAND WITHOUT FIGHTING HER.

That control will find its place among the hands and heads of the community that makes and uses the largest quantity of iron. A single decade of the system above described would suffice for placing us, in this respect, side by side with England. At the close of another, she would be left far behind, and we should then have vindicated our claim to that position in the world of which our people so often talk, and of the true means of obtaining which they so little think.

Hoping that the event may prove that the time for serious thought has now really arrived, and begging you to excuse my numerous trespasses on your attention, I remain, my dear sir, with great regard and respect,

Yours, faithfully,

HENRY C. CAREY.

Hon. SCHUYLER COLFAX.

PHILADELPHIA, February 18, 1865.

OUR RESOURCES.

It is of the resources of the Union, gentlemen, that I propose this evening to talk with you. By those who usually speak or write on that subject
we are constantly told of the vast extent of our yet unoccupied land, of the
great deposits of fuel and metallic ores by which our soil is underlaid, and
of the rapidly-growing numbers of our population; and yet, if we look
to Russia, Turkey, Canada, Mexico, or South America, the countries in
which such land most exists; or to that European one, Ireland, in which
the growth of population has been most rapid; we find among them precisely those in which land has the smallest money value, capital is most
rare, interest at the highest rate, and the workingman most nearly in the
condition of bond slave to the landholder or other capitalist. Turning
our eyes homeward and comparing the different portions of the Union, we
find, in the States south of the Potomac, the greatest natural advantages
coupled with a population whose natural increase has been even greater than
that of these Northern States; yet there it is that land has been cheapest,
that capital has least increased, that interest has been at its highest point,
and that the laborer has been most enslaved. Passing thence to the New
England States, we find that, though wholly destitute of natural advantages,
land is there scarce and high in price and man is free, while capital
abounds, and interest, though high when compared with certain parts of
Europe, is very low by comparison with almost any other portion of this
Western Continent.

Crossing the Atlantic and comparing two of the smaller kingdoms, near
neighbors to each other, Ireland and Belgium, both possessing great natural
advantages, we find differences closely approaching those which are here
observed. In the first, capital has been so scarce that, while holding the
laborer in a condition nearly akin to slavery, the middleman possessor of
money has been enabled utterly to ruin a large proportion of those who
formerly owned the land; in the latter, on the contrary, land commanding a
higher price than in any other part of Europe, and the use of money being
readily obtained at the lowest rate of interest. Turning next to the French
and Turkish empires, we find ourselves face to face with phenomena similar
in character and even yet more remarkable for their extent. The former
has no important natural advantages, yet is its land nearly on a par with
that of Belgium, while capital so much abounds that money is readily there

obtainable at moderate interest. The latter, on the contrary, has every conceivable natural advantage, fertile land abounding and the climate being among the best in the world, while fuel and metallic ores exist in great abundance; yet there it is that, of all Europe, land is cheapest, interest highest, and the laborer most depressed; and that, as a necessary consequence, the State is weakest.

Comparing Germany of the past and the present we meet with similar contrasts. Forty years since she exported wool and rags and imported cloth and paper, and then her people were poor and her land very low in price, while she herself was little better than a mere tool in the hands of foreign powers. Now, she imports both wool and rags and exports both cloth and paper; and it is as a necessary consequence of the changes that have been thus effected, that land and labor have greatly risen in price; that capital abounds and interest is low; and that she herself feels strong enough to set at defiance, as in the case of the Duchies she recently has done, the almost united will of Europe.

Having all these facts before us we are led necessarily to the conclusion that, with societies as with individuals, prosperity is far less due to the liberality of nature than to the use that is made of the bounties, large or small, of which they have been the recipients. The highly-gifted man, head of his class, throwing away his time and wasting his talents, dies in poverty, despised by all; while the patient industry of the fellow scholar to whom nature had been far less bounteous, enables him to attain to fortune, fame, and influence. Precisely so is it with nations, the question of their prosperity or adversity being dependent, mainly, not on the extent of nature's gifts, but on the use that is made of those which have been accorded.

Studying now the several communities above referred to, we find them susceptible of being divided into two well-defined classes, one of which, embracing Ireland, Turkey, Mexico, Canada, and the South American States, exports its products in their rudest state, leaving to others the work of changing their forms, and thus fitting them for consumption by the world at large. The other, embracing France, Belgium, and the *Zoll-Verein*, buys the raw products of other countries, combines them with those produced at home, and sends the two, thus combined, to every market of the world. In the first of these the price of land is low, capital is always scarce, and the capitalist is master of the laborer, whose condition is little better than that of mere hewer of wood and drawer of water for the middleman by whose aid he maintains his little commerce with the outer world.

Looking now homeward we find our Union itself equally susceptible of division, the South and West exporting raw produce and paying at the highest rate for the use of a very little money; the North and East meanwhile buying that produce, changing its form, and returning it to the original producers burthened with the heavy charges to which our Eastern friends have stood indebted for the large capitals which are always ready to be lent at rates of interest that, as I have already said, are moderate by comparison with those of the West and South, though high when compared with those of the European States to which reference has above been made.

Studying all the facts thus presented by so many important communities, we are led inevitably to the conclusion that the growth of capital is slow, and the price paid for its use high, in the direct ratio of dependence on strangers for finishing and distributing the products of the soil; while rapid in its growth and declining in its price in the ratio of the increase of that national independence which enables each and every nation to exchange directly, and without the need of foreign intervention, with each and every other. Admitting this, and all experience proves it so to be, then must the extent of national resources be mainly dependent upon the policy pursued, whether that which tends to promote or to repress the growth of that independence.

The questions asked by science are, "What are the facts?" and "Why are they so?" The first having above been answered, we come now to the second—"Why is it that poverty, high interest, and subjection of the laborer to the will of the capitalist are constant attendants of that course of policy which tends to limit nations to the two pursuits of labor in the field and labor in the shop—trade and agriculture?" To this an answer has recently been given by a well-known citizen of your State, one of the clearest-headed and most acute of economists, and late State Reporter—one to whom I gladly here acknowledge myself to have been indebted for many valuable suggestions—my friend Mr. Peshine Smith; and so well given that, although yet unpublished, I place it here before you, with his permission, in the words of his manuscript now in my possession, as follows :—

"Between the production of any commodity whatsoever, and its consumption, the interval, long or short, is one of inertness. So long as it so remains it stands a monument of human power and natural forces which, having expended themselves in bringing it into shape, slumber in suspended animation, not only communicating no impulse to that incessant activity which is the characteristic of vitality, but actually constituting a clog and obstruction that involves a draught upon the vital forces for the work of putting it again in motion. It is like an inorganic body contained within, and afflicting, an organism.

"The space to be overcome, and the time that must intervene before, by consumption, it evolves utility—thus becoming once again an instrument and a force—are co-efficients of its value, neutralizing in the same proportion the power of the community in which it so rests paralyzed. The growth of wealth, therefore, depends upon the rapidity of the societary circulation; not the speed with which products are transported in space, nor the frequency with which they pass from hand to hand; but the continuity of transformation through the immediate succession of actual consumption to production. This involves necessarily the concentration and interfusion of producers and consumers, the growth of wealth, and the diversification of employments."

Such being the theory, we may now compare it with the actual practice.

A bushel of wheat is produced representing, let us say, a dollar's worth of mental and physical force. The consumer being close at hand, the producer re-enters on the instant upon the possession of the whole capital that had been expended. Consumers not presenting themselves, the farmer stores it in his barn, losing so much interest. A neighbor offers to carry it for him, charging interest proportioned to the time that may reasonably be supposed likely to elapse before a consumer shall be found. A trader comes, and he now takes upon himself the burthen of carrying it, charging further interest. In this manner it passes from hand to hand and from city to city, finally finding a consumer in Lyons or Manchester, having on the road paid, in the mere form of interest, perhaps half the price at which it has at last been sold.

What is true of this single bushel is equally so of the hundreds of millions of bushels of wheat, rye, and Indian corn; of the thousands of millions of pounds of cotton; of the hundreds of thousands of hundred-weights of pork and beef, rice and tobacco, that are everywhere standing in barns, warehouses, wagons, cars, and ships, waiting the arrival of men prepared to give in exchange for them cloth, furniture, ploughs, harrows, and the thousand other commodities needed by the planters and farmers of the land. The whole constitutes a mass of petrified capital to be carried at the cost of the producer, and it is within the mark to estimate the amount so standing petrified at the present moment at five hundred millions of dollars, all of which bears interest. Turn back half a dozen years to the period of suspended animation that existed throughout the country before the war, and you will see that the amount of dead capital then carried must have greatly exceeded even a thousand millions. Can we then wonder at the high prices that, notwithstanding the wonderful gold discoveries of California and Australia, then were paid for the use of a little money by both our farmers and our planters? As I think, we cannot.

Let us now suppose that throughout the whole length and breadth of the land there had then, on the instant, sprung into existence, side by side with the producers, the number of consumers required for making an immediate market for the whole of this enormous mass, one offering in exchange personal service; another cottons; a third woollens; a fourth spades and hoes; and so on to the end of the chapter of the farmer's needs. At once, and almost as by enchantment, as in the case of the bottle of old wine made memorable by Webster's exclamation, the interest would have been stopped; the petrified capital would have sprung into activity and life; notes would have been paid; store debts would have been discharged; and the farmer would have found that instead of being dependent on the neighboring usurer for the means with which to buy sugar, tea, and coffee, he had in his hands a surplus ready to be applied to the purchase of all the machinery required for enabling him to double the produce of both his labor and his land. At what now might we estimate the gain to the community at large of this economy of capital? Most certainly the figure would be twice that of the mere saving of the 12, 15, 20, 30, or 40 per cent. to be paid throughout the country, and would represent many hundred millions. In the life of nations, as in that of individuals, it is thus in the rapidity of circulation and consequent economy of labor and interest that we are to find the surest road to wealth and power.

The case here supposed is precisely that exhibited in every country in which the consumer and producer are near neighbors to each other. The Southern traveller in New England asks, "Where are your barns?" and finds his answer in the fact then given him, that everything yielded by the land is consumed on the instant of production. So is it around our cities, the market gardener finding instant demand for all his products. So, too, is it in Belgium and in France; and therefore is it, that in those countries capital abounds, and that the services of money can always be commanded at the lowest rates of interest.

Whence, however, it will be asked, could have come the vast amount of labor required for giving this almost instant life to the enormous amount of capital so petrified? Before answering this question allow me to ask you to look to the extraordinary waste of human power that occurs in every country of the world in which, by reason of the absence of diversity of employment, there exists no regular and steady demand for it. Taking together all the countries I have named as exporters of raw products, Russia, Ireland, Canada, Mexico, and South America, it may well be doubted if the waste of force amounts to less than five parts out of every six; and yet, each and every portion of it represents some certain amount of capital in the forms of food, clothing, and shelter, expended for the support of life. Each dollar's worth of that capital, aided by the natural forces, is certainly capable of producing twice if not even thrice the quantity expended, and when it does so the community becomes from day to day more wealthy to the extent of the entire difference. When, on the contrary, the services of the laborer are not demanded, the community is impoverished to the whole extent of the consumption. Such being the case, it is easy to comprehend why capital should be scarce and interest high in all the countries that have last above been named.

Between labor and labor's products there exists the important difference, that while the latter can be preserved in the interval between production and consumption, the former cannot. The owner of capital petrified in the form of unconsumed wheat loses only interest; whereas, the owner of unconsumed labor loses capital, labor power being that one species of it which if not consumed at the moment of production is lost forever. The more instant the demand for human service, and the more rapid its circulation, the greater must therefore be the increase of power and of force, the law governing the social body being identical with that which we feel and know to govern the physical one, and which is embodied in the wish that "good digestion may wait on appetite and health on both."

The quantity of capital petrified in the form of raw products awaiting revivification in the years anterior to the war has, as you have seen, been estimated at much more than a thousand millions of dollars. Of how it was with capital in the form of muscular force we may form some opinion from the following passage from a Report of one of your charitable societies, exhibiting the state of things that here existed in December, 1855, nearly two years prior to the occurrence of the great crisis of 1857, as follows :—

"Up to the present, the Association has relieved 6,622 families, containing 26,896 persons, many of whom are families of unemployed mechanics, and widows with dependent children, who cannot subsist without aid. And as the season advances the amount of destitution will increase. Last winter it was three times as great in January as in December, and did not reach its height until the close of February."

This is the type of all the reports that might, in the years that followed, have been made throughout the Union. Look where we might, men and women were seen unemployed, because mines had been abandoned; furnaces put out of blast; mills and machine-shops closed; and farmers deprived of the power to make demand for labor because compelled to choose between storing their products on the one hand, or, on the other, selling them at the ruinous prices that then prevailed. Taking the whole country through, from North to South and from East to West, it may safely be asserted that two-thirds of the capital daily invested in the production of human force were then being daily wasted. Estimating now the national labor power as being equivalent to that of eight millions of men, and the power of production of that labor, properly aided by machinery, at but two dollars and a half per head, per day, the daily loss would have amounted to thirteen millions, or $4,000,000,000 a year. Capital in one form was thus being destroyed because other capital was standing petrified in the forms of corn, wheat, lumber, rice, and other commodities for which no market could be found; and therefore was it that, with the treasures of California at our command, money was scarce and high, and public and private credit at the lowest ebb.

Having thus shown what was the waste of interest and of that capital which took, necessarily, the form of physical and mental force, we may now for a moment look at the waste of things. The straw of France is valued at $150,000,000; but throughout the West it is destroyed because of the absence of that market for it which arises necessarily in all communities in which employment is diversified. The manure of England is valued at £100,000,000, and near our cities manure is greatly prized; but throughout that portion of the country which sends its products to market in the rudest forms there is a constant withdrawal of the elements of fertility, the consequence of which exhibits itself in a steady decline in the powers of the soil.

How enormous is the injury thus produced may be judged when it is known that more than a dozen years since it was stated, and by high authority, that our total annual waste " could not be estimated at less than the equivalent of the mineral constituents of fifteen hundred millions of bushels of corn." Well might the author of this statement exclaim, that " what with our earth-butchery and our prodigality we were every year losing the elements of vitality;" and that although " our country had not yet grown feeble from this loss of life-blood, the hour was fixed when, if the existing system were continued, the last throb of the nation's heart would have ceased, and when America, Greece, and Rome would stand together among the nations of the past!"

The reverse of this is seen in all those countries in which the producer and consumer are brought more near together.

With every stage of progress in that direction, the various utilities of the raw materials of the neighborhood become more and more developed; and with each the farmer finds an increase of wealth. The new mill requires granite, and houses for the workmen require bricks and lumber; and now the rock of the mountain side, the clay of the river bottom, and the timber with which they have so long been covered, acquire a money value in the eyes of all around him. The granite dust of the quarry is found useful in his garden, enabling him to furnish cabbages. beans, peas, and the smaller fruits for the supply of neighboring workmen. On one hand he has a demand for potash, and on another for madder. The woollen manufacturer asks for teazles, and the maker of brooms urges him to extend the cultivation of the corn of which the brooms are made. The basket-makers, and the gunpowder manufacturers, are rival claimants for the produce of his willows; and thus does he find that diversity of employment among those around him produces diversity in the demands for his physical and intellectual powers, and for the use of the soil at the various seasons of the year; with constant augmentation in the powers of his land and in its price.

Directly the reverse of all this becomes obvious as the consumer is more and more removed from the producer, and as the power of association is thus diminished. The madder, the teazle, the broom corn, and the osier cease to be required; and the granite, clay, and sand continue to remain where nature had placed them. The societary circulation declines, and with that decline we witness a constantly increasing waste of the powers of man and of the great machine given by the Creator for his use. His time is wasted, because he has no choice in the employment of his land. He *must* raise wheat, or cotton, or sugar, or some other commodity of which the yield is small, and which will, therefore, bear carriage to the distant market. He neglects his fruit-trees, and his potatoes are given to the hogs. He wastes his rags and his straw, because there is no paper-mill at hand. His forest-trees he destroys, that he may obtain a trifle in exchange for the ashes they thus are made to yield. His cotton-seed wastes upon the ground, or he destroys the fibre of the flax that he may sell the seed. Not only does he sell his wheat in a distant market, and thus impoverish his land, but so does he also with the very bones of the animals that have been fattened with his corn. The yield, therefore, regularly decreases in quantity, with constant increase in the risk of danger from changes of the weather, because of the necessity for dependence on a single crop; and with equally constant diminution in the powers of the man who cultivates it, until at length he finds himself a slave not only to nature but to those of his fellow-men whose physical powers are greater than his own. That it is density of population that makes the food come from the richer soils and thus enables men further to increase their power to command the various forces of nature, is a truth evidence of which may be found in every page of history; and equally true is it, that in order to the cultivation of those soils there must be that development of the latent powers of man which can be found in those communities only in which employments are diversified.

Combining together the various items of waste thus far referred to, we obtain an annual amount that counts by thousands of millions of dollars, and that well accounts for the fact that capital has here been always scarce and interest high; and that we have been compelled to look abroad for aid in the establishment of communications, promising always payment for its use at prices ruinously high, and then, when bankruptcy has come, finding ourselves compelled to submit to denunciations like the so often quoted one of the Rev. Sidney Smith; and yet, it is only at the threshold of this question of waste at which we have now arrived.

We have land in abundance without the power properly, or fully, to cultivate it. We have timber in abundance, but need the power required for bringing it to market. We have iron ore in abundance, but are deficient in power to convert it into axes, ploughs, rails, and engines; and yet in our beds of coal, vast beyond those of all Europe combined, we have an inexhaustible supply of that material a single bushel of which is capable of doing the work of hundreds of men. Why do we not mine it? Because we need the capital required for sinking shafts and purchasing engines; and yet, in the period to which I have referred there were more than a thousand millions of capital standing petrified at the expense of its producers, and we were wasting daily millions of that labor-capital whose application in this direction would have added so largely to the national wealth. How wonderful is the addition that may thus be made has well been shown in the results so recently attained in California, and still more recently in the oil regions of Pennsylvania and the adjacent States. Greatly more wonderful than both of these combined must have been the effects that would have resulted from the application to the development of our marvellous and almost universal resources in coal and ores of even so small a proportion as a single fifth of the labor capital that was being wasted on each and every day of the sad years to which I have referred—the years in which we paved the way for the leaders of the secession movement. To estimate the annual addition that would, in that quarter alone, and by means of that comparatively small economy, have been made to the national wealth, at $1,000,000,000, would be to remain very far indeed within the truth.

Failing to develop our mineral wealth we are led necessarily to a waste of the mental power for whose development we make such large expenditures on schools and colleges. Among the seven and thirty millions of whom the population of the Union is now composed, the variety of minds is on a par with the variety of faces, each and every one being better suited for some one occupation than for any other. To enable each to find that place in which he may most fully contribute to the growth of wealth and power, and to the promotion of the societary interests, there needs to be that diversification of pursuits which never can arise in a country that exports its products in the rudest state. In all such countries, the round man finds himself placed in the square hole, and the square man in the round one, each thus deprived of power to contribute his proper share to the advancement of the community of which he is a part. More than at almost any period of our history was this to be seen at the period of which I speak; and, as a necessary consequence, the proportion borne by non-producers, middlemen of every description, to producers was greater than in probably any other country claiming to rank as civilized. For want of the capital that then remained inert and useless, bearing interest at the cost of its producers, the mill, the mine, and the furnace were closed, and those who should have been furnishing for consumption all the various products of the earth found themselves compelled to become clerks and traders, lawyers and doctors, the claimants on the things produced thus increasing in number precisely as production diminished.

The power of accumulation, whether in the physical or social body, exists in the ratio of the rapidity of circulation. The circulation at the time of which I speak was sluggish in the extreme, and hence it was that, notwithstanding the vast receipts from California mines, capital was petrified, credit was impaired, and the rate of interest throughout the West great, as I believe, beyond all previous precedent. In the history of the civilized world there can, as I think, be found no parallel to the waste of physical and mental force that then was taking place. Seeing this, I then often told my friends that the tariff of 1846 was costing the country not less than $3,000,000,000 a year, but am now satisfied that I should have been much nearer the truth had I placed it at double that amount.

That waste, so far particularly as the 20,000,000 of the population of the Free States were concerned, was at its height throughout the whole period of Mr. Buchanan's administration. For the products of their agriculture there was almost literally no demand among the manufacturing nations of Europe, our exports of food in that direction in the three years that preceded the secession movement having averaged but $10,000,000. Corn in the West was then being used for fuel, and thus was its producer compelled to lose not only the interest upon his capital, but the very capital itself that he had thus invested. Labor power was in excess, and men were everywhere wandering in search of such employment as would enable them to purchase food. Mills and furnaces were abandoned, and so trivial was the domestic intercourse that the stock of a number of the most important roads of the country fell to, and long remained at, an average price of less than fifty per cent. For years we had been trying the experiment as to how large the outlay of labor could be made for the accomplishment of any given result, an experiment directly the opposite of that which is tried by every successful producer of corn or cotton, cloth or iron ; the effect exhibiting itself in the fact, that the community was paralyzed, and so wholly destitute of force that had the government then found occasion to call upon the whole 32,000,000 for a sum so small as even a single hundred millions, it could scarcely have at all been furnished.

Nevertheless, hardly had Mr. Buchanan left the seat of government when three-fifths of the nation, numbering but 20,000,000, commenced the erection of the grandest monument the world has ever seen; one that during the whole five years that have since elapsed has, on an average, required the services of more than a million of men, or more than five per cent. of the total population, male and female, sick and well, young and old. Not only have those services been given, but during all that time the men employed have been well clothed, abundantly fed, and furnished with transportation to an extent, and in a perfection, unparalleled in the history of the world. With them, too, have been carried all the materials required for making the edifice in whose construction they were engaged as durable as we know to have been the great pyramids erected by Egyptian monarchs. A wonderful work was it to undertake. More wonderful is it to see that it has been so soon and so well accomplished, to stand in all the future as the monument par excellence of human power.

Whence came the extraordinary force that we see to have been thus exerted? How was it that a people which in 1860 had been so very feeble could in the succeeding years have made donations to the extraordinary extent of a thousand millions of dollars a year ? The answer to this question is found in the fact that the conditions of national existence had wholly changed, activity and life having succeeded to paralysis, and the societary circulation having become strong and vigorous to an extent that had never before in any community been known. For the first time there was presented for examination a nation in which the demand for labor and all its products went ahead of the supply, enabling both farmer and planter to "stop the interest" upon capital that had so long been petrified in the crudest forms of agricultural production, and thus to enable them to make demand for the products of other labor applied to the development of our mineral wealth, and to the conversion into commodities fitted for human use, of the products of our hills and valleys, our farms and mines. The secret, gentlemen, of all the force that recently has been so well exerted—a force so extraordinary as to have astonished the world at large—is to be found in that simple principle to which I already have referred, evidence of whose truth is found in the books of every trader of your great city, and which is found embodied in words already given—the power of accumulation exists in the ratio of the rapidity of circulation.

What, however, was the force applied? Why was it that activity had so instantaneously succeeded to apathy—that life and energy had replaced the paralysis that had till then existed? Had these questions been put a year since, nine-tenths of our people would have said that it had been caused by the demands of the government and must terminate with their cessation; and yet, of all the vast body of men who might thus have answered there could not have been found even a single one who could have explained how the abstraction from other pursuits of the labor of a million of men, and the necessity for feeding and clothing them while engaged in the erection of such a monument as that of which I have spoken, could, by any possibility, have produced the extraordinary effects that have been here observed.

To attribute the activity and life then existing to the government demands is to substitute effect for cause. It was the force resulting from an activity of circulation wholly unprecedented in history that enabled the government to make the war, and that force existed in despite, and *not* as a consequence, of governmental necessities. That such was certainly the fact will, as I think, be clearly obvious when you shall reflect, that but for those necessities the whole million of men employed in building our great monument might have been employed in clearing land; sinking shafts; mining coal and ores and combining the two in the forms of lead, copper, and iron; making bricks and lumber; and thus furnishing supplies of raw materials to be converted on the spot into thousands of mills and shops, large and small, and into the cloth and iron, spades and shovels, coats and hats, required for supplying a population among whom the demand for mental and physical force so far exceeded the supply as to make it absolutely necessary to build engines by tens of thousands, and thus to substitute, to the annual extent of the power of tens of millions of men, the wonderful force of steam for that of the human arm. So applied, that same force would have produced annually of commodities in excess of what has been our actual production, at least $3,000,000,000, every portion of which would have been in the market seeking to purchase labor, thus greatly increasing the laborer's reward. The power of accumulation would, under such circumstances, have been more than trebly great, with steady decline in the rate of interest, and in the power of the capitalist to control the laborer's movements; freedom, wealth, power, and civilization, always growing with the growth of power to place the consumer by the side of the producer, and thus to increase the rapidity of the societary circulation.

That the wonderful activity of that circulation did not result from the necessities of the Government will, as I think, be clear to all who carefully reflect on the facts above presented. Whence, then, came it? From the adoption at Chicago, six years since, by the great Republican party, of a resolution to the effect that the produce of the farm should no longer be compelled to remain inert and losing interest while waiting demand in distant markets; that the capital which daily took the form of labor power should no longer bè allowed to go to waste; that the fuel which underlies our soil should no longer there remain to be a mere support for foreign rails; that the power which lay then petrified in the form of coal should everywhere be brought to aid the human arm; that our vast deposits of iron ore should be made to take the form of engines and other machinery to be used as substitutes for mere muscular force; and that all our wonderful resources, material and moral, must and should be at once developed. Such, gentlemen, was the intent and meaning of the brief resolution then and there adopted, to be at the earliest practicable moment ratified by Congress, as proved to be the case when the Morrill Tariff, on the memorable 2d of March, 1861, was made the law of the land. To that law, aided as it was by the admirable action of the Treasury in supplying machinery of circulation, we stand now indebted for the fact that we have, in the short space of five years, and at a cost of thousands of millions of dollars, erected the wonderful monument of which I have spoken; that we have, in those same years, produced more food, built more houses and mills, opened more mines, constructed more roads than ever before; and so greatly added to the wealth of the country that the property of the loyal States would this day exchange for twice the quantity of gold than could five years since have been obtained for all the real and personal property, southern chattels excepted, of the whole of the States and territories of which the Union stands composed.

The view thus presented of our power of accumulation throughout the period of Mr. Lincoln's administration differs widely from that which commonly is entertained; and yet, when you shall have reflected upon the facts which I shall now present, you will, as I feel assured, agree with me in the belief that it has not been overrated. It is probably true, as is so frequently asserted, that less than the average number of city houses has been built, but the growth of towns and villages in your vicinity has been great beyond all former precedent. Look, however, to the coal and iron regions —to the oil region of the Ohio and its tributaries—and to the wonderful mineral one beyond the Mississippi, and you will find that there have been there created homes for millions of men, their wives and children. Little cotton machinery, it is true, has recently been built, but you have more than doubled your power to produce both wool and woollen cloth. Rolling mills now exist capable of furnishing annually 750,000 tons of bars, while the power by means of which those bars are to be converted into ships, engines, and other machinery of transportation and production has more than doubled, and has, probably, even trebled. Factories have been created capable of supplying almost the world's demand for various instruments of production or defence; sewing machines on the one hand, pistols, rifles, and Parrott guns on the other. The quartz mills have been created to which we are now, as we are assured, to look for an immediate production of the precious metals to the annual extent of $200,000,000. For every engine five years since there are now, as I think, more than three at work. Throughout the vast fields of the west machines are everywhere doing the work that five years since was done by human hands. Fewer miles of railroad may have been constructed, but the rolling stock of all has been so much increased that the power of transportation throughout the loyal States has more than doubled. St. Louis presents to-day, as we are told, an amount of steam tonnage two-fifths greater than there existed before the war; and yet, so great has been the quantity of produce seeking to go to market that the Pennsylvania Central, at Pittsburg, within the present month, has been blocked by 2500 loaded cars, for the movement of which no power could be supplied. Look, then, in what direction we may, whether to the greater or smaller machinery of production, we witness an increase of quantity so great as fully to warrant us in the belief that, leaving wholly out of view the sums invested in loans to cities, counties, States, and to the general government, at no period has the power of accumulation been much more than half as great as it has been shown to be in the years of the great war that has now so happily terminated.

Adding together the capital that was only paralyzed to that which was absolutely wasted in the period of Mr. Buchanan's administration, we obtain an amount thrice greater than would, had it been so applied, have built and stocked as many mills as are in all Great Britain employed in the conversion of wool and cotton into cloth—as many furnaces as there are occupied in converting coal and ore into lead, copper, and iron—and as many mills as are now engaged in producing bars; to sink as many shafts as would have been required for giving to human labor all the aid that there is seen to result from a consumption of coal which is said to furnish power to an extent equivalent to that of six hundred millions of men; and to double the quantity and money value of our various products, to the great advantage of all our people, borrowers and lenders, employers and workmen, traders and manufacturers, builders of railroads and owners of ships, there being a perfect harmony of all real and permanent interests. A part, and but a small part, of that capital has, by means of a National Free Trade System, since been saved; and it is out of the saving that has thus been brought about that we have been enabled to give to the great work above referred to labor and commodities equal in their annual money value to the vast sum of $1,000,000,000.

In proof of the accuracy of the views above presented, I propose now to offer for your consideration a very brief review of our industrial history for the last half century, as follows :—

Half a century since, the second war with Great Britain came to a close, leaving our people well provided with mills and furnaces, all of which were actively engaged in making demand for labor and raw materials of every kind. Money was then abundant, labor was in demand, wages were high, and the public debt was trivial in amount.

Two years later came the system which looked to increasing our dependence on foreign markets and known as the British Free Trade one, and at once all was changed. Mills and furnaces were closed; labor ceased to be in demand; and poor-houses were everywhere filled. Money becoming scarce and interest high, land declined to a third of its previous price. Banks stopped payment. The sheriff everywhere found full demand for all his time, and mortgagees entered everywhere into possession. The rich were made richer, but the farmer and the mechanic, and all but the very rich, were ruined. Trivial as were then the expenses of the Government, the Treasury could not meet them. Such was the state of things that induced General Jackson to ask the question, "Where has the American farmer a market for his surplus produce?" The answer thereto, as given by himself, is so applicable to the present time that I give it here as proper to be read, daily and weekly, by every lover of his country throughout the Union :—

"Except for cotton, he has neither a foreign nor a home market. Does not this clearly prove, when there is no market either at home or abroad, that there is too much labor employed in agriculture, and that the channels of labor should be multiplied? Common sense at once points out the remedy. Draw from agriculture the superabundant labor, employ it in mechanism and manufacture, thereby creating a home market for your breadstuffs, and distributing labor to a most profitable account, and benefits. to the country will result. Take from agriculture in the United States six hundred thousand men, women, and children, and you at once give a home market for more breadstuffs than all Europe now furnishes us. In short, we have been too long subject to the policy of the British merchants. It is time we should become a little more Americanized, and, instead of feeding the paupers and laborers of Europe, feed our own, or else in a short time, by continuing our present policy, we shall become paupers ourselves."

To the state of things here described were we, in 1828, indebted for the first adoption of a National Free Trade System. Almost from the moment of the passage of the tariff act of that year, activity and life took place of the palsy that previously had existed. Furnaces and mills were built; labor came into demand; immigration increased, and so large became the demand for the products of the farm that our markets scarcely felt the effect of changes which then occurred in that of England; the public revenue grew with such rapidity that it became necessary to exempt from duty tea, coffee, and many other articles; and the public debt was finally extinguished.

The history of the world to that moment presents no case of prosperity so universal as that which here existed at the date of the repeal of the great national tariff of 1828. Had it been maintained in existence, not only should we have had no secession war, but at, this hour the South would exhibit a state of society in which the landowners had become rich while their slaves had been gradually becoming free, with profit to themselves, to their owners, and to the nation at large. It was, however, by successive stages, repealed in 1834, 1836, and following years, that repeal being accompanied by a constant succession of free trade crises, the whole ending in 1842 in a state of things directly the reverse of that above described. Mills and furnaces were closed; mechanics were starving; money was scarce and dear; land had fallen to half its previous price; the sheriff was everywhere at work; banks were in a state of suspension; States repudiated payment of their debts; the Treasury, unable to borrow at home even a single million at any rate of interest, was compelled to solicit credit at the doors of all the great banking houses of Europe, and to submit to finding that credit denied; and bankruptcy among merchants and traders was so universal that Congress found itself compelled soon after to pass a bankrupt law.*

Again, and for the third time, was the National System restored by the passage of the Tariff Act of 1842. Under it, in less than five years, the production of iron rose from 220,000 to 800,000 tons; and so universal became the prosperity that, large as was the increase, it was wholly insufficient to meet the great demand. Mines were everywhere being sunk. Mills were everywhere being built. Money was so abundant and cheap that the sheriff found but little work to do. Public and private revenues were great beyond all previous precedent, and throughout the land there reigned a prosperity more universal than had, in the whole history of the world, ever before been known.

Once more, in 1846, however, did the Serpent—properly represented on that occasion by British free traders—make his way into Paradise, and now a dozen years elapsed in the course of which, notwithstanding the discovery

* On the 12th of January, 1843, Mr. Walter Forward, then Secretary of the Treasury, reported to Congress the result of negotiations for a loan of $3,500,000; which negotiations were begun in April, 1842. But two bids had been made for this loan, one of 50,000 and one of 60,000 dollars; both at 96 per cent., for a six per cent. twenty years' stock. The Secretary in a special report to Congress said: "The repeated failures incurred in negotiating at home upon advantageous or creditable terms suggested the policy of sending an agent abroad for the purpose of endeavoring to effect a favorable negotiation in England or upon the Continent. Accordingly, a gentleman of the highest consideration for intelligence and integrity was selected for the purpose, and left the United States in July last. I regret to communicate that he has since returned without effecting the object of his mission."—*N. A. Review,* Jan., 1865.

of California mines, money commanded a rate of interest higher, as I believe, than had ever been known in the country for so long a period of time. British iron and cloth came in and gold went out, and with each successive day the dependence of our farmers on foreign markets became more complete. With 1857 came the culmination of the system, merchants and manufacturers being ruined; banks being compelled to suspend payment; and the treasury being reduced to a condition of bankruptcy nearly approaching that which had existed at the close of the free trade periods commencing in 1817 and 1834. In the three years that followed labor was everywhere in excess; wages were low; immigration fell below the point at which it had stood twenty years before; the home market for food diminished, and the foreign one proved so utterly worthless that the annual export to all the manufacturing nations of Europe, as has been already shown, amounted to but little more than $10,000,000.

Why was this? Why had not the foreign demand for food grown with the growth of our dependence on foreigners for cloth and iron? Because the British Free Trade System is in truth and in fact a monopoly one! Because it is based on the idea of stimulating competition for the sale of labor and thus enslaving the laborer; stimulating competition for the sale of the fruits of the earth, and thus enslaving every community that refuses to resist it!* At the moment of which I speak, notwithstanding the vast supplies of Californian and Australian gold, the money value of British labor had, on the average, scarcely at all increased, while foreign competition for the supply of food to the diminutive British market had reduced its price to a lower point than, as I believe, it had reached for half a century before.

The rebellion came, finding our people unemployed, public and private revenues declining, the Treasury empty, and the public credit greatly impaired. With it, however, came the power once again, and for the fourth time, to obtain a re-establishment of that National System required for protection of the men who had food and labor for which they needed to find a market. That protection has now endured for less than five years, and yet, as has been shown, so marvellous have been its effects that while it has enabled us to give to the government four thousand millions of dollars, it has so largely added to the value of land and labor that, notwithstanding the destruction of property in the South, the nation, as a whole, is this day almost twice as rich as it had been before.

---

* Of the amount paid by the British people for sugar, tea, coffee, and tobacco, not even one-eighth part reaches the poor people who produce those articles. The other seven-eighths are divided between the government and the middlemen, the former taking little short of a hundred millions of dollars. This it is that is called free trade! Under it the producer of cloth finds himself deprived of the power to buy sugar, while the sugar producer goes naked because unable to buy himself a shirt.

The history of the period thus reviewed may now more briefly thus be stated :—

The National Free Trade System, as established in 1813, 1828, 1842, gave, as that of 1861 is now prepared to give, to its British Monopoly successor—	The British Monopoly System, as established in 1817, 1834, 1846, and 1857, bequeathed to its successor—
Great demand for labor.	Labor everywhere seeking to be employed.
Wages high and money cheap.	Wages low and money high.
Public and private revenues large.	Public and private revenues small, and steadily decreasing.
Immigration great, and steadily increasing	Immigration declining.
Public and private prosperity great beyond all previous precedent.	Public and private bankruptcy nearly universal.
Growing national independence.	Growing national dependence.

Such is the history of the past. Let our people study it and they will, as I think, understand the causes of the prosperity of the present. That done, let them determine for themselves whether to go forward in the direction of individual and national independence, or in that of growing dependence, both national and individual.

THE TRADER who studies it can scarcely fail to see, that the more active the capital of the country, the greater the variety of pursuits, and the greater the demand for human service, the larger must be production; the greater must be the quantity of things to be exchanged; the less must be the necessity for resorting to trade as affording almost the only means of support; the less must be the competition among traders themselves; and the greater the probability of his securing independence for his children and himself.

THE MERCHANT can scarcely fail to see, that the greater the diversification of pursuits among our people, and the more we finish our products so as to fit them for consumption, the greater must be the variety of commodities with which to supply the world; the greater our demand for the products of distant countries; and the more numerous the markets open to his operations whether as a seller or a buyer.

THE SHIPOWNER can scarcely fail to see—

I. That the larger the demand for labor the greater must be the immigration of men who have labor to sell, and the greater the demand for ships:

II. That the more active the capital of the country the lower must be the average rate of interest, and the greater his power to compete with owners of foreign ships:

III. That the more active that capital the more numerous will be the finished commodities to be carried abroad; the greater the number of markets to which he can send his ships; and the greater the demand for sugar, tea, coffee, and raw materials of manufactures, products of countries which have no ships:

IV. That, on the contrary, the more sluggish that capital the higher must be the rate of interest; the more must we be limited to the export of raw produce; the fewer must be our markets; and the more must he find himself compelled to compete with the low rates of interest, and the low wages paid by owners of British and German ships:

V. That since the introduction of steam the question of navigation has become, and must from day to day more become, a mere question of the rate at which capital can be supplied; and, that if we are ever to resume upon the ocean the place so lately occupied, it can be only as a consequence of the pursuit of a policy tending towards bringing the consumer and the producer together, thereby quickening the motion of capital in the forms of food and of mental and muscular force, and thus promoting accumulation.

THE RAILROAD KING can scarcely fail to see—

I. That the more rapid the societary circulation the greater must be the quantity of men and things needing to be carried:

II. That the more rapid the development of our great mineral deposits, the greater must become the general supply of iron, and the more the tendency to a fall in price:

III. That all experience tends to furnish evidence of the facts, that foreign iron is always low in price when American iron masters are prosperous, and always high when American furnaces are out of blast:

IV. That, as a consequence, American railroads have always prospered when the internal commerce was rapidly growing; and have been always greatly depressed when in obedience to the orders of foreign traders that commerce has been sacrificed.

THE LANDOWNER can scarcely fail to see, that when capital is active interest is low and labor is in great demand; and that then it is that foreign capital and foreign labor tend, to his great advantage, here to seek employment.

THE FARMER can scarcely fail to see, that the greater the home consumption of his products the less must he be compelled to compete in England with the agricultural nations of Europe; the higher must be prices in that regulating market; and the higher must be those of the great domestic one.

THE MANUFACTURER of the East can scarcely fail to see, that the more our mineral resources are developed, and the more the people of the South and West give themselves to the production of the coarser kinds of cloth, the greater must be the demand upon himself for those more profitable of a higher order.

THE BANKER can scarcely fail to see, that all our financial crises, and all the losses thence resulting, have occurred in British free trade times; and that all that is needed for securing us against their recurrence in the future, is the thorough adoption of a policy tending to promote rapidity in the societary circulation.

THE PHILANTHROPIST can scarcely fail to see, that the more rapid that circulation the greater must be the tendency towards improvement in the condition of the laborer, black or white.

THE FINANCE MINISTER can scarcely fail to see, that the power permanently to contribute to the support of government has always existed, and must necessarily exist, in the direct ratio of the rapidity of the circulation.

THE BONDHOLDER can scarcely fail to see, that repudiation has always come as a consequence of an arrest of the circulation, and that perfect security for his children and himself can be found in one direction, and one alone; that which leads to more perfect combination among our people as a consequence of bringing the consumer and producer more and more near together.

The ECONOMIST can scarcely fail to see, that the British free trader seeks to place himself between all the producers and consumers of the world, and to enrich himself at their expense; and that the real road to national wealth and power lies in the direction of resistance to that system.

THE STATESMAN can scarcely fail to see, that our periods of national weakness have been always those in which consumers and producers have been becoming more widely separated, while our periods of strength have been those in which we have had a National System; as when, thirty years since, by aid of the tariff of 1828, we finally extinguished the national debt; as when twenty years since, by aid of the tariff of 1842, we resumed the payment of interest on our foreign debt; and as now, when we have just completed the erection of the greatest and most costly monument the world has ever seen, or perhaps will ever see.

THE MAN in whom there exists any feeling of national pirde can hardly fail to see, that the one great obstacle standing in the way of the permanent establishment of a sound National System has been the opposition of foreigners, and of that people especially which has recently been most active and most untiring in its effort to aid the South in breaking up the Union.

THE WHOLE PEOPLE can scarcely fail to see, that human force, mental and muscular, is the commodity which all have to sell; that it exhausts itself on the instant of production; that the more instant the demand for it the more is it economized, the greater is the power of production, the higher the rate of wages, the greater the power of accumulation, the lower the rate of interest, and the greater the tendency towards freedom and peace, both at home and abroad.

THE CHRISTIAN can scarcely fail to see, that the policy which tends towards increase in the rapidity of circulation tends necessarily towards increasing the reward of labor and effecting an improvement in the condition, material and moral, of the laborer; and that in advocating it he is aiding towards carrying into practical effect the great precept which lies at the foundation of Christianity, ALL THINGS WHATSOEVER YE WOULD THAT MEN SHOULD DO TO YOU, DO YE EVEN SO TO THEM.

The views thus presented differ widely from those taught to the world by that English school which holds that "the smuggler is the great reformer of the age;" and by those of its disciples who have recently throughout our southern coast carried their theories into practical effect. The cause of difference is to be found in this, that while the policy urged by it upon the outer world is directly the reverse of what is practised by every Manchester manufacturer, that National Free Trade policy to which we owe our recent great success and our present prosperity is in full accordance with the practice of every successful mechanic, manufacturer, and agriculturist throughout the civilized world. What is it that these latter desire? Is it not to economize human service? To that end are they not profuse in the application of food and clothing to the creation of machinery, thereby substituting the *products* of labor and capital for labor itself? Does not capital everywhere grow in the direct ratio of that substitution, and does not that growth make new demands for human labor, with constant tendency towards increased production, increase of wages, and increased ability to make still further substitution of capital for labor? To these questions there can be no reply but in the affirmative.

Nevertheless, when we study the writings of British economists, we find them filled with advice in reference to the saving of *products* in the form of money, leaving wholly out of view that *labor* is economized in the direct ratio of the rapid consumption of its products. Say to them that the waste labor of Ireland in a single year would more than suffice to give to the Irish nation mills and machinery for the conversion of all the cotton produced in America, and they reply by saying, that Manchester furnishes shirts to the Irish laborer more cheaply than could be done by men who should employ Irish labor and Irish fuel in making cloth for Irish wear. Prove to them, on the highest free trade authority, that in those parts of Russia in which employments are not diversified the condition of the free laborer is worse than that of the serf, and they ask your attention to the low price at which they supply coats and hats. Show them, as I myself did, some years since, to Mr. Cobden, that we were steadily giving more and more food and cotton in exchange for less and less gold, tin, copper, and iron, and they will reply, as he did to me, by asking, "Do we not now furnish iron cheaply enough to satisfy you?"

Talk with an American disciple of that school, of the pauperism that has always here existed in the British Monopoly times, and he replies, as recently was done by one of your own high authorities, by exhibits of the high prices of steel pens! Tell him that of all labor-saving machinery the precious metals are the greatest, and then invite his attention to the enormous rate paid for their use throughout the whole period of Mr. Buchanan's administration, and he will be likely to answer by showing at how low a price Britain had been willing to supply with cloth people who, unable to sell their labor, could scarcely purchase food! Need we then wonder that by that school the field of economical science has recently been so reduced in its proportions that it is now limited to the consideration of the mere acts of buying cheaply and selling dearly, having thus become a sort of shopkeeping science, the natural product of a policy that so long has tended, to use the words of Adam Smith, to the creation of a "nation of mere shopkeepers"? Scarcely so, as I think.

The one commodity, as we know, that all men have to sell is muscular and mental force, and that must be sold on the instant, or it is forever lost. The Irish people, on an average, waste nine-tenths of it, and while they shall continue so to do Ireland must remain in the pitiable condition in which she stands now before the world. Under the administration of Mr. Buchanan two-thirds of it were wasted here, and to that waste were we indebted for the pauperism of our people and the weakness of the government five years since. To the economy of it that resulted from the adoption of a National Free Trade System, and to that alone, do we stand to-day indebted for the wonderful changes we since have seen; and yet, strange to say, you have among you men of both intelligence and influence who are urging upon the country a return to that British Monopoly System which, under the mask of free trade, has not only paralyzed us on every occasion on which we have been subjected to it, but has ruined every friend that Britain has ever had, and every country that she has so long controlled as to give to it opportunity for proving the full extent of its capacity for mischief.

The world has been always word-governed, and so is it now, the word most in use for that purpose being that to which reference has above been made, to wit, "free trade." Such being the case, it may not be amiss here to inquire what it is that, as used, it really means. To that end let us examine the movements of the people here around us, and ascertain who among them it is that enjoy the most perfect freedom of trade; thus, in accordance with the true method of science, studying the near with a view to proper comprehension of the distant. Doing this, we shall be sure to find it among those who have the most direct relation with the consumers of their products. Take, for instance, the *Times*, *Tribune*, *Herald*, and *Post*, and see how entirely impossible it would be for any person, or persons, in any manner to control, to his own profit, their course of action. Ask their editors, and you will soon learn how fully they appreciate the fact that their success in the present and in the future is dependent wholly on themselves, and cannot be seriously affected by any outside action. Retailing the services of their journals, and the journal itself, their owners suffer little, if at all, at a time of crisis, nor do they ever figure among the creditors of bankrupts. Look, I pray you, throughout your city and see if you can elsewhere find any producing interest that is so entirely independent. As I think you cannot.

Take next those printers who, like the Messrs. Harper, make and sell their own books, and you will find a state of things precisely similar.

All that they need, as they well know, is good judgment in the selection of books, good taste in their manufacture, and sound discretion in the mode of bringing them to the knowledge and within the reach of the public.

Compare now with them the printer who works for publishers, the maker of printing paper, or the binder of books, and you will find a state of things most widely different. Perfectly familiar, throughout a large portion of my life, with everything connected with both paper and books, I can safely say that I know of scarcely any pursuits in which those engaged have been more dependent on the will of others, in which so few have accumulated fortunes, or in which there has existed less real freedom of trade. To what now is this to be attributed? To the simple fact that all the products of the labors of these men are required to pass through the hands of middle-men before they can reach the public. In common with all others, those middle-men rejoice when the demand for paper diminishes; when the raw materials of books accumulate; and when the necessities of their producers force them to sell at prices that yield no profit, and at credits so prolonged as to involve in risk of ruin all who are compelled to give them. The nearest approach to serfdom that I know to exist in civilized life is that of the men who are engaged in departments of manufacture whose products have yet to pass through several hands before they can reach those of the consumer.

Precisely so is it with nations. France finishes all her products, combining food, wool, and silk, and enabling the compounds readily to reach every country, every city, and every village of the world. Of all countries there is, therefore, none so independent. Hostile tariffs scarcely at all affect her commerce. Short crops, or wars abroad, affect her least; and for the reasons that her market is everywhere, and that such occurrences in one country find, to a great extent, their compensations in another. Her position in relation to the world at large is, therefore, precisely that of the proprietors of your journals. So long as both shall continue to furnish commodities better fitted than any other to meet the wants, or to gratify the tastes, of consumers, no laws that can be anywhere enacted can prevent them from supplying their accustomed markets.

Directly the reverse of this is what we find in those countries which export raw products. For them there is no market except in those countries which possess machinery of manufacture, wheat not being needed where there are no flour mills, nor cotton where there is none of the machinery required for spinning and weaving it. They *must* go where they *can*, and not where they would, their position being, therefore, precisely that of the printers and paper-makers above described. Thus limited in their markets they find themselves subjected to the will of those by whom these latter are controlled, by all of whom it is well known that the way to cheapen the commodities they need to purchase is to be found in working short time, diminishing the supply of money, and raising the rate of interest. In this manner are the people of all the countries that export raw produce kept in a state of dependence and made mere "hewers of wood and drawers of water" for men whose profits grow as theirs decline; and this is urged upon them by England as being a real freedom of trade. The day may come, and I cannot but hope that it soon will do so, when it shall be understood that its real meaning is monopoly; that the real free traders are those who advocate the National Free Trade System; that the road to civilization lies in the direction of that diversified industry which tends to bring the consumers into close relation with the producers; and that the raising of raw products for the supply of foreign markets is the proper employment of the barbarian and the slave, and of those alone.

Of all the communities that have at any time existed none has ever had in its hands so much power for good or evil as now is held by the one of which we are a part. With natural resources great almost beyond imagination we need only the labor and the capital required for their full development. For the one we do not need to look beyond those vast deposits of petrified power which lie beneath the soil, a single bushel taken from which is capable of doing the work of hundreds of men. Of the other the supply will be found in vast abundance whenever the nation shall come to learn, first, that corn and cotton unconsumed are so much dormant capital waiting only consumption to spring once again into activity and life; and, second, that labor power, mental and muscular, is so much capital that perishes on the instant of its production, and if not then consumed is lost forever.

We do not, therefore, need to seek abroad supplies of either capital or labor. Both, however, abound in various countries of Europe, and have always proved ready to come to us when we have pursued a policy tending to economize labor, to increase the supply of capital, and thus to lower the rate of interest—the immigration of both having largely grown under the National Free Trade policy of 1828, 1842, and 1861; and that of both having declined under the British Monopoly System established by the tariffs of 1834, 1846, and 1857. The more productive labor here the greater then must be the tendency towards emigration from Europe, and towards elevation of the laborer there. The greater the accumulation of capital and the more perfect the national and individual credit here, the greater must be the tendency towards export of European capital, and reduction of the rate of interest here. For the production of such results, beneficial to the world at large, we need but steadily to pursue that course which most stimulates the societary circulation; that one which tends most to enable the farmer and the planter to "stop the interest" on their products, and the laborer to find instant demand for the power he has to sell.

Such are OUR RESOURCES. Infinite in their extent, it is to their development thus far accomplished under the National Free Trade System that we have been indebted for our passage through a trial extraordinary far beyond any to which any nation of the world had before been subjected. The work, however, has but just begun. Let us continue onward in the same direction, and we shall find that the capital invested in the great monument of which I have spoken has proved as good an investment as that of the New York canals, the result of its erection having been that of giving to the loyal states the power to make themselves, and for the first time, really independent; as has already been the case to an extent that five years since could not have been anticipated. Let us so continue, and we shall find that the annual addition to the national capital, by means of labor and interest saved by individuals, will soon be fifty-fold greater than the amount of interest required to be paid from the treasury of the Government by which those individuals are represented.

In conclusion, allow me now to ask your attention to the great fact that commercial power has always gone hand in hand with that diversification of pursuits which has everywhere resulted from measures tending to the promotion of internal commerce. Athens, with her miners and manufacturers, governed the Grecian world. Carthage, largely manufacturing, controlled the commerce of half the then known world. Holland was mistress of the commercial world in those days when the people of the Rhine cities could boast, "that they bought of the stupid Englishman skins at sixpence and paid for them in tails at a shilling." England, wiser-grown, now does the same by us, and she it is that now controls the commercial world outside of Europe, leaving to industrial France the management of Europe itself. Such is the lesson taught by history, and we must now profit by it or abandon for ever the hope of occupying the proud position to which our natural resources so well entitle us. To it we never can attain so long as we shall continue to sell, as we so long have sold, whole skins for sixpence, accepting pay in tails at a shilling each. That is *not* the road towards civilization, power, and influence. That it *is* the one which leads to barbarism, weakness, and dependence, is proved by the experience of all communities that have travelled on it; and by none more thoroughly than our own. Should proof of this now be needed, let me ask you to study the present condition of the prostrate South, and see how readily the great Cotton King has been dethroned by the united efforts of the hammer, the spindle, and the loom. That done, turn your eyes to the west and study the recent prostration of almost the whole people of the great Mississippi Valley before a few insignificant capitalists, who were thus to be propitiated into giving to their obedient slaves an additional road to the British market. Those who desire to command the respect of others must learn to respect themselves; and that our people can never do until they shall first have learned that the road towards wealth and strength has, in all nations, and at all ages, been found to lie in the direction of bringing the plough, the loom, the anvil, and the ship to work in harmony with each other. Let them, gentlemen, once learn thoroughly that great lesson, and then, but not till then, will they be enabled to control and direct the commerce of the world.

THE

PUBLIC DEBT, LOCAL AND NATIONAL:

HOW TO PROVIDE FOR ITS DISCHARGE

WHILE

LESSENING THE BURTHEN OF TAXATION.

LETTER TO DAVID A. WELLS, ESQ.,
CHAIRMAN OF THE BOARD OF REVENUE COMMISSIONERS:

BY

HENRY C. CAREY.

PHILADELPHIA:
HENRY CAREY BAIRD,
INDUSTRIAL PUBLISHER,
306 WALNUT STREET.
1866.

LETTER TO D. A. WELLS, ESQ.,

CHAIRMAN OF THE BOARD OF COMMISSIONERS FOR THE REVISION OF THE
REVENUE LAWS.

DEAR SIR :—

BELIEVING the real and permanent interests of tax payers and public creditors to be in perfect harmony with each other, and that error in regard to one must be productive of injury to both, I have put on paper my views as to the proper mode of dealing with the principal of the public debt, and have now to ask of you to give to them that consideration they may seem to you to merit.

The amount required by the general government for current expenses, interest included, may be taken, as I suppose, at $280,000,000, and to meet that demand, with reasonable allowance for occasional drawbacks, it might be necessary so to arrange our revenue system as to warrant us in expecting from it ten or twenty millions more; say 290 or 300 millions. It has, however, been proposed that the annual sum of $200,000,000 be now, and in all the future so long as the debt shall continue to exist, set aside for payment of principal and interest alone—a proposition that, if adopted, will require that the revenue be so arranged as to enable us to look to it for fifty millions more, or in the whole at least 340, if not even 350 millions.

Two widely distinct modes of action are thus presented for consideration, by the one of which we should appear wholly to overlook the existence of the principal debt, while by the other we should appear to be making provision for its early annihilation ; and yet, after having given to the subject all the consideration demanded by its great importance, I have arrived at the conclusion that, while lessening by $50,000,000 the annual demand upon our people, the first of these is the one by which we should most speedily be relieved from all charge from either principal or interest of the great debt that has so recently and rapidly been created. My reasons for so believing shall now be given.

Widely different from any other recorded in history this was emphatically *a people's war*, waged for no purpose of conquest or of plunder, but purely and simply for that of perpetuating the Union and thus securing harmony of action throughout the vast territory over which now floats that star-spangled banner in whose defence has been expended so vast a quantity of both blood and treasure. As a consequence of this first great difference we find another and most essential one in the fact, that the contributions towards its maintenance, whether in the form of personal service or in that of the sinews of war, were in so large a proportion voluntary that the exceptions thereto scarcely merit the slightest notice. Men by hundreds of thousands sought the field of battle, while other men, their wives, and children, united in giving of their means, whether large or small, to the performance of the great work; the amount so given by individuals, at times directly and at others through the medium of sanitary and Christian commissions, or patriotic leagues, having reached, as there is reason to believe, an amount greater than the total receipts of the national treasury, those from loans included, during the period of Mr. Adams's administration, from 1825 to 1829, and that would now be undervalued in placing it at an hundred millions of dollars. States, counties, and cities united in the work, the amount voluntarily given by them having certainly exceeded $500,000,000. Of this large sum much was the produce of taxes specially imposed for maintenance of the war, the rest having been raised upon pledges of the credit of the various corporations, nearly all of which throughout the loyal States have proved themselves ever ready to make themselves responsible for whatsoever sums might seem required for enabling them to meet the demands of the general government. Taking then, at $600,000,000, the total amount of donations by individuals and corporations, it may, as I think, be regarded as nearly certain that 'one-half thereof, or $300,000,000, still remains a charge upon our people, involving payment of interest to the annual extent of little, if any, less than $20,000,000.

In some cases the debt still existing bears but small proportion to the total amount of contributions; whereas in others it is very large. In some, as I have seen it stated, no debt has been created; whereas in others the proportion actually discharged has been very small indeed. As a general rule, the more loyal the community the smaller is the proportion yet remaining to be paid.

The interest on this local war debt is probably little less than a seventh of that payable on the national debt. This would seem to be but a small proportion, yet is it really an enormous one when we reflect that the local governments have been stripped of nearly every source of revenue, except the lands and houses, mills, farmers and mines, that were before so heavily taxed for maintenance of schools and roads, poor-houses and prisons, and other matters with whose direction they stand charged. The effect of this now exhibits itself in the fact that local taxation has become almost trebly burthensome, and threatens to result in loss to owners of real estate little less than that which has been inflicted on those of the rebel States. Cases could readily be cited in which the proceeding even now falls little short of confiscation.

In others, where property has been but partially improved, the demands of the several governments absorb nearly the whole receipts, the burthen in every case becoming more and more severe with every step in the direction of appreciation in the value of that currency in which taxes must be paid. The farmer who in 1864 sold his corn for $1.50 per bushel, and his pork for $40 per barrel, finds it now, with prices in the East almost one-half reduced, much more difficult to pay the tax of transportation and those other taxes required for meeting the demands of those who have been so fortunate as to constitute themselves creditors of the general and local governments. How it must be in the future, if gold shall speedily become the standard, and if the price of food shall be reduced to   level with that of the diminutive British market, interest meanwhile having been carried up, as it is very like to be, to the rate that existed before the war, may, as I think, with certainty be predicted.*

* The average price of wheat in the London market, in 1863, as given in the Treasury Report, was $1.17 per bushel. That of the two succeeding years has been $1.02, or little more than half of the average for 1854 to 1857. Hams and bacon had, in 1863, already fallen from $11.50 to $7.20 per hundred-weight. Subsequently they participated with wheat in the further decline above exhibited. Throughout the two last years the average of wheat in the French markets has been about one dollar per bushel. The foreign demand for food having thus disappeared, the effect now exhibits itself in the facts here given as regards the corn of Illinois:—

"We understand that many of the people of Warren and other towns in the eastern part of the county are using corn for fuel. We had a conversation with an intelligent gentleman who has been burning it, and who considers it much cheaper than wood. Ears of corn can be bought for ten cents per bushel by measure, and seventy bushels, worth seven dollars, will measure a cord. A cord of wood, including sawing, costs $9.50, which is $2.50 more than the cost of a cord of corn, besides the fact that the corn produces more heat than the wood. If these statements are true (and we have no reason to doubt them), there is no fuel more economical than corn. The crop of corn this year is far beyond the demand."— *Galena Gazette.*

The British wheat crop of the last season having been deficient in both quality and quantity, prices in that market have slightly increased, the average of the first week of December, as given in the *Mark Lane Express*, having been $1.20 per bushel of 60 pounds. As a consequence of this, and of the cattle plague, there has been a slight demand for food of all descriptions for export to that market ; but how utterly contemptible it is when compared with the great domestic one is shown in the following table, exhibiting the receipts at New York since September 1, and the exports from that port to all the manufacturing nations of Europe :—

	Flour—barrels.	Wheat—bushels.	Corn—bushels.
Receipts . .	1,820,152	564,650	1,509,804
Exports . .	90,627	150,192	380,846

The prices obtained for the trivial quantity exported determine those of the whole crop, amounting to more than 1,200,000,000 of bushels. Had we made a market at home for all the food that we now export, the yield to our farmers on

Between the demands of the holders of private mortgages and public bonds on one hand, and those of transportation companies on the other, much of the real estate of the country will be very likely to pass through the sheriff's hands. The deficiency in the wheat crop of the past year has thus far saved the Western farmer, but when his eyes shall have once again been gladdened with the sight of crops so large as to make it necessary to look again to Europe for a market, he will certainly find it wholly impossible to meet the heavy demands that, if the local public credit is to be maintained, must then be made.* Even at the present moment some of the most important branches of our manufacturing industry, those which are making the largest demand for food, are wholly dependent for their continued existence on the fact that taxes on domestic products are payable in paper, while for payment of duties on competing foreign commodities the precious metals are required. Under such circumstances not only can there be no extension of such manufactures, but there is the greatest reason to apprehend that many of the establishments now in operation may be closed. With every step in that direction the farmer must become more and more dependent on those European markets which took of food from us, in the three years prior to the war, an average of but $10,000,000; and which, without our aid, are at present so over-supplied that bread may now be purchased at a price lower than has been known within the memory of any living man. Take from a dollar, the recent price in England of a bushel of wheat, the cost of freight from Illinois to Europe, the commissions, and all the heavy interest charged by various middlemen, and it will, as I think, be found that what will then remain to the farmer will scarcely enable him to live, leaving wholly out of view the payment of taxes required for meeting the demands of fortunate holders of city, county, State, and Federal bonds. At no time in the history of the country have the prospects of our farmers, if their dependence on European markets is to be maintained, been so bad as they are at the present hour.

To those who may doubt the accuracy of the views thus presented, I

the last year's crop would be greater than it is by not less than $600,000,000. . The difference is the price they pay for dependence on the dimunitive market of Britain. To make a market for wheat equivalent to the one now afforded by Europe, and thus to economize all that vast difference, would require but a few such iron works as that of Cambria, Pennsylvania, the annual consumption of flour by whose people is no less than 20,000 barrels.

* The wheat crops of the three past years, and the prices of wheat and wheat flour in the New York market, have been as follows :—

		Bushels.	Price of Wheat.	Price of extra Western Flour
1863	. .	179,000,000	$1 57 to $1 75	$6 40 to $7 40
1864	. .	161,0 0,000	2 35 to 2 70	10 25 to 10 50
1865	. .	149,000,000	2 30 to 2 80	8 50 to 8 80

beg now to suggest consideration of the following facts. Twenty years since, the British government determined that the true way to *protect* its manufacturers was to be found in the direction of giving them cheap food. Since then, it has been unceasingly engaged in the effort to induce all the other nations of the world to send to its little market food to be exchanged for manufactures, the effect exhibiting itself in the fact that the British farmer now receives far less for his wheat than he did before the discovery of California gold; that he pays more for nearly all the commodities he needs to buy; and that the British agricultural laborer of the present day is a poorer and more dependent being than was his predecessor of the days of Adam Smith. Anxious to follow in the free trade direction, the economists of France sought to prove to their farming fellow-citizens that they were being taxed for the benefit of manufacturers; that they themselves were not in any manner protected; and that what they needed was perfect freedom for the introduction of British and German manufactures. In the last six years various commercial treaties have been negotiated, all looking in that direction, and the result is seen in the existence of an agricultural crisis, the discovery of a remedy for which is tasking the skill of French economists. In forty years the production of wheat has nearly doubled, and now much exceeds the home demand. England recently has needed little, and as a consequence of this the French farmer, like his English neighbor, has obtained less for his food, while obliged to pay a higher price for all the articles he consumed. Of this cheap foreign food we are now importing annually, in the form of cloth, silk, and iron, to the extent of almost hundreds of millions of dollars; and it is with that food that our farmers are expected to contend in British markets, paying all the cost of transportation thereto. How, out of the trifle that will remain, can they by any possibility pay all the heavy taxes, local and general, to which they are now subjected? It cannot be done, nor will it be.

In our cities the burthen of the war debt is, for the moment, less severely felt; but when we look to the fact that in the one in which I write the city government has found it necessary to claim no less than four per cent. upon the assessed value of real estate, and that upon this are piled the demands of the State and those of the Federal treasury, these latter taking the form of income taxes, taxes on successions, taxes on consumption so arranged as to be twice, thrice, and sometimes, as I believe, five times over repeated before we reach the final product—this last then subjected to a tax of six per cent.—we find ourselves somewhat prepared for consideration of the question as to what must come to be the money value of city property when all the farmer's products shall come to be sold at gold prices corresponding with those now paid in England—when coupons issued at a time when gold was selling at nearly three to one are to be redeemed in gold at par—and when the price of money shall, as it probably will, range once again between 10 and 30 per cent.

The power to contribute to the support of government increases as the societary circulation becomes more rapid, and declines as it becomes more sluggish. What is its present state is well exhibited in an editorial of the *New York Tribune*, now but a few days old, from which the following is an extract :—

"The commercial reports from the West are not favorable, and the activity of the winter of 1864–5 has been replaced by a dulness which forbids the hope of profit to traders or forwarding companies. The millers are comparatively idle, and pork and beef packing is upon a reduced scale. In this vicinity the condition of business is not satisfactory, and the balance-sheets of merchants, like those of railroads, will show large figures, but reduced net income, and in numerous cases none at all."

Throughout the war the government has been in alliance with the land-owner, the trader, the manufacturer, the laborer, and the borrower of money, against the lender of money and the receiver of fixed income; and to that alliance has the country been indebted for all its recent successes, as well as for its present position among the nations of the earth. The time for these latter seems, however, to have now almost arrived. Already the price of money has advanced at least one-half, while that of some of the most important articles of food has almost as much declined. Thus far, however, the change is as nothing compared with that which would already have been experienced had not our people, despite all threats to the contrary, arrived at the conclusion that the day was yet far distant when the holders of city, State, and Federal coupons would be entitled to claim in gold both principal and interest, that gold to be the produce of taxes paid by farmers who were receiving for their wheat and their corn less of the precious metals than they had been accustomed to receive before the discovery of the mineral resources of California or Australia.

The local taxation is even now most severe, but its severity must increase with every step in the direction that above is indicated; and with each there must be a diminution of the power of both farmer and laborer to contribute to the Federal revenue. With each must come an increased demand for assumption by the Union of local debts that, for war purposes, have been contracted, thereby adding to the demands upon the Federal treasury at the very moment when already existing claims can only with constantly increasing difficulty be met. Will that demand be complied with ? Will the Union now assume the debts of the various States and corporations that have co-operated with it in carrying on the war ? That it would not do so has been my full belief. That it should not do this I am very certain, and for the reason, that the direct effect of such a course of action would be that of imposing upon those who have already taxed themselves and paid their contributions, for the benefit of those others who have depended almost entirely upon loans, trusting to the future to provide the means of payment.* For this reason, and perhaps for others that might be named, the local burthens will be allowed to remain a charge upon the local revenues, to be carried until their weight shall have become unbearable, and to bring in their train financial revulsion to be followed, certainly, by a political revolution the most complete.

Must all these things occur? Is it needed that such should be the results of the wonderful and most successful war that has just been closed? It is not! No such necessity really exists, yet must they certainly occur if we fail now to inquire into the cause of the change that already has been produced. Doing this, we find it in the fact that domestic taxes have been so piled up, one upon another, that the movement of the societary machine has become much impeded—the protection granted by the tariff of 1861 having now been so far nullified that in very many cases little of it now remains except that which results from difference in value between the gold in which duties are paid, and the paper which is receivable in discharge of internal taxes.† Trivial, even, as that protection has now become, the threat is held out daily, and in leading Republican journals, that it shall endure no longer; and it is as a consequence of this that furnaces and rolling-mills no longer increase in number; that faith in our future has no longer that existence which throughout the war was so fully manifested; that money is abundant and cheap for short loans, but scarce and dear for those permanent investments in the growing number of which is always found the evidence of that confidence without which no real prosperity can exist; that the societary circulation becomes from day to day more sluggish; that our dependence on foreign workshops now increases; that the efflux of gold becomes more rapid; that our foreign debt grows most rapidly; that we are paying on government

---

* The public debt of Ohio, notwithstanding her vast expenditures, is less at the present moment than it was five years since. That of New York has grown from $33,000,000 to $51,000,000. The total war debt of this latter State, including that of cities and counties, is stated at more than $80,000,000.

Some of the counties of Pennsylvania have raised by taxes nearly the whole amount that has been required for war purposes. Others have borrowed the major part, and are now paying interest thereon. It is little likely that those who have already paid will consent to assumption by the State of the debts that others have incurred.

† The taxes on materials used in the book manufacture, and on the books themselves, are stated at 15½ per cent., on the cost of publication. Add to these the taxes on fuel, machinery, &c. &c., and we shall obtain a total of not less than 20 per cent. As a consequence of this, American publishers are now having their books printed in England. Without a change of system this great department of manufacture must inevitably be ruined.

securities a rate of interest most disgraceful and that must prove ruinous; and that there is a daily increasing certainty of the continued subjection of our farmers to the will of that European people which has so effectually taught to the agricultural nations of the world the advantage of competition for the possession of its miserably diminutive market that wheat there now commands but a single dollar for a bushel of sixty pounds weight. In fewer words, the cause of all the change may be found in this, that the alliance between the National Treasury and the *employers* of money—farmers, laborers, and mechanics—has been dissolved. The tendency of all our present measures lies in the direction of raising the rate of interest, to the great advantage of *lenders* of money; and in that of enabling the receivers of interest on the various public debts to obtain from the farmer more food, from the workman more clothing, and from the laborer more labor, for less and less of money.

That is certainly the road to ruin, and if we shall persist in the determination to travel on it, all the sad results that have above been indicated must assuredly be realized. That we may avoid them, it is needed that we dissolve the existing alliance between those who have merely *lent* their money to cities, counties, States, and to the National Treasury, and renew that which has heretofore existed between those who have *given* their time—*given* their services—*given* their means—for the public use. To that end we need to abolish all those taxes which now so seriously impede the societary circulation; all those which tend so much to prevent the application of capital in the direction of that development of our internal resources which would give value to land and enable its owner more readily to bear the heavy burthens that necessarily have been imposed upon it for payment of interest on the vast amounts *given* to the public service; all those which tend in any manner to lessen the demand for labor, and thus diminish demand for the farmer's products.

Freed from the income tax, the landowner would find less difficulty in providing for the maintenance and improvement of roads and schools. Relieved of the burthen now resulting from taxes on hats and coats, shirts and shoes, he could more readily increase the number of his ploughs and harrows, cheapened as these latter then would be by the abolition of taxes on coal and iron and all their products. With every step in this direction, mines and furnaces, factories and rolling-mills, would become more numerous, making demand for all the produce of his land and thus diminishing the necessity for going to distant markets; abolition of taxes on transportation and on machinery of transportation meanwhile co-operating with the growing cheapness of bars and engines in giving him increased ability to determine for himself whether to sell in the distant one or in that which is near, and also to determine for himself by what road he would go to the market he might prefer—freedom of trade and freedom of man thus following, as it always does, in the train of an increased rapidity in the societary circulation and increase of the societary force.

Taking at $300,000,000 the amount required for payment of interest on the national debt and for maintenance of the national government, we have a sum that could readily be raised by duties on foreign merchandise, by taxes on cotton, tobacco, whiskey, beer, and some few other commodities, and by aid of stamps—at once and forever abolishing the tax on incomes and all those taxes on manufactures which now so greatly tend towards production of the state of paralysis above described.

The adoption of such a measure as this would, it may be said, have the effect of greatly protracting the time at which the national debt would be discharged. Not so, however. On the contrary, it is the road towards the most speedy annihilation of the debt, all experience having shown that a merely arithmetical increase in the rapidity of the societary circulation is followed by an almost geometrical one in the power to contribute to the support of government. Throughout the period of Mr. Buchanan's administration it would have been impossible by any means that could have been devised to obtain an annual amount of contributions thirty millions in excess of that which we see to have been collected. Nevertheless, throughout that of his successor our people furnished to State, county, city, and national treasuries an excess of almost $1,000,000,000 a year! Why was this? Because of a wonderful activity of the circulation. Let us maintain that activity, and we shall find ourselves enabled in less than twenty years to annihilate liabilities greater than those of industrial France, which now, notwithstanding her 37,000,000 of population, actually staggers under the weight of the mere interest upon her debt. Let us do that, *and it can be done,* and we shall have achieved a triumph more wonderful even than that of the extraordinary years through which we last have passed.

Before proceeding to show how it is that this may be done, let me call your attention to the fact that, while our population has been accustomed to duplicate itself in twenty-four years, our production has been supposed to increase twice more rapidly, and to quadruple itself in the time required for the duplication of the other. That the power to contribute to the support of Government increases in a ratio greatly more rapid even than production is proved by the experience of every period of our history in which the policy of the country has tended to the promotion of domestic commerce, as in that ending in 1835, when we finally extinguished the national debt; as in that from 1842 to 1848, when we so rapidly passed from the state of exhaustion into which we had been brought by the British free trade provisions of the tariff of 1834, and thus prepared ourselves for the expenditures of the Mexican war; and still more recently when, close upon the heels of the almost bankruptcy of Mr. Buchanan's administration, we passed so nearly instantly to a state of things in which we were enabled to give to the general and local governments an amount of contributions larger than had ever before been given by any people of the world. So, too, is it proved by the experience of Great Britain, the revenue of that country having, in the short period of twenty years, from 1842 to 1862, grown from £48,000,000 to £72,000,-000, notwithstanding the exemption from taxation of 1,119 out of 1,163 articles that had previously been subjected to import duties.

The close of next twenty years is likely to exhibit almost a duplication of our numbers, production meantime having at least quadrupled. That it may do so it is needed that we at once relieve ourselves from all those taxes which now so greatly impede the internal commerce, and which compel us to look abroad for so many commodities that should be produced at home. Let that be done, and the remainder, calculated now to yield $300,000,000, will grow with such rapidity as to enable us, before that time shall have arrived, to extinguish all of that debt which now bears interest.

What is needed for the accomplishment of that object, and all that is needed, is that stimulation of the societary circulation by means of which every man who has labor, or labor's products, to sell, shall be enabled on the instant to find a purchaser for his commodity, be it of whatsoever sort it may. To that end we need that producer and consumer shall, as far as possible, take their places by each other, as has been the case throughout the past four years to an extent that we never before had known. At the present moment their exchanges are everywhere impeded by a taxation which becomes from day to day more oppressive, and now closely resembles that which existed in Great Britain less than half a century since, described by the Rev. Sydney Smith in the following words :—

"Taxes were piled on taxes, until they reached every article which enters into the mouth, or covers the back, or is placed under foot; taxes upon everything which it is pleasant to see, hear, feel, smell, or taste; taxes upon warmth, light, and locomotion; taxes on everything on earth, and in the waters under the earth; on everything that comes from abroad or is grown at home; taxes on the raw material; taxes on fresh value that is added to it by the industry of man; taxes on the sauce which pampers man's appetite, and the drug which restores him to health; on the ermine which decorates the judge, and the rope which hangs the criminal; on the poor man's salt and the rich man's spice; on the brass nails of the coffin and the ribbons of the bride; at bed or board, couchant or levant, we must pay.

"The school-boy whips his taxed top; the beardless youth manages his taxed horse with a taxed bridle, on a taxed road; and the dying Englishman, pouring his medicine which has paid seven per cent. into a spoon that has paid fifteen per cent., flings himself back upon the chintz bed which has paid twenty-two per cent., makes his will on an eight-pound stamp, and expires in the arms of an apothecary, who has paid a license of a hundred pounds, for the privilege of putting him to death. His whole property is then immediately taxed from two to ten per cent. Besides the probate, large fees are demanded for burying him in the chancel; his virtues are handed down to posterity on taxed marble; and he is then gathered to his fathers, to be taxed no more."

This was a terrible picture when it was first presented, many years since, to the view of the people of England. Equally terrible, and equally true, is it now, when presented for our consideration; and yet, as I propose here to show, it is really as nothing when compared with the tax resulting from dependence on the diminutive demands of manufacturing Europe. That this may be properly appreciated, let us take the facts of the past few years in reference to the wheat crop, and the demand made upon us for wheat and flour for the supply of European markets. The harvests of both England and France, in 1858 and 1859, were abundant, as a consequence of which the demand made upon us by them for food of all descriptions, for the three years ending with 1860, amounted, as has been already shown, to an annual average of only $10,000,000. As a consequence, prices here were very low; the farmers were everywhere in debt; money was at the highest rates; and the whole agricultural interest of the North was in a condition of extreme distress. The rebellion came, cutting off the Southern demand upon the West; but, almost as by a special intervention of Providence, the British and French crops of 1860 and 1861 proved to be failures, and thus enabled us to find abroad the market then lost at home. Since then, their crops have been very large, while ours have been declining, as follows:—

	1863.	1864.	1865.
Wheat crop, bushels	179,000,000	160,000,000	148,000,000
Average price in New York	$1 66	$2 52	$2 55
Product	$298,000,000	$403,000,000	$378,000,000

The yield of this last year having been less than of the first by 31,000,000, the product has increased no less than $80,000,000. Had it been otherwise—had the crop grown gradually until it had reached in this last year 200,000,000, thereby producing a necessity for dependence on those European markets in which the price had fallen to a dollar—must not that of our Eastern markets have been lower than had ever before been known? Most certainly such would have been the case. Had it so been, could we anywhere have found the hundreds of millions of revenue that have been paid in the past twelve months? Could we anywhere now find those others upon which we are counting for the current year? Assuredly not! The farmers could have purchased neither cloth nor iron, nor could they have paid the taxes on their land. They and the national treasury have been saved from ruin by the deficiencies of our two last years' crops. Is it right that this dependence on the mere accidents of European harvests should be permitted longer to continue? Should we not, by creating a great home market, enable our financiers to make more certain calculations of revenue, such as are made in France and England? That we must do so if we would avoid ruin, and early ruin, I regard as absolutely certain.

Every yard of cloth—every bar of iron—every pound of coal—imported from Europe, represents so much foreign food. Of that food we now import to the annual extent of almost hundreds of millions of dollars, while Europe now takes of us almost none, and while the reports just now published in reference to the productiveness of French agriculture are rendering it daily more and more certain that, except in some very extraordinary cases, France cannot only feed herself, but also readily and cheaply supply any deficiency that may hereafter arise in Britain.* Such being the case, where are we in the future to look abroad for markets? Nowhere! Such markets do not exist, and if we do not now determine to create them for ourselves, there must arise a state of things in which it will become utterly impossible to collect the means of defraying even the current expenditures of the general and local governments.

So rapid, under the tariff of 1842, was the growth of the cotton manufacture, that in 1848 it was asserted by the editor of the *Charleston Mercury* that before the lapse of a dozen years the South would have ceased to export raw cotton. What was then prophesied may now, with moderate exercise of judgment, be fully realized. A judicious use of the taxing power, accompanied by provisions securing repayment of the tax when the cotton should be exported in a manufactured state, would, in a few short years, transfer here nearly the whole of this great branch of manufacture, thereby securing to the government a constantly growing revenue, and to the planter a certain price that could never again, as I am well

---

* WHEAT CROP OF FRANCE.

Average of five years ending in—					Bushels.	Per head.
1821	.	.	.	.	50,000,000	1.62
1826	.	.	.	.	58,000,000	1.82
1831	.	.	.	.	58,000,000	1.79
1836	.	.	.	.	67,000,000	2.01
1841	.	.	.	.	69,000,000	2.00
1846	.	.	.	.	74,000,000	2.09
1851	.	.	.	.	85,000,000	2.36
1856	.	.	.	.	81,000,000	2.28
1861	.	.	.	.	99,000,000	2.69

Low as, in 1863, was the price of wheat in England, the export from France to that country, of wheat and wheaten flour, was the equivalent of 800,000 barrels of the latter. In the succeeding years it must have been even more than this, as the French price was below the English one. Greatly manufacturing as she is, France supplies England with much more food than, agriculturists as we are, we sell to the whole of Europe.

satisfied, fall below 30 cents per pound.   Let us, then, determine to mine
our own coal and make our own cottons and our own iron, as we are now
producing nearly all the wool and most of the woollen cloths we need,
and we shall thereby make a market for food so great as not only to
relieve our farmers from all necessity for looking to Europe for markets,
but also make demand for all the food of Canada.   In the ten years ending
with 1864, Great Britain increased her produce of coal from 64 to 92
millions of tons.   Let us do as much, and we might readily do more, and
we shall thereby make at home such a market for the products of the farm
as will add to the money value of our land, North and South, East and
West, so many thousands of millions as will cause our present public debt,
local and national, to sink into insignificance.   Let us do that, and the
control of the commerce of the world will then have passed from the
eastern to this western side of the Atlantic, here forever to remain.

At the close, half a century since, of the great wars of the French
Revolution, England abolished her sinking fund and gave her undivided
attention to the measures required for increasing the power of production
and accumulation, and for thus reducing the rate of interest on public and
private debts, the results of that course of action exhibiting themselves in
the fact that, notwithstanding frequent and expensive wars, she now finds
herself prepared to enter upon the reduction of her debt. It was a great
example—one that should now be followed.   The more thoroughly it shall
be so, the greater must be the growth in the money value of both land and
man—the larger the reward of landowner and laborer—the greater the
growth of the productive power—the smaller the *proportion* required for
public purposes—and the more speedy the arrival of the period when we
shall not only have been relieved from the burthen of foreign debts, but
have become lenders to the outside world, as Great Britain so long has
been.   Then, and not until then, shall we have attained a real independence.

It may, and probably will, be said that the determination to adopt no
measures looking to instant reduction of the national debt would have
an injurious effect upon the price of our securities in Europe.   Should it
prove so to be, the nation would have reason to rejoice, however much
bill-brokers and bankers might find therein reason for lamentation.
Nothing but injury can, by any possibility, result from leading foreigners
to believe that the course we now pursue can ever end in resumption of
specie payments.   Every step we take leads in the direction of bankruptcy the most complete, to be followed by repudiation.   With each,
the rate of interest rises, to the great advantage of the money-lender of
the present, and great disadvantage of the laborer, the farmer, and the
mechanic—the men who need the aid of others' capital.   With each, the

price of food falls, to the great advantage of all whose income results from taxation of those to whose labor we stand indebted for both food and wool. With each, the holders of coupons and receivers of taxes are more and more enabled to live abroad, there consuming, to the annual extent of probably a hundred millions, French, British, and German food. With each, there is here diminished faith in our future, and diminished power to make a market at home for the various products of the land. With each, the *London Times* becomes more enthusiastic in its approval of our financial policy. Well it may do so, as it is precisely the one required for perpetuating our dependence on the capitalists of Britain. "In the eyes of the English," says that eminent philosopher, Mons. De Tocqueville, "that which is most useful to England is always the cause of justice. The man or the government which serves the interests of England has all sorts of good qualities; he who hurts those interests, all sorts of defects; so that it would seem that the *criterion* of what is right, or noble, or just, is to be found in the degree of favor or opposition to English interest."

English interests are to be served by heavy American taxation, and as that taxation becomes at every step of our present career more and more burthensome, it meets, of course, with English approval. When continuance in that course shall have led, as it certainly must do, to the reinstatement in power of the friends of Britain and of British free trade, the gentlemen who now direct our affairs may perhaps begin, but too late begin, to appreciate the magnitude of the error that is now so unhappily being committed.

Commending these views to your careful consideration,

I remain, with great regard,

Yours very truly,

HENRY C. CAREY.

PHILADELPHIA, January 3, 1866.

CONTRACTION OR EXPANSION?

REPUDIATION OR RESUMPTION?

LETTERS TO THE HON. HUGH M'CULLOCH,
SECRETARY OF THE TREASURY.

BY

HENRY C. CAREY.

PHILADELPHIA:
HENRY CAREY BAIRD,
INDUSTRIAL PUBLISHER,
306 WALNUT STREET.
1866.

LETTERS TO THE HON. H. M^cCULLOCH,

SECRETARY OF THE TREASURY.

LETTER FIRST.

DEAR SIR:—

FULLY agreeing with you, as I do, in regard to many most important questions of public policy, it is with great regret that I find myself so wholly differing in reference to the existence of that "plethora of paper money" of which you speak, and to which you now attribute the "large importation of foreign fabrics;" the "splendid fortunes realized by skilful manipulations at the gold room or stock board;" the "rise in the prices of the necessaries of life;" the increase in the number of "non producers;" and the most important fact that "productive industry is being diminished."

That this, to a considerable extent, is an accurate exhibit of the actual state of affairs I am not at all disposed to doubt, but were I even to admit its perfect accuracy the questions would still remain: Why are such the facts? Why is it that men are now unemployed who but a twelve month since were so fully occupied? Why is it that our foreign debt so steadily increases? To these questions you furnish one general answer, that "paper money" is too abundant; and that if we would bring about a more healthy state of things its quantity must be diminished. I, on the contrary, hold that no such "plethora" exists, and that the real cause of all this error must be sought for in a direction precisely opposite, there to be found in measures of contraction with which the country has been threatened; and fully do I believe that if we would bring about a more healthy condition of affairs it is required that we move in a direction exactly the reverse of that which you so recently have indicated.

Differing thus widely, one of us must be much in error. It may be that I am wrong, but until I can look at the facts in a manner very different from that in which they now present themselves to my mind, I must continue to believe that I am right. The error may, possibly, my dear sir, be with yourself, and if it can be shown that such is the case, you will, I am sure, rejoice at being so convinced. So believing, I propose, with a view to the determination of the question whether such "plethora" does or does not exist, to furnish here a comparison of the actual circulation of the three chief commercial countries of the world, France, Great Britain, and the United States; of the needs of each for such circulation; and of their power profitably to use it. Should the result of such comparison be that of proving that not only is our medium of circulation not in excess in its relation to population and production, but that it is greatly short in the proportion which it bears to both, then, as I most respectfully submit, will it be necessary to look in a direction opposite to that of "plethora of paper money" for the cause of error, and there, on further examination, perhaps it may be found.

Seven years since the coin in use in France was estimated at 4,880,-000,000 francs, or more than $900,000,000. Since then the quantity must have increased, the substitution of the convenient gold for the heavy and cumbrous silver coins that even then were still so generally in use having, as has been stated by a recent writer, had the effect of placing napoleons in pockets that before could carry only francs. Admitting, however, that the increase has been sufficient only to add to the coin in the hands of the public as much as before had been in the bank vaults, we have a hard money circulation of $900,000,000*
To which must now be added the "paper money" circulation, which may be taken at about . . 170,000,000†
_____
Giving a grand total of $1,070,000,000
Or nearly $30 per head.

The coin actually in use in Great Britain and Ireland was estimated a few years since at £60,000,000. Since then it must greatly have increased, but, claiming no allowance on that account, I put it here at the same figure, being the equivalent of only . . . $300,000,000
The "paper money" circulation of the past few years has varied between 37½ and 42½ millions. Taking the mean of these quantities we have the equivalent of about . . 200,000,000
To this must now be added a paper circulation of a character little known in this country, and consisting of promises of individuals, in the form of bills of exchange, to deliver money at a future day. Of these, large quantities are in constant circulation, returning finally to their payers covered with indorsements, sometimes 15, 20, and even more

_____

* From 1850 to 1865 the importations of the precious metals were in excess of the exportations to the extent of $334,000,000. The quantity held in 1852 was estimated by M. du Puynode at 3,500,000,000, or nearly $700,000,000.

† The amount in 1853 was only 395,000,000 francs. From that time it had grown with great steadiness until, in 1862, it had attained the figure of 869,000,000. In 1864 it was 804,000,000.

in number, and having throughout the whole period of their existence performed all the service that here is performed by bank notes. The whole quantity of bills of exchange outstanding at any given time was estimated, some years since, at £200,000,000, and must now be greatly larger. Allowing here but one-fifth of that sum to be used for purposes of circulation, we have the equivalent of   200,000,000

Giving a grand total of $700,000,000

Or but little less than $25 per head.

The actual circulation of the Union, as just now furnished by the Comptroller, we know to be $460,000,000, being $12.50 per head, or one-half of that of Great Britain and Ireland.* Compared with that of

---

* The amount of national bank notes in actual circulation on the
  1st day of October last, was $171,321,903
The amount of State bank notes in circulation at the same date,
  as appears by returns to the Commissioner of Internal Revenue, was 78,867,575

Making the bank circulation on the 1st day of October last . 250,189,378
The amount of legal-tender notes and fractional currency issued
  and outstanding on the 1st of October, 1865, was . . . 704,584,658
National bank notes in the hands of banks not yet issued . 19,525,152
National currency yet to be issued to banks 109,152,945

Making the aggregate amount of legal tender and bank notes in
  circulation as authorized to be issued to and by the banks 1,083,452,233
From which sum should be deducted, State
  bank circulation now outstanding that will be
  retired about as fast as national currency is
  issued to converted banks $78,867,575
Also the amount of "compound interest notes"
  converted into 5-20 bonds since the 1st of
  October last 44,417,329
                            123,284,904

The amount then left as the available currency of the country
  is 960,167,326
  In order to ascertain the amount of actual
active circulation on the 1st day of October
last, there should be deducted from the last
mentioned sum—
The amount of national currency delivered to
  banks, and not then in circulation . . $19,525,152
National circulation not delivered to banks . 109,152,945
Amount of legal-tender notes held by banks, including $74,261,847 compound interest notes, 193,094,365

    Carried forward $321,772,462 $960,167,326

France it stands in the ratio of but 5 to 12; and yet, for various reasons, we should be entitled to expect to find it bearing to population a larger proportion than in either one of those countries. Among these reasons are the following:—

First. To pay any given number of mechanics or laborers required, before the war, more than twice the quantity of circulation that would have been needed in France; and one-half more than would have been required in Great Britain. The war having been accompanied by the establishment of a National Free Trade System there came a greatly increased demand for laborers with so large an increase of wages that the quantity of circulation now required for paying any given number of hands must be taken at twice that needed by the latter and thrice that required by the former.

Second. The proportion borne by circulation to numbers tends rapidly to increase as population becomes more widely scattered, and as rapidly to diminish as men are enabled to come more near together. That this is so, is shown in the fact that thousands of millions of exchanges are weekly performed in New York and other great commercial cities without the necessity for using a single note; whereas, among a scattered people like our own, every exchange, large or small, necessitates the delivery of a given quantity of coin or "paper money." Such being the case, the 36,000,000 of our people, dispersed over a territory eight times more extensive than that occupied by the 37,000,000 of France, and twelve times greater than that of the United Kingdom, might fairly be expected to demand a circulation, per head, thrice greater than that of either of those countries; and yet, as has been shown, it is but half as great as that in use in the one, and much less than half that employed by the other. Is it then, my dear sir, to be believed that there is among us, really, any of that "plethora" of which you have spoken? As it seems to me did we need to find one it would be beyond the ocean that we should seek it.

Brought forward	$321,772,462	$960,167,326
Compound interest notes, other than those held by banks, mostly held as investments by insurance and trust companies and savings banks, less say $10,000,000 in actual circulation .	121,314,195	
Currency in the treasury of the United States,	56,236,440	
Total		499,323,097
Which will show the actual circulation to be		$460,844,229

This favorable exhibit of the amount of paper in actual circulation, is owing in a great degree to the accumulation of currency in the hands of the banks, in the absence of the great demands of the government for currency since the close of the war.—*Report of the Comptroller of the Currency.*

The grand error that, as it seems to me, we are accustomed to commit, is that which results from limiting ourselves to a comparison of the various periods of our own financial history, leaving wholly out of view the facts furnished by the history of other commercial nations. Thus, in the comparative view of our circulation given in your Report it is shown that it grew from $60,000,000 in 1830 to $140,000,000 in 1836; and from $58,000,000 in 1843 to $207,000,000 in 1860; but those facts are not supplied by means of which your readers might be enabled to judge as to whether or not even the largest of these figures was in excess of the absolute wants of the community—whether it did, or did not, indicate the existence of any " plethora of paper money." That it did not do so has seemed to me, and must now, as I think, appear to you, to be very certain. On the contrary, when compared with other commercial countries it furnishes conclusive evidence that the supply of the medium of circulation had always been deficient, and thus enables us to understand more accurately the real cause of the extraordinary activity of the societary circulation which prevailed throughout the war, and to which our people have been indebted for power to give to the government the thousands of millions of dollars required for enabling it to dictate the terms of peace.

Of all the phenomena exhibited during the wonderful war in which we have been engaged, among the most extraordinary are those connected with the transportation of vast armies and all the vast supplies by them required, throughout a country of such vast extent, and over roads scarcely any portion of which south of the Delaware could boast of more than a single track, that, too, supplied with rails of the poorest kind. Never in the world, even under circumstances far more favorable, has such an amount of transportation been effected—never so large an amount of public work so well accomplished. Precisely so has it been, and now is, with the machinery by means of which circulation is effected from hand to hand, no country having ever yet performed so large an amount of exchanges by means of a medium of exchange the supply of which was so utterly disproportioned to the amount of production, to the quantity of exchanges needed to be made, or to the number of people empowered to make them. So far from " plethora " having either then or at any previous time existed, the financial history of the Union presents an uninterrupted series of figures the study of which is calculated to excite surprise that so much has always been done when the supply of machinery by means of which alone it could be done, has throughout our whole experience been so deficient. No other people, with such means, could so well have effected the transportation of the war; no other could, with such a supply of the medium of exchange, have so well effected the exchanges of both war and peace.

Proposing in another letter to examine into the influence of "paper money" on the action of the past five years, I remain, meanwhile, with great respect and regard,

Yours very truly,

HENRY C. CAREY.

PHILADELPHIA, January 28, 1866.

LETTER SECOND.

DEAR SIR :—

HAD it been possible, on the 4th of March, 1861, to take a bird's-eye view of the whole Union, there would have been seen—

Millions of men and women wholly or partially unemployed, because of inability to find persons able and willing to pay for service :

Hundreds of thousands of workmen, farmers, and shopkeepers holding articles of various kinds for which no purchasers could be found :

Tens of thousands of country traders poring over their books seeking, but vainly seeking, to discover in what direction they might look for obtaining the means with which to discharge their city debts :

Thousands of city traders endeavoring to discover how they might obtain the means with which to pay their notes :

Thousands of mills, factories, furnaces, and workshops large and small, standing idle while surrounded by persons who desired to be employed ; and

Tens of thousands of bank, factory, and railroad proprietors despairing of obtaining dividends by means of which they might be enabled to go to market.

High above all these a National Treasury wholly empty, and to all appearance little likely ever again to be replenished.

Why was all this ? The laborer needing food, and the farmer clothing, why did they not exchange ? Because of the absence of power on the part of the former to give to the latter anything with which he could purchase either hats or coats.

The village shopkeeper desired to pay his city debts. Why did he not ? Because the neighboring mill was standing idle while men and women, indebted to him, were wholly unemployed.

The city trader could not meet his notes, because his village correspondents could not comply with their engagements. The doctor could not collect his bills. The landlord could not collect his rents ; and all, therefore, from laborer to landlord, were compelled to refrain from the purchase of those commodities to whose consumption the National

Treasury had been used to look for the supplies upon which it thus far had depended.

With all, the difficulty resulted from the one great fact already indicated in regard to the laborer. If *he* could have found any one willing to give him something that the farmer would accept from him in exchange for food—that the farmer could then pass to his neighbor shopkeeper in exchange for cloth—that that neighbor could then pass to the city trader in satisfaction of his debt—and that this latter could then pass to the bank, to his counsel, his physician, or his landlord—the *societary circulation* would at once have been re-established and the public health restored.

That one thing, however, was scarcely anywhere to be found. Its generic name was *money*, but the various species were known as gold, silver, copper, and circulating notes. Some few persons possessed them in larger or smaller quantities; but, the total amount being very small when compared with that which was required, their owners would not part with the use of them except on terms so onerous as to be ruinous to the borrowers. As a consequence of this, the city trader paid ten, twelve, and fifteen per cent. per annum for the use of what he needed, charging twice that, to the village shopkeeper, in the prices of his goods. The latter, of course, found it necessary to do the same by his neighbors, charging nearly cent. per cent.; and thus was the whole burthen resulting from deficiency in the supply of a medium of exchange thrown upon the class which least could bear it, the working people of the country—farmers, mechanics, and laborers. As a consequence of this, they shrunk in their proportions as the circulation became more and more impeded, while with those who held in their hands the regulation of the money supply the effect exhibited itself in the erection of those great palaces which now stand almost side by side with tenement houses whose occupants, men, women, and children, count by hundreds. The rich thus grew richer as the poor became more poor.

Why was all this? Why did they not use the gold of which California had already sent us so many hundreds of millions? Because we had most carefully followed in the train of British free trade teachers who had assured our people that the safe, true, and certain road towards wealth and power was to be found in the direction of sending wheat, flour, corn, pork, and wool to England in their rudest form, and then buying them back again, at quadruple prices, paying the difference in the products of Californian mines! Because we had in this manner, for a long period of years, been selling whole skins for sixpence and buying back tails for a shilling! Because we had thus compelled our people to remain idle while consuming food and clothing, the gold meanwhile being sent to purchase foreign food and clothing for the workmen of London and Paris, Lyons, Manchester, and Birmingham!

Why, however, when circulating notes could so easily be made, did not the banks supply them, when all around would so gladly have allowed interest for their use? Because those notes were redeemable in a commodity of which, although California gave us much, we could no longer retain even the slightest portion, the quantity required abroad for payment of heavy interest, and for the purchase of foreign food in the forms of cloth and iron, having now become fully equal to the annual supply, and being at times even in excess of it.* That demand, too, was liable at any moment to be increased by the sale in our markets of certificates of debt then held abroad to the extent of hundreds of millions, the proceeds being claimed in gold and thus causing ruin to the banks. To be out of debt is to be out of danger, but to be in debt abroad to the extent of hundreds of millions is to be always in danger of both public and private bankruptcy. *The control of our whole domestic commerce was therefore entirely in the hands of foreigners who were from hour to hour becoming richer by means of compelling us to remain so dependent upon them that they could always fix the prices at which they would buy the skins, and those at which they would be willing to sell the tails.* As a necessary consequence of this, the nation was not only paralyzed, but in danger of almost immediate death.

Such having been the state of things on the day to which I have referred, let us now look at the remedy then required. Let us, for a moment, suppose the existence of an individual with wealth so great that all who knew him might have entire confidence in the performance of what he promised. Let us then suppose that he should have said to the laborers of the country, "Go into the mills, and I will see that your wages are paid;" to the millers, "Employ these people, and I will see that your cloth is sold;" to the farmers, "Give your food to the laborer and your wool to the millers, and I will see that your bills are at once discharged;" to the shopkeepers, "Deliver your coffee and your sugar to the farmer, and I will see that payment shall forthwith be made;" to the city traders, "Fill the orders of the village shopkeeper and send your bills to me for payment;" to the landlords, "Lease your houses and look to me for the rents;" to all, "I have opened a *clearing house* for the whole country, and have done so with a view to enable every man to find on the instant a cash demand for his labor and its products, and my whole fortune has been pledged for the performance of my engagements;" and then let us examine into the effects. At once the societary circulation would have been restored. Labor would have come into demand, thus

---

* From November, 1849, to December, 1864, the gold shipped from California amounted to $694,908,923
Excess exports of the precious metals in the same period . 587,746,078

Balance $107,162,845

Allowing now but $7,000,000 for the annual consumption in the arts, the whole balance would have been thus disposed of.

doubling at once the productive power of the country. Food would have been demanded, and the farmer would have been enabled to improve his machinery of cultivation. Cloth would have been sold, and the spinner would have added to the number of his spindles. Coal and iron would have found increased demand, and mines and furnaces would have grown in numbers and in size. Houses becoming more productive, new ones would have been built. The *paralysis* would have passed away, life, activity, and energy having taken its place; and all these wonderful effects having resulted from the simple pledge of the one sufficient man that he would see the contracts carried out. He had pledged his credit and nothing more.

What is here supposed is almost precisely what then was done by the National Treasury, the only difference having been, that while in the one case the farmers and laborers had been required to report themselves to the single individual or his agents, the Government has since, by the actual purchase of labor and its products, and the grant of its pledges in a variety of shapes and forms, enabled each and every man in the country to arrange his business in the manner that to himself has seemed most advantageous. To the laborer it has said, "We need your services, and in return will give you that which will enable your family to purchase food and clothing." To the farmer, "We need food, and will give you that by means of which you can pay the shopkeeper." To the manufacturer, "We need cloth, and will give you that which will enable you to settle with the workman and the farmer." To the naval constructor, "We need your ships, and will give you that which will enable you to purchase timber, iron, and engines." In this manner it is that domestic commerce has been stimulated into life, the result exhibiting itself in the facts, that while we have in the last five years increased to an extent never known before the number of our houses and our mills, our mines, and furnaces, our supplies of food, cloth, and iron; and while we have diversified our industry to an extent that is absolutely marvellous; we have been enabled to lend, or pay, to the Government thousands of millions of dollars, where before, under the system which made us wholly dependent on the mercy of the wealthy capitalists of England, we found it difficult to furnish even tens of millions. The whole history of the world has presented no case of a financial success so perfect.

In the physical body health is always the accompaniment of rapid circulation, disease that of a languid one. Now, for the first time since the settlement of these colonies, have we had experience of the first. Every man who desired to work, found a purchaser for his labor. Every man who had labor's products to sell, found a ready market. Every man who had a house to rent, found a tenant. And why? Because the Government had done for the whole nation what Companies do for localities when they give them railroads in place of wagon roads. It had so facilitated exchange between consumers and producers, that both parties had been enabled to pay on the instant for all they had had need to purchase.

Important, however, as is all this, it is but a part of the great work that had been accomplished. With every stage of progress there had been a diminution in the general rate of interest, with constant tendency towards equality in the rate paid by the farmers of the East and the West, by the owner of the little workshop and by him who owns the gigantic mill. For the first time in our history the real workingmen—the laborer, the mechanic, and the little village shopkeeper—had been enabled to command the use of the machinery of circulation at a moderate rate of interest. For the first time had nearly all been enabled to make their purchases cash in hand, and to select from among all the dealers those who would supply them cheapest. For the first time had this class known anything approaching to real independence; and therefore has it been that, notwithstanding the demands of the war, the power of accumulation has been so great. The gain to the community from the economy of labor and labor's products has counted by thousands of millions of dollars, and it has been because of that gain that we have been enabled to furnish to the Government an amount of contributions so far exceeding anything of the kind that the world before had known.

The power of accumulation exists in the ratio of the rapidity of circulation, and it does so because the greater that rapidity the more complete is the economy of human force, the greater the production, and the more complete the economy of interest. That that power may grow a full supply of the medium of circulation is as much required as is a proper supply of railroad cars and engines. Without these latter there would be few exchanges between the East and the West, the North and the South; and without the former it is wholly impossible that there should be that rapidity in the exchange of human service to which alone must we look if we would have increase of production and of societary force.

The view above presented of our power of accumulation throughout the period of Mr. Lincoln's administration differs slightly from that which commonly is entertained; and yet, my dear sir, when you shall have reflected upon the facts which I shall now present, you will, as I feel assured, agree with me in the belief that it has not been overrated. It is probably true, as is so frequently asserted, that less than the average number of city houses has been built, but the growth of towns and villages has been great beyond all former precedent. Look to the coal and iron regions—to the oil region of the Ohio and its tributaries—and to the wonderful mineral one beyond the Mississippi, and you will find that there have been there created homes for millions of men, their wives and children. Little cotton machinery, it is true, has recently been built, but we have more than doubled our power to produce both wool and woollen cloth. Rolling mills now exist, capable of furnishing annually 750,000 tons of bars, while the power by means of which those bars may be converted into ships, engines, and other machinery of transportation and production has more than doubled, and has, probably, even trebled. Factories have been created capable of supplying almost the world's demand for various instruments of production or defence; sewing machines on the one hand, pistols, rifles, and Parrot guns on the other. The quartz mills have been created to which we are now, as we are assured, to look for an immediate production of the precious metals to the annual extent of $200,000,000. For every engine five years since there are now, as I think, more than three at work. Throughout the vast fields of the West machines are everywhere doing the work that five years since was done by human hands. Fewer miles of railroad may have been constructed, but the rolling stock of all has been so much increased that the power of transportation throughout the loyal States has more than doubled. St. Louis presents to-day, as we are told, an amount of steam tonnage two-fifths greater than there existed before the war; and yet, so great has been the quantity of produce seeking to go to market that the Pennsylvania Central, at Pittsburg, has recently been blocked by 2500 loaded cars, for the movement of which no power could be furnished. Look, then, in what direction we may, whether to the greater or smaller machinery of production, we witness an increase of quantity so great as fully to warrant us in the belief that, leaving wholly out of view the sums invested in loans to cities, counties, States, and to the general government, at no period has the power of accumulation been much more than half as great as it has been shown to be in the years of the great war that has now so happily terminated.

For all these successful results we stand indebted to the combined action of two great measures of the administration; *first*, the adoption of a national free trade system, by aid of which producers and consumers were to be brought to act together; and *second*, the adoption of a national system of circulation based entirely on the credit of the government with the people, and not liable to interference from abroad. Both were needed, and neither one could, without the other, have been productive of the great results that have been achieved. To the latter of them, however, you object, on the ground that it has caused an unnatural and injurious rise of prices; that it has lessened the disposition to exertion; and that it tends now to cause great diminution in the productive industry of the community. To all this I answer that, when carefully examined, the facts do not seem to me to sustain these objections, and that such is certainly the case I propose in my next to show, meantime remaining, with great respect,   Yours, very truly,

HENRY C. CAREY.

PHILADA., Jan. 30, 1866.

LETTER THIRD.

DEAR SIR:—

BEFORE proceeding to inquire into the changes of price so generally attributed to that "plethora of paper-money" of which you have spoken, it may be well to determine what, precisely, they recently have been. To that end, I give you here the actual prices of the New York market, as just now furnished by the *Merchants' Magazine,* for the closing week of the year which preceded the joint inauguration of Mr. Lincoln and of a national free trade policy, and for the corresponding week of the several years that since have passed, as follows :—

	1860.	1861.	1862.	1863.	1864.	1865.
Ashes	$5 00	$6 25	$8 50	$8 50	$11 75	$9 00
Flour, State . . .	5 35	5 50	6 05	7 00	10 00	8 75
Wheat, red . . .	1 38	1 42	1 48	1 57	2 45	2 05
Corn	72	64	82	1 30	1 90	95
Hay	90	77	85	1 45	1 55	75
Hops	25	20	23	33	40	50
Hemlock leather .	30	20	27	30	42	36
Lime	75	65	85	1 30	1 15	1 10
Pork, old mess . .	16 00	12 00	14 50	19 50	43 00	28 50
Beef, city mess .	6 00	5 50	.12 00	14 00	20 50	20 00
Hams	8	6	8	11	20	16
Lard	10	8	10	13	23	19
Butter	18	19	22	29	55	48
Cheese	10	7	12	15	20	18
Tallow	10	10	10	12	18	14
	$37 21	$33 63	$46 17	$56 05	$94 48	$73 11

From this list have been excluded cotton and naval stores, both of which, during the blockade, were so very high and have since so greatly fallen. For special reasons, however, many of these very articles might with equal propriety have been omitted. Of wheat, for instance, the crop of the last year was less by 12,000,000 bushels than that of 1864, that itself having been less by 16,000,000 than had been the one of 1863. This, of course, largely affects the present prices of both wheat and wheaten flour. Butter and cheese are higher than they would otherwise be, because of the very considerable diminution in the number of cows exhibited in the recent Report of the Commissioner of Agriculture. A corresponding diminution in the number of cattle generally, coupled with the existence of a cattle plague throughout a large portion of Europe, accounts for an increase in the prices of both beef and pork.* Allowing for all these circumstances, I would now, my dear sir, most respectfully beg you to reflect on the answers that might properly be given to the following questions, to wit :—

First. Comparing present prices with those which ruled before the war, is there here exhibited any increase that might not have taken place had there been no change whatsoever in the circulation ?

Second. Making the same comparison, and allowing for the fact that from the increased prices of 1865 is to be deducted the increased rate of freight, most of which has been rendered necessary by the heavy taxation of coal, iron, cars, engines, receipts, dividends, &c. &c., would the western farmer, except for the accidental circumstance of a deficient supply of wheat occurring simultaneously with the existence of a cattle plague abroad, receive to-day even as much in paper as he had before in gold ?

Third. Leaving wholly out of view, with the single exception of a cattle plague occurring simultaneously with a diminution in our own supply of cattle, all of the circumstances above referred to, would there, in the prices current, now be found as great a change for the better as we should have been warranted in expecting from the creation of that great internal commerce which had resulted from the adoption, in 1861, of a policy having for its object the bringing together of the producer and the consumer, to the great advantage of both ?

Fourth. Is there to be found in the above exhibit any evidence that the farmer now profits of the events of the past few years even to such extent as is absolutely required for enabling him to continue payment of the heavy taxes, local and national, now imposed ?

Fifth. Must not any attempt at further forcing down prices, with a view to compelling export of our products in exchange for gold, be followed by inability to pay the taxes and by financial and political ruin ?

Sixth. Do not all the facts above given show clearly, that what we really need is such a stimulation of the societary circulation as would cause that increased demand for all the products of the farm which would maintain their prices and diminish the necessity for employing our people in that which is the proper work of the barbarian and the slave, and of them alone, to wit, that of raising raw products for the supply of distant markets ?

Throughout the period of Mr. Lincoln's administration that circulation was active to an extent never before known in any country of the world, and to that activity, as has been shown, have we been indebted for power successfully to prosecute the war. How we have been indebted to

---

* So much has the demand for beef exceeded the supply, that, notwithstanding large imports from Canada, the number of cattle and oxen reported by the Commissioner of Agriculture is now nearly a million less then it was six years since.

increase in the supply of the medium of circulation for promoting that activity, and thus enabling us to supply the thousands of millions rendered necessary by the war, has been also shown. What have been the precise facts connected with the change of prices above exhibited I propose, in my next, to show, and have now to ask for them your careful consideration. Meanwhile, my dear sir, permit me here to say a word or two in regard to my own position. Throughout the war I have been a heavy sufferer under the legal-tender system, having been, as I still am, compelled to accept paper in place of the gold that honestly was due me, and to pay double or treble price for almost everything I required to purchase. My *apparent* interests are, therefore, all on the side of an early return to specie as the standard, but well do I know that my *real* interests are so closely bound up with those of my neighbors that what must be bad for them cannot be good for

Yours truly and respectfully,
HENRY C. CAREY.

PHILADELPHIA, February 3, 1866.

LETTER FOURTH.

DEAR SIR:—

At the close of 1860, the "paper money" circulation of the loyal States amounted to $150,000,000. Adding to this the precious metals then in actual use, the total circulation cannot materially have exceeded $250,-000,000.

The following summer witnessed a withdrawal of nearly the whole of the Western circulation consequent upon losses caused by the rebellion. The precious metals were still in use, but the tendency towards hoarding had greatly grown, and the total circulation, even after the issue of $50,000,000 of Treasury notes authorized by the law of July, 1861, had at the close of the year certainly much diminished.* The consequences of this exhibit themselves in the table heretofore given, in a reduction of about 10 per cent. in the sum of the New York prices, equivalent to at least 25 per cent. in those of the West.

The Act of February, 1862, authorized the issue of legal tender notes to the extent of $150,000,000
That of July, 1862 . . , ... 150,000,000
Adding now to this for the bank notes in circulation . 100,000,000

We have at the close of the year a total of . . . $400,000,000

---

* Even as late as December, 1862, the State bank circulation, as given in the annual report, was but $97,000,000.

exhibiting an addition of scarcely less than 60 per cent. ; and yet, the increase in the sum of prices, as has been shown, was but from $37.21 to $46.17, or $8.96 ; and of this trivial augmentation two-thirds are seen to have resulted from an increased demand for the beef required for supplying the hundreds of thousands of men engaged in the effort at maintenance of the Union. There is, certainly, here no difference that might not as readily have taken place under a moderate extra demand from abroad, had the circulation remained entirely unchanged.

In March, 1863, there was authorized a further emission of legal tender notes, the amount of which was now to be carried up to $450,000,000

The fractional currency issued may then have reached   20,000,000

The State bank circulation, as returned to the Comptroller, was $147,000,000, to which must now be added that of the banks from which no returns had been received, giving a total of probably not less than   155,000,000

National bank circulation probably   5,000,000

To which must here be added interest bearing legal tenders issued in the last quarter of the year, and all then in circulation among the people, estimated at   60,000,000

Total circulation Dec., 1863 .   .   .   .   .   **$690,000,000**

In three years the circulation had thus almost trebled, and with what effect on prices ? The $37.21 of the dull and lifeless period which followed the election of Mr. Lincoln had been replaced by the $56.05 of the period of life and animation of December, 1863, showing an aggregate difference of $18.84, nearly two-thirds of which are found in the two articles of beef and pork, the army demand for both of which had been so immense. Here again there is found no increase that, under circumstances otherwise similar, might not properly have been looked for, had gold remained the standard.

With 1864, we have no increase of circulation except that which resulted from additional issues by State and National banks. What was the extent of the former I have no means of knowing, but see no reason for believing that it was very great. Of National bank notes, the total quantity supplied to the first of October had been $65,000,000; but, as shortly after stated in your annual Report, they were "to a considerable extent" merely a substitution of National for State currency. In all cases, the institutions receiving notes found themselves compelled by law to retain on hand one-fourth of the amount in legal tenders, which were thus withdrawn from circulation, and constituted an offset so large as almost to neutralize the issues to the new banks that had been then created. The interest bearing legal tenders may somewhat have increased, but, having been steadily withdrawn from circulation as they grow in value, the increase cannot have been very great. Further than this, the high price of gold having withdrawn from it all the private hoards of the country, the hoarding of " greenbacks" had not only now commenced, but had made such progress as to constitute an important element in the estimate here, for the close of the year, to be made of the " paper money" then outstanding. Allowing for all these circumstances, the highest estimate of the circulation that could now be made would scarcely, as I think, exceed $750,000,000, giving an increase of 60 millions, or from eight to nine per cent.

In the mean time, however, the field throughout which this " paper money" was to be diffused had greatly been enlarged. At the close of 1863 there had been, except near New Orleans, scarcely a foot of ground south of the Potomac, the Ohio, or the Missouri, that was securely held; and of the expenditures in the field by far the larger portion was being made at points that were but very little further southward. Now, however, all had changed, the seat of war having been transferred to the vicinity of the James, the Alabama, and the Savannah. Adding to this the fact that the States of Colorado, Nevada, and Montana were being rapidly created; while Nebraska and Minnesota were as rapidly increasing in the numbers of their population; it will be seen that the surface over which a medium of circulation was required must have been, to say the least of it, one-half greater than it had been at the close of the previous year. Making now allowance for all these facts, it is, as I think, safe to say, that the proportion borne by circulation to the need for it, *had in that year been diminished at least a fourth ;* and yet, within that year the $37.21 of 1860, and the $56.01 of 1863, had become the $94.45 of 1864. Thus are we presented with the extraordinary facts, that while the circulation was being increased prices had but slightly risen; whereas, now, when, in practical effect, it had been materially reduced, they had risen with great rapidity; showing, and very clearly, as it appears to me, that the extraordinary changes we recently have witnessed have not been caused by increase of circulation, and that it is not in the direction of its diminution that we are to look if we desire to bring about resumption.

The real cause of all this extraordinary rise, in the face of a diminution in the proportion borne by circulation to the need for it, is found in the following paragraph of the Comptroller of the Currency, to wit :—

" By a gold valuation of our imports and exports, the balance that has accrued against this country during the four years previous to the 30th day of June last, including the interest on American securities held abroad purchased within that time, and also taking into due consideration the difference between our own standard and that of foreign gold (9⅜ per cent.), has been $308,000,000."

This, of itself, would be sufficient to account for all the rise of gold, and rise of " paper money" prices, that occurred in 1864 ; and yet, thereto must now be added a sum almost, if not even quite, as large, for covering the expenditures of our travellers in Europe; the interest on stocks and bonds held in Europe before the war; the freights, and the under-valuations of imports. It is safe, as I believe, to estimate our expenditures abroad as having exceeded our exports to the annual extent of $150,000,000, or, in the whole, $600,000,000. The only commodity in which this balance could be paid was gold, the price of which naturally rose until it had so thoroughly emptied all the hoards of the country, public and private, that scarcely any now remains except what is indispensably necessary for the payment of interest by, and of duties to, the Government.

It fell with the opening of southern ports and the emancipation of cotton, and with it fell, too, the prices of each and all of the commodities in the list above presented. Is there, however, to be found any evidence that the "plethora of paper money" had controlled the prices of our various products? None, whatsoever! On the contrary, the changes are precisely such as must, under similar circumstances of supply and demand, have occurred had the idea of a legal tender note had no existence. The total difference between the sum of the prices of 1860 and 1865 is $35 90, of which three-fourths, even, are here found in the articles of pork and beef, leaving but $9 40 for all the others. Hay, for "paper money" is cheaper than when it was payable in gold. Wheat commands now far more gold than it did in 1864. Why? Because the crop proved short! Butter remains high because cows have become far less numerous. Oats are scarcely higher than they were five years since. Corn has fallen to half the price of 1864, because the crop has been very large. Such are the results, when we compare the New York prices, increased as they are by the present enormous charges for transportation, but when we look West, we find that corn is being used for fuel, while wheat is in some places selling at 40 cents, and oats at only eight! That such prices must, in a great measure, deprive the western farmer of power to contribute to the Federal revenue would seem to be very clear; yet is there an unceasing cry for further reduction, that cry coming, too, chiefly from men who are most urgent for "thorough taxation," speedy resumption, and prompt discharge of the public debt! Could the editors to whom we are indebted for such advice be persuaded to study carefully the facts above presented, they could scarcely, as I think, fail to see that further travel in that direction must lead to public bankruptcy, political revolution, and a perpetuity of "paper money" as the exclusive medium of circulation.

That "paper money" is democratic in its tendencies may readily be seen by all who study the fact that it is scarcely at all used by the great operators in foreign merchandise of whom you have spoken, or by the stock board operators to whom you yourself, my dear sir, have referred.

Thousands of millions pass and repass among such people without the aid of a single note; whereas, among the small operators of our cities—the workmen of our factories—the laborers in our fields—the farmers and miners of the West—there exists an absolute necessity for *a letter of credit*, in the form of a bank or treasury note, to be used on the occasion of each and every exchange of commodities or services that is made. A war upon what is called "paper money" is therefore a war upon the poor in favor of the rich; and that the war being made upon it has precisely that effect is proved by the fact, that the western farmer is now being impoverished by reason of such a reduction in the price of corn and oats that the former is being used as fuel while the latter is being sold at 8 cents per bushel, houses and lots in the neighborhood of Wall Street commanding at this moment prices such as had never before been heard of. That such a war *can* have no end other than that of political revolution the most complete is so absolutely certain that, regarding as I do the future of the country and that of the administration as being inseparably linked together, I feel it a matter of positive duty most respectfully to ask that you should once again examine this question with a view to satisfying yourself that at no time in our history has there existed any such "plethora of paper money" as that of which you speak; and, that the supply of the medium of circulation is not only not in excess, but is, at this moment, so far below the real needs of our people that any attempt at further reduction must be attended with financial and political dangers of the most serious kind.

In another letter I propose to show what are the relations between "paper money" and societary force, and meanwhile remain, my dear sir, very respectfully and truly,

Yours,

H. C. CAREY.

Philadelphia, February 5, 1866.

LETTER FIFTH.

Dear Sir:—

Of all the phenomena of the physical world there is none so wonderful, none whose action is so entirely beyond the reach of observation, as is that of electricity. At times it makes its existence manifest, as when it performs the very trivial act of shattering a tree or destroying a life; but when engaged in the wonderful work of aiding in the production of universal vegetable and animal life, its operations are so entirely invisible to the eye that few among the thousand millions of the population of the earth could, even now, be induced to believe in its existence.

As it is with electricity in the physical world so is it with money in the social one, the vigor and importance of its operations being in the inverse ratio of the manifestations of its existence. At every purchase and every sale of the thousands of millions of sales and purchases made in the higher commercial ranks of a great city, *the money passes, yet is it never seen.* Passing downward we find, at each successive stage of the descent, the manifestations of its existence becoming more abundant, as the operations become more trivial, the *letter of credit* " greenback" here, and bank-note there, becoming more and more required in every exchange of labor or its products. Arriving at the lowest stages, we find ourselves among a people indisposed to use these latter for even the smallest sums, and greatly preferring the copper coin to the three or five cent note—*the diminutiveness of the exchange keeping steady pace with the constantly growing materiality of the instrument required for its performance.*

So precisely is it as we pass from our great and populous cities towards those regions of the West in which States are being formed whose total population scarcely exceeds that of single wards of Philadelphia or New York, the societary movement becoming at each and every step less and less rapid, and the necessity for a material representative of value more and more urgent, until at length we reach those regions in which, to the present hour, no bank has yet been tolerated—no "greenback" used for purposes of circulation—and perhaps no contract made that could be otherwise redeemed than by actual delivery of the precious metals. As a consequence of this it is, that while cheapening gold throughout, the world, the price there paid for the use of machinery of circulation is higher than in any other community of the world claiming to rank as civilized. The societary movement of the distant West is therefore, in this respect, nearly on a par with that of the lowest and least productive portion of our city population, credit, circulation, and the substitution of mental for muscular power, travelling always hand in hand together, and thus producing increase of societary force.

The substitution of circulating notes for coin constitutes an important step in the progress of civilization ; and yet, a further and more important one would still remain, to wit : that of so elevating the whole population of a country as to enable the little people, those who work, to do as do those great ones who profit of their labors, performing all their exchanges without the aid of any material representative of the money to be paid.* That, of course, could never be accomplished, and the idea is here suggested merely with a view to calling you attention to the fact, that it is *in that direction lies the road towards real civilization.* Sufficient

---

* In no part of the world is this so nearly accomplished as in New England. Nowhere does there exist in such perfection the machinery of circulation. Nowhere is it obtained at so small a cost.

will it be for us if we shall take the first great step by bringing up our whole people, the near and the distant, the inhabitants of Atlantic cities and western territories, to a full comprehension of the advantage to be derived from the steady and regular use of the *letter of credit* known to the world as the "greenback;" or that other one known as the national bank note. At times, the feeling of a necessity for this has produced an effort in that direction as when, in 1835, the paper circulation had reached $100,000,000; and again, in 1856, had attained to double that amount, to be, however, in both cases followed by collapse and ruin. Why was this? Because of an excess of circulating *notes*? Assuredly not, for, with a widely scattered population whose need for a tangible representative of money was then *thrice greater* than that of the European manufacturing nations, the amount in actual use was *not even one-third as great*, per head, as that we see to be required in both France and England. The real cause of the fearful changes to which you have referred is found in this, that, while requiring our people to regard the precious metals as the basis of all their contracts, we had overlooked the one great fact, that those metals travel always *from* semi-barbarous countries *to* those which are civilized; *from* those in which the rude products of the earth are cheap, *to* those in which they are dear; *from* those whose people, like our own, are employed in selling their soil in the forms of corn and cotton, *to* those which bring from abroad rude products and thus enable themselves to create a real agriculture; and *from* those in which labor is performed by the unassisted human arm, *to* those in which coal and iron ore are so utilized as to give to each and every individual the service of willing slaves who do the work, requiring in return neither meat nor drink, neither clothes nor shelter from the weather. *The raising of raw products for distant markets is the proper work of barbarous communities, and none such has ever yet, nor ever will, maintain a specie circulation.*

The collapses came in 1837 and 1857, and with what effect? Who were they that then most severely suffered? Was it not the people of the West, from whose midst the circulating note so wholly disappeared, driving them back to that barter system from which they but then had made an effort to escape? Who profited? Was it not the wealthy of our cities, in whose hands then centred nearly all the circulating medium of the country? Assuredly was it so, and thus were the rich of the East made richer while the poor of the West were made poorer than they had been before. With the opening of the rebellion there came, throughout almost the entire West, a third collapse, and with precisely the same results, ruin to the man who was in debt, and increase of wealth to the already wealthy owner of New York and Boston lots and houses.

Now again has there been made a great effort towards enabling our western friends to accomplish that great step on the road towards civilization which consists in substituting *letters of credit* for material money, thereby imitating, in a very small degree, the mode of operation of the great men, and great centres of the world; the work this time having been undertaken by a corporation of whose solvency none could doubt, offering, as it did, a mortgage on the whole property of the Union as security for the performance of its engagements. With what effect on this occasion? With that of stimulating the societary action to a degree that in all the world had never before been known, and so stimulating production as to have enabled us not only to lend to the Government thousands of millions; not only to make to it *donations* of service and of commodities to an amount scarcely less than $200,000,000 a year; but simultaneously therewith to add to the wealth of the country to an extent that finds no parallel in the records of mankind.

Such a result, my dear sir, might have been expected to bring with it an almost universal conviction that we had at last *stumbled* upon the real road to progress; that in a great deficiency of the machinery of circulation had been found the essential cause of many of the most serious difficulties of the past; and, that it would be desirable to proceed onward in the same direction, stimulating production and gradually placing our people in a position to accumulate such a store of the precious metals as would enable each and every man to determine whether to content himself with individual promises such as, in the great marts of commerce, have now so entirely superseded the circulating note—to demand the note—or, still further, to insist upon the delivery of the coin itself. Such is the point at which we should desire to arrive—such the one at which we should arrive, could our people but be persuaded once to see that the substitution for coin of the circulating note is one of the evidences of advancing civilization; that its convertibility into coin is dependent on the maintenance of a system that shall cause the inward current of the precious metals to exceed the outward one; and, that to attempt resumption in face of a system that not only makes demand for all the produce of California mines, but year after year adds hundreds of millions to our foreign debt, is a course of action that must result in financial revulsion, to be followed by political revolution the most complete.

Journalists, however, my dear sir, tell us that circulating notes cause speculation; that speculation causes men to travel about when they should be in the field or workshop; that if we would stop this "speculation" we must rid ourselves of the "plethora of paper money" under which we are supposed to suffer; and, that the way towards financial and political salvation is to be found in sending abroad bonds with which to purchase such supplies of the precious metals as will enable each and every man to determine for himself the sort of money in which he will be paid.

What, however, is this "speculation" that is the cause of so much evil? The lad going forth from school "speculates" with himself whether it will be best for him to become a farmer or a trader. Arrived at man's estate, he "speculates" as to whether he can be best employed in mining coal, making cloth, smelting iron ore, sinking shafts, building mills, erecting furnaces, making roads, or buying treasury bonds. These things he does only after carefully "speculating" as to the direction in which he is to look for the largest return to his labor or his capital, or both. He is *speculating for a rise*, as is every employer of capital, every really useful man amongst us. He desires that money may be abundant, and that the charge for its use may be small. With *that class* of speculators—farmers, laborers, mechanics, manufacturers, road makers, and others—the National treasury has been allied throughout the past few years, and from that alliance has come the power successfully to prosecute the great war that has just now closed. To those "speculators" stand we now indebted for the facts, that our railroad facilities are twice greater than they were five years since; that our furnaces are capable of producing more than 1,200,000 tons of iron, and our rolling mills annually 750,000 tons of bars; that houses have grown in number in full accordance with the growth of population; that oil wells have been developed capable of supplying the home demand and giving us annually 30,000,000 of gallons for export; that the supply of food has grown from less than a thousand millions of bushels, to more than twelve hundred millions; that the supply of wool has grown to more than a hundred millions, woollen mills having meanwhile grown to such extent as still to need from abroad large supplies; and, that in almost every department of manufacture we have made in the midst of an expensive war, a progress such as is without a parallel in the whole history of the world. Such having been the works of *speculators for a rise*, is it, my dear sir, possible to feel surprised that the alliance between them and the treasury which subsisted throughout the whole period of Mr. Lincoln's administration, should have proved to the latter so highly advantageous?

There is, however, another class of men, who, while building no houses, making no roads, opening no mines, erecting no furnaces, stand always ready to purchase them at the sheriff's hands. These men, being *speculators for a fall*, desire that money may be scarce and interest high; and with them it is that the Treasury, wholly unintentionally on your part as I am very certain, is now allied. With them, too, if we may judge from the bill that is now before the House, it seeks to form a still more close alliance. It is, however, the alliance with sin and death, and can lead to no result other than that of financial and political ruin. Worse than to Hercules was the poisoned shirt of Nessus has at all times proved the contact with such men. Worse than in any other nation it has ever been, must it prove with us.

The consequences of this alliance exhibit themselves in the facts that while, on unquestionable security, money abounds and is very cheap in Wall Street, it is very dear to all who seek to use it in any manner likely to increase production. Railroad stocks and bonds are cheap. City bonds, paying six per cent. interest, sell at 90 per cent. Cities pray to be permitted to pay 7 per cent. Treasury bonds, paying in gold 6 per cent., command in market less than par. Scarcity of money presses into market the seven-thirties, men who helped the government in the day of its need now finding themselves compelled to sell at heavy loss, thereby aiding in building up the fortunes of those who throughout the war have ".speculated" for a fall, and have witnessed with regret the triumph of loyalty over treason that has been secured. Step by step, with every movement in this direction, the societary movement becomes more sluggish, with steady increase in the number of men who seek employment and cannot find it.

Simultaneously with decline here in the demand for labor comes advice from Illinois, that so low has fallen the price of food that farmers are "holding indignation meetings," at one, at least, of which, it has been proposed to plant in the coming season but half the land that had been planted in the years that have lately passed. Paralysis of the farm goes thus hand in hand with that of the workshop, and must result in paralysis of the party that has so successfully made the war, and that now requires of us that we should do that which no other nation ever yet has done, to wit: maintain a specie circulation while exporting little or nothing beyond the rudest products of agricultural and mining labor.

Cheap money—low interest—enabled our working men to prosper, built up that party, carried us through the war, and gave us our present position before the world. That dear money—high rates of interest— will swamp both the party and the country, is the firm conviction of, my dear sir,   Yours very respectfully,

                                             HENRY C. CAREY.

Philadelphia, February 5, 1866.

LETTER SIXTH.

Dear Sir:—

The farmer—having throughout the war given his own services, thereto adding perhaps the life or lives of his son or his sons, to his country's cause—finds, now that victory has been achieved, that he is compelled to accept for his oats 8 cents, and for his wheat 40 cents, while corn so much abounds that burning it has become more advantageous than carrying it to market. Seeking the cause of this, he turns to journals eminent for their Republicanism, there to find that there exists a " plethora of paper-money;" that the prices of food are too high to permit that it should go abroad in search of gold by help of which to achieve resumption; that he and his neighbors have become "speculators;" and that the way to salvation for the country lies through such a war upon this "paper-money" as will have the effect of compelling his neighbors and himself to sell their food and their wool at prices to be fixed by other "speculators" in Chicago or Cincinnati, representatives of great capitalists of New York or Liverpool who have not only withheld from the government all aid, but have given their best efforts for accomplishing the dissolution of that Union in whose behalf he has made such heavy contributions. Severely feeling the effect of this, he applies to the Republican editor for a corresponding reduction in the price of his journal, receiving for answer the assurance that paper, wages, taxes, and rents remain so very high, that war prices must continue to be maintained. Asking next for a reduction of his taxes, he learns that the public debt is large; that the interest is great; that the people who have *lent* greenbacks when gold was at two and a half for one are anxious for such a fall of prices as may enable them to double their consumption of food and clothing; that the public debt must be diminished; and that, for all these reasons, the full war rate of taxation must not only be maintained, but may be much increased.—Unable to sell his corn, he seeks to convert into money the certificate he holds as representative of little savings placed in the public funds at a time when necessity compelled the Treasury to court the aid of little people like himself, but finds that he can do so only at a loss of two, three, or even five per cent. Failing here, he seeks to borrow the trifle that he needs, but receives for answer that, money having become so scarce as to have raised the Chicago rate of interest to two per cent. per month, it is no longer to be lent in the country at any price.—Seeking to buy a shirt, he finds that prices have but slightly fallen. Inquiring the cause of this, he learns that cotton manufacturers are making profits that are almost fabulous. Why, then, he inquires, do they not increase the number of their mills? To this he receives for answer, that the men of enterprise throughout the country have had positive Republican assurance that the "plethora of paper-money" shall be brought to an end; that the price of food shall be made to fall; that labor shall once again be cheap; and that, under such circumstances, none dare now to risk the building of either mills or furnaces.

The laborer, too, finds that since the day on which he volunteered his services for the war great changes have been brought about. Then, there were two men ready to purchase service where there was but a single one seeking to sell it. Now, however, all has changed, the sellers having become more numerous than the buyers. His wages having fallen, he seeks reduction of his rent, instead of which he receives notice that it has been advanced. Inquiring the cause of this, he learns that there has been, and is, a "plethora of paper-money;" that food and wages have been too high; that contraction is the order of the day, and that prices must be reduced; and that, until they shall have been so reduced, none can risk their means in building either houses, mills, or furnaces. "Speculators," as he is assured, have already built more furnaces and rolling-mills than are now required. "Speculators" have brought into cultivation so much land, that corn can no longer find a market. "Speculators" have sunk so many wells, that the price of oil has greatly fallen. "Speculators" have made so many roads, that railroad stocks have become mere drugs in the market. "Speculators" have taken so many treasury bonds, that they can no longer hold them. "Speculators" for a rise—working-men—men who *employ* money—those who have carried the country through the war—have been becoming too independent. The time, as he learns, has now arrived for those who "speculate" for a fall—for those who have money to lend—those who have *not* helped the government in its time of need—those who are to reap the harvest when the "plethora of paper-money" shall have ceased to exist, and when we shall have returned to those "good old times" of the Buchanan administration, throughout the whole course of which the Treasury could never have commanded the use of a single hundred millions at any reasonable rate of interest.

At all this the wealthy capitalist rejoices, receiving ten or twelve per cent. where before he had only five or six, and buying at heavy discounts the bonds of those who had helped the government when its existence had been most endangered.

The wealthy manufacturer goes on his way rejoicing in the idea that the danger of increased domestic competition has passed away.

The receiver of fixed income rejoices in the idea that decline in the price of gold now enables him to live abroad and profit by the lower rents and lower prices of continental Europe.

The British manufacturer rejoices in the knowledge that he is from day to day becoming more and more "master of the situation," and more and more enabled to dictate the prices at which he will buy, and those at which he will sell.*

The Copperhead, knowing well that to an activity of circulation without parallel in the history of mankind the government has been indebted for power to make the war, now rejoices in the gradual spread of a *paralysis* that in every stage of its progress is more and more preparing tax-payers to seek a change of rulers.

Throughout the war, as has been shown, the National Treasury had for

---

* "We know of manufacturers in the linen trade who have been making as much as £1,000 per day in goods chiefly for the American market, and such was the demand for their goods that they were masters of the situation, and in the matter of terms they naturally dictated their own."—*Sheffield Iris*, Jan. 12, 1866.

its allies the men who worked—*those who sought to rise*—those to whom it was desirable that money should be cheap; and to that alliance have we been indebted for all our past success. Now, the alliance is with those who do not work—those who, *having risen*, have money to lend—those who desire that food and labor may be cheap, and money dear. To the former we have stood indebted for power successfully to make a war unparalleled in its demands for blood and treasure, and for the existence of a faith in our future such as had never before been witnessed in any country of the world. To the latter stand we now indebted for the facts that faith in the future is gradually passing away; that the burthen of taxation is becoming more and more severe; and that preparation is now being daily made for a financial and political revolution that must result in causing us to forfeit all the advantages that, in the brief period of Mr. Lincoln's administration and at the cost of so many thousand millions, had been acquired.

Believing that careful examination must result in satisfying you that without a change of system the hopes of those who have opposed the government, and the worst fears of those who have throughout sustained it, must all be fully realized, I remain, my dear sir, with great regard,

Yours, very truly,

HENRY C. CAREY.

PHILADELPHIA, Feb. 8, 1866.

LETTER SEVENTH.

DEAR SIR:—

ON a former occasion it was shown that the *tangible* machinery of exchange of France was in the ratio of $30 per head, and that of Great Britain in that of $25; whereas with us it now stood at not over half of this latter quantity. When, however, we come to compare it with the surface over which such machinery is needed to be used, we find, as I propose here to show, differences so exceedingly great as fully to warrant the assertion heretofore made, that no people other than our own could, by any possibility, have effected so large an amount of exchanges while having been allowed the use of so really trivial a quantity of the machinery by aid of which alone they could be made.

Thirty years since the circulation of France, then altogether specie, was estimated at more than $600,000,000, or three thousand dollars per square mile. It now exceeds $1,000,000,000, or more than *five thousand dollars per mile*. At the first of these dates, her annual exports scarcely exceeded $100,000,000, or three dollars per head; but they since have nearly trebled.

In the same time the machinery of circulation of Great Britain has been so much improved that the necessity for the use of coin, or of any other *tangible* evidence of the existence of the power of purchase, has much diminished; and yet, with every step in that direction there has been an increase of the quantity thereof in daily use. At the present moment it bears to the surface over which it needs to be used nearly the same relations as does that of France, being certainly not less, and probably greatly more, than *five thousand dollars per square mile ;** each successive stage of the increase therein having been accompanied by a growth of foreign commerce fully corresponding with that observed in France.

Such being the facts, to what extent do they correspond with the teachings of the learned men who, following blindly in the steps of Hume, so confidently assure us that every increase in the quantity of money used tends to render a country worse as one in which to buy, though better as one in which to sell? Do they not, on the contrary, prove directly the reverse of this? Do they not show clearly that every increase of power to command the use of machinery of circulation is attended with improvement in the condition of a country, *both as sellers and as buyers?* That such is the case can no more be questioned than can the existence of the facts, that light invariably follows the rising of the sun and absence of light his disappearance. Nevertheless, all our practice, as it is proposed now to show, has been in direct accordance with the teachings of learned Thebans who have thus far failed, and yet do fail, to recognize the existence of the great principle, that *the power of accumulation exists in the ratio of the rapidity of circulation.*

Looking now homeward we find that thirty years since, say in 1835-6, the quantity of circulating notes here in use did not exceed, and was probably considerably short of, $120,000,000. Adding to this the little specie then in use, we obtain an amount that certainly could not have much exceeded $170,000,000. The surface then wholly, or partially, occupied, was about 500,000 square miles, and the total circulation must have averaged about *three hundred dollars per mile*, or *one-seventeenth of that now used in France and England.* Shortly before, by aid of a *National* free trade tariff, our public debt had been extinguished, but at that date the effect of a *British* free trade policy had commenced to exhibit itself in the cessation of all disposition to build mills, all effort at development of our mineral resources; and, in the purchase abroad, on credit, of the cloth and iron that should have been made among ourselves. One year later, our foreign credit having become exhausted, there arose a demand so great for the precious metals to go abroad, that banks were compelled so far to curtail their loans that, to avoid the production of an universal

---

* A recent writer states the amount of the precious metals in actual use, and exclusive of that in the bank vaults, at $400,000,000. This would give a total circulation, per square mile, of more than $6,000.

bankruptcy, they themselves at length suspended payment. For all this, as we then were told by Mr. Van Buren, had we been indebted to a "plethora of paper money;" whereas, we now most clearly see, that in *actual amount* it had been less than is at this moment the "paper money" of France, in which a note is rarely seen. Some years later, the precious metals having wholly disappeared, the total circulation of the country was but $60,000,000, the equivalent of three dollars and a half per head, or *one hundred and twenty dollars per square mile* of settled territory. As a consequence of this, the societary circulation had almost ceased, the laborer having been unable to find a market for his labor; the planter and the farmer having been compelled to sell their products at prices lower than had ever before been known; and the general rate of interest having meanwhile attained a point that till then had been almost unexampled. The sheriff expelled the landholder, and an outraged people followed suit by expelling that one of their Presidents who stands now in history as the man by whose advice had been commenced, and by whom had been carried out, the first of our crusades against "paper money;" that executive magistrate who bequeathed to his successor such a condition of the national treasury as made it necessary to send to Europe agents empowered to borrow money, not even a single dollar of which could be then obtained.

Twenty years later, in 1856, the surface occupied having then been nearly trebled, the quantity of circulating notes in use amounted to $200,000,000. California had, meantime, given us hundreds of millions of gold, nearly the whole of which had gone to Europe to pay for cloth and iron that should have been made at home. Some little had, however, here remained, and adding now that little to the circulating notes, we obtain a total of probably $300,000,000, the equivalent of $10 per head, or *two hundred dollars per square mile*. The $200,000,000 of foreign debt of Mr. Van Buren's day had meanwhile grown to $500,000,000, as a necessary consequence of which our credit had become again exhausted. Banks then again stopped payment, and then again were we told that to a "plethora of paper money" had been all our troubles due. Now again did the internal commerce perish, the laborer finding himself unable to sell his labor, or to purchase food and clothing. Now again did the price of money rise to such a height as had scarcely before been known. Now again did the sheriff everywhere expel the farmers and the landholders. Now again, too, did the people expel a President who stands in history as the man who had aided and abetted Mr. Van Buren throughout his crusade against the democratic "paper money;" the one who, notwithstanding all the vast treasures that by California had been supplied, bequeathed to his successor a National Treasury without a dollar, and a public credit so impaired that on a mortgage of the whole property of the Union but the most trivial sums could, by any effort, be obtained; and those too at a rate of interest so high as to be worthy of the weakest and most contemptible countries of Europe, and of them alone.

Three years later, at the close of 1863, the circulation had risen to more than $600,000;000, the surface over which it was needed to be used having, because of secession, meantime declined to less than half. To the population of the loyal States it stood in the ratio of about $30 per head; but to surface it was only *six hundred per mile*. As regarded the former it had risen nearly to a level with that of France and Britain; but as to the latter, it yet stood, as compared with them; in the relation of but *one to eight*. The increase, as compared with 1835, had scarcely been greater than that of France and not a third as great when considered with reference to the growth of population; yet had it so stimulated the societary circulation as to enable us not only to furnish to the government, as loans or revenue, nearly a thousand millions a year; but also to make to it *donations* to an extent that had never before in all the world been known—wealth and power meantime growing among our people with a rapidity so great as not only to have astonished ourselves, but also amazed the world.

With the close of another year we arrive at the last session of Congress to find that body much embarrassed by the questions—*First*, as to how, with an empty treasury, to pay the hundreds of millions then required for discharge of its contracts with soldiers in the field, and with contractors at home who had supplied the food, the clothes, and the transportation that had so much been needed; and *second*, how to guard our people against the dangers to which the internal commerce might find itself exposed on a sudden change from war to peace. Taxes on that commerce had been so heaped up that, in many cases, the foreign manufacturer had been placed almost exactly on a footing with the domestic one; while in very many of them almost the only protection left consisted in the fact, that internal duties were payable in paper, while for those on imports gold was still required. Two causes for embarrassment being thus presented for consideration, it was needed that they should be so disposed of as carefully to protect both the people and the government throughout the long period that must intervene before Congress should be again assembled. In what manner was this done? Let us see.

The claimants on the Treasury did not demand payment. All they asked was, that Congress should authorize the Secretary to give to each and every of them promissory notes, payable at its own pleasure, and bearing no interest; but of such a character as would facilitate their use for the support of families, and for the payment of debts. This *they had a right to demand*, and no honest man in private life could have ventured to refuse it. Congress, however, did refuse to grant the modest application, and for the reason that it feared that such a course of action might have the effect of raising the price of gold, that rise to be, perhaps, followed by a general rise of other articles. Had it, however, studied the facts given by me in a former letter, it must have seen that there had really been very little change in the prices of our products other than that which it had been the object of the tariff of 1861 to produce, as a consequence of the creation of a great domestic market. Labor had been in great demand, and the laborer fully paid. All had had it in their power largely to consume, and the farmer profited of the liberal demands of the artisan, the loyal party of the north meanwhile profiting of the farmer's votes, and the country of the inducements thereby offered to immigration. Failing to see these things, and failing, too, to see that "honesty" was always "the best policy," Congress adjourned, leaving soldiers and their families, contractors and their creditors, to wait the slow process of borrowing money at high rates of interest; when, with a word, their demands could have been so discharged as greatly to have stimulated our internal commerce, while enabling the Treasury readily, and at low rates of interest, to obtain the balance. The erroneous and dishonest course of action then adopted now costs the country more than $20,000,000 in annual interest, its effect meanwhile having been that of causing a waste of productive power greatly larger than our present enormous revenue. Thus have the people been doubly taxed, with corresponding diminution in their power to aid the government; and *therefore it is that the Treasury finds itself now reduced to look to foreign bankers for the help so greatly needed.* Of all the financial blunders ever made it stands now forth as one of the worst. Why it should have been made was that Congress then had, as few of our people have even now, no proper appreciation of the fact, that *of all the commercial nations of the world our own is the one that is worst supplied with the machinery of circulation—that machinery for the use of which men are accustomed to pay interest.*

From that time to the present, the whole tendency of the national action has been in the direction of lessening the supply of that machinery and increasing the price paid for its use, the result now exhibiting itself in the facts, that while in the intervening period we have increased by one-half the number of people who need its services; while we have more than doubled the surface over which it must be used; while throughout the additional surface there is a total absence of such machinery; we have by a full third reduced the quantity in use; the present actual amount being but $460,000,000, the equivalent of $12 50 per head of the population, and of less than $300 per mile of wholly or partially occupied surface, the proportions being thus less than half of those above exhibited as having existed in the prosperous days of the close of 1863.

How this is now affecting our internal trade is shown in the following figures exhibiting the receipts of free State produce at New York in the month of January for this and the two past years:—

	1864.	1865.	1866.
Ashes, bbls.	1,399	937	540
Wheat flour, bbls.	315,906	173,451	100,564
Corn meal, bbls.	35,699	42,405	26,954
Wheat, bush.	10,507	5,819	28,137
Rye, "	5,657	2,382	2,405
Oats, "	284,726	219,469	159,414
Barley, "	63,603	29,751	35,532
Peas, "	687	5,131	2,585
Corn, "	160,039	142,680	178,651
Pork, pkgs.	45,826	36,326	17,311
Beef, "	28,384	25,939	3,261
Cut meats, pkgs.	40,966	18,024	4,245
Butter, pkgs.	40,028	67,828	42,413
Cheese, "	15,096	25,018	6,300
Lard, tcs. and bbls.	10,658	14,872	10,167
Lard, kegs .	1,683	94	2,031
Whiskey, bbls. .	36,802	6,199	7,383
Petroleum, galls.	55,452	41,694	98,062

The above is copied from a journal whose editors have, of all, been most urgent that the "greenback" circulation should be withdrawn with a view to reduction of prices and extension of our power to supply with rude produce the distant markets of the world—"thorough taxation" being meantime maintained with a view to extinguishment of the public debt, and thereby "killing the goose" in the vain hope of "finding the golden egg." How far the foreign commerce of the port profits by this course of action is shown by the following comparison of the monthly exports taken from its columns :—

	1864.	1865.	1866.
Ashes—Pots, bbls.	478	516	502
Asbes—Pearls, bbls.	21	58	10
Beeswax, lb. .	38,381	32,549	38,001
Wheat flour, bbls.	166,768	126,906	117,318
Rye flour, "	409	. . .	120
Corn meal, "	12,987	14,366	7,235
Wheat, bush.	1,282,313	43,834	58,226
Rye, "	105	141	25,427
Oats, "	1,353	7,560	18,733
Peas, "	37,831	6,047	7,761
Corn, "	10,999	30,835	551,320
Candles, bxs.	10,577	16,403	6,527
Coal, tons .	1,313	3,071	455
Hay, bales .	1,886	4,479	6,088
Hops, "	3,929	3,844	107
Lard, galls. .	10,509	2,947	2,182
Linseed, galls.	1,564	2,578	466
Pork, bbls. .	14,876	12,222	8,396
Beef, "	2,679	4,776	1,991
Beef, tos. .	12,844	7,217	4,673
Cut meats, lb.	15,745,514	4,354,303	2,193,678
Butter, lb.	3,317,125	2,166,137	239,837
Cheese, "	2,743,334	4,834,989	1,538,742
Lard, "	3,265,832	2,954,660	2,423,345
Tallow, lb. .	4,193,548	3,674,420	1,285,170
Petroleum, galls. .	1,321,517	630,031	3,086,194

The more abundant the machinery of transport the greater will be the quantity of goods transported, and the less the charge for transportation to the great advantage of producer and consumer, and to the great benefit of the governing power. The more perfect the supply of the machinery of exchange the more prompt and numerous will the exchanges be, and the lower the rate of interest, to the great advantage of both public and private revenues. At the present moment this latter is greatly short, and hence the existence of a *paralysis* by means of which we are, as it is asserted, to reach *resumption*. To me, however, it appears to be the road by which most speedily to attain the point of a disgraceful and wholly unnecessary *repudiation*.

Believing that careful study of the facts must result in satisfying you of the accuracy of the views thus presented, I am, my dear sir, with great respect and regard,

Yours truly,
H. C. CAREY.

PHILADELPHIA, February 10, 1866.

CONCLUSION.

DEAR SIR:—

Influential Republican journals, by many supposed to represent the views of the Administration, are proving daily to the men of intelligence and enterprise—those " speculators" who have created the mills, furnaces, and mines to which we have stood indebted for power to make the war— that not only must they no longer rely upon the co-operation of the national authorities, but that they may count securely upon their opposition or oppression.

Appealing constantly to the ignorance, but never to the intelligence, of their readers, they denounce such men as belonging to a class whose ruin should afford just cause of triumph to all who in the past few years have sought to aid their country's cause.

Crippling those who had commenced the creation of new mills and furnaces, they have already closed many of those that had been throughout the war at work, and are now most effectually preventing the undertaking of any new enterprises tending towards development of our mineral wealth, or towards increase of our industrial forces.

Therefore is it:

That we are largely and rapidly diminishing the demand for human service, and lessening the power of the laborer, the mechanic, and the miner to claim reward for labor; this too being done at the very time when thousands and tens of thousands of able-bodied men have been, and are being discharged from the public service; the very time, too, when active and earnest men are engaged in an effort to draw from Europe the supplies of men required for enabling us to develop our vast resources :

That we are lessening the demand upon the farmer for the fruits of the earth, and compelling him to increased dependence on foreign markets :

That there is a decline in the power of our people to maintain with Britain that competition for the production and sale of cloth and iron to which alone can we look for such reduction of their prices as may compensate the farmer for the burthens of the war :

That, while reducing the prices of food and labor, we are largely and rapidly raising the general rate of interest, thereby enabling those who *do not* work to profit at the cost of those who *do :*

That we are making taxation more and more burthensome while lowering the rate of exchange to the great advantage of those who prefer to expend their incomes abroad rather than do the same at home :

That we are thus daily making it more impossible that our mills and furnaces should supply the domestic market; that those who "live at ease" should apply their means to the advantage of those who labor; that ships should be built to enter into competition with those of Europe; that we should in time of peace extend, or even maintain, that independence to which we have been indebted for recent success in war.

As consequences of all this, we are—

Supporting abroad, at an estimated annual cost of $100,000,000, a hundred thousand of our people engaged in consuming foreign food and paying for foreign labor :

Enabling foreigners to deluge our markets with cloth and iron in the production of which have been consumed hundreds of millions of bushels of foreign food :

Maintaining those foreigners in a monopoly of the carrying trade between this and Europe, and thus compelling our own people to the exclusive use of ships that represent both foreign labor and foreign food :

Increasing in every manner that can be devised the demand for the capital and the skill of Europe while destroying demand for the wonderful mechanical skill of people at home :

Raising the prices of all the things we need to buy, money included, while lowering those of all that we need to sell, stocks and bonds not excepted :

Buying now, annually, to the extent of hundreds of millions of dollars more than we have, or are like to have, to sell :

Exporting every ounce of gold yielded by California :

Increasing daily the necessity for going abroad to beg for loans, and thus adding to a foreign debt that now already exceeds a thousand millions of dollars :

Selling abroad at little more than half price bonds that must, at full prices, be redeemed in gold :

Paying thereon, on the security of the whole property of the Union, a rate of interest unknown to any really civilized people of the world; and more than thrice the rate at this instant paid by that British government with whom we should be now contending for control of the commerce of the world:

Compounding interest by borrowing the money with which to pay it, and thereby doubling its amount in less than half a dozen years.

Such being our present course of operation, it may be not improper here to ask the questions: "Why it is that such things should now be done?" Why is it that we have so entirely abandoned the policy that carried us so triumphantly through the war? Seeking a reply thereto, we find it in the fact, that our eyes are closed to the existence of a very simple principle whose perfect truth has recently been so fully demonstrated as to make it absolutely marvellous that it should now be doubted—that principle being embraced in the following words: to wit, THE POWER OF ACCUMULATION EXISTS IN THE RATIO OF THE RAPIDITY OF THE SOCIETARY CIRCULATION.

Throughout the war that circulation steadily increased in its rapidity, and for the reason that a really *national free trade policy* created demand for labor and its products, a really *national system of circulation* meantime giving to the internal commerce facilities of exchange such as it never before had known. Since the peace, however, we have been travelling backward, and undoing all that had so well been done—piling up taxes on one hand, while, on the other, not only refusing to our people the power to create for themselves machinery of circulation, but actually *frightening home* that which previously had been furnished; doing this, too, to such extent that *the quantity now in use bears to the exchanges needed to be performed a proportion that, with the exception of the closing years of our most calamitous British free trade periods, is less than has ever yet been known.*

The periods thus referred to are the following:—

I. That one which followed the conclusion, in 1815, of *political peace* with Britain, to be followed by that *industrial war* which was proclaimed by Messrs. Brougham, Hume, and other British *liberals*, when they announced in Parliament their determination to "strangle in the cradle" the then growing manufactures of America and of Europe; that one in which British hostility to American industry produced a general paralysis like to that which is now again so rapidly approaching, and thus enabled General Jackson, by aid of his admirable letter to Dr. Coleman, to reach the presidential chair:

II. That one in which bankruptcy of the treasury and general ruin of our working men paved the way for expulsion of Mr. Van Buren from the chair of state:

III. That one in which public and private bankruptcy, civil war, and almost universal ruin, were exhibited to the world as the bequest of Mr. Buchanan, on his retirement from public life, to the people to whom he had stood so much indebted.

From all this we speedily recovered, doing so by aid of a *national* free trade tariff, and a *national* medium of circulation. *To* all of it we are now returning, having, by means of internal taxes, almost re-enacted the *British* free trade tariff, and being now engaged in frightening out of use even the existing circulation. Let us so continue, and we shall soon be called to witness a political revolution quite as thorough as were those which drove to private life the two of our public men who, of all others, had placed themselves most fully on record as opposed to progress in the direction of that substitution for coin of the circulating note by means of which the farmer, the laborer, and the mechanic are brought more nearly on a level with the great men who live at their expense—those who build palaces by aid of the performance of exchanges to the extent of thousands of millions without the use of a dollar of coin, and almost without being required to use a single note.

For all this the remedy, my dear sir, is clearly indicated by your present action in reference to the fractional currency, of which, as we are informed, nearly half a million per week has recently been sent to the Southern States. The people of those States needing such notes they are at once supplied. Why, however, should they be denied the use of notes of larger size, say of one, two, five, ten, or twenty dollars? Why, even, deny them those of a hundred or a thousand dollars? Why compel them, when selling bales of cotton, to accept payment in notes of less than a single dollar? Why not at once furnish them with facilities of exchange by means of which they may be enabled promptly to discharge each and every engagement they need to make? Why not do the same with the people of the West, thereby enabling the farmer to extend, instead of, as now, diminishing his cultivation? Why not place it in the power of our whole people to do as they did two years since, deal for cash with one another? The simple question that, so far as this question of credit is concerned, is now to be settled, is, whether throughout the whole country our people shall be buying and selling on credit, the poor man everywhere paying to the rich the ten, twenty, or even thirty per cent. demanded for the use of money; or, whether the treasury shall make itself the general debtor to such extent as may enable all to deal for cash, thereby placing the poor man more nearly on a level with the rich one. Adopting this latter course the treasury will give us once again those facilities of exchange to which we have stood indebted for that wonderful rapidity of circulation by means of which labor and capital were so much economized as to have enabled us to *donate* to the treasury hundreds of millions, while *lending* it thousands of millions. Adopting the former, we shall rapidly return to the position in which, by reason of sluggishness of the circulation, labor and capital were *annually* wasted to an extent greater than the whole cost of four years of the most expensive war the world has ever seen. By means of the one, we shall so deepen the water as to enable the treasury ship to float securely, while advancing steadily in the direction of *resumption;* whereas, by adopting the other, the water must from day to day be made more shallow, until at last there will remain to us, as our only port, that of *repudiation.*

That we may hereafter move in the one here first indicated, all that is needed is that the treasury shall make itself once again "master of the situation," controlling banks and brokers—excellent servants, but the worst of masters—instead of being controlled by them. To that end, let it give full consideration to the great fact, that, notwithstanding the density of population and consequent diminution of necessity for the use of any tangible machinery of exchange, *the coin alone* in actual use, in Great Britain, *is nearly equal in amount to the total quantity of that machinery here allowed for a population greatly larger, and scattered over almost a continent.* Let it remark the fact that, trivial as our allowance now is, the public mind is kept in a state of continual alarm by means of threats of measures of contraction. Let it reflect, that the more perfect the supply of that machinery by means of which alone exchanges are made *from hand to hand,* the more rapid must be the increase in the quantity of that required for making exchanges from place to place. Let it see that the injurious effect of deficiency in the supply thereof increases geometrically as distance from the great centres of commerce increases arithmetically, with constant tendency towards production, throughout the South and West, of that irritation which, if permitted once again to grow as it has in time past done, must result in final dissolution of our Union. Let it see, that in supplying that machinery it is therefore doing what is most required for producing harmony throughout the Union, while diminishing the taxation required for payment of interest on the public debt. Let it then grant to the men of the South, as regards exercise of the power to create banks, and to supply themselves with machinery of exchange, the same freedom that has been already granted to the loyal people of the North. Let it see that with the reincorporation of the South, and consequent extension of the field of commerce, there has arisen a necessity for exchanges greatly more numerous than were required to be performed when, two years since, there was found employment for a circulation greater by almost one-half, than that which now exists. Finally, let it see that the time has come for granting to our people facilities of exchange equal, at least, to those required during the war; and, that by so doing it will at once, and forever, bring to a close the practice of *shinning it* from day to day by aid of those "temporary loans" and "certificates of indebtedness" by means of which banks and brokers, at the cost of public creditors, are enabled to make enormous profits, the treasury meanwhile paying for the privilege of thus postponing payment of its debts, to the extent of little less than a dozen millions per annum.

Let these things be done, and then will there at once reappear that *faith in our future* by means of which we had been enabled to make our way through the wonderful war that has just now closed. Let them be done, and activity and energy will at once replace the paralysis that now so much exists. Let them be done, and there will no longer be *a daily waste of capital and labor greater in amount than the total public revenue.* Let them be done, and at once our people will recommence the building of houses, mills, and furnaces, thereby making demand for the services of the laborer and the products of the farm. Let them be done, and the public revenue will so much increase as to enable you to dispense at once with all those taxes which now so much impede our internal commerce. Let them be done, and the world will soon cease to witness the extraordinary spectacle of a country flaunting the Monroe Doctrine in the eyes of foreign sovereigns, its people meantime besieging every little banking house in Europe, seeking thence to draw some small supply of the "sinews of war." Let them be done, and we shall at once re-enter upon competition with Britain for control of the commerce of the world. Let them be done, and great prosperity will enable our people to more and more retain the produce of California mines; and thus, with profit to all and injury to none, gradually to prepare for that resumption which both you and I so much desire to see achieved. Let them be done, and we shall not only cease, by the export of bonds, to increase our dependence on Europe, but shall gradually buy back those now held abroad, and thus increase our independence. Let them be done, and the great republican party will continue to control the movements of the great Ship of State. Let them be done, and the East and the West, the North and the South, will become from day to day more thoroughly knit together, the Union thenceforward marching steadily forward towards the occupation of that position which its wonderful natural resources, and the extraordinary intelligence of its people so well entitle it to claim, to wit, that of leader of the civilization, and controller of the commerce of the world.

Let them be *not* done and paralysis, to be followed by financial ruin, must pave the way for the destruction of that great party which has carried us through the war, but which, by reason of *deficiency of courage*, has thus far failed to give to the country that prosperity in peace for which it so well had fought, and had so largely paid. Let them be *not* done, and there will be growing discord, ending in final dissolution of that glorious Union in whose behalf so many have fought, bled, and suffered. Let them be *not* done, and the public debt of the Union will, in the estimation of the world, and that at no very distant period, stand side by side with that of the Confederate States.

The question, my dear sir, now before you for determination is, in my belief, the most momentous one ever yet submitted to the decision of a single individual. We have just now closed a little internal difficulty, leaving yet for settlement the one great question as to whether the world is, in all the future, to be subjected to that *British* and *anti-national* system which has for its especial object that of enabling bankers and brokers to enslave the farmers and laborers of the outside world; or, whether the Union shall now place itself in the lead of the now agricultural nations for resistance to that system, and for relief of the agriculturists of the world from the oppressions under which they so long have suffered. Contraction, by means of which the price of money is being so rapidly carried up, looks in the first of these directions and must result in giving the victory to England. Expansion, by means of which there shall be re-established the alliance between the treasury and the employers of money — farmers, laborers, artisans, and "speculators" — looks in the second, and will give the victory to us—health, wealth, strength, and the power of accumulation growing always with growth in the rapidity of the societary circulation.

It may, however, be said that gold will rise in price. That for a brief period it must do so is very certain. So soon, however, as that rise shall have produced the effect of lessening the importations by which we now are being inundated, and so soon as we shall have established a small counter-current of bonds, it will fall again—that fall continuing until we shall have placed ourselves in a position to retain at home the produce of California, thereby enabling ourselves quietly and profitably to resume the use of the precious metals.

Begging you now, my dear sir, to excuse my repeated trespasses on your attention, and earnestly hoping that you may be guided to a right decision, I remain, with sincere regard and respect,

Yours very truly,

HENRY C. CAREY.

PHILADELPHIA, February 17, 1866.

POSTSCRIPT.

Dear Sir :—

In one of the journals of the day I find an article on the subject of prices that seems to me worthy of being made the subject of a postscript to the letters with whose perusal I have already troubled you. It is as follows :—

"The advance in house rents and in the price of stores and business places in the large cities, is attracting general attention. At New York the rents paid, and the prices at which favorable locations find purchasers, are subjects of almost daily newspaper comment. The same disposition to run into high figures is observable here and in all cities, and carries with it, to the observant mind, wholesome admonition of the end to which it points. At New York, in some fashionable quarters, the proposed rise in rents for first-class dwellings is, in many cases, from fifty to seventy-five per cent., houses on the Fifth Avenue renting as high as $12,000 a year, while in other localities dwellings which last year rented for $3,000 are now let for $4,000. The rents of stores are correspondingly increased. A store in Broadway, 150 by 25 feet (four stories high), was rented last spring for $40,000 a year. Previously for five years the annual rental was but $13,000. The lease of a corner store, for $12,000, expires next spring, and the owner has fixed on $42,000 a year for the future. The half of a fourth floor, 25 by 100 feet, was rented a few days ago for the sum of $3,000. A corner basement on Broadway rents for $7,000 a year. The *Journal of Commerce* mentions the following case, illustrative of the same extravagant tendency of prices :—

"'A dry goods firm have rented a store for the current year at $15,000. The owner called on them a few weeks since to ask their intentions for another year. They expressed a wish to remain if the terms were agreeable. He offered to treat them fairly, and suggested that $40,000 per annum for a three years' lease would be a reasonable advance. They indignantly refused to treat, and he left. After a few hours' search for another place, they concluded to pocket their indignation and accede to the terms. Calling on the owner for this purpose, they learned that they were too late, the premises having been leased for three years at $50,000 per annum. A further search left them hopeless of securing anything more eligible, and they have purchased the lease of the new parties for a bonus of $10,000. We do not see how these enormous rents are to be met ; but we suppose it " will all come right in the end." In the words of a graphic oracle of the market, " if everybody thinks somebody is going to smash, nobody had better tell anybody about it.'"

"We think with the *Newark Advertiser* that it is impossible that the condition of affairs disclosed in these extracts can long continue. There is certainly nothing in the present position of the business of the country to justify such an exorbitant appreciation of real estate values. Already an apprehension is beginning to prevail in some business circles that a crash, induced by natural causes, cannot be much longer postponed; and in any event, it is obvious that should Congress authorize a policy of contraction by the national treasury, a speedy check must be given to the present reckless extravagance of prices."

The "reckless extravagance" here exhibited is, as we are assured, to be checked by "a policy of contraction." In opposition to this, however, we have the fact, that it *follows* a "contraction" that has been for months in progress—one so serious that it has now reduced the "paper money" circulation to an amount actually less, per head, than is the *coin alone* of Great Britain, leaving wholly out of view the hundreds of millions of her "paper money," and the thousands of millions of credit money by means of which she is enabled to transact countless millions of business without the need of either coin or notes. Such being the case, may it not, my dear sir, be possible, that the "reckless extravagance" here referred to comes as the *natural consequence* of a "contraction" that has largely raised the rate of interest throughout the country—that has greatly diminished general confidence—that has caused the present paralysis—and that threatens destruction of the internal commerce; and that the real remedy is to be found in the pursuit of a course of measures tending to the restoration of confidence, such as I have already indicated. That it is so you will, as I think, be prepared to admit when you shall have accompanied me in a brief review of the various phenomena by which the crises of 1837 and 1857 had been preceded, as follows :—

By aid of our first really *national* tariff, that of 1828, the country had, in 1832, been brought to a state of prosperity such as had never before been seen, and the public revenue had so greatly grown as to make it necessary to wholly free from impost duties tea, coffee, and very many articles of general use. Still, however, the revenue grew, and so largely grew as to require that, in order to the absorption of the balance in the treasury, the three per cents., held in Holland, should be extinguished. As a consequence of this, the year 1835 saw the country wholly free from public debt, and almost, if not even entirely, free from foreign liabilities of any description, whether those of States or of individuals. The seed, however, of a great and destructive foreign debt had been already planted, and was destined soon to yield a most abundant crop of fruit. By the compromise tariff of 1833 it had been provided, that all duties on foreign merchandise should biennially be reduced until, in 1842, we should attain the point of a perfectly horizontal tariff of 20 per cent. From that date the population and its demand for cloth and iron steadily increased, but the growth in number of mills, furnaces, and mines wholly ceased; and with every step in that direction there came a decline in the demand for domestic labor, and in the domestic commerce. With each, it became more necessary to obtain abroad commodities that should have been made at home. Importations, therefore, grew rapidly, and the more they grew the greater here became the waste of labor and of capital. The more that waste the greater became the necessity for looking to Atlantic cities as the only places in which to make exchanges, with constant increase in the rents of city stores and dwellings until, at length, in the spring of 1837, they had attained a point higher than had ever before been known. The day of settlement was then, however, close at hand, our foreign credit having, even then, somewhat declined. It came soon after, bringing with it almost the annihilation of city rents, which were not again to attain the point from which they then had started, until after the restoration of the domestic commerce by means of the protective tariff of 1842. *The real and permanent interests of city proprietors are thus shown to be in perfect harmony with those of mill, mine, and railroad owners, and of those who look for food and clothing to employment in such works.*

Coming now to a later period, we find that at the date of the discovery of California gold another *British free trade crisis* had been close at hand. For a time the influx of that gold staved it off and caused great increase in the rapidity of the societary circulation, the effects of which, as regarded our industrial interests, are clearly shown in the following figures representing the quantity of anthracite coal then sent to market :—

1850 . . . 3,321,000 tons.	1854 . . . 5,831,000 tons.
1851 . . . 4,329,000 "	1855 . . . 6,486,000 "
1852 . . . 4,899,000 "	1856 . . . 6,751,000 "
1853 . . . 5,097,000 "	1857 . . . 6,431,000 "

From 1850 to 1856, as here is seen, there was a steady upward movement. The downward one, however, had now commenced, and as a necessary consequence of that paralysis of the domestic commerce which here exhibits itself in the prices of railroad shares :—

	1852–3.	December, 1856
Baltimore and Ohio	96	84¼
Boston and Worcester	105	83¾
New York and Erie	85	61½
Cleveland and Pittsburg	93	56¼
Michigan Southern	118	88¼
Pennsylvania Central	93	94½
Camden and Amboy	149	124
Boston and Maine	102	77½
Total	843	670
Average	105⅜	83¾

A thousand millions of property had been thus one-fifth deteriorated. Why? Because, that labor was then everywhere being wasted. Because, that mills and furnaces were ceasing to work, and mines were being abandoned. Because, that artisans and miners were wandering everywhere in search of employment, coal meanwhile selling in this city for $3 50 per ton of 2,240 pounds, or little more than now is charged for transporting it less than a single hundred miles on its road to market. Because, that credit was then gradually passing away, the price of money in our cities meantime ranging between 10 and 20 per cent. Importations, however, were immense, and the foreign debt steadily increased, the prices of city lots and rents of city houses meanwhile growing with its growth until at length they attained a height that, even in 1837, had never before been reached.

Thus far, as we see, the parallel is perfect between the periods preceding the great crises of 1837 and 1857, domestic paralysis, pauperism of our people, waste of capital and labor, and destruction of the value of mill, mine, furnace, and railroad property, having gone hand in hand with augmentation of the already enormous foreign debt, and increase in the price of city lots and rents of city stores and warehouses. May the parallel be yet further carried out? Assuredly it may. In both, the foreign credit soon became exhausted. In both, city lots and houses fell with a rapidity greater even than that which had marked their rise, crushing in their fall all whose property had been mortgaged, and thus enabling "speculators" for a fall to profit at the cost of those who had "speculated" for a rise, the rich being thus made richer as the poor became poorer. In both, banks stopped payment. In both, importations ceased. In both, the public revenue passed almost away, leaving the national ship high and dry amid the shoals of bankruptcy. In both, the people marked their appreciation of the public servants by expelling from offices nearly the whole of those, from doorkeeper to President, who, by their war upon the domestic credit and domestic commerce, and by their alliance with those "speculators" for a fall who had built no railroads, sunk no mines, and employed no labor, had aided in bringing about a state of affairs so ruinous to working men of all descriptions, farmers and laborers, miners and artisans—and so utterly destructive of the national character and the national power.

Now again, in 1866, do we find the parallel to the periods that preceded the great crises of 1837 and 1857. Now again, has the domestic commerce become greatly crippled. Now again, are mines, mills, and furnaces idle. Now again, has capital so invested ceased to yield to their owners even the smallest profit.* Now again, does decline in the consumption

---

* To this cotton and woollen mills furnish exceptions. Why they do so was shown in my fifth letter.

of coal furnish evidence of decay of our industrial interests. Now again, do artisans pace our streets vainly seeking to find demand for services they would gladly render.* Now again, has railroad property fallen, and, notwithstanding our great increase of numbers—notwithstanding the vast advantages enjoyed throughout the war by northern roads—notwithstanding the present enormous rates of freight—so greatly fallen, that they do not now command, in "paper money," even the prices at which they sold when the early supplies of California gold were so stimulating our domestic commerce as largely to increase the demand for coal. In proof of this I give here again the prices of the above-named roads, as follows:—

	1852-3.	February, 1866.
Baltimore and Ohio	98	112½
Boston and Worcester	105	131
New York and Erie	85	82
Cleveland and Pittsburg	93	81½
Michigan Southern	118	71½
Pennsylvania Central	93	111¾
Camden and Amboy	149	118
Boston and Maine	162	118¾
Total	843	827
Average in gold	105⅜	
Average in greenbacks		103⅜

Now again, however, have importations. grown, and grown to such a height as to have caused astonishment even in the minds of those excellent British free traders who did the smuggling of the war. Now again does the foreign debt increase at an appalling rate. Now again does the domestic credit disappear, with large advance in the rate of interest. Now again do influential journalists, supposed to represent the views of the administration, stand side by side with "speculators" for a fall, denouncing those "speculators" for a rise to whom we had been indebted for power to make the war; just as, in 1833, we had to such men been indebted for ability to extinguish the public debt; and as, in 1845, we had owed to such the power once again to pay interest on the State and other debts then held abroad. Now again, too, have the prices and rents of city lots and houses attained prodigious elevation—having risen to a point as much exceeding that attained in 1857 as does the wonderful rapidity with which we now are adding to our foreign debt exceed that exhibited in '37 and '57. Then, the annual addition counted by tens of millions only. Now, it counts by hundreds of millions.

The parallel between the preparations for a crisis being thus complete, may it not now, as to results, be fully carried out? Assuredly it may,

---

* Ten days since an advertisement for hands to work in a machine shop of this city, brought more than *three hundred applications*. Since then, hundreds who were then at work have been discharged.

with the difference only, that when the crash shall come it will be more thorough and complete than any the world has ever known. Why? Because our banks stand to-day on public stocks and bonds, and nothing else. Because our foreign debt is being contracted on the faith of treasury promises, compliance with which is wholly dependent upon receipts from taxation of a domestic commerce now, and rapidly, becoming so entirely paralyzed that it is likely soon almost to cease to have existence. To a large extent those taxes have, in the past year, *been paid out of capital;* but to a larger one must they soon cease to be paid at all. So soon as these results of our present policy shall have become a little more clearly visible, the foreign credit must pass away, and with it the power to collect, in any manner, whether from the foreign or the domestic commerce, sufficient even to meet the annual demand for interest; leaving wholly out of view the thousand millions of floating debt, *payment* of which must then be made—acceptance of other bonds being entirely optional with the holders of those which now exist.

The high city rents of 1836 and 1856 were followed by bankruptcy of banks and merchants, ruin to the farmer, and pauperism to the laborer. Owing little or nothing, the treasury escaped with little more than loss of revenue. Those of 1866 must bring in their train bankruptcy of *the one universal debtor*, that national treasury into which our people have so freely poured so large a portion of the profits of the past few years. The former crises were followed by political revolutions the most complete. The one now impending, if it shall be allowed to come, must bring with it disunion and repudiation, and thus enable the South to achieve in peace the end for whose attainment they made the war.

The cause of all the evil now existing, and all that now is threatened, is to be found in the fact that threats of a resumption that, under existing circumstances, is clearly seen to be entirely impracticable—one that never can take place until we shall at least *begin* to retain the produce of California mines—have wholly annihilated that *faith in the future* to which we have been indebted for past success. If we would avoid the dangers with which we are now threatened—if we would maintain the Union—THAT FAITH MUST BE RESTORED. To that end we now need clear and distinct action on the part of Congress tending towards remedy of that great mistake of the last session, referred to in my seventh letter, which has already cost the country a waste of capital and labor to the full extent of the $600,000,000 then ordered to be borrowed, leaving still that vast amount a burthen to be carried. Let that error be now corrected. Let the treasury borrow *from the people* the $200,000,000 that they will most gladly lend on notes bearing no interest, therewith discharging the floating debt by which it is embarrassed, and for which it now is paying, of annual interest, little less than $12,000,000. Let it arrest the export of California gold by retaining in its vaults all that is not required for payment of the demands of public creditors. Let it abolish all those taxes by which the domestic commerce is being now destroyed, and it will speedily find itself enabled once again to feel itself "master of the situation," which now it certainly is not.

Nothing that could here be mentioned would so much rejoice our whole people as would a knowledge of the fact that Congress had decided to *permit* them—poor and rich, great and small—to unite in lending to the treasury the sum of $200,000,000, receiving in exchange simple promises of repayment at the pleasure of the borrower. Effecting *such* a loan, the treasury would be at once enabled to accumulate a store of gold, and thus, while enabling our people more readily to pay the diminished taxes, begin to move in the direction of resumption. Selling bonds abroad, in the hope of being able to re-import the gold of California, is but the direct and certain road to *repudiation.*

Let the men who made the war now unite together in giving activity to the circulation and life to the people, and they will find themselves sustained, while the Union will be maintained. Let them continue onward in the present false direction and both must be forever lost.

Once more apologizing for this further trespass upon your time and attention, I remain, my dear sir,

Yours faithfully,

HENRY C. CAREY.

PHILADELPHIA, February 17, 1866.

THE NATIONAL BANK AMENDMENT BILL.

REPRINTED FROM THE NORTH AMERICAN AND UNITED STATES GAZETTE,
April, 1866.

THE existing national bank system having proved in some respects seriously defective, it is proposed to amend it, a bill for that purpose being now before the Senate. Whether, should it become a law, it will tend towards correction, or increase, of existing error, it is our purpose here to inquire.

Of all the banking institutions of the world those of New England have been the most regular in their action. Why? Because, of all, they have traded most on their own proper means, and least on those of other people, their average excess of loans beyond their capitals having rarely exceeded sixty per cent. In some of the States, indeed, that average has, for long periods of years, been under forty per cent.—southern and western banks having meanwhile traded beyond their capitals to the extent of one, two, and even three hundred per cent. The larger the proportion borne by the base of a building to its height, the greater must necessarily be the tendency towards stability; and it is for the reason that the foundations of eastern banks have been broad as compared with their elevation that the people of New England have had a currency so stable, and have enjoyed the advantages of the banking system in more perfection, and at smaller cost, than any other of the communities of the world.

For all this they have been indebted to that freedom of competition which has resulted from the facility with which bank charters have been obtained—New England legislators having generally shown themselves to be of the opinion that the more numerous the shops at which money, coffee, cloth, or iron could be bought or sold, the more accurately would the supply of those commodities be proportioned to the demand, and the more moderate the charges of those by whom the work was done. New York, a colony of New England, has followed in the same direction, granting full power to create banks any and everywhere, provided only that those who desired to issue circulating notes should first deposit security with the State.

Out of the two systems has grown our present national banking law, nominally free, yet less free than either because of its having given us a procrustean bed in which to lie, limiting, as it does, to $300,000,000, or little more than $8 per head of the present population of the Union, the amount of capital that may be applied to the trade in money, while leaving to the owners of those few millions full power to trade to the extent of thousands of millions, and thus creating a sort of inverted pyramid. As a consequence of this it is, that we now see banks dividing 20 and 25 per cent. where before they were well content with 8 or 10—the danger of revulsion increasing geometrically as the figure which indicates the dividend increases arithmetically.

The remedy for all this would be found in the existence of a power to convert into banking capital money standing on deposit to the credit of individuals, whether by creation of additional banks, or by enlargement of the foundations of those already in existence. That remedy existed under the New York system, but it has no existence in that national one of whose freedom we so much boast, but which is, in this respect, greatly inferior to the one for which it has been substituted.

New York insisted upon security for the payment of circulating notes, but it granted perfect freedom as to the quantity that might be issued, leaving to the people to determine for themselves whether they would carry their money balances in their pockets, or leave them on deposit in the banks. Here, again, the national system is much inferior, security having been insisted on while freedom has not been granted.

The national system as it now exists is a monopoly one, there being no power to create a single rival to existing banks. It compels capital to lie idle and unproductive to its owners, thus increasing the profits, and the power for evil, of those to whom the monopoly has been granted. Setting no limits to the exercise of that power its tendencies are in the direction of general instability, to be followed by financial crises that cannot fail to prove more severe than any of those by which we have in the past been so much afflicted.

Does the proposed amendment look to the correction of any of these evils? It does not. On the contrary, it tends to extend, to perpetuate, and to intensify them. More than half the Union being as yet unsupplied with those very necessary institutions called banks, it proposes to grant to that vast extent of country power for their establishment to the pitiful extent of $15,000,000, or somewhat less than a single dollar per head—thereby giving to the *whole* Union just five per cent. more than, three years since, was granted to *less than half* of it, thus making the monopoly even more complete. With every step in that direction the system must become more unstable, yet are these restrictions imposed by legislators who sincerely desire to produce the reverse effect.

Twenty years since, Sir Robert Peel gave to the people of England a banking law so bad that, now its defects have come to be recognized, it is to be regarded as somewhat wonderful that any one could, even for a moment, have supposed that it could be made to work. That it has not worked we know from the fact that the bank has already twice been forced to ask for interference of the government as the only means of preventing an actual stoppage of payment. How it has operated as regards public and private interests, and the movement of commerce, is well exhibited in an able article in the last number of *Blackwood's Magazine,* from which we take the following paragraph, closely descriptive of what is already occurring among ourselves.

"The Bank of England now charges 8 and 9 per cent. in circumstances where previously it used to charge 4½. As a natural consequence the dividends of banks have risen almost to a fabulous extent, and the profit of financial companies and of all other parties who deal in money has proportionately increased. On the other hand, as an equally necessary consequence, the price of the funds is steadily falling, and railway shares and the profits of all other kinds of industrial enterprise are proportionately depressed. The increased rate which railway and other companies have to pay on their debentures, and which traders have to pay for their bills, tends to neutralize the increased business which most of them are carrying on. The stock of banking and financial companies is raised in value, while that of mercantile and industrial companies tends to be lowered, by this recent change in the practice of the Bank of England—a change which it is impossible to check as long as the present system of monopoly is allowed to exist."

The most serious defects of the British law have been carefully copied in our own, but the danger to be apprehended here was less, and for the reason that the system was supposed really to mean free banking. Now, however, after having legislated out of existence all the State banks, it is proposed to limit the banking capital of half a continent, with a population already far exceeding that of Britain, to an amount that is less than the mere liabilities of two only of the many joint-stock banks of London,* and thus to create a monopoly more complete even than that which now so much excites the ire of the English people—doing this, too, in a country whose population doubles in little more than twenty years, and whose production, and consequent need of the facilities of exchange, should increase at least twice as fast..

The British government is indebted to the Bank of England £14,000,000 or $70,000,000. To that amount the latter may issue circulating notes without providing gold with which to meet them; but, for every additional pound in circulation it must have a sovereign in its vaults. To the extent of tens of millions, or even hundreds if it will, it may incur liabilities, and the money thus obtained may be re-lent at any rate of interest. The day arriving when many of those to whom it stands indebted call for payment, it endeavors to contract its loans, and thus makes money scarce. This contraction being long continued panic comes, with increased demand for notes,† until at length its circulation, in excess of $70,000,000, stands on a level with its gold. From that instant everything is at a dead-lock, and further movement becomes impossible. Its creditor, with thousands or tens of thousands at his credit, asking for notes receives for answer that the power of issue has been exhausted, the circulation having already reached a level with the gold. Failing to obtain paper, he asks for gold, then learning that, large as is the quantity in the vaults, it is all, by law, required there to remain as security for the circulation. The bank would now stop payment did not the government, as it always has done, and always must in future do, now step in and authorize the violation of a fundamental condition of its charter—the most absurd of all the conditions ever inserted in the charter of a banking institution. Absurd as it is, it had, at the time of its adoption, the almost unanimous approbation of that British public to which we are so much disposed to look for instruction in all financial and commercial matters. It was then regarded as the great financial invention of the age.

Such being the state of things in the moneyed centre of Europe, we may now look homeward and study our own great national system, taking for examination a bank of $1,000,000 capital that has commenced its operations by handing over to the Treasury public securities to that whole amount, receiving in exchange $900,000 of circulating notes. Of these, it exchanges $225,000 for legal tenders, to be always kept on hand. It now borrows from its neighbors, sometimes at low interest, at others at none, repayable on demand, to the extent of $5,000,000, calling this *deposits*. The total sum at its command is now $5,900,000, of which it lends to its customers $5,000,000. Money, however, coming

---

* The liabilities of the Bank of England exceed $200,000,000. Those of the London and Westminster, and of the Union, both joint stock banks, are stated in *Blackwood's Magazine* to be each of nearly equal amount, making a total for those two alone, of nearly $400,000,000.

† A run upon the bank is always for notes, never for gold.

soon after into more demand, its creditors require payment of perhaps half the amount now standing to their credit, or $2,500,000. In turn it calls upon its debtors, who may pay, or may not. If they do, it meets its engagements. If they do not, when asked for notes, it must reply that its power of issue has been exhausted, its circulation having already attained the full amount, or $900,000. When asked for "greenbacks," it must of course reply that all the lawful money in its vaults is by law required there to remain as security for its circulation. Powerless for the sale of securities deposited with the Treasury—powerless for the use of its lawful money—powerless for further issue of its notes—it finds itself now compelled to press more hardly on its debtors, producing panic and thereby increasing the demand upon itself by those who own the millions standing to their credit on the books. Ruin now ensuing, the world accepts the fact as evidence of the necessity for inventing some new contrivance by means of which we may in future avoid the dangers incident to the existence of a "plethora of paper money." Nevertheless, *throughout the whole of this performance* "paper money" has furnished not even the slightest evidence of its existence, the people, relying on the government for its redemption, having continued to employ it precisely as they before had done. Of the few national banks that yet have failed, the proportion of their notes that has been presented for redemption has been, as we have seen it stated, small beyond any conception that could previously have been formed.

We have a free banking system in which there is really no freedom, having thus practically reproduced the idea of the tragedy of Hamlet, with the part of Hamlet omitted by particular desire. We have adopted the system of New England and New York, omitting its fundamental idea, that of leaving to the people themselves the determination of the question as to whether or not they need to create additional shops at which money may be bought and sold; whether or not the capital they employ in the trade shall count by hundreds of thousands, millions, or tens of millions. We have created a monopoly more complete than that of the Bank of England, and in constructing a code of laws for its government have borrowed that ridiculous and absurd idea of Sir Robert Peel, by means of which that great institution has been twice reduced to beg for an Order of Council providing for its temporary repeal, as the only mode of enabling it, with millions of gold in its vaults, to escape the disgrace of actual bankruptcy.

For a remedy for all this we must look in the same direction that, under the State bank system, our New England friends have looked, to wit, that of FREEDOM. The more the people shall, in this important matter, be allowed to govern themselves, the less will be the accumulation of unemployed capital in the banks; the more reasonable will be bank dividends; the more will the whole community profit by their existence; and the less must be danger of revulsion. The more thorough the monopoly shall be made, the more will be the tendency towards large bank dividends, to be followed by financial crises; and the more will the state of things among ourselves approximate to that now existing in Britain, so well described in the passage from Blackwood already given.

To all this the "skilful financier"—the man so often quoted in money articles—objects, believing that the monopoly now established is a good and proper thing; that large bank dividends are greatly preferable to small ones; and that the less the tendency to stability in the monetary movement, the more abundant must be the chances of accumulating fortune for himself. The legislator, little familiar with the subject, finding himself assured that increase in the number of banks tends towards the production of a " plethora of paper money," closes his eyes to the fact that the more perfect the monopoly the greater must be the power to overtrade by means of the use of the ·unemployed capital of others; and, as in the case of the bill now before the Senate, gives us a system of law for our government in all the future, so narrow and illiberal, and so unworthy of the age, as to furnish proof almost conclusive that it must for its paternity have been indebted to some of the "financiers" above described—men belonging to that class which profits by having labor cheap and money dear.

Before the war our total paper circulation was but $200,000,000, or about $6 per head; and yet, insignificant as was its amount, it was the habit of our people to attribute to the use of "paper-money" nearly all the financial troubles then resulting from the maintenance of a commercial policy that had compelled us to look abroad for cloth and iron, and to give in exchange therefor nearly all the produce of California mines. The amount of labor and its products needing to be circulated was large, while the machinery of circulation was so trivial in its quantity as to make it, throughout three-fourths of the whole country, almost entirely inaccessible; as a consequence of which the barbarous system of barter was everywhere throughout the West and South in general or partial use; debt was universal; and the price paid for the use of a little money, to both foreign and domestic usurers, was exorbitant to a degree unknown in any other commercial country of the world.

The war came, and swept from existence a very considerable portion of the Western banks, their circulation having been secured by the deposit of bonds of Southern States. With the war, however, there came a necessity for the use of power by the General Government, and the "greenback" now made its appearance on the stage—giving us, for the first time in our history, an amount of circulation fairly adequate to the performance of the great work of circulating the labor, and the products of the labor, of our vast and widely-scattered population. To these were next added circulating notes bearing interest, and intended gradually to be taken up for investment; and, lastly, national bank notes, the amount of which was, by law, limited to $270,000,000.

Leaving out of view the interest-bearing greenback, nearly all of which have already disappeared from circulation, the amount now authorized of notes of every description but little exceeds $700,000,000, nearly 10 per cent. of which is, by law, required to be locked up in the vaults of national banks, precisely as the absurd British law, heretofore described, locks up the British gold. Far more than this is, however, habitually retained by them, while very much is hoarded, the result being that, at this hour, the total amount of actual circulation for 35,000,000 of people, dispersed throughout half a continent, is less than $500,000,000; whereas, according to recent statements, Great Britain, with a much smaller population, condensed within a space less than double that of the New England States alone, has in daily use, wholly exclusive of that retained in bank vaults, *coin alone* to the extent of $400,000,000, being nearly as much per head as our people are now allowed for total circulation.

This would certainly seem to be so small as wholly to preclude the idea that inflation could thence result; yet are all the efforts of legislators turned in the direction of its reduction, Congress having just now authorized the Secretary to cancel "greenbacks" at a rate that will, in five years, reduce them to half their present amount; and the Senate now proposing to co-operate with him by means of a law under which the bank circulation must, in the same period, be reduced to nearly the point at which it stood in 1860, although the population will then have increased at least a third, while the production should at the very least have trebled. A proper pendant to the bill before that honorable body would, as we think, be one by which it should be provided that each and every railroad in the country should reduce the number of its cars and engines, with a view to ascertaining if the products of 1870 could not be transferred from place to place by aid of the same machinery by which that work had been done ten years before. Were such a measure suggested, it would be regarded as being supremely ridiculous; yet would it be even less so than is the suggestion that we should now return to the same machinery of exchange from hand to hand by aid of which the work had been so very poorly done in 1860.

What renders this course of action the more extraordinary is, that the mere collection and distribution of our present enormous revenue makes demand for an amount of circulation one-half, at least, as great as the whole quantity that before the war had been permitted to exist. While thus increasing the demand for machinery of exchange the Treasury strains every nerve in the effort to diminish the supply and thus to raise the rate of interest, to the serious injury of all who need to borrow, itself included. The higher that rate the smaller must be production, the greater the need for maintaining the present oppressive taxation, the less the revenue, and the greater the necessity for competing in the market with individuals who look to banks for supplies of money. The whole is thus a great financial blunder.

The country was promised free banking. It has obtained nothing but subjection to a monopoly that it is now proposed to make more complete and permanent than anything of the kind that has ever yet existed in the Union. It did obtain a moderately proper supply of the machinery of exchange, but even that is now to be withdrawn; this, too, at a moment when every man of common sense in England is awaking to a perception of the errors of the British law that we have so closely copied. That our readers may better appreciate the working of the present system outside of the large cities, we pray them to accompany us in a short examination of its operations in the neighboring county of Schuylkill, to which they are indebted for so large a proportion of the heat and power they daily need to use.

Saturday being pay day, and the pay being monthly, the close of each successive week brings with it a necessity for the means of distributing among miners and laborers the proceeds of the vast quantities of coal that have been sent to market. The money for this purpose stands at the credit of the operator but the means of distribution can be found nowhere, and miners and laborers go unpaid because banks have no power to issue notes without the assent of the Comptroller, and Congress refuses to permit that he should give it. Why, then, it is asked, do they not create more banks? Why do they not enlarge the capitals of those already in existence? Because of the fact that Congress has granted a monopoly of the privilege of banking, of which certain individuals have already obtained the country's share, the amount of which it is to the interest of "skilful financiers" to retain unchanged. Because Congress has decreed that the privilege of furnishing "paper-money" shall be confined to the few that have obtained that monopoly of the banking power by means of which they are enabled to make double and treble dividends. Because Congress fails to see that all our recent success has resulted from the facts that protection on the one hand, and the "greenback" on the other, made great demand for labor, and thus enabled the poor to contend with the rich for the privilege of aiding in carrying out the war to the successful conclusion at which it finally arrived.

"Plethora of paper-money," however, being the form of words now most in use, that, we are assured, is the cause why labor is high and certain commodities are dear. Those, however, of our readers who may have studied the facts in regard to Egypt that we recently have laid before them, can scarcely fail to see that the rise of prices there, consequent upon increased demand for cotton and for labor, and upon a cattle plague, has been even more remarkable than any that has been here observed; and yet Egypt is emphatically a hard-money country, "greenbacks" being there unknown.*

Leaving the far East, and turning our eyes towards the far West, we find the state of facts in the flourishing Territory of Utah to be as is here described in a letter of recent date from Salt Lake City:—

"You have tight money markets sometimes in the East. I have read of how semi-savage nations 'barter.' I saw it cited, as a curious fact, in the newspapers, that in Georgia eggs are used as small change; but in Utah I see around me a people, a prosperous people, doing the business of life almost without any

---

* "Arriving late in 1862, she found no difficulty in securing for her exclusive use, on her voyage up the Nile, 'an excellent boat,' with captain, steersman, eight men, and a cabin-boy, for the trivial sum of $120 per month. This seems very low, yet is it in perfect accordance with nearly every other demand then made upon her purse. Everything was then cheap. A year later, October, 1863, she writes her friends that she has 'just bought blankets, but they are much dearer than last year,' and that 'everything is almost doubled in price.' In October, 1864, she says: 'The dearness of all things is fearful here; all is treble, at least, what it was in 1862–63; but wages have risen in proportion. A sailor who got 60 piasters a month now gets 300. All is at the same rates—clothes, rents, everything. Cairo is dearer than London, and Alexandria dearer still, as I believe—at all events, as to rents.' Four months later, a common boat hand is described as getting three napoleons a month, while butter commands the enormous price of 3s., or 72 cents, per pound.

"Why was all this? Had the Pasha issued any 'greenbacks?' Had gold gone up, and 'paper-money' down? Assuredly not, Egypt being so emphatically a hard-money country, that paper is there nowhere in use. The cause of all this change is readily found in the fact of the existence of a cotton famine, by means of which there had been made demand so great for that important product of Egyptian land and labor as to cause coin to flow in from every quarter of Europe, and thus to produce a 'plethora' of gold, the effects thereof exhibiting themselves in changes of prices precisely similar to those which have occurred among ourselves, and which now stand charged to the absence of that same hard money whose presence elsewhere was, as we see, producing so much disturbance.

"Why, however, had the prices of butter, and of animal food generally, so greatly risen? For reasons precisely similar to those which have been here observed, the scarcity of cows and oxen. Here, we have had to feed millions of men bearing arms, as a consequence of which our cattle are, North and South, a third less in number than they were six years since. There, a plague had just reduced to less than half the stock of cattle, and had thus produced, in the prices of meat and butter, precisely the effects that the 'skilful financiers,' who now desire that interest may be high and wages low, find it convenient to attribute to a 'greenback' circulation."

money at all. In Salt Lake City itself, right in the line of travel, there is some money; but in the country settlements, which radiate thence into every valley and by every watercourse for a hundred miles, it is literally true that they have no circulating medium. Wheat is the usual legal tender of the country. Horses, harness, vehicles, cattle, and hay are cash; eggs, butter, pistols, knives, stockings, and whiskey are change; pumpkins, potatoes, sorghum, molasses, and calves are 'shinplasters,' which are taken at a discount, and with which the saints delight to pay their debts (if it is ever a delight to pay debts). Business in this community, with this currency, is a very curious and amusing pastime. A peddler, for instance, could take out his goods in a carpet-bag, but would need a 'bull' train to freight back his money. I knew a man who refused an offer to work in the country at fifty dollars a month because he would need a 'forty-hundred wagon and four yoke of oxen' to haul his week's wages to the whiskey-shop, theatre, &c., on Saturday evening. That was an inconvenience, truly. And yet the farmers in the country towns suffer from an exactly opposite grievance. They cannot keep their big sons from sneaking into the granary at night, and taking off a half bushel or so of wheat, carrying it to the dram-shop, and having a 'high.' When a man once lays out his money in any kind of property, it is next to impossible to reconvert it into money. There is many a man here, who, when he first came into the valley, had no intention of remaining but a short time, but soon got so involved that he could never get away without making heavy pecuniary sacrifices. Property is a Proteus, which you must continue to grip firmly, notwithstanding his slippery changes, until you have him in his true shape. Now you have him as a fine horse and saddle; presto, he is only sixty gallons of sorghum molasses; now he changes into two cows and a calf, and before you have time to think he is transformed into fifteen cords of wood up in the mountain canon; next he becomes a yoke of oxen; then a 'shutler' wagon; ha! is he about to slip from you at last in the form of bad debts?"

It is in the face of facts like these, now occurring not only in Utah, but throughout the South and Southwest, the West and Northwest, that our "skilful financiers" venture to assure us that there is a "plethora of paper-money;" that there are too many banks and bank-notes; and that we must return to the good old state of things that existed a few years since, when labor and its products to the extent of millions per day were wasted for want of means of circulation.

What the country really needs is that its people should be allowed the exercise of some little of the power of self-government. Congress has made an exceedingly stringent law for the government of banks. That having been done, let the people now make banks when and where they please, as was the case under the New York system. In reply to this, it will be said that banks will become too numerous; but, as it appears to us, the people are better judges than Congress by any possibility can be as to their actual needs in that respect, as well as in that of dry-goods shops or railroads.

A multiplicity of banks will, it will be said, lead to a "plethora of paper-money." On the contrary, it is when banks are most numerous that there is the smallest power to maintain an extended circulation. New England uses paper more exclusively than any other part of the world; and yet, so little is the power of its banks to profit by the issue of notes, that the dividends of its banks are smaller than in any other portion of the Union. Let Congress carefully study the working of the New England system, and it will give us something very different from the miserable bill that is now before the Senate.

The system now established will prove an excellent one, provided that the one element in which it is so entirely deficient, that of freedom, be now supplied. Let that not be done, and it will prove to be the most unstable and injurious that has been yet devised.

THE NATIONAL POLICY.

TRACTS FOR THE TIMES---NUMBER 2.

SUBJECT:

BRITISH FREE TRADE,

HOW IT AFFECTS THE AGRICULTURE AND THE FOREIGN COMMERCE OF THE UNION.

CONDUCTED BY JOHN WILLIAMS,

EDITOR OF "THE IRON AGE."

NEW YORK:
THE OFFICE OF "THE IRON AGE,"
80 Beekman Street.

CHICAGO:
JOHN A. NORTON, BOOKSELLER AND PUBLISHER,
AND AGENT FOR THE WRITINGS OF HENRY C. CAREY,
126½ Dearborn Street,
1866.

OFFICE OF THE IRON AGE,

80 BEEKMAN STREET, New York.

The following articles, from the pen of HENRY C. CAREY, Esq., LL.D., have been published in THE IRON AGE; but believing their more general circulation at this time may be of utility in removing the very common misapprehension which prevails as to the effect of depending upon a foreign market for the breadstuffs we produce, I have printed them in the present form.

I commend their study to every man who would understand the inevitable consequences which must result from a persistence in the present unwise policy advocated by the champions of British Free Trade amongst us. The letter of Mr. Langley, which is also printed, contains facts which are very significant in this connection.

JOHN WILLIAMS,

Editor THE IRON AGE.

BRITISH FREE TRADE.

WHY DO WE IMPORT WHEAT AND WHEATEN FLOUR?

Twenty years since crops abroad were short, causing famine in Ireland, and making great demand on us for supplies of food. As a consequence of this, our exports of "breadstuffs" trebled in a single year, the nineteen millions of the fiscal year 1846 becoming fifty-seven in that of 1847. The then Secretary of the Treasury was Mr. Robert J. Walker, author of the tariff of 1846, under which British free trade had, just before the close of the latter year, become the law of the land. Greatly elated at the increased foreign demand for food, he placed the whole to the credit of his free trade policy, and, at the opening of Congress in December, 1847, furnished that body with an estimate of our foreign commerce in the future, based upon the idea that each and every succeeding year was to exhibit changes similar to the one which had then occurred. The total domestic exports having grown in 1847 from $101,000,000 to $150,000,000, those of 1848 were to reach $222,000,000, and those of 1849 $329,000,000, the essential part of this extraordinary increase to be in the form of "breadstuffs," with which we were, in his belief, to supply the European world.

Of the time that since has passed, more than ten years were spent under the free trade *regime* established by the author of these predictions. During four of the remaining years we had the highly improved free trade tariff of 1857, under which Southern slave-owners were steadily gaining the predominance which finally prompted them to an effort at independence which led to war. Since then, we have been feeding millions of men engaged in an effort at maintaining the authority of the Union and restoring domestic peace.

Throughout the whole of this long term of years the British free trade system has had a fuller and fairer trial than had here ever before been given to any other system whatsoever. Through-out the whole of it the inventive faculties of our countrymen have been given towards facilitating extraction of the soil and its trans-port to distant markets, increase in the number of reaping and threshing machines having kept steady pace with increase in the number of miles of railroad, and in the number and power of engines, each and every step in this direction having been in per-fect harmony with the magnificent free trade predictions of 1847. What, however, is the point at which we have now arrived? Have we reached, or even approached, the port towards which the national ship was supposed to be then directed? Has the great foreign demand for food arisen? Had it done so, has there been any growth in our power to meet it? Nothing of the kind. So far the reverse is it, that not only have we now almost wholly lost the great natural market that has in all the past been furnished by the West Indies and South America, but are now dependent on France for supplies of wheat, and likely so to become to an extent greater than now exists. As a consequence of this, flour rises here with a rise in the price of that only commodity, Cali-fornia gold, with which we now pay for foreign food—wheat now commanding here a price that is almost thrice as great as has been that of France for the past three years.

How must it be in the years that are ahead? To obtain an answer to this question we must begin by studying the past. At the date of the prediction above referred to, the average crop of wheat might have been taken at 126,000,000 bushels, giving 5¾ per head of the population. In 1860, it was 5½ per head. Last year, that of the loyal States was 148,000,000, and the total prob-ably a little more than 165,000,000, or less than 5 per head. This year, so far as can now be judged, it can scarcely exceed 160,-000,000, or 4½ per head; while the actual British consumption is 6 per head. Taking, then, into consideration the present rapid increase of population, it seems to us quite clear that instead of giving "breadstuffs" for iron, we shall be compelled to give gold, and very much of it, too, in exchange for food.

Of the causes of this extraordinary state of things we shall speak in another article.

WHY ARE WE NOW GIVING GOLD FOR WHEAT?

In our last it was shown that whereas twenty years since our average crop of wheat gave 5¾ bushels for each individual of our population, it has since been gradually declining in its proportion, until it now stands at little more than 4; and, that to this it is due that not only have all past British free trade predictions in relation to supplying the world with "breadstuffs" been thus falsified, but that we have now become importers instead of exporters of the materials of bread. That our readers may understand the cause of this we give the following facts, from a very valuable work of recent date.*

Kentucky, Missouri, and Tennessee are best adapted to corn, and wheat cannot be regarded as the great staple of any of them. Cotton is the staple of the last, the others being unsurpassed for raising stock, and there being no reason whatsoever why they should give much attention to the wheat culture. North Carolina raises some wheat, but south or southwest of that State, both soil and climate are adverse to its production.

"Indiana, Illinois, and 'the far West,' are," says our author, "pointed to us as the great wheat regions, to which we are to look for wheat to supply the world. The common idea," as he continues, "is that this whole region is peculiarly adapted thereto, but this, like many other popular theories, may not be strictly correct. The prairie soil—the virgin soil of the West—when first broken up generally produces good wheat. But virgin soil will not last; like virgin beauty it becomes old and faded with age. It consists of friable mold, and when by cultivation and exposure to the atmosphere it becomes completely pulverized and then covered with surface water, as much of it frequently is, the frost will heave the wheat out of the ground, and it is winter-killed. If the plants are so fortunate as to escape winter-killing, this friable mold, when dry, is an almost impalpable powder, and the high prairie winds will blow it from the roots of the plants, exposing them to the dry and parching rays of the sun, and then what winter has spared the summer kills."

As a consequence of this it is that we find Solon Robinson, the well-known agricultural editor, telling his readers that wheat is "the most precarious crop in the west;" Mr. Ellsworth, of Indiana, an extensive farmer and able agriculturist, meanwhile writing as follows:

"After a full consideration of the subject, I am satisfied that stock raising, *at the West*, is much more profitable than raising grain. The profits of wheat appear well in expectation, on paper, but the prospect is blasted by a severe winter—ap-

---

* *The Wheat Plant*, by J. H. Klippart, Corresponding Secretary of the Ohio Board of Agriculture, Cincinnati, 1860.

pearance of insects—bad weather in harvesting, in threshing, or transporting to market; or last, a fluctuation in the market itself."

Throughout New England "much labor," says our author "may produce small crops, but all, we believe, will agree that it is not, and cannot be, a wheat-producing section."

What then remains ? Only the States north of the James and the Ohio, and east of Indiana. Among them stands out most conspicuously Virginia, as possessing advantages for the wheat culture nowhere else exceeded. What has there been the course of affairs is shown in the following extract from a discourse delivered some twelve years since by one of her most distinguished citizens :

"How many of our people do we see disposing of their lands at ruinous prices, and relinquishing their birth-places and friends, to settle themselves in the West; and many not so much from choice as from actual inability to support their families and rear and educate their children out of the produce of their exhausted lands —once fertile, but rendered barren and unproductive by a ruinous system of cultivation."

Maryland and Delaware are exhausted and unproductive, and thus do we find ourselves reduced to Ohio and Pennsylvania, New York and Southern Michigan, in reference to which our author speaks as follows :

"Ohio stands at the head of all the wheat-growing States in the aggregate of her production. Her crop in 1850 was 28 millions of bushels. * * * The geological survey of the State gives the reason, and confirms the statement, that 'a large mixture of clay in the soil is necessary to the perfect growth of wheat,' and that the absence of it from the soil of the prairies of the West would prevent them from ever becoming permanently good wheat-producing sections.

"Thus, the reports of the geological survey of Ohio show the soil to be clayey,' ' clayey loam,' and ' clay sub-soil,' and it produces 16¼ bushels to each inhabitant ; while Indiana, with a richer soil, produces only 8¼ bushels, and Illinois, with a still richer soil, only 7 to each. Virginia, Maryland, and Delaware, as well as New York, were formerly great wheat-producing sections. But many parts of New York, that formerly produced 25 bushels to the acre, do not now average over 5 bushels ; and many parts of Maryland, Virginia, and Delaware, that formerly produced abundantly, will not now pay the cost of cultivation. EXHAUSTION is written all over them, in language too plain to be misunderstood.

"Ohio has reached her maximum of wheat production, and, if not retrograding, is at least stationary. [The crop of 1860 was but 15 millions, or little more than aalf that of 1850.] Thirteen bushels to the acre may be set down as an average production, and this average must continue to grow rapidly less, till, like the exhausted lands of Virginia, her soil will not produce enough to support the cultivator, unless an improved system of husbandry is introduced to increase its fertility, One great source of deterioration in exhausting our soils, has been in the manufacture of potash, and the exports of it to foreign countries, or to our manufactories. In this way our soil has been robbed of an ingredient without which no plant can mature, and no cereal grain form. As our forests have disappeared, this source of deterioration must be cut off, but a serious injury has been inflicted, which nothing can cure but the refurnishing of the potash to the soil. How it can be done, is the great inquiry for our farmers.

"The export of our flour has been another source of exhaustion to the soil, in taking away from it the phosphate of lime that is necessary to give plumpness to the kernel.

"This exhaustion can be more easily remedied by the application of bone dust. For many years the English farmers have carried on a large traffic in old bones, paying five dollars a ton for them. This has stimulated many to gather them up, and even rob the battle fields of Europe of the bones of their brave defenders, to enrich the wheat fields of England. By this course, the fields of England have been made more productive, while the countries from which the bones are taken have been permanently injured by their loss.

"The English, too, have sent to every island of South America to procure niter, n the form of guano, to fertilize their fields, while the American not only imports little or none, but negligently wastes that which nature forces on them.

"*The idea of skinning the soil of our wheat-growing sections, with a view of abandoning them soon and going West to procure new and fertile wheat land, must itself be abandoned, as we are on the western verge of the permanently good wheat-producing section.*

"Our only resource now is to preserve our wheat lands where they are not exhausted, and to restore them where they are. Under judicious and scientific tillage, the lands of England, that have been under cultivation for hundreds of years, now produce twenty-five bushels to the acre. This is done by a liberal use of lime, plaster, clover, and a judicious rotation of crops. In wheat-raising, this rotation is clover and corn. Peas, beans, turnips, beets and carrots, all furnish a good rotation, and good food for sheep, which are good on wheat land. In fact, the culture of wheat and raising of sheep should go together. *The rotating crops furnish food for the sheep, and the sheep furnish the best of manure for wheat land.* All the manure derived from the sheep should be carefully preserved for enriching their land. It is highly concentrated, and prepares the land for a generous crop of wheat at a small expense. The manuring agent consumes the crop that gives the land rest from wheat culture, and prepares the soil for another crop of wheat."

Such were the facts, and such was the advice given seven years since. Turning back, however, to the Patent Office Report of a few years earlier date, we find the presentation of a state of things almost precisely similar, closing with an estimate by its writer, Dr. Lee, a high agricultural authority, that it "would be improper to estimate *the total annual waste of this country at an amount less than equal to the mineral constituents of* 1,500,000,000 *bushels of corn.* To suppose," as he continues, "that this state of things can continue, and we as a nation remain prosperous, is simply ridiculous. We have as yet much virgin soil, and it will be long ere we reap the reward of our present improvidence. It is merely a question of time, and time will solve the problem in a most unmistakable manner. With our earth-butchery and prodigality, we are each year losing the intrinsic essence of our vitality. Our country has not yet grown feeble from the loss of its life-blood, but the hour is fixed when, if our present system continue, the last throb of the nation's heart will have ceased, and America, Greece and Rome will stand together among the ruins of the past. The question of economy should be, not how much do we annually produce, but how much of our annual production is saved to the soil. Labor employed in robbing the earth of its capital stock of fertilizing matter is worse than labor thrown away. In the latter case, it is a loss to the present generation—in the former, it becomes an inheritance of poverty for our successors. Man is but a tenant of the soil, and he is guilty of a crime when he reduces its value for other tenants who are to come. after him."

Almost at the moment when these words were being written, the Finance Minister of the Union was amusing our people with calculations having for their object to prove that an agricultural people we were, and as such must remain, and that if we would but adopt in full the British free trade doctrines, the time would speedily arrive when our annual exports of "breadstuffs" would count by hundreds, if not even thousands, of millions of dollars! Since then we have, with slight exception, been moving steadily in the direction towards which he pointed—inventing machines for facilitating the tearing out of the soil, and making roads for its transportation to the distant market; the result now exhibiting itself in the Agricultural Report for the present month, in which we find it stated that "*the prospect on the first of June* was for *seventenths of a crop.*" How entirely the facts there presented, in reference to the wheat-producing powers of the Western States, are in accordance with those given by the author of the excellent volume to which we have referred, will be seen by those who read the following extract:

"The total yield of wheat in Ohio and Indiana appears to have suffered most from winter-killing. A prospect for thirty-four per cent. of a crop of winter wheat in Indiana is sufficiently discouraging. An increase of four tenths of the average growth of spring wheat will afford some relief, and ought to bring up the average to half a crop. Ohio is reported at four-tenths for winter wheat, with two and a half-tenths more for spring wheat than usual. A very little better prospect for winter wheat than Indiana, and not quite so large an increase of spring wheat will give about the same result—half an average crop.

"Illinois, now our greatest wheat-growing State, promises seven-tenths of a crop of winter wheat. As the spring wheat, which is the main dependence for a crop in portions of the State is nearly as good as usual, at least three-fourths of a crop of that should be expected in that State. In Wisconsin, the winter wheat is reported at six and one-third tenths, with one and three-fourths more spring wheat than usual, which should secure three fourths of an average crop for this State. In Iowa the appearance of winter wheat is nine-tenths; spring, ten and three-fourths tenths; breadth of the latter·sown, twelve and one-eighth tenths. This should give at least an average crop for Iowa. In Missouri a prospect for a full crop of winter wheat is reported with one-half tenth or five per cent. more than the usual breadth of spring wheat, looking nearly as well as usual at this season of the year."

In our next we propose to show how widely different has been the course of affairs in countries whose policy has been to bring consumers and producers nearer together, and·thus to make a market on the land for all its products.

WHY FRANCE NOW EXPORTS WHEAT.

Forty years since, under a system of long continued, steady and thoroughly effective protection, France supplied the outer world with silks, cottons, linens, woolens, and other products of her various industries, to ·the extent of 500,000,000 francs or...$100,000,000

Fifteen years since, under the same highly protective system, her exports had reached the amount
   of......................................·............$250,000,000

Six years since, under the same system, they had
   attained the extraordinary hight of.............$400,000,000

Then it was that there was negotiated between England and France a commercial treaty providing for the abrogation of antiquated prohibition and restrictions, and which, therefore, was heralded forth as a British free trade measure. In reality, however, it gave to France a system more intelligently protective than any now existing in any other country of the world; one under which the export of domestic products has already risen to the extraordinary hight of nearly..................$600,000,000

Such having been the result of efficient protection in a country possessing little coal or iron ore, no gold or silver mines, and no cotton fields; one in which schools have been few, armies great, taxes heavy, and population almost stationary; let us now compare it with that which has been obtained in another country in which, in the same period, population has trebled, while schools have been sextupled; one in which coal and iron ore exist to an extent elsewhere entirely unequaled; one that has controlled the cotton commerce of the world; one capable of supplying the world with sheep's wool; and one that possesses the most profitable gold and silver mines the world has ever known; to wit, these United States:

Forty years since our domestic exports had risen to
  nearly...................................... $70,000,000
Ten years later they were.......................... 100,000,000
Twenty years since they amounted to............ 150,000,000
Six years since, in the year before the breaking out
  of the rebellion, they were, exclusive of specie... 300,000,000
For the fiscal year just now completed they are es-
  timated at a gold value not exceeding.......... 260,000,000

Compared with the growth of population, the movement has therefore been as follows:

	1825.	1860.	1865.
French Exports, per head	$3	$11	$16
American " "	6	9	7

Under intelligent protection the first have more than quintupled, while under British free trade the second, exclusive of specie, have scarcely at all increased. This is certainly an extraordinary exhibit, but, extraordinary as it is, it is in perfect accordance with the teachings of those eminent men, who, from the days of Hamilton, have sought to teach our people that it was in efficient protection we were to find the real road towards an extensive foreign commerce and real freedom of trade. France has done what Hamilton, Clay, and Jackson urged as proper to be done; and, as a necessary consequence, her export of the products of her soil has grown at a rate more rapid than the world till now has ever known. We have followed in the direction indicated by our British free trade masters, and the result exhibits itself in the fact, that our foreign commerce is this day little more per head than it had been in the disastrous decade that followed the close of the great wars of the French Revolution.

France imports raw materials, combines them with her own food, and then exports them in a finished form. We export our soil in the various forms of potash, cotton, pork, and wheat, and then re-import them in a finished form. The first is always importing manure, while the second is always exporting it. The results of these different modes of operation exhibit themselves in the fact that France, with a stationary population and limited territory, has, in half a century, carried up her wheat crop from one hundred and fifty to three hundred millions of bushels—from less than five bushels per head to fully eight; whilst we, with a erritory unlimited and a population rapidly growing in numbers and intelligence, have passed downwards from nearly six bushels per head in 1846 to little more than four in 1866.

At the present moment wheat so abounds in France that prices are lower than have almost ever before been known, and there exists an agricultural crisis. Referring thereto, and endeavoring to console the farmers in their troubles, the *Journal des Economistes,* the most radical free trade journal in Europe, speaks as follows :

"That which, above all, agriculture claims is the multiplication of markets, its greatest need being that of a non agricultural population. The prosperity of that of Britain is almost wholly due to the great part that manufactures there perform. What is it that presents itself to view in our poorest provinces ? A people thinly scattered a nd almost entirely rural; not working within reach of a market; consuming on the spot their own local productions; with few or no towns, no industry, and no commerce beyond that which is strictly necessary for satisfying the limited wants of their inhabitants. There, the poor proprietor divides the produce with miserable tenants, the inevitable result of agriculture without a market. Our manufacturing departments, on the other hand, are by far the best cultivated, and for that reason the most productive. There, our agriculture has proved her ability to realize by other means, but in an equal degree, the wonders of English husbandry. *Wherever a large centre of consumption is formed the neighboring farmers are the first to profit by it. This law is infallible, and allows of no exception ; and thus is explained the enormous value of land near to the great cities of the world.* In proportion as markets are defective, agriculture is compelled to feed, in some sort on itself; the division of labor, or the adaption of culture to the soil, being thus forbidden, it then labors not for profit, but merely to live, and must content itself with wheat, rye, or some other cereal, at any price, let the result be what it may, Ruinous as is this course of proceeding, the farmer has no choice. New markets being opened, a new state of things arises—production, in view of profit, of commodities to suit the market. Agriculture then changes its character; it is transformed, and becomes itself industrial."

" The real reason for decline in the price of wheat is not " says the journalist in continuation, "difficult to discover; it is simply the excess of its production. Within half a century agriculture has made immense progress, and most especially within the last fifteen years. To-day it turns against itself, improvement in the cultivation of corn lauds by better rotation, manuring and subsoil plowing—conversion of silicious land, formerly devoted to rye, to the production of wheat—improvement of lands—clearing of forests—extension of drainage and liming—having, one and all, borne their fruits. 'The production of wheat has doubled in half a century, increasing from an annual average of fifty millions of hectolitres (22 gals.) to that of one hundred millions. Not only has agriculture become more productive, but it has also largely gained in security. The frequency of high prices formerly was due to bad cultivation; climacteric conditions in our day exert less influence on the yield. The harvest of 1863 was 111,274,000 hectolitres, more than double that of 1820, notwithstanding a season in many respects less favorable.''

France protects her farmers by making a market in the land for each and all of its almost infinite variety of products. As a consequence *she exports,* in the various forms of silks and satins, cottons and woolens, paper, perfumery, chemicals, flour, locomotives, &c., &c., *food alone to an amount greater than that of our total commerce with the outside world.* Receiving in exchange the gold of California and Australia, she maintains a special circulation, while exhibiting her independence of British movements by keeping the rate of interest at less than half of that demanded by the Bank of England.

We, on the contrary, compel our farmers to dependence on poor and distant markets, and to destruction of the powers of the soil they need to cultivate. As a consequence, we import both cloth and iron, and have no wheat to sell. The daily increasing adverse balance is settled for with bonds whose interest must be paid in gold. Owners of the most productive mines in the world, we use paper because of inability to command the services of the precious metals. The Western farmer borrows money at a rate of interest thrice greater than that paid by his French competitor, and then mortgages his farm to his British free trade masters as security for the price of rails required for enabling him still more rapidly to destroy the powers of the soil. Those rails are laid over land that abounds in coal and ore, the conversion of which into rails and castings would, by giving him a market, quadruple the value of his farm. In default of that market his land is sold by the sheriff, he himself, meanwhile, going to the polls to vote, perhaps, a copperhead British free trade ticket.

With a territory of very small extent, and wholly destitute of natural advantages, France, by means of the protection accorded to her farmers, is enabled, through her *Credit Mobilier,* to grant aid to railroads throughout Europe, and now to extend her operations in that direction to some of those among ourselves. With a territory ten times larger, and twenty times more abounding in the natural elements of wealth, the people of these United States exhibit themselves throughout the civilized world as beggars for the aid required for enabling them to purchase the iron required for giving them new facilities for distributing, in the forms of corn, cotton, and tobacco, their soil among the civilized communities of Europe. We are, nevertheless, accustomed freely to boast the universal intelligence of our people!

THE SUPPLY OF BREADSTUFFS.

[The following letter by Mr. W. H. Langley, an extensive miller of Gallipolis under date of June 10th, 1866, will be read with deep interest by those who are considering the serious subject of our prospective supply of breadstuffs. The writer states:

Let us examine how our supply will stand for the coming year. The Agricultural Bureau at Washington, in its report for November, 1865, says the crop of wheat for the year

1863 was	179,404,036
1864 was	160,695,823
1865 was	148,522,829
From the last deduct for deficiency in quality	14,068,694
Net crop in 1865	134,454,135
On hand of crop of 1864, at harvest time, 1865	26,241,698
Total, 1865	160,695,833

Now this is the quantity we should have had on hand last year at harvest, and, from all the information I have been able to get, I am well satisfied that the whole of it will be exhausted before any of the new crop will be in market. I was fully convinced at harvest last year that we had a very short supply of breadstuffs to last us through the ensuing year, and on several occasions through last fall and winter wrote to my friends in the Eastern cities, saying that if gold declined to par, it could have but a temporary effect on breadstuffs, that is, wheat flour, and claimed that the supply in the country was so small that we had none to spare for export, and that prices must continue to advance until it reached a point that would admit of importation from foreign countries, or until we raised another and a better crop than for the last two years. Being engaged in the manufacture of flour, principally for shipment to the eastern cities, and the crop of 1865 around us being almost a total failure, and not much better for 1864, we either had to go from home to buy wheat, or let our mill stand. The latter we did not wish to do, as we had established a good and large trade for our brands of flours, in the eastern cities, and did not like to lose it, and knowing that our brands would always command the best price going, and believing that owing to much of the wheat in the country being poor, light, damaged, and unsound, if we could succeed in getting high grades of old wheat, of the crop of 1864, to keep running, we could make money, for we thought such grades as it would make must be higher relatively than other grades. And in pursuance of this belief we went into the Cincinnati market, and for the last six months or more I think we have bought full three-fourths or more, of all the choice old red and white wheat that came into that market, and, until recently, succeeded in getting enough of such to keep our wheels in motion about three-fourths of the time. More recently, finding that old winter wheat has become very scarce, especially for choice grades, we have turned our attention to Minnesota spring wheat, extra and choice quality, and have bought from 60,000 to 70,000 bushels of it, which we are now making into a very nice flour of choice quality, for spring-wheat flour. Thus far the result of the venture has been far more favorable than we anticipated, and, while there are a dozen of mills along the river, from Pittsburgh to Louisville, I do not know of one that has been so constantly in motion as ours, or that has done more than a local trade. Owing to the high price of wheat, the difficulty of keeping up a supply, and the relative lower price for common and medium grades of flour east, millers would not take the risk of buying wheat and making flour for shipment east. Many of them preferred letting their mills stand, while others ran just so much of the time as was necessary to supply the local demand. Being thus engaged in the business, we have fully understood the necessity of being correctly and fully advised of the state of the stocks in the country, and of the prospects for a supply from the growing crops, and have made it my business, since last harvest, to get all information on the subject possible; and principally with that object in view have made eight trips from this point to the eastern cities in that time—each trip from here down the river to Cincinnati, remaining there from one to six days each trip—while there picking up all information I could get. From there passing up through the central part of the State to Pittsburgh, embracing all opportunities that presented themselves to gather information as to stocks in the country, prospects for growing crops, &c., returning sometimes by the same route, and sometimes via Baltimore, through Delaware and Maryland, to Wheeling or Parkersburgh, then by the river home, thus having an opportunity of seeing and hearing from much wheat-growing territory. Have just returned from one of those trips east, and after posting up all information collected, and from my own observation, I arrive at the following conclusion :

1. That the stock of wheat and flour in the country is so nearly exhausted that it cannot last longer than new wheat makes its appearance, if that long. 2. That the States of New Jersey, Pennsylvania, Delaware, Maryland, West Virginia, Kentucky, Ohio, Indiana, Illinois, Wisconsin, Tennessee, and Georgia, will not, under any circumstances, have over one-third of an average crop, and even that is yet subject to many casualties between this and harvest. What New Jersey, Delaware, Maryland, lower part of Illinois and Eastern Pennsylvania will have in excess of this quantity, will be far more than lost in the balance of the dis-

tricts named. The quantity under one-third of an average crop in the State of Ohio alone will be far greater than the excess over one-third named in the districts above. This county will not produce half as much as the seed sown, so say many of our best farmers. A large portion of the farmers throughout the Western States are now buying their bread, a thing they were never known to do before; but they did not raise enough last year to seed and to bread them until this harvest, and I know some who have already commenced buying wheat and flour for next year's supply, and have had applications from some farmers for seed for next fall's sowing, saying there would not be half enough in this county for seed next fall, to say nothing about bread. It is too early yet to make any reliable calculations about the growing spring wheat crop, which, owing to late heavy frosts and other causes, was later in sowing than usual. Though, from the information I have, there has been more than the usual quantity of spring wheat sown, much of the ground sown in fall and winter wheat having, after the failure of that, been plowed up and spring wheat sown on it. The average of the spring wheat crop of 1865, I believe, is considered to have been a very good one, and will not probably be any better, if as good, this year. It has certainly not had as favorable a start as last season. Last year it was sown early, this year very late, some of it as late as the 10th of May. The agricultural report from Washington for February, 1865, gives the crop for the following States for 1864 as follows :

States.	Bushels.
New Jersey	1,582,113
Pennsylvania	12,523,404
Maryland	6,487,946
Delaware	1,054,916
Kentucky	3,882,275
Ohio	20,407,503
Indiana	22,321,376
Illinois	33,371,173
Wisconsin	14,168,317
Total crop for 1864	115,799,071
In the nine State named above deduct estimated crop for this year	38,599,690
Estimated deficiency in the nine States this year, as compared with the year 1864	77,199,381

Now, as shown above, or is claimed by the Cincinnati Chamber of Commerce, the crop of 1864 was considered an average crop, which was, as reported by

Commissioner Newton.............................160,695,823

And as shown above was the quantity we should have
had on hand last harvest, for the consumption of
the current year, which 'I claim will be exhausted
before the new crop is ready for market. Deduct
from this average crop the deficiency this year, estimated for the nine States above named......... 77,199,389

83,496,434

Giving us for the use of the country for the next year, 83,496,434
bushels against 160,695,223 bushels consumed in the current
year, or the coming crop deficient in wheat and flour for the consumption of the next year, 77,199,389 bushels. Where is that
deficiency to come from? Can Europe supply it? I think not;
for if my information is correct, several of the countries of Europe
produced less than an average crop of wheat last year, and I have
not heard of any large surplus in any country in Europe. Much
of their crop of last year was, like our own, very inferior in quality, and secured in bad condition. I know many will say if we had
not wheat enough for the consumption of this country, we must
eat corn. I would say to those that thousands of the citizens of
the West have been using corn bread for months past that never
used it to any considerable extent before, and that there are thousands in the West that have not had as much as a pound of flour
in their houses for some weeks past. This increased consumption
of corn and also potatoes is beginning to tell on the price of these
articles throughout the West. Potatoes are very high at all
points, and corn is advancing in most of, the corn-producing sections of the West. I am told that in the interior of this county
corn suitable for bread is selling freely at $1 per bushel, and is
becoming very scarce. Along the rivers and large creeks, where
the great surplus of corn is produced, the price has advanced
within thirty to forty days 25 to 33 per cent., becoming scarce at
many points, and still advancing, and the fact of such high prices
for wheat and flour at present, and in prospect, must have the
effect of driving thousands to the use of anything that will answer
as a substitute for flour, and as a natural consequence must
greatly enhance the value of all such articles of food.   *   *   *
Since commencing the above I have received several items of information that fully sustain my opinion of short supplies and the
deficiency in growing crops.

REVIEW OF THE DECADE 1857–67.

BY

H. C. CAREY.

PHILADELPHIA:
COLLINS, PRINTER, 705 JAYNE STREET.
1867.

CALLED upon to furnish a Preface to a new edition of one of the German translations of his work on Social Science, its author has availed himself of the opportunity thus presented for comparing with his theory the facts that have occurred in the remarkable decade that has elapsed since the date (1857) of its first appearance.

PHILADELPHIA, June 22, 1867.

REVIEW.

§ 1. DESIRING fully to understand and properly to appreciate the men around us we study their antecedents, and thereby, in some measure, qualify ourselves for predicting their probable future. So is it, too, with nations. That we may understand the direction in which they are moving, whether toward civilization, wealth, and power, or toward barbarism, poverty, and weakness, it is needed that we compare their present with their past and satisfy ourselves as to whether their policy has tended in the direction of developing those qualities which constitute the real MAN, the being made in the image of his Creator, fitted for becoming master of nature and an example worthy to be followed by those around him, or those alone which he holds in common with the beasts of the field, and which fit him for taking place among men whose rule of conduct exhibits itself in the robber chieftain's motto, "that those may take who have the power, and they may keep who can."

Such was the design of the work that is now to be reproduced, and to which its author has been requested to furnish this present preface. That by such a mode of inquiry, and such alone, could he have expected to arrive at anything approaching to correct results, will be obvious to all who reflect how wholly useless would be any calculations as to the time or place of arrival of a ship based upon a mere statement of her actual position at any given moment, unaccompanied by information as to the rate of movement in the past, or the direction in which she was heading in the present. A decade having now elapsed since the date of the observations that then were taken and the predictions that then were furnished,-and the various ships of state having steadily been moving in their various directions, opportunity is now afforded for further observations with a view to determining how far their several movements have been in accordance with the anticipations that then were made, and for thus subjecting to the severe test of actual practice the principles upon which the work itself was based. That it is which its author proposes now to do, but, preparatory thereto, he desires to ask the reader's attention to a brief exposition of the gradual development to which, and almost insensibly, he has been led, of the grand idea of the UNITY OF LAW, so soon, as he believes, to be adopted as the necessary complement of the great one so recently developed, but already so almost universally admitted, that of UNITY OF FORCE.

The first step, so far as regarded Societary Science, ever made in that direction, consisted in furnishing *a theory of value* so simple that, in the words of one of the highest authorities in economical science, "there could not arise a case in which a man should determine to make an exchange in which it would not be found to apply."*

Up to that date, amid the many suggestions as to the "nature, measure, and causes of value," there had been none, to quote again from the same high authority, that had not proved to be "liable to perpetual exceptions." The law then furnished was that of *the labor saved*, the limit of value being found in *the cost of reproduction*.† Subsequently adopted by an eminent French economist,‡ it has been made known to tens of thousands who had never seen, or even heard of, the work in which it first was published.

Simultaneously therewith was demonstrated the existence of a natural *law of distribution* applicable to any and every case that could by any possibility occur, whether between the landlord and his tenant, the laborer and his employer, the lender of money and its borrower, the owner of ships and the man who sought to freight them. Likewise adopted by M. Bastiat, and characterized by him as "the great, admirable, consoling, necessary, and *inflexible* law of capital,"§ it constitutes the second step in the direction of proving that in each department of the social relations there is perfect unity, and that the whole are as much subjected to law, absolute and inflexible, as are those of inorganic matter.

Ten years later, another step in the same direction is found in the proof that then was furnished, that in the great work of developing the powers of the earth at large man had always, and necessarily, pursued a course identical with that he is seen to have pursued in reference to each and every of its parts, passing from the poorer to the richer soils precisely as he had passed from the use of stone to that of copper, from copper to iron, and thence to steel; and from the use of mere human power as the exclusive means of transportation, through the ox and the horse, the cart and the wagon, until at length he had reached the railroad car."‖ Here again we have a unity of law and a harmony among men, directly

---

* "Carey, and after him Bastiat, have introduced a formula *à posteriori*, that I believe destined to be universally adopted; and it is greatly to be regretted that the latter should have limited himself to occasional indications of it, instead of giving to it the importance so justly given by the former. In estimating the equilibrium between the cost to one's self and the utility to others, a thousand circumstances may intervene; and it is desirable to know if there be not among men a law, a principle of universal application. Supply and demand, rarity, abundance, etc., are all insufficient, and liable to perpetual exceptions. Carey has remarked, and with great sagacity, that this law is the labor saved, *the cost of reproduction*—an idea that is, as I think, most felicitous. It appears to me that there cannot arise a case in which a man shall determine to make an exchange, in which this law will not be found to apply. I will not regard it as equivalent, unless I see that it will come to me at less cost of labor than would be necessary for its reproduction. I regard this formula as most felicitous; because, while on one side it retains the idea of cost, which is constantly referred to in the mind, on the other it avoids the absurdity to which we are led by the theory which pretends to see everywhere a value equivalent to the cost of production; and, finally, it shows more perfectly the essential justice that governs us in our exchanges."—FERRARA: *Biblioteca dell' Economista*, vol. xii. p. 117.

† CAREY. Principles of Political Economy, vol. i., Philad., 1837.

‡ BASTIAT. Harmonies Economiques, Paris, 1850.   § Ibid.

‖ Carey, Past, Present, and Future, Philad., 1848.

opposed to that discord which resulted necessarily from the idea that whereas, in regard to all the *parts* of the earth out of which machines were made man, was always passing from the poorer to the better with steady improvement in his condition, when he came to the occupation of the *whole* he pursued a course that was entirely different, passing always, and necessarily, from the richer to the poorer soils, and thus bringing about a state of things in which a constantly increasing portion of the human race must "regularly die of want." On that occasion, it again was shown that unity of the law by which the whole was governed tended necessarily and certainly towards harmony among those for whose use the earth had been created.

Further reflection having led him to the conclusion that the laws which thus far had been exhibited were but parts of a great and harmonious system instituted for the government of matter in all its forms, whether those of coal or iron, fish or birds, clay, corn, oxen or men ; that the Creator of the Universe had not been obliged to institute different laws for government of the same matter ; that the physical and social laws were, therefore, one and the same ; and, that the idea of *unity of law* must, at no distant day, become as clearly susceptible of proof as is now so rapidly becoming that of *unity of force;* he availed himself in the work of which the present is a condensation,* of the familiar phenomena of heat, motion, and their effective forces in the physical world, for illustration of corresponding facts and forces in the societary one—the result having been that of showing that, with societies as with individual men, physical and mental development, health, and life, had always grown with growth in the rapidity of circulation and declined as the circulation had been arrested or destroyed.

§ 2. In the decade that has since elapsed the accumulated contributions of leading physicists have gone so far towards demonstration of the doctrine of the correlation and conservation of the forces known in their several distinctive manifestations as heat, light, electricity, magnetism, and chemical affinity, that it may be now regarded as entirely established. The new philosophy resolves all these subtle agencies into modes of motion, asserting that they are all capable of mutual conversion ; that they are one and the same force, differing only in its manifestations and effects ; that their various mutations are rigidly subjected to the laws of quantity ; that the force of the form assumed is the precise equivalent of that which disappears ; and, therefore, that every manifestation of force must come from some pre-existing equivalent force, and must give rise to some subsequent and equal amount of force in another form. Originating with Count Rumford and Sir Humphrey Davy, this grand idea was left to be rounded into its present fulness and symmetry by a host of men of the present day, among whom may here be mentioned Grove and Helmholtz, Meyer, Faraday, Liebig, and Carpenter.†

The identity and convertibility of these subtlest of forces have abundantly justified the analogies which had thus far been assumed between

---

* Principles of Social Science, 3 vols., Philad., 1857–59.

† The several writings of these authors on this subject have been collected and published by Professor Youmans, with an introductory preface, to which the author here acknowledges his obligations.

the heat and motion of matter and the forces of societary life, but the choice of electricity, as the preferable analogue, would give us now a greatly larger and happier application of the correspondence. Retaining all the persistency of the heat into which it is convertible, it presents a far more striking resemblance to the brain power which is its correspondent in societary life. So striking indeed is it, that when in the world of mind we desire to express the idea of rapid action of the societary thought and will, we find ourselves driven, and that necessarily, to the physical world for the terms to be employed, availing ourselves of those of electricity and magnetism.

So universal is this force that all the combinations and decompositions, all the processes of dissolution and reconstruction, are effected through its agency. In organic structures, vegetable and animal, that agency is intimate, pervading, and essential. Between it and the nerve force physiologists scarcely find a trace of difference, except that of absence of subjection to the human will. Ever present, it serves to vitalize the globe, and in its most obviously manifest movements, as in those which as yet are most inscrutable, it stands for the best correspondent to mental and moral action that imagination could devise.

Franklin, assuming that the fluid was simple, or uncompounded, gave the names positive and negative to its modes of manifestation. Other philosophers have preferred the names vitreous and resinous, thereby suggesting the idea of a compound nature in the fluid, and all the analogies seem to favor this presentation of the case. A mere disturbance of electrical equilibrium might perhaps explain the movements of lightning in the atmosphere, but certainly does not at all account for electric affinities of the positive and negative manifested in the various processes of chemistry.

Rubbing and rubbed bodies acquire opposite electricities, the contact and interaction requiring the sort of co-relation which subsists between an acid and an alkali. That contact is combination, not mere aggregation—distinctive individuality being here, as in every department of societary life, the condition of perfect association.

Substances assume vitreous or resinous electricity in adjustment to the conditions or capacities acting or acted upon. Woollen cloth is strongly vitreous with zinc, but with gold or iron it is resinous. Such mutations occur in all electric bodies, varying in their intensities, also, under the influence of diversely related substances. Here, again, do we find a beautiful analogy to the law of societary association—an infinitely varying adaptation to, and influence upon, the infinitely varied individualities required for giving rapidity to the societary circulation.

This force of immeasurable and resistless energy flows silently, gently, imperceptibly, through perfect conductors, supplying its currents of vitality to the whole organic world. Disturbed, resisted, or misdirected, it blasts and crushes, on the contrary, every obstacle encountered in its course; and here, again, do we find a perfect correspondence to the social force. The actual relation of each and every member of a community, as giver and receiver, teacher and learner, producer and consumer, is positive and negative by turns and relatively to every difference of function and force in his associates, the whole mass constituting a great electric battery to which each individual contributes his pair of plates. Perfect circulation being established, as a consequence of perfect development of all the various individualities, the economic force flows smoothly through every member of the body politic, general happiness and prosperity, improved mental and moral action, following in its train. When, however, by reason of failure on the part of those charged with exercise of the co-ordinating power of the State, the circulation is obstructed, capital misused, and labor abused, the gentle vital force is converted into thunderbolts, whose existence is made manifest by the presence of consuming fires. The broken balance rushes by a pathway of ruin to regain its equilibrium, the war of elements thus presented being the correspondent of the strife engendered by resistance to the laws of human life.

The production of electricity, or its excitation for use, requires order and relations that are full of suggestiveness to those who desire fully to understand the conditions upon which, alone, there can be a prosperous and permanent societary life. Zinc and copper plates, promiscuously piled, are mere rubbish, powerless as the fragments of any other waste. Let them, however, be connected in orderly alternation, and the range may continue indefinitely with increase of latent force, ready upon the instant when the circuit shall be completed to gather together at one extremity the whole accumulated negative, and at the other the whole accumulated positive, and thus present an active force sufficient to bind and unbind the elements of matter; to penetrate to the innermost parts of their constitutions; to subdue their resistance to its will; to shatter to atoms the largest masses; or to enable man to hold instant converse with his fellow men throughout the earth.

Turning now to the societary organization we find the precise parallel to all this, poverty and weakness being the lot of all those communities in which, as in Turkey and in Ireland, the human plates are promiscuously piled, and in which, as a necessary consequence, there is little or no circulation, wealth and power, on the contrary, growing everywhere in the ratio in which each and every pair of plates is placed in proper relation with each and every other; the vitalized circuit being thus established throughout the entire mass and made to bear, with the concentrated energy of the whole, upon every object of general interest. For the establishment of such order and consequent production of such action it is, that men, as is now being shown in all the new communities of the southern and western hemispheres, are led to grant to certain individuals exercise of the power of co-ordination, a course of proceeding directly opposed to the doctrine of *laisser faire*. The more this power is exercised in the direction of promoting rapid circulation among the plates of which the great battery is composed the greater is the tendency to development of an inspiration and an energy closely resembling the service of the lightning of heaven subdued to human use. The more the reader shall make himself familiar with the wonderful force of which, even yet, so little is known, the more, certainly, must he be struck with its extraordinary correspondence with the life forces that govern the destinies of the race, and the more must he be led to arrive at the conclusion that the author has not erred in taking it as the force required for illustrating social action, and for aiding in the study of social science.

§ 3. "To Nature," says Professor Tindall,* "nothing can be added;

* Heat considered as a Mode of Motion.

from Nature nothing can be taken away; the sum of her energies is constant, and the utmost man can do in the pursuit of physical truth, or in the applications of physical knowledge, is to shift the constituents of the never-varying total, and out of one of them to form another. The law of conservation rigidly excludes both creation and annihilation. Waves may change to ripples, and ripples to waves—magnitude may be substituted for number, and number for magnitude,—asteroids may aggregate to suns, suns may resolve themselves into florae and faunae, and florae and faunae melt in air,—the flux of power is eternally the same. It rolls in music through the ages, and all terrestrial energy,—the manifestations of life, as well as the display of phenomena, are but the modulations of its rhythm."

We have here, according to Dr. Faraday, "the highest law in physical science which our faculties permit us to perceive, that of the conservation of forces." But recently discovered, it seems now to have become the crown of the edifice of that great system of law by means of which harmony is secured throughout the whole range of matter, from the coral insects which build up islands that are to form the nuclei of continents to the innumerable suns, with their attendant planets, of which the universe is composed.

By *unity of force*, and *unity* and *universality of law*, is here intended that persistency of impulse and constancy of action in the multiform substances and subjects of natural law, which is found to follow them through all their mutations of form and modifications of office, exhibiting an infinite variety of phenomena, yet without any change of essence or of intrinsic qualities and necessary tendencies in action. The cohesive attraction which produces and maintains the forms of material things, though apparently controlling, cannot be regarded as the abolition, or the temporary suspension, of that law of gravity which governs all masses of matter at all distances; for it is not so destroyed or suspended. It clings to every atom as persistently and permanently as the existence of the atom itself, for it is a condition of its existence. The disintegrating force of gravitation abides, and is as active in the integrity of the resistant forms of things as it is when displayed in their decomposition. Nay, cohesive attraction thus exhibiting an apparent opposition to, or difference from, the attraction of the planet, is probably the very same force acting with greater effect by virtue of the greater proximity of the atoms in the defiant form; just as an under-ground water-current descends from its source in one hill, and ascends from beneath the intervening valley to the crest of the neighboring height, pressed upward to its point of issue by the very same force which carried it downwards from its spring-head. In a multitude of familiar instances we in like manner learn to find unity and even identity, where, in appearance, we seem to see diversity and opposition.

It is certain that every atom of matter must carry with it through all changes of form and action the entirety of the properties which make it what it is; else the earth and the universe would have no constitution, and could not be the subject of any law.

This doctrine is not fate, but fact; not materialism, but order, organism, law, government. In its extension to all its subjects it trenches neither upon life, liberty, will, morals, religion, nor responsibility; it only affirms that the matter in man, as in the rest of the universe, is subject to positive, permanent, and universal rules of action, and that all of his functions which involve material agencies and relations, fall under the laws which arise out of their constitution. If by the terms mind, spirit, or immateriality, *nothingness* is meant, all inquiry, and with it all discussion is at an end, for of nothing we know nothing: but if mind is a something, a substance, an entity, it too must have a constitution and laws, and neither its will nor liberty is lawless. And surely we are safe in saying that if mind bears any relation to matter or substance, however transient in duration, it cannot be even conceived of as totally exempt from, or unfurnished with, such answering or correlative powers and properties as are necessarily required to qualify it for such co-ordinated existence and reciprocal action.

The unity of which we speak, as in all other instances in which the idea is used among men, is not identity or sameness, but the harmony of correspondence—unity by relation, fitness, or co-operation, effected by such continuity of character and force of all substances through all spheres of being, and all adaptations of use as alone can constitute a *universe* of the atoms and individualities which it embraces—of that one entire system "whose body nature is, and God the informing soul."

Physiologists exhibit the functions of human life as divided into individual, or vegetable, on the one hand, and relative on the other; the organs of the first of these classes being uniformly single, while those of the latter are as uniformly double and symmetrical There are two kinds of blood to be circulated, and for each there is a heart, the two being joined together as by a party wall, but not in any sense, as with the eyes and ears, a pair, of which each performs the same office. The life of relative functions consists in their connection with, and their action upon, the physical and societary world; and it is by means of that action that the real MAN is gradually developed. Deprived of these there would remain nothing proper to the man, and he could have no existence beyond that of a mere vegetable life—such a life as would be that of a solitary individual placed in the heart of the rich prairies of this Western continent. Of self-government—of the exercise of will— he could have none whatsoever, nature being there all-powerful, and he himself being weakness personified. Let him have a companion, and at once his proper human life is awakened; the opposing electric states of consumers and producers, givers and receivers, teachers and learners, having been induced, just as air awakens the quiescent lungs, and as light kindles and informs the eye, the real MAN then coming into existence, just as, by reason of association with his fellow-man, he is enabled to feel that he really has A WILL, and has ceased to be the absolute slave of nature.

The closer and more intimate the contact of these men, and the more rapid the circulation of ideas and services, the greater is the tendency toward development of the faculties peculiar to each, toward further combination, further friction, and further rapidity of circulation. Other men, their wives and children, now arriving, the phenomena are with each and every step in this direction repeated and intensified, human force steadily growing at the cost of Nature, and man obtaining by slow degrees that exercise of Will so entirely at first denied. Population steadily increasing, there arises that diversification in the demand for human force which leads to new developments of the various faculties of each and every member of the association, but in order to such development there must be that orderly arrangement which we see to be required in a galvanic battery, producers and consumers—the electric poles—being brought in close relation with each other. The closer those relations the more rapid becomes the circulation, and the more the power of self-government. The greater that power the more rapid is the growth of man's ability to compel Nature to yield in full abundance all the things required for maintenance and enjoyment of life and for further development of human force; and the more rapid the growth of that feeling of responsibility which scarcely at all exists in the barbarian, the slave, or the pauper of civilized life. The more these great questions shall be studied the more will it become obvious that man —the real MAN, capable of the exercise of Will and responsible for his actions—holds his existence in virtue of laws of universal force and effect, and, that the teacher who fails to familiarize himself with them, and with their bearing on societary and Christian life, fails in the performance of his duty to his Creator and to his fellow-men.*

§ 4. For the production of a sound state of morals it is indispensable that there be that freedom of the will which results from having power to direct to human service the wonderful forces of nature. That such power may exist it is as indispensable that there be in the societary body that same orderly arrangement of the positives and negatives— producers and consumers—which is seen in every well organized factory, in every properly appointed ship, in the administration of every well conducted road. To that end it is needed that there be such prompt and vigorous exercise of the power of co-ordination as may be required for removing obstacles to the societary circulation, and for enabling each and every of the millions of pairs of plates of which the battery is composed to be put in relation with each and every other. How wonderful is at times the effect of such action is shown in the case of Spain, as exhibited in chapter ix. of the present volume, and yet further in the following passage from a recent work describing the same period there referred to, that in which the discovery of the compass and of the art of printing, and the establishment of order throughout the kingdom, combined for producing the electrical effect that is here described:

"The human mind is like a hive. The dormant mass seems dead; but shake it and you will find that it is alive. Another shake—and your ears are struck by a low and confused hum—a murmur of discontent perhaps at its repose being disturbed—and then comes out a flight of

---

* "We must improve the sanitary condition of the people. Until this is done, no civilizing influence can touch them. The schoolmaster will labor in vain; the minister of religion will labor in vain; neither can make any progress in the fulfilment of their mission in a den of filth. Moral purity is incompatible with bodily impurity. Moral degradation is indissolubly united with physical squalor. The depression and discomfort of the hovel produce and foster obtuseness of mind, hardness of heart, selfish and sensual indulgence, violence and crime. It is the home that educates the family. It is the distinction and the curse of barbarism that it is without a home; it is the distinction and the blessing of civilization that it prepares a home in which Christianity may abide, and guide, and govern."—BAKER. *The Common Nature of Epidemics.*

thoughts, which, like busy bees, scatter far and wide, some distilling honey, and others checking intruders with their sharp stings. It is not astonishing that, in such a reign, during which the mind and soul were so much excited, literature, the arts, and sciences should have acquired such a prodigious development, particularly when fostered by the favor of a princess who patronized them with fond love and intelligent appreciation. Pompey had boasted that, if he stamped his foot, armies would spring up from the bosom of Italy. At the gentle beckoning of Isabella, there sprang up in Spain a host of men who distinguished themselves as theologians, jurists, historians, physicians, astronomers, naturalists, lyrical and dramatic poets, linguists, musicians, and successful explorers through the whole range of human knowledge."*

Compare with this the present poverty, the famines, the wretchedness, the demoralization of Ireland, of India, of Turkey, and then inquire into the causes of the existence of so deplorable a state of things, and it will be found that it results from the fact that their people exercise no Will— that the several nations are mere creatures in the hands of others that allow no power of self-government. Turn then to the advancing countries of Europe, and see that they become more moral in the proportion that they acquire self-direction, and that the power for such direction grows in the precise ratio of the judicious exercise of the power for so co-ordinating the various forces of society as most effectually to bring into connection the opposing electric poles, and thus most to stimulate the rapidity of the societary movement.†

§ 5. Self-reliance, and the power to command the confidence of others, grow with growth in the habit of self-government. To the individual who has them in possession they constitute forces always applicable to his service, and as much constituting portions of his capital as do the skill of the mechanic, the scientific knowledge of the chemist, or the learning of the judge. Both grow and extend themselves throughout a community in the direct ratio of that judicious exercise of the co-ordinating power which is required for removing obstacles to association, and for enabling producers and consumers—the positives and negatives of the great battery—to put themselves in close relation with each other and thus to make prompt demand for all the human forces that are from hour to hour produced.

---

* GAYARRÉ. Philip the Second, p. 322.

† That the scientific method of inquiry is inadequate, and inapplicable to the higher study of man, is a widely prevalent notion, and one which seems, to a great extent, to be shared alike by the ignorant and the educated. Holding the crude idea that science pertains only to the material world, they denounce all attempts to make human nature a subject of strict scientific inquiry, as an intrusion into an illegitimate sphere. Maintaining that man's position is supreme and exceptional, they insist that he is only to be comprehended, if at all, in some partial, peculiar and transcendental way. In entire consistence with this hypothesis is the prevailing practice; for those who, by their function as teachers, preachers and lawgivers, profess to have that knowledge of man which best qualifies for directing him in all relations, are, as a class, confessedly ignorant of science. There are some, however, and happily their number is increasing, who hold that this idea is profoundly erroneous; that the very term "human nature" indicates man's place in that universal order which it is the proper office of science to explore; and they accordingly maintain that it is only as "the servant and intepreter of nature" that he can rise to anything like a true understanding of himself.—YOUMANS. Lecture on the Scientific Study of Human Nature.

That this is so will be seen on careful examination of the operations of all those communities of Europe whose policy tends to give to its farmers so much of self-government as results from exercise of power to choose between a domestic and a foreign market. That the reverse of this exists in all the cases in which producers and consumers become more widely separated—that the moral force declines as the circulation becomes more and more obstructed—will be seen on study of the past and present course of things in Ireland, India, Turkey, and all other countries in which, by reason of failure to exercise the co-ordinating power, the men who cultivate the land become more and more dependent on distant markets, and more and more deprived of power to determine for themselves whether to sell in the near or distant one. Poor, wretched, and wholly dependent on the will of others, they and all other countries similarly situated, furnish abundant proof of the accuracy of the *North British Review,* (March, 1867) in asserting that it is only "in the free development of the natural forces, whether of morality, intelligence, or of material wealth," that the "balance of power" will be found, and, that "it will be always held by the country which, in proportion to its powers, has economized its material resources to the highest point, and acquired the highest degree of ascendency by an honest and constant allegiance to the laws of morality in its domestic policy and in its foreign relations."

That "balance" has for a long period been mainly held by France and England, the two nations that, of all others, have been most persistent in their determination so to exercise the power of co-ordination as to bring into close relation their own producers and their own consumers, and thus to establish orderly relations among the many millions of human positives and negatives of which their populations have been composed; although now, of all, the most determined to urge upon others rejection of the policy they have so long pursued. The reason for this may perhaps be found in the fact that that "balance" tends to pass into other hands, and for the Eastern continent into those of a people of Central Europe which stands now indebted for the power it has so lately manifested to its adoption of that system which had been elsewhere seen to tend so largely to the development of all "the natural forces, whether of morality, intelligence, or national wealth"—that one under which man has been most enabled to obtain perfect exercise of the power to will, and that under which, for that reason, he himself has become most moral, and credit most developed.

§ 6. In the author's definition of capital first given, mental and physical force were alone included. To this, as the reader will see (chap. xxxiii), is now added that moral force to which is due the existence of a credit system that has in all advancing countries assumed such large proportions, although but recently it had, in most of them, so slight existence.

Since the publication of that work a very voluminous writer has given to the world a new system, an essential feature of which is found in the assertion that "credit is capital, and debts are wealth."* Were this so, the man whose expenses so far exceeded his income as to render it necessary with each succeeding year to place a mortgage on his paternal acres, would be steadily adding to the wealth of the community; while his provident neighbor, of equal means, whose income and expenditure

* McLeod. Dictionary of Political Economy, article, Credit.

were regularly made to meet, would not. Were it so, the community that maintained large armies, and thus produced a necessity for making large additions to its funded debt, would be adding largely to the country's wealth ; whereas, its more modest neighbor, occupied in paying off existing liabilities, would be, with each successive day, so far as govermental action was concerned, becoming poorer than before !

Wealth grows with growth in the power to command nature's services. Its existence manifests itself—

Not in the possession of telegraph poles and wires, but in the *power* thence obtained for speedy transmission of ideas :

Not in the railroad track, its cars and engines, but in the *power* thence obtained for cheap and speedy transportation of men and merchandise :

Not in the circulating note, but in the *power* thence obtained for making a single piece of gold do the work for which, in its absence, an hundred might be needed :

Not in the debt itself, but in the evidence thereby offered of the existence of a moral force, giving *power* to contract the debt.

At first, Mr. McLeod's suggestions attracted considerable attention, but since that time have so far passed away that they would not now be mentioned were it not that the author deems it proper to show that they differ wholly from those he has above propounded.

These things premised, we may now enter upon that review of the past decade to which he has above referred.

§ 7. Ten years since the author expressed the opinion that Germany, whose "national sin for the last two centuries," according to Chevalier Bunsen, " had been poverty, the condition of all classes with few exceptions"—Germany which but thirty years before had been held to be so greatly overpopulated as to warrant the suggestion of a resort to infibulation as the only remedy,*—then already stood "first in Europe in point of intellectual development," and was " advancing in the physical and moral condition of her people with a rapidity exceeding that of any other portion of the Eastern hemisphere."†

Since then, an empire has been created embracing a population little short of 40,000,000, among whom education is universal ; with a system of communications not excelled by that of any other country, with the exception of those provided for the very dense populations and limited territories of England and of Belgium ; with an internal commerce as perfectly organized as any in the world, and growing from day to day with extraordinary rapidity ; with a market on the land for nearly all its products, and, as a necessary consequence, with an agricultural population that grows daily in both intelligence and power; with a mercantile marine that now numbers more than 10,000 vessels ; with a public treasury so well provided that not only has the loan authorized at the close of the late war remained unused, but that it has been at once enabled to make large additions to the provision for public education; and with private treasuries so well supplied as to enable her people not only with their own means to build their own furnaces and factories and construct

---

* WEINHOLD. *Von der Uebervolkerung in Mittel Europa.* Halle, 1829.—He proposed that *infibulation* should be established by law, and accomplished by means of soldering up all males at their 14th year, and so retaining them until they could prove that they had the means required for supporting a family.

† Principles. Chap. xxiv. § 11.

their own roads, but also to furnish hundreds of millions to the improvident people of America, to be by them applied to the making of roads in a country the abundance of whose natural resources should long since have placed it in the position of money lender, rather than that now occupied of general money borrower.

How rapid has been, and now is, progress in the mechanic arts will be seen on an examination of the following facts in regard to iron. In 1850, the product of steel was valued at $350,000. Ten years later it had reached $1,400,000. Five years still later, having meantime endowed the world with the great gift of the Bessemer process, the figure reached was $10,000,000. In 1850, the total value of pig and wrought iron was but $15,000,000; whereas, in 1865, it had grown to $55,000,-000, and all this vast increase was but preparation for new and further movements in the same direction, arrangements, as we are told, having recently been made for great extension of operations.

Seeking for a high condition of morals or manners, in either England or America, no inquirer would be led to look to the mining regions of either the one or the other. Should he, however, be led to turn to Germany, he would find in a highly interesting little work recently published,* that there 10,000 miners could be congregated together at a festival, and without the slighest drunkenness or disorder, either in the day or the night that followed.

Referring to the general social condition of that country the author says :—

"If I ever turn philanthropist, it will be my object to promote all innocent amusements in my ill-used native land, where it now appears to me that our working class are the most abject and degraded slaves compared to the people here—slaves to a hopelessly hard master—not an individual, but an enormous dominant mass of money."†

Comparing it with Scotland, the land she had left behind, she speaks as follows :—

"Here are no 'gentry' to patronize or tyrannize—no one from whom anything is to be hoped; every one is dependent on his own industry alone. Add to this that all are educated compulsorily; every child goes to school; and any one will plainly understand how immeasurably superior in intelligence the working people here are to those at home."‡

How great is the tendency to union among the working people thus described is shown in the fact that whereas in 1859 there were but 183 co-operative associations, in 1865 there were 961, 839 of which were outside of the Austrian empire. More than half of these were "people's banks," the others having been formed for various purposes of production, or for facilitating purchase and consumption.

Out of the shattered fragments that five and thirty years since passed with the world as Germany, there has already been created the most important empire of Europe; one whose power for self-defence exhibits itself in the fact that it has just now given to the world the greatest improvement ever made in regard to the production of that metal in the abundance of whose use is found the highest evidence of civilization; and in that other most important one that, with only an equal

* A Summer in the Hartz Forest. Edinburgh, 1865.
† Ibid., p. 272.   ‡ Ibid., p. 275.

population, the number of young men that annually attain the age fitting them for military duty exceeds that of France by the large number of 68,000,* the mere surplus being sufficient for meeting the wants of war, should unfortunately, at any time, war be needed.†

To what now, has this all been due? To the quiet and simple operation of the protective features of the system of the Zoll-Verein, long regarded by the author as the most important measure of the century, and among the most important ever adopted in Europe. Under it labor was everywhere economized. Under it, the positives and negatives of a whole nation were brought into communication with each other, and thus has been created a great battery of 40,000,000 pairs of plates throughout which there is now a rapidity of circulation scarcely elsewhere, on so large a scale, exceeded, and destined ultimately, in all probability, to produce effects throughout the Eastern continent fully equal to any that may, by even the most sanguine, be hoped for in this Western one.

The lion and the tiger—the Cæsars and Napoleons of the animal world—leave behind no evidences of their ever having existed. The little coral insect creates islands that endure forever. So is it like to be with that great monument just now, and at the trivial cost of a single week of battles, erected to the memory of FREDERIC LIST and his associates, the humble laborers to whom the world at large stands indebted for the formation of the Zoll-Verein.

---

* RAUDOT, in the *Gazette de France.* Quoted in the *Zeitschrift* of the Prussian Statistical Bureau, for 1866, p. 129.

† The following passage, bearing as it does upon the two great events of the decade, is given in illustration of the importance of that moral element whose development follows necessarily in the train of measures tending to bring into communication the positives and negatives of society—producers and consumers—and thus to quicken the societary circulation.

"The plain, simple, unvarnished truth I take to be, that the Prussians uniformly defeated the Austrians because, man for man, they were better and stronger soldiers. They were not so well drilled, they were worse dressed, they were not so rapid in their movements, they were far less soldier-like looking; but they were much more ready to encounter danger, they were animated with a far higher and more intelligent courage. Physically they were stronger, stouter, and more powerful men than their opponents; mentally they were immeasurably superior to the mixed hordes of Croats and Bohemians and Hungarians arrayed against them. They knew, or fancied they knew—which comes to much the same thing—what they were fighting about; they had a strong sense of duty; they were steady, orderly, God-fearing men. From the highest general to the lowest private, they had learned how to obey; and they had implicit confidence that their officers, whether able or not, were prepared to do their duty also. All estimates of the men I have yet seen seem to me to leave out of sight the power of what I may call the religious element of the Prussian army. You may call it superstition, or bigotry, or fanaticism, as you choose; but no person who has studied the subject carefully can deny that the Prussian soldiers had a sort of reliance in their own cause, as being that of duty and religion, which was entirely wanting amongst the Austrians. The phrase of 'Holy Prussia,' about which we in England have laughed so often, when it was used by the King in his addresses to his people, had a real meaning and purport for the Prussian peasant. And so the Prussian armies, in my judgment, conquered for much the same reason that the Puritans conquered the Cavaliers, the Dutch conquered the Spaniards, and the Federals conquered the Confederates—because they were more in earnest, more thoughtful, more willing to risk their lives for a principle, whether false or true, more imbued with a sense of duty." DICEY. *Battle Fields of* 1866.

So *will* it be, provided that those charged with exercise of the power of co-ordination shall always recollect that progress in the past has been a consequence of vigorous local action ; that that action tends to increase in vigor as agriculture becomes more and more a science; that agriculture is the last of all the pursuits of man to attain its full development; that upon that development depends the growth of mind and morals among the people, and of strength in the state; that the obstacle thereto is found in the oppressive tax of transportation ; and that relief therefrom is to be obtained in no manner other than that of the pursuit of such measures as are required for bringing into close relation with each other the many millions of societary positives and negatives—producers and consumers, teachers and learners, lenders and borrowers—and thus providing for constant and rapid increase in the societary circulation.

§ 8. Five and thirty years since, Germany and the American Republic exhibited states of things directly antagonistic, the one to the other. The first was divided and disturbed, its internal commerce in every way embarrassed, its people and its various governments very poor, and with little hope in the future except that which resulted from the fact that negotiations were then on foot for the formation of a Customs Union, which, five years later, was accomplished. In the other, on the contrary, everything was different, the internal commerce having been more active than had ever before been known, the public treasury filled to overflowing, the national debt on the eve of extinction, and capital so much abounding as to make demand, for the opening of mines, the building of houses and mills, and the construction of roads, for all the labor power of a people that then numbered thirteen millions.

The cause of these remarkable differences was to be found in the facts, that, up to that time, Germany had wholly failed to adopt such measures of co-ordination as were needed for establishing circulation among the 30,000,000 of pairs of human plates of which her society was then composed; whereas, the Congress of the American Union had, four years before, and for the first time, adopted measures having for their object development of all the powers physical, mental, or moral of its population, all the wealth of its soil, and all the wonderful mineral deposits by which that soil was known to be underlaid. The one had failed to bring together the producer and consumer of food and wool, and had remained dependent upon traders in distant markets. The other had just then *willed* that such dependence should, at no distant time, come to an end ; that producers and consumers should be brought together ; and there had thence already resulted an activity of circulation and an improvement in physical and moral condition, the like of which had never before been known to be accomplished in so brief a period.

Three years later (1835), the two countries are once again found totally opposed, Germany having adopted the American system and thus provided for freedom of internal commerce, America simultaneously adopting that which to Germany had proved so utterly disastrous, and which had been then rejected. Thenceforth the one moved steadily forward in the direction of creating a great internal commerce, doing this by means of a railroad system which should so bind together her whole people as to forbid the idea of future separation. The result with the one already exhibits itself in the quiet creation of a powerful empire. The other meanwhile has constructed great roads by means of which it has been enabled to export its soil, in the forms of tobacco, corn, and cotton, to distant markets, and thus to destroy the power to maintain internal commerce—the result obtained exhibiting itself in a great rebellion that has cost the country, North and South, half a million of lives, the crippling of hundreds of thousands of men, and an expenditure of more thousands of millions than, properly applied, would have doubled the incomes of its whole people, while making such demand for human force, mental, moral, and physical, as would, in a brief period, have secured the establishment of universal freedom, with benefit to all, white and black, landowner and laborer. Such have been the widely different results of two systems of public policy, the one of which looks to introducing into society that proper, orderly arrangement which is found in every well conducted private establishment, and by means of which each and every person employed is enabled to find the place for which nature had intended him ; the other meanwhile, in accordance with the doctrine of *laisser faire*, requiring that government should abdicate the performance of its proper duties, wholly overlooking the fact that all the communities by which such teachings are carried into practical effect now exhibit themselves before the world in a state of utter ruin.

At the date of the first publication of the work of which this volume is a condensation, this latter system had, with the exception of the brief and brilliant period, 1842 to 1847, prevailed throughout the American Union for more than twenty years, and its results, in causing waste of labor, waste of raw material, waste and misdirection of mental power, moral and political demoralization, and steady growth of the pro-slavery belief, were therein fully and freely exhibited.* At that moment, closely following on the wonderful discoveries of Californian and Australian treasures, its political sea was, to all appearance, calm and unruffled, and its financial skies were bright, yet did the author not hesitate to predict that political and financial crises were even then close at hand. Scarcely had his book been given to the public eye when there broke upon the world the great financial crisis of 1857, the most destructive, and, to merchants generally, the most unlooked for of all that stand on record. Following on this there came the prostration necessarily consequent upon an almost entire destruction of the societary circulation that had been thus produced. So very sluggish was it, notwithstanding the continuance of vast receipts from California mines, that capital was petrified,† credit was impaired, and the rate of interest throughout the West great beyond all previous precedent. In the history of the civilized world there can with difficulty be found a parallel to the waste of physical and mental force that then was taking place. Seeing this, the writer was led to believe that the policy of *laisser faire* was costing the country not less than $3,000,000,000 a year, and he has as yet seen no reason for doubting the accuracy of the view that is thus presented.

That waste was at its height throughout the whole presidential period which preceded the rebellion. For the products of Northern

* See Principles of Social Science, Philadelphia, 1857, Chapters xxvi. to xxix.
† See note to page 10.

agriculture there was almost literally no demand among the manufacturing nations of Europe, the exports of food in that direction in the three years that preceded the secession movement having averaged but $10,000,000. Corn in the West was then being used for fuel, and thus was the producer compelled to lose not only the interest upon his capital, but the very capital itself that he had thus invested. Labor power was in excess, and men were everywhere wandering in search of such employment as would enable them to purchase food. Mills and furnaces were abandoned, and so trivial was the domestic intercourse that the stock of a number of the most important roads of the country fell to, and long remained at, an average price of less than fifty per cent. For years the country, under the system of *laisser faire*, had been trying the experiment as to how large an outlay of labor could be made for the accomplishment of any given result, an experiment directly the opposite of that which is tried by every successful producer of corn or cotton, cloth or iron ; the effect exhibiting itself in the fact that the community was paralyzed, and so wholly destitute of force that had the government then found occasion to call upon the whole nation for a sum so small as even a single hundred millions, it could scarcely have at all been furnished.

The day of trial that had been predicted was, however, close at hand, three-fifths of the nation, numbering 20,000,000, then finding themselves called, without a moment's notice, to the suppression of a rebellion the most remarkable that the world had yet seen ; a work that during a period of five years required, on an average, the services of more than a million of men, or more than five per cent. of the total population, male and female, sick and well, young and old. Not only were those services given, but during all that time the men employed were well clothed, abundantly fed, and furnished with transportation to an extent, and in a perfection, unparalleled in the history of the world. With them, too, were carried all the materials required for making, as it may be hoped, the monument to freedom in whose construction they were engaged as durable as we know to have been the great pyramids erected by Egyptian monarchs.

Whence came the extraordinary force that we see to have been thus exerted ? How was it that a people which, in 1860, had been so very feeble could in the succeeding years have made donations to the extraordinary extent of a thousand millions of dollars a year ? The answer to this question is found in the fact that the conditions of national existence had wholly changed, almost perfect circulation having been established throughout a gigantic battery of 20,000,000 pairs of plates, activity and life having succeeded to paralysis, and the societary movement having become strong and vigorous to an extent that had never before in any community been known. For the first time in the history of the world there was then presented for examination a nation in which the demand for labor and all its productions went ahead of the supply, enabling both farmer and planter to stop the interest upon capital that had so long been petrified in the crudest forms of agricultural production ; and, as a necessary consequence, to make demand for the products of other labor applied to development of the mineral wealth that so much abounded, and to the conversion into commodities fitted for human use, of the products of hills and valleys, farms and mines. The secret of all the force that was then so well exerted—one so extraordinary as to have astonished the world at large—is to be found in that simple principle, evidence of whose truth is found in the books of every trader and the records of every nation, and which is found embodied in words already given—the power of accumulation exists in the ratio of the rapidity of circulation.

What, however, was the force applied? Why was it that activity had so instantaneously succeeded to apathy—that life and energy had replaced the paralysis that had till then existed? By most persons answers to these questions would be given in the assertion that it had been caused by the demands of the government and must terminate with their cessation; and yet, of all who thus might answer there would not be found even a single one who could explain how the abstraction from other pursuits of the labor of a million of men, and the necessity for feeding and clothing them while engaged in the erection of such a monument, could, by any possibility, produce the extraordinary effects that had been here observed.

To attribute the activity and life then existing to the government demands is to substitute effect for cause. It was the force resulting from an activity of circulation wholly unprecedented in history—one precisely similar to that observed on occasion of every connection of the positives and negatives of any other great electric battery—that enabled the people, *not* the government, to make the war; and that force existed in despite, and *not* as a consequence, of such demand. That such was certainly the fact will be clearly obvious to the reader when he shall reflect, that but for those demands the whole million of men so employed might have been employed in clearing land, sinking shafts, mining coal and ores and combining the two in the forms of lead, copper, and iron; making bricks and lumber, and thus furnishing supplies of raw materials to be converted on the spot into thousands of mills and shops, large and small, and into the cloth and iron, spades and shovels, coats and hats, required for supplying a population among whom the demand for mental and physical force so far exceeded the supply as to make it absolutely necessary to build engines by tens of thousands, and thus to substitute, to the annual extent of the power of millions of men, the wonderful force of steam for that of the human arm. So applied, that same force would have produced annually of commodities in excess of what was then the actual production, to the extent of thousands of millions of dollars, every portion of which would have been in the market seeking to purchase labor, thus greatly increasing the laborer's reward. The power of accumulation would, under such circumstances, have been more trebly great, with steady decline in the rate of interest, and in the power of the capitalist to control the laborer's movements; freedom, wealth, power, and civilization, moral, and intellectual, always growing with the growth of power to place the societary plates—producers and consumers—in close relation with each other, and thus to increase the rapidity of the societary circulation.

That the wonderful activity of that circulation did not result from governmental necessities will be clear to all who carefully reflect on the facts above presented. Whence, then, came it? From the re-adoption by the people of the Free States of the ideas, that exercise of the co-ordinating power was first among the duties of the government; that the produce of the farm ought no longer to be compelled to remain inert and losing interest while waiting demand in distant markets; that the capital which daily took the form of labor power ought no longer be allowed to go to waste; that the fuel which underlaid the soil ought no longer to remain to be a mere support for foreign rails; that the power which lay then petrified in the form of coal ought everywhere to be brought to aid the human arm; that the vast deposits of iron ore should be made to take the forms of engines and other machinery to be used sa substitutes for mere muscular force; and that all their wonderful resources, material and moral, ought and must be at once developed. Such was the intent and meaning of the nation when the Morrill Tariff, ou the memorable 2d of March, 1861, became the law of the land. To that law, aided as it was by the admirable action of the Treasury in supplying machinery of circulation, does the world stand now indebted for the fact that the people of America, in the short space of five years, and at a cost of thousands of millions of dollars, were enabled to retrieve the downward steps of more than twenty years; to establish freedom throughout the land; and to save from destruction a nation of more than 30,000,000 that, by long practice on the pernicious doctrine of *laisser faire*, had been brought so near the verge of ruin that its escape therefrom constitutes now the most remarkable event in the history of the world.

Adding the capital that was only paralyzed to that which was absolutely wasted in the presidential period that preceded the war, we obtain an amount thrice greater than would, had it been so applied, have built and stocked as many mills as are in all Great Britain employed in the conversion of wool and cotton into cloth; as many furnaces as there are occupied in converting coal and ore into lead, copper, and iron; and as many mills as are now engaged in producing bars; to sink as many shafts as would have been required for giving to human labor all the aid that there is seen to result from a consumption of coal said to furnish power to an extent equivalent to that of six hundred millions of men; and to double the quantity and money value of production, to the great advantage of all, borrowers and lenders, employers and workmen, traders and manufacturers, builders of railroads and owners of ships, there being a perfect harmony of all real and permanent interests. A part, and but a small part, of that capital was, by means of a National Free Trade System, then saved; and it was out of the saving that thus was brought about that the country was enabled to give to the great work above referred to labor and commodities equal in their annual money value to the vast sum of $1,000,000,000.

Was that, however, all it gave? That such was not the case is proved by the extraordinary voluntary contributions that throughout the whole period were made of time, mind, and material means for promotion of the comfort of those who were in the field, as well as of those whom they left behind—contributions that are as little to be paralleled as is the magnitude of the work then needed to be performed. The more that this history shall come to be studied the more will the student be led to the belief that moral as well as material force constitutes capital; that both grow with growth in the rapidity of circulation; and that growth in this latter is wholly dependent upon discreet exercise of the power granted by the people for so directing the societary movement as gradually to remove the many obstacles standing in the way of perfect association and combination.

Among the most remarkable facts of the decade may here be mentioned the admirable conduct of millions of negro men suddenly set free, and the equally admirable conduct of a single American citizen in donating many millions to be applied to their education, and to various other benevolent purposes in both Great Britain and the United States.

Since the close of the war the Union has been unfortunate in having for its Finance Minister a man who has profited little by the experience of the past few years, and now appears to think that the shortest way to extinction of the national debt is to be found in stoppage of the societary circulation. As a consequence, all that has been gained during the war is being lost in time of peace. To what extent the losses are to be carried, or how long this system is to be endured, none now can venture to predict.

§ 9. Annihilating at a single blow the local institutions of France, the Revolution gave to the world, in lieu of the historic names of Burgundy and Brittany, Anjou and Languedoc, those of Cantal, Doubs, Lot, and eighty others, none of which in any manner connected their people or themselves with the eventful past. *Pays d'Etat* and *Pays d'Election* alike disappeared, and with them all the local life that had resulted from local exercise of power in reference to social action of high importance.* Paris, thenceforth, was to issue the decrees in virtue of which schoolhouses might be built, or roads constructed, and Préfets sent therefrom would see to their execution. Since then, the general tendency has been in the same direction—that of political centralization'; but, as at no period has it been so decided as since the establishment of the second empire, advantage may here be gained from studying the course of things in the last decade with a view to see how far it tends towards establishing the accuracy of Mirabeau's idea, that "Capitals were necessities," but that "if the head were allowed to grow too large, the body would become apoplectic and waste away"—one of the most important that could at the present time be offered for both European and American consideration. Should the facts now to be presented tend towards proving its perfect truth, then may we find therein an explanation of the causes to which must be attributed the remarkable change that so recently has occurred in reference to the place occupied by France in the eyes of Europe, if not even in those of the world at large.

Wars, causing large expenditures, are centralizing in their tendencies. Since the creation of the second empire, the moneys paid annually into the Treasury at Paris, to be thence distributed, have increased in amount more than $60,000,000, while interest on the debt has increased about $22,000,000, indicating an enlargement of the principal to the extent of probably $550,000,000, such being the natural products of the numerous

* See Principles of Social Science, vol. iii. p. 227.

wars, Crimean, Chinese, Cochin Chinese, Italian, and Mexican, in which the empire has been so steadily engaged.

Looking always outward, the empire has been steadily engaged in efforts at increasing external commerce, sometimes by enlargement of its remote possessions, at others by means of foreign treaties, and thus following in the footsteps of its British neighbor. When, however, we look to the arrangements for promoting internal commerce and thus giving life to the various local centres, we are met at once by the fact that France, the country that, with Belgium, constitutes the great highway of the world, with a population of 38,000,000, a territory containing 200,000 square miles, an army of 600,000 men, a fleet that costs little less than $50,000,000, and a taxation yielding $350,000,000 annually, has but 8000 miles of railroad, a quantity little greater than is now possessed by the three adjoining States of Pennsylvania, New York, and New Jersey, with a population of 8,000,000, and a territory of 100,000 square miles.*

* The following passage from a recent speech in the *Corps Legislatif* exhibits the effects of the system above described :—"Farmers had been recommended to raise less corn, to form pasture lands. That advice was very easy to give; but to put it in practice resources were required which agriculture could not always command. What, then, were the remedies to be applied to the sufferings and embarrassments of agriculture ? Nobody wished to see the price of bread raised; the duty of the farmer was to produce as much corn as possible at the lowest possible price. But to contend with foreign competition the existing legislation would require to be modified. All the great works promised by the Emperor should be executed without loss of time, whether relating to the canals, railways, rivers, or vicinal and departmental roads. The water courses were also in a very deplorable state. Boats coming from the sea, and only drawing a yard of water, were unable last summer to ascend to Paris; and the canals opening into the Seine were in a similar condition. The works to be executed to improve the navigation of the Seine between Paris and the sea would cost six millions, but they would produce a saving in the price of transport of seven millions a year. The same may be said of other rivers. The government should modify its system of public works by concentrating them on five or six principal routes; the navigation of the great streams should be first attended to; then the canals, and those improvements should be executed, not simultaneously, but one at a time, so that the sums expended might be rendered productive at once. (Hear, hear.) Agriculture should be relieved of some of the heavy imposts with which it is burthened. When the great economic reform was carried out, customs duties which weighed on industry were sacrificed to the amount of a hundred millions. Agriculture has, nevertheless, the same right to relief as manufactures. (Assent.) When the enterprises in which the country is engaged are brought to a close the surpluses should be applied to the amount of fifty millions or more to remove some of the burthens from the farmer. The land tax and registration dues paid by the rural districts amount to about four hundred millions. But while awaiting a reduction in the charges, an equality between foreign and French corn may be established by imposing a duty of two francs per hectolitre on the former, for before a hectolitre of French produce has left the farm it has paid at least two francs of taxes. Agricultural credit must also be established on new bases. The government has, indeed, made several attempts to do so, among others that of the foundation of the Credit Foncier Company, which has lent a great deal of money to the towns, but has rendered but slight services to the growers. A drainage fund was also established, and the Legislative Body voted a sum of one hundred millions, but not more than one million three hundred thousand or one million four hundred thousand francs have been lent to agriculture." The direct effect

Examining these latter, we see how ill they are even yet provided with the means of local communication, and to how great an extent their existing roads have been constructed with exclusive reference to outside commerce. Such being the case, how obvious and excessive becomes the French deficiency when we find that, as compared with the territory of the great highway of the world, their needs are, even now, better supplied in the ratio of two to one, and as compared with population that of almost five to one.

New England, *not* a highway for any portion whatsoever of the exterior world, but possessing a large internal commerce, has 1000 miles of railroad for every million of her population, whereas France has little more than 1000 for every 5,000,000. In the one, local life and activity increase with a rapidity nowhere else exceeded. In the other, the reverse effect is from year to year being more and more produced, the attractions of the capital steadily increasing, while those of minor towns and cities as steadily decline.*

Railroads are necessarily centralizing in their tendencies, but when to this is added, that the Imperial Government has been, and perhaps still is, engaged in transferring to the capital the monuments and records of the past, and thus diminishing the attraction of local centres, while incessantly engaged in enlarging and beautifying Paris, and thereby making it more and more desirable as a place of residence, the cause of the general lifelessness of local centres throughout the empire may readily be understood.

Why, however, is it, the local roads remain unmade? That it was otherwise before the revolution in the provinces which were then allowed the exercise of power for self-government, is seen in the answer to the king, made by the States of Languedoc, to the effect that they needed no aid from government for the completion or maintenance of any works of public utility whatsoever, feeling themselves perfectly competent for doing all the work required to be done.† Then, however, those people exercised a Will of their own. Now, they are subjected to that of men whose homes are found in the great central city, and who, while ever ready to aid in the construction of roads leading to and from it, feel but little interest in the cross-roads required for giving life to the smaller towns and cities, and thus bringing into closer connection the many millions of positives and negatives—producers and consumers, lend-

---

of the extremely imperfect system of internal communications is to prevent the people of Northern France from supplying the South with food, and the indirect one that of compelling its export to England, and thus reducing the price in the regulating market of the world. The two chief trading nations of the world are thus united in the effort to depress the prices of food and raw materials of every kind.

* "What *can* induce you to stop at Dijon?" Such was the question addressed to the author by an eminent French economist, after hearing that he proposed to spend a day in that city which for centuries had been the splendid capital of the Burgundian dukes, and as such the centre of power and rival of Paris for capital of the kingdom! There are fifty towns and cities in Germany in regard to which no German would think of putting such a question. In France, outside of the few trading cities, there is scarcely even a single one.

† DE TOCQUEVILLE. *L'Ancien Régime. Appendix.*

ers and borrowers—of which the population of the empire, outside of a very few principal cities, now stands composed.

Prior to the revolution of 1848, the lenders and borrowers of various cities and towns, after overcoming many obstructions, had been enabled to come together for the formation of banks of discount and deposit. At that date, however, centralization triumphed, all local banks being then closed, and the power for corporate banking, as well as for the issue of circulating notes, being limited to the Parisian stockholders who own the few millions constituting the capital of the Bank of France. Financial and political centralization have thus gone hand in hand together.

In the decade ending 1861 the total increase of numbers was 930,000, of which no less than 531,000 were found in Paris alone, while of the small remainder the greater part were found in Bordeaux, Marseilles, and other principal cities. In all of them air and light are scarce, the proportion borne in Paris by population to space, as stated by Mons. Duval in his *Reflections on the Census of* 1866,* being nearly thrice greater than is the case even in London, and yet greater in the others. Such, says Mons. Duval, are the results of frequent wars, and of the pressure of taxation.†

As a consequence of all this it is, that population now grows so slowly that two hundred years would be required for its duplication. How far this tends to affect the position of France as regards other powers is shown in the fact, that while the number of young men annually attaining the age required for military service is stated at only 315,000, that of the newly-formed German empire is no less than 383,000, the tendency towards profitable connection of agricultural and mechanical pursuits being, in this latter, more complete, and the supply of light and air, therefore, more abundant.‡

Throughout the physical world the more rapid the motion, the greater is the force. So, too, is it in the social world. Centralization, tending as it does towards wider separation of the societary positives and negatives, tends necessarily to arrest of the one and destruction of the other. At no period has the tendency in that direction been so great as in the years of the second empire; and if we now see that France is gradually losing the position she so long had held, we may find in it confirmation of the predictions of Mirabeau as to the injury that must inevitably result from "drawing all the talent of the kingdom to Paris, and leaving to the provincials no chance of reward or motive of ambition," thereby placing them "in a state of dependence" and converting them "into an inferior class of citizens."§

Such is the present tendency of imperial action. Let it be continued, and it will become safe to predict that France will never regain that influence over European thought and action she so long had exercised.

* Republished in the *Zeitschrift* of the Prussian Statistical Bureau, 1866, p. 128.

† In the five years ending 1866, the increase was 680,000, of which a third were found in eight principal cities, nearly two-fifths of the departments meanwhile exhibiting a decrease of numbers. The ratio of increase in less than a third of one per cent. per annum, or one-ninth of that of the American Union.

‡ For the better course of things in Central Europe generally, see LE PLAY, *La Reforme Sociale*, vol. i. p. 430.

§ Quoted by De Tocqueville, *L'Ancien Régime*, chap. vi.

§ 10. The onward progress of Russia, as a consequence of measures tending towards bringing together the producers and consumers of the empire is exhibited, in this last decade, in the great measure of emancipation so happily effected.

Turkey, on the contrary, steadily adhering to the policy which looks to perpetuation of the farmer's dependence on foreign markets, and to increase of the taxation of trade and transportation, has steadily declined, the "sick man" passing slowly forward toward the grave, doing this, too, in despite of numerous proclamations of changes in the constitution, each of which, in succession, as the world has been assured, was to produce effects so important as to insure revivification of the empire.

Little more than a dozen years since France and England, the two leading nations of Europe, formed an alliance having for its object the defence of Turkey against Russia, and the continued maintenance of the former in its then existing condition of subjection to the will of foreign traders. That subjection has been continued, and, as a necessary consequence, Turkey has become greatly weaker while Russia has become as greatly strengthened. In this state of things the former is again menaced by the latter, but, as her allies have no desire to repeat the lesson of 1854, she seems destined now to find that not a single stranger gun will be fired in her defence, and thus to give to the world further evidence of the fact that the man, or the nation, who would command the aid of others, must show by proper management of his own proper household that his need of help is likely to be a declining, and not an increasing, one. Such, even in Turkey, would speedily be the case could those who are charged with the management of affairs be made properly to appreciate the idea that strength and power grow with growth in the rapidity of circulation, and that the circulation becomes more rapid as the positives and negatives of society are brought into closer relation with each other.*

§ 11. Turning now to the British dependencies, we find in Canada, as has above been shown in Turkey, efforts at the correction of *economical*

---

* For the maintenance of anarchy throughout this unfortunate empire the ruling powers of Europe require that their consuls shall be invested with authority in reference to all cases in which their subjects may be interested. What is the effect of this *imperium in imperio*, and what the character of the magistracy thus created, are thus shown in a recent work entitled *The East and the West*, a series of papers edited by the Hon. Henry Stanley, a gentleman closely allied to distinguished members of the late Administration, and one whose long residence, in official capacities, in Greece and Turkey had fully qualified him properly to appreciate the atrocities perpetually practised upon the people of the East whom it pleases those of the West to treat as mere barbarians. "What is, moreover, the machinery actually at work for carrying out the obligations of these treaties? Consuls having the power of magistrates, but without legal training or social *status*, with no police to speak of to carry out their orders, or to cause them to be respected. The Consuls themselves are either traders or adventurers, or persons who have failed in other professions. In the Levant many Consuls are pluralists—that is, they represent, in their own persons, several Powers. On official reception-days, such a Consul pays several visits successively to the Governor, merely going out of the room to change his decorations, and having himself again announced as Consul of another country: such an official is named in Levantine French, 'Un Consul de plusieurs potences.'"

error by frequent change in *political* forms; but here, as there, wholly unsuccessful. Attributing former difficulties to political separation, the upper and lower provinces were thrown together, but with so small effect that, notwithstanding the great abundance of rich and unoccupied territory, the past few years have placed in strong relief the fact, that not only can the province not secure the many settlers who come by the St. Lawrence, but that it cannot even retain its native population. Repetition of old troubles requiring repetition of remedies we have just now a further political change, leaving wholly out of view the great economical one needed for bringing into close connection the producers and consumers of the country, as, to a certain extent, has been done in the adjoining more attractive States. When that course shall have been adopted; when Canada, passing from a state of dependence, shall begin to have *a will* of her own; when the present stagnation shall have given way to that activity which always follows in the train of rapid circulation amongst the societary positives and negatives; then, but not till then, will she have the force required for freeing herself from the humiliating necessity for asking parliamentary guarantees of loans to be created for the purpose of further facilitating export of the soil in the form of agricultural products of the rudest kind. Then, and not till then, will she begin properly to appreciate the fact that the raising of raw materials for foreign markets is the proper work of the barbarian and the slave, and of them alone.

Passing now to Jamaica, we find the decade to have furnished new evidence of the great truth, that freedom proclaimed by law is of small avail when unaccompanied by measures tending toward production of that diversification of pursuits which results from bringing producers and consumers into close relation with each other. Thirty years since the colored people of the island were declared to have been emancipated, yet has civilization made but little progress with either blacks or whites. For this the reason mainly is, that so adverse is British policy to any measures tending to the production of real freedom, that up to a recent period, as it yet may be, such were the arrangements of the British revenue system that the poor producers found themselves wholly deprived of power for so far diversifying their employments as even to be enabled to subject their own sugar to the first and simplest processes of refinement. The result exhibits itself in the fact, that oppression has recently been followed by an insurrection in the suppression of which there have been perpetrated "cruelties of which," says the London *Times*, "it is impossible to speak without shuddering."* Such occurrences strike un-

---

* "It is now certain that scores, and perhaps hundreds, of prisoners were flogged before being hung, and often before being tried. It is certain that some, though it is uncertain how many, were compelled to run the gauntlet, after being flogged, through a crowd of brutal spectators, who were allowed to insult them or pelt them as they pleased. It is certain that several, at least, were shot or hung without the pretence of a trial, at the caprice of an officer or subordinate. It is certain that Mr. Ramsay, the Provost Marshal, stands charged by a multitude of witnesses, black and white, with excesses for which a parallel must be sought among the infamous eccentricities of Oriental despots. It is certain, at least—for the statement rests on the authority of the resident magistrate at Bath—that he flogged with his own hand fifteen men who had never been sentenced, and were to be sent before the court-martial at Morant Bay.

pleasantly of course, for the moment, upon the British mind, but they are then again forgotten, only to be revived on the occurrence of some new atrocity, proper study of which could scarcely fail to satisfy every man sound in mind and heart that the system which looks towards making Britain "the workshop of the world," is, of all the forms of tyranny ever devised, the one that, *par excellence*, tends to the establishment of slavery as the normal condition of the man who needs to work, and to the destruction of all moral feeling among those by whom the workers are employed. Should this be doubted, they would find evidence thereof that might tend to satisfy them, by turning to Lady Duff Gordon's charming little book on Egypt and there seeing the effect produced on a high-minded and admirable woman by the conduct of her countrymen towards the Arabs, as preparation for treatment of the poor Hindoos over whom they were so soon to exercise their powers of government.* Had Lady Gordon written a little later she might have added, in a note, that the question of woman-flogging in Jamaica, by officers and gentlemen bearing commissions in the British service, had been set at rest by the admission of Captain Hole, of the 6th Foot, that he had ordered women to be flogged by the soldiers under his command, and had stood by to see it done.

Boasting of British freedom, but in Egypt holding that "nothing can be done without forced labor"—their fellow-countrymen meanwhile clinging to human slavery in America as the only course by means of which to secure abundant supplies of cheap cotton—these men arrive in India, fully prepared for participation in the work of *civilizing* a people of whom, at an earlier period, Sir Thomas Munro, perhaps the highest Indian authority, emphatically declared, that in regard to all the essential characteristics of civilization they " were not inferior to any civilized people in Europe." What is their general course of action towards the impoverished people by whom they find themselves at once surrounded, is thus described, in a speech in Parliament, by Earl Russell :

"That very morning he had received a long letter from Sir F. Bruce, lamenting the insolence and disregard of Chinese customs and feelings, which were exhibited by Englishmen in that country. He lamented their want of courtesy, and improper behavior to the Chinese, whom they regarded as an inferior race. He (Earl Russell) was afraid the same was the case in Japan. But conduct of that kind was not exhibited to the Chinese and Japanese alone ; for he found,

---

It is probable, moreover, that men were bribed with the hope of life—a hope not always realized—to betray their accomplices ; that persons accused of crimes were refused permission to call witnesses in their defence, and that some were executed, the only proof of whose guilt was their being found wounded. These are things which cannot be dismissed with common-places about the dire necessities of war, and the unfairness of scrutinizing retrospectively through a microscope the proceedings of men confronted with an overwhelming danger. They are acts, not military, but judicial, done for the most part after armed resistance had ceased, and when there was nothing to prevent a deliberate separation of the innocent from the guilty."—*Times.*

* " What chokes me is to hear Englishmen talk of the stick as being the only way to manage Arabs."—*Letters from Egypt*, 1863–65, p. 105.

" It is really heart-breaking to see *what* we are sending to India now. The mail days are dreaded. We never know when some brutal outrage may excite ' Mussulman fanaticism.' They try their hands on the Arabs in order to be in good train for insulting the Hindoos."—*Ibid.*, p. 309.

in a book recently published, that the same kind of conduct was practised towards the Indian race. He could not but lament that more courteous conduct was not shown by our countrymen, and that they did not pay more regard to the habits and customs of people, whom they were pleased to regard as a race inferior to their own."*

To those familiar with statements in regard to India similar to those here referred to by Lord Russell, that at various times have appeared in British journals, the occurrence of the great event in Indian history of the last decade, must have afforded as little cause for surprise as did 'the horrible circumstances which followed the suppression of the rebellion, thus described in a recent article (January, 1867) of the *Westminster Review:*

"A historian of some promise has said that he knows nothing in early English history, except William's devastation of the North, that approaches the horrors that our troops have committed in putting down the Indian revolt, a judgment that appears to be confirmed by Captain Trotter's statement, p. 284, when, speaking of Lord Canning's clemency, he says:

"'When the gallows, the cat, the torch, were threatening to blot out the last distinctions between guilt and innocence, to turn whole districts into grave-yards, deserts, haunts of beggared or fear-stricken outcasts, it was time for some voice of power to cry out upon the folly, the savage meanness, of overdone revenge. In thirteen days alone of June and July, one commissioner had sent to the gibbet forty-two wretches guilty, all save one murderer, of nothing worse than robbery, rioting, or rebellion. Some of them paid with their lives for having goods or money—even bags of copper half-pice—about which they failed to give any plausible account. In less than six weeks up to the 1st of August, some hundred and twenty men, of whom none were Sepoys, and only a few were of higher rank than villagers, servants, policemen, had been hanged by the civil commissioners of one county alone. Of course, in many cases, the evidence against the prisoners seemed strong only to minds that saw all objects through a film of blood. *Of the numbers arrested, not one in ten appears to have escaped some form of punishment, not two to have escaped the gallows.*'

"This is the way in which Englishmen sometimes recommend their civilization and illustrate their Christianity in British dependencies, not without sympathetic applause from excitable compatriots at home."

The picture here presented would be more complete had it been accompanied by an estimate of the value of the booty obtained in Hindoo cities, together with a list of the chief officers who participated in division of the spoil.

Of all men the thorough trader, whether in slaves or merchandise, is most merciless. Of all pursuits there is none so well calculated to deaden, if not utterly to destroy, all the best feelings of the human heart as is a thorough devotion to trade; and yet, when seeking a definition of political economy, we turn to the most recent work of an eminent French economist, we find it there described as being the science which treats only of buying and selling, or in other words, of Trade!

But a few years previous to the occurrence of the Indian rebellion there occurred in Denmark a very serious one, the suppression of which was followed by no occurrence prejudicial to either the life or the limb of any of the parties who had been engaged therein. Since then there has occurred on this Western continent the greatest rebellion on record,

---

* The East and the West; or, our Dealings with our Neighbors. Edited by the Hon. H. Stanley. London, 1866.

yet has the last State prisoner been but now discharged and left to wander throughout the world at his own perfect pleasure. The reader who may now compare American conduct towards Jefferson Davis with the British treatment of the unfortunate Nena Sahib, hunted as he was like a wild beast, may be led, perhaps, to doubt the civilizing tendencies, whether as regards the foreign master or the native slave, of a system which leads its advocates to talk to the poor Hindoo of a religion whose base is found in the grand idea of doing to others as they would that others should do to them, while tendering with one hand the piece of shoddy cloth, and directing with the other the bayonet required for retaining in "festering and compulsory idleness" the "vast heaps of humanity that now encumber the soil of India,"* and that should be employed in converting wool into cloth.

Shortly previous to the rebellion the post of Finance Minister of India was tendered to Mr. Wilson, long editor of the *Economist,* and by him accepted. Thorough free trader as he had always been, but little study on the spot was required for satisfying him that a change of policy had become entirely indispensable, and for leading him to the adoption of measures tending towards protection of the yet remaining manufactures of that magnificent but impoverished country. For this he and the new policy were forthwith denounced in the most unmeasured terms, and such pressure was brought to bear upon the Indian government as to forbid continuance of the trivial protection that had been allowed. Since then, India has profited largely by diminution of the supplies of American cotton, yet has the world been now again compelled to read of famines, of destruction of life, of general demoralization, such as flow necessarily from a system that looks to compelling the poor cultivator to exhaust his land by sending its produce, in its rudest state, to foreign markets, and such as are here described :—

"The crop fails again, and the peasant sees that it is death instead of ruin which now threatens him. Rice is unprocurable within a hundred miles, and would cost him a shilling a pound to bring it into his village. The cattle are killed, but not eaten ; the seed-corn is consumed ; the family is reduced to a few potatoes, or jungle berries, or fish, and of these eats only once in two days. The children die one by one, the weakest first, and then the aged, and the women—kinsfolk, wives, sisters, dropping daily, till the few who are permitted by Hindooism to bury the dead are overtaxed, and life seems to each man ended for him. Then the men give way slowly ; they have been starving quietly for months, till they are worn to that horrible aspect which Sir S. Barker has sketched in one of his chapters, an aspect under which human beings look like enlarged spiders, and men have no calves and no thighs, and no flesh whatever on the head, and no strength even for the commonest household duties. * * * * * There is no rich man, the absence of a perpetual settlement prohibiting agricultural wealth, the nearest European is forty or fifty miles away, and the

---

* CHAPMAN. Cotton and Commerce of India.
"The missionary has lately entered into such close partnership with the trader that the people of the countries they wish to 'open up' must be in doubt whether it is our Bibles or our broadcloth, our cotton or our Christianity that we most desire to force upon them, and the attempt to compel them to accept a spurious Christianity and shoddy manufactures by means of bayonets and cannon is not likely to be permanently successful."—*Free Press,* London, April, 1866.

solitary hope is the far-off and impersonal "Shirkar," the State. If that does not help, the village perishes. This has been the scene repeated for five months in all the villages of Orissa, of a province that is of the area of England and Wales, with a population estimated at five millions. Hundreds, it is quite possible, thousands, of villages have been so situated, have, there seems no reason to doubt, so perished, more especially in the hilly and jungle-covered interior. Where a town existed the people fled to it, till in Balasore they dropped dead of hunger at the rate of 126 a day, and the magistrate reports that he was compelled to leave them unburied for three days—equivalent to three weeks in England—for there were not enough of low caste men to bury. The European assistants found the dead all along the roads with the dogs feeding on their bodies. They could do nothing, for money could not purchase food; they themselves were importing bread from Calcutta, and rice could only be shipped in sufficient quantities by the State, and even then, the cattle being dead, could only be carried into the interior by driblets. Imagining the entire crop to have failed twice in Ireland, and the sea closed against imports, we may gain some idea—an imperfect one—of the misery spread over Orissa, where, except the crop, the people have absolutely nothing, *their old salt manufacture having been suppressed.*"

The salt manufacture, one that had endured for ages, had been suppressed. Why? That salt might be made scarce, and that the government might be enabled to realize large revenue from the sale of a limited quantity of that indispensable article of food! That its price might be high, and that the product of British mines might be enabled to compete in Indian markets with that of Hindoo laborers! Great was the rejoicing in Britain when the salt manufacture was prohibited, and when the people of Orissa were thus driven from an industry that, had it been maintained, might have sufficed for preventing the immolation of a million of its unfortunate inhabitants at the shrine of British free trade.* In this manner it is that *civilization* has been diffused throughout British India in the last decade.

The people of Australia, having found that under the system of *laisser faire* the country was rapidly becoming "a huge sheep-walk;" that "their farmers could no longer struggle in the face of discouragement and disaster;" that "their youth were growing up in a state of semi-barbarism, without education, without employment, and without hope for the future;" that "their manufactories were falling into decay, their capital was idle, and the whole body in the saddest state;" determined two years since on the adoption of measures such as seemed to be required for bringing together the societary positives and negatives—producers and consumers; a course of action in which they naturally found themselves opposed by all the birds of prey among them—all those who profited by means of buying wool cheap and selling dear the cloth the shepherds needed.

What has thus far been the result of this change of policy we are not advised, but the mere fact that the people are so far awake that a large

* The report of the Famine Commission of India is severe in its condemnation of the Board of Revenue. The Commissioners estimate the mortality in Orissa and Midnapore as certainly not less than one-fourth of the whole population, but state that they have no trustworthy statistics of the whole population of the province. The statistics vary from three and a half to five millions, which would make the mortality from three-fourths of a million to a million and a half, in an area of twenty-eight thousand seven hundred and thirty-six square miles, or half that of England and Wales.

majority has already pronounced in its favor furnishes evidence that the day cannot be now far distant when Australia must decide on having *a Will* of its own, and thus bring to a close its dependence on distant men who, desiring that the Australian farmer may obtain the smallest price for the things he needs to sell, and pay the largest for those he needs to buy, seek by all the means in their power to promote increase of competition for the *sale* of wool and for the *purchase* of cloth.

Such is the sad condition of the several principal dependencies of Britain at the close of the second decade of a system that was, as we were assured, destined to bring about "the moral regeneration of the world."[*] How it is with the Central Power itself we may now inquire.

§ 12. Turning now to the United Kingdom, we find the last dozen years to have presented to view wars with both Russia and China, a rebellion in India, a war in the South Pacific, an insurrection in Jamaica, and one at home, this last having occurred in that only portion of the civilized world in which a nation has been seen to be steadily passing out of existence without the aid of either guns or gunpowder, a sacrifice on the altar of trade.

The same period has furnished two monetary crises, both so severe as to have compelled the Bank to place itself in a situation to require absolution at the hands of Parliament. Add to them two periods of paralysis following these crises—a cotton famine that brought to the verge of starvation tens, if not hundreds, of thousands of poor working-people— a pauperism that now numbers in England and Wales alone, a million of subjects[†]—and a public expenditure that has grown from little more than fifty to seventy millions[‡]—and we have the chief occurrences of little more than the second decade of a system that was, as we were confidently assured, to give to the laborer happiness and comfort, to the society a steadiness of action and an economy of administration such as thus far had not been known, and to the world at large universal peace.

The more continuous and steady the action of an engine the greater is the force obtained, and the more the reason to expect continuance of its profitable existence. In the case of the sócietary machine every step towards proper co-ordination of its various parts—consumers and producers, borrowers and lenders—tends towards acceleration of motion and increase of the force obtained; towards equality of fortune and of rights; towards development of the individualities of each and all, with growing power of self-government, and growing sense of accountability here and hereafter, freedom and responsibility going always hand in hand together, and the machine itself tending more and more to assume the form that assures its permanence.[§] Wars, crises, strikes, lock outs, and all other causes of unsteadiness in the societary action, tend to produce precisely the reverse effects, fortunes becoming more and more unequal, and the land more and more monopolized, a state of things that was well exhibited half a century since when, at the close of the great

[*] DUNCKLEY. Charter of the Nations, p. 413.
[†] January 1, 1854, the number of paupers in receipt of relief was only 818,822.
[‡] The total expenditure for the year ending January 5, 1854, was but £51,174,839.
[§] See chap. xxii., section 8.

French war, rapid changes of political and financial position so greatly increased the power of the already rich to become possessors of the properties of thousands of small proprietors to whom those changes had brought entire ruin. Even then, however, there yet remained a fourth, if not even a third, of the 200,000 proprietors of the days of Adam Smith; but so great have been since the changes, and so unsteady the societary movement, that progress has been steadily made in a false direction, and to so great extent as to have warranted Mr. Bright in saying that one-half of England and Wales was then, a year since, owned by 150 persons, while of the land of Scotland a half was held by ten or a dozen persons. In the former, the whole number of proprietors, large and small, has sunk to 30,000, or less than a sixth of what it had been a century since.

With every step in that direction the place of the small proprietor, so much regarded and respected by Adam Smith, comes to be filled by the day laborer entitled to claim of the landlord, or his tenant, little beyond the minimum of food required for support of life.* With each there is increased tendency towards total separation of the laborer from the land. By the last census there was shown, in 821 parishes, a diminution in the number of houses to an extent exceeding 3000, the number of persons to be accommodated having meanwhile become 16,000 greater. As a consequence of this it is, that recent parliamentary reports exhibit a state of things so frightful as regards drainage, ventilation, the crowding of large families into single rooms, and the fearful immorality thence resulting, not only fully confirming the views presented in the body of this work, but actually going ahead of them and thus presenting a condition of manners and morals utterly disgraceful to any country claiming to rank as civilized.

"The order of the peasantry, a country's pride," says D'Israeli, "has vanished from the face of the land." Seeking their descendants we find them in receipt of from two to four dollars a week, a part of which goes for rent of a miserable dwelling,† the wife meantime earning sixpence

---

* In connection with the theory of Mr. Ruskin and some English political economists, that a British laborer is entitled to wages which will support him, and that the value of a day's labor is at least what a day's food and a night's lodging cost, the English estimate of how much, or rather how little, food and money will support human life in that country is curious. The Fen district laborers, for instance, get from six to fifteen pence per day, and as they generally sleep in barns, or under ricks and hedges, and have no lodging to pay for, and wear no clothes "to speak of," and are mostly young and not over healthy people, with limited appetites, their small earnings are supposed to be sufficient to buy their daily food. Respectable farm-laborers with families are presumed to be well paid at from six to twenty shillings a week for their labor, and they live on these small wages.—*Evening Post.*

† "The customary rate of wages in the South of England is from eight to nine shillings, two dollars to two dollars and twenty-five cents, subject to a deduction of one shilling or twenty-five cents per week for the rent of a cottage, where that luxury is indulged in. It is common for cottagers to have an allotment of land, which they cultivate for themselves in evening hours, and for which they pay rent at the rate of about three dollars per half acre yearly, the crop being worth about ten dollars above the rent, if the man takes time enough out of his hours of rest to cultivate it thoroughly. The laborer furnishes his own tools, which cost him at least one dollar and seventy-five cents yearly. Men also earn about twenty dollars additional for piece-work during harvest.

a day by working in the fields, and the children, by thousands, making part of "gangs" such as are here described :—

"The gang system," as recently exhibited in Parliament, "in brief is this: In the Fen districts, covering nearly a million of acres of the richest land in England, Huntingdonshire, Cambridgeshire, Nottinghamshire, Norfolk, Suffolk, and in parts of the counties of Northampton, Bedford, and Rutland, about seven thousand children, from five years of age and upwards, besides persons of both sexes of from fifteen to eighteen years of age—are employed in gangs numbering from fifteen to twenty laborers in each gang, under a master, and in a condition differing from slavery only because it is infinitely worse.

"The gang-master is almost invariably a dissolute man, who cannot get steady employment as a laborer with any decent farmer. In most instances he actually purchases the labor of the children from poor parents ; he sells this labor to farmers, pays the gang what he pleases, and puts the profit in his pocket. For seven or eight months in the year these gangs are driven, often seven or eight miles a day, to farms where they work at planting, weeding, picking, stone-gathering, and like labor, from half-past five in the morning to seven or eight o'clock in the evening. The gang-master is paid by the day or by the acre; and he pays the little children from fourpence to sixpence per day, while the older lads and girls receive from nine to fifteen pence. The master, for driving his hands to the field and for keeping them up to their work, which he does with a stick, makes an estimated profit of a pound sterling, or thereabouts, a week.

"There is testimony to show that hundreds of the younger children are carried home in the arms of the older lads every night. From working breast-high in wet grain many of the children are crippled for life by rheumatism, while others contract the seeds of ague, pleurisy, and consumption. Cases are given where little girls, four years old, have been driven through these long, terrible days of work. The most pathetic pictures presented by Mr. Wilberforce of colonial slave-driving forty years ago, make the British West Indies seem almost an Arcadia in comparison with the Fen districts in England to-day.

"This exhibition, shocking as it is, is by no means the most frightful phase of the gang system. The gangs are under no moral restraint whatever. Oftentimes at night both sexes are huddled together in barns, where, among the older boys and girls, the most shameful events naturally follow. Clergymen and other respectable witnesses testified to the Commission of Inquiry that the gang laborers are 'beneath morals.' They have no consciousness of chastity, and do not know the meaning of the word. Medical directors of infirmaries state that gang girls, as young as thirteen years, have been brought to them to be confined. Their language and conduct are so depraved that dozens of parish clergymen, surgeons, and respectable laboring people, declared to the commission that the introduction of any gang labor in any village extinguishes morality." —Evening Post.

Turning now to Ireland we find the country of "popular famines," from which all fly who can find the means for so doing, and from which so many did fly in the last decade that the diminution of population was nearly 800,000. Of all countries there is none that has been subjected to so many experiments, almost all having been already tried except the single one which really is needed—that one which has made of the little

They work during eight months of the year from seven o'clock until five, with a half-hour for breakfast and an hour for dinner, making nine and a half hours. In winter they work from six to five, with one hour for dinner, making ten hours of labor. If a pressure of work extends the time of labor an hour or two, no extra compensation is commonly given beyond an extra mug of ale or cider."

Corresponding with this we find, in the Northern portion of the United Kingdom, a third of the whole population of Scotland living in houses of a single room.

Belgium one of the most thriving countries of the world*—the bringing together of societary positives and negatives, producers and consumers, givers and receivers, borrowers and lenders.

Throughout the United Kingdom the increase of population was, in round numbers, 1,500,000, one-third of which was found in and near London, and another in Liverpool, Manchester, Birmingham, Glasgow, and five other cities; leaving for the kingdom at large but the remaining half million.

In the decade the disproportion of the sexes had much increased, the 704,000 excess of females of 1851 having grown to 870,000 in 1861, no allowance being made in either case for army, navy, or seamen in the merchant service.

Driven from the land, many emigrate, leaving behind those who from sex, age, or infirmity of health, are unfitted for the labors of clearing and cultivating American or Australian lands. More, however, place themselves in that limited portion of Britain in which are found the cities of London and Liverpool, Manchester and Birmingham, transferring to property in their vicinities the money value lost by the lands they had left. The result exhibits itself in the enormous wealth of ducal owners of almost entire counties, and of millionaire proprietors of city lots and houses, side by side, as the *Times* has recently told its readers—

"With crowds of men jostling, striving, almost fighting each other, for admission, not to see a favorite actor or hear a popular preacher, or to witness a prize fight or rat bait, but to gain the privilege of breaking hard stones, in a cold, muddy yard attached to the parish workhouse, for the reward of three-pence and a loaf of bread. These men," it adds, " are not clad in the usual stone-yard apparel ; they wear good coats—rags are scarcely to be seen. They are men who, not very long ago, were earning from $6 to $13 weekly, to whom the very mention of the workhouse would have been contamination; and here they struggle and wrestle for its most meagre advantages." Comparisons are added of the relief afforded to the poor. "During the winters of 1865-6 the average daily number of laborers in the Poplar stone-yard, attached to one of the London poor-houses was 200, but in the week ending January 9th, 1867, the daily average was over 1000. In the last week of 1866, that poor-house gave outdoor parochial relief to 4340 persons, as compared with 1974 in the last week of 1865. This establishment," it says, " is now giving relief to its utmost capacity, and this fact, together with the announcement that nearly all the funds have been drawn out of the London savings banks—the working classes having been from four to six months without regular wages—shows that at present there is greater distress in London than has been known for a long time."

Turning now to another high authority, the *Saturday Review*, we find the effects of instability thus exhibited :—

" London Street contains no less than 250 families, no one of which, however numerous, occupies, as a rule, more than one room. Father, mother, and, it may be, six or seven children, somehow contrive to sleep together in one bed, and, in the absence of sheets and blankets, which are being taken care of by the pawnbroker, probably find some compensation for the discomfort of overcrowding in the luxury of animal warmth—a luxury all the more prized from the difficulty, in cold weather, of procuring it anywhere but in bed. The plan is cheaper for the moment than either blanket or coals, and unhappily the British

* "Belgium is Paradise Regained for everybody except the dogs in the carts, and even for them the supply of bones is perennial." FISHER. *Food Supply of Western Europe.* London, 1866.

laborer has yet to learn how much more it costs him in the long run. Enter one of these rooms at random, and the chances are that you find it tenanted by a dock-yard laborer, who, like the engineer in the *Pall Mall Gazette*, made quite enough to keep himself and family in what they consider comfort until he was thrown out of work. Now, all the work he can get is the dignified employment for Lord Palmerston's *Civis Romanus* of oakum picking at the work-house, and this procures each hungry child a slice of bread. If the wife is a good needle-woman, she can earn 4½d. a day, by nine hours of shirt making; so long, that is, as her health stands one of the most trying, both mentally and physically, of all sedentary occupations. This pays the rent. A family fortunate enough to be able thus to provide for bread and shelter, the stoic's two necessaries of life, can secure its superfluous luxuries by a little begging, a little borrowing, and a good deal of pawning. The wife in that case does not sacrifice more than half her petticoats, and the husband is not obliged to be in bed while she washes his one shirt."

On a recent occasion the Archbishop of York referred to the sad con-dition, physical, mental, and moral, of an extensive district of London, closing his statement with the following facts :—

"Not half the Gentile adults can read. Half the women cannot handle a needle. Our Mothers' Meeting has seventy members, half of whom, though living with men and having families, are unmarried, and this is the proportion throughout the Gentile district. . Nine families out of ten have but one small room in which to live, eat and sleep. Not one family in six possesses a blanket or a change of clothing. Not one in four has any bedding beyond a sacking, containing a little flock or chopped straw (a miserable substitute for a mattress). Not one in twenty has a clock—not one in ten a book. . Many of the houses are in the most wretched condition of dirt and filth—walls, ceilings, floors, and staircases broken and rotting. Drunkenness, brawling, blasphemy, and other sins are fearfully prevalent."

Speaking of one of the London poorhouses a journalist tells his readers of "naked misery wallowing in its filth, of human creatures massed together more disgustingly than hogs in a stye," thereto adding that the Poor Law Commission had expressed regret at having no power to compel remedy of the "disgraceful nuisance."*

Why is it that such things are ? Because the policy of England looks to underworking the local manufacturers of the world—to driving the poor Hindoo from the loom to the field—and for that reason needs low priced labor. Because man is there daily more and more regarded as a mere instrument to be used by trade. Because, according to a writer in the *Times*, "every advance on the present rate of wages is a certain retrograde step in the direction of Protection. Let Freetraders, then," as he adds, "take care that in advocating the 'rights of labor' they are not digging a grave for free trade."

It is thus the *trade* that is to be protected, *not the people.*

The position of England is now a very unfortunate one. So long as she controlled in a great degree the supply of coal and iron for the world, and monopolized the use of steam, she remained almost mistress of the world. Just, however, as intelligence becomes more and more dissemi-

---

* Since writing the above the author has had, for the first time in many years, occasion to visit the asylum provided by the city in which he lives for its blind and its lame, its lunatics and its drunkards, its infants and its aged, dependent on the public for support, and has been greatly gratified at witness-ing the scrupulous neatness everywhere evident, and the manifestation through-out of a Christian charity scarcely to be believed by those who have not seen it.

nated the sceptre passes from her hands. France and Belgium are rivalling her with regard to engines, and even in her own market. Germany passes ahead of her in reference to steel, and America furnishes locomotives that command the admiration of Europe at the Paris exhibition. Steam gave her power to make the law of the ocean, but steam in other hands has now, in effect, destroyed that British navy upon whose creation hundreds of millions have been wasted.* With every step elsewhere made in the development of mind her power has declined, and the tendency in that direction must increase with wonderful rapidity should success attend the present efforts at substituting fluid hydro-carbons, readily susceptible of transportation, for the bulky and expensive solid the supply of which for the world has so long been almost monopolized by Britain.

Little more than half a century since Britain dictated the law of the ocean, doing then the same on the land, and doing it by means of armies that compared favorably with those of any country in the world—the joint contributions of Ireland, the Scottish Highlands, the *statesmen* of northern English counties, and little proprietors everywhere. Forty years later, shortly before the opening of the last decade, it was with difficulty that she raised the little force required for service in the Crimean war. To-day, judging from statements in the public journals, it is found almost as difficult to keep on foot the forces required for maintaining order in Ireland and India. Seeking now the cause of the remarkable change that, as regards both quantity and quality, has so obviously occurred, we find it in the facts, that famine and pestilence have combined for rendering Ireland a place so entirely unfit for human occupation as to threaten its abandonment by all but those who by reason of disease, decrepitude, and poverty, are deprived of power to emigrate;† that the Highlanders, so long renowned for feats of arms, have been displaced by flocks of sheep; that the important class of small proprietors, intermediate between the mere laborer and the great landlord—that class which furnished Cromwellian armies and since has given to the country so large a portion of its most valuable men—has been replaced by the mere day laborer, recipient of wages in the factory or in the field.‡ The source of supply having been thus dried up, diminution of mental, moral, and physical force now presents itself as the necessary consequence.

That her position before the world of Europe has greatly deteriorated

* "Our great wooden fleet, so long the pride of Britain, the terror of the world, lies stored up in Portsmouth harbor, of no earthly use in maintaining any maritime contest. Those noble three-deckers, such as the Duke of Wellington, would be sent to the bottom by a single gun carrying a three hundred pound ball. We have, at one blow, virtually lost the fleet which had been growing up for two hundred years."—SIR A. ALLISON.

† In the six years ending 1863, the quantity of land in cultivation diminished to the extent of 350,000 acres. Last year, 1866, the diminution was 129,000, emigration having carried off 102,000 persons, a larger proportion of whom than usual were males.

‡ "Great Britain is the only country of the world in which the majority of the inhabitants subsist on wages, and consequently there is no other country in which the government by the greatest number would be so dangerous to property."—*Saturday Review.*

has been fully shown by one of her own ablest writers, Mr. Matthew Arnold.* The reason for the change he has described may be found in the expression of Mirabeau hereinbefore quoted, to the effect, that "when the head is allowed to grow too large, the body becomes apoplectic and wastes away"—the state of things precisely that has, under the system denounced by Adam Smith, grown up in Britain. The head is there found in a small district embracing perhaps a fifth of the United Kingdom, the body extending throughout the world and embracing hundreds of millions of people, all of whom have been so wholly deprived of the exercise of *Will* that, as in the case of the salt manufacture of India, they have been compelled to remain idle when they would have wished to work, and to buy from abroad commodities the raw materials of which they have seen going to waste at home.

England's essential difficulty is to be found in the entire absence of *a national conscience.* "In the eyes of her people," says M. de Tocqueville, "that which is most useful to England is always the cause of justice," the *"criterion* of what is right, or noble, or just," being "to be found, in the degree of favor or opposition to English interests." Such being her standard it affords no cause for wonder that she should, in her foreign relations, have adopted the Jesuit maxim that "the end sanctifies the means," publicly proclaiming that "the smuggler was the great reformer of the age; that the illicit trade in opium must be maintained even at the cost of stirring up anarchy among the hundreds of millions of Chinese people; and that, in the interests of trade, it was needed to break up the Union of these American States, even at the cost of setting at defiance well-known principles of public law.

That the "balance of power" may continue to be held by any nation there is required, as the reader has seen in a passage already quoted from the *Westminster Review,* not only development of its material resources, but also "an honest and constant allegiance to the laws of morality in its domestic policy and in its foreign relations." How far that condition is being even now complied with is shown in the following passage from a recent work already more than once referred to :—

"With regard to the foreign jurisdiction, it may be said that this system is the chief cause of wars, and that it is inexpedient for any State to incur the risks of war for the sake of securing license and impunity to the criminal class—for well-behaved people do not require the intervention of the consuls. Earl Grey has set forth in the House of Lords, what has been generally admitted, that our war with China, undertaken for the purpose of enforcing the importation of opium, weakened the government of China, so as to produce the anarchy which now desolates that country. Lord Grey pointed out last session that the foreign jurisdiction was producing the same effects in Japan, by stimulating the license of the European community, who find themselves released from all restraint; that this trampling upon the self-respect of the Japanese must lead to war; and that, after much bloodshed and expenditure, we shall perhaps reduce Japan to a state of anarchy like that we have brought about in China."†

* *Cornhill Magazine,* February 10, 1866, article *My Countrymen.*
† The East and the West, or our Dealings with our Neighbors.

The "balance" of material power is no longer in Britain's hands. That what yet remains of moral influence must speedily pass away will be obvious to all who reflect on the fact that the moral feeling of the world has been and is now being daily more and more offended—

By the spectacle of overgrown wealth at home side by side with a destitution the most complete :

By the pro-slavery tendencies of a system that at home produces a necessity for cheapening labor, and has elsewhere led to advocacy of negro slavery as the only mode by which to obtain cheap cotton :

By the spectacle of a neighbor nation—one that in the past had given to Britain her ablest statesmen and most distinguished soldiers—now passing rapidly out of existence :

By the tyranny over hundreds of millions of Asiatics, feeble as they are, that is daily exercised, and recently so well described by Earl Grey in the passage that has above been given.

Of all, however, that has occurred throughout the decade, there is nothing that, equally with the alliance between the governing portion of the British people and that portion of the American one which was engaged in the effort to establish a slave republic, has tended to destroy that moral force which constitutes so essential a portion of the capital of an individual or a nation.

"A nation," says a reflecting British writer, "which resists in principle the just social impulses natural to its history and position—which discourages those honorable social emotions with which men regard the proceedings of men—is sure to find, sooner or later, that the forces which she has thus kept back from their regular modes of expansion have found outlets and channels within her own borders less regular, and therefore more perilous and uncertain. Adherence simply to negative precepts [*laisser faire*] seldom obtains in any sphere of policy without being, in a greater or less degree, the mark of all the rest. And it is so here. * * * We fail to set to work with will and indomitable resolution at the task of relieving Ireland from anarchy. We fail to perform, or even to see clearly the pressing necessity of performing, the positive duty of devising some means, and means there must be somewhere in the minds of men, for finally uniting Ireland to ourselves and removing our heaviest reproach in the eyes of Europe. We are innocent, again, of wishing the poor and ignorant any ill, but there is no sign of a diligent and determined national action to ameliorate their condition and diminish their numbers. And so on throughout all the spheres of government. To that watery self-satisfaction which comes of the discharge of negative duties we are entitled. * * * An energetic, full-blooded, and generous initiative is no more seen. Under our present set of social conceptions it is forever impossible. The idea of the two great functions of the State is torpid or extinct. The nourishment of a strong and harmonious national life, in the first place ; in the second, the maintenance of a wise, unselfish, and upright international life ; these are the two ideas at present fatally wanting in English policy. * * * If anybody thinks that we are playing that powerful and beneficent part in our relations with Europe to which our material strength and moral disinterestedness entitle us, or rather which they demand from us, let him reflect that the counsels which Lord Stanley is said to be pressing both at Berlin and Paris count for about as much as if they came from the cabinet of Sweden or of Portugal."—MORLEY. *Fortnightly Review*, May, 1867.

More than thirty years since there was in Britain what was called a "Reform," but it was limited to changes of *form*, leaving the *policy* untouched. The result is seen in the facts here given. Now again, there is to be a great reform. Will it, however, prove more successful than the former one? Most certainly not, if the cheap labor system is to be maintained. Not, if the laws of morality are to be, as now, daily set at defiance in the treatment of the 500,000,000 of Asiatics so much subjected to British influence. Not, if all the poor and weak communities of the world are to be driven, at the point of the bayonet, to confining themselves to the work of raising raw produce for distant markets, the proper work of the barbarian and the slave, and of them alone. Not, if Britain shall continue to have for her motto, in all international relations, that "the end sanctifies the means." Not, certainly, if British policy shall continue to set at defiance, as it now daily does, that great law of Christianity which teaches that duty to our Creator and to our fellow men demands that we do unto others as we would that they should do unto us.

§ 13. The decade whose history has above been sketched is of all recorded in the world's annals the most remarkable, yet are the changes there exhibited but preparation for new and greater in the future—such changes as must not only greatly affect the relative positions of the communities that have been named, but also the future of all mankind. Their character will, as the writer thinks, be clearly obvious to those who may have studied his "Principles," published ten years since, and with their aid have studied this review of what has since transpired. To all such it must be plain—

That the system which looks to having but one "workshop for the world" is unchristian, and can but little longer be maintained:

That England has passed her zenith, and that, in common with Tyre, Carthage, Venice, Holland, and all other merely trading communities that had preceded her, she is destined, and that at an early day, to take her place among the great powers of the past:

That France, under the centralizing system of the empire, must inevitably follow in the same direction:

That, in accordance with a great law from the study of which we learn that the richest soils are always last to be brought under cultivation, the great powers of the future must be Germany, Russia, and these United States:

That, to the end that they may attain the position now so clearly within their reach, it is essential that they recognize the facts, that agriculture is the great pursuit of man and therefore always last to attain development; that for attainment of that development it is indispensable that there be a proper co-ordination of the societary positives and negatives, producers and consumers being brought in close proximity with each other; that the closer their relations the greater must be the rapidity of circulation; and that—

THE MORE RAPID THE CIRCULATION THE MORE THOROUGH BECOMES THE DEVELOPMENT OF THE CHRISTIAN MAN, THE MORE RAPID THE GROWTH OF WEALTH, AND THE GREATER THE SOCIETARY FORCE.

§ 14. Materialism, elsewhere described as the " Philosophy of declining Systems," is the essential characteristic of that one which seeks to make of Britain the single " workshop of the world." Looking to the *things* produced, and the wagons, cars, and ships by which they are carried, it wholly rejects consideration of the beings by whom they are produced. Regarding trade as the one thing needful it sanctions all the immoralities by which traffic may be promoted, careless of the fact that their constant perpetration tends necessarily towards sinking man to a level with the brute.

Looking always to development of the real MAN Adam Smith denounced the "mercantile system" upon which Britain so long has practised. Following in the same direction the, system here given presents to view the grand and harmonious laws by means of which it was provided that man should ultimately become master of nature—master over himself—a being capable of the exercise of Will and fitted to "look through nature up to nature's God"—becoming daily more and more conscious of the facts, that duty required him to do to others as he would that they should do unto him ; and, that for the proper use of the power with which he had been intrusted he must hold himself responsible, here and hereafter, to his fellow men and to the great Author of his being. For the accomplishment of that object the societary laws were instituted, and thus was society made the instrument by means of which man—the real MAN—was to be developed, to become the subject of that higher branch of knowledge which treats of the human soul and its relations, and known as psychological science.

Quite recently the author has made acquaintance with Oersted's work, entitled " Soul in Nature,"* and has been greatly gratified to find that, starting from a point directly opposite, so illustrious a philosopher had been led to arrive at the same conclusions, to wit, that "the laws of nature hold good throughout the universe ;"† and that, as "the truths of natural science continually approach nearer those of Religion," both "must at last be united in the most intimate connection."‡

---

* London, 1852. Of this eminent man, Sir John Herschell, now thirty years since, at a meeting of the British Association, spoke as follows :—
"In science there was but one direction which the needle would take, when pointed towards the European continent, and that was towards his esteemed friend, Professor Oersted. He knew not how to speak of him in his presence without violating some of that sanctity by which, as an individual, he was surrounded. To look at his calm manner, who could think that he wielded such an intense power, capable of altering the whole state of science, and almost convulsing the knowledge of the world. * * * * The electric telegraph, and other wonders of modern science, were but mere effervescences from the surface of this deep recondite discovery, which Oersted had liberated, and which was yet to burst with all its mighty force upon the world. If he were to characterize by any figure the advantage of Oersted to science, he would regard him as a fertilizing shower descending from heaven, which brought forth a new crop, delightful to the eye and pleasing to the heart."
† Ibid., p. 92.   ‡ Ibid., p. 109.

ERRATUM.—Page 12, line 16 from foot—*for* " national" *read* " material."

RECONSTRUCTION:

INDUSTRIAL, FINANCIAL, AND POLITICAL.

LETTERS

TO THE

HON. HENRY WILSON,
SENATOR FROM MASSACHUSETTS.

BY
H. C. CAREY.

PHILADELPHIA:
COLLINS, PRINTER, 705 JAYNE STREET.
1867.

LETTERS TO THE HON. HENRY WILSON,

SENATOR FROM MASSACHUSETTS.

LETTER FIRST.

DEAR SIR:

In the recent Address at Saratoga your hearers were told that you were "accustomed to take hopeful views of public affairs;" that "during the darkest hours of the war" you had had "faith in the country, faith in our democratic institutions," and had "never doubted the result;" that, "since the close of the war," we had had "trials quite as severe,", but you had "never had any doubt" that that result was "to be a great and united nation." Continuing on in the same direction, you spoke as follows:—

"We have passed through a bloody struggle. I am among those who believe that it was inevitable—that it was one of the great wars of the human family. It was a struggle on this continent between the democratic ideas of the Declaration of Independence and the system of human bondage, and in such a contest there could be no doubt of the result. We who stood by our country, and the cause of liberty, justice, and humanity, have triumphed. We have triumphed at a fearful cost. We are proud and strong; we have lifted the country toward the heavens; we are a greater people than ever before. We have destroyed human bondage; we have subjugated and conquered a brave and heroic portion of the country, and now the great work is done, I am for welcoming them back with warm and generous greetings, trusting that the causes of all our troubles have passed away forever, and that hereafter in the future we shall be friends and brothers as we were in the morning of the Republic."

The anticipations here presented are most pleasant and agreeable, and gladly would I accept them as likely to be realized were it possible for me so to do. That I do not, is due to the plain and simple fact that sad experience is now teaching the farming and mining States that for them the only "result" thus far recently achieved has been that of a change of masters, Massachusetts having, so far as regards material interests generally, taken the place of South Carolina, and New England at large, in reference to some of high importance, that of the States so recently in rebellion. Power has gone from the extreme South to the extreme North, and the sectionalism of to-day is likely, as I think, to prove quite as injurious as has already proved that of the past.

This, I pray you, my dear sir, to believe, is said in no unfriendly spirit. No one more than I respects the great mass of the people of Massachusetts. Few have given more full expression to their admiration of the estimable qualities by which New England people generally are so much distinguished. It is because of my respect for them, because of my desire for their continued happiness and prosperity, that I desire now, through you, to ask consideration of the facts, that they now exercise a political power wholly disproportioned to their numbers; that the State in which I reside, with *two* Senators, has a population nearly equal to that of New England with *twelve* Senators; that, as a consequence, the Senate, as regards economical questions generally, is now in frequent conflict with the House; that the day is at hand when there will be a dozen States, each one of which will outnumber all New England; that abolition of slavery has removed the difficulties which so long had stood in the way of union between the Centre and the South; that of all the States there are none that, for that reason, should so studiously as your own avoid suspicion of improper use of power; that to enable the East to maintain its present political position there is needed a most discreet, most careful, most magnanimous exercise thereof; and that, for want of that care, for want of that discretion, for want of that magnanimity, the Union is to-day, in my belief, more endangered than it had been in the years by which the war had been immediately preceded.

That you will *now* believe this I do not at all expect. Neither did I expect Mr. Dallas to believe me when, less than ten years since, in answer to a question as to when the Capitol would be completed, I told him that it would be "just about the time when the Union would be dissolved." "Nothing," as I then added, "could stand against a system which, like that of the tariff of 1846, made Liverpool the centre of exchange among ourselves and with the world at large, and made of our railroads mere conduits to be used for carrying to Britain the soil of the country in the form of wheat, corn, tobacco, and cotton. It would," as I continued, "ruin any country of the world." Of this he did not *then* believe a single word. Nevertheless, two years afterwards, when *too late*, he did believe it. So, as I fear, will it be with your constituents and yourself. They will believe nothing of the danger until the ruin shall have come, as, without a change of policy, come it must, and before the close of the next decade.

An enlightened foreigner, one who had had abundant opportunities for studying our people, said of them, but a few years since, that "none so soon forgot yesterday." Nothing was ever more truly said. Rarely, if ever, do we study the past. We never, in any manner, in our public affairs, profit by experience, whether our own or that of others. Be the question before us what it may, great or small, it is treated precisely as if none such had, here or elsewhere, ever before arisen; and hence it is that our movements so much resemble those of a blind giant, daily forced to look for advice to the one-eyed dwarfs by whom we are surrounded. Were it otherwise—could our people, North and South, East and West, but be persuaded to study a very little of *their own* history—could it, do you think, be made to pay for Britain to employ so many of her people, Irish and English, Christian and Hebrew, in the work of teaching them the advantage to be derived from maintaining and increasing their dependence upon a country whose movements were becoming daily more irregular and uncertain; whose power for self direction was diminishing with each succeeding year; one that to-day had not, outside of this Union, a friend on earth; one that had already passed its zenith, and for the reason that the societary ruin by which she was surrounded was in the direct ratio of the reliance of others on her friendship? Seeking evidence of this, let me beg you to look to Ireland, the land of "popular famines;" to Turkey, with which she has for centuries been in close free trade alliance; to Portugal, once the most valuable of her customers; to India, in which the millions who formerly were occupied in the cotton manufacture, are now "festering in compulsory idleness;" to China, brought to a state of anarchy by means of wars made for maintaining the illicit opium trade; to Japan, likely, according to Earl Grey, soon to be reduced to the condition in which China now exists; to Australia, now little more than a great sheep walk, whose occupants, in default of any market for their products, are now again converting their flocks into tallow; to New Brunswick and Nova Scotia, both abounding in coal and ores, while compelled to import all the iron they use; and finally, to Canada, whose population has for the past few years been steadily passing to the land of the stars and stripes, seeking there the *protection* denied to them at home. Look where you may, you will find prosperity to exist *in the inverse ratio of the connection with Britain.* Look even to France and see that loss of position before the world has gone hand in hand with her adoption of the British system. Seeking evidence of these decaying tendencies, you may with advantage turn to the last *Edinburgh Review*, finding therein a proposition for military alliance between the two countries as the only mode of preventing further loss of caste.

Britain has been long engaged in building an inverted pyramid; but at no period has her progress in that direction been so rapid as within the last twenty years, the free trade period. The important class of small landholders so much admired by Adam Smith— that class which so long had constituted the right arm of British strength—has now almost entirely disappeared, half of the land of England being owned by 150 men, and half of that of Scotland by a single dozen. So, too, is it in regard to all industrial pursuits, a perpetual series of crises having crushed out the smaller and more useful men, and all the processes of mining and manufacture having passed into the hands of the few whose vast fortunes had enabled them to profit by the ruin of the lesser men by whom they had been surrounded. In consequence of this it is, that British society daily more and more exhibits the phenomena of squalid poverty side by side with enormous wealth; precisely the state of things that, under the free trade and pro-slavery policy, had, before the war, obtained throughout the Cotton States. To these latter it brought the weakness that has recently been so well exhibited. To the former it has brought the decay of influence that has, on a recent occasion, led a reflecting British writer to say to his countrymen that "the counsels which Lord Stanley is said to be pressing both at Berlin and Paris, count for about as much as if they came from the cabinet of Sweden or Portugal;" than which nothing could be more true—Britain having no longer a place in the European system. To enable her to maintain a place anywhere she must break up this Union, and to the consciousness of this has been due the fact that, with the exception of the mere laboring class, nearly the whole body of the British people has exhibited itself before the world as advocate of a system which has human slavery for its corner-stone, and as ready to make any sacrifice of honor or of conscience, public or private, that might be needed for securing its permanent establishment. Thus far she has failed; but, having now before her only the choice between, on the one hand, the disruption of our Union, and, on the other, her own descent from the position she so long has occupied, we may be quite assured that no effort will be spared that may seem to tend towards accomplishment of the former.

To prevent this would be an easy task could our people but be persuaded to study a very little of the past, with a view to an understanding of the present, and to preparation for the future. That you at least, my dear sir, may be induced so to do, I propose in another letter to present for your consideration a brief view of the mode by which preparation had before the war been made for accomplishment of the ruin from which we so recently have escaped, meantime remaining, with great regard,

Yours, truly,

HENRY C. CAREY.

Hon. HENRY WILSON.

PHILADELPHIA, Aug. 20, 1867.

LETTER SECOND.

DEAR SIR:—

Before prescribing for removal of fever the skilful physician seeks to ascertain why it exists, varying his treatment with variation in the cause discovered. The quack treats all fevers alike, and kills his patients. What is true with regard to physical evil is equally so with reference to social disease, it being essential that we understand the ultimate cause of error before we write the prescription for its cure. In the case now before us you charge all our recent troubles to the existence of slavery, but your Address furnishes no answer to the previous question, *Why had it been that slavery had so rapidly grown in power?* Studying the matter more carefully you will, I think, find that, like the fever, slavery had been the mere symptom, and that if you would now prevent its recurrence, if you would really and permanently establish human freedom, you must begin by eradicating the cause, just as you would remove trouble of the head by treatment of the stomach. In no other way can permanent reconstruction be secured. Of that you may rest assured.

That you, my dear sir, may arrive at a proper understanding of the ultimate cause of our recent troubles, look around you in Massachusetts and satisfy yourself that it has been precisely as pursuits have been more and more diversified, *precisely as competition for the purchase of labor has increased,* that the weak have been rising to a level with the strong, that the woman has been coming more near to an equality with the man, the man himself more and more acquiring the power of self-direction. Look again, and see that diversification of employment has always grown most rapidly in periods of protection against the working of the British monopoly system, and that then it has always been that the capitalist has been obliged to seek the laborer. Look then further, and see that it has been in periods of British free trade, so-called, but really monopoly, that the laborer has lost the power of self-direction and has been obliged to seek the capitalist, and then determine for yourself which has in the North proved the road to freedom.

Turn next south, and see that slavery had grown in power just as the land had become more and more monopolized, as the little proprietors more and more disappeared from the stage, as the laborer everywhere found himself more and more compelled to limit himself to the single pursuit of raising raw material for the supply of distant markets, the proper work of the barbarian and the slave,

and of those alone., That done, you will, as I think, better understand why it has been that freedom had tended upward in all that
portion of the country that had accepted the idea of protection,
and downward in those that had resisted it. There is but one
road to freedom, peace, and harmony, and that is found in such
diversification of pursuits as leads to enlargement of domestic commerce, and stimulation of the societary circulation.

British policy looks to arrest of the circulation of the world by
means of compelling all raw material produced to pass through its
little workshop. It is a monopoly system, and therefore it is that
poverty, disease, and famine, all of which unite for the production
of slavery, are chronic diseases in every country wholly subjected
to British influence.

Therefore, too, has it been that British agents have been always
in such close alliance with the slave-holding aristocracy of the
South ; and that, throughout the late war, British public opinion
has been so nearly universally on the side of the men who have
publicly proclaimed that slavery was to be regarded as the proper
corner-stone of all free institutions.

British free trade, industrial monopoly, and human slavery, travel
together, and the man who undertakes the work of reconstruction
without having first satisfied himself that such is certainly the fact,
will find that he has been building on shifting sands, and must
fail to produce an edifice that will be permanent. So believing,
and seeing in your Address nothing that indicates a proper appreciation of the fact that it is to a diversification of our pursuits, *alone,*
we are to look for permanent establishment of human freedom and
national independence, for permanent reconstruction of the Union,
I am led to ask you to accompany me in an examination of the
real causes of the rebellion that is proposed now to make. Let
these be ascertained, and you may then safely proceed in the great
work in which you are so actively engaged, but not before. Without this you will be prescribing for permanent dissolution, and not
for reconstruction.

Within the last half century, compelled thereto by the general
ruin that has in each and every case resulted from permitting
the advocates of pro-slavery and British monopoly ideas to dictate
our course of action, we have three times sought to establish
domestic commerce and thus to achieve a real independence. In
each of these the country almost at once revived, commerce became
active, labor came again into demand, and prosperity reigned
throughout the land. Throughout each and every of them, however, British money has been lavishly applied to the work of teaching the vast advantage to be derived from coming again under the
British yoke; from again submitting to be compelled to make all
our exchanges with the world at large in a single, distant, and
diminutive market; and from thus uniting with British traders in
the work of preventing the growth of human freedom. As a consequence of these teachings, and of the constant stimulation in that

direction by the advocates of human slavery as it existed in this western world, the tariffs of 1828 and 1842 were allowed an existence of less than five years each, the general result having been, that of the last five and forty years by which the war had been preceded, there had been less than ten in which our policy had tended in the direction of human freedom and national independence.

Brief as had been the existence of the first of these tariffs its close found the country so far advanced in the right direction that the foreign debt, public and private, had been entirely discharged. Nevertheless, but seven years of the then re-established British monopoly system with its perpetually-recurring financial crises; its destruction of internal commerce; its annihilation of confidence; and its paralyzing effects in destroying the demand for labor; sufficed for plunging the country more deeply in debt than it ever before had been, and for making us more than ever dependent upon the chances and changes of a market that, more than any other, is governed by men who find their advantage in bringing about those sudden upward and downward movements by means of which they are themselves enriched, their humble dependents throughout the world being meanwhile ruined. The end in view is *trading despotism*, of all despotisms the most degrading to the unfortunate beings subjected to it. The name by which it is generally known is that of *British free-trade*—a freedom that carries with it slavery in the various forms of war, poverty, famine, and pestilence, and for emancipation from which, as has so well been proved in Ireland, its unfortunate subjects can find but a single road—that one which terminates at the grave. Of all, it is the meanest, most selfish, most soul-destroying; yet are its advocates among ourselves found among those who most profess a belief in human freedom.

Under the tariff of 1842 we resumed the road towards independence, commencing discharge of the heavy obligations incurred in the seven years of the monopoly system, and so rapid was our progress in that direction that but a single decade would have been required for the attainment of perfect emancipation. That, however, did not suit the admirers of, and believers in, human slavery, either at home or abroad. The system was to be broken down, and to that end our farmers were assured that if they would but consent to re-establish Liverpool in its old position of centre of the Union, at which the farmer of Illinois should make all his exchanges with his neighbor of Tennessee, our grain exports would speedily count by hundreds, if not even by thousands, of millions of dollars. The ridiculous absurdity of all such calculations now exhibits itself in the fact, that our average export to Britain of wheat and flour, for the last ten years, has been but the equivalent of little more than 10,000,000 cwts., or 16,000,000 bushels. It is, however, the business of British agents—that for which they are so well paid—to deceive and cheat our people. Should you desire new evidence to this effect, look, I pray you, to the fact, that the British Free-Trade League, which holds its meetings in New York, and which is supported by contributions of British traders, has just now refused the offer of their American opponents to institute a free discussion, by means of which all might be enabled to see both sides of the question. No journal in foreign pay ever, by any chance, permits its subscribers to see the argument in favor of industrial independence. No *American* journalist would hesitate for a moment to enter into any arrangement by means of which all should be enabled to see the argument *pro* and *con* on this important subject.

From the date of the re-establishment in 1846 of the British monopoly system we went steadily forward destroying the domestic commerce, increasing our dependence on Liverpool as a place of exchange with all the world, and augmenting our foreign debt, until all at once the inevitable result was reached—that of dissolution of the Union. That no other could have been arrived at will, as I think, be clearly obvious to you when you shall have studied the facts that will now be given.

Under the free-trade system, with its constantly increasing dependence on the most unstable and irregular market of the world, proper development of the abounding mineral wealth of the Central States was entirely impossible. As a consequence of this, nearly the whole increase of Northern population was forced to seek the prairie lands of the Northwest and West, there to employ themselves in tearing out the soil and exporting it, in the form of wheat or corn, to markets of the East, home or foreign; and thus, as far as in their power lay, increasing competition for *the sale* of food, and of all other raw materials they had to sell, while increasing competition for *the purchase* of iron, and all the commodities they had need to buy—that being the especial object of the monopoly system established by Britain, and now given to the world as tending to the promotion of freedom of commerce. As a further consequence, the Slave States of the Centre, unable to develop and mine their numerous and abounding ores, were compelled to send their people south; and thus did we, from day to day, increase the weight and power of the *extreme North* and the *extreme South*, while depopulating and weakening the Centre.

That you may fully understand the effects of this, and how it had been that secession had gradually become not only possible but inevitable, I pray you now to take up a railroad map of the Union, and mark the fact that *all our great roads are merely spokes of a wheel whose hub is found in Liverpool.* Those of them which have most tended to acquire strength and weight are those which have found their terminations north of Pennsylvania, and south of Virginia. With each and every stage of movement in that direction it became more and more impracticable that the two extremes could hold together, until at length they parted company in 1861. That such was the tendency of the British monopoly system, and that such must certainly be the result, had long been clearly obvious to me, when, less than ten years since, I told Mr. Dallas, then in London, that dissolution of the Union would come about the time when the Capitol should be completed. In this I erred, the building being not even yet quite finished. Whether or not, when it shall be so, it will be the Capitol of all the existing States, is very doubtful. Without a decided change of policy *it certainly will not*, the centrifugal force of the system now advocated by Massachusetts being too great to defy resistance.

What is it, my dear sir, that now so closely binds together the New England States? Is it not their *network* of roads. Could they now by any possibility be torn asunder? Certainly not. Could there be any difficulty in accomplishing this were there but two great parallel roads leading through Boston and Portland to Liverpool? Not in the least. Sectionalism would then be as rife in New England as it has been throughout the extreme south and extreme north. Mr. Lincoln saw clearly that the Mississippi was the cross-tie that had held the Union together, and therefore did he urge the making of another through the hills, recommending a road that should pass through Kentucky and East Tennessee. Congress refused the little aid that had been asked for, yet did it never hesitate at granting enormous quantities of land in aid of roads across the continent. So long as our legislation on all economic subjects shall continue to be sectional in its tendencies it is wholly vain to hope for permanent reconstruction. Had Mr. Lincoln's advice been taken, Kentucky would now, in all probability, be a republican State.

Having thus shown the sectional and pro-slavery tendencies of the British monopoly system, I propose now to ask your attention to the manner in which *construction* has been elsewhere accomplished, believing that when this shall have been properly understood there will be less difficulty about measures of *reconstruction*.

I remain yours, &c.,

HENRY C. CAREY.

Hon. Henry Wilson.

Philadelphia, Aug., 1867.

LETTER THIRD.

DEAR SIR:

Ten years since I expressed the belief that Germany, whose "national sin for the last two centuries," according to Chevalier Bunsen, "had been poverty, the condition of all classes, with few exceptions"—Germany, which thirty years before had been held to be immensely overpopulated—then already stood "first in Europe in point of intellectual development," and was "advancing in the physical and moral condition of her people with a rapidity exceeding that of any other portion of the Eastern hemisphere."

Since then, an empire has been constructed embracing a population little short of 40,000,000, among whom education is universal; with a system of communications not excelled by that of any other country, with the exception of those provided for the very dense populations and limited territories of England and of Belgium; with an internal commerce as perfectly organized as any in the world, and growing from day to day with extraordinary rapidity; with a market on the land for nearly all its products, and, as a necessary consequence, with an agricultural population that grows daily in both intelligence and power; with a mercantile marine that now numbers more than 10,000 vessels; with a public treasury so well provided that not only has the late war left no debt behind, but that it has been at once enabled to make large additions to the provision for public education;* and with private treasuries so well supplied as to enable her people not only with their own means to build their own furnaces and factories and construct their own roads, but also to furnish hundreds of millions to the improvident people of America, to be by them applied to the making of roads in a country the abundance of whose natural resources should long since have placed it in the position of money lender, rather than that now occupied of general money borrower.

The course of things on the two sides of the Atlantic has thus, as we see, been entirely different. On the one side there has been

---

* "Shocked as the Chamber was at the extent of the Budget, yet the Liberal party received with applause the announcement that a half million thalers was expended in order to increase the salaries of the teachers in the public schools. 200,000 thalers were devoted especially to the teachers of primary schools, a small sum, it will be said, for the teachers of a nation of twenty millions; but the sum, in relation to the end proposed, is not so small as it at first sight seems. The primary schools are exclusively connected with the communities, and must be tolerably well maintained by the latter. And this sum is appropriated only to those communities which are too poor to pay the teachers sufficiently."—*Tribune Correspondence.*

a quiet and peaceful movement that has ended in *construction*. On the other a constant series of feuds, that has resulted in a need for *reconstruction*. Why it is that results so widely different have been obtained I propose now to show you.

Five and thirty years since, Germany and the American Union exhibited states of things directly antagonistic, the one to the other. The first was divided and disturbed, its internal commerce in every way embarrassed, its people and its various governments very poor, and with little hope in the future except that which resulted from the fact that negotiations were then on foot for the formation of a Customs Union, which shortly after was accomplished. In the other everything was different, the internal commerce having been more active than had ever before been known, the public treasury filled to overflowing, the national debt on the eve of extinction, and capital so much abounding as to make demand, for the opening of mines, the building of houses and mills, and the construction of roads, for all the labor power of a people that then numbered thirteen millions.

The cause of these remarkable differences was to be found in the facts, that, up to that time, Germany had wholly failed to adopt such measures of co-ordination as were needed for establishing rapidity of circulation among the 30,000,000, of which her society was then composed; whereas Congress had, four years before, and for the first time, adopted measures having for their object development of all the powers, physical, mental, or moral, of its population, all the wealth of its soil, and all the wonderful mineral deposits by which that soil was known to be underlaid. The one had failed to bring together the producer and consumer of food and wool, and had remained dependent upon traders in distant markets. The other had decided that such dependence should, at no distant time, come to an end; that producers and consumers should be brought together; and there had thence already resulted an activity of circulation and an improvement in physical and moral condition, the like of which had never before been known to be accomplished in so brief a period.

Three years later (1835), the two countries are once again found totally opposed, Germany having adopted the American system and thus provided for freedom of internal commerce, America simultaneously adopting that, which to Germany had proved so utterly disastrous, and which had been then rejected. Thenceforth the one moved steadily forward in the direction of creating a great domestic commerce, doing this by means of a railroad system which should so bind together her whole people as to forbid the idea of future separation. The result already exhibits itself in the quiet creation of a ·powerful empire. The other meanwhile has constructed great roads by means of which it has been enabled to export its soil, in the forms of tobacco, corn, and cotton, to distant markets, and thus to destroy the power to maintain internal commerce—the result obtained exhibiting itself in a great rebellion that has cost the country, North and South, half a million of lives, the crippling of hundreds of thousands of men, and an expenditure of more thousands of millions than, properly applied, would have doubled the incomes of its whole people, while making such demand for human force, mental, moral, and physical, as would, in a brief period, have secured the establishment of universal freedom, with benefit to all, white and black, landowner and laborer. Such have been the widely different results of two systems of public policy, the one of which looks to introducing into society that proper, orderly arrangement which is found in every well-conducted private establishment, and by means of which each and every person employed is enabled to find the place for which nature had intended him; the other, meanwhile, in accordance with the doctrine of *laisser faire*, requiring that government should abdicate the performance of its proper duties, wholly overlooking the fact that the communities by which such teachings are carried into practical effect—those whose dependence on Britain is a growing one—now exhibit themselves before the world in a state of utter ruin.

Turn now, if you please, to a railroad map of Germany, and see how wide is the difference between it and a similar map of the Union. Instead of a few great railroad lines leading out of the country, and having for their objects the *compulsion* of the people of close adjoining States to go abroad to make exchanges—Tennessee and Alabama going to Manchester and Liverpool to exchange with their neighbors of Indiana and Illinois—you find a perfect network, by means of which every town throughout the whole extent of the new empire is enabled peacefully and cheaply to exchange with each and every other. Look again to the journals of the day, and see that it has been just now determined that every town of 1500 inhabitants shall at once be put into telegraphic communication with each and every other. Turn then your eyes homeward, and see that while Congress has been willing to grant aid to telegraphic communication *outside* of the Union, it has never, so far as I can recollect, been willing to do anything *inside* of it. That domestic commerce by means of which the most powerful empire of Europe has been constructed, and in little more than a quarter of a century, is here considered wholly unworthy of Congressional notice.

The difference between the two countries consists in this, that the one has been making a piece of cloth, warp and woof, all the parts of which become more firmly knitted together from day to day; the other, meanwhile, having made nothing but warp, the filling having been forgotten. The strength of the one has been recently strikingly manifested in the determination of Southern Germany, in defiance of French interference, to adhere anew to the Zollverein.* The weakness of the other now manifests itself

* "The leaders of the 'South German national party' in Bavaria, Wurtemburg, Baden, and Hesse-Darmstadt, have decided to hold a meeting at

in the necessity for interference, on the part of Massachusetts, with the internal affairs of Texas and Louisiana. With our eyes always directed to Liverpool our whole policy is made sectional, and not national, and until it shall be changed it is as certain as that light follows the rising of the sun, that there can be no permanent reconstruction.

The great backbone of the Union is found in the ridge of mountains which commences in Alabama, but little distant from the Gulf of Mexico, and extends northward, wholly separating the people who inhabit the low lands of the Atlantic slope from those who occupy such lands in the Mississippi valley, and its constituting a great free-soil wedge with its attendant free atmosphere, created by nature herself in the very heart of slavery, and requiring but a slight increase of size and strength to enable its inhabitants to control the southern policy, and thus to bring the entire South into perfect harmony with the North and West, and with the world at large. That you may fully satisfy yourself on this head, I ask you to take the map and pass your eye down the Alleghany ridge, flanked as it is by the Cumberland range on the west, and by that of the Blue Mountains on the east, giving in the very heart of the South itself a country larger than all Great Britain, in which the finest of climates is found in connection with land abounding in coal, salt, limestone, iron ore, gold, and almost every other material required for the development of a varied industry and for securing the highest degree of agricultural wealth; and then to reflect that it is a region which must necessarily be occupied by men who with their own hands till their own land, and one in which slavery could never by any possibility have more than a slight and transitory existence. That done, I ask you to determine whether or not I am right in the assertion that the South is clearly divided into three separate portions, two of which have desired to move in the direction of perpetual human slavery, while the third, inserted between them, has been, and is, by the force of circumstances, necessarily impelled towards freedom.

Admitting now that the policy of '42 had been maintained; that rapid circulation had made such demand for labor as to cause the annual importation of miners and laborers to count by hundreds of thousands, if not almost by millions; that all the wonderful min-

Stuttgart in the beginning of August, with the object of forming a league, in conjunction with the Prussian liberals, for achieving the unification of Germany. This decision is supposed, on good authority, to have been precipitated by overtures lately made by France at Carlsruhe, Munich, and Darmstadt, with the object of preventing the acceptance by the South German States of the Prussian proposals for a restoration of the Zollverein. These overtures, it is said, were made in a very dictatorial tone. The conduct of the French diplomatic agents in this matter has greatly provoked the South German Liberals, and has produced so strong a feeling against France in the South German States that even the Ultramontanes no longer venture to continue their advocacy of a French alliance against Prussia."

eral resources of the country above described had been placed in course of development; that roads had been made by means of which Cincinnati and Savannah, St. Louis and Charleston, Boston and Mobile, had been enabled freely to exchange together; that the country south had been gradually creating a network of roads, by means of which coal and iron miners, farmers and weavers, had been enabled to exchange their products; admitting, I say, all these things, would not the wealth and strength of the people of the hills have, long since, so far outweighed those of the men of the flats, as to enable the former to control and direct the movements of the States? Would not that domestic commerce have given us freedom for the negro, harmony and peace among the people, and love for the Union among the States? Would it, under such circumstances, have been possible to *drive* the southern people into secession? That it would not, you can scarcely, as I think, fail to admit. Whensoever we shall have a fixed policy, tending gradually towards giving to our whole people such a network of roads as now knits together the New England States; whensoever there shall be real freedom of trade between Georgia and Illinois, Carolina and Iowa; whensoever the people of the interior generally shall be enabled to prosper under a system which stimulates domestic competition for the *purchase* of all they have to sell, and for the *sale* of all they need to consume; then, but not till then, will the freedom of the so recently emancipated slave become something more than a mere form of words; and then, but not till then, will there be good reason, my dear sir, for believing in the realization of your agreeable anticipations.

Slavery *did not* make the rebellion. British free trade gave us sectionalism, and promoted the growth of slavery, and thus led to rebellion. Had Mr. Clay been elected in 1844, all the horrors of the past few years would have been avoided. Why was he not? Because free-trade stump orators of New York and Massachusetts, professing to be opposed to slavery, could not believe him radical enough to suit their purposes. They, therefore, gave us Messrs. Polk and Dallas, and by so doing precipitated the rebellion, for the horrors and the waste of which, North and South, they are largely responsible before both God and man. Judging, however, from recent letters and speeches, they are now willing to take the responsibility of the next secession movement, giving us at one moment the extremest anti-slavery doctrines, while at the next advocating that British free trade policy which had always commanded the approbation of southern slaveholders, and which has reduced, or is reducing, to a condition closely akin to slavery, the people of every community that has been, or is, subjected to it. Unable to see that any system based on the idea of cheapening the raw materials of manufactures, the rude products of agricultural and mining labor, tends necessarily to slavery, they make of themselves the pro-slavery men, *par. excellence*, of the world.

To what extent the policy of your State has, since that time, been in accordance with the teachings of such men, I propose in another letter to examine, meanwhile, remaining

Yours faithfully,

HENRY C. CAREY.

Hon. H. WILSON.

PHILADELPHIA, Aug. 26, 1867.

LETTER FOURTH.

DEAR SIR:—

Forty years since, at the date of the agitation for the passage of that protective tariff of 1828, by means of which the country became first emancipated from the control of foreign money-lenders, the people of Massachusetts, as represented in Congress, were full believers in the advantages of the British free-trade system. Fourteen years having elapsed, during one-half of which they had, under protection, enjoyed the advantages derived from a peaceful and most profitable extension of domestic commerce; the other half having, on the contrary, furnished a series of free-trade and pro-slavery crises, ending in almost universal bankruptcy, and in an exhaustion of the national credit so complete that, after having, in 1835, finally extinguished the public debt, it had just then been found impossible to borrow abroad even a single dollar; Messrs. Choate and Sprague, representing Massachusetts in the Senate, are found gladly co-operating with Archer of Virginia, and other enlightened Southern Whigs, in the passage of the act of 1842, under which the consumption of iron and of cottons was, in the short space of less than half-a-dozen years, almost trebled; the country, meanwhile, resuming payment of its foreign debt, and re-acquiring the credit which it had required but a similar period of British free-trade so entirely to annihilate.

The protection granted by the tariff of '42, full and complete as it was, enabled Massachusetts—and for the first time—to compete in foreign markets for the sale of cottons. It enabled, too, the South to engage in their manufacture; and so rapid had, in 1848, been its progress, that Mr. Rhett, of the *Charleston Mercury*, was thereby led to predict, in a letter to Mr. Abbott Lawrence, that before the lapse of another decade, it would have ceased to export raw cotton. The prediction was one not likely to be so early realized, but even its half realization would have spared us all the cost in life, limb, and property, of the late rebellion, while it would so far have advanced the slave towards freedom as to have relieved the existing Congress from all the necessity for those measures of reconstruction of which you speak, and in which you have been, and are, so actively engaged.

The repeal of the act of 1846 was followed by a political revolution which placed General Taylor in the Presidential chair, and gave, or seemed to give, to the friends of American labor, and American interests generally, power for re-establishing protection. Forthwith a convention was held at Newport for the purpose of deciding what it was that needed to be asked for. The result of its deliberations was given to me a fortnight later by the then recognized head of the cotton interest of your State, in the few brief words: "We do not desire any protection that will stimulate domestic competition." To put this into other words, it was to say:—

"We do not wish that the South or West should engage in manufactures, for that would make competition for the *purchase* of cotton, and raise the price of the raw material."

"We do not desire that the South or West should become manufacturers, for that would produce competition for the *sale* of cloth, and reduce our profits."

"The tariff of 1846 having already closed the few mills of the Centre and the South, we do not desire any tariff that could have the effect of reopening them, or of causing new ones to be erected."

"That tariff having broken down our competitors, has given us a monopoly, and we desire to keep it. Nevertheless, we desire to have the duties increased some five or ten per cent., for that would benefit us, and would not suffice for producing domestic competition either for purchase of the raw material, or for the sale of finished goods."

It was a very narrow view of the question, wholly rejecting, as it did, the idea of any harmony between the interests of the producers and consumers of cotton. It was the right British idea, then first, as I think, naturalized in this country, and from that time forward, as I propose to show, made the rule of action of your representatives in both houses of Congress. It was the pro-slavery idea, common sense teaching that "raw materials" represent agricultural and mining labor, and, that whatever tends to increase competition for their sale, and thus to reduce their prices, tends directly to the subjugation of the laborer, black or white, to the will of those by whom his labor is directed. Wherever raw materials are low in price, man, be his color what it may, and whether found in Ireland or India, in Jamaica or Alabama, in Canada or Illinois, is little better than a slave, the only difference being in the form in which the master's whip presents itself for examination. The well-fed negroes of the South were, ten years since, less enslaved than were those Irish people so accurately described by Thackeray as "starving by millions." The Russian serf, paying *obrok* to his master, and comfortably supporting his wife and children on the proceeds of his labor, was far more master of his actions and himself than this day are the small remnant of those Pennsylvania miners that, in April, 1861, threw aside their tools and rushed to the nation's rescue, finding themselves, as they do, wholly without the employment by means of which they might be enabled to obtain better supplies of food and clothing. Competition for the purchase of labor *makes* men and women free. The ballot-box is useful as a means of *perpetuating* freedom. In your Address I find much in reference to this latter, but in regard to the former, and infinitely the most important, you are, as is much to be regretted, wholly silent.

The election of Mr. Cobb, in 1849, as Speaker of the House, threw the committees into the hands of the Democrats, and your manufacturers, as a consequence, wholly failed to obtain that small additional protection for which they so steadily had asked; just as much as, but no more than, would give security to themselves, while not in any manner "stimulating domestic competition" for purchase of cotton, or for the sale of cloth.

At the next step we find a coalition between British iron-masters and a self-constituted committee of three, having for its active head an ex-member of Congress from Massachusetts, since then presiding officer in one of the Republican conventions. This committee was, for a commission, to procure repeal of all duties on railroad iron, and return of much of those already paid. The movement failed; but for three years the sword of Damocles was held over the heads of all those engaged in the production of coal and iron, and at a cost to the mining interests of the country at large greater than would now suffice for buying and paying for all the cotton and woollen mills of your State, and all the towns in which those mills are placed.

Two years later the East proposed to the West, that, as compensation for granting it free wool, free raw material, and pro-slavery economic policy generally, it would itself generously consent to sacrifice the interests of its late co-laborers of the mining centre—of that section to which alone it had been indebted for the triumph of Whig principles in 1848. The proposition, in the form of an amendment to the appropriation bill, was strongly advocated by a distinguished Massachusetts member, shortly afterwards raised to the speakership, and it finally passed the House. It was defeated in the Senate, having there, on the last day of the session, been talked to death; this, too, in defiance of all the efforts of Massachusetts manufacturers, and of the readiness by them manifested to buy, and *pay for,* the silence of those engaged in the patriotic work.*

The first of these periods had been given to the closing of

---

* Should conclusive evidence on this subject be desired, it can at any hour be supplied.

existing rolling-mills, and preventing the building of others. In the second, it was claimed that because the mills were idle that, for that reason, the work of destruction should be further carried forward.

Simultaneously with these operations came the Canada reciprocity scheme, having for its object the cheapening of all the raw materials of manufacture that could be obtained from the country beyond the Bay of Fundy and the St. Lawrence, barley, wool, wheat, and coal, included. Wholly misunderstood, it passed the House, and was on the eve of becoming a law by means of senatorial action when I myself, for the first time, opened the eyes of Mr. Clay and other leading senators to the injurious, and even destructive, tendencies of the measure. From that hour the case became so hopeless that, as I think, the bill never afterwards came up for consideration. The election of Mr. Pierce, and consequent return of the pro-slavery party to power, brought about a change, however; it having then become to the South most clearly obvious that for preventing annexation of the British Possessions there was but a single remedy—that of granting to the Provinces all the advantages of being in the Union, while requiring of their people the performance of none of the duties, the bearing of none of the burdens, of American citizens. Such was the true intent and meaning of the treaty that then was negotiated, and that was carried through the Senate by aid of the combined pro-slavery and trading States, Massachusetts and New York steadily uniting with Carolina for preventing any change in the period for which it was to endure, and unanimously recording their votes against limiting it to one, two, three, and so on to nine years. To force through the House a bill providing for carrying it into effect was now the difficulty. That the work was done all know, but of the character of the means resorted to for having it done, few know who have not had the advantage I have had of hearing it fully described by one of the most honored and honorable members of the House. As in the case of the amendment to the appropriation bill above referred to, it seemed to be held that "the end"—the cheapening of raw materials at whatsoever cost to the farmers, miners, and laborers of the Union—"sanctified the means;" and "sanctified" them even in the eyes of men who long had found their chief employment in lecturing their fellow-citizens on the unchristian character of American slavery, and on the necessity for giving freedom to the Southern producers of those raw materials in the cheapening of which they found themselves so steadily engaged.

That this had been from first to last a Boston measure, is, of course, well known to you, as you must have seen the circulars asking subscriptions for moneys to be paid to the men who had succeeded in placing Canadians in a position far better than that occupied by our own citizens.

Close upon this followed the nomination of General Fremont,

another British free-trade measure forced upon the States of the Centre by extremists of the North and East. In the course of the campaign the agents of British makers of cloth and iron were, on one occasion, greatly gratified by a speech made in front of the New York Exchange by a gentleman of Massachusetts, who, in his character of Speaker of the House, had, but a few months previously, appointed committees entirely satisfactory to that portion of the body which had had full belief in *American* free-trade, and in the idea that every step in the direction of diversified industry tended towards emancipation for the laborer, black and white, foreign and domestic.

Coming now to 1857, we find the Ways and Means Committee, by its chairman, Mr. Campbell, of Ohio, reporting a bill for reduction of the revenue, somewhat satisfactory to the people of the Centre and the West. Wholly changed by a senatorial pro-, slavery committee, with Mr. Hunter, of Virginia, at its head, it was then advocated by yourself, my dear sir, in a speech in which occurs the following passage, to wit:—

" The people of New England, Mr. President, and especially of Massachusetts, are very extensively engaged in the manufacture of articles in which wool, hemp, flax, lead, tin, brass, and iron are largely consumed. It is for their interest that the duties on these articles should be merely nominal, or that they should be duty free."

The opposition to this pro-slavery and cheap raw material substitute of the Virginia senator was very vigorous, Mr. Seward taking therein a very decided part. So doubtful, at length, became its adoption, that its friends found it necessary to telegraph your colleague, Mr. Sumner, advising him that without his vote the friends of freedom for the American mining and agricultural laborer, and of independence for the American Union, would probably succeed in accomplishing its rejection. He came, then presenting himself for the first time in the session, still suffering under injuries caused by the attack of a Carolinian opponent of the doctrine of diversified interests; and he then and there united with Virginia, Carolina, and Mississippi in a vote, the true intent and meaning of which was, that the farmers, miners, and laborers of America, black and white, should, in all the future, be mere "hewers of wood and drawers of water" for Southern slaveholders and British and Eastern capitalists.

On more than one occasion I had said to your Colleague that while he had spoken much of freedom, his senatorial votes on industrial questions had thus far always been given on the pro-slavery side. Meeting him in Paris shortly after the one last above recorded, I could not refrain from congratulating him on having so far recovered from the effects of Carolinian brutality as to have been enabled to unite with Carolinian senators in a vote for perpetuation of slavery throughout the South. In the true Christian spirit he had returned good for evil.

The passage of that act brought about a crisis, whose effect was that of almost total stoppage of cotton and woollen mills throughout the country north and south. For the moment Massachusetts suffered some little inconvenience, but she soon after resumed operations, and with great advantage to herself, her rivals in the Central, Southern, and Western States having been irretrievably ruined. The danger of "domestic competition" had disappeared, and the manufacturing monopoly had become assured.

The years that followed exhibited an almost total prostration of the various industries of the country, yet was it determined by the leaders of the Republican party, North and East, that the platform to be adopted at Chicago should be a mere repetition of that of 1856, all "new issues" to be entirely ignored. On the Committee of Resolutions there was, however, one member who was determined that the question of protection should be squarely met, and he therefore notified his fellow-members that if they did not then and there adopt a resolution to that effect they should be compelled to fight it on the following day on the floor of the convention. In that he, representing New Jersey, was sustained by the member from Delaware, and the debate terminated by the adoption of a resolution in the following words, the reading of which, on the succeeding day, was followed by a storm of applause from the assembled thousands, the like of which has had no parallel on this Western Continent:—

"That, while providing revenue for the support of the General Government by duties upon imports, *sound policy requires such an adjustment of those imposts as to encourage the development of the industrial interests of the whole country;* and we commend that policy of national exchanges which secures to the workingmen liberal wages, to agriculture remunerating prices, to mechanics and manufacturers an adequate reward for their skill, labor, and enterprise, and to the nation commercial prosperity and independence."

Such is the history of the decade. It is the history of a constant war by Massachusetts upon the greatest of all the national interests—a war for sixpences, carried on at an annual cost to the mining and farming regions of the country five times greater than the receipts of California gold—a war more than half the cost of which was paid by Pennsylvania. To the Union at large its cost consists in this, that had Massachusetts fully, fairly, and honestly exerted her influence in the opposite direction, the iron manufacture of the Border States would probably have made such progress as to have prevented their secession, and thus prevented all the injury, as regards both property and life, they have been made to suffer.

Of what has since occurred I shall speak in another letter, meanwhile remaining,

Yours, very truly,
HENRY C. CAREY.

Hon. Henry Wilson.

LETTER FIFTH.

Dear Sir:—

By the adoption, as part of its platform, of the resolution given in my last, the Republican party pledged itself to a policy the reverse of that advocated by yourself in 1857; one which looked to "stimulation of competition" for the purchase of raw materials, labor included; one which would "stimulate domestic competition" for the sale of finished commodities; one based on the idea, apparently unknown to our Massachusetts friends, that protection to the miner, by giving him means of purchase, is, in effect, protection to the maker of cloth; and that protection to consumers of his products is, in effect, protection to the farmer, there being a perfect harmony of interest among all the members of the social body.

Less than a year later, Congress redeemed the pledge then given, enacting into law the determination of the many thousands present at the Chicago Convention, a protective tariff having received the assent of Mr. Buchanan on the day before his quitting office. By it full protection was secured to the cotton manufacturer, and this was *then* most gladly accepted by the men of Massachusetts, the Cotton States having left the Union, and the danger of "stimulating domestic competition" having altogether ceased.

For means to carry on the war an internal revenue, however, came soon after to be required, and, as usual, the mining interest was made to suffer; taxes being piled upon iron at its every stage from the pig to the engine, while duties on the most important of all its products, railroad bars, were subsequently so diminished that the difference between contributions by the domestic and foreign article fell to little more than that which resulted from the fact that gold was required for the latter, while greenbacks sufficed for the former.

So long as the war endured, and the premium on gold continued large, this latter furnished all the protection which seemed to be required. With the peace, however, this so far died away as to produce a necessity for such change in the tariff as would tend to counteract the nullification of protection caused by demand, for public use, for contributions on almost every article at every stage of manufacture. To this end the Secretary of the Treasury appointed a Commission, upon whose report was based a tariff bill which finally passed the House in the second week of July, 1866, and was on the following day received in the Senate. A senator from Iowa forthwith moved that its consideration be postponed until the following December; and in the debate on this motion you yourself, as representative of the manufacturing interests of your State, spoke as follows:—

" I shall vote, Mr. President, to commit this bill to the Committee on Finance, with instructions to report early in December. I shall so vote because I believe the permanent interests of the whole country demand that the adjustment of the tariff should be made after the most thorough examination, research, and care. Congress cannot take too much time, nor devote too much attention, to the proper adjustment of a measure that so deeply concerns the revenues of the Government and the varied productive interests of the country. * * *

" What I objected to the other day, and what I object to now, is, that New England should be singled out and charged with the sin of the paternity of this measure. While the representatives of Massachusetts and of New England have voted on general principles for this bill, they have so voted with a great deal of hesitation, doubt, and reluctance. They saw what was clear to the comprehension of gentlemen of ordinary intelligence, that this measure imposed increased duties upon raw material, increased largely the cost of production, and subjected the manufacturing and mechanical interests of their section to the censure and hostility of those who spare no occasion to manifest their hostility to that section of our country."

Here, as ever, "cheap raw material" is, as you see, the one object to be accomplished. Pending the existence of the reciprocity treaty Nova Scotia coal had come in free of duty, and Boston capitalists had, as it is understood, become largely interested in the properties by which it had been supplied. The treaty having been abrogated, the special protection they had so long enjoyed was now to cease, and the fact that this new tariff bill did not provide for continued import of coal duty free, constituted the main objection to it. Here, as everywhere, the mining interests were made the object of attack; "cheap raw materials," whether "lead or tin, brass or iron," being, as you had told the Senate in 1857, essential to your constituents. Who, however, would, in this case of coal, have paid 'the duty? The manufacturers? Not one cent of it. The man who *must* go to market *must pay the cost of getting there*, as is so well known to the farmer of Iowa who sells for a few cents a bushel of corn that in Massachusetts would command almost a dollar. The price of coal is fixed by the domestic supply, and to that the importer must conform, whatever may be the cost of transportation, or charges of the revenue. The Boston owners of coal mines would have been required to pay the duty fixed by the bill before the Senate, yet was no effort spared for inducing the people of Massachusetts, and of New England generally, to believe that it was a tax to be paid by *them*.

In the division that ensued we find extremists of the North and South combined for destruction of the common enemy, the miner and the laborer—Massachusetts and Kentucky voting together for postponing a measure having for its object the "stimulation of domestic competition" for purchase of the rude products of mining and agricultural labor; and New York and Massachusetts giving all the votes required for securing postponement of this important bill to another session.

At the next session a bill, nearly similar, passed the Senate; and now we find in the House a near approach to the senatorial action of the previous year. The majority of the latter was decidedly favorable to protection, and the state of the country demanded that it should be given. By no direct action could the bill be defeated; but here, as everywhere, there were indirect modes of accomplishing that which directly could not be done. Its management fell into the hands of a representative of Boston capitalists, and the result exhibits itself in the prostration of the industrial interests of the country; and in the fact, that not only do we export all the gold received from California, but that we are running in debt to Europe to an annual amount little less than $200,000,000. In this way it is that we are carrying into practical effect "the democratic idea of the Declaration of Independence," making our people from day to day more dependent on the capitalists of Massachusetts and of Europe.

It may be asked, however, if the Boston capitalist engaged in the cotton manufacture does not suffer equally with those elsewhere engaged in other industrial departments? He does not. Having secured an almost entire monopoly, all he desires is that nothing shall be done that will "stimulate domestic competition;" and to that end, as I understand, New England men have shown themselves inflexibly opposed to the granting of any more protection than that which they themselves required, or little more than that now allowed them. With them capital abounds, interest is low, and machinery exists in great perfection. Just now, they suffer in some small degree; but they find their compensation in the fact that, as before in 1848, and again in 1857, their competitors in the purchase of cotton and sale of cloth, are being ruined beyond redemption. In this State nearly all the mills have been already stopped, and the effect of this well exhibits itself in the fact that Eastern journalists now tell us, that "factory cloths are easy, with an upward tendency in prices, the stocks in first hand in all New England not exceeding 150,000 pieces." The more frequent the crises, the more dangerous the trade; and the more the free-trade cry can be raised, as is now being done throughout New England, the less is the danger of "domestic competition" for the purchase of cotton and for the sale of cotton cloth; and therefore is it that Eastern cotton manufacturers have been enabled to build up the immense fortunes that we find recorded. The system here pursued by them closely resembles that of the great British iron-masters, as below described; the latter being as much intent upon having a monopoly of the supply of iron to the world as are the capitalists of Boston upon monopolizing that of cottons for the Union.

" The laboring classes generally, in the manufacturing districts of this country, and especially in the iron and coal districts, are very little aware of the extent to which they are often indebted for their being employed at all to the immense *losses* which their employers voluntarily incur in bad times, in order *to destroy foreign competition, and to gain and keep possession of foreign markets.* Authentic instances are well known of employers having in such times carried on their works at a loss amounting in the aggregate to three or four hundred thousand pounds in the course of three or four years. If the efforts of those who encourage the combinations to restrict the amount of labor and to produce strikes were to be successful for any length of time, the great accumulations of capital could no longer be made *which enable a few of the most wealthy capitalists to overwhelm all foreign competition in times of great depression,* and thus to clear the way for the *whole trade* to step in when prices revive, and to carry on a great business before *foreign* capital can again accumulate to such an extent as to be able to establish a competition in prices with any chance of success. *The large capitals of this country are the great instruments of warfare against the competing capitals of foreign countries,* and are *the most essential* instruments now remaining by which our manufacturing supremacy can be maintained; the other elements—cheap labor, abundance of raw materials, means of communication, and skilled labor—being rapidly in process of being equalized."

For "iron and coal" read cotton, and for "foreign competition" read "domestic competition," and you will have an almost perfect history of Massachusetts policy for the last twenty years.

Such, as I understand it, is the true history of your State in relation to the question of *real* freedom of trade, *real* freedom for the men who labor, *real* love for the whole Union, and *real* tendency towards enabling freedmen of the South in any manner to profit by the "bloody struggles" through which they and we have so lately passed; and which you here describe as the "struggle on this continent between the democratic idea of the Declaration of Independence and human bondage." The one great object to be accomplished has been that of having "cheap raw materials" at whatsoever cost to the miner and laborer, black or white; and to that end there has been coalition with Canada and Carolina against the West; with Nova Scotia and the South against the Centre; with any and everybody, indeed, that could be made to contribute towards placing the State you represent in the same position as regarded the Union as is now occupied by Britain in reference to the world at large. If it has, in any of its parts, been misrepresented, I shall be most glad to give publicity to any correction that may seem to be required. Postponing, for the present, all remarks thereon, I shall, in another letter, present for your consideration a similar review of the action of this State as representative of the mining interests, of all others the most important in, and to, the Union : meantime remaining,

Yours, faithfully,

HENRY C. CAREY.

HON. HENRY WILSON.

PHILADELPHIA, Sept., 1867.

LETTER SIXTH.

DEAR SIR:—

The cotton manufacturer, at a time of serious crisis, discharges some of his hands, putting the rest on half or quarter time and holding himself ready, on the instant when danger shall have ceased, to go ahead and reimburse himself for all that he had lost; doing this by means of higher prices consequent upon the suppression of "domestic competition" that had been brought about.

With those engaged in supplying fuel all is widely different. Mines must be kept free from water whether coal is shipped or not, and pumping is an expensive process. Timbers decay, iron rusts, and both need to be replaced. Coal that should be mined, but for which no market can be found, now falls, and tracks become encumbered—the general result being, as I have always understood, that the difference to the operator from maintaining a mine in idleness on one hand, or full work at the other, is so small as scarcely to be imagined by those not familiar with mining operations. Stoppage to him, therefore, is almost utter ruin. To go ahead is little worse, and therefore is it that the mining record of the State furnishes an exhibition so appalling of the ruin of active, intelligent men to whose energetic action the country has stood indebted for the cheap fuel now in daily use; that fuel to which your State, as well as all New England, owes the development of its manufacturing industry; and that by means of which, alone, we have so recently been enabled to maintain the great blockade, and to pass successfully through the war.

The mine and the furnace, bases of the industrial pyramid, are always the first that are, by reason of absence of demand for their products, compelled to stop. They are, too, always and necessarily last to resume operations. The tariff of 1842 was, so far as the value of coal property had been concerned, wholly inoperative until the autumn of 1844, at which time the manufacturers of Massachusetts, profiting by that annihilation of "domestic competition" for the purchase of cotton or the sale of cloth which had resulted from repeated British free-trade crises, had more than repaid themselves for all the losses they had suffered. So has it lately been; the first two years of the tariff of 1861 having enabled your people to make enormous fortunes, coal meanwhile remaining almost as stagnant as before. The war was more than half over before the occurrence of any essential change in the value of coal property or the profits of coal shippers. Were we now to have a restoration of the societary circulation, several years would be required for restoring the coal region to anything approaching to life and vigor; Massachusetts meanwhile accumulating hundreds of millions of dollars, and going on her way rejoicing. The need of the miner for regularity of the social movement as much exceeds that of the manufacturer as that of the latter exceeds that of the keeper of a grog-shop.

To a great extent, however, the damage done can never be repaired. Mines having been allowed to fill up, coal has been abandoned. The little that could be readily obtained has been dragged out and sent to market, leaving enormous masses to go to waste. To such an extent has this been the case that it is now safe to say, that for *each* ton that has gone to market, *three* have been utterly wasted. Therefore is it that although the whole quantity shipped in more than forty years scarcely exceeds, if indeed it equals, eighteen months' supply for Britain, a very considerable proportion of the region has been entirely exhausted, and very much of it so scratched over as to have caused damage that can never be repaired. The industrial history of the world may be searched in vain for any so wanton waste of wealth, happiness, and national power, as has, by aid of the combined efforts of British and Eastern free-trade believers in "cheap raw materials," and in the advantages of cheap labor, been perpetrated in the coal region of Pennsylvania.

For all these reasons the mining regions of the country—those regions of which Pennsylvania is the representative—require more than any others, such a policy as tends to make of that Declaration of Independence to which you have referred, something more than a mere form of words—such an one as tends to give steadiness of action to the societary machine. Has Massachusetts policy tended in that direction? Look, I pray you, to the exhibit thereof presented in my last, and satisfy yourself if much of the instability of the last twenty years has, or has not, thence resulted; and if the question might not now be fairly put as to whether, even to-day, the danger to the Centre of close political connection with an almost exclusively trading community like that you represent, looking, as it has always done, exclusively to the cheapening of raw materials at the cost of their producers, is not fully as great as has ever been that of a connection with planting communities like those of Alabama or Mississippi. To my mind it appears to be even greater, and it is my belief that conviction to this effect will, without a total change of Massachusetts policy, at no distant day force itself upon the minds of the people of the central and mining States.

To the Union at large the development of Pennsylvania coal mines has been worth thousands of millions of dollars. To that it has been due that you have found yourself enabled to say in your Address that "we have triumphed;" that "we are proud and strong;" that "we have lifted the country towards the heavens;" that "we are a greater people than ever before." But for Pennsylvania anthracite not one word of this could now be said. The cause of the North would this day be "the lost cause," had the chance of war closed the sources from which the coal has been derived; and yet, so far as relates to the persons who have supplied the means required for its development, *it would have been very far better if not a ton of anthracite had ever been found in the State;* or, if found, it had been left where it had first been placed. Had the whole anthracite region, and the improvements of every kind in and leading to it, on the 1st of January, 1861, been appraised at the price in money it would have then commanded, and to the sum then obtained had there been added all the rents and dividends to that day received, the gross amount would not, in my belief, have even been equal to two-thirds of the money that had been given to the work of development, *leaving wholly out of view any price originally paid for the land itself.* It had enriched all but those who had done the work.

Half a dozen years having since elapsed, it might be well, perhaps, for you to pay a visit to the region, and satisfy yourself as to its present condition and its prospects in the future. Doing this, you would find thousands of men, victims of the "cheap raw material" system, wholly unemployed, and very many whose wives and children stand much in need of increased supplies of food and clothing. Looking to the machine shops to which you had been indebted for power to close the southern ports against blockade-runners, you would find them idle. Inquiring for the mechanics, you would learn that not only had they long been unemployed, but that there existed little prospect of demand for the services they so much desired to render. Passing around among the mines, you would be told that where they had not been utterly abandoned, their maintenance had, for a long time past, been rapidly eating up all the profits on the coal supplied to the various workshops by means of which republican armies had been enabled to achieve the great "triumph" of which you speak. Asking for the remnant of the troops which, on receipt of the first advice of danger, and in advance of the men of Massachusetts, had so promptly rushed to the rescue, you might, as I think, find that their wives and children had become candidates for poor-house quarters. Having carefully studied all these things, you might next, perhaps, inquire what had been the effect of paralysis so perfect upon the owners of all this vast property, valuable as it had been supposed to be. In answer, you might be told, that you had before you, in a single valley, 70,000 acres, richer in coal than any other in the world, nearest of all to market, and best supplied with roads; which yet would give to their unfortunate proprietors little more than would be required for paying the additional war taxes, leaving wholly out of view those required of old for education, maintenance of the roads, and other local purposes. Such, in my belief, is the actual fact.

Taking now a bird's-eye view of the whole region, you might, on full reflection, be led to the conclusion that the vote of last year in favor of the Massachusetts system, that one which looks to the cheapening of raw materials and to the establishment of a single market for the Union, had cost, to it alone, a sum more than, if so applied, would purchase all the cotton and woollen mills of your State, and all the houses of the people that in them were employed.

Let the people of Massachusetts now, for a moment, change places with those of this State, finding themselves and their property so placed, and then reflect what would probably be *their* modes of thought and action. Might they not be led to think that further political connection with us was a thing to be dreaded, and not desired. Might they not be disposed to inquire into the effects that had resulted from an improper accumulation of power in the hands of 3,000,000 at one extremity of the Union? Might they not begin to see that sectionalism at the North was as greatly to be dreaded as sectionalism at the South? Might they not be led to arrive at the conclusion, that the work of reconstruction could not be regarded as having been achieved so long as the whole nation should be required to aid in the construction of an inverted pyramid, the little apex of which was to find its place among the mills of Lowell and of Manchester? Might they not, finally, be brought to a *determination* that what really was needed was not so much *reconstruction* as the *construction* of a true pyramid, with a base so broad as to enable it to cover every part of that great farming and mining region—the richest in the world—which, with exception of that small portion of the mere surface occupied by extremists North and South, is co-extensive with the Union, and embraces all its territories from the Lakes to the Gulf, and from the Atlantic to the Pacific? I think they would. If, then, such would probably be, when so placed, their modes of thought, what *should be now* the modes of thought and action of those who really own the State, and who so long have found themselves, as between the upper and the nether millstone, ground between the rival States of Carolina and Massachusetts?

Leaving you to reflect on the answer proper to be given to this important question, I remain, for the present,

Yours, faithfully,

HENRY C. CAREY.

HON. HENRY WILSON.

PHILADELPHIA, September 10, 1867.

LETTER SEVENTH.

DEAR SIR:—

Massachusetts is the type of that portion of our population which has its home north of the 41st parallel, and which, more than any other, finds in trade the chief occupation of life. In like manner, in Pennsylvania is found the type of that which occupies the territory between 39° 30' and 41°, and with which farming and mining, and the conversion of the rude products of both, make most demand for physical and mental force. Of that force, she is, and has always been, the representative, and therefore has it always been, that as she has gone so has gone the Union. What has been her course in the past, and what are her claims in the present for occupation of a position so important, it is proposed now to show.

The Constitution, as completed by the Convention of 1787, gave great satisfaction to the smaller States, placing them, as it did, on an equal senatorial footing with the larger ones, and securing them against that absorption by these latter which had been not a little dreaded. Would, however, Massachusetts be content to accept as an equal in political power the little Rhode Island? Would Virginia be so by Delaware? or Pennsylvania by the little State beyond the Delaware?

First to answer this question was Pennsylvania, the call of a Convention for the purpose of considering the Constitution having been issued almost instantly on learning that the general Convention had completed the work intrusted to its hands. First, with exception of little Delaware, she ratified it, doing this by the large majority of two to one, and thus setting an example of magnanimity which was but very slowly followed. First of the large States to follow was Massachusetts, but her action long remained in doubt, and the majority was but 19 in a body of 355. Some months later came the Virginia Convention, and here the doubt was greater still. Ratification was, however, at length effected by the meagre majority of 10 out of 160. From the first New York had been opposed to union, and the signature of but one of her representatives in the Convention, that of Hamilton, is appended to the Constitution. Very late in taking it into consideration, the opposition in the State Convention proved then so fierce as to make it in the highest degree doubtful if ratification could be at all obtained. When, however, it had been ascertained that nine States, the necessary number, had at length given in their adhesion— that formation of the Union could in no possible manner be prevented—that power had already been given to a Federal government that might be used coercively—then, and not till then, was ratification obtained; and yet, by little more than a bare majority, the ayes having exceeded the noes by only three.

But for the prompt and decided action of Pennsylvania the Union would not have been formed. But for her steady adhesion since it could not have been maintained. By the one she earned the title of the Keystone State; by the other she has, as I propose to show, vindicated her claim thereto.

Five and twenty years later we find in Massachusetts the first attempt at secession, followed a few years after by Carolina nullification of the law, as preparation for further and more decided action. On both occasions Pennsylvania stood unflinchingly by the Union. From that hour the question of its further maintenance rested with her, and *her alone*. Had she been willing to abandon her Northern friends, she might, as is well known, have made her own terms. Offers of every kind were made to her. Always faithful, she treated them with that contempt they merited, and the records of Congress would, as I think, be searched in vain for evidence that she had ever, even for a moment, been willing to profit herself at the cost of any whatsoever of the great national interests. The greatest of all, the maintenance of the Union, was in her especial keeping; and on that head she now stands before the world with a record that is without a parallel in the world.

First at the ballot-box in 1860, she, by the vast majority given to Gov. Curtin, decided the question between Messrs. Lincoln and Breckinridge. First again at the ballot-box in the dark hours of 1863, she saved the Union at a time when both New York and New Jersey had passed under the control of sympathizers with the rebellion. Had she then failed, the Union would have perished.

First in the field in 1861, her hardy miners preceded, by a single day, the men of Massachusetts. First to appreciate the importance of prompt exertion, she raised and equipped an army of sixteen thousand men, of whom not so much as a fifth returned from the field unharmed. Placing at the head of her divisions the best officers of the State, she tendered them to the nation, and had they been as promptly accepted as they had been promptly raised, the result of the Bull Run battle would have been widely different.

First to appreciate the importance of social organization, the loyal men of her commercial capital set the example of forming themselves into a League for controlling and directing the public opinion of the State—and with what effect I need not tell you. Leaving wholly out of view its other important services, it stands now alone as an association of individuals that had, at their own private cost, placed ten full regiments in the field.

First to feel that every private, of whatsoever State, was to be regarded as the people's friend, that city fed, and kindly cared for, every man of the many hundreds of thousands who passed from north to south, or from south to north.

Alone in the possession of anthracite, whose development had caused the ruin of most of those concerned therein, she furnished nearly all the motive power that maintained the blockade; that kept in operation all the mills and shops from which the Union obtained its rifles and its cannon, its cloth and its ships, and most of its internal revenue.

Alone in the possession of furnaces and rolling-mills in quantity sufficient for doing the greatly needed work, their owners, then so recently denounced by Eastern friends as little better than public robbers, supplied nearly all the iron needed by mills and shops throughout the Union.

Without Mr. Lincoln, without Stanton or Grant, without Meade or Sheridan, without any other State, the war might, perhaps, have been brought to a successful conclusion. Without HER no war could have been maintained for even a single hour. Had Lee succeeded at Gettysburg, he would have controlled the sources of national power, and the war would have been ended. Then, as ever, as Pennsylvania went, so has gone the Union. As she may in future go, so *must* the Union go; all the obstacles that have, till now, stood in the way of combined Central and Southern action having been removed.

Having thus shown what had been her course in the recent eventful years, allow me now to ask that you should re-read my last, and satisfy yourself as to what has been her compensation. Look at her abandoned mines! Look at her closed-up rolling and spinning-mills! Then, I pray, re-peruse the adverse speeches that have been made in Congress in reference to her interests; *interests a hundred-fold greater in national importance than some of those in regard to which our Eastern friends have been accustomed to be so eloquent.*

Leaving out of view, however, her own private interests, it is her duty, as GUARDIAN OF THE UNION, to look to those of the whole people, North and South, East and West, and satisfy herself what has thus far been the result of a commercial policy whose tendencies have all been in the direction of giving to the East an entire monopoly of the cotton manufacture, while depriving the most important portions of the Union of all power to avail themselves of the vast mineral wealth in which their territories so much abound. Doing this, as she *must* now do, she meets with the striking facts in regard to cotton cloth, and iron, that will now be given :—

Twenty years since the domestic consumption of cotton had reached 600,000 bales, being the equivalent of . . . . . . pounds 250,000,000
The import of foreign cottons was then about
40,000,000 yards, equal, probably, to pounds 6,000,000

Total, 256,000,000

The population was then about 20,000,000, and this would

give a total consumption of more than 12 pounds per head; and a growth, in five years of full and complete protection, of fully 70 per cent.

Last year the domestic consumption required, as I am informed, 700,000 bales. This year it will need but little more than 600,000. Taking it, however, at even 650,000, we obtain, say, . . . pounds 270,000,000
The import of the first four months of the year was 20,000,000 yards; at which rate we should have for the year 60,000,000, the equivalent of probably . . . pounds 10,000,000

Total, 280,000,000

Within this period we have mined of the precious metals to the extent of some twelve or fifteen hundred millions of dollars. Nevertheless, instead of an increase, we have large decrease, the consumption, per head, having fallen *from twelve pounds down to eight;* the quantity being little more than it had been when the pro-slavery tariff of 1846 came into practical operation. Such have been the results of the policy which has looked to the cheapening of raw materials; to the discouragement of "domestic competition" for their purchase; and to the practical subjugation of the miners, farmers, and laborers engaged in their production! The Massachusetts system has in view nothing beyond enrichment of the capitalist, while that of Pennsylvania tends towards giving to labor that real freedom which results from growing competition for its purchase. Of the two, which, my dear sir, has most tended to "destroy human bondage?"

In 1842 our production of iron was about 220,000 tons, and our total consumption, of foreign and domestic, about 300,000. Five years later, the production, as stated by Mr. Walker, and as subsequently confirmed by the iron-masters themselves, was 700,000. The import was then about 100,000, giving a total of 800,000, and an increase, under thorough protection, in the five years that had then elapsed, of 167 per cent.

Twenty years have since passed, throughout a large proportion of which it has pleased the representatives of Massachusetts to array themselves on the side of cotton-planters, slave owners, railroad monopolists, and all other opponents of real freedom, against the people of the mining regions of the country, the result now exhibiting itself in the following facts, to wit: that the average product of the last three years has been but 1,100,000 tons; that the quantity this year made will be less than that of the last by 200,000 tons; that the import of the year will probably reach 200,000, in payment for which we are sending by every steamer all the gold yielded by the Pacific and Mountain States; that the total consumption of the year will, in actual quantity, be but 65 per cent. greater than that of 1847, although our population has almost doubled; that the consumption per head, which had more than doubled in the protective years from 1842 to 1847, has now fallen to less than it then had been; and that, as the consumption of iron furnishes the best of all tests of advancing civilization, we must have gone forward rapidly under protection, and have been retrograding ever since its abandonment in 1847.

In facts like those here presented, in relation to both cotton and iron, there is found, as it seems to me, no evidence that we are likely long to have to boast "that we are a greater people than ever before;" or that "hereafter, in the future, we shall be friends and brothers as we were in the morning of the Republic." Had the tariff of 1842 been maintained, we should be now making of the one 4,000,000 tons a year, and consuming or exporting in the shape of cloth, 3,000,000 bales of the other; the nation becoming *really* great, the colored population of the South, meanwhile, peacefully advancing with profit to themselves and their owners towards a freedom far more perfect than that which, at the cost of hundreds of thousands of lives, and thousands of millions of property, they have as yet obtained.

To all this, however, in the eyes of the capitalists of New and Old England, there would have been one objection, to wit, that it would have greatly raised the prices of raw materials throughout the South—land, labor, and the rude products of both. It would have made a market on the land for both food and cotton, and would so have facilitated consumption of the latter that the price would never have been below $80 per bale. It would have made throughout the South that competition for purchase of human force, physical and mental, which would have "destroyed human bondage." It would have made throughout the Centre and the South a network of roads that would have tied together all the States of the Union just as now are bound together those of the little and compact New England. Giving us, quietly and profitably to all, an universal freedom, we should have gone gently ahead towards the *construction* of a "more perfect Union," and would have been spared the present necessity for *reconstruction.*

You speak of the "warm and generous greetings" with which the South will now be welcomed. What is there needed is, however, something more than a mere form of words. The ballot-box is of little use for filling the stomach, or for repairing roads. The South sees the price of cotton steadily falling, until it has now, in Liverpool, reached ten-pence, the equivalent of twenty-eight cents. Why is this? Because, under the industrial and financial policy now advocated by Massachusetts, the domestic consumption, instead of rising this year, as it should have done, to 1,100,000 bales, has fallen to 650,000, at a cost to the South, on a crop of 2,500,000 bales, of $100,000,000.

Such, my dear sir, are the "greetings" thus far given by Massachusetts to Carolina, Georgia, and Alabama. Let those of the future be of the same character, and the day will not then be far distant when you and your fellow-citizens will find yourselves compelled to the conclusion that you had been quite in error when you had said that "all our troubles had passed away forever." British free-trade built up slavery and made the rebellion. Let it be maintained, and it will defeat all your efforts at reconstruction.

Yours, very truly,
HENRY C. CAREY.

HON. HENRY WILSON.

PHILADELPHIA, Sept., 1867.

LETTER EIGHTH.

DEAR SIR:—

The *greatness* of our country, of which, in common with so many of its people, you so recently have spoken, is, as you see, being manifested not only by a diminished power over our own mineral deposits, but by a diminution in the ratio of consumption, whether of domestic or foreign production, to population. Why is it that such has been, and now is, the case? Is it because of any deficiency in the quantity of ores at our command? That you may yourself answer this question, I here, leaving this State wholly out of consideration, present you with an account, by a recent traveller, of some of the midland counties of Virginia, as follows:—

"I have rambled over the best portions of Goochland, Fluvianna, and Buckingham Counties, mixed freely with their people in all conditions of life, and witnessed an amount of mineral wealth of which you in the North have not the remotest conception—an amount of wealth quite equal to, if not in some instances surpassing anything to be found in California. I know that much of what I am about to tell you may be received with incredulity; but facts are stubborn things, and nothing is easier than for those who may doubt me to come here and look with their own eyes.

"That Virginia contains the precious metals every geologist and mineralogist has long been aware; and there can be but few intelligent readers who are ignorant of the fact that enormous fortunes have been extracted from isolated places of wide reputation—such, for instance, as the London Mine, in Buckingham County, in this State. But very few, I venture to say, know the vast amount of treasure which runs through Virginia in her entire length—a distance of not less than two hundred miles, by at least sixty miles in width.

"In that magnificent belt of richness, revealed to her by the same mighty convulsion which heaved the Blue Ridge chain of mountains from her womb, are to be found, in the greatest abundance, gold, silver, copper, iron, platinum, cinnabar, lead, plumbago, tin, coal, roofing-slate of the most durable kind, marble of the rarest beauty and perfection, and a variety of other valuable mineral substances—such as gypsum, limestone soapstone, hone-stone, equal to anything Turkey ever produced—too long for enumeration."

What is here said of these few counties is almost equally true in reference to the whole uplands of the South, fuel and ores, and especially iron ore, abounding to an extent wholly unknown in any other country of the world; and it is in behalf of that region of marvellous mineral and metallic wealth, as well as in her own, that Pennsylvania has asked protection. The idea of preventing the growth of "domestic competition" for the purchase of ores, or for the sale of iron, finds, as I am happy to say, no place in *her* record.

Among the richest of the States in these respects is Alabama, fuel abounding and her ores being fitted, as I understand, for production of iron fully equal in quality to the very best obtained in Pennsylvania.

Crossing the Mississippi, we find in North Louisiana, according to a report recently made to the Legislature by the Hon. Mr. Robertson,

"Iron ore so abundant as absolutely, at some points, to obstruct agriculture. Vast heaps of rich ores may be seen piled up in the fields. In De Soto and West Nachitoches is a vast field of granular and argillaceous ores, many miles in extent. This iron field lies north and northeast of Pleasant Hill, and all the necessary concomitants for the successful manufacture of iron are to be found in convenient proximity and in great abundance. A large portion of Claiborne and Bienville is an immense iron bed. Jackson and Winn are also rich in their beds of iron ore. The superficial surface ores, brown hematite and granular, of these parishes, would supply hundreds of furnaces for years to come. Seven miles east of Minden is a rich field of iron, lying for miles around the base of Fort Hill, a huge hill which rises above the surrounding country in three distinct and broad terraces. Around the outer edges of these terraces are natural embankments of arenaceous boulders, each embankment some seven or eight feet in height. This bed of ore extends to within four miles of Minden on the northeast, and from that point it may be continuously traced through Mount Lebanon, and nearly to Sparta, in Bienville parish. The region around Mount Lebanon is peculiarly rich in valuable ores."

From the iron mountain of Missouri to the near neighborhood of the Gulf such ores abound, and in a profusion of which the European world has no conception, yet is our consumption, per head, less than it had been when Congress, under the lead of Mr. Walker, abandoned the road towards freedom for all, black and white, to re-enter upon that pro-slavery one to which we had been indebted for the numerous crises which had occurred between 1837 and 1842.

These are striking facts, and such as would, in any other country, command the consideration of men professing to be statesmen. Here, however, they are not regarded as sufficient to offset the demand for cheap iron made by Massachusetts makers of pins or penknives who fail to see that the greater the "domestic competition" for the sale of their raw material, the cheaper must it become, and the greater the growth of the domestic commerce the more must be the demand for both pins and knives.

Turning now to France, badly supplied with ores, and compelled to look for coal to Belgium and to Britain, we find the domestic production and total consumption, foreign and domestic, in the last six years, to have grown as follows :—

	PRODUCTION.		CONSUMPTION.	
	Pig—tons.	Iron—tons.	Tons.	Tons.
1860 . . .	880,000	560,000	935,000	500,000
1861 . . .	890,000	672,000	1,030,000	550,000
1862 . . .	1,070,000	700,000	1,270,000	788,000
1863 . . .	1,150,000	790,000	1,330,000	790,000
1864 . . .	1,175,000	795,000	1,270,000	735,090
1865 . . .	1,191,000	848,000	1,320,000	810,000

With no perceptible increase of population, the average increase of these quantities is about 50 per cent. In twenty years of British free-trade, and its attendant crises, our own has retrograded in its ratio to numbers, when it should have quite quadrupled. Seeing all this, I find myself unable to see how we can fairly make the boast, that " we are greater than we ever were before."

It may be said, however, that is the free-trade period, and so it *will* be said by those who find their profit in blinding our people's eyes to the fact that French free-trade meant merely the passage from prohibition to highly protective duties; and, that the protection this day enjoyed by those engaged in developing the mineral resources of France, is fully equal to that given by our tariff of 1861, before internal taxes had so nearly nullified the little that had been granted. In proof of this permit me to refer you to the following comparative table :—

NAMES OF ARTICLES.	Quantities.	French duties under the Reciprocity treaty in American money.	U. S. duties under the Morrill tariff.
Iron, pig, and old cast iron · .	ton.	$4 39	$6 00
Iron, old broken wrought . .	ton.	6 35	6 00
Iron, bar	ton.	13 68	15 00
Iron, railroad	ton.	13 68	12 00
Iron, sheet	ton.	25 41 to $31 28	20 to $25
Iron manufactures; pipes and solid columns . . .	ton.	8 30	11 20
Iron manufac.; heavy wrought	ton.	17 58	20 00
Iron manufactures; small wares	ton.	29 39	22 40
Iron manufactures; cut nails .	cwt.	97¾	1 12
Iron manufactures; wr't nails	cwt.	1 46½	2 24
Iron manufactures; anchors, chains, cables . . .	ton.	19 54	30 to $33
Iron manufactures; tubes of wrought iron, large . .	ton.	25 40	44 80
Iron manufactures; tubes of wrought iron, small . .	ton.	48 85	44 80
Steel in bars of all kinds . .	lb.	1 3-10c.	1¼ and 2c.
Steel in sheets above 1-12th of an inch thick . . .	lb.	2c.	2c. and 15 ℔c.
Steel in sheets under 1-12th of an inch thick . . .	lb.	2⅝c.	2½ and 15 ℔c.
Steel tools in pure steel . .	lb.	3⅓c.	30 ℔ cent.
Steel sewing needles . .	lb.	8¼ to 17½c.	20 ℔ cent.

Of far more importance, however, than any moderate difference in the amount of duty, is the fact that in France development of the mineral resources of the country is held to be a matter of national importance. *Canaille* like those, jew and gentile, gratuitously supplied by England for teaching our legislators how to obtain cheap iron, are there not tolerated, Frenchmen having too much self-respect to permit such interference in their domestic arrangements. The iron man of France can, therefore, go confidently ahead, making the large investments required for facilitating cheap production. Here, on the contrary, *as if with a determination that iron never shall be cheap*, the sword of Damocles is always held suspended over him, and he perishes at last for the simple reason that no one dares to lend him the amount required for making the improvements that are needed. Had our legislation in the past exhibited anything like common sense, or real national feeling, we should have now no need for measures of reconstruction.

How rapid has been, and now is, the German progress will be seen on an examination of the following facts: In 1850, the product of steel was valued at $350,000. Ten years later it had reached $1,400,000. Five years still later, having meantime endowed the world with the great gift of the Bessemer process, the figure reached was $10,000,000. In 1850, the total value of pig and wrought iron was but $15,000,000; whereas, in 1865, it had grown to $55,000,000; and all this vast increase was but preparation for new and further movements in the same direction, arrangements, as we are told, having recently been made for great extension of operations.

Five and thirty years of protection have sufficed for constructing the greatest empire of Europe—a true pyramid, based upon the mineral and metallic resources of the State. The same five and thirty years have been by us expended in the effort to create an inverted pyramid with its apex resting upon the cotton and woollen mills of Massachusetts; and with such success that, after expending thousands of millions of dollars, wasting property to the amount of other thousands of millions, and destroying lives to the extent of hundreds of thousands, we are now engaged in an effort at *reconstructing* the rickety edifice, taking no note of the fact that its permanent existence would be in opposition to all experience, as it would be certainly opposed to all the teachings of science.

Were it this day possible so to raise the duties on iron, and commodities of which iron is the chief component, as to make them almost prohibitive, at the same time giving assurance that, despite the claims of pin or penknife-makers, the protection so granted should endure for even one decade; were it possible, I say, to do this, the close of that period would see iron cheaper here than elsewhere in the world; we should then export iron instead of gold; and then it might be possible to speak with truth of our existing *greatness*.

Three and thirty years since, when the protective tariff of 1828 had enabled us to extinguish the whole national debt, even that which bore an interest only of three per cent.; when the treasury was full to overflowing; when, for the first time, we had achieved a real independence; when immigration was for the first time growing rapidly; then, and then only, could we honestly have made any claim to greatness. Seven years later the country was so utterly without credit that the same bankers who had been paid, at par, a loan at three per cent., utterly refused to lend a single dollar at six per cent. Where was *then* our free-trade *greatness*?

Five years later, the tariff of 1842 having meantime *reconstructed* the country, we had become strong enough to dictate law in the halls of the Montezumas, and to add California to the Union. Then, for the second time, might there have been made some little claim to the idea of greatness. Little more, however, than a dozen years of British free-trade next sufficed for rending the Union asunder and placing both the parts at the feet of Britain.

Two years since, when protection and the greenback at home, and British hostility abroad, had combined for promoting material and moral independence, and had enabled us to pass safely through the war, we might again have laid some claim to be considered "great."

Where, however, are we now? We have a *bigger* country, having added Walrussia to our territories. We have a larger foreign debt than any country of the world. We pay a higher rate of interest than any other with claim to be considered civilized. We produce more of the precious metals than any other, and so perfect is our independence that not a dollar of either gold or silver can be retained. We have the *friendship* of England, and it clings to us as pertinaciously and destructively as did the poisoned shirt of Nessus to the shoulders of Hercules. Having closed our rolling-mills, we now import iron at the monthly rate of $2,000,000, and pay for it in gold-bearing bonds. Having closed our glass-houses, we now import whole cargoes of coal and sand in the shape of window-glass, and pay for them in the gold of California. Having destroyed the demand for coal, we are now destroying the powers of the land itself by which that coal is yielded. Having reduced the consumption of cotton to little beyond the point at which it had stood twenty years since, and having thus compelled so large an export as to have already reduced the British price to ten-pence, we have imposed a tax upon our reconstructed brethren of the South, of probably $100,000,000, and this at a time when they specially need our aid.

Such are the evidences, as they present themselves to my mind, of the *declining greatness* achieved since the peace. Believing that before the close of another decade, if the Massachusetts policy be maintained, you will see the country arrive at a condition even worse than that of 1861, at that perfection of littleness which, forty years since, was exhibited by what is now the *really* great and powerful Germanic empire, I remain, with much regard,[*]

Yours, very truly,

HENRY C. CAREY

Hon. Henry Wilson.

Philadelphia, Sept., 1867

LETTER NINTH.

Dear Sir:—

Half a century since the vast country west and north of the Ohio, with its extraordinary wealth of soil, that soil, too, underlaid to an extent elsewhere unknown with coal and ores, contained but half a million of inhabitants. From that time to the present its population has gone on increasing until it numbers now a dozen millions; yet, during nearly all that time has it been required by the allied Southern and Eastern States, that its farmers should altogether fail to profit of the great mineral treasures by which they had been everywhere surrounded, and by aid of which they would long since have been enabled to create a great domestic industry and a varied agriculture. The one desired that food might be low in price that they might cheaply feed their negroes; the other desired " cheap raw material" of every kind, that they might obtain and maintain a monopoly of the cotton manufacture. Compelled thus to go abroad for iron, all the materials of which lay beneath their own proper land; compelled, too, to send their wool abroad to be returned in the form of cloth—the people of that vast territory have found themselves limited in their cultivation to those white crops of which the earth yields but little, and which, for that

------

[*] Since writing the above I have received a very interesting account of the mining operations of Belgium, giving the following facts :—

From 1850 to 1863 the increase of production was as follows—

Of coal, per cent.	100
" mineral, per cent.	100
" forges and mills, per cent.	300
" foundries, "	250

In proportion to the numbers of her people Belgium now produces eight times as much coal as France, between twice and three times as much as Prussia, only one-fourth less than Great Britain, and the quantity doubles every fifteen years. This, too, occurs in a country whose coal fields scarcely exceed in their extent those of our anthracite region alone, and whose population increases so very slowly that a century and a half would be required for its duplication.

reason, could alone bear carriage to distant markets. Green crops, of which the earth yields by tons instead of bushels, and by means of which the soil is best prepared for white ones, have, as a rule, been interdicted, the cost of transportation to distant cities having been greater than the prices that could be obtained when those cities had been reached. The place of consumption being far distant from that of production no manure could be returned upon the land; and, as a necessary consequence of this, it became yearly poorer than before. The greater its poverty the more imperious became the necessity for change of place, and thus it has been that a few millions of people have been scattered over a surface capable of feeding half the population of the earth. The more they scattered the more did they become subjected to damage to their crops resulting from winters of so intense a cold as to compel them to postpone to spring the sowing of their various seeds. The more they scattered over the prairies the greater became their need for fencing, and for their own protection against the winter's blast, and the greater became the difficulty of bringing from a distance the lumber so much required. The more they scattered the more were they compelled to place their dependence on a single crop, and the greater their losses resulting from excess of moisture or of heat. The more they scattered the greater became the need of roads, and the greater the difficulty of obtaining iron, the ores of which, and the fuel with which to smelt them, lay beneath their feet; they themselves, meanwhile, wasting annually a larger amount of force, physical and mental, than would have been required for erecting furnaces, forges, and rolling mills, in quantity sufficient to supply with iron all the people who could then, or now, be found between the Rocky Mountains and the Atlantic.

The single form that agricultural improvement has taken throughout almost the whole territory has been that of machinery for facilitating the reaping of the crops, large or small, that have been yielded by land from which the soil has been, and is being, annually carried off to distant markets. With every such *improvement* less and less has been consumed at home, the result exhibiting itself in the fact, that the average yield of wheat by the originally fertile soil of Ohio, Indiana, and Illinois, scarcely exceeds, if indeed it equals, a dozen bushels to the acre.

Twenty years since Britain offered to the world, as consideration for abandoning all further efforts at industrial independence, a repeal of her Corn Laws, thereby granting to them the great boon of supplying her few and impoverished artisans with food. Germany, nevertheless, went straight ahead, and so did France, developing their mineral resources, and thus making a market on the land for all its products, the result exhibiting itself in the fact that not only has their consumption of iron increased twice, if not even thrice, more rapidly than the numbers of their respective populations, but that they have fairly distanced Britain in the importance of their inventions, the beauty and the excellence of their iron fabrics. With us the course of things was different; we having promptly swallowed the bait that had so skilfully been proffered. Abandoning the policy of freedom under which our domestic consumption of cotton and our domestic production of iron had, in the short space of four years, almost trebled, we returned to the pro-slavery British free-trade system, the result exhibiting itself in the facts that not only do we now consume less iron per head than we did twenty years since, but that our consumption of cotton is scarcely more in quantity than it then had been.

During nearly the whole of this long period Massachusetts has cried aloud for cheap raw materials, whether corn or cotton, coal, tin, lead, or iron, and to the end that they might be "cheap" she has coalesced with British iron-masters in waging systematic war upon the greatest of all national interests, coal and iron. The result, so far as regards the first, exhibits itself in the fact that, with beds of fuel so vast and rich as to be without a parallel in the world, the quantity this year mined will scarcely exceed, if, indeed, it equals, the *addition* made to the British quantity as compared with that of seven years since.

Such having been the price paid for the privilege of underworking the British agriculturist and supplying the British artisan with "cheap" American food, we may now, for a moment, look to see to what extent the end in view has been obtained.

At the date of the repeal of the Corn Laws the import of wheat into Great Britain, as given in an article just now published, was 1,141,967 quarters, or, in round numbers,

about . . . . . . bushels	10,000,000
By 1850 it had grown to	44,000,000
In 1858 it was	43,000,000
" 1860 "	59,000,000
" 1861 "	70,000,000
" 1862 "	93,000,000
" 1865 "	48,000,000
" 1866 "	60,000,000

Of these enormous quantities how much have we, owners of what we had been accustomed to look upon as the granary, *par excellence*, of the world, on an average of the last ten years, supplied? Just *sixteen millions*, that being the mess of pottage for which Mr. Secretary Walker sold our birthright, and that being the great trade in whose behalf our Massachusetts friends require that we close our mines and furnaces, and import, duty free, our railroad bars! For every dollar's worth of food that we send to Britain, France sends, as I think, three or four. Why? Because France avails herself of her mineral resources, few and poor as they are, and thus creates a real agriculture! Because, refusing to profit of the almost inconceivably vast mineral wealth at our command, we compel our farmers to export their soil to distant markets, with daily diminution in the power of the land to yield return to labor! Because French policy tends to "stimulate domestic competition" for purchase of the rude products of the field, and for the sale of finished commodities! Because, with us, the extreme North and the extreme South have always been united in a policy whose object has been that of compelling the West to look South or East, and not homeward, for any market for its products. Because the pin and pen-knife makers of the East can command the votes of Massachusetts, at the cost of those who mine the coal and produce the iron by means of which blockades have been maintained.

The "cheap raw material policy" having now, with slight exception, prevailed for twenty years, let us for a moment inquire into the progress thus far made.

In the first four months of the present year the total of our domestic exports was, in round numbers, $184,000,000, the equivalent of $120,000,000 in gold.

Of this Cotton furnished	.	.	.	$108,000,000
Gold	.	.	.	19,000,000
Coal-oil and oil-cake	.	.	.	6,000,000
Tobacco	.	.	.	6,000,000
Breadstuffs and provisions	.	.	.	22,000,000
Lumber, rosin, and turpentine	.	.	.	6,000,000
Whale-oil	.	.	.	1,000,000

Making a total of $168,000,000,

the products of little else than the rudest labor, and leaving but $16,000,000, the equivalent of $11,000,000 in gold, as the representative of an amount of industrial capacity that has no equal in the world, and that ere this, under a system tending to "stimulate domestic competition," would have placed us in a position to convert the whole of this food and cotton into cloth; to give to the world $50,000,000 per month of commodities whose production would be tending daily towards stimulating into full activity all these faculties for whose development we maintain our public schools.

Men and nations, my dear sir, become greater as they more and more acquire the power of self-direction. France finishes all her commodities, and can go with them *where she will.* We, more enlightened as we think ourselves to be, send forward all our products in their rudest form, and go with them *where we must.* The one requires the world to come to her, and *determines the price they must pay;* the other, always seeking buyers, piles up her goods in Liverpool and Havre, and leaves to French and English manufacturers the power to determine *at what prices they will consent to take them.*

In all this you may see proof that "we are really greater than we ever were before." If growing dependence on the will of foreign traders can be taken as evidence of growing greatness, then are you wholly in the right. If growing independence is to be taken as such evidence, then are the Germans in the right, and the policy they pursue is precisely the antipodes of that now advocated by the literary and political representatives of Massachusetts.

Yours, truly,

HENRY C. CAREY.

HON. HENRY WILSON.

PHILADELPHIA, April, 1867.

LETTER TENTH.

DEAR SIR:—

Even before the war a great change had already commenced in regard to the sources from which the northern supplies of cereals were to come, Tennessee and North Carolina furnishing large supplies of wheat greatly superior in quality to that grown on northern lands, and commanding higher prices in all our markets. From further south, and almost to the Gulf, we now learn from an important public document before referred to, that—

"Wherever the United States cavalry camped in Louisiana, during the war, wheat, rye, oats, and barley sprouted from the seed scattered where they fed their horses, and, when undisturbed, headed finely and ripened well—*the extraordinary size and weight of the wheat and barley heads showing that the soil was peculiarly adapted to their growth.* A gentleman, residing in the swamps of Assumption, assures me," says its author, "*that he has raised wheat and rye for twenty-two years, and that he has never had a failure; both grains frequently made forty bushels to the acre.* I have cited these instances to show that wheat has been raised, time and again, under all sorts of circumstances, and on every kind of soil in Louisiana."

In other cases as many as 60 bushels to the acre have been obtained. It ripens in May, and its market value may be judged from the facts that while—

"The daily quotations show that Southern flour, raised in Missouri, Tennessee, and Virginia, brings from three to five dollars more per barrel than the best New York Genesee flour; that of Louisiana and Texas is far superior to the former even, owing to the superior dryness, and the fact that it contains more gluten, and does not ferment so easily. Southern flour makes better dough and maccaroni than Northern or Western flour; it is better adapted for transportation over the sea. and keeps better in the tropics. It is therefore the flour that is sought after for Brazil, Central America, Mexico, and the West India markets, which are at our doors. A barrel of strictly Southern flour will make twenty pounds more bread than Illinois flour, because, being so much dryer, it takes up more water in making up. In addition to this vast superiority of our grain, we have other advantages over the Western States in grain growing. Our climate advances the crop so rapidly that we can cut out our wheat six weeks before a scythe is put into the fields of Illinois; and being so near the Gulf, we avoid the delays in shipping and the long transportation, the cost of which consumes nearly one-half of the product of the West. These advantages, the superior quality of the flour, the earlier harvest, and the cheap and easy shipment, enable us absolutely to forestall the West in the foreign demand, which is now about 40.000,000 of bushels annually, and is rapidly increasing, and also in the Atlantic seaboard trade. Massachusetts, it is calculated, raises not more than one months' supply of flour for her vast population. New York not six month's supply for her population, and the other Atlantic States in like proportion. This vast deficit is now supplied by the Western States, and the trade has enriched the West, and has built railroads in every direction to carry towards the East the gold-producing grain. We can, if we choose, have a monopoly of this immense trade, and the time may not be far distant when, in the dispensation of Providence, the West, *which contributed so largely to the uprooting of our servile system and the destruction of our property, will find that she has forced us into a rivalry against which she cannot compete, and that she will have to draw not only her supplies of cotton, sugar, and rice, but even her breadstuffs from the South.*"

Is it, however, for breadstuffs alone that the North is likely, with our present exhaustive cultivation, to be compelled to look to the South? It is not; the sweet potatoe, which can be grown on "every acre in Louisiana," and of which the yield, even at present, "averages 200 bushels to the acre," having, during the war, been fully tested in feeding hogs, and having, quantity and quality of the pork considered, been found, *pound for pound*, fully equal to Indian corn, of which the average yield of the States north and west of the Ohio is less than a third as much. With careful cultivation it has been known to yield more than 600 bushels, or six times as much as can, with equal care and close to Eastern markets, be obtained of the great staple of the North, thereby enabling those who are in the future to cultivate those rich Southern lands wholly to supersede the Northwest in the work of supplying animal as well as vegetable food to the people of the tropics and of Europe.

Sixty acres to the hand, it is said, may be cultivated in grain. Combining with this the raising of cotton the effect of diversification of agricultural pursuits is thus exhibited:—

"With one-fifth of our former labor, it is, therefore, clearly practicable to put every inch of cleared land under cultivation. Thus, under the present system of labor, a cotton or sugar plantation of 600 acres would require 100 hands to cultivate it exclusively in either cane or cotton, for two years' experience has taught us that five acres to the hand is all that can be successfully accomplished in these crops, while twelve or fifteen active hands will suffice to cultivate and take off fifty acres of cotton and 450 of wheat, rye, or barley, by the aid of the well-tried, improved implements in every-day use at the North and West, and at much less expense for teams than would be required if cotton alone were planted."

Turning now to fruits, we find the State under consideration, which is, however, to a great extent the type of the whole of those bordering on the Gulf, to be capable of yielding "in unusual proportion nearly all those of the other States," and very many of the tropical ones.

"Oranges, superior to those of the West Indies, are grown in all the lower portion of the State, and are rarely hurt by the frost. The trees attain, in some places, a great size. I measured one at Lake Charles, in Calcasieu, eleven years old, which was over thirty feet in height, and, at a foot above the ground, was three feet five and a half inches in circumference, and which, I learned, had produced near 2,500 oranges the past season, one of which weighed eighteen ounces. Bananas have been largely cultivated during the last ten years, and now adorn every dwelling. Citrons, mespilas, lemons, jujubes, pomegranates, guavas, and even pine apples, are cultivated in all Lower Louisiana, while the fig, the pear, the apple, the peach, the plum, the apricot, the nectarine, the quince, the cherry, the almond, and every variety of grape and currant, grow in every part of the State. Dewberries, blackberries, mulberries, gooseberries, huckle or whortleberries, strawberries, and raspberries, are found as wild and indigenous fruits. The peaches, pears, and figs of Louisiana are peculiarly sweet and luscious. Fruit-raising is one of the most remunerative employments."

Hops may be seen "growing thriftily and bearing abundantly." The State is "prolific in native dye-plants." In its forests abound "nearly every variety of tree known in the United States." For cattle raising it is perhaps the finest country of the world. Turn, therefore, in which direction we may, we find that nature has provided for that diversification of demand for human service for which we look in vain amid the fields of northern States. Seeking for it in these latter, we find ourselves compelled to look below the surface, and there alone; yet there it is that Massachusetts, anxious to protect her pin and pipe makers, insists that it shall not be sought.

The war has already made great changes, yet are they, as it would seem, but preliminary to greater in the future, as you will see by the paragraphs that follow :—

"Vast numbers of freedmen could be hired for one or two months at a time, for liberal day wages. This system is in conformity with their ideas and notions of work; they reluctantly contract for a year. Rye, barley and buckwheat have been tried in Louisiana. Barley and buckwheat are both natives of a southern climate, and flourish remarkably well here. *In Texas, during the past year, the papers state that eighty-five bushels of barley were made to the acre in Central Texas.* Sixty bushels could easily be made here, and as it is superior to the northern barley for brewing, the fourteen breweries of New Orleans would alone consume vast quantities of it. *Barley, as compared with corn, is a better food for stock, particularly work stock,* as it is muscle producing and does not heat the system like the oil or fat producing property of corn, *and while it produces three times as much to the acre, of grain, the stock consumes all of the straw.* A hand can cultivate much more ground in barley than corn, and it needs no working after planting. Grain growing would not only be profitable to the planter, but it would build up New Orleans, and make her the greatest city on the continent. What New Orleans lacks is a summer trade; her business has been heretofore compressed into six or eight months. After the cotton and sugar crops had been received and disposed of, the merchants and tradesmen had nothing to do. Most of them went North with their families, leaving New Orleans a prey to epidemics, when a small portion of the very money which they had earned in New Orleans, and were spending so lavishly abroad, would have perfected sanitary measures, which would have protected her from the epidemics. During this season of inactivity nearly all branches of business are suspended; the merchant must, however, pay house rent, insurance, clerk's hire and other incidental expenses; must lose interest on his investments, and have his goods and wares damaged by rust, dust, moth and mould. If the cultivation of grain were begun and encouraged around New Orleans, grain would pour in during the month of May, and the summer months, and would fill up this fatal hiatus in our trade.

"The merchant would be compelled to reside here in summer as well as winter, and he would be forced on his own account to lend his time and money towards building up the city and improving its health.

"Every branch of business would be kept up then throughout the whole year, and *our own steamships would supply the countries south of us with provisions, and we should not, as now, be compelled to import coffee by way of Cincinnati.* Northern and European emigrants, knowing that our grain growing was more profitable than at the North, and that *they could grow grain without working during the summer months in that sun they have been wrongfully taught to dread, would flock to our lands; and of course, where provisions and all other necessaries of life would be cheap, manufactures would necessarily spring up, to work up the raw materials so abundant here.* I have thus lengthily urged the cultivation of the cereals, because I find so little is known among the most intelligent, as to the capabilities of our State in this respect, and because, too, I think that therein lies the true secret of recuperation and permanent prosperity for our people. It is a business which all classes of agriculturists may profitably engage in, from the poor farmer of the pine hills to the rich planter of the coast. It is a business in which every landholder, lessee, laborer, mechanic, manufacturer, tradesman, merchant, ship-owner, and, indeed, every citizen, is deeply interested, as it is a question of large profits and cheap bread, and the State of Louisiana and the United States have a deep concern in it, as large owners of land in the State. I have placed grain first in the list of productions, for looking to the future, *I am sure that grain will become our leading staple, and that New Orleans is destined to become the leading grain market of the world.*"

Such being the Southern anticipations, the question now arises, are they likely to be realized? That you may yourself answer this question, I ask you now to look again at the West and Northwest and see—

First, that as a consequence of that Massachusetts policy which requires that raw materials of every kind, coal, lead, and iron not excepted, shall be low in price, the West has thus far been wholly deprived of power to bring the miner and the manufacturer to the side of the farmer, and thus to relieve its producers from the burthensome and destructive tax of transportation.*

Second, that, as a necessary consequence of this, the powers of the soil have gradually diminished and are diminishing, with constantly increasing necessity for scattering over more widely extended surfaces, with steadily augmenting tax for commissions and for freights, and constantly increasing exposure to loss resulting from excess or deficiency of moisture, from excessive heat or cold.

* At the moment at which I write I find notice of sales of corn in Iowa at 8 cents per bushel, yet does the State abound in ores whose development would make demand for all the food that could be raised.

Nearly twenty years have now elapsed since the then head of the Patent Office, an eminent agriculturist, estimated our "annual waste" of the mineral constituents of corn, under the "cheap raw material" system, at the equivalent of 1,500,000,000 bushels of corn, and told the nation that if such "earth butchery" were continued, the hour would soon arrive when "the last throb of the nation would have ceased, and when America, Greece, and Rome would stand together among the ruins of the past." From that hour to the present, with but slight exception, we have moved in the same false direction, the result now exhibiting itself in the fact that the great West, the "granary of the world," has so little food to spare that the whole amount of our export is much less than is now required for payment of the mere interest upon debts contracted .in Europe for cloth and iron that should have been made at home. This present season has been a fine one for the farmer, and for months past have we been assured that it would in a great degree compensate for the short harvests of the past two years; but the actual result now presents itself in the following passage from the *Tribune* of the day on which I write :—

"Advices from the West in regard to wheat are unsatisfactory. An extra yield has ceased to be talked about, and the fact is apparent that it threshes out poorly in comparison with the estimates before harvest. Measurement shows 12 and 14 bushels where 25 per acre were expected, and the increased breadth sown will scarcely make up for the deficit in yield. So far as wheat is concerned, cheap bread cannot be realized from the crop of 1867, nor are the prospects better for corn at the present moment. Already Western experts are buying old corn on speculation, paying $1 25 per bushel, against 83 cents in September, 1866. This state of things is in marked contrast with the general expectations forty days since, and will modify many business calculations then made. Instead of an abundant harvest of wheat and corn to make cheap bread, and consequently cheaper labor, high prices appear inevitable, with all the attendant disasters. Instead of a crop which would tax the rolling stock of railroads to their utmost, and enable them to clear their books of floating debt, managers are brought face to face with the fact that there is not an average crop, and that its transportation will yield little profit. To traders this changed appearance of the crop is of vital importance. Instead of a full crop to be used in the payment of old debts and in exchange for new commodities, producers from this year's labor promise to be left where old debts must be neglected, and new purchases made sparingly."

Need we desire better evidence than is here furnished that the raising of raw produce for the supply of distant markets is the proper work of the barbarian and the slave, and of those alone? I think not. Twenty years of the Massachusetts system—that one which claims for its own people all the protection they need, while denying it to the people of the Centre, the West, and the South— that one which refuses to "stimulate domestic competition" for the *purchase* of raw products, or the *sale* of finished ones—have sufficed for so reducing the power of the whole body of loyal States to maintain commerce with the outer world that *their whole exports, gold and bonds excepted, scarcely more than suffice for meeting the demands of Europe for interest and freights*—leaving but little for payment even of the travelling expenses of our people, now amounting to scarcely less than $100,000,000 per annum.

The remedy for all this has been provided by nature, which has underlaid the soil with coal and ores, but Massachusetts wars upon the miner and thus compels the farmer still further to exhaust the soil by sending wool and corn in their rudest forms to distant markets, there to be exchanged for other wool and corn in the forms of cloth and iron.

At the South nature has provided for removal of all existing difficulties, having placed the farmer in such position that not only is he nearer to the great markets for his products in their original forms, but that he may convert his wheat and his sweet potatoes into cotton, into pork, oranges, or any other of the numerous fruits above referred to, for all of which he finds an outlet in the various markets of the world. Seeing these things, and seeing further, that its whole upland country presents one of the most magnificent climates of the world, can it be doubted that the day is at hand *when emigration to the South and Southwest must take the place now occupied by emigration to the West, and when power is to pass from the poor soils of the Northeast to those richer ones which now offer themselves in such vast abundance in the Centre, the South, and the Southwest?* As I think, it cannot. In my belief the time is fast approaching when northern intelligence will be everywhere found engaged in teaching southern men how they may be best enabled to square their long-running account with the men of Massachusetts; and when almost every town and village of the South will be found offering protection to the makers of pins and pipes, nails and bars, tubs and buckets, shoes and cloths, in the manner here described as having but now occurred in Maine :—

"The town of St. Albans, Somerset County, Me., recently voted to exempt from taxation, for the space of ten years, any sum not less than ten thousand dollars that might be invested in any permanent manufacturing business."

That such is now the tendency of the Southern mind is clearly obvious. Look where we may throughout the South and Southwest, we meet with evidence of the facts that their people have profited of the experience of the past few years, and that they now see the necessity for making themselves independent of the North. The Report now before me everywhere urges the development of the vast mineral resources of the country—the establishment of furnaces and forges—the erection of cotton-mills—and closes with a proposal for the establishment of a Bureau specially charged with carrying these ideas into full effect, and authorized to offer premiums to those who may engage therein. Such is now the feeling of every Southern State, and such will certainly be its course of action.

The day for all this is at hand. Is Massachusetts preparing for it? Is she making home so attractive as to lessen emigration? Is she not, on the contrary, under the "cheap raw material" system, now expelling more rapidly than ever before her native population, replacing it with one greatly inferior drawn from distant lands, and thus lowering the standard of all? Of this there can be no doubt whatsoever.

How may this be prevented in the future? How may she be enabled to maintain her position, prospering in common with the South, the West, and the Centre? To enable us to obtain the answer to this question let us now for a moment study the widely different policies of France and England.

The one has been engaged in *protecting* herself, never having warred upon the rival industries of other countries. To that end she has always sought, as she is now seeking, to place herself in the lead of the world as regards artistic development, and this is now as much exhibited in her iron works as it so long has been in the factories of Lyons and St. Etienne. Selling much skill, and but little raw material, she cares little how much this latter costs, and can, therefore, afford to permit the rest of the world to pursue the course of action that leads to freedom.

The other, on the contrary, has been steadily engaged, not only in preventing elsewhere the growth of diversification in the modes of employment, but in destroying it wherever it previously had existed. To that end she has been competing with the lowest priced labor of the world. Selling mere brute force, and much raw material, she cares greatly about the cost of this latter; and, in the effort to cheapen it, she has become the promoter of slavery, whether black, white, or brown, in every region of the world. Her words, like those of Massachusetts, are words of freedom, but her policy, again like that of Massachusetts, is that which tends to put the whip in the hands of the slave-driver, whether in the bank or on the farm, in the factory or on the plantation, be the color of the slave what it may.

The one becomes from day to day more independent of the tariff regulations of the world. The other becomes from hour to hour more dependent, and hence it is that she now seeks so anxiously to make amends for her discreditable conduct during the recent war. Hence, too, it is that she now pays so liberally all the men amongst ourselves, home grown and foreign, who employ themselves in teaching our people the *advantage* to be derived from tearing out and exporting the soil, and carrying it thousands of miles over lands so filled with coal and iron ore that the match thereto can be found in no other country of the world.

Of these two policies, the one tending towards elevation of the laborer, the other toward his depression—the one toward national independence, the other toward national dependence — which is it that has thus far been followed by Massachusetts? Is it not the "cheap raw material" one—that one which tends towards subjugation of the laborer and perpetuation of the national dependence ? That it is so cannot be questioned, nor can it be doubted that it is in this direction we must look if we desire to find the cause of the change now occurring in reference to the character of her population. Let that change go on as it now is going, and the day will not be distant when she will find that her day of power is over, and that she must be content to take her place among the great trading communities of the past. Holland was once all powerful, but the hour is now at hand when she will take her proper place as merely one of the provinces of the great Germanic Empire.

Desiring to retain her place in the Union, Massachusetts should at once awake to the fact that her policy has been selfish and illiberal, and that it can end nowhere but in ruin. Let her then promptly recognize the existence of a harmony of interests among all the portions of the Union, and let her see that the more the southern people can be led to convert their cotton into yarns and cloth the greater must be the demand upon her for those finer goods she may so soon be prepared to furnish. Let her follow in the train of France, making demand for taste and brains instead of muscle, and she will then retain her native population. By that course, *and that alone*, will she be enabled to retain her influence, and to regain, in the commerce of the world, that position which, under the "cheap raw material" system, she has to so great an extent already lost.

She has been long engaged in making bitter enemies, and they abound in nearly every quarter of the Union. Let her now, by manifesting a *real* love for freedom, a *real* love for the Union, a *really* national spirit, seek to convert those enemies into friends. Fully believing that if she fail so to do she will herself be the greatest sufferer,   I remain

Yours faithfully,

HENRY C. CAREY.

Hon. HENRY WILSON.

PHILADELPHIA, Sept., 1867.

LETTER ELEVENTH.

DEAR SIR :—

Seeking to obtain financial reconstruction we must begin by an industrial one, it being wholly impossible that we should ever again avail ourselves of the services of the precious metals so long as our commercial policy shall continue to impose upon us a necessity for not only exporting the whole produce of California, but of sending with it gold-bearing bonds to the annual extent of almost hundreds of millions of dollars. In like manner must both industrial and financial reconstruction precede the political one that is to have any, even the slightest, chance of permanence. The former are the bases on which the latter must rest, and therefore is it that I so much regret your having in your Address so wholly excluded both from notice.

The industrial question having been now to some extent examined, although not by any means exhausted, I propose next to ask your attention to the financial one, as follows:—

In speaking of the currency it is usual to refer to that portion of it only which takes the form of circulating notes, leaving wholly out of view that which exists in the shape of credits to individuals on the books of banks, and which have been, and always must be, the real causes of financial crises. By a recent report now before me of the condition of the national banks, the amount of those credits was about $500,000,000, the whole of which large sum, with the exception of about $100,000,000 remaining in bank vaults in the form of specie or legal tender notes, had been lent out and was then bearing interest. The difference, $400,000,000, constituted the currency created by banks, and liable at any moment to contraction, at the will of bank directors.

Again, the daily creation of currency in those forms in which it comes before the clearing houses, amounts, in this city and New York alone, to more than $30,000,000.

The persons chiefly contributing to the creation of this latter form of currency number by hundreds, and with many of them the daily amount counts by hundreds of thousands. In like manner some few hundreds of persons control institutions to which the country stands indebted for the former, and thus it is that we obtain what may properly be characterized as the *aristocratic* form of currency creation; that form which seems most to please our legislators and our finance ministers, as, not only do they wholly fail to inquire into the expediency of leaving so much power in the hands of private individuals, but *to them*, precisely, is it that they always look for advice as to the further measures needed to be pursued. The shepherd thus asks of the wolf how he may best provide for the safety of his sheep, the wolf giving for answer precisely such advice as promises most to enable him to gobble up the flock with comfort to himself.

For the poor sheep there is provided a currency which takes the tangible form of circulating notes; that one by means of which the shop-keeper is enabled promptly to pay the farmer, the workman to pay the shop-keeper, the employer at once to pay his workmen, and the merchant to pay on the instant the manufacturer. This is the *democratic* form of currency, and therefore is it that it has been always so much vituperated by that sham-democracy which has clamored so loudly in behalf of hard money and British free-trade. It is, too, that form in which it is being now maligned by that portion of the republican party which so much believes in maintaining protection at that point precisely which seems best to suit the purposes of Massachusetts, as nowhere "stimulating domestic competition" for the purchase of those raw products she

needs to buy, or for the sale of those finished ones she needs to
sell. In this she is doing little more than imitating the action of
that democracy of the past which has so frequently sought the
prohibition of notes below ten or twenty dollars, and has so uniformly ended by bringing about impoverishment of the people,
the ruin of merchants, the stoppage of banks, the repudiation of
State debts, the creation of *shin-plasters*, and the almost utter
bankruptcy of the national treasury itself.

The years previous to the war were, throughout the West and
South, marked by an exaggeration of the almost ruinous state of
things by which the crisis of '57 had been attended. The farmer,
desiring to sell his potatoes, his fruits, his corn, was required to
accept "store pay," or retain his produce on his hands unsold.
The miner, in like manner, was required to accept "orders" on
store-keepers who fixed prices to suit themselves. The little Western farmer, desiring to mortgage his farm to obtain the means with
which to improve it, was required to pay two or three per cent.
per month, or even more. Everybody was in debt, not from want
of property, but because of the absence of any medium of circulation by aid of which the coal operator and the farmer could be
enabled to pay the store-keeper, and the latter to buy for cash in
the cities with which he dealt.

The war gave us in the "green-back" the machinery by means
of which labor could promptly be exchanged for food and fuel,
cloth and iron, and at once all was changed. Forthwith the
societary circulation became rapid, and with every step of progress
in that direction the nation acquired strength. To the tariff of
'61, to the "greenback," and to the State in which I write, have
we been indebted for power to make the war, and therefore, perhaps, it is, that the whole period of peace has been characterized
by an incessant war upon them, each and all.

Next in order came the establishment of a national banking
system, in itself a good measure, but so very bad in its details
that, if they be not corrected, it must inevitably bring about a
separation of the trading States of the North and East from the
producing States of the Centre, West, and South.

Requiring a deposit of the whole capital as security for redemption of the circulation, it throws the banks on circulation and
deposits for power to perform the services for which they were intended. Taxing them heavily it thus produces a necessity for
over-trading, and for thus causing that inflation of which our
eastern friends so much complain, but which they will be the last
to remedy, for the reason that they themselves so largely profit by
it. By a recent statement now before me, the joint capital of
the national banks is shown to be . . . $418,000,000
while the amount of their interest-bearing investments is 1,122,000,000
thus closely approaching three to one.

Turn back now, I pray you, twenty years, and study the operations of the banks in your own vicinity, those which have most

freely furnished circulation, and have most uniformly met their obligations. Doing this, you will find that while the loans of Rhode Island institutions rarely exceeded their capitals to the extent of *a third*, those of your own State rarely went beyond *a half*, or fifty per cent. In both, the banking system presented true pyramids, with elevation that was slight in proportion to their bases; whereas, the national one gives us an inverted pyramid the greatest breadth of which is found in the air, and which may, therefore, be readily toppled over.

Why is this so? Because this latter is *a great money monopoly*, for the especial benefit of the Trading States. Limiting the amount of circulation to $300,000,000, it by that means limits the capital to be applied to the great money trade—*the most important of all trades;* and does so for the reason that outside of the cities the deposits are so very trifling in amount.

A monopoly having been thus created, we may now inquire who they are that profit by it. Doing this, we find that the Eastern States, with perhaps a twelfth of the population, have had granted to them above a third of this monopoly power; that New York, with an eighth of the population, has almost a fourth; that this State, with a population nearly as large as that of New England, has been limited to little more than an eighth; that to Ohio, Indiana, and Illinois, with a population far more than twice as great as that of New England, there has been allowed little more than a third as much; and, that for the vast region beyond the Mississippi and south of the Delaware and the Ohio—containing more than two-fifths of our population—there has been allowed *just one-ninth;* or less than is *daily manufactured* in New York and Philadelphia.

Do the people of New England, my dear sir, find that they have too much of the machinery of circulation? Do those of New York? Do they not, on the contrary, frequently complain that the notes cannot be found that are needed for the work to be performed? How then must it be with this State whose needs have been supplied to but little more than a third of those of the New England States? How must it be with Ohio and her immediate neighbors? How, above all, must it be with the almost thirty States and territories that with a present population *four times as great* as that of New England, are allowed banking powers and privileges *less than a third* as great.

The money shop is denied them. The power to create local circulation of any kind is denied them. Pressed thus to the wall, one southern city made an effort to provide for enabling its own people to make exchanges with each other, but then down came Congress with a tax of, I think, ten per cent. upon such local circulation. In this manner it is, my dear sir, that our northern and eastern friends, luxuriating in their full supply of banks and circulating notes, are furnishing the "warm and generous greeting" of which you so recently have spoken.

As a consequence of this it is, that New York and New England are now enabled to lend circulating notes on the best, security, at the south, at two per cent. per month; and that southern people now pay, regularly, three, four, five, and even, as it has been stated, ten per cent. per month, for the use of little pieces of paper issued by northern and eastern banks for the private profit of their stockholders. Such *may* be the road to permanent reconstruction, but if it is, I, for one, must say, that it does not so to my mind present itself. Bad as is all this, we are promised that it shall, for the unfortunate people outside of the Trading States, yet be worse. Up to this time they have had the advantage of some portion of the " green-back" circulation, but of that they are, as our Finance Minister insists, to be gradually, but certainly deprived. The circulation, as he gravely assures us, is quite too large, and contraction is to be, as he so long has desired that we should understand it must be, the order of the day. This the West resists, and moves the House that further strengthening of the money monopoly of the trading States, New York and New England, be dispensed with. The vote being taken, but sixty-five votes are found adverse to the motion, and of these there are from

New England and New York 38
All other States . . . ⌊ . . 27
———
Total 65

The majority, favorable to the doctrine of equal rights among the States, numbers 95
Of these there are from

New England and New York 13
All others 82

The vote for the resolution outside of the Trading States is therefore more than three to one. Were the question now to be taken, it is doubtful if even a single adverse vote could be found south or west of those States. Outside of them the treasury system has scarcely a friend. Why should it have ? In no country of the world is the supply of currency so small when compared with the commerce for whose service it is needed.

Of the " green-backs" the amount at present existing is but $370,000,000
Of national bank-notes there are less than . . 300,000,000
———
$670,000,000

Of these the quantity always in bank, or in the treasury, and thus out of circulation, is never less than 170,000,000
———
Leaving but . . . $500,000,000

for the service of nearly 40,000,000, scattered over a whole continent. Of this the little New England has, legal tenders included, more than a fourth, leaving the balance for the service of the less fortunate portion of our population. One of two things is certain: either New England has thrice too much, or the rest of the country much too little. The former does not think she has more than she needs, and will relinquish none. Neither will she agree to any increase elsewhere. On the contrary her people, in and out of Congress, lecture the unfortunates who have not the happiness of residing east of the Hudson, after the following fashion :—

"If the people of this country could be made to see that the present expanded currency is not a blessing but a curse; that it is one of the most unequal and burdensome of taxes; that it gives undue value to capital as compared with labor, thus pressing most heavily on the working classes, tending to make the rich richer and the poor poorer; that it stimulates speculation (which is gambling under a less offensive name) by turning the most active and ambitious men from the occupations of production to those of exchange, from mechanics and farmers into brokers and middlemen; that it drives men from the country into the cities, in the hope of sudden wealth, and because it is thought more respectable to buy and to sell than to labor with the hands; that it subverts all true notions of value and produces such constant fluctuations as to make honest industry insecure of its rewards; if the people can be made to see all these evils, and will open their eyes to the enervating, demoralizing consequences, they will patiently and cheerfully submit to the temporary hardships which are involved in reducing this redundant currency to its normal proportions; they will by all their influence strengthen the hands of Congress and of the Secretary of the Treasury, that the day may be hastened when this country shall again conduct its domestic and foreign dealings on the basis of the only currency which can render trade secure—that of the precious metals."

The author of this, my dear sir, is one of your own constituents—one of those who, in common with the rest of the New England people, have secured for themselves a fixed and certain allowance of currency more than three times greater than is, by law, now allowed to nearly thirty States and Territories, with a population five times greater, and standing greatly more in need of tangible machinery of circulation. Do you, however, find in it any suggestion that the monopoly now existing shall be in any manner modified; that the power already obtained over the currency shall in any way be lessened? Not in the least. It says to the Centre, the South, and the West, surrender a part of the little we have left you, and let our monopoly be rendered more complete, and more than this it does not say.

The day, however, for all this is past. Massachusetts must determine voluntarily to abandon the idea of manufacturing, money, and trading monopolies, or she will raise such a storm in the Centre, the West, and the South, as will compel her so to do. Fully believing this, and as much believing it to be the duty of Pennsylvania, as Keystone and Guardian of the Union to take the lead in a movement to that end, I remain,

Yours very truly,

HENRY C. CAREY.

Hon. H. Wilson.

Philadelphia, September, 1867.

LETTER TWELFTH.

DEAR SIR :—

The Fort Wayne decree of Secretary McCulloch, likely to prove of far more enduring importance than the Berlin and Milan decrees of the Emperor Napoleon, is now nearly two years old. As it stands it constitutes the great financial blunder of the age, having already, by the paralysis of which it has been the cause, cost the country more than the whole amount of the national debt. Let its policy be persevered in and it will constitute the greatest in history, for *it will have cost the Union its existence.*

Gladly hailed by the capitalists and bankers of your State, and by the gentlemen who represent them in Congress, *contraction* has, from that day to the present, been the burden of their song. What, however, was it that they desired to see contracted? Any portion of the $100,000,000 of circulation that they had so promptly appropriated to their own especial use? Any part of the $170,000,000 appropriated by the combined Trading States, New York and New England? Certainly not. That for whose *contraction* they have since so loudly clamored constituted nearly the whole machinery of exchange throughout the Producing States with their present population of 30,000,000, likely very soon to be 50,000,000. For these, their unfortunate *subjects*, there was to be allowed in all the future the fixed amount of $130,000,000, or, even now, but *four dollars* per head; the compact New England, whose need, per head, for some tangible medium of circulation, was not one-half as great, meanwhile luxuriating in a circulation of *thirty* dollars per head, and finding even that not to be at all in excess of its actual wants.

On a former occasion, as you may recollect, it was shown that your State, in its anxiety for commercial reform, had magnanimously and liberally offered to the West, in exchange for what it claimed to need, a surrender of the rights of its late allies of the Mining Centre. What then was done has now been repeated here, her anxiety for financial reform having led her to insist upon a total surrender of the rights of the Producing States, and the member for Lynn having uniformly taken the lead in insisting that such surrender should be made. A monopoly of the money power had been obtained, and it was to be maintained even at the cost of reducing the whole people of the Producing States, loyal or disloyal, to the condition here described as now existing in the Mormon State :—

"Wheat is the usual legal tender of the country. Horses, harness, vehicles, cattle, and hay are cash; eggs, butter, pistols, knives, stockings, and whiskey are change; pumpkins, potatoes, sorghum molasses, and calves are 'shinplasters,' which are taken at a discount, and with which the Saints delight to pay their debts (if it is ever a delight to pay debts). Business in this community, with this currency, is a very curious and amusing pastime. A peddler, for instance, could take out his goods in a carpet-bag, but would need a 'bull' train to freight back his money. I knew a man who refused an offer to work in the country at fifty dollars a month because he would need a forty-hundred wagon and four yoke of oxen to haul his week's wages to the whiskey-shop, theatre, &c., on Saturday evening. * * * When a man once lays out his money in any kind of property, it is next to impossible to reconvert it into money. There is many a man here who, when he first came into the valley, had no intention of remaining but a short time, but soon got so involved that he could never get away without making heavy pecuniary sacrifices. Property is a Proteus, which you must continue to grip firmly, notwithstanding his slippery changes, until you have him in his true shape. Now you have him as a fine horse and sadddle; presto, he is only sixty gallons of sorghum molasses; now he changes into two cows and a calf, and before you have time to think he is transformed into fifteen cords of wood up in the mountain canon; next he becomes a yoke of oxen; then a 'shutler' wagon; ha! is he about to slip from you at last in the form of bad debts?"

Place, I pray you, the people of Massachusetts in this position, and determine for yourself how they would think and *act*. Study the picture, for it is a tolerably accurate one of that which now prevails throughout a large portion of the Centre, South, and West.

To the hour at which was issued that most unfortunate and ill-advised decree there had still remained in existence most of that *faith in the future* by means of which we had been carried safely through the war. From that hour it began to pass away, and with each successive day there has been seen an increased desire to *centralize* in the trading cities the disposable capital of the country—hoarding with banks and bankers, trust and deposit companies, at small interest, the means that otherwise would have been employed in opening mines, building furnaces, mills, or ships, mining coal, or making cloth. From that unfortunate hour works of national importance were abandoned, mills and factories commenced to contract their operations, coal tended more and more to become a drug in the market, and the demand for labor to decline. From that hour money tended to accumulate in all those cities, and to become more and more inaccessible to men by which it could be made to create demand for human service. From that hour the poor tended to become poorer and the rich to become richer, till, as now, the Boston capitalist obtains twice the war rate of interest, the little Western farmer, as is shown by the following passage from a money article of the day on which I write, meanwhile gradually returning to the enormous rates of the period before the war:—

"At the West rates of interest are, as usual, far in advance of our home figures. *An agency has been established in Boston, within a very short time, for negotiating first-class Western mortgages at ten per centum.* In Cincinnati the bank depositors have to pay from eight to nine per centum, and the lowest street rate is ten per cent. Two per cent. a month is not a very uncommon figure out West. In the southwest the rates of interest would appear enormous to even the eyes of the sharpest Eastern note-shaver. *In Memphis three to five per centum a month are common figures."—Press.*

Such being the state of things in the green wood, what will it be in the dry? When the Secretary made his speech denunciatory of the best currency the people had ever had, the legal-tenders stood at $400,000,000
On the first of last month we had . . . 369,164,344

Reduction in 22 months $30,835,156

There are yet, therefore, to be withdrawn nearly $370,000,000. When that shall have been done may we not hope to hear of agencies in the Eastern States for negotiating first-class Western mortgages at more than double the rate above described? That we shall do so, I feel quite assured.

The money monopoly already here established is, I am well satisfied, the worst at present in existence in any country claiming to rank as civilized; yet is it now seriously proposed to make it from day to day more complete, and thus to establish a subjection to the money power of our whole people, black and white, without a parallel in financial history.

We are, however, gravely told that it is in this manner alone that we are to be enabled to return to the use of the precious metals. What has been our progress in that direction, in two years of paralysis throughout which the Secretary has been unremitting in his efforts at contraction, will be seen on an examination of the following figures, representing millions of dollars :—

	Oct. 1865.	Oct. 1866.	July, 1867.
Banking capital . . .	393	403	418
Interest-bearing investments .	1,020	1,060	1,122

Twenty-five millions have thus been added to the base, a hundred meanwhile to the superstructure, and the edifice having more and more assumed the form of an inverted pyramid that may at any moment be toppled over. So must it continue to do for every hour of the future in which the McCulloch-Massachusetts system shall continue to be maintained, the direct effect of paralysis being that of giving increased power to banks and bankers, and all others of the class which controls and regulates that portion of the currency which has been designated as *aristocratic*, and from which our crises always have come and must always come.

To the $100,000,000 of the incorporated banks may now, as I doubt not, be added half as much, additional to the quantity that had been usually controlled by individuals, and by institutions other than banks, in those war days when the public policy tended to favor those who had money to borrow and labor to sell, instead of, as now, favoring those who have money to sell and labor to buy.' That $150,000,000, *centralized in the few trading cities, does more to produce that which it is the fashion of the day to call inflation than would be done by five times the amount of greenbacks scattered among the* 30,000,000 *of people inhabiting the Producing States.*

By its help it is that money is made cheap to the British iron-master who places his products in the public stores, while made so dear to the coal-miner that he becomes bankrupt by reason of inability to borrow at two per cent. per month. By its means the country is flooded with foreign iron requiring for its payment $2,000,000 per month of California gold. By its means our people are being from hour to hour more compelled to look to the large cities as the only places at which exchanges can be made, and the more they are so compelled the higher becomes the taxation of the Producing States for maintenance of owners of New York and Boston hotels and houses. The higher that taxation, and the poorer the people of the Producing States, the greater becomes the ability of owners of city property to live abroad, and thus to swell the amount of *travelling bills* that have already reached so high a figure as to require for their payment a sum equal to nearly the whole amount of the exports of the loyal States, leaving little beyond gold and bonds with which to pay for foreign merchandise consumed at home. Study carefully these facts, my dear sir, and you will find little difficulty in understanding how it is that the Massachusetts policy is now compelling us to go abroad to borrow money, on the security of the State, at almost thrice the rate of interest paid by Britain.

According to Mirabeau, "capitals are necessities, but," as he added, "when the head grows too large the body becomes apoplectic and wastes away."—British free-trade, and Massachusetts determination to resist any measure tending to promote "domestic competition," have combined to make of the little territory east of the Hudson a head so large that we are threatened with precisely the state of things above described. The "waste" is now going on, and, unless the system be resisted, must so increase as to produce financial, moral, and political death; that, too, despite all your efforts at political reconstruction.

Prices, however, it is insisted, must be reduced. So were we told two years since by men who did not trouble themselves to study the fact that years were needed for enabling us to restore our stock of hogs and cattle, cows and horses, even to the point at which it had stood before the war. So are we now told by others who do not care to see that constant exhaustion of the soil of the West and Northwest has made our supplies of food more precarious than they had ever been before.* That some prices must

---

* The average quantity of certain articles that passed the New York canals in the three seasons 1848, 1849, and 1850, closely following the

have been reduced is shown by statements of the *Tribune* in reference to the number of persons now wholly unemployed in New York city. That others have been reduced you may find on visiting our mining region, where men who are not wholly unemployed are compelled to accept half war prices in return for labor, while paying almost war prices for the food consumed by their families and themselves. Petroleum has become so complete a drug that most of the wells have been abandoned, and the men who therein had been used to labor have been dismissed. Cotton, by reason of the closing of our mills, has been piled up in Liverpool until it, too, threatens to become as great a drug as it had been in the good old British free-trade times when British manufacturers could pick and choose at five pence. Contraction is, throughout the Producing States, putting down the price of American labor and its products, while putting up the prices of money, cotton cloth, and various other things that Massachusetts has to sell, yet has the process but begun. It is carrying into full effect the idea that, so far as I am informed, was first broached in the Newport Convention twenty years since, that "domestic competition" must be prevented, whether for purchase of raw materials or sale of finished goods; and with the further addition, that there is not in the future to be allowed, throughout the Producing States, any competition with the trading States for the sale of money. The monopoly of that important trade is now in the hands of these latter; and that it is to be rigorously maintained has been proved by Massachusetts action throughout the last Congress.

The tax on cotton being specific, the lower the price the more burthensome does it become. The McCulloch-Massachusetts policy has largely reduced its price while doubling the rate of interest paid by its producer, yet is the tax collected. Such being one of the "warm and generous greetings" extended to our erring brethren of the South, the question now arises as to how many such will be required for producing resistance in a form that, when it shall come, *as come it must*, will result in perfect achievement of the object.

Taxes are heavy. Collected in the Trading States, they are finally paid in those Producing States to which it is now proposed to allow a circulation of *four dollars* per head, the people of New England meanwhile jealously retaining their *thirty dollars* per

passage of the pro-slavery tariff of 1846, and in the first half of the present and the past seasons, is as follows :—

	Seasons of 1848, '49, '50.	Half seasons, May 1 to July 31, 1865, '66, '67.
Flour, barrels	3,224,000	148,000
Wheat, bushels	3,126,000	1,500,000
Corn, "	3,700,000	4,300,000
Pork, barrels	69,000	5,000
Beef, "	87,000	2,400

In that time the population, chiefly occupied in tearing out and exporting the soil, must have more than quintupled.

head, and lending out the surplus to the Centre, South, and West at prices varying, as we see, between ten and fifty per cent. per annum. Moving in this direction, how long, my dear sir, will it be before we shall attain a perfect reconstruction? Shall we not sooner reach a new rebellion? I think we shall.

Throughout the war we were steadily congratulated on the facts, that the certificates of public debt were nearly all held at home— that the number of small bond-holders was immense—that we had thus an important security for punctual payment of the interest. Since the peace all this, however, has been changed, the great object now sought by the Treasury, and by our Massachusetts friends, to be attained, being low prices for human service and for all the rude products of mining and agricultural labor. The lower those prices the greater becomes the necessity for selling the little fifty dollar bond in which had been invested the savings of a year, and the greater the centralization of certificates of public debt in the hands of Eastern and European capitalists. Going ahead under the McCulloch-Massachusetts system, the time must soon arrive when nine-tenths, or more, of this interest will need to be paid north and east of Pennsylvania, in the Trading States and in Europe; the Producing States meanwhile paying nearly all the public taxes, and thereto adding two, three, if not even five, per cent. per month, for the use of circulating notes so liberally allowed to our New England friends. Should this system be maintained, might it not lead to non-payment of the interest? I think it would.

On occasion of the dedication of the Gettysburg Cemetery, Mr. Lincoln declared that this was "a government of the people, by the people, and for the people;" and in this most of my fellow-citizens of the Centre are in full accord with him. They do *not* believe that it is a government of the Centre, the West, and the South, by the North and East, and for the special benefit of the trading States. Well will it be for the people of these latter if they can at an early date arrive at the conclusion that Mr. Lincoln had been right and that their whole policy, directly opposed thereto as it has been, had been a most unwise one!

Mr. McCulloch's policy has been one great mistake, and it has proved a most costly failure. Seeing, that the law had created a monopoly of the money power; that while it limited the base of the edifice it set no limit to the elevation; that with every hour it was becoming more top-heavy and more in danger of being toppled over; seeing all this, I say, he should have asked of Congress an extension to the people of the Producing States of all those powers which had been so fully granted to the trading ones, and he should have then encouraged the creation of local institutions for the service of the 30,000,000 of people who are now so unjustly, and unconstitutionally, made mere hewers of wood and drawers of water for their brethren of the northeast. So doing, he would have prevented that accumulation of capital in trading centres which has been so freely used for speculation in commodities of first necessity, to the heavy loss of those by whom they were needed. So doing, he would have been aiding in the construction of mills and furnaces, and in the cheapening of cloth and iron. So doing, he would have made a home market for the hundreds of millions of bonds that have already gone to Europe, each new bank becoming a holder thereof to the whole extent of its circulation. So doing, he would have tied the States together, and would have been bringing about the "more perfect union" that we had all so much desired. Not having so done, he has brought about a state of things so purely sectional that it must, *and should*, provoke resistance.

At this moment circulating notes are very scarce in Eastern cities. Why? Because of the help demanded by their poor clients of the South and West for movement of their very little crops. Why, however, cannot the Producing States help themselves? Why not, like Massachusetts, *make* such notes? Why, bone and sinew of the country, and ultimate payers of nearly all the taxes, as they certainly are, should they be held in such complete dependence? Because they are being made mere puppets whose strings are to be pulled at their master's pleasure! To make the thing complete, it is now required only, that the "greenback" be annihilated, and that all banks south and west of the Hudson be required, as it is meant they shall be, to place in New York City lawful money with which to redeem their notes. Thereafter, the wolves may, at their entire convenience, devour the poor and unfortunate sheep, *as it is proposed they shall do.*

More than any other State is Pennsylvania representative of the 30,000,000 of the Producing States: more than with any other, therefore, is it for her, in the existing state of things, to study her rights and her duties. So doing, she finds that to herself she owes it to insist that her citizens be placed on a precise equality with those of the Eastern States. To the Centre generally, to the South, Southwest, and West, she owes it to *demand* for them now, as in all the past she has done, the enjoyment of all the rights and privileges she claims for her people and herself. To the whole Union she owes it to *demand* the abandonment of that monopoly system which now threatens to defeat all efforts at reconstruction. To the world at large she owes it to interpose in behalf of the impoverished Southern people, and more especially of those colored men who are now threatened with a money tyranny more injurious in its effects than the slavery from which they have but now been rescued.

Such are her duties. That they will be performed I feel well assured. Fully believing that you, were you one of her citizens, would desire that they should be so, I remain

Yours, very truly,

HENRY C. CAREY.

Hon. H. Wilson.

Philadelphia, September, 1867.

LETTER THIRTEENTH—AND LAST.

DEAR SIR :—

England believes in buying raw materials at low prices and selling finished goods at high ones. It is her *one* Article of Faith; that one her belief in which has brought about a necessity for reconstruction at home and abroad, in England herself and all her dependencies. France, under the imperial regime, has been following in the British footsteps, with daily growing necessity for a reconstruction the day for which cannot be now remote. Both are declining in influence, and thus are furnishing new evidence of the fleeting character of trading power. Our trading States take Britain for their model, and so rapid is their progress in the false direction that, while still dreaming of *reconstruction*, they are already face to face with a *dissolution* which, if allowed to come to pass, will prove a permanent one.

Germany and Russia, producing States, desire that raw materials should be high in price and finished commodities cheap. So do our Centre, South, and West. Natural allies of the two advancing countries of Europe, our fast friends throughout the war, these latter may safely leave the Trading States to their alliance with those declining ones which so gladly gave their countenance to the rebellion, and which now so clearly see that maintenance of their own political power is dependent wholly upon preventing permanent reconstruction here.

The tendencies of the two portions of the Union are thus, as we see, in opposite directions, and most especially must this be so now that the war has on one side *removed* the obstacle that had prevented combined action, while on the other it has *created* trading, manufacturing, and moneyed monopolies of fearful power. Can they in any manner be brought to act together? Will the Trading States cordially ally themselves with the Producing ones for the gradual, but certain, abolition of these monopolies? Will they agree upon a system that shall promote, and not prohibit, "domestic competition"? Upon the answer to be given to these questions now hangs the determination as to whether we are, or are not, to have a permanent political reconstruction embracing the whole of the existing States.

Prior to the Chicago Convention of 1860 it had, as I have already said, been determined by the Trading States that the platform, like that of 1856, should be confined to politics alone, leaving wholly unexpressed the desires of the people in reference to national questions of high importance. It was a British free-trade plot, well arranged, but the defeat it met was thorough beyond example. From that time to the present the Republican party, in imitation of the old Democratic one, has been playing fast and loose with the question then decided, advocating British free-trade in one State and American free-trade in another; and so, as I just now read, it is proposed that it shall continue to do in all the future. The arrangements for all this are, as I doubt not, very perfect, but *the scheme will fail*. Of that you may rest assured. The next convention, like that of 1860, will find itself compelled either to indorse or repudiate the monopolies of which I have spoken; to be for or against the doctrine of equal rights; to be American or English; to be for or against that industrial independence without which any attempt at financial or political reconstruction is a useless waste of time and words. In 1860, men who had to that time been strenuous advocates of British free-trade and industrial dependence, found themselves compelled to join in the tumultuous demonstrations of joy at the reading of that resolution by which the party placed itself on the side of American independence. So, I feel confident, will it be again. Powerful as are the Trading States, there will, on that occasion, be found not even a single man so poor as to do reverence to the monopolies that the war has given us, or has so much strengthened.

Such is my firm belief, yet it may prove that the Trading States exercise a greater amount of influence than I anticipate, and that the advocates of high freights, dear money, dear cloth, and cheap raw materials, whether "wool or hemp, coal or iron," succeed in obtaining an indorsement of the policy of Massachusetts capitalists. Admitting now, for a moment, that such should be the case, what, in your opinion, would be the course of the people of your State were they to be at once transferred to the hills and valleys of Pennsylvania? Might they not, do you think, be disposed to invite *a Conference of the Producing States*? Might they not, in that invitation, show that the Trading States had had but one end in view, that of compelling the producing ones to make all their exchanges through the ports of New York and Boston, and through the mills of Old and New England? Might they not show that to the trading monopoly which had so long existed there had now been added a monopoly of the money power by means of which its holders had already become enabled to tax, almost at discretion, the people of the Producing States? Might they not show that every effort was now being made so to strengthen that monopoly as to render it tenfold more oppressive than as yet it had become? Might they not show that while the real wealth and strength of the country was to be found in the Producing States, their agents, the merely Trading States, had now become so confident as to have ventured to defy resistance? That done, might they not proceed to say—

That throughout a large portion of the Producing States, but most especially in the South and Southwest, there existed a wealth of soil, and a mineral wealth, without parallel in the world:

That what was needed for the development of both was population:

That immigration had always grown with great rapidity in periods of protection, while it had always decreased in those of British free-trade:

That to enable the people of Europe readily to reach the rich lands of the Centre, the South, and the West, it was indispensable that their owners should themselves be enabled freely to communicate with the whole outside world through the various ports that fringe the coast from the Delaware to the Rio Grande:

That to enable northern people to pass from the now exhausted lands of the West and Northwest, and thus obtain power to participate with their owners in the development of rich Southern lands, it was indispensable that roads should be made leading North and South, and not, as now, exclusively East and West:

That to the end that such roads might be made, and such ports be used, it was indispensable that measures should be adopted for enabling Southern and Western men to mine their own coal, smelt their own ores, and make their own cloth:

That the one great object always held in view by the Trading States had been that of preventing, throughout the South and West, the application of capital and labor to the work of manufacture, and thus preventing any growth of "domestic competition" for either the purchase of raw materials or the sale of cloth:

That to the trading and manufacturing monopolies which had so long existed there had now been added a money monopoly of fearful power; one whose continued maintenance could have no result other than that of making the people of the Producing States mere hewers of wood and drawers of water for those who had so long been employed in forcing themselves into the position of being their exclusive agents:

That the real power was in their own hands, and that it rested wholly with themselves to determine whether their exchanges should in future be performed in the cities north of the Delaware or south of it:

That the time had arrived for exercise of that power, and that by the adoption of proper measures they could, if they would, compel the transfer to the South and West of a large portion of the machinery now in use in the Trading States:

That to the end of arriving at some clear understanding by means of which the Producing States should be enabled to establish an equality of rights; to secure to themselves free communication with the outer world; to obtain for themselves a proper supply of the machinery of circulation; to be freed from the present ruinous charges for the use of circulating notes; to proceed peacefully and quietly in the development of the vast resources placed by nature within their reach; to obtain that real freedom of trade which can exist in no country that exports raw produce; to establish that diversity in the demand for human service by means of which, alone, can the freedman be enabled to profit by the act of emancipation; and, finally, to secure that the Union, when reconstructed, shall be permanent; this conference had been invited.

Having read the above, allow me, once again, to ask that you place yourself and your constituents in the position of the people of Pennsylvania, feeling yourselves the proper representatives of great national interests whose development in other countries has brought wealth to the people and power to the State. Study then with them the history of our past legislation, and see how little creditable have been the influences, foreign and domestic, that have prevented such development. Study with them the consequences, and see that our supplies of food become more and more irregular as we become more dependent on other nations for cloth and iron. Study with them our monetary system, and see that nearly all the power that the States at large have lost has now become closely monopolized and mainly held in a few trading States. Study with them the results that even thus far have been realized, and then see with them that the strengthening of that monopoly, now so strongly urged, must result in grinding to powder the whole people of the Centre, the South, and the West. Study all these things, and then, I pray you, answer to yourself the question as to whether you would or would not, under such circumstances, hold that you would be failing in your duty to them, to the nation, and to the cause of civilization, if you did not strongly urge the adoption of the course of action that has above been indicated. That you would I feel well assured.

Will it, you may ask, be adopted? If so, will Pennsylvania find herself among allies or enemies?

To the first I confidently answer in the affirmative. To the second, that, unlike Massachusetts, Pennsylvania has no enemies.

Penn and his successors had a great mission on this Western Continent which, thus far, has been well performed. First to provide by legislative action for emancipation of the colored race, they simultaneously with New York emancipated the weaker sex from the Common Law tyranny in regard to rights to property. First to recognize the perfect equality of the States, large and small, they, in effect, made our present Union. Occupying a frontier State, and the only one liable to invasion, they stood, materially and politically, the bulwark of that Union throughout the late rebellion.— The crowning act yet remains to be performed, in now interposing between the Trading and Producing States for the purpose of bringing about that harmony of action without which the Union neither can, nor *ought to be*, maintained; and for the further purpose of making of the Declaration of Independence something more than the mere form of words that it has thus far been. For such interposition their State stands fully qualified, her record being as bright and as free from any taint of selfishness as that of any other community whose history has been recorded. She has not now, nor has she ever had, any interest that is not common to twenty other States. Never has SHE abandoned her friends.* Never has she made demand for anything to be enjoyed by herself alone. In regard to the production of iron she stands now as far above all other States as does your State in regard to cottons, yet does she insist on that perfect protection which must aid in development of the wonderful mineral resources of the country from the Lakes to the Gulf, and from the Atlantic to the Pacific. For herself, therefore, she asks nothing. For the Union she asks, and will insist upon, that harmony and peace which must result from proper appreciation of the fact, that while it is quite in the power of the Producing States to change their places of exchange and their agents, it is not in the power of the Trading States to find elsewhere such patient milch-cows as they have thus far proved themselves to be. To make the demand therefor has now become her duty, and so great has become the dissatisfaction—I might use a stronger word—at the extreme selfishness of eastern friends, that were the question of its performance now submitted to a vote, it would command the assent of four out of five of the whole people of the State.

Might not, you may ask, a movement like that I have indicated, lead to another civil war? Certainly not. To the great natural resources of the hill and mountain country was the South indebted for power to maintain the recent war. To the more developed resources of the mountain country of the North have we stood indebted for power to extinguish the rebellion. When the whole mountain region shall be of one mind it will be found that the people of the flats can make no war. As Pennsylvania has gone so has always gone the Union. As she now goes, so will it go. She does now go for abolition of monopolies, Northern, Eastern, and British, and it may be well for our Republican friends of the trading States to know that the days of their existence have been already counted, and have been found to be very few in number.

Ten years since, after the occurrence of the great financial crisis

---

[*From the "Globe,"* Feb. 24, 1855.]

* "The manufacturers of Massachusetts were willing to assent to a reduction of manufactured articles for the reason *that it was accompanied by a still greater reduction* on raw material. * * * *

"The way to break down protection is to strike at it in detail; by detaching from its support interests that are willing to be detached."—Mr. BANKS, of Massachusetts.

"When, sir, the effort was made to detach the Pennsylvania representatives by appeals to their peculiar interests, what did you see? When we were told that ample protection would be given to the iron interest if we would strike a fatal blow at the interests of other States, the united delegation from Pennsylvania, Whigs and Democrats, answered: No!"—Mr. HOWE, of Pennsylvania.

of 1857, but in advance of his first message, I addressed Mr. Buchanan a private letter in which he was told that persistence in the policy of his predecessor would result in his own ruin and that of his party, and in dissolution of the Union. Of course he did not believe of this even a single word, it being a rule with our public men never to believe in anything until too late. That letter is, however, a tolerable history of what has since occurred. Now, my dear sir, I do the same by you. You, as I fear, will do as Mr. Buchanan did, not believing what has been predicted. Within the next decade those predictions will have become history, and your fellow-citizens may then find reason to regret that, like Mr. Buchanan, you had not believed, until *too late.*

Begging you to excuse my repeated trespasses on your kind attention, I remain, with great regard,

Yours truly,

HENRY C. CAREY.

HON. H. WILSON.

PHILADELPHIA, September 30, 1867.

POSTSCRIPT.

Since writing the above I find the following in the *New York Times:—*

THE REPUBLICAN PARTY—ITS GREATEST PERIL.

The warning of the Maine election came not a moment too soon for the welfare of the Republican party. The West furnishes abundant indications of the danger it encounters as a consequence of the determination of cliques and factions to foist upon it issues quite foreign to the recognized objects of its organization. Senator Grimes's vigorous protest against the attempt to make the prohibitory tariff a test of party orthodoxy, receives the indorsement of the leading Republicans of his State. Gen. Baker, Adjutant-General, and one of its most influential men, writes "that if the tariff lobby succeed in interpolating into the creed of the Republican party a prohibitory tariff plank, and making that the issue, the Republican party of the Northwest will be smashed to atoms." Strong as the statement is, we are persuaded that it does not transcend the truth. Throughout the Northwest the Republican press is unanimous in its denunciation of the combinations which try to manipulate the action of Congress on the tariff question; admitting the necessity of high duties in existing circumstances, but resisting any assertion of the prohibitory principle in the interest of classes.

History is constantly repeating itself. The above is but a new edition of the advice given to the party in 1860, and given by all the British free trade journals, the *Times* included. How it was then answered by the Convention we all now know, and my readers have been informed as to the reasons why the answer had been such as secured the election of Mr. Lincoln.

For a present answer I beg to offer the following paragraphs from the London correspondence of the same *New York Times*, just two days later in date :—

"The correspondents of English papers give melancholy accounts of dull business in commerce and manufactures in America; but the remedy for this is so easy, as pointed out in a *Times* leader, that it is only necessary to call an extra session of Congress and adopt it. You have only to remove all restrictions upon Free Trade. Repeal all duties upon imports, and every ship-yard would be alive with workers, every factory in full operation, and the whole country prosperous and happy. But the trouble is that nobody in America knows anything about political economy. Under the actual tariff, it is said that American manufacturers are undersold by those of England and Germany—a Free Trade would bring all right again. It happens, however, that England, with Free Trade, is scarcely building any ships, and that she is in serious danger from Continental competition. How is this muddle to be disposed of? With Free Trade, half the laboring population in England lives upon wages just above the point of starvation, with no resource in sickness or old age but the workhouse, and Ireland is in a state of chronic poverty and discontent. With Free Trade, there is a perpetual war between capital and labor, and the enormous burden of pauperism is increasing. Americans may be ignorant of political economy, but I cannot see that the English are overburdened with wisdom, or that the practical results of their system are of a very enticing character. The workingmen of England believe in protection, and the English colonies practice it, to the great annoyance of the theorists at home.

"After all, Free Trade is a proved impossibility. Parliament is constantly interfering with what, according to our philosophers, should regulate itself. The Poor Law system is itself a protective measure. So are all the laws limiting the hours and ages, and regulating the conditions of labor. We have acts of Parliament forbidding the employment of women in coal-pits, where, a few years ago, they worked naked like brute beasts; acts forbidding the employment in factories of children of twelve years; and, during the last session, laws have been passed for the protection of children in the numerous trades and in the agricultural gangs which would disgrace Dahomey. There is need of abundance more of such interference. In the black country, north of Birmingham, there is a large population engaged in making nails by hand labor—especially horse-shoe nails. On an average, three females are employed in this work to one male. I wonder if, in all America, there is one female blacksmith. Even the strongest-minded of the advocates of woman's rights have not claimed for women the trade of a blacksmith. But here little girls from seven to nine years old are set to work, and kept at work as long as they can stand, hammering at the anvil, roasting by the forge, blacked with soot, never seeing school-house or play-ground, but employed their whole lives making horse-shoe nails for a bare subsistence. Absolute Free Trade sets women and children to work at forge and mine and reduces wages to the lowest possible standard; and that is the system against which humanity protests, and with which Parliament, in spite of theories, finds it necessary to interfere. Free Trade, as ultimated in England, is the most debased ignorance, the most abhorrent cruelty, the most disgusting vice, and the most heart-breaking misery, that can be seen in any country, calling itself civilized and Christian."

RESUMPTION No. 1.

In his first report to Congress, December, 1865, Mr. Secretary McCullough told that body that the currency was in excess, and that prices were too high ; that the former must be contracted and the latter reduced ; that the debt was burdensome and dangerous, and needed to be paid ; and that, to the end that he might be enabled so rapidly to proceed in the work of payment as to complete it within thirty years, he desired to have appropriated to the discharge of principal and payment of interest an annual amount of $200,000,000. That done, he was of opinion that the day of resumption would prove to be not far distant.

In his second report (December, 1866), after expressing great regret that Congress should, so far as regarded the non-interest-bearing portion of the debt, have limited his contractive powers to $4,000,000 per month, and that he should thus have been "prevented from taking the first important step towards a return to specie payments," he urged that for the present fiscal year his powers should be so extended as to enable him to cancel circulating notes at the rate of $6,000,000 per month, and thereafter at the rate of $10,000,000 per month until the whole should have been extinguished. These things done, he believed that we should be ready for resumption in July, 1868, if not even "at a still earlier day."

The views thus presented had previously been given to the world in his Fort Wayne speech, made more than two years since. Throughout those years every effort has been made to put a stop to exchanges of property for labor. From day to day the world has been assured that prices were yet quite too high ; that they must and would fall ; that those who now built ships or houses, furnaces or factories, would find that they had given for them far more than they then were worth ; and thus has the sword of Damocles been held suspended over the heads of our people until a paralysis has been produced that is scarcely less complete than were those which accompanied the financial crisis of 1837 and 1857. Purchases are now made only from day to day, or from hour to hour, none desiring to be caught with merchandise on hand when the day of final settlement shall have been reached. Prices fall steadily, but the lower the price the stronger is the belief that there is yet before us a still lower deep, and the more the desire to refrain from supplying even the most necessary wants until the lowest deep shall have been arrived at. Threats of early resumption having brought us to this sad condition, it is now, in sheer despair, suggested that we should almost at once take the great leap, making public declaration that at an early day the Treasury would be prepared to redeem with gold its obligations of any and every kind, and that from and after that day the banks would be required, on pain of forfeiture of their charters, to do the same. The Rubicon would then have been passed ; the lowest point would then have been reached ; men would then begin again to buy and sell ; commerce would then become active ; mills and furnaces would then be built ; and prosperity would then again become the order of the day. So, at least, we are assured by those journals which advocate the Secretary's policy, and most especially by some of those of New York and New England.

The proverb, however, advises that you look before you leap, and that is what, for the benefit of our readers, we propose now to do, presenting for their consideration, to the best of our ability, an exact statement of the position at which, at the close of the second year of the contractive policy, we have arrived, and leaving to them then to judge for themselves how far it would be expedient to take the extraordinary leap that, in accordance with all the past teaching of the Secretary and his friends, is thus proposed.

The public debt is now, in round numbers, $2,500,000,000. Of this only $2,100,000,000 as yet bear interest, but to that amount there should this year be added $72,000,000, and next year $120,000,000, until at length in 1870 the whole should draw interest payable in gold, and making demands upon the Treasury to the annual extent of $150,000,000. The present demand, admitting that resumption had now taken place, would be but $126,000,000, but to this would have to be added diplomatic expenses, maintenance of fleets abroad, and payment for Walrussia, Samana, and other territories that have been or may be purchased, the whole making little if any less than $140,000,000, to be gradually increased until it shall reach $155,000,000, if not even $160,000,000.

For obtaining the gold thus needed the Treasury is now wholly dependent on receipts from customs duties, the average of which, as shown by the Treasury report, but little exceeds forty per cent. To enable us to receive from that source the sum of $140,000,000, we need to import foreign merchandise to the declared extent of nearly $350,000,000.

To this must now be added a sum sufficient to cover the under valuations, the smuggling, and the passengers' baggage, this last alone amounting to very many millions. By many, ourselves included, it is believed that these involve an additional hundred millions, but we shall content ourselves with taking them at only $60,000,000, giving $410,000,000 as the annual amount of merchandise that must be imported to enable the Treasury to obtain from that source the gold required for enabling it to meet the gold demands upon it.

Nearly the whole of our intercourse with Europe, and very much of it with the rest of the world, being now maintained by means of foreign ships, we need now to add to the above, for freights and passage money, not less than $10,000,000. It may be twice that amount, but we are content to place it at the one we thus have named, giving so far a total of $420,000,000.

To this must be added the expenses of our absentees, travelling and resident, sometimes estimated at $100,000,000. We, however, are satisfied to place them at $60,000,000, by adding which to the amount above given, we obtain as payable abroad, $480,000,000.

Adding next for dividends on stocks held abroad, and for interest on public and private debts, only $60,000,000, we obtain a total of $540,000,000 payable in foreign countries, and in gold. How is this vast demand to be met? Let us see!

Exclusive of gold and cotton, our exports, valued in greenbacks, for the fiscal year 1866, amounted to $189,000,000

For the second half of the present fiscal year they were $83,000,000. Taking the same amount for the first half, we have a total of   166,000,000

It is little likely that those of the present year will be greater, but we are content to estimate them at   190,000,000

Contraction having closed many of our cotton mills, while forcing very many of them to work short time, the domestic demand for the raw material has so far declined that the price has fallen to less than 18 cents, or about $80 per bale of 450 pounds.

Of the last crop we exported 1,216,000 bales, yielding, probably, little short of $200,000,000. The present one, as now reported by the Bureau of Statistics, will give but 1,568,000 bales, of which we should retain, even with the present diminished consumption, 650,000. This would leave less than 1,000,000 for export, giving $80,000,000 as the amount to be added to the miscellaneous list, and making our total exports, gold excepted, $270,000,000.

Converting this into gold, we obtain less than $190,000,000 with which to meet demands that, as has been shown, exceed $500,000,-000.* For the balance we *must* give either gold or bonds. As regards the first, however, the same influences are at work to prevent extension of mining operations throughout the centre, the west, and the south. Paralysis forces capital back to the commercial cities, and gold mines remain unworked that under a different system would even now be yielding tens of millions. Coal and cotton, gold and iron, feel thus alike the benumbing effects of a policy that to us appears the most vicious that has ever been proposed by any finance minister the world as yet has seen.

Under such circumstances, what would be the value of a declaration on the part of the Treasury of its ability to resume payment in specie of its obligations? Would any sane man believe that it could do so for even a single week? If none such could or would do so, could resumption have any effect other than that of distributing among private hoards the gold now hoarded in

---

* It is positively asserted that the report above referred to is wholly incorrect, and that the cotton crop will exceed 2,000,000. Should this prove to be the case, the addition in gold to be made to our exports may be $25,000,000, giving a total of $215,000,000.

Treasury vaults? That done, to what quarter would the Secre-tary look for means with which to meet demands for interest?

This question is submitted in the hope that some of those who now so strongly advocate the Secretary's policy may be induced to explain how it is that, in their belief, resumption may be first attained and then maintained   C.

RESUMPTION No. 2.

The Secretary's friends seem unwilling to exhibit the process by means of which, in their belief, resumption may be either attained or maintained. They do not explain how it is to be—the age of miracles being supposed to have passed away—that, in the face of an annual deficit in our transactions with foreigners which now counts by hundreds of millions, and that grows with each succes-sive year, we are to be enabled to retain among ourselves the produce of our mines with a view to resumption of the use of the precious metals. They have little relish for calculations other than those furnished by the Treasury, no two of which seem to be much in harmony with each other. They shriek "resumption," at the same time threatening that if the legislative authority shall in any manner interfere with the Secretary's plans, "the movement will be delayed at least by Executive interposition." It is thus threatened that if Congress shall, as it certainly must, arrive at the conclusion that continuance in the policy of contraction can have no result other than that of repudiation, the President will interpose his veto, in the hope and belief, as we suppose, that he may be thus enabled to succeed in placing the loyal and the rebel debts on a level with each other. To accomplish this would cer-tainly please him much, and none are laboring more to gratify him than are those professed friends of resumption, and professed opponents of Executive usurpation, by whom this threat has but now been uttered. How far Congress will find itself disposed to afford him such gratification we have yet to see.

The New England States, as represented in Congress, are urgent for an early return to specie payments. Why? Because, with little more than *a twelfth* of the population, they have secured to themselves more than *a third* of the great money monopoly that, under the new banking law, has been created! Because, to those States, small as they are, there has been granted an average circu-lation of no less than seventeen millions! Because, the large amount of capital that has been there allowed to be invested in banking prevents necessity for the over-trading that exists in the less favored States of the centre, the south, and the west! Be-cause the channels of commerce are there so abundantly filled with notes of every size as almost to annihilate demand for either legal tender notes or the precious metals! Because, but very few millions would suffice for supplying all their needs; and because those millions would, on the day of resumption, be at once obtained from Treasury vaults! Because, being creditor States, they desire that all existing claims shall be paid in gold, the commodity of highest value! Because, being purchasers of wool, cotton, and other raw material, they desire that the agricultural and mining States may find themselves compelled to accept the lowest prices! For all these reasons the votes of eastern members are almost unanimously favorable to the Treasury policy of contraction.

Equally unanimous in their opposition to it are the people occupying the vast Territory south of the Delaware and the Ohio and west of the Mississippi, fifteen millions in number, and likely soon to be thirty millions. Why? Because, to their thirty States and territories, with *two-fifths* of our total population, there has been allotted but a *ninth* of the great money monopoly that now exists. Because, while the average circulation allotted to the little New England States is more than $17,000,000, that allotted to their States and Territories scarcely exceeds a single million! Because, by reason of the monopoly that has been created they now find themselves almost entirely dependent on legal tenders for machinery of circulation! Because, to give them gold by means of which they should be placed upon an equal footing with the highly favored eastern States, would require more than thrice the quantity now in Treasury vaults! Because, even now, they gladly pay from two to five per cent. per month for the use of circulating notes issued by eastern banks, for the private profit of their stockholders! Because, with every step in the progress of contraction, the price of money tends to rise, and that of wool or cotton tends to fall! Because, even now they find themselves ground as between the upper and the nether millstone! Because, being debtor States, they prefer to pay in the commodity that was receivable at the date of contraction of the debt! Because, being sellers of raw products, they do not desire to be thrown on the "tender mercies" of eastern traders, leaving to them to fix the prices at which they will receive those products. For all these reasons the people of two-thirds of the States and territories of the Union, rightly believing that the Treasury policy can have no result other than that of making them mere hewers of wood and drawers of water to their more favored brethren of the east and north, are to a man opposed to it.

Before the war, with a banking capital of 85 millions, the New England States had a circulation of 34 millions. To-day, with 145 of the one, they have 103 of the other—this latter having more than trebled in the short space of seven years. Thus well provided at home, they find themselves ready to dispense with Treasury notes.

With an almost equal population and almost equally engaged in other than agricultural pursuits, Pennsylvania's share in the great money monopoly is but little more than a third as great, whether as regards either capital or circulation. Therefore is it that she is more dependent on the use of Treasury credit, and quite determined to resist the policy of contraction.

Before the war, Georgia had 16,000,000 of capital and half that amount of circulation. To-day, she is most graciously allowed to have two of the one and one of the other.

Before the war, Missouri had nine of capital and eight of circulation. To-day, greatly growing as she is, she is most kindly permitted to have four of the former and two of the latter. Need we then wonder that her people, as well as those of Georgia, see in the Treasury policy nothing but absolute subjection to the will of eastern capitalists and utter ruin to themselves? Most extraordinary would it be did they fail so to do!

The tendency towards resumption thus exists in the precise ratio of the presence of those substitutes for the precious metals which almost annihilate the demand for gold. On the other hand, the opposition to it exists in the direct ratio of such absence of those substitutes as makes those metals the almost exclusive medium of circulation. Such being the case, the road towards specie payments would seem to lie in the direction of placing the centre, the south, and the west as nearly as possible in the same position with the eastern States, giving them notes of every denomination, and thereby lessening the demand for gold. Directly the reverse of this, however, the Secretary insists that they shall now surrender the legal tender notes, and make almost exclusive use of gold and silver. Whence, however, are these to come? Paralysis, caused by Treasury action, forbids development of their mining interests, and mines remain unworked that, under other circumstances, would furnish the supplies that are now so greatly needed. Thus is it that the Secretary is busily engaged in burning the candle at both ends, diminishing the supply of the very commodity by means of which, almost alone, he insists that the people of those numerous States and territories shall make exchanges of food for labor, of labor for cotton, cloth and iron. This *may* be the road towards resumption, but to us it seems more like that which finds its end in repudiation.

Study the Secretary's policy where we may, we obtain the same results. The seven-thirties make no demand for gold. Compound interest notes make none. Legal-tenders make none. That they may be enabled so to do, it is needed that the form of debt be changed, and that gold-bearing certificates, fitted for exportation, be issued in their stead.

That is the work on which the Secretary is now engaged, his whole energies being given to the manufacture of bonds for European markets. With each successive bond exported there arises a new demand for gold with which to pay abroad the interest. With each there is increased facility for importing cloth and iron that should be made at home. With each there is increased demand for gold with which to pay the duties. With each there is a diminution in the product of oil and cotton sent to distant markets.

In all times past it has been held that the road towards resumption lay in the direction of diminishing demand for the precious metals, while increasing the supply thereof. All this, however, is to be now unlearned, the Secretary having discovered that the more the supply can be diminished and the demand increased, the sooner shall we attain the much-desired end. It may be that it will thus be reached, but if it shall be so, there will thus be furnished conclusive evidence that the age of miracles has returned.

C.

[From the National American.]

INDUSTRIAL RECONSTRUCTION OF THE SOUTH.

LOUISIANA held its first grand State fair under conduct of the Mechanics and Agricultural Fair Association, on the 26th November, 1866. We have the report of its proceedings, including premium essays and addresses, and have read it with unmingled pleasure, not unfrequently heightened by surprise. One of the orators goes at large into what he styles "The causes which led to southern subjugation; and the means by which the South may be restored to prosperity and power." On a rapid examination of statements and arguments, we find nothing said and nothing omitted that a picked representative of northern opinions could improve. He traces the conquest of the South to the superior economic policy of the North—to the difference of the industries of the two sections, from which resulted all the difference of power to make and maintain the war. The hope of restoration he necessarily puts upon the frank acceptance of her situation by the South, and such change of industrial and commercial policy as shall make her self-supplying and self-supporting. In a word, she must diversify her productions, agricultural and manufacturing, after the model of the Northern States; and she must educate her whole people, white and black, rich and poor, up to the point of qualifying them all for their respective functions in society. Moreover, she must actively encourage the immigration of foreign mechanics and mariners, with the double purpose of making her own manufactures, and securing the domination of the white race in the social and political systems. Of which last-named motive we need say nothing, for we care nothing about a side issue of this sort. Only let them do the right things, and then the things will take care of themselves, and of their political and social issues

Altogether, it is with uncommon pleasure that we find these people growing wise, as well as earnest, in reconstructing themselves. Among the essays read at this Fair is a very brief one on "Raising Swine in Louisiana," by Judge Robertson, whose remarkable report upon the resources of Louisiana, made to the Legislature in January last, may have come under the notice of some of our readers.

The points made by the Judge are substantially these: owing to the difference of climate hogs are at least doubly more prolific in Louisiana than in Ohio or Illinois; always producing two litters in the year against one in the colder North, and bringing them to maturity with great certainty. Owing to the same cause they need no housing in the winter, and can find roots and grasses, green and fresh, for pasturage all the year. The average yield of the sweet potato there is 200 bushels to the acre, and twice as many can be raised. This root is found to make pork equally as fast as the like weight of corn; giving an average of 200 to the potato against an average of thirty bushels of corn, as the yield of food; the culture of the former being at the same time much less expensive than of the latter. Barley there averages fifty bushels to the acre, while at the North and West it is but little over twenty; it is far superior to corn in giving body and frame to the hog, and it comes so early in the season that it may be used in raising the young pigs, and preparing the stock for fattening. Louisiana produces, besides potatoes and barley for hog feed, a semitropical abundance of peas, pumpkins, peanuts, squashes, peaches (!) and Jerusalem artichokes. The Judge concludes by saying that he believes hog raising to be far more profitable for that region than either cotton or sugar planting; that they have every advantage over the Northwest in the competition; that they have salt better and cheaper; that their hams and bacon are equal to any in the Union; that they abound in the woods used for packing; and, being situated at the mouth of the Mississippi, they have the immense advantage of a short and cheap inland transportation; and, finally, that they can and will supply the world's markets with this great article of export.

It is really pleasant to the head and heart of a sound political economist to see the South thus turning her back upon the causes of all her troubles, and setting the example to the Northwest of a sound and healthy system of industrial enterprise; entering upon a course of diversified production which, of itself, will compel the Northwest to adopt a like progressive and secure economic policy. Cotton having lost its provinces, corn will be obliged to live at home. For both, the system of hazardous dependence upon distant regions is broken up forever. Let all parties take notice and prepare.

THE

FINANCE MINISTER, THE CURRENCY,

AND

THE PUBLIC DEBT.

BY

H. C. CAREY.

———————

PHILADELPHIA:

COLLINS, PRINTER, 705 JAYNE STREET.

1868.

THE FINANCE MINISTER AND THE CURRENCY.

§ 1. "In all the cities and towns throughout the country checks upon credits in banks and bills of exchange have largely taken the place of bank notes. Not a fiftieth part of the business of the large cities is transacted by the actual use of money, and what is true in regard to the business of the chief cities is measurably true in regard to that of towns and villages throughout the country. Everywhere bank credits and bills of exchange perform the office of currency to a much greater extent than in former years. Except in dealings with the government, for retail trade, for the payment of labor and taxes, for travelling expenses, the purchase of products at first hand, and for the bankers' reserve, money is hardly a necessity. The increased use of bank checks and bills of exchange counterbalances the increased demand for money resulting from the curtailment of mercantile credits."—*Report of the Secretary of the Treasury on the State of the Finances for the Year* 1867.

The Secretary here clearly recognizes the existence of two descriptions of currency, an inferior and a superior one—the former composed of notes which circulate on the faith of moneyed institutions, the latter of checks and drafts based on bank credits, and circulating on the faith of individuals. That this latter, being the superior one, tends to supplant the former, we are here assured; and that such is the natural tendency of monetary affairs is proved by all experience. The real need for circulating notes exists, therefore, always in the inverse ratio of the use of checks, drafts, clearing houses, and all other of the various contrivances for dispensing with the services of either the precious metals or the circulating note.

Between these two descriptions of currency there are these important differences, to wit:—

That the note represents actual property of the parties by whom it is issued, that property having been deposited in the Treasury as a security for its redemption; whereas the credit represents property temporarily deposited in the banks, and liable to be claimed at any instant:

That, while the note cannot be so used as in any manner to change its relation to the total currency, the credit may be, and habitually is, so used as to *duplicate* its relation thereto—A, the actual owner, and B, the temporary user thereof, both exercising equal power of purchase and equal power to create a currency of checks or drafts—that superior one with the growth of which there should be diminished need for circulating notes :

That, as the inferior currency yields no interest to its *holder*, all desire to circumscribe within the narrowest limits the quantity to be kept on hand:

That, as the superior one yields interest to its *makers*, banks and bankers seek as far as possible to increase it by lending out all the moneys placed with them on deposit :

That, as the people at large find their interest promoted by limiting the use of circulating notes the quantity in actual use changes, under ordinary circumstances, so slowly as scarcely to be perceived ; whereas, the quantity of credits, dependent as it is upon the arbitrary will of banks and bankers, changes from hour to hour, and with a rapidity that sets at defiance all calculation :

That, consequently, it is the power to create the superior currency, that based on mere credits, which demands to be regulated by law ; and *not* that inferior one which is based on property, and which finds its proper regulation in the need for its use by the masses of the people.

These things premised, we may now study the course of things under the State bank system, taking as its type the returns of 1860, as follows, the figures representing millions :—

	Capital.	Circulation.	Capital and circulation.	Investments.	Excess investm'ts.
Total amount . . .	422	207	629	807	178
New York and New England .	235	73	308	443	135
All other States and Territories	187	134	321	364	43

The first thing that strikes us on an examination of this table is the entire harmony of the facts here presented with the theory of the Secretary, and with the general impressions on the subject, the proportion of circulating notes to capital and business having been very small in those States in which a credit currency most abounded, and very large in those in which such credits were least abundant. With a bank capital of but $235,000,000, New York and New England had the use of $178,000,000 of credits created by banks for their own use and profit, being nearly two and a half times the amount of their circulation. With a capital only one-fifth less, the remaining people of the Union appear to have enjoyed the advantages of the superior currency to the extent of but $43,000,000, and their banks to have been dependent upon the profits of circulation to an amount equal to three-fourths of their whole capital, being about twice that of the trading States above enumerated.

The total currency created by banks for their own profit appears to have been as follows :—

New York and New England, with a population of 7,000,000, and a

wealth, as returned by the census, of $3,707,000,000, had credits based
upon moneys temporarily in banks to the extent of . . $135,000,000
Circulation 73,000,000

Total $208,000,000

The remaining States, with a population exceeding twenty-four millions,
and a wealth of $11,558,000,000, or more than thrice greater, had a bank-
created currency thus composed, to wit :—

Credits $43,000,000
Circulation 134,000,000

$177,000,000

In the one case banks might have lived and prospered, even had they
been wholly deprived of the profits of circulation. In the other, outside
of a few cities, no bank deprived of those profits could have existed for
even a single hour.

Fully enjoying the advantages of both the people of the one could
generally have the use of money at about the legal rate of interest.
Limited almost entirely to the circulation, and that itself in many cases
limited by absurd restrictions, those of the other were accustomed to pay
twice, thrice, and even four times that rate. With the one prompt payment was a thing of general occurrence. With the other, debt was almost
universal, not because of want of property, but because throughout a large
portion of the country there existed neither credits, circulating notes, nor
any medium of exchange whatsoever.

Such having been the state of things seven years since, under the State
bank system, we may now examine the working of the, so-styled, national
system, with a view to see if it has tended to correction or to exaggeration of the difficulties that then existed.

§ 2. Under the State bank system, as has been shown, the distribution
of credits and circulation among the States was very nearly in accordance
with the Secretary's present teachings. How far it is so now, under this,
so-called, national one, organized by the Secretary himself, it is proposed
here to show.

By the report of the Comptroller, just now published, the following
was the state of things in October last, two years having then elapsed
since the date of the Secretary's decree issued at Fort Wayne, by which
the public were advised that "paper money" was too abundant, that
speculation must cease, and that "contraction" must be the order of the
day, the figures, as before, representing millions :—

	Banking Capital.	Circulation.	Capital and Circulation.	Investments.	Excess Investments.
Total	420	297	717	1103	386
New York and New England .	260	173	433	677	234
All other States and Territories	160	124	284	326	152

The total circulation had, in seven years, increased 90,000,000, but instead of finding that increase in those parts of the country in which credit least abounded and circulating notes were most needed, we find the whole of it, and even 10,000,000 more, to have been distributed by the then Comptroller, and now Secretary, to those very States in which credits were most abundant and a paper circulation least required.

Comparing now the bank-created currency of the two periods, we obtain the following figures :—

	1860.	1867.	Increase.
New York and New England, present population 7,000,000—			
Credit currency	135	234	
Circulation	73	173	
Total	208	407	199
Other States and Territories, population 30,000,000—			
Credits	43	152	
Circulation	134	124	
Total	177	276	99

In the first, population could have but very slightly grown. In the other it had increased to the extent of many millions, and yet, while nearly two hundred millions had been added to the one, less than one hundred had been secured by the latter. Such has been the working of a system that is styled national, but that is not only sectional as regards the North and the South, but also as regards the Centre and the West as against the North and the East.

In the intervening period the necessities of our people for a general medium of circulation had grown south and west of New York thrice more rapidly than in the country north and east of the Delaware. In many of the older States, poorly supplied before, the check and draft currency had wholly disappeared. Throughout the West new territories had been settled, and new States had been created, in which credit had as yet obtained no foothold whatsoever. Nevertheless, in the vast region south and west of New York, with four-fifths of the total population of the Union and two-thirds of its wealth, the quantity of circulation granted by the financier who has so much complained of the "plethora of paper money" has been, as here is shown, $10,000,000 less than it had been when Kansas was but beginning to be settled, and when many of the present States and territories had scarcely yet found a place on any map whatsoever.

Circulating notes are least needed where credit currency most abounds. Such is the Secretary's present text. Cities, then, are the places at which banks least need to avail themselves of the privilege of furnishing circulation. That such was the practice under the State bank system is well known to all. How it is now, under the one organized by the Secretary himself, and how his system compares with that he had found established, is shown by the following figures, representing, as before, millions :—

	Capital.	Circulation.	Capital and Circulation.	Loans.	Excess of Loans.
October, 1860.					
New York . .	69	10	79	123	44
Boston . . .	35	7	42	64	22
Philadelphia .	12	3	15	27	12
	116	20	186	214	78
October, 1867.					
New York . .	75	35	110	241	131
Boston . . .	42	24	66	101	35
Philadelphia .	16	11	27	59	32
	133	70	203	401	198

Of $90,000,000 addition to the currency in that form of which the Secretary is now so generally accustomed to speak as "paper money," no less than $50,000,000 are here shown to have been given, and given, too, by himself as Comptroller of the Currency, to those three communities in which, by his present showing, circulating notes had been least required; $10,000,000 having at the same time been *withdrawn* from the country south and west of New York, embracing States and Territories almost forty in number, with a population numbering little less than 30,000,000, and growing by millions annually, the needs of all for some general medium of circulation being, man for man, thrice greater than those of the people of the cities whose past and present have been above described. The Secretary's theories, as given in the passage of his report heretofore quoted, are excellent. Can he now explain why it is that his practice has been so different?

The bank-created currency of those cities at the same periods may thus be stated :—

	1860.	1867.
Credits based on loans of moneys at the credit of individuals	80	*198
Circulation . . . . . . : . . .	20	70
	100	268

* This is probably much less than the truth, there being checks and "cash items" that to some extent must have borne interest. Opposed to them there are surplus funds which are additions to capital. The one would probably balance the other.

The Secretary denounces speculation, and professes to be earnest in his desire to put it down. Nevertheless, here, *in the very centres of speculation*, three great trading cities, we have, under a system organized by himself, an *increase* of currency amounting to $168,000,000, or within little more than $60,000,000 of the *total* quantity that, excluding Philadelphia, is allowed to all the States and Territories of the Union south and west of New York, with four times the population and with twice the wealth of New York and New England. Not content, even, with this, the great opponent of speculation and of " paper money" has been unwearied in his efforts still further to deplete the centre, the west, and the south, and to perfect the centralization already so far established, by compelling all their banks to provide in one alone of them funds for redemption of their circulation, after having already provided for the same by deposits in his own hands at Washington. A better provision for the maintenance and extension of the speculative spirit, so often and so bitterly denounced by himself, could scarcely have been devised.

The 50,000,000 additional circulation thus injected into the great centres do more to cause what it is the fashion of the day to style " inflation" than would be done by 500,000,000 of the one, two, and five dollar notes required " for the retail trade, for travelling expenses, and for the purchase of products at first hands," those purposes for which money is really, in the Secretary's view, to be regarded as a " necessity." By whom, however, were they so injected ? By the Secretary himself, in his capacity of Comptroller of the Currency ! He, therefore, it is, who is to be regarded as the great " inflationist;" yet does it please him to style as such all those who fail to see that the resumption of specie payments can by any possibility be attained by means of measures tending to total destruction of the societary circulation.

" Capitals," said Mirabeau, " are necessities, but if the head is allowed to grow too large, the body becomes apoplectic, and wastes away." That, precisely, is what is here occurring, the whole tendency of the Secretary's system being in the direction of causing accumulation of blood in and about the societary heart, to the utter destruction of circulation throughout the body and the limbs. Hence it is that property in New York city has attained such enormous prices, and that we are now daily called upon to read of the " unparalleled advance" that, according to the *Tribune*, has taken place in the adjoining States, New Jersey and Connecticut. Passing outward, however, into Pennsylvania, we find a totally different state of things, miners and farmers being thrown altogether idle, and the depression there being quite as little to be " paralleled" as is the advance in the States so liberally patronized by our consistent Finance Minister.

To find his system working in full perfection we need, however, to look further south—to Georgia, Carolina, and Alabama. Doing this, we find the same *Tribune*, the especial advocate of his most unphilosophical and most exhaustive system, speaking to its readers in the words that follow :—

"A correspondent, writing from Hinesville, Liberty County, Georgia, says: 'A sale has taken place at this county seat that so well marks the extreme depression in the money market that I send you the particulars: Colonel Quarterman, of this county, deceased, and his executor, Judge Featter, was compelled to close the estate. The property was advertised, as required by law, and on last court day it was sold. A handsome residence at Walthourville, with ten acres attached, out-houses, and all the necessary appendages of a first-class planter's residence, was sold for $60. The purchaser was the agent of the Freedmen's Bureau. His plantation, four hundred and fifty acres of prime land, brought $150; sold to a Mr. Fraser. Sixty-six acres of other land, near Walthourville, brought three dollars; purchaser Mr. W. D. Bacon. These were all *bona fide* sales, It was court day, and a large concourse of people were present. The most of them were large property owners, but really had not five dollars in their pockets, and in consequence would not bid, as the sales were for cash.' In Montgomery, Alabama, lots on Market Street, near the Capitol, well located, 50 feet by 110 feet, averaged about $250 each. The Welsh residence on Perry Street, two-story dwelling-houses, including four lots, sold for $3500; Dr. Robert M. Williams was the purchaser. The same property in better times would not have brought less than $10,000. The Loftin Place, near Montgomery, containing 1000 acres, was recently rented at auction for forty cents an acre. The same lands rented the present year for three dollars an acre. About thirty real estate transfers were recorded in Nashville last week; prices were low. In Portsmouth, Virginia, a house and lot, formerly of the Reed estate, situated on the south side of County Street, near the intersection with Washington, was recently sold to Mr. Ames for $750. A building lot at the intersection of South and Bart Streets, brought only $125. A portion of Woodland, the late Judge John Webb Tyler's estate in Prince William County, Virginia, has been purchased by Mr. Delaware Davis, of New Jersey, at $20 an acre."

The more the blood is driven to the heart the more do the limbs become enfeebled, and thus greater becomes the liability to paralysis, to be followed by death. The Secretary has been, and still is, driving all the blood of the Union into the States and cities of the north and east, and with every step in that direction the circulation becomes more and more torpid and the paralysis more complete.

§ 3. Of the agricultural departments of France a very large proportion are steadily declining in population, the main reason therefor, as given in a highly interesting paper recently published,* being to be found in "a total absence of that power to supply themselves with circulating notes which elsewhere results from the presence of banks or other establishments of credit, or that of individuals whose signatures to such notes command the public confidence."

Agriculture, for this reason, fails in those districts to obtain the aid of capital, except on conditions so onerous as to be ruinous to the borrower.

* Journal des Economistes, September, 1867.

Just so has it always been throughout more than half the Union; the farmers of the Mississippi Valley, and the planters of the South and Southwest having been compelled to pay for the use of circulating notes twice, thrice, and often even five times the rate of interest paid by their brother agriculturists of New England and New York.

So did it continue to be until the needs of war compelled the Treasury to do that which it should long before have done, furnish a national machinery of circulation, by means of which the farmer might be enabled to buy and sell for cash, and to pay in cash his mason and his carpenter; thereby, and for the first time in our history, enabling these latter in their turn to acquire that feeling of real independence which results from exercise of power to choose among contending shopkeepers that one which would most cheaply supply the cloth, the coffee, or the sugar required by their families and themselves. At once the whole position of affairs was changed; the needy farmer and laborer, begging for credit, disappearing from the stage, and the anxious trader, begging for their custom, taking their place. It was a revolution more prompt, more complete, and more beneficial than any other 'recorded in financial history; its direct effect having been that of supplying the inferior, the most useful, and the least dangerous currency to those portions of the country which, while abounding in labor and in natural wealth, were as yet too poor to command the services of that superior one by which, in the course of time and in accordance with the Secretary's present teachings, it was to be replaced.

Of all the machinery of commerce there is none which renders so large an amount of service as that which facilitates exchanges from hand to hand. The more it abounds the more rapid is the circulation, and, as in the physical body, the greater are the health, the strength, and the force. It is, however, the one that is always last obtained, and most difficult to be retained. In furnishing it gratuitously to the centre, south, and west, the Treasury rendered a larger amount of service to our whole people than it would have done had it given the gratuitous use of railroads whose *cost* would have been twice as great as its own *amount*. That service was found in the increased demand for labor, to the great advantage of those who had it, in its various forms, for sale—the farmers, mechanics, and laborers of the Union. To some extent, however, it damaged those who made no profitable use of their own physical or mental faculties— annuitants, mortgagees, and other persons in the receipt of fixed incomes.

That, however, is the necessary result of beneficial changes of every kind, all such improvements manifesting themselves in an elevation of the labor of the present at the cost of accumulations of the past—the rate of interest always falling as labor becomes more productive. Instead, however, of so regarding it, those who suffered have, of course, insisted that it had been nothing but "a forced loan;" that, for that reason, it should, at the earliest possible moment, be repaid; and that the whole people should, for their benefit, be deprived of all the vast advantage which, under pressure of the war, had been so promptly gained. By whom, however, had the loan been made? Had it not been by the whole body of the people? Assuredly it had, and that same body had been the recipient of its products.

It had been simply the one great corporation of the Union combining with its members for obtaining, free of charge, the use of machinery of inestimable value, in default of which the societary circulation had previously been so much and so frequently arrested as to cause waste of labor to an annual amount twice greater than the circulation that had thus been furnished. It was that corporation combining with its members for their relief from the oppressive taxation of usurious capitalists, money-lenders on the one hand, and traders on the other. Of those who made the loan none complain. None suffer; there being not even a single one who cannot, on the instant, be reimbursed, obtaining from his neighbor property of value fully equal to that which he had given for his share of this, so-called "loan." What they do complain of is that, while willing to extend their loans, and to do so without charge of interest therefor, they are not permitted so to do; and here they complain with reason.

The Secretary insists, however, that this is only "paper money," of which there exists, in his opinion, so great a "plethora," that, at any sacrifice, this loan must be repaid. Seeking this "plethora," we look to the South, and find plantations being almost given away, because of the almost entire absence of currency of any description whatsoever. Turning next to the Mississippi Valley we find currency so scarce that manufacturers and traders pay for its use twice and thrice the usual rate of interest; farmers, meanwhile, finding difficulty in obtaining it on any terms whatsoever.

Coming now to the centre, we find it to be so little superabundant as to compel the employment of bank certificates—a sort of bastard "paper money" that otherwise would not be used. Passing thence to the North and East, the centre of speculation, and therefore, perhaps, in both the past and the present, so largely favored by a finance minister who professes himself opposed to "speculation," we find an abundance, and perhaps even the "plethora" of which he has so much and so frequently complained. Taking, however, the whole Union, we find that of this terrible "paper money" the quantity in actual circulation cannot be estimated at more than five hundred millions of dollars, or little more than a dozen dollars per head. With less than half the need of it per head, France has a circulation of thirty dollars for each individual of her population; and yet, with even this large supply, her agricultural districts are even now actually perishing for want of some representative of money to be employed in the effectuation of exchanges. Of all the countries of Europe there is none in which there exists in such complete abundance that superior currency which, as the Secretary assures us, and as we know to be the fact, tends to supplant the circulating note, as is the case in Britain. Yet even there do we find the circulating medium, per head, to be twice as great in quantity as among ourselves. Nevertheless, with these facts before him, and in direct opposition to his own most recent teachings, the Secretary assures us that it is to the excess of "paper money" we are to look when desiring to find the "obstacle" which stands in the way of "a return to a stable currency!"

Scotland, as stated in the article above referred to, has for each 5000 of her population a place at which money operations may be transacted. Nevertheless, there is no country of Europe in which circulating notes are so generally used. This, according to the Secretary, should make of it a good place to sell in and a bad one in which to buy; there yet is none in Europe better in which both to sell and to buy.

Jersey, one of the little Channel islands, with a population of 55,000 gathered together in a space less than half that embraced within our city limits, has no less than seventy-three places at which monetary affairs may be transacted; and yet, with all this vast machinery for supplying the superior currency, her people use of notes, none of which are of less than $5 value, more than $400,000, or almost $8 per head. Add to this the gold and silver that must necessarily be used, and we obtain a larger proportion than is now in use by a people of little less than 40,000,000, scattered over half a continent, among by far the larger portion of whom there exist none of those appliances by means of which, in more advanced communities, the use of money, whether the precious metals or the circulating note, is so much economized. Excluding New York and New England, and allowing for the general absence here of those means, the circulation of Jersey is *ten times* greater per head than that of nearly forty of our States and Territories; and yet, not only does this little island enjoy the highest degree of prosperity, but there is not a spot in Europe in which excess of currency stands less in the way of both buying and selling with advantage. The facts and the Secretary's theory do not, therefore, harmonize with each other. So much the worse, he will probably reply, for the unfortunate facts.

It is, however, as he says, an irredeemable currency, and therefore an "obstacle" to resumption. The first of these assertions is true, and here we are happy once again to agree with the honorable Secretary. Whether or not it really constitutes *the* obstacle, and whether or not the Secretary's movements tend to remove that which is certainly the real one, we may now inquire.

§ 4. By the present banking law it is required that before any association of capitalists, large or small, shall commence supplying their neighbors with machinery by means of which they may be enabled readily to make their various exchanges, they shall lend to the government an amount one-ninth greater than that of the circulating notes with which they desire to be supplied; and that the bonds they are thus required to buy shall be placed in the Treasury, to be there held as security for payment of the notes.

That done, and the notes received, it is then required that with these latter they shall purchase a certain proportion of Treasury notes payable on demand, to be held by them as further security for the payment on presentation of any portion of their own circulation. Further, in the event of failure of payment, their stockholders are made to a certain extent individually liable for any ultimate deficiency of assets, whether as regards the holders of notes, or the owners of credits on the books.

Having thus defined the terms on which the several portions of the country might be enabled to furnish their various neighborhoods with machinery of circulation, and having provided such restrictions as rendered it most difficult so to do except in rich and populous districts, it might have been supposed that then it would have been everywhere left to the people themselves to decide whether they would, or would not, have among themselves institutions of credit empowered to supply them with circulatory notes. Not so, however, the law providing that whensoever such circulation shall have been anywhere issued to the extent of $300,000,000, all power for further issue shall cease, and thus establishing a monopoly in the hands of those who first had taken possession of the little that had been granted.

Compliance with these conditions was easy in those communities within which credit institutions already largely abounded, and in which, by the Secretary's own showing, circulating notes least were needed, to wit, New York and New England. Most difficult, however, must it prove in all of those in which such notes most were needed, to wit, the centre, the west and the south, those in which the superior currency of checks and drafts least existed. Most of all was it easy in those large cities in which, as shown by the Secretary himself, "not a fiftieth part of the business is transacted by the actual use of money;" and in which, as he further says, "except in dealings with the government, for the retail trade, for the payment of labor and taxes, for travelling expenses, the purchase of products at first hands, and for the banker's reserve, money is hardly a necessity." Of all this the Secretary must have been then perfectly aware, and so having been, it became his duty, in his then capacity of Comptroller of the Currency, so to act as to secure to the States and Territories least provided with the superior currency the largest possible share of the limited quantity of the inferior one that has been thus allowed. Directly the reverse of this, however, we find him to have added $100,-

000,000, to the previously existing circulation of those States in which credits most existed, and $50,000,000 to that of the three cities in which circulating notes were least of all required ; while actually diminishing by $10,000,000 the allowance to the whole country south and west of New England and New York. Had it been his especial desire to produce the inflation of which he has since so much complained, he could have chosen no better mode of operation.

By this course of action there was established a monopoly of money power without a parallel in the world ; that monopoly, too, created by the Secretary himself in those very centres of speculation in which each additional.million does more to produce "inflation" than could or would be done by any ten millions scattered throughout the pockets of the farmers and laborers of the east, the west, the south, or the southwest.

The counterbalance to this monopoly was found in the existence of a machinery of circulation that had been created by the people themselves for the purpose of enabling each and all of them readily to exchange their services and products. The one tended towards enabling capitalists of the cities to compel the interior more and more to depend on them for performance of all their exchanges, and thus to give them more complete control over the farmer and the laborer. The other, on the contrary, tended towards enabling farmers and laborers to exchange among themselves, freed from the control of city capitalists ; and for that reason, perhaps, it has been that our Finance Minister has been so unwearied in his efforts to drive it from the stage.

For the accomplishment of that object he and his particular friends have done their utmost towards destroying the confidence of our people in each other, and in the country's future. From day to day has "contraction" been insisted on, accompanied by the assurance that prices must be made to fall ; that property of any description whatsoever bought to-day might be valueless to-morrow ; that mines opened, furnaces or houses built, this year, must prove in the next to be worth far less than they had cost. Raids have been made upon banks. Interest-bearing securities have been withdrawn from them for the express purpose of compelling them to heap up greenbacks in their vaults. Factories and furnaces have been closed that might and would have consumed hundreds of thousands of tons of coal and bales of cotton. Mines have been abandoned, and manufacturers have been ruined. Paralysis has been brought about through the whole extent of the Union, and all these things have been done to the ends that the people might be deprived of a circulating medium created by themselves and for themselves ; that the monopoly of the extreme North and East might be perfected ; and that the "speculator" might in this manner be driven from existence. To what extent these latter have been attained, we may now inquire.

From the report of the Comptroller just now issued we learn that on the first of January, 1867, the loans on private security by the banks of New England and New York were $404,000,000, and that nine months later not only had there been *no contraction*, but there had been an actual *increase* of their amount.

At the first of these dates they held $297,000,000 of interest-bearing public securities. At the last, their amount had fallen $14,000,000, the whole effect of a nine months' vindictive warfare having been that of compelling them to disgorge *public* securities yielding them an annual interest of probably $800,000. Placing against this the higher interest that lenders had, by means of the Secretary's aggressive policy, been enabled to secure, the balance in favor of the banks would probably count by millions, for all of which they had been indebted to the policy announced in the celebrated but unfortunate Fort Wayne decree. The policy that carried us through the war favored those who had labor to sell and money to borrow. That of the Secretary favors those who have money to lend and labor to buy; and hence it is that the societary circulation becomes daily more and more impeded, and that the Treasury daily loses power.

Throughout the North and East there was certainly a plethora of currency needing to be corrected. Has the Secretary, with all his efforts, succeeded in making this correction? On the contrary, he has not only proved himself utterly powerless in that direction, but has, by largely withdrawing that machinery on which, almost alone, were dependent the people of more than half the Union, made the centres of speculation relatively far more powerful than they had ever been before. To what extent this course of action has tended towards facilitating resumption may be now examined.

§ 5. The Secretary's policy of "contraction," as has been shown, has been fully operative in all those portions of the Union that did *not* enjoy the benefits of that superior currency of checks and drafts which, as he informs us, have so largely "taken the place of bank-notes," and that, for that reason, most needed such notes, the national circulation having been reduced more than $70,000,000, without provision of local currency to take its place. It has been wholly inoperative in all those centres of speculation in which "not a fiftieth part of the business is transacted by the actual use of money," the "plethora" still existing just where the Secretary had himself created it, monetary starvation being, meanwhile, the lot of two-thirds of the whole population of the Union, and their position, relatively to the highly speculative North and East, undergoing daily deterioration. In this state of things it is that the Secretary has graciously announced his determination to postpone resumption for another year, giving to banks and bankers to July, 1869, for preparing to "face the music." More simple, and more in accordance with what, as we think, he must have known to be his real position, would it have been had he at once announced a postponement to the Greek *kalends*, a day whose arrival was never to be apprehended. That under the present system it never *can*, by any possibility, arrive, will be clear to all who shall take the trouble to study the existing relation of banks and people, banks and State, as it will be now exhibited.

On the first of October last the debts of banks to individual
depositors amounted to $538,000,000
Their debts to banks and bankers, a very considerable
proportion of which was from city to country banks, and
bearing interest, were 112,000,000
Circulation 300,000,000
_____
$950,000,000

On the same day they held of legal-tender notes, of various
descriptions $157,000,000

Let us now suppose that notice had then been given them to be prepared on the first of January to face their creditors and meet their obligations. Such preparation would, of course, have involved the calling in of hundreds of millions of loans, attended with bankruptcy of thousands if not even tens of thousands of miners, manufacturers, traders, "speculators," and others interested in the general business of the country, to be followed by a general failure of institutions whose stockholders were all, to a greater or less extent, liable for payment of their debts. Would the banks have done this? Assuredly not, if any other course were open to them. Would there then have been any other? Most assuredly there would. They might then have chosen between bankrupting the Treasury with large profit to themselves therefrom, or becoming themselves bankrupt with still greater loss; the one course simple and readily pursued, the other difficult and trying to the consciences of all who might, even for a moment, think of its adoption.

On the day thus supposed to have been appointed, the first of January, the Treasury was owner of $88,000,000 of gold. On that day the banks held probably the same amount as in October of Treasury obligations redeemable in gold—to wit, $156,000,000. By presenting little more than half of these for payment, they would at once empty the Treasury vaults, while still retaining nearly $70,000,000, every dollar of which would be from that moment receivable at the custom-houses, though not necessarily receivable by the claimants of interest on the public bonds. From that hour the Treasury would be bankrupt, as interest could be no longer paid. Is it, then, the banks that need to be protected against the State, or the State that needs, by continuing the suspension, to be protected against the banks? Assuredly it is this latter.

Would, however, the banks so have acted? Most certainly they would. They held then, as they now hold, in their own hands the means of protection against a policy that is both insane and vicious; and had they failed to use it, they would have fully earned the censure of their fellow-citizens and of the world at large.

The debts due to depositors by the banks of New England and New York, and those of the three chief Atlantic cities, exceed $500,000,000. Add to this their circulation, and we obtain an amount little short of $700,000,000, to meet which they hold somewhat more than $100,000,000 of Treasury obligations payable on demand, a quantity very insufficient for meeting their creditors, but quite sufficient for enabling them to hold the Treasury itself in check. There is thus at the heart of the system, and centre of the "speculation" so much denounced by the honorable Secretary, a force that can at the shortest notice be brought to bear upon him, and against which he would find himself as utterly powerless as did Canute when he undertook to check the rising of the tide. In establishing the great money monopoly of the East and North, the Secretary did but create a monster, a sort of monetary Frankenstein, armed with power to control himself, the author of its unfortunate existence.

That the Secretary knows and feels all this is proved by his extreme anxiety to be authorized to go abroad to beg for loans, and to dress up his securities in a manner calculated to please the fancies of the little capitalists of France and Germany, Switzerland and Holland. His fellow citizens are anxious to lend him all he needs, and wholly free of interest. Rejecting all such aid he, placed in the direction of a community possessing greater mental and mineral resources than any other, seeks to be allowed to peddle his wares in all the towns and villages of Europe, and thus to present in fullest relief the miserable state of weakness to which, by means of a policy the most narrow and unstatesmanlike, our people and our government have been reduced.

Closing his eyes to the fact that throughout the whole of his ministerial life we have been exporting bonds by *tons weight*,* the Secretary now urges that he be permitted to create new bonds, to be exchanged for gold by means of which to effect resumption. Simultaneously with this we have an estimate of customs revenue for the realization of which we must, allowing for frauds of various kinds, import more than $400,000,000. of foreign merchandise. Add to this freights, interest, and expenses of our

---

* One of the agents charged with care of the foreign mails has stated recently, to one of our diplomatic representatives in Europe, that *each and every trip* throughout the last two years he had carried registered letters containing bonds the weight of which varied between 60 and 300 pounds. This is for but one of the several weekly lines of steamers, and to estimate the total quantity at but 150 pounds per week, would give *a ton weight per quarter*. It is in the face of this that it is now gravely proposed to create a new loan specially for Europe.

people resident or travelling abroad, and we obtain a gold demand for
Europe of fully $550,000,000 ; or more than twice the amount of all
the tobacco, oil, cotton, and other products we have for export. In our
relations with foreign countries there is an annual deficit of hundreds of
millions to be paid in gold or bonds, and it is in the face of this great
fact that the Secretary proposes to go abroad to purchase the gold by
means of which he is to be armed with power for controlling a great monopoly which but for himself would never have had existence. With every
step in this direction he is still further weakening both the people and
the State, and making new preparation for our arrival at that goal toward
which, from the hour of his taking the direction of our finances, we have
been tending—that of bankruptcy of the Treasury and final repudiation
of the national debt.

Had the Secretary studied our financial history, he would have seen
that whenever the societary circulation had, as in the protective periods
ending in 1835 and 1847, been rapid, the *many* who had had need to
labor and to borrow had been strong for their contest with the *few* who
had need to purchase labor and had money to lend ; and, that then, and
then only, had the nation been strong for the assertion of its proper place
among the Powers of the world.

It was the *many* who made the recent war. It was they, and not the
few, who gave the government power for suppressing the rebellion. Almost from the hour, however, of the appointment of our present Finance
Minister the alliance between the many and the Treasury ceased to exist,
and hence the present weakness of the State. From that hour there has
been an incessant effort at strengthening the *few* for their contest with
the *many*, and hence it is that such large fortunes have been accumulated
by those connected with Treasury operations, the whole people meanwhile suffering under a necessity for paying greatly increased rates of
interest, and banks and bankers building palaces while laborers and their
families perish because mines and mills stand closed, their owners having
been almost, even when not altogether, ruined.

The road in which the Secretary demands that we now travel finds its
termination in repudiation. That such is the case is proved by all the
recent movements. If, then, the holders of our bonds desire that the
national honor be maintained, let them insist upon such a change of
policy as shall tend towards early restoration of the societary circulation.

§ 6. The societary circulation becomes more rapid, men become more
prosperous and more free, and the State grows in wealth, strength, and
power, as the circulating note, readily exchangeable for coin, takes more
and more place of the coin itself. Still more rapid is the growth of all
as that higher currency of credits, upon which are based the checks, the
drafts, the clearing-houses, and other machinery for economizing the use

of money, tends to supplant both the metals and·the note; every move.
ment in that direction as much indicating progress as does the substitution
of the wagon for the pack-horse; the locomotive, in its turn, supplanting
both horse and wagon. For speed and economy the highest form of cur.
rency almost emulates the electric telegraph, the circulating note finding
its correspondent in the postman of modern days, and the precious metals
in the messenger of olden times, when the public postman had as yet
scarcely made his appearance on the stage.

Electricity and steam need the curb. So does the highest form of cur.
rency. The wagon horse needs the spur. So does that description of
currency which takes the form of circulating notes. Crises, public and
private, come when the former is left wholly uncontrolled. Stagnation
and weakness follow in the train of measures preventing development in
direction of the latter. That such is the case is proved by every page of
our financial history, yet do our legislative records present a constant
series of efforts for prohibiting the use of the note and thus compelling
use of the metals, a course of proceeding just as philosophical as would
be one that should look to forbidding wagons lest they might lessen the
demand for pack horses. Time and again has it been proposed that our
people should be prevented from giving or taking any note of less denomi.
nation than $10 or $20. As often have they been forbidden to avail them.
selves of the services of any that should be less than $5; and yet, despite
of all opposition, the note has held its ground and grown in public favor.
Not only so, but it must continue so to do, despite the recent declaration
of our honorable Secretary that to all systems under which "circulating
notes are issued" he finds such "grave objections," that "if there were
none in existence in the United States he would hesitate to recommend
or to indorse the most perfect that had ever been designed."

Greatly admiring the *credit* which so supplants both the note and the
metals that the use of either almost ceases to be "a necessity," he thus
strongly opposes the note which constitutes the intermediate step between
the metals and the credits. Unable to recommend the dangerous wagon,
he greatly admires the safety and celerity of the locomotive and its train.
Common sense, however, teaches that as the wagon is useful as prepara.
tion for the engine, so the note is needed as preparation for the credit, and
that both are evidences of advancing civilization.

Beyond the Atlantic there is no country that has so much as Scotland
tended towards substitution of the readily-transferable note for the slow.
moving metals, yet is there none that less has suffered from financial crises
of her own creation. Directly the reverse of this, we find in England a
constant series of regulations as to who might, or might not, issue notes,
and as to the minimum value of such as might be issued, the whole at last
culminating in an absurd and preposterous system that has, in its little
more than twenty years of existence, given to the world no less than three

financial crises, each more severe than that by which it had been preceded; and the last so greatly so that recovery therefrom has scarcely as yet commenced. By that law it was provided that the curb should be used where the spur had most been needed, leaving at the mercy of banks and bankers that higher currency, created for their own especial use and profit, in relation to which control was really required, while checking and controlling that inferior one with the use of which all seek to dispense as far as is consistent with the convenient effectuation of their exchanges. Such having been its necessary tendencies, the extraordinary expansions and contractions that have attended its brief existence offer no cause for wonder.

At home, in the New England States, there was presented for examination a banking system directly the reverse of that of England, the most free, the most natural, and therefore the most stable and useful, of any the world had ever known. Nowhere had currency been so cheaply furnished. In none had redemption been so uniform. Instead, however, of studying it, the originators of our present system studied carefully that of England, finally adopting it, with the addition of new and burdensome restrictions in reference to that inferior currency which most was needed, and leaving, as in England, wholly unchecked that superior one to which we had in all the past been indebted for every financial crisis with which the country had been afflicted.

Bad as was this law itself the danger that it threatened was intensified by the organization under it that followed, the then Comptroller of the Currency, and now Secretary, having applied the spur in all those portions of the country in which the curb had theretofore been needed, while reserving this latter for those of them in which institutions of credit least existed, and in which their careful nurture was most required. Hence the situation in which he now finds himself, face to face with a great monopoly whose power increases with each and every of his efforts at its limitation.

Desiring now to reach resumption we must wholly change our system, ceasing to use the spur in that only portion of the country in which the curb is needed, the north and east, and declining to apply this latter in the centre, the south and the west; in all of which the prosperity of the people and strength of the State would greatly be promoted by increased facilities of exchange.

Circulation demands to be re-established throughout the Union, and to that end we need to calm down the excitement which exists in close neighborhood of the heart; at the same time adopting measures tending to stimulate the body and the limbs that are now so nearly torpid. That such measures may be adopted it is needed that our legislators begin to appreciate the folly of a system that leaves to banks, bankers, and "speculators" the entire and absolute control of that superior currency whose power for good or evil so closely resembles that of electricity, while re-fusing to permit the miner and the laborer, the mechanic and the farmer to determine for themselves how much of the inferior one they will carry in their pockets.

The road by which we now travel is, to the people at large, a painful one, and one by which resumption never can be reached. That by which we should travel, though somewhat long, would be travelled joyfully by all but those who are now financially and politically so largely profiting by the general distress. The Treasury forces have been long arrayed on the side of these latter, and hence the weakness of the people and the State. It is for Congress now to see that this no longer be the case.

THE FINANCE MINISTER AND THE NATIONAL DEBT.

§ 1. The Secretary's theory in reference to the currency, as has been shown, is in direct conflict with his practice; the former most earnestly teaching that the need for circulating notes everywhere exists in the *inverse* ratio of the use of checks, drafts, and other machinery for economizing money of every kind; the latter, on the contrary, giving such notes in the *direct* ratio of the existence of that superior currency which, as the Secretary himself informs us, everywhere tends to super-sede the note. So too, as will now be shown, is it with reference to the public debt, his teachings being in the direction of maintaining in-violate the public faith, the tendency in the opposite direction of the public mind becoming, and that necessarily, more and more rapid as his policy is more fully carried out. Like the boatman, he is always looking in one direction while rowing in another.

Seeing clearly that such *is* the present tendency, and correctly appre-ciating "the great interest and alarm excited by the doctrines recently promulgated," the Secretary has, in his recent voluminous and most feeble report, devoted much space to a lecture on the absolute necessity for pay-ing the debt in gold, both principal and interest. Replying thereto, Con-gress might, as we think, with great propriety ask of him to show how far his own measures in the past had tended toward diminishing the amount of interest now to be paid; toward lessening the present burthen of the debt; toward increasing the general power to contribute to the revenue; toward strengthing the hands of that loyal portion of our people to which we had been indebted for suppression of the rebellion, and to which alone the holders of our public securities can now, or in the future, look with any confidence for disposition to carry into full effect the contracts of the war. Admitting that this were done, let us now look to see what are the figures in relation to present burthens that must be given in the reply that would then be made.

In October, 1865, the total debt was $2,808,549,000, of which $1,162,-000,000 were payable in gold. The total interest was $133,000,000, of which $67,000,000 were gold, and $66,000,000 currency. Admitting now that the character of the debt had remained unchanged, and taking the price of gold at 140, the quantity of lawful money to-day required for payment of interest on that amount of debt would not exceed $150,000,000.

In October, 1866, the debt, deducting money in the treasury, had been reduced to $2,551,000,000, of which the gold portion had been increased to $1,342,000,000. Here was a large reduction and yet the interest paid thereon appears to have grown to $143,751,000, the gold portion of which must have been $78,000,000. Estimating as before this gold at 140, it would amount to $109,000,000, adding to which the currency portion, $66,000,000, we obtain as the amount of lawful money then required for satisfaction of demands for interest the sum of $175,000,000.

In October last the debt had been further reduced, and then stood at but $2,491,000,000, the gold portion of which had grown to $1,775,000,-000. Almost three hundred millions less in quantity it now requires for the payment of interest, as stated in the report, page 43, no less than $152,515,640, being nearly $20,000,000 more than had been needed before reduction of the principal had been commenced. Of this the gold portion is $105,000,000, being the equivalent of $147,000,000 lawful money. Adding now to this the currency portion, say $47,000,000, we obtain as the total amount of lawful money this year required for satisfaction of claims for interest no less a sum than $194,000,000, being $44,000,000 more than had been needed when the debt, as stated by the Secretary himself, had been $266,000,000 greater. Adding further the interest on these $266,000,000, we obtain $210,000,000 as the amount that would to-day be payable on the same amount of debt which had existed at the date of the celebrated decree which announced "contraction" as being the order of the day; and by means of which confidence, public and private, has been so far destroyed, and the societary movement so thoroughly paralyzed, that the payment of even half of this enormous amount would be far more burthensome than would have been that of the whole on the day on which the Secretary entered on his most destructive career.

At the date of that mischievous and most unfortunate decree there were still outstanding compound interest notes, payable in 1867 and 1868, to the extent of $159,000,000. The interest on these, so far as paid, may be estimated at $20,000,000; and to that extent is the growth of currency interest accounted for. There is in this, however, nothing to account for the fact that the interest hereafter to be paid, all of it in gold, stands at $130,000,000, or within $3,000,000 of the sum actually paid in the fiscal year 1866, when the debt stood at its very highest point. We are thus presented with the fact that the Secretary proposes in the next fiscal year to divide among bondholders $130,000,000 of gold, now worth in lawful money more than $182,000,000; whereas the amount of such money required at the time when the debt amounted to $2,808,000,000, had been but $150,000,000. In all other countries the public credit improves with diminution of the need for loans. Here, under our admirable system of finance, it seems, on the contrary, to deteriorate as the debt is more and more diminished.

The remarkable fact is thus presented, that precisely as the paralysis becomes more general—precisely as labour and all its products fall in price—precisely as lawful money becomes more valuable in the hands of those who hold it—precisely as it becomes less and less attainable by those who need to get it—precisely as taxation becomes more and more burthensome—precisely as these phenomena become more general throughout the land, the quantity of lawful money required for satisfaction of the claims of bondholders increases; the poor being thus made poorer while the rich are being made richer, and banks, bankers, and treasury agents building palaces, while mills and mines are being closed and working men and women deprived of power to obtain either the food or the clothing required by their families and themselves.

On an average·the prices of labor and its products are at least a third less than had been the case at the date on which the Secretary announced to Congress and the people his determination to enforce "contraction." The $182,000,000 lawful money of to-day would therefore purchase almost as much as could have then been bought with $300,000,000. As but half this latter sum, or $150,000,000, was then required, it is clear that the burthen of taxation for payment of interest has, except among the bondholders themselves, by means of the Secretary's policy been fully doubled. Hence it is that the cry has become so general for discharge of the principal in lawful money. Hence it is that the word repudiation is now so freely used! That it shall soon become universal all that is needed is that the Secretary shall be allowed by Congress to go ahead in the substitution of gold bonds for greenbacks, for compound interest notes, and for all other securities that make no demand for gold, whether for principal or for interest.

The amount of gold to be paid in the next fiscal year, for various purposes will exceed $140,000,000. To enable the Treasury to obtain that quantity our importations, allowing for frauds of various kinds, *must* exceed $400,000,000. Adding to this interest payable abroad, travelling expenses and freights, we obtain a sum exceeding $500,000,000, and perhaps reaching $550,000,000. Against this we have exports in the last fiscal year amounting in currency to $385,000.000, and in gold to $231,000,000, leaving little less than $300,000,000 to be paid in either gold or bonds.

The day for the sale of bonds abroad is fortunately approaching its close, and with every step in that direction there must be diminished power to import foreign merchandise, accompanied by diminution of Custom-House receipts. With each there must be diminution of treasury power for controlling prices, that diminution keeping steady pace with the increased necessity for gold growing out of a constant substitution of gold bonds for those whose demands upon the Treasury are limited to lawful money. Such being very decidedly the tendency of affairs, the probability is great that the $130,000,000 required for the coming fiscal year will represent much more than $200,000,000 in lawful money; and little less than thrice the quantity of commodities generally that could, in the autumn of 1865, have been purchased with the $150,000,000 of lawful money that were then required for discharging all the claims for interest.

The late holders of 7.30 currency bonds are now receiving gold equivalent to 8.50 lawful money. But for the interference of Congress, such would now be the case with most of the present holders of legal-tender interest-bearing notes. Such it *will* be with all those whose notes cannot be included within the $50,000,000 of three per cent. certificates. The perfection of modern financiering is, to all appearance, to be found in raising the rate of interest, in increasing the burthen of the public debt, and in annihilating the power of the people to contribute to the public revenue.* The financial system that carried us through the war, looked, on the contrary, to reduction of the rate of interest, and to stimulation of the societary circulation.

Were it not for the Secretary's profession of desire to maintain the public faith we should be much disposed to believe that, determined upon bringing about repudiation, he had arrived at the conclusion that the shortest road thereto lay in the direction of making the debt from day to day more burthensome. Certain it is that had such been his wish, he could have chosen no better course of operation than that he has so consistently pursued almost from the hour that he was so unfortunately placed in the direction of the national finances.

* The most efficient and persistent advocate of the Secretary's plans for raising the rates of interest is found in the New York *Tribune*, whose teachings of the day on which we write are as follows:—

"The Secretary of the Treasury, if he has any surplus, should use it in paying off $46,244,780 of compounds, and $23,265,000 of three per cent. certificates—together $69,509,780; and if he has no surplus, should sell six per cent. gold bonds enough to pay them as they mature. Congress and the Secretary should lose no time in undoing the financial blunder made during the rebellion. The first step should be the funding of every currency obligation with gold-bearing bonds, leaving nothing to be cared for next December but its 'due-bills,' called legal tender."

§ 2. Prior to the breaking out of the rebellion Congress had been accustomed to define very accurately the course to be pursued in the negotiation of loans and in the discharge of public debt, and to require that in all cases there should be the most perfect publicity in regard thereto. With the war, however, there came, here as elsewhere, many changes, the exigencies of the case having made it necessary to leave very much to the discretion of the distinguished man who then, so honorably to himself, discharged the duties of the place now filled by Mr. Secretary McCulloch. Peace having returned, it might have been supposed that his successor would gladly have sought, as far as possible, to relieve himself from responsibility, taking the orders of Congress rather than promulgating his own decrees. Directly the reverse of this, however, he has, on every occasion, whether as regarded contraction or expansion, sale of gold or cancellation of greenbacks, negotiation of loans or discharge of liabilities, demanded to be invested with full authority, and has, with all his energies, resisted every effort at limitation of his powers. Such having been, and such being now the case, there would seem to be propriety in showing, to some small extent, how power has been exercised in the past, with a view to proper understanding of what may be looked for in the future.

The last hours of the XXXIXth Congress were marked by the enactment of a law having for its object limitation of the Secretary's contractive force. To the end of compelling the banks to absorb the greenbacks then in circulation he had announced a determination to convert all the "interest-bearing notes into five-twenty bonds," and had already so far proceeded in the act that of the $217,000,000 issued there had remained outstanding, at the date of his report, less than $160,000,000. Of these a large amount would become payable on the first of October 1867, and thenceforward to August, 1868, and it was greatly feared that while limited in his *direct* contraction of the currency to $4,000,000 per month, he might, *indirectly*, bring about one thrice greater in amount. That he might be prevented from doing this Congress instructed him to issue three per cent certificates to the extent of $50,000,000, at the same time authorizing the banks to take and hold them, as they before had held the interest-bearing notes, as part of their reserve. Such was the second act of congressional rebellion—the second repudiation of that financial system which looked to increasing the wealth and strength of the already rich while depriving those who had labour to sell of all power to provide food and clothing for their families and themselves.

Sullenly accepted by the Secretary, he, from the hour of its passage, persistently refused to give any *public* notice of his intentions in regard to execution of the law that had been thus enacted. Would he issue the notes and thus prevent necessity for contraction ? Would he refuse to issue them and thus compel contraction ? Such were the questions that for the nearly seven months which passed between the second of March and the first of October 1867, occupied the minds of banks and bankers, borrowers and lenders. As the day approched on which this important question *must* be determined, anxiety increased, and what were its effects is shown in the following statement of the rate of loans and discounts throughout September :—

	Sept. 9.	Sept. 16.	Sept 23.	Sept. 30.
Call loans	3 @ 4	4 @ 6	7 @—	6 @—
Loans on Bonds and Mortgage . .	6 @ 7	6 @ 7	6 @ 7	6 @ 7
A 1, indorsed bills, 2 mos. . .	6 @ 6½	6 @ 6½	7 @ 7½	7 @ 7½
Good indorsed bills, 3 and 4 mos. .	6½@ 7½	6½@ 7½	8½@10	8½@10
" " single names .	9 @10	9 @10	10 @—	10 @20
Lower grades	11 @15	12 @18	12 @20	12 @20

"The stringent tendency of the money market," says the *Merchants' Magazine*, from which we take this table, "causes a sudden realizing movement at the Stock Exchange, and stocks held at the beginning of the month with much confidence in a rise corresponding to the improved earnings of the roads, were sold at a decline ranging from 5@10 per cent."

To calm the excitement then existing—to relieve the public mind—to save from bankruptcy hundreds of most useful citizens—to maintain in employment tens of thousands of working men and women—all that was then required was *a single word* from the Secretary to the effect that he meant certainly to obey the law ; but, *that word was never uttered.* Why was it not ? Why had it not been uttered even six months earlier ? Why had our whole people been kept so long in ignorance in reference to a matter of such vast importance ?

The first of October at last arrived, bringing with it an absolute necessity for announcement of the fact that the Secretary, having always regarded the act as "mandatory," had then no power to avoid its execution. At once the public mind was relieved, and men went on their way rejoicing in the belief that bankruptcy might be avoided without necessity for adding to the enormous sacrifices they had already made.

The Secretary professes to be deadly hostile to "speculation," yet here do we find him compelling nearly the whole societary world to give itself during many weary months to the work of "speculating" as to whether he would or would not comply with the provisions of a law that had been enacted with a view to limit his powers for mischief. We say *nearly the whole*, it being scarcely to be supposed that there did not exist some one or more persons fully cognizant of the fact that he had arrived at the conclusion that the law had been so worded as to leave to him no choice whatsoever ; and that, for that reason, it *must* be carried into full effect. Were there any such persons ? If so, they were in possession of a secret worth very many millions. Having seen the cards they could safely "speculate," doing this by aid of a studious silence on the part of an officer of the government who ought to have known that retention of so important a secret must inevitably have the effect of inducing suspicion that he himself had profited of the "speculation" he had so freely and so persistently denounced; and whose self respect should have taught him that, like Cæsar's wife, he was bound to be not only pure but unsuspected.

In the whole history of the government there can be found no single case in which a secret has been more perfectly, if even so perfectly, guarded. Down to the moment *at which silence could be no longer kept* the bank officers of this and other cities were kept in ignorance as perfect as could have been the case had it been a decision of the French or English government that had been awaited. That others, and those others in close relation with the treasury, were not so ignorant would seem to be fully proved by the magnitude of the purchases that, as generally understood, then were made.

Starting now from the day on which the public mind had been relieved, and the "speculators" had been thus placed in a position to realize large profits on their extensive purchases, we may now study the course of things from that date to the present time. To that end the following table is submitted, showing—

I. The total amount of currency in the treasury;

II. The amount thereof deposited in the banks;

III. The quantity of notes withdrawn from circulation by being placed in the various sub-treasuries; and

IV. The gold on hand after deducting the gold notes then outstanding.

	Oct. 1.	Nov. 1.	Dec. 1.	Jan. 1.
Total currency	31,813,000	22,458,000	37,486,000	25,770,000
On deposit	22,434,000	23,590,000*	23,000,000†	23,000,000†
In Sub-treasury notes	9,379,000		14,486,000	2,770,000
Gold	88,000,000	97,000,000	82,000,000	88,400,000
	97,379,000	97,000,000	96,486,000	91,170,000

The remarkable fact is here presented, that while the whole quantity of money, gold and paper, in the various sub-treasuries but slightly varies, the difference of proportions is enormously great, notes being withdrawn from circulation as gold is sold, and gold reappearing as paper is again permitted to go abroad. Closely following the announcement that the three per cent. certificates were really to be issued, and at the very moment

* This is the amount that was on deposit on the last day of October, whereas the quantity in the treasury is for the first of November. This may, perhaps, account for the fact that the former appears to be somewhat in excess of the latter.

† These are estimates, there being no published account of later date than October 31st. The amount appears, throughout the year, to have varied between 22 and 25 millions.

when the "speculators" of September had such substantial reason for desiring that money should be abundant, we find the sub-treasuries to have been entirely stripped of notes, while gold was being rapidly accumulated. October passed, November now presents another change, gold being sold and notes to an enormous extent withdrawn; that withdrawal, too, made at the moment when large amounts were being called for at the west and south for removal of the crops, and the rate of interest being thus carried even higher than had been the case before the issue of certificates.

	Nov. 1.	Nov. 8.	Nov 15.	Nov. 22.	Nov. 30.
Call loans	6 @ 7	6 @ 7	6 @ 7	7 @—	7 @—
Loans on bonds and mortgage	—@ 7	—@ 7	—@ 7	—@ 7	—@ 7
A 1, indorsed bills, 2 mos. .	7 @ 9	7 @ 9	7 @ 8	8 @—	7½@
Good indorsed bills, 3 and 4 months	9 @12	9 @12	8 @12	8 @12	8 @12
Good indorsed bills, single names	11 @12	11 @12	11 @12	11 @12	11 @12
Lower grades	15 @25	15 @25	15 @25	15 @25	15 @25

December now, as we see, presents another change, gold being piled up as notes are paid out, money being made again abundant, and "speculators" of the previous month being now again afforded opportunity to realize their profits. What may have been the movement in the month that since has passed we have no present means of knowing; but, as money is now *permitted* to abound, it may fairly be assumed that in that time little gold has been sold, and but few notes have been withdrawn.

Studying the facts above presented the reader must, we think, be forcibly reminded of the well-known game of the pea and the thimble, commonly known as thimble-rig. Of those who play it there is always one *who knows exactly where the little joker may be found*, and he it is who profits by the " speculation." So, as it would seem, is it in all our present treasury arrangements, there being always some one who knows under which thimble the golden pea may certainly be found, and whether he may safely play the part of bull or bear; and hence it is that fortunes are being now so largely and so rapidly accumulated by all of those concerned in the various treasury manipulations.

§ 3. The suggestion has been made by some evil minded persons that political reasons had had much to do with the extraordinary financial movements of September and October last, money having been made exceedingly scarce and men in thousands having been deprived of power to earn subsistence for their families and themselves, at the very moment when elections in the great central States were already close at hand. What truth there may be in this none but the Secretary himself can certainly tell, but sure it is, that had he desired to produce general dissatisfaction he could scarcely have chosen any more suitable course of action than that here exhibited as occurring in the few weeks which preceded the second Tuesday of October last, as follows:—

BEFORE ELECTION.	AFTER ELECTION.
Menaced suppression of $50,000,000 of legal tender notes :	Announced emission of $50,000,000 of three per cent. certificates :
Large sales of gold :	Gold sales stopped :
Temporary suppression of $9,000,000 circulating notes :	Actual emission of $9,000,000 of circulating notes :
Contraction universal and crisis imminent :	Inflation general, and fear of crisis removed :
Bears and money lenders rejoicing :	Bulls and borrowers rejoicing :
Mills and mines being closed, and working men despairing of both the present and the future.	Miners, manufacturers, and working men more hopeful.

How the treasury action first above described was then regarded, is shown in the following paragraph from the *Merchants' Magazine* of October last, and particularly in the sentences here italicized :—

"The money market during September exhibited the activity usual at the fall season. The demand for currency, to move the crops at the West, has been unusually large, owing not only to the abundance of the yield, but equally to the high prices of breadstuffs and the anxiety of the farmers to realize. The receipts of grain at the lake ports have been about double the quantity for the same period of 1866 ; and the Western banks have been taxed to their utmost in satisfying the wants of the movers of this large amount of products. The discounting and rediscounting of produce paper, and the withdrawal of the balances of Western banks have caused an outflow of currency, legal tender and bank, of probably fully $25,000,000 within the month ; and at the close the efflux continued in undiminished volume. *The financial operations of the Government have also had an important bearing upon the course of the money market. At one period its sales of coin and of bonds largely exceeded its disbursements in the purchase of seven-thirty notes, resulting in a temporary withdrawal of currency from the banks which, together with the westward drain, and the calling in of funds from some of the national depositories, had the effect of producing a very sharp stringency, and a full 7 per cent. rate on demand loans.* The city merchants have suffered inconvenience from this condition of things. As the banks could employ their balances at 7 per cent. on call they have been indifferent about discounting, and have confined their operations in paper to the best of their depositors. Large amounts of choice paper have been thrown upon the street at 7½ @ 9 per cent. ; while fair average names have sought buyers in vain at much higher rates."

Looking only at the movement by which the elections had been preceded the political idea would certainly seem to have some foundation ; but when we study the whole ground as above exhibited, and estimate the number of millions that might have been, and perhaps were, realized by parties, individual and incorporated, who had stood behind the scenes selling gold and heaping up greenbacks; gathering large commissions and controlling free of interest the public moneys; investing those moneys in bonds and stocks preparatory to the upward movement that must inevitably follow disclosure of the important and closely guarded treasury secret; the idea becomes in a high degree absurd. Still more so does it appear when we take the month following the last of the fall elections, finding in November the "contractive" screw turned again and to such extent as in that short period to have converted into paper no less than $15,000,000 of treasury gold; all this, too, having been but the prelude to an "inflation" that, in the month directly following, converted into gold nearly all the treasury paper. Seeing the vast pecuniary advantage that must have resulted from such manipulation of the public funds, none but the most maliciously disposed could possibly be led to find therein any evidence of the Secretary's desire to interfere in mere politics.

The Secretary's friends, including, of course, all those of both political parties who stand behind the scenes, justify this course of action, asserting it to be his duty to cause money to abound at intervals in order to obtain good prices for the gold bearing bonds he seeks to sell; and then to cause it to become scarce that he may obtain at low prices the paper-bearing securities he seeks to buy; a very comfortable doctrine, certainly, for those who know *the precise moment at which they themselves may buy and sell.* Less comfortable, however, is it for that outside public which finds itself robbed at one moment by being forced to sell to the well-informed; and then again robbed at the following one by means of an artificial expansion of the causes of which, as well as of the contractive movement *meant to follow,* it is kept in utter ignorance.

At the great European gaming establishments, Baden, Homburg, and others, the laws of the game establish an advantage to the bank by means of which, notwithstanding occasional heavy losses, it *must,* in the long run, come out winner. Outside of this all is fair, and players have not the slightest fear that dice will be cogged, that cards will be packed, or that *well-informed* employees will be found betting on their own private account. Here, on the contrary, each successive treasury report furnishes evidence that the cards *had been* packed, while the rapidly accumulating fortunes of treasury friends and agents give proof conclusive that *they,* at least, had not been kept in ignorance.

Desiring now to compare the Secretary's practice with his theory we turn to his report for December, 1866, and there read as follows, the italics being our own:—

"Under these circumstances, feeling sensible of the great responsibility of his position, the Secretary has deemed it safer and better for the country to act according to the dictates of his own judgment, carefully regarding the condition of the markets and of the treasury, rather than to take his direction from those who, however intelligent and able, were under no official obligations to the government, and might be less accurately advised in regard to the actual state of its financial affairs. *He has regarded a steady market as of more importance to the people than the saving of a few millions of dollars in the way of interest; and observation and experience have assured him that, in order to secure this steadiness in any considerable degree, while business is conducted on a paper basis, there must be power in the treasury to prevent successful combinations to bring about fluctuations for purely speculative purposes."*

Here, as elsewhere, the theory is excellent, but when we compare it with the practice, it is found that the last sentence of this passage would very accurately describe the latter had it told us that the treasury must have "power for the *promotion* of successful combinations to bring about fluctuations for merely speculative purposes."

The Secretary bitterly opposes all that "speculation" which manifests itself in the opening of mines, or the building of mills and furnaces. Of all the financial ministers the world has yet seen, those alone excepted by whom Louis Napoleon has been surrounded, there is, nevertheless, none who has more favored that class of "speculators" which profits by causing the "fluctuations" he here professes himself desirous to prevent.

§ 4. "The debt is large, but *if kept at home,* as it is desirable that it should be, with a judicious system of taxation, it *need not be oppressive.*"—*Report on the Finances, Dec.* 1865.

Such was the Secretary's theory at the opening of the Thirty-ninth Congress, but little more than two years since. Nevertheless, almost before the ink had dried with which it had been written, and certainly before there had elapsed even a single month, he had become most urgent with Congress to permit him to manufacture bonds expressly calculated for European markets. Most wisely, permission was refused, Congress having been then of the opinion that the debt, if *not* "kept at home," *must* become "oppressive;" and that it would become more and more unbearable as it became more and more the property of absentees, whether foreign or domestic.

One year later, in the Secretary's Report of December, 1866, we find him addressing Congress in these words:—

"Our importations of goods have been increased by nearly the amount of the bonds which have been exported. Not one dollar in five of the amount of the five-twenties now held in England and upon the continent has been returned to the United States in the form of real capital. But if this were not a true statement of the case, the fact exists, as has already been stated, that some three hundred and fifty millions of government bonds—not to mention State and railroad bonds, and other securities—are in the hands of the citizens of other countries, *which may be returned at any time for sale in the United States, and which, being so held, may seriously embarrass our efforts to return to specie payments.*"

The theory here propounded is admirable, but what was to be its writer's practice? Did this latter look towards bringing about a state of things that should enable the smaller holders among ourselves to retain the bonds yet remaining in their hands? Did it look to abolition of that great money monopoly in the creation of which the writer himself had taken so large a part, and by means of which the domestic market for bonds, as security for circulating notes, has been limited to little more than $300,000,000? Did it in any manner tend toward lessening the power of foreign creditors over all our movements? Nothing of the kind! Directly the reverse, the Secretary asked that

"He should be authorized to issue bonds, not having more than twenty years to run, and bearing a low rate of interest, payable in England or Germany, to be used in taking up the six per cents now held abroad, *and in meeting any foreign demand for investment that may exist.* The question now to be considered is not," as he continued, "how shall our bonds be prevented from going abroad—for a large amount has already gone, and others will follow as long as our credit is good, and we continue to buy more than we can pay for in any other way—but, how shall they be prevented from being thrown upon the home market, to thwart our efforts in restoring the specie standard? The Secretary sees no practicable method of doing this at any early day, but by substituting for them bonds which, being payable principal and interest in Europe, will be less likely to be returned when their return is the least desired."

Here, as everywhere, we find the Secretary's practice to be in direct conflict with the theory so well presented in his report. Finding this latter excellent, and having no faith whatsoever in the former, Congress again refused the permission for which he had thus again applied.

Another year having now rolled round we are favored with a new report, containing not even a single word in reference to the exceeding dangers to be apprehended from the existence of a foreign debt for the mere interest on which there are now required sixty millions of gold dollars, and most probably a quantity greatly larger. Equally silent is he seen to be in regard to his favorite idea of manufacturing bonds expressly calculated for captivating the fancies of the little capitalists of Continental Europe—theory and practice being, apparently, alike forgotten. Not so, however, the whole scheme promptly reappearing in another shape, demanding $20,000,000 for meeting the expenses incident to carrying it into full effect; and threatening, like the celebrated horse of Amy Darden, to be ridden year after year into our legislative halls until, as in that memorable case, Congress shall, from sheer exhaustion, be led to grant the power for which the demand had been so persistent.

Meanwhile the Secretary has not failed to use all the power with which he had been, unhappily, invested; nor is he likely to do so in the future. The foreign market requires gold-bearing bonds, and will take nothing else. Seven-thirties cannot, therefore, go abroad. So, too, is it with legal-tenders and compound-interest notes. To fit them for exportation they must be converted into five-twenties, a work to be accomplished at any cost. So well has it been accomplished that these latter have gone by *tons weight* across the Atlantic, and so rapidly as effectually to have prevented any rise of price, and to have caused a national loss of probably a hundred millions.

Common sense might have taught the Secretary that the more cotton, wheat, bonds, or any other commodity, forced upon the foreign market, the lower *must* be the price abroad and at home. Equally might it have taught him that the more he increased the necessity for gold the higher must · be its price. Setting at naught, however, all its teachings, he has glutted Europe with the one, while so increasing his need for the other that he now *dares not* to do anything tending to prevent increasing the foreign debt. Bonds *must* be sold that gold may be made to flow into the treasury·through the custom-house; and any failure to find further foreign markets for securities must, and certainly *will*, be followed by failure to pay the gold interest the Secretary now so freely promises.

Those promises can be redeemed only on condition of an import of merchandise that, after deducting other demands abroad which constitute first mortgages upon our exports, leaves a balance of hundreds of millions to be paid in either gold or bonds. The more we send of the latter the lower will be their price, and the higher will be the rate of interest; and yet, strange to say, the Secretary fancies that it is by means of travel in that direction we are to reach resumption !

With each new bond manufactured by the Secretary, in defiance of his own teachings, for exportation, it becomes more uncertain as to when, if ever, we shall resume the use of the precious metals. With each it becomes more certain that the road in which he would have us travel finds its termination in bankruptcy of the treasury, and final repudiation of the public debt.

§ 5. Of the many lessons taught us by the war the most important was that from which we learned that the national strength had grown, and must continue to grow, with the growth of self-dependence. Mining our own coal, smelting our own ores, and making, wearing, or using our own iron and cloth, swords and guns, ships and engines, but little difficulty was experienced in meeting the large demands of the government for labor and its products of any and every kind, accepting, in return, its promises to pay in money at a future day; doing all this too not only without the aid of British capitalists, but in direct defiance of their predictions that the debt thus being contracted neither could nor would ever be discharged. For the first time in our history we found ourselves released from all dependence on foreign banks and bankers.

Throughout the war the societary circulation had been rapid to a degree never before known in any country of the world. Labor had, therefore, been so productive as to have enabled thousands and tens of thousands of working men and women to accumulate little capitals; and so absolute was their faith in the public promises of future payment that they gladly placed their little earnings in the treasury, to be used for prosecution of the war. Confidence of the people in their government so far begot confidence in each other that throughout the whole range of the loyal States it made itself manifest in the great fact, that in the rate of interest paid by poor and rich, by the weak and the strong, the owner of the little workshop and the proprietors of the great railroad, the man of the East and his correspondent in the West, there was a nearer approach to equality than had here ever before been known.

With return of peace and the accession to power of the present Secretary it came, however, to be discovered that, however well-intentioned might have been his predecessors, their whole movement had been grievously erroneous and must be at once retraced. Machinery of exchange had been too abundant, and the supply thereof must be contracted. The community had become too largely indebted to its individual members, and the debt must at the earliest moment be diminished, preparatory to being, and at an early date, entirely discharged. Lenders had been placed at a disadvantage as compared with borrowers, and needed now to have their grievances redressed. That all this might be done—and done, too, at a time when States, counties, cities, and individuals were yet struggling under heavy burthens resulting from voluntary contributions to the extent of hundreds of millions—it was needed that prices should be everywhere diminished, taxes meanwhile being maintained at their greatest height; the Secretary thus demanding that the people's candle should be burned at both ends, with a view, perhaps, to determination of the important question as to how long, under such circumstances, it could be made at all to last.

So it has been burnt until mines, mills, and workshops have to so great an extent been closed that hundreds of thousands of working-men, their wives and children, have been deprived of bread; their owners, meantime, having been wholly deprived of revenue.

So it has been burnt until the domestic consumption of cotton has been to so great an extent diminished as to *force* upon the country that increase of dependence on foreign markets which has reduced its price to less than the cost at which it could be reproduced.

So it has been burnt until confidence has so nearly disappeared that working-men, the really useful portions of society, find themselves compelled to pay thrice, even when not quadruple, the rate of interest.

So it has been burnt until long loans on individual credit have almost entirely given place to loans "on call," on the security of government bonds.

So it has been burnt until our dependence on foreign banks and bankers has become more complete than at any former period.

So it has been burnt until the Secretary has become entirely dependent

on imports resulting from the sale of bonds abroad for means with which
to pay the daily growing interest on the public debt.

So it has been burnt until from almost the whole interior comes advice
of entire inability to meet the just demands of city merchants.

So it has been burnt until the picture presented in all our cities has
become that described in the following paragraphs cut from journals of
the day:—

DESTITUTION IN PHILADELPHIA.—Unusual destitution is prevailing this winter
among a class which has hitherto been comparatively free from want. We refer
to respectable mechanics with their families, and work-women of every kind, such
as have never before needed alms. Rev. Mr. Long, the Bedford Street missionary,
whose specialty it is to relieve poverty, declares that the misery among the
respectable poor, who are the last to beg, is heart-rending. Those who are able and
willing to contribute alms, which will be employed in the most judicious manner,
may send them to this gentleman, No. 619 Bedford Street. There is at present
especial need in this severe weather for shoes and garments.

"The report of the NEW YORK ASSOCIATION for improving the condition of the
poor, shows that during the month of January the number of the needy classes
was greater than in the corresponding one of any year save January, 1855. Great
as is the present destitution, the Association fears it will become even greater, as
the month of February is always found to be the most trying for the poor. Compared with the past winter, there has been, up to the present time, a decrease of
$5411 in its receipts. This fact finds an explanation in the existing business
depression, which not only causes increased want to be relieved, but contracts
one of the main sources of that relief. In addition to this cause, the Association
has not been favored as usual with special donations; and, although no public
appeal has as yet been made, it has become necessary to do so. The total number
of families assisted during the month was 4943, and of persons 18,123. The
amount expended in relief was $13,021.14, and the number of visits amounted
to $8712."

The Boston *Traveller* says: "Such has become the increased demand for soup
at the station-houses that it has been found necessary to procure sixty-gallon ket-
tles instead of those holding only forty gallons, which were first put in use. Yesterday several of our first men tested the quality of mutton soup provided, and
pronounced it capital, and good enough for anybody."

Such having been the results obtained, we may now, for a moment,
study the Treasury process by means of which so disastrous a state of
things has been produced.

Throughout the war, confidence being universal, capital was freely
scattered through the country to the great advantage of farmers, miners,
manufacturers, and working-men of every kind. To compel its withdrawal and to raise the current rate of interest that confidence needed
to be destroyed, and to that end it was required that we should have successive shocks, such as have already been described—gold being sold at
one moment and paper withdrawn, the latter being again pushed out as
the former was heaped up—until it should become manifest that none but
the very rich could hope to prosecute their operations to a successful ter-

mination. To what extent this system has been carried throughout the past half year has been already shown, and its effects in forcing capital back on the great centres of speculation are here described:—

"The monetary irregularities connected with the arbitrary withdrawal of a large portion of the circulation caused the banks throughout the country to hold an ample amount of their funds constantly in readiness for sudden emergencies; and the suspension of the process, having removed these dangers, has left the interior banks free to employ an enlarged proportion of their money with their New York correspondents. This accumulation of deposits, however, is to be regarded as indicating an unusual contraction of business operations, which is another of the injurious consequences of an unnatural process of contraction."—*Circular of Clews & Co., New York, Feb. 7.*

The general alarm of September last, consequent upon large sales of gold, and refusal of the Secretary to give any *public* notice of his intentions in regard to the three per cent. certificates, caused a reduction of the deposits of the associated banks of New York, from 195 to 178 millions. In October, when the Secretary gave out paper and heaped up gold, they rose again to $187,000,000. Sales of gold and absorption of paper, in November, forced them down at the opening of December, to $174,000,000. Giving out of paper and retention of gold carried them up again, until, on the 4th of January, they had reached $187,000,000; and on the 1st of the present month, no less an amount than $213,000,000, or about $10,000,000 in excess of anything that had before been known. Such have been, and such still are, the movements of a finance minister who professes himself opposed to "speculation," and gravely asks for power to be used in preventing "*successful combinations to bring about fluctuations for purely speculative purposes.*"

By all this *somebody* profits. That the general public does not would seem to be proved by the following from the same Circular to which we have been indebted for the paragraph given above:—

"In financial circles there is a very general feeling of dissatisfaction at the bearing of the public debt upon the rate of interest. There is now held on this side of the Atlantic, about $1,400,000,000 of United States gold-bearing bonds, the larger portion of which yield interest equal in currency to 8 to 8¼ per cent. This high rate of interest upon such an enormous aggregate of investments has a tendency to keep capital aloof from productive employments, and naturally compels borrowers to pay more for the use of money than they can afford. The prevalence of high prices and the heavy taxation of products tend directly to reduce the net profits upon business; and, as an offset to this diminution of profits, money should be procurable at a proportionately lower interest. But so long as the Government is paying such exorbitant rates, this desideratum is impossible of attainment. Should this condition of things be long continued, the mercantile interest must be ultimately seriously impoverished, and the progress of the country retarded."

Who, then, *does* profit by all these contrivances for raising the rate of interest—for improving the condition of those who live without labor—

and for destroying public and private credit? The answer to this question is found in the fact that there are always certain persons who know
exactly *when to buy and when to sell*, and who *do* buy and *do* sell at precisely the time when profit is certain to result therefrom. For the benefit of
such persons, and not that of the people at large, is, to all appearance, the
Treasury now administered; and if such a course of administration shall
not have the effect of bringing about final repudiation of the debt, it will
need to be recorded as one of the most wonderful facts in financial history.

How all this affects the general power to contribute towards payment
of either principal or interest of the debt, may be understood by those
who study the following figures, representing the state of the Treasury at
the opening of the year, and on the first of the present month:—

	January.	February.
Currency	$25,770,000	$25,578,000
On deposit [estimated] .	23,000,000	23,000,000
In Sub-treasury . . .	$2,770,000	$2,578,000
Gold	88,400,000	68,862,000
Total . . .	$91,176,000	$71,440,000

With no diminution whatsoever of the debt there is, as here is shown, an
actual loss of $20,000,000 in the means with which to meet it. Deducting
this from the payments of the month, $42,700,000, we obtain as the actual
revenue less than $23,000,000, or the equivalent of $270,000,000 for the
year; and even that obtained at the cost of sacrifices on the part of tax
payers that find no parallel in any portion of our financial history. Seeking compensation therefor, the unhappy sufferers must be content to find it
in the fact that to banks, bankers, and Treasury agents the system has
proved so largely profitable that they now propose to establish in Washington a journal charged with the especial duty of advocating that policy
under which the many are being deprived of bread, while the few become
daily richer; that one under which the burthen of the debt increases with
every hour; that one which tends to carry us forward, and with daily increased rapidity, towards final repudiation.

§ 6. "The Secretary of the Treasury holds despotic power over the material
interests of the country, and it is now known by the disclosures made, beyond
truthful denial, that the authority he holds has been used, ignorantly or by
design, to promote private ends at public cost.

"It is an error to suppose that the Secretary is deprived of the power of contraction or inflation of the currency. He may sell bonds or gold at his pleasure,
privately; collect the proceeds of sale in currency, withhold it from circulation,
and thereby reduce it temporarily, as certainly as if the notes were cancelled;
and then, by payments from the Treasury, inflate again.

" Prior to the war, the uniform practice of the Government was to offer to public
competition the bonds of the United States, and awarding them to the highest
bidder. Then no secretary would have dared to sell bonds without special
authority, and by public sale. The employment of brokers was unknown, and
transactions, such as have been reported, would have insured prompt inquiry and
condemnation.

"The exigencies of the war appeared to justify another course of action, and
many thoughtful and experienced men saw its dangers, and warned the public of
the threatening peril; but they warned in vain, and that which was intended to

be only temporary, became the established practice, and the prevalence of a remarkable and unaccountable apathy in regard to the financial interests of the country, doubtless protected the officials and their friends from the investigation which now is being instituted. Encouraged by the indifference referred to, and stimulated by the hope of vast additional gains, the famous 'Sherman Funding Bill' was conceived; a scheme doubtless the product of much thought and of many minds, fertile in expedients, and skilled in the art of applying language to conceal and not express their thoughts and designs."

In the views thus expressed by the able author of an anonymous paper just now published nearly all will now fully coincide. Entire as was its confidence in the integrity of the then finance minister, and fully as that confidence has been justified by the fairness and openness of his conduct throughout the war, Congress certainly, and greatly, erred in granting to any one, however honest or however able, an exercise of power so absolute as was that granted to Mr. Chase. Necessity alone could at all have justified such a course of action. With the close of the war that necessity ceased, and thenceforth should there have been a change the most complete, publicity being enforced and the finance minister of the day, be he whom he might, being thus freed from the suspicion that must necessarily arise when hundreds of millions are negotiated with a privacy so perfect as to have given no little color to the charge that millions, if not even tens of millions, had been made so to pass into the hands of the negotiators as almost entirely to defy detection.*

Mr. Chase and his immediate successor courted publicity; whereas, their successor, the present Secretary, so entirely avoids it that, outside of a certain magic circle, few pretend even to guess at the shuffling of the cards till the game has throughout been played, and the winnings bagged. The former always used words calculated to "express," and *not* to "conceal their thoughts and designs"—never saying *black* when they really meant *white*. With the latter all is different, his teachings and his practice being uniformly in conflict with each other, black meaning always white, and *vice versâ*, as will now be shown.

Professing publicly a desire to prevent inflation and stigmatizing as "inflationists" all who fail to see the public advantage that is to result from building up the fortunes of banks, bankers, treasury agents, and all others within *the ring*, we find him privately injecting tens of millions into those great centres of speculation in which single millions do more toward producing the inflation he affects to deprecate than could be done by tens of millions of legal tenders given to the Centre and the West:

Professing publicly a desire to bring about financial stability we find him privately exchanging millions and tens of millions of gold for the "paper money" he so much dislikes; and then again as suddenly, and as privately, reconverting millions of this greatly despised "paper money" into gold:

Publicly professing a desire to prevent "speculation" he is constantly

---

* "The administration of the Treasury Department under Secretary M'Culloch reminds one of the rebuses which appear in certain ambitious periodicals, with the provoking note—'Solution in our next.' It is a perpetual rebus which keeps us all guessing wildly day and night, until the appearance of the next monthly exhibit from the Department puts us out of our pain by furnishing the solution.

"Everybody guessed the rebus for May. The blunder of the Department was so enormous that nobody needed to wait for the June statement to learn that thirty millions of gold had been thrown away at 15 @ 20 per cent. below the market, and that somebody had thereby realized a neat little profit of three or four millions."—*Harper's Weekly.*

and privately engaged in bringing about the changes desired by speculators, so well succeeding that the chill and the fever now follow each other with a rapidity wholly unparalleled in our financial history:

Publicly professing a desire to prevent "successful combinations to bring about fluctuations for purely speculative purposes," the chief business of the Treasury now, to all appearance, consists in privately organizing such combinations:

Publicly professing a desire to keep the debt at home, the private arrangements all tend towards compelling small holders to part with their little property, and thus to furnish the bonds required for foreign markets, and for facilitating those imports by aid of which, alone, the Secretary can at all hope to obtain the gold whose payment he now so freely promises.

The regular recurrence of this opposition between theory and practice may, perhaps, be attended with some disadvantages; but, on the other hand, it has the recommendation that when we desire to know what it is that the Secretary means privately to do we need only to seek for the opposite of that which publicly he recommends as proper to be done.

Looking thus always one way while rowing in another the Secretary furnishes a subject for "speculation" the like of which the financial world, here or elsewhere, till now, has never seen—a whole people "speculating" as to how it is that the cards are being shuffled. Detectives innumerable hover about his path, at one moment announcing that 10-40's are being smuggled into circulation, and at the next that offers for millions of the same had been privately refused. Closely following public efforts at stimulating offers of 7-30's comes the announcement that the Secretary had privately ceased to purchase. On one day we learn that gold had been gradually smuggled out; while on the next it is suggested that, determined to hold the gold operators in check, the Secretary has determined to make no further sales. These things may, or may not, be true, but there is always one set of men *that certainly knows*, and that gains by all the movements, those looking to contraction as well as those by means of which "inflation" has so frequently, so privately, and so profitably to the ring, been brought about.

In thus privately arranging for so many hundreds of millions, and thus exposing himself to suspicions so injurious, the Secretary may, perhaps, be misled by the belief that he is rendering public service, and that, Curtius like, he is sacrificing himself for his country's good. If so, it being wholly wrong to accept such sacrifice, Congress should at once prohibit private arrangements of any kind whatsoever, and insist on the most perfect publicity being given to every financial operation, large or small. By so doing it would relieve the Secretary as regards the future, but what of the past? Must he forever be exposed to charges of the malevolent to the effect that he had been prompted by private reasons to the enormous changes above described as having occurred in the past half year? Assuredly not. Congress would seem bound now to afford him opportunity for showing that in all those extraordinary movements he had proved himself as pure as had been either of his distinguished predecessors. Justice would seem to require that he should, too, be allowed the fullest opportunity for showing that there is not the slightest reason for the belief, now so universal, that the exits and the entrances of the Treasury are so carefully guarded as entirely to prevent effectuation of any public arrangements in regard to disposal of the public revenues.

The financial despotism now here established cannot be paralleled in any civilized country of the world. Determined to maintain it in its full effect, and utterly careless, apparently, in regard to reputation, the Secretary has resisted with all the force of eloquence and of patronage, every attempt at limitation of his power, or at restoration of publicity in his course of operation. Congress has, however, now rebelled, having prohibited further reduction of the greenback currency, and provided for deposit in the sub-treasuries of nearly all the public moneys. So far it has done well, but further steps are needed. The Secretary ought to be instructed to furnish greenbacks to the banks in payment of the many millions that the interest-bearing notes exceed the 50,000,000 of three per cent certificates. The effect of such a measure would be only that of causing the banks to retain their reserves in notes not bearing interest. It would make little, if any, addition to the currency, while it would save the annual $2,000,000 of gold that would otherwise be required for payment of interest on the five-twenties with which the Secretary proposes that they be replaced. It would, too, greatly limit his power to manufacture gold bonds for exportation, than which there are few things to be so much dreaded.

Further, the Secretary should be forbidden to make any further sales of gold, and should be thus deprived of all power for disturbing the money market in the way that has been above described. For this there are however, other and important reasons as will readily be seen by those who mark the fact that the sale abroad of bonds is steadily declining, and with it the power to purchase that foreign merchandise to whose import, alone, we are to look for the gold required for payment of interest on the bonds the Secretary has already so profusely manufactured. The day is now near at hand when custom-house receipts must fail to meet the gold demand; when the small amount that thus far has been hoarded will be greatly needed; and, when the value of the declarations now being made in regard to perfect maintenance of the public faith will be severely tested. What is the present tendency of affairs is shown in the fact that Pennsylvania sixes, payable principal and interest in lawful money, are preferred, at equal prices, to treasury obligations that are payable, principal and interest, in coin that now sells at 140; and that, without a total change of system, must at no distant date command a very much higher price.*

What the country now needs is restoration of that confidence of our people in each other, and of the whole body of the people in the honest management of their financial affairs, which so fully existed down to the date at which the present Secretary entered upon their management; both of which have now so entirely disappeared. To that end it is indispensable that Congress resume the control that so fully existed before the war, dictating orders and not accepting them, as has recently been so much the case. Let that body tell the Secretary what to do and how to do it; let it prohibit, under heavy penalties, such private arrangements as have been above described; and there will be then reason for hoping that the day may yet come when a people who thirty years since paid off, at par, a debt bearing but three per cent. interest, may cease to be compelled to beg for money in all the markets of Europe, gladly paying for the use thereof *little less than thrice that rate.*

---

* Seven-thirties convertible into gold six per cent. bonds sell at 107½, State bonds, payable in 1881, commanding 108½ to 109.

SHALL WE HAVE PEACE?
PEACE FINANCIAL, AND PEACE POLITICAL?

LETTERS

TO THE

PRESIDENT ELECT OF THE UNITED STATES:

BY

H. C. CAREY.

PHILADELPHIA:
COLLINS, PRINTER, 705 JAYNE STREET.
1869.

SHALL WE HAVE PEACE?

DEAR SIR:—

LET us have peace! In these brief words you express the unanimous wish of the loyal portion of the nation, North and South, and of whatsoever shade of color. It is the one great and preponderant desire of all that portion of our population which, at the close of a tedious and destructive war, has now succeeded in placing in the presidential chair the man to whom they had been most of all indebted for suppression of the armed rebellion. That there should be peace, and that it should be permanent, is to the true interest of all, whether loyalists or rebels, and it is in the interest of all that I now propound the great question, *Shall we have peace* —not a temporary one to be maintained by aid of military force, but such a peace as shall tend, day by day and year by year, so to bind together and consolidate the different portions of the Union as to render absolutely impossible a recurrence of scenes of war and waste like to those through which we so recently have passed? *Can* we have such a peace? For answer to this I have to say that such an one has recently, and on the largest scale, been established in Central Europe, and that all now needed among ourselves is that we study carefully what has there been done, and then imitate the great example which has there been set us.

Five and thirty years since, Germany presented to view a collection of loose fragments, most of which were mere tools in the hands of neighboring powers, France or England at one hour, Russia or Austria at another. A state of civil war had for centuries been the chronic condition of the country, and, as a necessary consequence, poverty, and such poverty as in our loyal States is entirely unknown, had, with but few exceptions, been the condition of all classes of her people.

Brief as is the period which has since elapsed, an empire has been there created embracing a population little short of 40,000,000, among whom education is universal; with a system of communications that, with the exception of those provided for the very dense populations and limited territories of England and Belgium, is not excelled by that of any other country; with an internal commerce as perfectly organized as any in the world, and growing from day to day with extraordinary rapidity; with a market on the land for nearly all its products, and, as a necessary consequence, with an agricultural population that grows daily in both intelligence and power; with a mercantile marine that now numbers more than 10,000 vessels; with a public treasury so well provided that not only has it made the recent war without need for negotiating loans, but that it has at once made large additions to the provision for

1

public education; and with private treasuries so well supplied as to enable its people not only with their own means to build their own furnaces and factories and construct their own roads, but also to furnish hundreds of millions to the improvident people of America, to be by them applied to the making of roads in a country the abundance of whose natural resources should long since have placed it in the position of money lender, rather than that now occupied of general money borrower.

To what now, has this all been due? To the quiet and simple operation of the protective features of the system of the Zoll-Verein, the most important measure of the century, and among the most important ever adopted in Europe. Under it labor has been everywhere economized. Under it, the producers and consumers of a whole nation have been brought into communication with each other, and thus has been created a great society which is destined ultimately, in all probability, to produce effects throughout the Eastern continent fully equal to any that may, by even the most sanguine, be hoped for in this Western one.

§ 2. Five and thirty years since, Germany and the American Union exhibited states of things directly antagonistic, the one to the other. The first was divided and disturbed, its internal commerce in every way embarrassed, its people and its various governments very poor, and with little hope in the future except that which resulted from the fact that negotiations were then on foot for the formation of a Customs Union, which, shortly after, was accomplished. In the other, on the contrary, everything was different, the internal commerce having been more active than had ever before been known, the public treasury filled to overflowing, the national debt on the eve of extinction, and capital so much abounding as to make demand, for the opening of mines, the building of houses and mills, and the construction of roads, for all the labor power of a people that then numbered thirteen millions.

The cause of these remarkable differences was to be found in the facts, that, up to that time, Germany had wholly failed to adopt such measures of co-ordination as were needed for establishing circulation among its 30,000,000 of population; whereas, our Union had, five years before, and for the first time, adopted measures having for their object development of all the powers, physical, mental, or moral, of its people, all the wealth of its soil, and all the wonderful mineral deposits by which that soil was known to be underlaid. The one had failed to bring together the producer and consumer of food and wool, and had remained dependent upon traders in distant maikets. The other had just then willed that such dependence should, at no distant time, come to an end; that producers and consumers should be brought together; and there had thence already resulted an activity of circulation and an improvement in physical and moral condition, the like of which had never before been known to be accomplished in so brief a period.

But little later (1835), the two countries are once again found totally opposed, Germany having adopted the American system and thus provided for freedom of internal commerce, America simultaneously adopting that which to Germany had proved so utterly disastrous, and which had been there rejected. Thenceforth the former moved steadily forward in the direction of creating a great domestic commerce, doing this by means of a railroad system which should so bind together her whole people as to forbid the idea of future separation. The result already exhibits itself in the quiet creation of the most powerful empire of Europe. The latter meanwhile has constructed great roads by means of which it has exported its soil, in the forms of tobacco, corn, and cotton, to distant markets, and has thus diminished its power to maintain internal commerce—the result obtained exhibiting itself in a great rebellion that has cost the country, North and South, half a million of lives, the crippling of hundreds of thousands of men, and an expenditure of more thousands of millions than, properly applied, would have doubled the incomes of its whole people, while making such demand for human force, mental, moral, and physical, as would, in a brief period, have secured the establishment of universal freedom, with benefit to all, white and black, landowner and laborer. Such have been the widely different results of two systems of public policy, the one of which looks to introducing into society that proper, orderly arrangement which is found in every well conducted private establishment, and by means of which each and every person employed is enabled to find the place for which nature had intended him; the other, meanwhile, in accordance with the doctrine of *laisser faire*, requiring that government should abdicate the performance of its proper duties, wholly overlooking the fact that all the communities by which such teachings are carried into practical effect now exhibit themselves before the world in a state of utter ruin.

§ 3. Studying now our American railroad system, we find the great trunk lines to be, so far as regards the North and the South, purely sectional, all of them running east and west and the whole constituting a collection of spokes in a great wheel whose hub, wholly controlled by men like Laird and other workers in aid of the great rebellion, is found in Liverpool. As a consequence of this it had been that our dependence on such men had become more complete as those great lines had increased in number, and with every such increase our financial crises had become more frequent and more severe. Prior to the war a single turn of the British screw had sufficed for ruining thousands of those who had invested their means in the opening of mines, the building of furnaces or factories, and for thus crushing out the most important portions of our domestic commerce. With each such crisis there came increased necessity for scattering our people over the land, and for limiting ourselves to that single species of employment which is the essential characteristic of semi-barbarism—the raising of raw produce for the supply of distant markets. From year to year the tide of white emigration rose, following always the lines of road and canal of the extreme North, and carefully avoiding the Central States. Simultaneously, south of Mason and Dixon's line, a black emigration depleted the Centre, Virginia and Kentucky, Maryland and Delaware, furnishing the bone and the muscle required for consumption in the fields of Mississippi and of Texas. As a consequence of this, the extreme

South and the extreme North grew steadily in the proportions borne by them to the whole system, until at length, as an unavoidable consequence, the body broke in two, with serious danger of seeing the parts forever separated.

Why was this? For the simple reason that the revenue tariff policy so long and so steadily pursued had effectually prevented development of the wonderful mineral resources of Maryland, Virginia, North Carolina, and the whole column of States extending west of these, embracing hundreds of millions of acres the like of which had elsewhere no existence. Had our policy been different—had we strengthened the centre—there would have been such a growth of domestic commerce that roads would have been made running north and south, northeast and southwest, southeast and northwest, thereby so tying together the various parts of the Union as to render it wholly impossible that the idea of secession should continue to have existence. *Had that centre been strengthened, as it should have been the slave would have been becoming gradually free, independence would have been fully established, we should have had no rebellion, and we should have been spared the mortification of feeling that the solution of the question as to whether or not the Union could be maintained rested almost wholly in the minds of men like Russell and Napoleon.*

Turning now to a railroad map of Germany, we find that each and every part of that now greatest of all European empires has been, and is daily being, more and more brought into communication with each and every other as direct and cheap as is now the case in our little New England States. Bavaria and Wurtemberg on the south, Mecklenburg and Westphalia on the north, are now so tied together that separation, under any circumstances, has become a thing to be no longer thought of. That this was so was clearly shown at the close of the recent war, the sovereigns of southern Germany having been compelled, notwithstanding the solicitations of France and Austria, not only to maintain but even to strengthen their relations with the *Zoll-Verein.* Peace and harmony within—strength for resistance to attack from without—material and mental wealth—political and industrial independence—all had grown together with the growth of that domestic commerce which with us has so studiously and carefully been destroyed.

Widely different would be now the state of Europe had Southern and Northern Germany been accustomed to do as we have done, making all their exchanges with each other through the medium of Paris and Lyons, Liverpool and Havre. Had they done so, the great German empire could never have had existence. Had we *not* done so—had we *not* continued Liverpool as the hub of our great political wheel—we should have escaped an expenditure of hundreds of thousands of lives, and of thousands of millions of dollars. For all that waste we stand this day indebted to the men who gave us the tariffs of 1846 and 1857 in lieu of that highly protective one of 1842 under which the nation was so rapidly achieving a real independence; and by means of which the reward of labor had so much increased that, and for the first time, immigration began to count by hundreds of thousands.—*Desiring now to prevent a recurrence of that waste, we must have a policy capable of giving us the great domestic commerce for which nature has so well provided as the basis of the greatest foreign commerce the world ever yet has known.*

§ 4. The difference between the two systems consists in this, that while Germany has been unremitting in her efforts to make a piece of cloth, warp and woof, America has limited her efforts to the making of warp alone, the filling having been entirely omitted. The one has sought increase of domestic commerce, creating a great network of roads, and bringing consumer and producer more nearly together; the other, meantime, has looked exclusively abroad, wholly overlooking the fact that each and every step tended to the further separation of producer and consumer, and to the further diminution of power to maintain commerce of any kind, either abroad or at home.

The road toward perfect peace, perfect union, perfect freedom of trade, and perfect political independence, lies through the establishment of perfect industrial independence. It is the one on which Germany for forty years has travelled; the one which we, and just at the moment when its vast advantages were being proved, so often have abandoned. It is the one on which we *must* travel if we would have peace.

President Lincoln's attention having been, at the opening of the war, called to the view that is here presented, he recommended to Congress the making of a road through Kentucky to and through East Tennessee, to connect with other roads leading to South Atlantic ports. Had that suggestion been adopted, Kentucky would this day be a loyal State, and Tennessee would be now engaged in works of development causing such an emigration from the North as would be giving to her loyal people a power of control such as would insure the maintenance of peace. Had it been adopted, another road would probably have been suggested, leading from the Northeast to the Southwest, the two tending to bring about between the North and the South the same intimate relations which now exist between the East and the West. Rejected by Congress, an opportunity was thus lost that with difficulty will again be found. Twenty millions spent in the manner that Mr. Lincoln would have advised would have given us an emigration southward that would have effectually controlled the men who are now assuming the direction of the movements of Georgia, Alabama, and Mississippi. Those few millions would before this time have produced results that would now be cheap at hundreds, if not even thousands of millions.

Long persistence in a policy directly the reverse of that which has in so short a period built up the great German empire, has given us a rebellion, and that rebellion has led to a state of things wholly adverse to the maintenance of a permanent peace. So must it continue to be unless the national government can now be brought to co-operate with loyal Southern men for production of a change. Unaided, the people of the Centre, the South, and the Southwest cannot make the roads that are now most needed, and without which there can be no security for the maintenance of such a state of things as would warrant Northern men in opening Southern mines, in building furnaces or factories, by means of which the consumers and producers of the South might be brought together. Can they have such aid? Apparently they cannot, millions upon millions being lavished upon Eastern and Western roads which, useful as they may eventually prove to be, tend now to intensification rather than to obliteration of the sectional feelings under which we have already so greatly suffered. Such roads need comparatively little help from government, Eastern capitalists being always ready for any measures tending to bring trade to the great cities, European or American, of the Atlantic coast. Northern and Southern roads—roads tending toward development of the extraordinary mineral wealth of the Central States—roads tending to enable the cotton of the South to reach mills and factories in the West—do need it, and for the reason that those capitalists are not yet so far enlightened as at all to appreciate the idea that the larger the domestic commerce the greater must be the power to purchase those finer commodities for which the Centre, the West, and the South are accustomed to look to Philadelphia and Baltimore, New York and Boston.

An expenditure for such purposes, involving an annual demand upon the Treasury for less than half a dozen millions, would add five times that amount to the annual public revenue, while giving to the domestic commerce a development that would add countless millions to the money value of labor and land, and by promoting immigration from abroad would do more for elevation of the down-trodden people of the eastern continent than ·has been done by all its sovereigns from the days of Charlemagne.

That we may have permanent peace, and that the desire of all loyal men may thus be realized, it is needed that our people be brought to understand that between the various portions of the Union there is a perfect harmony of real and permanent interests, all profiting by measures looking to establishment of perfect political and industrial independence, and all suffering from those which tend to prolong a dependence upon those foreign communities that hailed with so much joy the action of the men who initiated the great rebellion.

Throughout the world the tendency towards peace, freedom, and independence has grown as consumers and producers have been brought more nearly together, as the societary circulation has become more rapid, and as land and labor have become more productive. That peace may be here maintained—that all may really enjoy equality of rights—that the Union may be perpetuated—and, that the country may enjoy a real independence—we *must* have a system that shall tend towards enabling our whole people to make their exchanges with each other freed from the interference of foreign ships, or foreign merchants.

In another letter I propose to show the bearing of the measures above proposed upon the condition of the recently enfranchised people of the south, and through them on the Union at large, meanwhile remaining, with great regard and respect,·

Yours truly,

GEN. U. S. GRANT.   HENRY C. CAREY.

PHILADELPHIA, November 5, 1868.

LETTER SECOND.

DEAR SIR:

Little more than sixty years since the German people were in a condition so nearly akin to slavery that the chief difference between them and the colored people of our Southern States consisted in the fact, that while these latter could, the former could not, be sold at the horse block like other chattels. On the other hand, while the American slave had a positive money value that made it desirable to grant protection to children in their infancy, and to men and women in their age, the Germans had no such value except when, as with the Hessian sovereign of our Revolution, their masters could find opportunities for selling them by regiments as food for powder. Badly fed, badly clothed, wretchedly poor, and with no poor-laws by aid of which they might be enabled to demand assistance in case of illness, few, very few indeed, could command even the trifling means required for enabling them to seek abroad the subsistence denied to their families and themselves at home.' Some few did then occasionally cross the Atlantic, but most generally as "redemptioners," liable to sale in open market for as many years of service as were then required for payment of their passages.

Such was the state of things throughout Germany when the disastrous campaign of Jena (1806), closely succeeding that of Ulm (1805), followed as it was by the almost entire subjugation by France of the German people, first awakened Prussian statesmen to an appreciation of the fact that if Prussia would ever resume her place in the family of nations she must look to the elevation of her whole people, and bring to a close her dependence on an effete landed aristocracy whose utter worthlessness had so recently been entirely proved. Prompt and energetic, the great man (Baron Stein) who then stood in the lead of Prussia, found himself before the close of another year prepared to announce arrangements by means of which the land was to become divided between those who theretofore had held it as property, and those by whom it had been cultivated, these latter passing at once from the condition of mere tenants at will to that of free proprietors. Thenceforth the Prussian peasant stood before the world as a freeman, and the effect of this was fully shown when, but a few years later, the Sovereign found it necessary to call to his aid the whole body of his people for expulsion of the French, and for liberation of that which then had become for them really a Fatherland.

The years which followed that expulsion were, however, years of British free trade, sad and sorrowful years, in the course of which there was little demand for German labor except so far as it was needed for that work of barbarism, the raising of raw produce for consumption in distant markets; years in which wool, rags, and wheat went abroad to be exchanged for other wool, rags, and wheat, converted by foreign labor into cloth, paper, and iron; years in which there was furnished daily evidence that poverty of the people and weakness of the government grew with every increase of distance between the producers and consumers of a nation. Nominally, the Prussian people had become free, but practically they were so entirely under the control of foreign traders that they profited little of that freedom.

Sad experience having soon and thoroughly satisfied Prussian statesmen of the absolute necessity for bringing consumers to the side of producers, and thus relieving farmers from the burdensome and oppressive tax of transportation, the year 1818 witnessed the establishment of a tariff that was thoroughly protective, and that looked to the establishment of a great domestic commerce. Not content, however, with the slight step which had thus been made, they in the years that followed spared no efforts for bringing about an union of the various States of Germany on the footing of an entire freedom of internal intercourse similar to that which had so long existed in our American Union. Fiercely opposed in this by British agents, public and private, no less than seventeen years were required for its accomplishment; but the year 1835 at length witnessed the formation of that complete Customs Union which still exists, and to which the world at large stands indebted for the creation of a great empire which now stands first in Europe for the development, moral and material, of its people, and for the influence it exercises over the movements of the Eastern Continent.

Stein gave to the Prussian people that freedom which has everywhere been seen to result from division of the land, but to make it permanent, to extend it throughout Germany, and to prevent the retrograde movement which must inevitably have resulted from persistence in a policy which separated producers from consumers, and which looked to constant exportation of the soil in the form of rude products, it was needed that another great man, List, should make his appearance on the stage. At the cost of both property and life he did the work, and if we now seek his monument, we shall find it in the remarkable empire that has so recently appeared upon the European stage, described in my former letter.

Following the example set by Prussia, Russia, by dividing her land among those who previously had owned or cultivated it, has made one great step towards the establishment of freedom for her whole people. Thus far, however, the Emperor seems to have failed to see that there can be no real freedom for men who are compelled to waste their labor and to exhaust their soil by sending its products in their rudest forms to foreign markets. The day must, however, come when his eyes will be open to that great fact, and then, but not till then, will it be that the benevolent desires of those who had labored in the cause of Russian emancipation will stand a chance of being fully realized.

2. Failing altogether to profit by the great examples that had thus been set us, we have proclaimed emancipation while leaving all the l nd in possession of its opponents; and have given the right of

suffrage to men who, as the recent election has proved to be the case, must exercise it in a way to please their late masters, or forfeit power to obtain bread for their wives and children. So far as regards public lands, the Homestead Law happily places all on an equal footing, but outside of this the union man, white or black, seems likely to enjoy no rights whatsoever.

As a slave the black man had a large money value, and it was greatly to the interest of planters to provide carefully for the women and the children, much of the year's profit arising from increase of *stock*. Now, having lost all such value, and having ceased to be mere chattels, the men are shot down by hundreds, while women and children perish for want of medical assistance. How small is the chance in this respect for black republicans may be seen from the following description of affairs as they exist in relation to whites in Edgecombe county, North Carolina, at the present moment:—

" Cases are frequently reported to me of physicians refusing to attend the sick, because their relatives were republicans, or expressed their intention to vote for Grant and Colfax. One man came into my office and told me that his little boy died on Monday for want of medical aid. No physician in the part of the country where he lived would attend the boy, because he was a radical; one storekeeper kept him from eight o'clock in the morning until two o'clock in the afternoon, and would not sell him anything, because he persistently said he would vote for Grant. One man asked me to send for a northern physician, because the faculty of this country would not attend his wife, and she was at the point of death. Did I tell you about the affair in Wilson county a few weeks ago? The authorities, all Rebels, and equal to Ku-Klux, arrested a colored man named Grimes, on the charge of burning a barn, but Grimes proved himself to any reasonable and unprejudiced mind *perfectly innocent*. But he is the leader of the Union League, and they wanted to rake him up, as he had made a severe speech against them and in favor of the radicals the day before. A delegation of colored men came for me twenty miles. I went. I asked for a hearing for Grimes in my presence. It was not granted. I offered to bail him. This offer was rejected. A Rebel drew his revolver on me in the court-house behind my back. Some one more prudent stopped his shooting. I left telling them I would have Grimes out, and the next morning they released him to prevent my having the gratification of doing it, so I was told. Grimes wouldn't promise them to vote for Seymour and Blair, but the next day he raised a company and went to the Raleigh Convention."

Nominally free, the condition of the blacks, in such a state of affairs, must be far worse than it had ever been before.

3. Nominally free, but really enslaved, the Irish people, long before the year (1846) of the great famine, were described by Thackeray as "starving by millions;" and by another high authority as having before them only the choice between "land at any rent on one hand, or starvation on the other." Famine and emigration having since largely reduced their number, and measures of confiscation having transferred a large portion of the soil from Irish to British hands, they now tell us of an increased prosperity of the Irish people; but on studying the real facts of the case we learn, that " at no period has their hold upon the land been so feeble and precarious as now;" that "the control of landlords over their tenants is practically absolute;" that "they can and do make by-laws on their estates which place the tenant for all practical purposes in a state of serfdom;" that "by those rules marriage has been known to be forbidden without license of the agent;" that "tenancy from year

to year is reduced by the contrivance of an annual notice to quit to actual tenancy at will;" and that "in some estates a receipt for rents is never given without a printed notice to quit on the back of it."*

The negro slave of our Southern States, more fortunate than the Irish one, had an actual money value, and of so great amount as to make it highly profitable for his owner to feed, clothe, and house him, to provide medical attendance, to care for his children, and generally to do nearly as well for him as he would for for his horses or his cattle. So absolutely valueless, on the contrary, has been the Irish slave that population has been declared to be "a nuisance," to be abated by means of any and every measure of oppression that could be devised; and when starvation had been followed by pestilence, this latter has been hailed as having, in the providence of God, been sent as a means of relieving the land from the burden of supporting so many useless mouths.

4. Such being Irish freedom, we may now advantageously study the condition of the agricultural population of England with a view to see what there has been and now is the effect of a monopoly of the land such as we have permitted to remain in our Southern States. Doing this, we find that whereas but recently we were told that it was to the south of England we were to look for the greatest agricultural degradation, when we turn our eyes to the Eastern counties we meet with the state of things here described:—

"'The gang system,' as recently exhibited in Parliament, in brief is this: In the Fen districts, covering nearly a million of acres of the richest land in England, Huntingdonshire, Cambridgeshire, Nottinghamshire, Norfolk, Suffolk, and in parts of the counties of Northampton, Bedford, and Rutland, about seven thousand children, from five years of age and upwards, besides persons of both sexes of from fifteen to eighteen years of age—*are employed in gangs numbering from fifteen to twenty laborers in each gang, under a master, and in a condition differing from slavery only because it is infinitely worse.*

"The gang master is almost invariably a dissolute man, who cannot get steady employment as a laborer with any decent farmer. In most instances he actually purchases the labor of the children from poor parents; he sells this labor to farmers, pays the gang what he pleases, and puts the profit in his pocket. For seven or eight months in the year these gangs are driven, often seven or eight miles a day, to farms where they work at planting, weeding, picking, stone-gathering, and like labor, from half-past five in the morning to seven or eight o'clock in the evening. The gang-master is paid by the day or by the acre; and he pays the little children from fourpence to sixpence per day, while the older lads and girls receive from nine to fifteen pence. The master, for driving his hands to the field and for keeping them up to their work, which he does with a stick, makes an estimated profit of a pound sterling, or thereabouts, a week.

"There is testimony to show that hundreds of the younger children are carried home in the arms of the older lads every night. From working breast-high in wet grain many of the children are crippled for life by rheumatism, while others contract the seeds of ague, pleurisy, and consumption. Cases are given where little girls, four years old, have been driven through these long, terrible days of work. *The most pathetic pictures presented by Mr. Wilberforce of colonial slave-driving forty years ago, make the British West Indies seem almost an Arcadia in comparison with the Fen districts in England to-day.*

"This exhibition, shocking as it is, is by no means the most frightful phase of the gang system. The gangs are under no moral restraint whatever. Often-

---

* Morison. Irish Grievances shortly stated, pp. 33, 35. London, 1868.

times at night both sexes are huddled together in barns, where, among the older boys and girls, the most shameful events naturally follow. Clergymen and other respectable witnesses testified to the Commission of Inquiry that the gang laborers are 'beneath morals.' They have no consciousness of chastity, and do not know the meaning of the word. Medical directors of infirmaries state that gang girls, as young as thirteen years, have been brought to them to be confined. Their language and conduct are so depraved that dozens of parish clergymen, surgeons, and respectable laboring people, declared to the commission that the introduction of any gang labor in any village extinguishes morality."
—*Evening Post.*

Turning now to the west of England we find a state of things entirely in harmony with this, as may be seen by all of those who care to study the memoir of Canon Girdlestone, read before the British Association in August last.

The *Edinburgh Review*, just now published, questions the accuracy of some of the Canon's details, but admits that British agricultural laborers have before them no future but that of the slavery of the poor house—a slavery worse than that of our southern negroes in the past.

5. So long as the great Scottish proprietors could sell to the government the blood and bones of their subjects, creating regiments to be officered by sons and nephews, brothers and cousins of their own, everything was done to encourage increase of Highland population. That branch of the slave trade having, however, ceased to exist, and the slave having no longer a money value, people whose forefathers had for centuries occupied millions of acres have, by thousands and tens of thousands, been expelled from their little holdings, under circumstances of atrocity wholly without a parallel. The latest exhibit of these well-known atrocities, is given in the last (October) No. of the *Westminster Review.* The most prominent actors therein are found in the *liberal* families of Stafford and of Sutherland. Their most distinguished advocate is found in the *liberal* Duke of Argyle, so well known as author of the *Reign of Law*, which has passed through so many and so large editions.

6. The British and Irish people above referred to are really enslaved, although the law refuses to permit their being sold as chattels, and although the world is accustomed to speak of them as free. In what then does real freedom consist? Let us see!

Friday, on Crusoe's island, found no competition for the purchase of his services, and was, therefore, glad to sell himself on terms dictated by the man who could, if he would, both clothe and feed him, thus becoming the latter's slave. Had the island contained other Crusoes, their competition would have enabled him to make his selection among them all, exercising thus that power of self-government by which the freeman is distinguished from the wretched slaves above described.

Will you buy? Will you sell? The man who has a commodity, and must sell, is forced to ask the first of these questions; obtaining, for that reason, twenty or thirty per cent. less than what might be regarded as the fair market price. His neighbor, not forced to sell, waits for the second, thereby obtaining more, perhaps, than the ordinary price. Such being the case with commodities that can be kept on hand waiting for a purchaser, to how much greater extent must it not be so in reference to that labor power which results from the consumption of food, and which *cannot be held over for even a single instant.* The trader takes the market-price for his oranges, great as may be his loss; he stores his iron, waiting for a better market. The farmer sells his peaches on the instant, low as may be the price; but he holds his wheat and potatoes, waiting for an advance. The laborer's commodity being yet more perishable than oranges or peaches, the necessity for its *instant* sale is still more urgent.

The farmer and the merchant having stored their sugar, or their wheat, can obtain advances, to be returned when their commodities are sold. The laborer can obtain no advance upon his present hour, his commodity perishing on the instant of production. It must be at once either sold or wasted.

Further, the merchant may continue to eat, drink, and wear clothing, his stock meanwhile perishing on his hands. The farmer may eat his potatoes, after failing to sell his peaches. The laborer must sell his potential energies, be they what they may, or perish for want of food. In regard to no commodity, therefore, is the effect resulting from the presence or absence of competition so great, as in relation to human force. Two men competing for its purchase, its owner becomes a freeman. Two others, competing for its sale, become enslaved. *The whole question of freedom or slavery for man is, therefore, embraced in that of competition."*

The more varied the employments, the greater is the tendency towards having the miner, the weaver, the spinner, the mason, and the carpenter, take their places by the side of the farmer; the greater becomes the competition for purchase of labor; the more does the land tend to become divided; the greater is the money value of labor and land; the more perfect is the farmer's independence; the higher is the state of manners and morals; and the more perfect becomes the freedom of the whole people of whatsoever sex or age. In no part of the world is there at this moment so much competition as in New England for the *purchase* of labor, and in none, consequently, are its people so absolutely free. In none claiming in any manner to rank as civilized, has the contrary tendency so much existed as in Ireland. In none, therefore, has there been so universal a competition for the *sale* of labor; the consequences exhibiting themselves in the fact, that the occupant of land is now more than ever before a mere slave, holding his existence at the pleasure of the man who claims to own the land.

7. Thus far our measures of emancipation have resulted in giving to the negro slave just the same amount of freedom that has so long been enjoyed by the Irish slave, to wit, that he may, if he will, marry and beget children; that those children may not forcibly be taken from him; and that, although he may with impunity be shot or otherwise maltreated, he cannot be exchanged by his master against any given quantity of money. Wholly dependent for employment upon the men who own the land his situation is almost precisely that of the great mass of the Irish people, as here described by one of the most distinguished of English authors;—

"In a country in which every one who can find a landlord to accept him can be a farmer, and scarcely any one can be a laborer; where the three only alternatives are the occupation of land, beggary, or famine; where there is nothing to repress competition and everything to inflame it—the treaty between landlord and tenant is not a calm bargain, in which the tenant, having offered what he thinks the land worth to him, cares little whether his offer be accepted; it is a struggle like the struggle to buy bread in a besieged town, or to buy water in an African caravan. It is a struggle in which the landlord is tempted by an extravagant rent; the agent, by fees or by bribes; the person in possession, by a premium to take him to another country; and rivals are scared away by threats or punished by torture, mutilation, or murder. The successful competitor knows that he has engaged to pay a rent which will swallow the surplus, beyond the poorest maintenance for his family, that with his trifling stock he can force the land to produce. He knows that if he fails to pay he must expect ejectment, and that ejectment is beggary."—Senior. *Journals, Conversations, and Essays relating to Ireland, London,* 1868.

To four millions of people similarly situated we have given the right to vote in accordance with the orders of their masters, at the same time giving to those masters the right of representation in Congress for each and every one of them, thereby making a most important addition to the power that to the present time has been so much misused.

What is the use now to be made of the tremendous power thus accumulated in their hands is shown by the recent proceedings in Georgia and Louisiana. A year hence it will be the same elsewhere, and the day is not far distant when, if the national authorities do not interfere, the whole body of the States south of Mason and Dixon's line, with the possible exception of Tennessee, will be found engaged in a new, but peaceful, rebellion that must this time prove entirely successful, controlling Congress and placing in the presidential chair some man whose claim to that high office results from participation in the accursed rebellion so lately crushed.

Clearly seeing that such is likely to be the case, loyal Southern men are crying aloud for immigration, the rebel portion of the population meantime everywhere notifying Northern men that if they would save their lives they must flee the land, and thus preparing for a new rebellion in which they will be most heartily supported by all the rebel sympathizers of Northern States. Just now I have heard of the final expulsion, even from Eastern Tennessee, of a body of Scotchmen who had been sent there with a view to the introduction of the culture of long-wooled sheep.

8. The remedy for all this is to be found in creating competition with the landholders for purchase of negro labor, and thus giving to the slave that freedom which results from power to choose between employers in the field, in the mines, and in the workshop.

Why is it, however, that such competition had not long since existed? For the reason that our legislators have wholly failed to see that throughout the world freedom had come, *not as the result of mere proclamations,* but as a consequence of that diversification in the demand for human service which enables each and every individual to find the employment for which he had been intended, and for which he was most completely fitted. Look where they might they would have seen that slavery existed as a consequence of exclusive dependence on labors of the field. Correction of this, bringing with it freedom for all would have resulted from permanent maintenance of the protective tariff of 1842, as under it both the centre and the south would have been filled with furnaces and factories, thereby trebling the money value of land while greatly elevating the man who worked it. Great properties would gradually have become divided; the little proprietor—the man "whose touch," says Arthur Young, "turns sand into gold"—would long before this have made his appearance on the stage; the harmony of all real and permanent interests would have been hourly becoming more fully recognized; immigration would have attained proportions much greater than any it yet has seen; and the wealth and power of the Union would be thrice greater than now they are.

So rapid under the tariff of 1842 was the growth of Southern manufactures that in 1848 the editor of the *Charleston Mercury*, Mr. Barnwell Rhett, was led to predict that before the lapse of another decade the South would have ceased to export raw cotton. Unfortunately, however, for his prediction the South had just before placed the knife to its own throat by giving us the revenue tariff of 1846 in place of the protective one of 1842. From that hour Southern manufactures declined, with corresponding increase in the growth of that barbarous feeling which found its culmination in the atrocities of the late rebellion.

For the suppression of that rebellion we needed a million of men in arms. For prevention of the one that is now proposed, we need, and that at once, great armies of men and women carrying with them spades and ploughs, spindles and looms, sewing-machines and steam-engines, geographies and Testaments, and all other of the machinery by aid of which the people of the North have been becoming more prosperous and more free. For enabling such armies to move, and for giving them security while employed in carrying into full effect the great work of emancipation, we need that the government should, at the earliest moment, take measures for creating, and for placing in loyal hands, great lines of road by means of which the North and the South, the Northeast and the Southwest, the Northwest and the Southeast, should have between them communications as safe and rapid as those already existing between the shores of the Atlantic and the waters of the Mississippi.

To do this thoroughly and thus to bring the people now occupying the borders of the Hudson, the Delaware, and the Ohio, into direct and rapid communication with those of the Savannah and the Rio Grande, would involve an annual cost, as interest on the amount expended, less than would be required for maintenance of half a dozen regiments of men in arms; and yet, while preventing all future necessity for raising such regiments, it would so add to the productive power of the nation that the growth of wealth would soon be seen to be twice greater than at any former period.

With that growth would come division of the land, always a consequence of improvement in the means of communication and exchange. Freedmen, now wholly dependent upon planters for food and clothing, would find in road makers and furnace men competitors with their recent masters for purchase of their services, and would soon be seen accumulating little capitals by aid of which they might be enabled to enter upon and improve the little tracts secured to them by the Homestead Laws, and through many of which these roads would run. The already rich would be made richer by means of the increased value given to their properties, the now down-trodden negro race meanwhile becoming from hour to hour more free and independent. Harmony and peace would take the place of existing discord, and the various parts of the Union would become as thoroughly united as already are those of the great German Empire so recently created.

Let it now be understood that men and women who give themselves to the work of Southern development both can and will be sustained by all the powers of the government, and the negro will become really free, while the nation will become as really independent. Let this not be done, and the negro will be re-enslaved; the Union will be split up into fragments, as so recently has been the case with the great empire which now stands in the lead of Europe; and the men who have so nobly carried us through the late rebellion will have to regret that their labors have resulted in leaving the country in a condition far worse than that which had existed when Fort Sumter had been first assailed.

Earnestly hoping that a result very different from this may yet be reached, I remain,   Yours, very respectfully and truly,
      GEN. U. S. GRANT.   HENRY C. CAREY.

PHILADELPHIA, November 9th, 1868.

LETTER THIRD.

DEAR SIR:—

AN eminent foreigner, speaking of our countrymen, characterized them as "the people who soonest forget yesterday," and that nothing could be more accurate is shown by the facts which I propose now to give, as follows:—

The revenue tariff period which followed the close, in 1815, of the great European war, was one of great distress both private and public. Severe financial crises bankrupted banks, merchants, and manufacturers; greatly contracted the market for labor and all its products; so far diminished the money value of property as to place the debtor everywhere in the power of his creditor; caused the transfer of a very large portion of it under the sheriff's hammer; and so far impaired the power of the people to contribute to the revenue that, trivial as were the public expenditures of that period, loans were required for enabling the Treasury to meet the demands upon it. Under the protective tariff of 1828 all was changed, and with a rapidity so great that but few years of its action were required for bringing the country up to a state of prosperity the like of which had never before been known, here or elsewhere; for annihilating the public debt; and for causing our people wholly to forget the state of almost ruin from which they so recently had been redeemed.

Returning once again, as a consequence of this forgetfulness, to the revenue tariff system, the troubles and distresses of the previous period were reproduced, the whole eight years of its existence presenting a series of contractions and expansions, ending in a state of weakness so extreme that bankruptcy was almost universal; that labor was everywhere seeking in vain for employment; that the public credit was so entirely destroyed that the closing year of that unfortunate period exhibited the disgraceful fact of Commissioners, appointed by the Treasury, wandering throughout Europe and knocking at the door of all its principal banking houses without obtaining the loan of even a single dollar. Public and private distress now compelling a return to the protective system we find almost at once a reproduction of the prosperous days of the period from 1829 to 1835, public and private credit having been restored, and the demand for labor and its products having become greater than at any former period.

Once again, however, do we find our people forgetting that to the protective system had been due the marvellous changes that were then being witnessed, and again returning to that revenue tariff system, to which they had been indebted for the scenes of ruin which had marked the periods from 1817 to 1828, and from 1835 to 1842. California gold now, however, came in aid of free trade theories, and for a brief period our people really believed that protection was a dead issue and could never be again revived. With 1854, however, that delusion passed away, the years that followed, like those of the previous revenue tariff periods, having been marked by enormous expansions and contractions, financial crises, private ruin, and such destruction of the national credit that with the close of Mr. Buchanan's administration we find the treasury unable to obtain the trivial amount which was then required, except on payment of most enormous rates of interest.

Once again do we find the country driven to protection, and the public credit by its means so well established as to enable the treasury with little difficulty to obtain the means of carrying on a war whose annual cost was more than the total public expenditures of half a century, including the war with Great Britain of 1812. Thrice thus, with the tariffs of 1828, 1842, and 1860, has protection redeemed the country from almost ruin. Thrice thus, under the revenue tariffs of 1817, 1835, and 1846, has it been sunk so low that none could be found "so poor as do it reverence." Such having been our experience through half a century it might have been supposed that the question would be regarded now as settled, yet do we find among us men in office and out of office, secretaries and senators, owners of ships and railroads, farmers and laborers, denouncing the system under which at every period of its existence, and most especially in that of the recent war, they had so largely prospered—thereby proving how accurate has been the description of them above referred to, as "the people who soonest forget yesterday."

Such being the case, it seems to me that it might be well to show what was the actual state of affairs throughout the country in the revenue tariff years immediately preceding the war, and thereby enable railroad owners to study what had been the effect upon their interests that had resulted from the cry of cheap iron; ship owners to see that the decay of their interests had been the necessary result of a system under which internal commerce had been destroyed; laborers to see why it had been that labor had then been so super-abundant and so badly paid; farmers to see why it had been that their farms had then been so deeply mortgaged; secretaries to see why it had been that the public credit had then been so nearly annihilated; and all to see why it had been that the pro-slavery power had so largely grown as to have warranted the south in ven-turing on the late rebellion. To that end, I shall now present two letters written in 1858, and addressed to our then president, Mr. Buchanan, respectfully asking you to remark the predictions that further continuance in the same direction must result in financial and political ruin, and in our being driven from the ocean, all of which we now see to have been so fully realized.*

"Civilized communities—those communities, Mr. President, which have obtained that freedom of domestic intercourse which, as you have seen, we so sorely need—follow the advice of Adam Smith, in exporting their wool, and their corn, in the form of cloth, at little cost for transportation. Thus, France, in 1856, exported silks and cloths, clothing, paper, and articles of furniture, to the extent of $300,000,000; and yet the total weight was short of FIFTY THOUSAND TONS—requiring for its transport but forty ships of mode-rate size, and the services of perhaps 2000 persons.

"Barbarous, and semi-barbarous countries, on the contrary, ex-port their commodities in their rudest state, at heavy cost for trans-portation. India sends the constituents of cloth—cotton, rice, and indigo—to exchange, in distant markets, for the cloth itself. Brazil sends raw sugar across the ocean, to exchange for that which has been refined. We send wheat and Indian corn, pork and flour, cot-ton and rice, fish, lumber, and naval stores, to be exchanged for knives and forks, silks and cottons, paper and China-ware. The total value of these commodities exported in 1856—high as were then the prices—was only $230,000,000; and yet, the American and foreign ships engaged in the work of transport were of the capacity of SIX MILLIONS, EIGHT HUNDRED AND TWENTY-TWO THOUSAND TONS, —requiring for their management no less than 269,000 persons.†

"In the movement of all this property, Mr. President, there is great expense for transportation. Who pays it? Ask the farmer of Iowa, and he will tell you, that he sells for 15 cents—and that, too, payable in the most worthless kind of paper—a bushel of corn that, when received in Manchester, commands a dollar; and that he, in

* These letters form part of a series entitled " Letters to the President of the United States on the Foreign and Domestic Policy of the Union and its Effects as exhibited in the Condition of the People and the State." Phila., 1858.

† This is the total tonnage that arrived from foreign countries, in that year. A small portion was required for the exportation of manufactured commodi-ties, but it was so small as scarcely to require notice.

this manner, gives to the support of railroads and canals, ships and sailors, brokers and traders, *no less than eighty-five per cent. of the intrinsic value of his products.* Ask him once again, and he will tell you that while his bushel of corn will command, in Manchester, 18 or 20 yards of cotton cloth, he is obliged to content himself with little more than a single yard—*eighty-five per cent. of the clothing power of his corn having been taken, on the road,* as his contribution towards the tax imposed upon the country, for the maintenance of the machinery of that "free trade" which, as you, Mr. President, have so clearly seen, is the sort of freedom we do *not*, at present, need.*

"The country that exports the commodity of smallest bulk, is almost wholly freed from the exhausting tax of transportation. At Havre—ships being little needed for the outward voyage, while ships abound—the outward freights must be always very low.

"The community that exports the commodities of greatest bulk, must pay nearly all the cost of transportation. A score of ships being required to carry from our ports the lumber, wheat, or naval stores, the tobacco, or the cotton, required to pay for a single cargo of cloth, the outward freights must always be at, or near, that point which is required to pay for *the double voyage ;* and every planter knows, to his cost, how much the price of his cotton is dependent upon the rate of freight.

"In the first of these, Mr. President, employments become from day to day more thoroughly diversified ; the various human faculties become more and more developed ; the power of combination tends steadily to increase ; agriculture becomes more and more a science ; the land becomes more productive ; the societary movement becomes more stable and regular ; and the power to purchase machinery of every kind, whether ships, mills, or the precious metals, tends steadily to augment.

"In the last, the reverse of this is found, the pursuits of men becoming less diversified ; the demand for human faculty becoming more and more limited to that for mere brute force, or for the craft by which the savage is so much distinguished ; the power of association tending to decline ; agriculture becoming less and less a science, and the land becoming more and more exhausted ; the societary movement acquiring, more and more, the fitfulness and irregularity of movement you have so well described as existing among ourselves ; and the power to obtain machinery of any kind tending steadily to diminish.

"The first of these, Mr. President, may be found in the countries of Central and Northern Europe—those which follow in the lead of Colbert and of France. All of these are gradually emancipating themselves from the most oppressive of all taxes, the tax of transportation. All of them, therefore, are moving in the direction of growing wealth and power, with correspondent advance in civilization and in freedom.

"The last may be found in Ireland, India, Jamaica, Portugal,

* "Thirty-one independent States enjoying a thousand advantages and carrying on a mutual free trade with each other. *That* is the 'free trade' that we really want."—BUCHANAN.

Turkey, and these United States—the countries which follow in the lead of England. All of these, are becoming more and more subjected to the tax of transportation. All of them, therefore, are declining in wealth and power, in civilization, and in freedom.

"In the first, the land yields more and more with each successive year—with constant increase in the power of a bushel of wheat, or a pound of wool, to purchase money. In the last, the land yields less from year to year, with constant tendency to decline in the price of food and cotton. The first import the precious metals. The last, export them. The first, find daily increase of power to maintain a specie circulation, as the basis of the higher and better currency supplied by banks. The last, are gradually losing the power to command a circulation of any kind, and tending more and more towards that barbaric system of commerce which consists in exchanging labor against food, or wool and corn against cloth.

"We may be told, however, Mr. President, that in return for the eighty-five per cent. of his products that, as we see, is paid by the farmer of Iowa, and by the Texan planter, we are obtaining a magnificent system of railroads—that our mercantile marine is rapidly increasing—that, by its means, we are to secure the command of the commerce of the world, &c. &c. How far all this is so, we may now inquire. To me, it certainly appears, that if this be really the road to wealth and power it would be well to require the exportation of wheat instead of flour, paddy in place of rice, cotton in the seed, corn in the ear, and lumber in the shape of logs, rather than in that of furniture.

"Looking, first, to our internal commerce, we find a mass of roads, most of which have been constructed by help of bonds bearing interest at the rate of 6, 8, or 10 per cent.—bonds that have been disposed of, in the market, at 60, 70, or 80 per cent. of their nominal value, and could not now, probably, be re-sold at more than half the price at which they orginally had been bought. Half made, and little likely ever to be completed, these roads are worked at great expense, while requiring constant and great repairs. As a consequence of this it is, that the original proprietors have almost wholly disappeared; the stock being of little worth. The total amount applied to the creation of railroads having been about $1,000,000,000, and the average present money value scarcely exceeding 40, if even 30, per cent., it follows that $600,000,000 have been sunk, and with them all power to make new roads. Never, at any period of our history, have we been, in this respect, so utterly helpless as at present. Nevertheless, the policy of the central government looks steadily to·the dispersion of our people, to the occupation of new territories, to the creation of new States, and to the production of a necessity for further roads. *That, Mr. President, is the road to physical and moral decline, and political death, as will soon be proved, unless we change our course.*

"The railroad interest being in a state of utter ruin, we may now turn to the shipping one, with a view to see how far we are likely, by its aid, to obtain that command of the commerce of the world so surely promised to us by the author of the tariff of '46·

Should that prove to be moving in the same direction, the fact will certainly afford new and stronger proof of the perfect accuracy of your own views, Mr. President, as to the sort of freedom we so much require.

"In a state of barbarism, person and property being insecure, the rate of insurance is high. Passing thence towards civilization, security increases, and the rate of insurance declines, as we see it to be so rapidly doing, in reference to fire, in all the advancing countries of Europe. Our course, in reference to shipping, being in the opposite direction—security diminishing, when it should increase—the rate of insurance steadily advances, as here is shown:—

Rates of Insurance upon American Ships.

	1846.	1858.
To Cuba	1½ per cent.	1½ to 2 per cent.
" Liverpool	1¼ "	1½ to 2 "
" India and China . . .	1¾ "	2¾ "
To and from Liverpool, on packet-ships, annual rates . .	5 "	8 "

" To what causes, Mr. President, are we to attribute this extraordinary change? May it not be found in the fact, that the more we abandon domestic commerce, and the larger the amount of taxation imposed upon our farmers for the maintenance of transporters, the greater becomes the recklessness of those who gain their living out of that taxation? Look back to the last free trade period—that from 1837 to 1841—and you will find phenomena corresponding precisely with those which are now exhibited, although not so great in magnitude. At present, the utter recklessness—the total absence of conscientious feeling—here exhibited, is such as to astonish the thinking men of Europe. Railroad accidents have become so numerous as scarcely to attract even the momentary attention of the reader, and the loss of life becomes greater from year to year. Steamers are exposed to the storms of the lakes that are scarcely fit to navigate our rivers Ships that are unfit for carrying insurable merchandise, are employed in the carriage of unfortunate passengers, they being the only commodity for whose safe delivery the ship-owner cannot be made responsible. Week after week the records of our own and foreign courts furnish new evidence of decline in the feeling of responsibility which, thirty years since, characterized the owners of American ships, and the men therein employed.

" Look where we may, Mr. President, on the sea or on the land, evidences of demoralization must meet our view. 'Stores and dwellings'—and here I give the words of a New York journal—'are constructed of such wretched materials as scarcely to be able to sustain their own weight, and with apologies for walls which tumble to the ground, after being exposed to a rain of a few hours' duration, or to a wind which possesses sufficient force to set the dust of the highways in motion. Entire blocks of edifices are put up, with the joists of all so connected with each other, as to form a complete train for the speedy communication of fire from one to another. Joists are built into flues, so that the ends are exposed to becoming first heated, and then ignited by a flying spark. Rows of dwellings and warehouses are frequently covered with a single roof, which has not, in its whole extent of combustible material, a parapet wall, or other contrivance, to prevent the spread of the flames in the event of a conflagration.'

" The feeling of responsibility, Mr. President, grows with the growth of real civilization. It declines with the growth of that mock civilization, but real barbarism, which has its origin in the growing necessity for ships, wagons, and other machinery of transportation. The policy of the central government tends steadily towards its augmentation, and hence it is that American shipping so steadily declines in character, and in the proportions which it bears to that of the foreigners with whom we are required to place ourselves in competition.

" Two years since, we were told, that our shipping already exceeded 5,000,000 tons; that we had become the great maritime power of the world; and, of course, that this great fact was to be received as evidence of growing wealth and power. Last year, however, exhibited it as standing at only 4,871,000 tons, and future years are likely to show a large decrease—ships having become most unprofitable. More than four-fifths of the products of Western farms and Southwestern plantations, are, as we have seen, taken for the support of railroads and ships; and yet, the roads are bankrupt, while the ships have done little more, for some years past, than ruin the men who owned them. Such being the case, it seems little likely, that it is by means of sailing ships we are to acquire that control of the commerce of the world, so confidently promised when, in 1846, we were led to abandon the policy which looked to the creation of a domestic commerce as the true foundation of a great foreign one. What are the prospects in regard to that higher description of navigation which invokes the aid of steam, will be shown in another letter."

That letter will be given in my next, and, meanwhile, I remain with great respect,

Yours very truly,

GEN. U. S. GRANT.   HENRY C. CAREY.

PHILADELPHIA, December 10, 1868.

LETTER FOURTH.

DEAR SIR:—
Steam is rapidly superseding sails, and the day is fast approaching when the latter will almost entirely have disappeared from the ocean; yet are we at this moment nowhere in the race. The time has been when we built ships for carriage of the produce of other lands, but the day has now arrived when we are almost wholly dependent on British and German steamers for commerce with the world, and for carriage of our own. Why this is so can, I think,

be readily understood by all who care to study the state of things that existed ten years since, the date at which the following letter —being the second of those referred to in my last—was addressed to President Buchanan:—

"Every improvement in the construction of a ship tends to lessen the proportion borne by her tonnage, to the weight of the commodities to be moved. Every improvement in the quality of the commodities moved, tends to augment the proportions borne by the money value transported, to the tonnage of the ships required for its transportion. Here, Mr. President, is a simple principle by aid of which we may, perhaps, be enabled to arrive at some conclusion in reference to the tendency of our present policy—progress towards civilization having, everywhere, manifested itself in a diminution in the proportions borne by the machinery of transportation, to the value of the things transported.

"In the first year which followed adoption of the Compromise revenue tariff, that of 1834–5, we sent abroad, cotton and tobacco, food and lumber, to the amount of $92,000,000; and in that year, the shipping, domestic and foreign, that cleared for foreign ports, amounted to 2,030,000 tons. Six years later, in 1840–41, when the strictly revenue provision of that tariff had but begun to operate, we exported, of the same rude products, $98,000,000—the quantity of shipping clearing from our ports having, in the same period, risen to 2,353,000 tons. Two years since, after ten years experience of the revenue tariffs of 1846 and 1857, the total value of those exports was $230,000,000, while the quantity of shipping leaving for foreign ports amounted to little less than seven millions of tons—the increase in the former, in twenty-years, having been but 150 per cent., while that of the latter had been but little short of 350 per cent.

"If there is, Mr. President, any single proposition in social science that cannot be disputed it is *that wealth, civilization, and power, increase in the ratio of the diminution of the machinery required for performing the work of transportation.* On the turnpike, a single horse performs the work that before had been done by two; and, on the railroad, a single car transports as great a weight as, at first, had been done by hundreds of horses and men, carts and wagons. With every movement in that direction, land acquires money value, and man becomes more free. With each and every one in the opposite direction, the value of land declines, and man becomes more and more enslaved.

"The first and heaviest tax, Mr. President, to be paid by land and labor is that of transportation; and it is the only one, to which the claims of the State itself are forced to yield precedence. Increasing in geometrical proportion as the distance from market increases arithmetically, therefore it is, that agreeably to tables recently published, corn that would produce at market $24.75 per ton, is worth nothing at a distance of only a hundred and sixty miles, when the communication is by means of the ordinary wagon road—the cost of transportation being equal to the selling price. By railroad, under ordinary circumstances, that cost is but $2.40—leaving to the farmer $22.35, as the amount of tax saved to him by the construction of the road; and if we now take the product of an acre of land as averaging but a ton, the saving is equal to interest, at 6 per cent., on $370 an acre. Assuming the product of an acre of wheat to be twenty bushels, the saving is equal to the interest on $200; but, if we take the more bulky products—hay, potatoes, and turnips, it will be found to amount to thrice that sum. Hence it is, that an acre of land, near London, sells for thousands of dollars, while one of equal quality may be purchased in Iowa, or Wisconsin, for little more than a single dollar. The owner of the first enjoys the vast advantage of the endless circulation of its products—taking from it several crops in the year and returning to it at once, a quantity of manure equal to all he had abstracted; and thus improving his land from year to year. He is *making* a machine; whereas, his western competitor, forced to lose the manure, is *destroying* one. Having no transportation to pay, the former can raise those things of which the earth yields largely—as potatoes, carrots, or turnips; or those whose delicate character forbids that they should be carried to distant markets; and thus does he obtain a large reward for that continuous application of his faculties, and of his land, which results from the power of combination with his fellow-men.

"In the case of the latter, all is widely different. Having heavy transportation to pay, he cannot raise potatoes, turnips, or hay, because of them the earth yields by tons; as a consequence of which, they would be almost, even when not wholly, absorbed on the road to market. He may raise wheat, of which the earth yields by bushels; or cotton, of which it yields by pounds; but if he raise even Indian corn, he must manufacture it into pork before the cost of transportation can be so far diminished as to enable him to obtain a proper reward for labor. Rotation of crops being therefore a thing unknown to him, there can be no continuity of action in either himself or his land. His corn occupies the latter but a part of the year, while the necessity for renovating the soil, by means of fallows, causes a large portion of his farm to remain altogether idle—although the cost of maintaining roads and fences is precisely the same as if every acre were fully occupied.

"His time, too, being required only for certain portions of the year, much of it is altogether lost, as is that of his wagon and horses, the consumption of which latter is just as great as if they were always at work. He and they are in the condition of steam-engines constantly fed with fuel, while the engineer as regularly wastes the steam that is produced, a proceeding involving heavy loss of capital. Further stoppages of employment, both for his land and for himself, resulting from changes in the weather, are consequent upon this limitation in the variety of things that may be cultivated. His crop, perhaps, requires rain that does not come, and his corn, or cotton, perishes of drought. Once grown, it requires light and heat, but in their place come clouds and rain; and it and he are nearly ruined. The farmer near London, or Paris, is in the condition of an underwriter who has a thousand risks, some of which are maturing every day; whereas, the distant one is in that of a man who has risked his whole fortune on a single ship. Having made the voyage she arrives at the entrance of her destined port, when striking on a rock, she is lost, and her owner is ruined. Precisely such is the condition of the farmer who, having all at risk on his single crop, sees it destroyed by blight, or mildew, almost at the moment when he had expected to make his harvest. With isolated men, all pursuits are extra-hazardous. As they are enabled to approach each other and combine their efforts, the risks diminish, until they almost altogether disappear. Combination of action thus makes of society a general insurance office by help of which, each and all of its members are enabled to secure themselves against almost every imaginable risk.

"Great, however, Mr. President, as are these differences, they sink almost into insignificance compared with that which exists in reference to maintenance of the powers of the land. The farmer distant from market is always selling the soil, which constitutes his capital; whereas, the one near London not only returns to his land the refuse of its products, but adds thereto the manure resulting from consumption of the vast amount of wheat brought from Russia and America—of cotton brought from Carolina and India—of sugar, coffee, rice, and other commodities yielded by the tropics — of lumber and of wool, the products of Canada and Australia—not only maintaining the powers of his land, but increasing them from year to year.

"The more perfect the power of combination, the greater is the yield of the land; the higher are the prices of the rude products of the soil; the smaller is the bulk of the commodities to be transported; and the larger are the proportions borne by their value to the machinery required for their transportation. That, Mr. President, is the road towards civilization; but it is, also, the very opposite of the road that we ourselves are travelling, *the quantity of machinery required for the work of transportation increasing with a rapidity far greater than that which marks the growth of money values.* This latter being the certain road towards barbarism, we need look but little further for the causes of the decline in morals, wealth, and power, now so rapidly in progress throughout the Union.

"Power to command the use of improved machinery grows with the growth in money value of the things requiring to be transported, the farmer, whose proximity to the mill enables him to send his grain to market in the form of flour being far more able to contribute to the improvement of roads, than his fellow-farmer who is forced to send it in that of wheat. It diminishes as the things to be transported decline in value, and hence the weakness of countries like Portugal, Turkey, and India, that are becoming more and more dependent on distant markets. It diminishes with us, *and hence it is that our dependence on foreign countries, even for efficient means of transportation, so rapidly increases.*

"More than twenty years have now elapsed since the arrival of the *Great Western* steamer, and the establishment of the fact that we might avail ourselves of the power of steam for passage of the broad Atlantic. For nearly all that time we have been struggling to obtain steam communication, by means of American ships, with

Europe, the government aiding in the effort to the extent of many millions. What, however, has been the résult of all our efforts? Ship after ship has been lost, until confidence in American steamers has almost disappeared, and with it the lines of steamers. The Collins line, as it still is called, now dispatches a single ship per month, and that, too, chiefly owned in Europe. The Havre line dispatches a monthly ship. The Bremen line has wholly disappeared. Mr. Vanderbilt has yet three ships engaged in the European trade, but the recent accident to one of them can scarcely fail to be felt injuriously by all, annihilating the little confidence that previously had existed. *The day is fast approaching, Mr. President, when no single steamer carrying the American flag will float upon the ocean, except government ships, and the very few private ones engaged in the coasting trade, in which foreign competition is wholly interdicted.* Such being the facts, and such the prospects, is it probable that we shall long maintain that superiority on the ocean which so certainly existed at the time when the general government entered upon the career of centralization? It would seem not. Beaten in agriculture, and beaten in manufactures, we are likely to be even yet more thoroughly distanced in regard to ships; and for the reason that our policy tends steadily towards lessening the value of the commodities seeking to be transported.

"The French policy—looking, as it does, to the emancipation of land and labor from the tax of transportation—is directly the reverse of ours. We tax ourselves for maintenance of the millions of tons of shipping required for transport of merchandise to be given to France, in exchange for millions upon millions of tons of food and other commodities, so reduced in bulk that their weight, in tons, is counted by thousands. Freed by that reduction *from all the cost of transportation*, France is enabled to invoke the aid of steam, and to such extent, too, that the arrivals of her own steamers, in her own ports, amounted in 1856 to no less than 8000 tons per week, and more than four hundred thousand in the year.

"France, Mr. President, is carrying out your own most excellent views in regard to commercial policy—laying a broad foundation of domestic commerce, as a means of obtaining the largest power of intercourse with the outer world. We, on the contrary, are destroying the domestic commerce, in the vain hope of thereby building up a great foreign one. Why have we no steamers running to Rio, to Buenos Ayres, to Montevideo, to Valparaiso, to Lima, or Australia? Because we have little to sell, except those rude products which the people of Brazil or Chili cannot use, and do not need to buy. Before they can do so those commodities must pass through the looms of Manchester or Mulhausen, and hence it is that nearly all our intercourse with the world is burthened with costs of transportation so enormous that our farmers are generally poor, although themselves owners of the land. In search of trade we fit out expeditions against Japan, involve ourselves in disputes with Paraguay and Buenos Ayres, explore African and South American rivers, and maintain an enormous diplomatic establishment throughout this continent; and yet have scarcely anything to sell, except to the people of France and England.

"What we need, Mr. President, is that real free trade which consists in maintaining direct intercourse with the world at large; but that we cannot have so long as we shall continue to export our commodities in their rudest state. The farmer who has but one mill at which to grind his grain has no freedom of trade. The miller and the baker have it, they being free to sell to whom they please. Our farmers and planters have none of it, being compelled to send their products to the distant mills before they and their neighbors can make exchanges, even among themselves. They need, as you so well have seen, that real free trade which would enable the planter of Mississippi to exchange with the farmer of Illinois, receiving cloth, lead, and iron in exchange for sugar and cotton. *That*, as you so well have said, is the free trade we want. That we may have it, we must diversify the employments of our people; we must enable them to combine their efforts; we must *relieve our farmers from a tax of transportation greater than is required for maintaining, ten times over, all the armies of Europe;* we must enable ourselves to pay our debts to the land, and thus obtain a real agriculture, in place of the system of spoliation that now exists; we must establish a balance of trade in our favor, enabling us to retain the precious metals and to maintain the real specie currency that you so much desire to see established. Those things done, we shall be able to command the use of machinery of exchange of the highest order—fleets of steamers taking the place of sailing ships, and the use of money becoming obtainable without the payment of a higher interest than is paid in any other country of the world claiming to be held as civilized. Such, Mr. President, is the real road to wealth and power; but, as you have seen, all our movements are in the reverse direction."

Forty years since the now great Germanic Empire owned less than a thousand ships. Two years since the number had already more than tenfold increased, and the day seems near at hand when it will again be greatly increased by the inclusion of Holland within the limits of that wonderfully growing Empire. Occupying now the first place on the land of Europe, it is being rapidly prepared for occupying one almost as distinguished on the ocean; and for thus perfecting a change of position wholly without parallel in the annals of the world, to have been accomplished in so brief a period.

To what, then, has all this been due? To the simple fact that enlightened German men have looked to the creation of a great domestic commerce as foundation on which to build a great foreign one, exchanging with the world at large cloth and paper instead of, as formerly, sending wheat, rags, and wool to the limited market of England. Then, the whole cost of transportation was borne by poor and wretched German farmers. Now, it is borne by those American and Australian farmers to whom Germany sends cloth and paper to be exchanged for wool and cotton.

Germany can now have that real free trade which results from finishing commodities and sending them, so finished, to all the ports of the civilized and barbaric world. We, on the contrary, have had that British free trade which has required that our farmers and planters should make nearly all their exchanges with the outer world in the single and diminutive market of England. They have sought the establishment of industrial independence, while we have sought a perpetuation of that industrial dependence in the face of which there can be no freedom for either man or nation.

Let me now pray you, my dear sir, to study the Reports on Commerce and Navigation, and to mark the fact that, while cotton stands alone in quantity, oil stands almost alone in the fact that we send it abroad fit for use. Turn next to the oil column, and see that with regard to it, and it almost alone, we have that real free trade which results from power to make direct exchanges, sending it to every part of the civilized world. Turn next to the cotton column, and see that it gives us little or no commerce except with England, France, and Germany, a score or two of ships being fully able to transport all that goes to other countries.

Germany has been building a true pyramid, of which a real agriculture was to be the basis and a foreign trade the apex. We have been building an inverted one, subjecting our farmers and planters to a tax of transportation so oppressive that the top-heavy edifice at length toppled over and came near burying all under the ruins.

So long as we shall insist upon limiting ourselves to the export of raw produce—the proper work of a semi-barbarous population—our exchanges must continue to be mainly made with those European countries which have already possessed themselves of steam navigation; and so long must we continue in our present state of helpless dependence. Whenever we shall have determined to export cloth instead of cotton, iron in place of corn, and machinery in the place of tobacco; whenever we shall have made ourselves industrially independent; then, and not until then, shall we regain that place on the ocean which we had occupied in the days when the now powerful Germany was a collection of scraps and fragments of territory, controlled in turn by France and England, Austria, or Russia.

To the development of her internal resources was England indebted for that control of the ocean which warranted her in saying that "not a sail but by permission spreads." So long as she held it there was there but little peace. Desiring now to enable our people peacefully and freely to communicate with the whole outer world, we shall find that the road by which we are to move in that direction leads through the establishment of such perfect protection as will enable us fully to develop the wonderful mineral resources by which, more than by anything else, our Union is distinguished from all other countries of the world. How that protection is to affect our growth in numbers I propose to show in another letter, meanwhile remaining, very respectfully, yours,

HENRY C. CAREY.

Gen. U. S. Grant.

Philadelphia, Dec. 10, 1868.

LETTER FIFTH.

DEAR SIR:—

That peace may prevail throughout the States recently in rebellion, and that harmony may be established among the various portions of the Union, it is indispensable that throughout the South and Southwest employments be diversified; that the habit of association and combination for useful purposes be enabled to arise; that mines be opened and furnaces built; that the wonderful natural resources of the country lying between the Potomac and the Rio Grande be developed; that the market be brought home to the farmers and planters of that great region of country; that between the various portions of the Union there be provided means of cheap and rapid intercourse; and, finally, that we establish among ourselves that great internal commerce to which Germany, as has been shown, stands now indebted for the commanding position she so speedily, by aid of the protective policy, has taken among the nations of the world.

That to such development it is we are to look for peace is from hour to hour becoming more clearly obvious to the people of the Southern States, and hence it is that each successive day brings with it new evidence of their anxious desire for promotion of immigration. West and Northwest, however, we find competition therein with the South and Southwest, millions upon millions of acres, capable of contributing on the largest scale to the comfort and happiness of our people, lying there wholly idle, even in states that have already long been represented in the councils of the Union. To meet all these demands we need to import *that only commodity which Europe stands prepared to give to us without demanding gold in payment—those only machines that increase in number and power the more they are usefully employed*—MEN, WOMEN, AND CHILDREN. What, however, are the circumstances under which such machines, more valuable than any engines, are most led to find a market among us for their service? Let us see!

Prior to the establishment of the first really protective tariff, that of 1828, immigration had been altogether insignificant, that of the whole decade ending in 1829 having given us little more than 100,000 persons. So soon, however, as that tariff had commenced to take effect immigration began to rise, and so strong and rapid was its growth that four years later it had already reached the extraordinary figure of 65,000, that large number of persons having been attracted by the great demand for labor which protection had created. Protection having been then abandoned, we find immigration to have become unsteady and irregular, the mean number for the decade ending in 1844 having been but 70,000. No sooner, however, had the tariff of 1842 become fairly active than we find the effect of protection exhibiting itself in the rapid rise of immigration from 74,000 in 1844, to no less than 234,000 in 1847—thus furnishing proof conclusive of rapid increase in the demand for, and compensation of, all human service. Under the revenue tariff of 1840–41 two men had everywhere been seeking employ. ment at the hands of one employer. Under that of 1842 all had changed, employers having everywere been compelled to seek for labor, and liberally to pay for the service needed to be rendered.

The discovery of California gold deposits furnished a new va. riety of employment with large, but temporary, increase in the power to pay for labor, and under that stimulus immigration con. tinued to increase until, in 1854, it passed beyond 400,000. Thence. forward, however, under the unhappy influence of the revenue tariffs of 1846 and 1857, it rapidly declined until in 1860–61 it had fallen to 112,000, or little more than its amount twenty years before. British free trade now gave us rebellion with further decline of im. migration, which stood in 1861–2 at less than 70,000. Secession, however, gave, and most happily gave, to the loyal States the power of self-protection, and now we find the effect of the protective tariff of 1861 in the following figures exhibiting the number of persons who in the succeeding years were hither led to seek a market for their labor, to wit:—

1862–3	.	.	.	.	.	.	139,170
1863–4	.	.	.	.	.	.	193,754
1864–5	.	.	.	.	.	.	180,679
1865–6	.	.	.	.	.	.	330,725
1866–7	.	.	.	.	.	.	311,994

Extraordinary as is the growth here exhibited, it is far from pre. senting the entire truth, the number of persons who have trans. ferred themselves from the unprotected British colonies to our protected States having been so large that were it added to the figures shown above, the total for the last three years would probably exceed a million.

The production of that million of people had cost the States of Europe at least A THOUSAND MILLIONS OF DOLLARS, yet did they furnish them in free gift to our Union. Had they given as much in engines, or other machinery, it would have been regarded as a wonderful addition to the wealth of the country; and yet, engines wear out with use, whereas men and women double and quadruple themselves, the quantity of such machinery increasing more rapidly in almost the exact proportion in which their services are made available to the purposes of the nation.

2. By aid of the protective tariff of 1842 immigration, as we see, more than trebled itself in the short period from 1844 to 1847, having been carried up from 74,000 to 234,000. Had that tariff been maintained, and had we continued to mine our own coal, smelt our own ores, and to make our own lead, copper, and iron, it would, with the aid of California gold discoveries, have been carried beyond half a million, and it would have since stood there, at the least, *giving with the natural increase a population ten millions greater than we have at present.* Forgetting, however, as they have always done, the troubles from which they had so recently been redeemed, our people had twice again repudiated

protection, and had thus reduced immigration, in the whole period of Mr. Buchanan's administration, to an average of 134,000, or little more than half a million in all. The revenue tariff policy of Mr. Walker and his friends then gave us a rebellion that has cost us, white and black, so great a destruction of life that more than all the immigration of Mr. Lincoln's period of presidential life was required to make amends for it.

Of all the legislative acts on record there is scarcely one that has worked an amount of injury so large as that which has resulted from the repeal of the tariff of 1842, forced upon the country by Mr. Walker and his friends. But for them our population would be now, at the least, one-fourth greater than it is at present, and our wealth more than twice as great! But for them, we should long since have achieved a perfect industrial, financial, and political independence! But for them iron would be so cheap that we should be consuming millions of tons, while exporting it to half the world!* But for them we should have had no civil war! But for them the slave would have been gradually becoming free, while his master would have been becoming rich! But for them harmony would now prevail throughout the Union, and the stars and stripes at this moment be floating over the largest mercantile marine the world had ever seen! But for them the demand on Europe for men, women, and children, to take part in the great work of developing our wonderful resources, would be now so great that capital would be everywhere seeking labor, while labor would be everywhere dictating to capital the terms on which it could be allowed to have its aid. That protection and freedom travel hand in hand together is proved by all the facts of our history, and the man who strikes at the former cannot claim to be otherwise than an enemy to the latter.

3. In accordance with the habit of the time, my dear sir, I have spoken of protective tariffs on one hand, and revenue tariffs on the other; and yet, when you shall have studied the facts which will now be given, you will, as I think, find yourself convinced that *the real revenue tariff is a protective one,* the free trade tariff, so called, being the one that so far depletes the treasury as naturally to bring about the state of weakness and of bankruptcy which now exists in each and all of the communities of the world that have found themselves unable or unwilling to defend themselves against the British free trade system.

In the four years by which the passage of the semi-protective tariff of 1824 had been preceded the customs revenue averaged but $16,000,000, and trivial as were the expenditures of that period, they so far exceeded the revenue as to make it necessary to borrow $10,000,000 in 1824 and 1825. In the four years 1826-29, with only semi-protection, the customs revenue rose to $22,000,000, and the necessity for borrowing wholly passed away. Under the really protective tariff of 1828 it rose to $26,000,000, and the public debt was then extinguished. The revenue tariff, so called, of 1840-42

---

* Of railroad iron alone our import in the present year will exceed 270,000 tons, and yet we have here such beds of coal and ore as are found in no other part of the civilized world.

gave but $15,000,000, and the treasury became literally bankrupt— money and credit having wholly disappeared. The protective tariff of 1842 gave $26,000,000 a year, and we found then no difficulty in raising all the money required for making the war with Mexico which terminated in the acquisition of California. Under the revenue tariff of 1857, with fifty per cent. more of population than had existed in the period of the tariff of 1842, we obtained but $47,000,-000, notwithstanding the wonderful addition to our resources resulting from discovery of California gold and Nevada silver.

Comparing now the protective tariff of 1828 with the revenue one of 1857, we find that notwithstanding the introduction of the railroad and the discovery of California treasures, the custom revenues had little more than doubled, while the population had more than a hundred and fifty per cent. increased. Comparing, again, the product of the free trade tariff of 1857 with the protective one of the last three years, we find that, although the population had grown but 25 per cent., the customs revenue had more than trebled. Such being the facts, the truth of the following propositions would seem to be now entirely established :—

First, That the more perfect the protection to domestic industry and the larger our strides toward industrial and political independence, the greater is the power of our people to contribute to the customs revenue:

Second, That the more domestic commerce is left unprotected, and the greater our industrial dependence, the smaller must be the customs revenue, and the greater the tendency toward bankruptcy of the people and the States.

Third, That the true road to freedom for man, to wealth, power and independence for the nation, lies through the pursuit of a policy which looks to the establishment of a great domestic commerce as the basis of a commerce with the outside world far greater than any we yet have known.

In face of all these facts, however, we are told, my dear sir, and by men claiming to be regarded as friends of freedom, that "from protection to serfdom there is but a single step, and that but one other is required to carry us on from serfdom to slavery. These three," as we are further assured, "are but links in the chain by means of which controlling spirits are enabled to confiscate, for their own proper benefit, the time, the forces, the labor, the capital, the liberty, and the rights of the great masses of their thus subjugated countrymen." Such being the views that, in a great variety of forms, are put forth daily by those who believe that, despite our recent unhappy experience, we should once again resume that course of action to which we stand indebted for all the losses of property and life inflicted by the late rebellion, it seems to me that it might be right and proper for you to ask of them to furnish answers to questions like the following, to wit:—

Why is it that, if protection be really adverse to freedom and to the general prosperity of our people, immigration always grows with such rapidity when protection is most complete?

Why is it that, if British free trade is really favorable to freedom, men who previously had come among us with intent to stay, have always then so largely re-emigrated to Europe?

Why it has been that in the last few years hundreds of thousands of Canadians have abandoned their free trade country, and have preferred to settle in these benighted and protected States?

Why it is that of the emigrants who arrive at Quebec and Montreal, and who have the choice between free trade on the one hand and protection on the other, nearly all prefer to take the latter, selecting homes in our Western States?

Why it is that Nova Scotia and New Brunswick are almost in a state of rebellion, because of their feeling of the absolute necessity for a closer connection with these protected States?

Why is it that nearly the whole population of Ireland would desire to fly from British freedom of trade and seek for homes in this now partially protected country?

Why is it that British emigration to Australia diminishes, and that to us increases, almost precisely as our protective policy is made more and more complete?*

Why is it that Australia, after a most severe political contest, has just now elected a protectionist parliament?

Why is it that when we build furnaces and open mines railroads are always profitable to their owners, and capital is easily obtained for the construction of new lines of road?

Why is it that when mines and furnaces are abandoned, railroad property so far declines that it becomes impossible to obtain the means for building further roads?

Why is it that financial crises, resulting in the ruin of trade, are the *never failing* accompaniments of the British free trade policy?

Why is it that such crises *never* occur in periods of protection?

Why is it that the deposits in our saving funds increase in times of protection, and diminish in those of British free trade?

Why is it that sheriff's sales are so numerous in British free trade times, and so few in number in those of protection?

Why is it the revenue tariff periods always end in almost total failure of public revenues and almost total bankruptcy of the treasury?

Why is it that protective tariffs are so favorable to increase of public revenue, and to reduction of the public debt?

Why is it that a protective tariff now produces annually nearly as much revenue as was obtained by aid of a merely revenue one in the whole period of Mr. Buchanan's administration?

Why is it that the Republican party—the party of liberty, of

					To Australia.	To the United States.
*	1861	.	.	.	23,728	49,764
	1862	.	.	.	41,843†	58,706
	1863	.	.	.	53,054†	146,815
	1864	.	.	.	40,942†	147,042
	1865	.	.	.	37,282†	147,258
	1866	.	.	.	24,097	161,000
	1867	.	.	.	14,466	159,274

† In these years emigration was unnaturally stimulated by temporary increase of demand for Australian wool, consequent on failure in the supply of American cotton.

equal rights, of intelligence, and of sound morals—is so generally favorable to the protective policy?

Why is it that British free trade doctrines are so universally popular among men who believe in the divine origin of slavery.— among sympathizers in the late rebellion—among foreign agents— among ignorant foreigners—and among the dangerous classes throughout the Union?

Why is it that, now that the South diversifies its industry by raising its own food, it obtains as much for 2,000,000 bales of cotton as before it had received for 4,000,000?

Why is it that when the refining of our oil, and fitting it for consumption, gives us now almost our only real free trade, the same results would not be obtained, and, on a much larger scale, by finishing our cotton and fitting it also for consumption?

Why is it that Belgium, the most prosperous little country in Europe, so earnestly adheres to protection?

Why is it that Russia, after a ten years' trial of British free trade, exhibits herself as a constant borrower throughout western Europe?

Why is it that Sweden is now in a state of so great suffering, after nearly a decade of British free trade?

Why is it that France, in making her last treaty with England, established a tariff more intelligently protective than our own?

Why is it that the maker of that treaty, Mons. Chevalier, had been led to tell his countrymen that—

"Every nation owes it to itself to seek the establishment of diversification in the pursuits of its people, as Germany and England have already done in regard to cottons and woollens, and as France herself has done in reference to so many and so widely-different kinds of manufacturing industry. Within these limits," as he further says, "it is not an abuse of power on the part of the Government; on the contrary, *it is the accomplishment of a positive duty so to act at each epoch in the progress of a nation, as to favor the taking possession of all the branches of industry whose acquisition is authorized by the nature of things.* Governments are, in effect, the personification of nations, and *it is required that they should exercise their influence in the direction indicated by the general interest, properly studied, and fully appreciated.*"

Why is it that Germany, the country that has most persistently carried into effect the policy thus recommended, now stands in the lead of Europe, although so recently a mere collection of loose fragments, ready to be moved about in whatsoever direction might be most agreeable to France or England at one moment, Russia or Austria at another?

Why is it that British policy, that policy whose imitation is urged upon us by all the advocates of that revenue tariff system which has so invariably resulted in destruction of the revenue, has so entirely crushed out of existence the whole race of those small British proprietors, "whose touch" according to Arthur Young, "turned sand into gold?"

Why is it that the British agricultural laborer has, by means of that policy, been reduced to a condition so nearly akin to slavery as to have before him no future but the poor house?

Why is it that all the countries of the earth which find themselves compelled to submit to the, so called, free trade policy now urged upon the world by British traders, are this day in little better than a state of ruin ?

You have said, my dear sir, Let us have peace! Peace comes everywhere with general demand for labor; with good wages; with large demand for products of the farm, the furnace, the factory, and the plantation; and all these come with protection. Let us have protection, and let that protection be so definitively adopted as to give to all a perfect confidence in its continued maintenance, and all your wishes for the establishment and perpetuation of peace will be fully realized.

Greatly hoping that such may prove to be the case, I remain, very truly and respectfully, yours,　　HENRY C. CAREY.

GEN. U. S. GRANT.

PHILADELPHIA, Dec. 17, 1868.

LETTER SIXTH.

DEAR SIR:—

More than anything else whatsoever the country needs financial peace. Shall we have it? On the answer to this question depends, as I think, the decision as to whether or not the public faith is to be maintained—whether or not the Union is to be perpetuated.

Forgetful always, even of the events of yesterday, our people are particularly so in reference to financial questions, and therefore is it that we are now required to witness so many absurd attempts at bringing the country back, so far as regards machinery of circulation, to the point at which it had stood at the opening of the great rebellion. Scheme follows scheme, their authors wholly overlooking the facts, that the long period from 1815 to 1860, *with exception alone of the brief and happy periods of protection under the tariffs of 1828 and 1842*, had presented a constant series of financial crises, bringing ruin everywhere to unfortunate debtors, while enabling wealthy creditors largely to augment their already enormous fortunes; that in that period there had been no less than four general bank suspensions; that throughout the Centre and the West, the South and the Southwest, the average rate of interest had been higher than in any other country of the world, claiming to rank as civilized; that the money value of property everywhere had been almost wholly dependent on the condition of the English money market; that railroad proprietors, manufacturers, miners, and furnace men had, on repeated occasions, seen their property almost wholly swept away; that in each successive revenue tariff period a large portion of the lands and houses of the country had changed owners under the sheriff's hammer; and, finally, that rebellion was but the natural consequence of a system by means of which the Bank of England had been enabled, by a single turn of the screw, to withdraw from the country nearly the whole of the little specie basis on which our circulation has rested, thereby paralyzing the societary movement, and depriving both government and people of the means required for their support. What was the real state of things at the opening of the rebellion will now be shown, as follows:—

Had it been possible on the 4th of March, 1861, to take a bird's-eye view of the whole Union, the phenomena presenting themselves for examination would have been as follows:—

Millions of men and women would have been seen who were wholly or partially unemployed, because of inability to find persons able and willing to pay for service.

Hundreds of thousands of workmen, farmers, and shopkeepers would have been seen holding articles of various kinds for which no purchasers could be found.

Tens of thousands of country traders would have been seen poring over their books seeking, but vainly seeking, to discover in what direction they might look for obtaining the means with which to discharge their city debts.

Thousands of city traders would have been seen endeavoring to discover how they might obtain the means with which to pay their notes.

Thousands of mills, factories, furnaces, and workshops large and small, would have been seen standing idle while surrounded by persons who desired to be employed; and

Tens of thousands of bank, factory, and railroad proprietors would have been seen despairing of obtaining dividends by means of which they might be enabled to go to market.

High above all these would have been seen a National Treasury wholly empty, and to all appearance little likely ever again to be filled.

Why was all this? The laborer needing food, and the farmer clothing, why did they not exchange? Because of the absence of power on the part of the former to give to the latter anything with which he could purchase either hats or coats.

The village shopkeeper desired to pay his city debts. Why did he not? Because the neighboring mill was standing idle, while men and women indebted to him were wholly unemployed.

The city trader could not meet his notes, because his village correspondents could not comply with their engagements. The doctor could not collect his bills. The landlord could not collect his rents; and all, from laborer to landlord, found themselves compelled to refrain from the purchase of those commodities to whose consumption the National Treasury had been used to look for the supplies upon which it thus far had depended.

With all, the difficulty resulted from the one great fact already indicated in regard to the laborer. If *he* could have found any one willing to give him something that the farmer would accept from him in exchange for food—that the farmer could then pass to his neighbor shopkeeper in exchange for cloth—that that neighbor could then pass to the city trader in satisfaction of his debt—and that this latter could then pass to the bank, to his counsel, his physician, or his landlord—the *societary circulation* would at once have been re-established, and the public health restored.

That one thing, however, was scarcely anywhere to be found. Its generic name was *money*, but the various species were known as gold, silver, copper, and circulating notes. Some few persons possessed them in larger or smaller quantities; but, the total amount being very small when compared with that which was required, their owners would not part with the use of them except on terms so onerous as to be ruinous to the borrowers. As a consequence of this, the city trader paid ten, twelve, and fifteen per cent. per annum for the use of what he needed, charging twice that to the village shopkeeper, in the price of his goods. The latter, of course, found it necessary to do the same by his neighbors, charging nearly cent. per cent.; and thus was the whole burthen resulting from deficiency in the supply of a medium of exchange thrown upon the class which least could bear it, the working people of the country—farmers, mechanics, and laborers. As a consequence of this they shrank in their proportions as the societary circulation became more and more impeded, while with those who controlled the money supply the effect exhibited itself in the erection of those great palaces which now stand almost side by side with tenement houses, whose occupants, men, women, and children, count by hundreds. The rich thus grew richer as the poor grew poorer.

Why was all this? Why did they not use the gold of which California had already sent us so many hundreds of millions? Because we had most carefully followed in the train of British free trade teachers who had assured our people that the safe, true, and certain road toward wealth and power was to be found in the direction of sending wheat, flour, corn, pork, and wool to England in their rudest form, and then buying them back again, at quadruple prices, paying the difference in the products of Californian mines! Because we had in this manner, for a long period of years, been selling whole skins for sixpence and buying back tails for a shilling !* Because we had thus compelled our people to remain idle while consuming food and clothing, the gold meanwhile being sent to purchase other food and clothing for the workmen of London and Paris, Lyons, Manchester, and Birmingham!

Why, however, when circulating notes could so easily be made, did not the banks supply them, when all around them would so gladly have allowed interest for their use? Because those notes were redeemable in a commodity of which, although California gave us much, we could no longer retain even the slightest portion, the quantity required abroad for payment of heavy interest, and for purchase of foreign food in the forms of cloth and iron, having now become fully equal to the annual supply, and being at times even in excess of it. That demand, too, was liable at any moment to be increased by the sale in our market of certificates of debt then held abroad to the extent of hundreds of millions, the proceeds being claimed in gold, and thus causing ruin to the banks. To be out of debt is to be out of danger, but to be in debt abroad to the extent of hundreds of millions is to be always in danger of both public and private bankruptcy. *The control of our whole*

* In the days of the Stuarts England exported raw materials and imported finished products, and the people of the Rhine countries ridiculed them as fools who sold whole skins for sixpences and bought back the tails for shillings.

domestic commerce was therefore entirely in the hands of foreigners who were from hour to hour becoming richer by means of compelling us to remain so dependent upon them that they could always fix the prices at which they would buy the skins, and those at which they would be willing to sell the tails. As a necessary consequence of this, the nation was not only paralyzed, but in danger of almost immediate death.

Such having been the state of things on the day of Mr. Lincoln's inauguration, let us now look at the remedy that was then required. Let us, for a moment, suppose the existence of an individual with wealth so great that all who knew him might have entire confidence in the performance of what he promised. Let us then suppose that he should have said to the laborers of the country, " Go into the mills, and I will see that your wages are paid ;" to the millers, " Employ these people, and I will see that your cloth is sold ;" to the farmers, " Give your food to the laborer and your wool to the millers, and I will see that your bills are at once discharged ;" to the shopkeepers, " Give your coffee and your sugar to the farmer, and I will see that payment shall forthwith be made ;" to the city traders, " Fill the orders of the village shopkeeper, and send your bills to me for payment ;" to the landlords, " Lease your houses and look to me for the rents ;" to all, " I have opened a *clearing house* for the whole country, and have done so with a view to enable every man to find on the instant a cash demand for his labor and its products, and my whole fortune has been pledged for the performance of my engagements ;" and then let us examine into the effects. At once the societary circulation would have been restored. Labor would have come into demand, thus doubling at once the productive power of the country. Food would have been demanded, and the farmer would have been enabled to improve his machinery of cultivation. Cloth would have been sold, and the spinner would have added to the number of his spindles. Coal and iron would have found increased demand, and mines and furnaces would have grown in numbers and in size. Houses becoming more productive, new ones would have been built. The *paralysis* would have passed away, life, activity, and energy having taken its place, all these wonderful effects having resulted from the simple pledge of one sufficient man that he would see the contracts carried out. He had pledged his credit and nothing more.

What is here supposed is almost precisely what was done by Mr. Lincoln and his administration, the only difference having been, that while in the one case the farmers and laborers had been required to report themselves to the single individual, the Government had, in the other, by actual purchase of labor and its products, and the grant of its pledges in a variety of shapes and forms, enabled each and every man in the country to arrange his business in the manner that to himself had seemed most advantageous. To the laborer it had said, We need your services, and in return will give you that which will enable your family to purchase food and clothing. To the farmer it had said, We need food, and will give you that by means of which you can pay the shopkeeper. To the manufacturer it had said, We need cloth, and will give you that which will enable you to settle with the workman and the farmer. To the naval constructor it had said, We need your ships, and will give you that which will enable you to purchase timber, iron, and engines. In this manner it was that domestic commerce has been stimulated into life, the result exhibiting itself in the facts, that while we increased to an extent never known before, the number of our houses and ships, our mills, mines, and furnaces, our supplies of food, cloth, and iron; and while we diversified our industry lo an extent that was absolutely marvellous; we were enabled to tend or pay to the Government thousands of millions of dollars, where before, under the system which made us wholly dependent on the mercy of the wealthy capitalists of England, it had been found difficult to furnish even tens of millions. The whole history of the world presents no case of a financial success so perfect.

In the physical body health is always the accompaniment of rapid circulation, disease that of a languid one. Now, for the first time since the settlement of these colonies, had our people had experience of the first. Every man who had desired to work, had found a purchaser for his labor. Every man who had had labor's products to sell, had found a ready market. Every man who had had a house to rent, had found a tenant. And why? Because the government had done for the whole nation what companies do for localities when they give them railroads in place of wagon roads. It had so facilitated exchange between consumers and producers, that both parties had been enabled to pay on the instant for all they had had need to purchase.

Important, however, as is all this, it is but a part of the great work that had been accomplished. With every stage of progress there had been a diminution in the general rate of interest, with constant tendency towards equality in the rate paid by farmers of the east and the west, by the owner of the little workshop and by him who owned the gigantic mill. For the first time in our history the real workingmen—the laborer, the mechanic, and the little village shopkeeper—had been enabled to command the use of the machinery of circulation at a moderate rate of interest. For the first time had nearly all been enabled to make their purchases cash in hand, and to select from among all the dealers those who would supply them cheapest. For the first time had this class known anything approaching to real independence; and therefore had it been that, notwithstanding the demands of the war, capital had so rapidly accumulated. The gain to the working people of the Union thus effected, had been more than the whole money cost of the war, and therefore they had cheerfully paid their taxes, while so many had been enabled to purchase the securities offered by the government.

Further than all this, we had for the first time acquired something approaching to a *national independence*. In all time past, the price of money having been wholly dependent on the price in England, the most important intelligence from beyond the Atlantic was that which was to be found in the price of British securities on the Exchange of London. With each arrival, therefore, our railroad shares went up or down because the Bank of England had seen fit to purchase a few Exchequer bills, or had found it necessary to part with some of those it previously had held. In all this there had been a change so complete that the price of British Consols had ceased entirely to enter into American calculations. The stride, in this respect alone, that had been made in the direction of independence, was worth to the country more than the whole money cost of the great war in which we are now engaged.

Throughout the war the government allied itself with the great body of the people, those who had money to borrow, interest to pay, labor and labors' products to sell, comprising nineteen-twentieths of our total population; and hence it was that the war resulted in success so entirely complete. Since then there has been a constant effort at separating the government from that great class, and bringing it into close alliance with that very trivial one, so far as numbers go, which profits by high rates of interest and low prices of labor and labors' products; and hence it is, that there has recently been so much danger of seeing control of the country pass into the hands of those who, North and South, had participated in the rebellion. To that end the greenback, *everywhere claimed as the people's money,* has by those in high places been denounced, small as is the quantity, when compared with the real need for it. To that end there has been an unremitted effort at leading farmers, laborers, and mechanics, to the belief that it had been a "forced loan," by means of which they had been daily robbed; that it had been, and still remains, "a dishonored and dishonorable currency," by the use of which they themselves were "becoming demoralized;" that as a consequence of its use they were "in danger of losing that sense of honor which is necessary for the well-being of society;" that to its continued use they had been indebted since the war for "instability of prices, unsteadiness in trade," and a variety of other ills, whose general effect is, as we are assured by no less an authority than that of our Finance Minister, that of "filling the coffers of the rich," while making the country absolutely "intolerable to persons of limited incomes."

The person to whom we are just now indebted for this last and worst description of the evils under which we labor, may, my dear sir, certainly be classed among those who most entirely discharge from their memories all recollection of yesterday's events. Had it been otherwise with him he would have seen that, with exception of the years of the protective tariffs of 1828 and 1842, the whole of the period from 1815 to 1860 had exhibited a succession of changes infinitely greater and more injurious to both people and government than any that had been known since the greenback had been issued; since the nation first assumed performance of the duty of furnishing a basis for our monetary transactions not liable to be withdrawn at any and every moment of change in the policy of the Bank of England, as had been the case in all those periods at which we had pretended to maintain the use of the precious metals, while pursuing a revenue tariff policy which compelled an export of the whole gold produce of California.

Less forgetful than the Secretary, those who have labor to sell and money to buy, the vast majority of our people, cling to the existing state of things, and anxiously desire to witness a restoration of that financial peace which had prevailed at the moment when the former, in his memorable Fort Wayne speech, fulminated his declaration of financial war. From that hour he has been in close alliance with the money lending class, receivers of interest, and livers on incomes, with them asserting that circulating notes were greatly in excess of the public needs; that the national honor demanded a substitution of gold for notes; and that suppression of the latter would be followed by such increased supplies of the former as would at once fill the vacuum thus created; thereby doing all in his power toward destroying that faith in the future to which we had been indebted for success in war, and to which we must be indebted for power to resume should resumption ever again be brought about.

How absurd are such assertions, and how little they are calculated to bear examination, will, as I think, become obvious, my dear sir, when you have reflected on the following facts:—

With a population scarcely larger than our own, grouped together on a surface less than that of half a dozen of our States and therefore having far less need than ourselves of any material medium of exchange, France has a circulating medium one-half greater than is allowed to us.

With a still more compressed population, and one far more accustomed to effecting exchanges without the use of any species of money whatsoever, Great Britain and Ireland use more than twenty dollars per head.

With less than forty millions of people, scattered over almost a continent, *and therefore standing thrice as much in need of some material medium of circulation,* we are allowed far less than is given in either France or Britain. When, however, we look to those portions in which population is dense, and money by comparison little needed, we find them using more than either France or England, the actual circulation of New England being more than thirty dollars per head.

Looking next South and West, we find in many of the States and territories hardly even a single one, and with scarcely the smallest chance that more than one will ever be allowed them. To assert, under such circumstances, that there is any excess of circulation, is so utterly absurd as to make it almost doubtful if the géntleman who writes treasury and currency reports, and those others who make resumption speeches, can really believe the strange assertions they have been used to make. To seek, by means of action in the direction such men now indicate, a resumption of specie payments, must result in failure so complete as to postpone any real resumption for half a century to come.

What the country really needs is an increase, and not a decrease, in the machinery of circulation. That, however, as we are assured, will readily be obtained if the circulating notes can only be suppressed. Create a need for the precious metals, and they will be sure to come. Why, however, is it, that it is precisely where circulatory notes most abound, in New England, Old England, France, and Belgium, that gold and silver are most attracted? Why is it, that in the almost total absence of circulating notes, the precious metals have so entirely disappeared from Georgia and Alabama, North and South Carolina? Why is it, pending the existence of the state of affairs here below described, the precious metals fly from *Utah* and its immediate neighborhood?

"You have tight money markets sometimes in the East. I have read of how semi-savage nations 'barter.' I saw it cited, as a curious fact, in the newspapers, that in Georgia eggs are used as small change; but in Utah I see around me a people, a prosperous people, doing the business of life almost without any money at all. In Salt Lake City itself, right in the line of travel, there is some money; but in the country settlements, which radiate thence into every valley and by every watercourse for a hundred miles, it is literally true that they have no circulating medium. Wheat is the usual legal tender of the country. Horses, harness, vehicles, cattle, and hay, are cash; eggs, butter, pistols, knives, stockings, and whisky, are change; pumpkins, potatoes, sorghum, molasses, and calves, are 'shinplasters,' which are taken at a discount, and with which the saints delight to pay their debts (if it is ever a delight to pay debts). Business in this community, with this currency, is a very curious and amusing pastime. A peddler, for instance, could take out his goods in a carpet-bag, but would need a 'bull' train to freight back his money. I knew a man who refused an offer to work in the country at fifty dollars a month because he would need a 'forty-hundred wagon and four yoke of oxen' to haul his week's wages to the whisky-shop, theatre, &c., on Saturday evening. When a man once lays out his money in any kind of property, it is next to impossible to reconvert it into money. There is many a man here, who, when he first came into the valley, had no intention of remaining but a short time, but soon got so involved that he could never get away without making heavy pecuniary sacrifices. Property is a Proteus, which you must continue to grip firmly, notwithstanding his slippery changes, until you have him in his true shape. Now you have him as a fine horse and saddle; presto, he is only sixty gallons of sorghum molasses; now he changes into two cows and a calf, and before you have time to think he is transformed into fifteen cords of wood up in the mountain canon; next he becomes a yoke of oxen; then a 'shutler' wagon; ha! is he about to slip from you at last in the form of bad debts?"

The following passage from a letter just received from Iowa, shows how completely the financial policy of our Financial Minister tends to place the many who have to borrow at the mercy of the few who are able to lend :—

"When the banks have money to loan it can be borrowed for 10 per cent. interest per annum; but sometimes, and very often, they are short and refuse to loan except to their daily customers. Then the occasional borrower is thrown upon the tender mercies of money men, many of whom indeed are bankers, and is forced to pay 30 and sometimes 40 per cent. This is, of course, done in an underhand way, so that the law cannot reach the extortioner, but it could not be done *at all* if we had circulation enough."

The picture here presented is that of the whole country south and west of Pennsylvania, yet are we daily treated with prescriptions for financial cure based upon the idea of making more and more scarce that machinery of circulation for use of which poor men are already paying 30 or 40 per cent. per annum!

Careful study of the facts here given might, perhaps, satisfy our Finance Minister, that the more thoroughly the channels of circulation are supplied with the cheaper commodity, as is now the case in all New England, *the greater is the power to purchase the precious metals and the less the need for them*. What is now most required is an increase of the former and a diminution of the latter, every step in that direction tending towards reduction of that premium on gold, of which complaint is made.

That such reduction may be brought about, there must be a restoration of that confidence which the Secretary has so studiously labored to destroy. Such restoration may be looked for when our reformers shall have determined to study a very little of that past, which they have so evidently forgotten. Studying it, they will be led to see that, with the single exception of the protective periods above referred to, at no time in our history has the price of gold, as measured in corn or cotton, cloth or houses, farms or furnaces, remained so steady as in the four years through which we have just now passed.

Within those years we have closed a war which was costing three millions a day, and have entered upon a state of peace the cost of which is less than half a million; and yet, sudden as was the change, the bankruptcies and sheriff's sales have not been a fifth as great in number as those produced in nominally specie-paying, and really British free-trade, times, in a single year. Never in the whole history of the world has so great a change been so little felt; and the reason why it has been so is, *that the substratum of our whole monetary system consisted of a commodity for which there was no demand in foreign markets.*

That we should at all times hold in mind that resumption must eventually be reached, is not at all to be questioned. That it may be so reached as to give us increased prosperity, it must be sought in a direction very different from any yet indicated by our many monetary reformers, whether editors, senators, or finance ministers.

What that direction is I propose to state in a future letter, and meanwhile remain, with great regard and respect, yours truly,

HENRY C. CAREY.

Philadelphia, December 21, 1868.

LETTER SEVENTH.

DEAR SIR :—

The cheapest, most effective, and most important of all the machinery by means of which property is enabled to pass from hand to hand, and thus to become *current*, is found in *the credit* and *the check* by whose aid thousands of millions pass in Wall Street with less use of any material medium of circulation than among the Rocky Mountains would be required for arrangement of transactions counting by hundreds, or by thousands.

Next to them comes *the circulating note*, the most generally useful, the most harmless, and the most calumniated of all the labor saving machinery ever invented by man.

Last of all—the most cumbrous, most expensive, and least effective of all the machinery of circulation in use among people claiming to be civilized—come the precious metals themselves, and for that reason, probably, the most admired by such financiers as our actual President and his Finance Minister, the two uniting in denouncing the circulating note as the inferior currency by means of which the superior one, consisting of the metals themselves, is, as they assure us, driven out of use.

When, however, the honorable Secretary comes to compare the working of *the credit* and *the note*, he assures us that so far is the inferior note from expelling the superior credit, that it is this latter which is continually thrusting the former out of use, in the manner that here is shown :—

"In all the cities and towns throughout the country checks upon credits in banks and bills of exchange have largely taken the place of bank notes. Not a fiftieth part of the business of the large cities is transacted by the actual use of money, and what is true in regard to the business of the chief of cities is measurably true in regard to that of towns and villages throughout the country. Everywhere bank credits and bills of exchange perform the office of currency to a much greater extent than in former years. Except in dealings with the government, for retail trade, for the payment of labor and taxes, for travelling expenses, the purchase of products at first hand, and for the bankers' reserve, money is hardly a necessity. The increased use of bank checks and bills of exchange counterbalances the increased demand for money resulting from the curtailment of mercantile credits."—*Report of the Secretary of the Treasury on the State of the Finances for the year* 1867.

This is all perfectly true. The superior currency of *the check* and *the credit* tends to lessen demand for the inferior *note*, just as the locomotive lessens demand for the wagon—the *note* in its turn displacing the precious metals just as the wagon displaces the mule and the pack-saddle. Any attempt, therefore, at driving *the note* from use, with a view to compel increased use of the metals, is as much in opposition to the progress of civilization as would be a law forbidding use of the telegraph with a view to compel increased use of the facilities of intercourse furnished by the post office and the railroad train.

The great labor-saving machine is *the credit*. The next is *the circulating note*. Last come *the metals*, by means of which men are enabled to pass from the slow and costly operation of barter to the more rapid one of purchase and sale. Why then do not all men prefer the cheap *credit* even to the slightly expensive *note?* For the reason that credit itself can have no existence among a poor and widely scattered population. It abounds in England and New England, but has no existence in the regions of the Rocky Mountains and Rio Grande. Why, then, do these latter not even adopt *the note?* For the reason that they are not yet so far advanced in civilization as to have among themselves either individuals or corporations capable of making notes such as would readily be received in exchange for property of any description whatsoever. *The need for such notes, proportioned to the exchanges required to be made, is a thousand times greater than it is in Wall Street;* and it exists everywhere in the precise ratio of the absence of the check, the draft, the clearing house, and all other of the various contrivances for dispensing with the services of either the precious metals or the circulating note.

Between these two descriptions of superior currency there are these important differences, to wit:—

That *the note* represents actual property of the parties by whom it is issued, that property having been deposited in the Treasury as scurity for its redemption; whereas *the credit* represents property temporarily deposited in the banks, and liable to be claimed at any instant:

That, while *the note* cannot be so used as in any manner to change its relation to the total currency, *the credit* may be, and habitually is, so used as to *duplicate* its relation thereto—A, the actual owner, and B, the temporary user thereof, both exercising equal power of purchase and equal power to create a currency of checks or drafts —that superior one with the growth of which there should be diminished need for circulating notes:

That, as the inferior of these two currencies—*the note*—yields no interest to its *holder*, all desire to circumscribe within the narrowest limits the quantity to be kept on hand:

That, as the superior one—*the credit*—yields interest to its *makers*, banks and bankers seek as far as possible to increase it by lending out all the moneys standing to the credit of their customers:

That, as the people at large find their interest promoted by limiting the use of *circulating notes* the quantity in actual use changes, under ordinary circumstances, so slowly as scarcely to be perceived; whereas, the quantity *of credits*, dependent as it is upon the arbitrary will of banks and bankers, changes from hour to hour, and with a rapidity that sets at defiance all calculation:

That, consequently, *it is the power to create the superior currency, that based on mere credits, which demands to be regulated by law;* and *not* that inferior one which is based on property, and which finds its proper regulation in the need for its use by the masses of the people.

These things premised, we may now study the course of things under the State bank system, taking as its type the returns of 1860, as follows, the figures representing millions:—

	Capital.	Circulation.	Capital and circulation.	Investments.	Excess investm'ts.
Total amount	422	207	629	807	178
New York and New England	235	73	308	443	135
All other States and Territories	187	134	321	364	43

The first thing that strikes us on an examination of this table is the entire harmony of the facts here presented with the theory of the Secretary, and with the general impressions on the subject, the proportion of circulating notes to capital and business having been very small in those States in which a credit currency most abounded, and very large in those in which such credits were least abundant. With a bank capital of but $235,000,000, New York and New England had the use of $135,000,000 of credits created by banks for their own use and profit, being nearly twice more than the amount of their circulation. With a capital only one-fifth less, the remaining people of the Union appear to have enjoyed the advantages of the superior currency to the extent of but $43,000,000, and their banks to have been dependent upon the profits of circulation to an amount equal to three-fourths of their whole capital, being about twice that of the trading States above enumerated.

The total currency created by banks for their own profit appears to have been as follows:—

New York and New England, with a population of 7,000,000, and a wealth, as returned by the census, of $3,707,000,000, had credits based upon moneys temporarily in banks to the extent of $135,000,000
Circulation 73,000,000

Total $208,000,000

The remaining States, with a population exceeding twenty-four millions, and a wealth of $11,558,000,000, or more than thrice greater, had a bank-created currency thus composed, to wit:—

Credits $43,000,000
Circulation 134,000,000

$177,000,000

In the one case banks might have lived and prospered, even had they been wholly deprived of the profits of circulation. In the other, outside of a few cities, no bank deprived of those profits could have existed.

Fully enjoying the advantages of both the people of the one could generally have the use of money at about the legal rate of interest. Limited almost entirely to the circulation, and that itself in many cases limited by absurd restrictions, those of the other were accustomed to pay twice, thrice, and even four times that rate. With the one prompt payment was a thing of general occurrence. With the other, debt was almost universal, not because of want of property, but because throughout a large portion of the country there existed neither credits, circulating notes, nor any other general medium of exchange whatsoever.

Such having been the state of things seven years since, under the State bank system, we may now examine the working of the, so-styled, national system, with a view to see if it has tended to correction or to exaggeration of the difficulties that then existed.

§ 2. Under the State bank system, as has been shown, the distribution of *credits* and *circulation* among the States was very nearly in accordance with the Secretary's present teachings. How far it is so now, under this, so-called, national one, organized by the Secretary himself, it is proposed here to show.

By the report of the Comptroller, just now published, the following was the state of things in October, 1867, two years having then elapsed since the date of the Secretary's declaration of war upon circulating notes issued at Fort Wayne, by which the public were advised that "paper money" was too abundant, that speculation must cease, and that "contraction" must be the order of the day, the figures, as before, representing millions:—

	Banking capital.	Circulation.	Capital and circulation.	Invest- ments.	Excess in- vestments.
Total.	420	297	717	1103	386
New York and New England	260	173	433	677	234
All other States and Territories	160	124	284	326	152

The total circulation had, in seven years, increased 90,000,000, but instead of finding that increase in those parts of the country in which credit least abounded and circulating notes were most needed, we find the whole of it, and even 10,000,000 more, to have been distributed by the then Comptroller, and now Secretary, to those very States in which credits were most abundant and a paper circulation least required.

Comparing now the bank-created currency of the two periods, we obtain the following figures :—

	1860.	1867.	Increase.
New York and New England, present population 7,000,000—			
Credit currency	135	234	
Circulation	73	173	
Total	208	407	199
Other States and Territories, population 30,000,000—			
Credits	43	152	
Circulation	134	124	
Total	177	276	99

In the first, population could have but very slightly grown. In the other it had increased to the extent of many millions, and yet, while nearly two hundred millions had been added to the one, less than one hundred had been secured by the latter. Such has been the working of a system that is styled national, but that is not only sectional as regards the North and the South, but also as regards the Centre and the West as against the North and the East.

In the intervening period the necessities of our people for a general medium of circulation had grown south and west of New York thrice more rapidly than in the country north and east of the Delaware. In many of the older States, poorly supplied before, the check and draft currency had wholly disappeared. Throughout the West new territories had been settled, and new States had been created, in which credit had as yet obtained no foothold whatsoever. Nevertheless, in the vast region south and west of New York, with four-fifths of the total population of the Union and two-thirds of its wealth, the quantity of circulation granted by the financier who has so much complained of the "plethora of paper money" has been, as here is shown, $10,000,000 less than it had been when Kansas was but beginning to be settled, and when many of the present States and territories had scarcely yet found a place on any map whatsoever.

Bad as is this exhibit, and much as such a state of things must tend to prevent the approach of financial peace, that presented by an examination of the operations of our chief commercial cities is infinitely worse, as I propose to show in another letter, meanwhile remaining, very truly and respectfully, yours,

GEN. U. S. GRANT.   HENRY C. CAREY.

PHILADELPHIA, Dec. 25, 1868.

LETTER EIGHTH.

Dear Sir:—

Circulating notes, as the Secretary assures us, are least needed where credit currency most abounds. Cities, then, are the places at which banks least need to avail themselves of the privilege of furnishing circulation. That such was the practice under the State bank system is well known to all. How it is now, under the one organized by the Secretary himself, and how his system compares with that he had found established, is shown by the following figures, representing, as before, millions:—

OCTOBER, 1860.

	Capital.	Circulation.	Capital and circulation.	Loans.	Excess of loans.
New York . . .	69	10	79	123	44
Boston . . .	35	7	42	64	22
Philadelphia . .	12	3	15	27	12
	116	20	136	214	78

OCTOBER, 1867.

	Capital.	Circulation.	Capital and circulation.	Loans.	Excess of loans.
New York . . .	75	35	110	241	131
Boston . . .	42	24	66	101	35
Philadelphia . .	16	11	27	59	32
	133	70	203	401	198

Of $90,000,000 addition to the currency in that form of which the Secretary is now so generally accustomed to speak as "paper money," no less than $50,000,000 are here shown to have been given, and given, too, by himself as Comptroller of the Currency, to those three communities in which, by his present showing, circulating notes had been least required; $10,000,000 having at the same time been *withdrawn* from the country south and west of New York, embracing States and Territories almost forty in number, with a population numbering little less than 30,000,000, and growing by millions annually, the needs of these for some general medium of circulation being, man for man, thrice greater than those of the people of the cities whose past and present have been above described. The Secretary's theories, as given in the passage of his report heretofore quoted, are excellent. Can he now explain why it is that his practice has been so different?

The bank-created currency of those cities at the same periods may thus be stated:—

	1860.	1867.
Credits based on loans of moneys at the credit of individuals	80	[1]198
Circulation	20	70
	100	268

[1] This is probably much less than the truth, there being checks and "cash items" that to some extent must have borne interest. Opposed to them there are surplus funds which are additions to capital. The one would probably balance the other.

The Secretary denounces speculation, and professes to be earnest in his desire to put it down. Nevertheless, here, *in the very centres of speculation*, three great trading cities, we have, under a system organized by himself, an *increase* of currency amounting to $168,-000,000, or within little more than $60,000,000 of the *total* quantity that, excluding Philadelphia, is allowed to all the States and Territories of the Union south and west of New York, with four times the population and with twice the wealth of New York and New England. Not content, even, with this, the great opponent of speculation and of " paper money" has been unwearied in his efforts still further to deplete the centre, the west, and the south, and to perfect the centralization already so far established, by compelling all their banks to provide in one alone of their funds for redemption of their circulation, after having already provided for the same by deposits in his own hands at Washington. A better provision for maintenance and extension of the speculative spirit, so often and so bitterly denounced by himself, and for preventing resumption either now or at any future time, could scarcely have been devised.

The 50,000,000 additional circulation thus injected into the great centres do more, my dear sir, to cause "inflation," than would be done by 500,000,000 of the one, two, and five dollar notes required "for the retail trade, for travelling expenses, and for the purchase of products at first hands," those purposes for which the money is really, in the Secretary's view, to be regarded as a "necessity." By whom, however, were they so injected? By the Secretary himself, in his capacity of Comptroller of the Currency! He, therefore, it is, who is to be regarded as the great "inflationist;" yet does it please his friends to style as such all those who fail to see that resumption of specie payments can by any possibility be attained by means of measures tending to total destruction of the societary circulation.

" Capitals," said Mirabeau, " are necessities, but if the head is allowed to grow too large, the body becomes apoplectic, and wastes away." That, precisely, is what is here occurring, the whole tendency of the present monopoly system being in the direction of causing accumulation of blood in and about the societary heart, to the utter destruction of circulation throughout the body and limbs. Hence it is that property in New York city has attained such enormous prices, and that we are now daily called upon to read of the "unparalleled advance" that, according to the *Tribune*, chief advocate of prompt resumption as it is, has taken place in the adjoining States, New Jersey and Connecticut. Passing outward, however, south and west, we find a totally different state of things, miners, and laborers being thrown altogether idle, and the depression there being quite as little to be "paralleled" as is the advance in the States so liberally patronized by our consistent Finance Minister.

To find his system working in full perfection we need, however, to look further south—to Georgia, Carolina, and Alabama. Doing this, we find the special advocate of the Secretary's most unphilosophical and most exhaustive system, speaking to its readers in the words that follow :—

"A correspondent, writing from Hinesville, Liberty County, Georgia, says: 'A sale has taken place at this county seat that so well marked the extreme depression in the money market that I send you the particulars: Colonel Quarterman, of this county, deceased, and his executor, Judge Featter, was compelled to close the estate. The property was advertised, as required by law, and on last court day it was sold. A handsome residence at Walthourville, with ten acres attached, out-houses, and all the necessary appendages of a first-class planter's residence, was sold for $60. The purchaser was the agent of the Freedmen's Bureau. His plantation, four hundred and fifty acres of prime land, brought $150; sold to a Mr. Fraser. Sixty-six acres of other land, near Walthourville, brought three dollars; purchaser Mr. W. D. Bacon. These were all *bona fide* sales. It was court day, and a large concourse of people were present. The most of them were large property owners, but really had not five dollars in their pockets, and in consequence would not bid, as the sales were for cash.' In Montgomery, Alabama, lots on Market Street, near the Capitol, well located, 50 feet by 110 feet, averaged about $250 each. The Welsh residence on Perry Street, two-story dwelling-houses, including four lots, sold for $3500; Dr. Robert M. Williams was the purchaser. The same property in better times would not have brought less than $10,000. The Loftin Place, near Montgomery, containing 1000 acres, was recently rented at auction for forty cents an acre. The same lands rented the present year for three dollars an acre. About thirty real estate transfers were recorded in Nashville last week; prices were low. In Portsmouth, Virginia, a house and lot, formerly of the Reed estate, situated on the south side of County Street, near the intersection with Washington, was recently sold to Mr. Ames for $750. A building lot at the intersection of South and Bart Streets, brought only $125. A portion of Woodland, the late Judge John Webb Tyler's estate in Prince William County, Virginia, has been purchased by Mr. Delaware Davis, of New Jersey, at $20 an acre."

The more the blood is driven to the heart the more do the limbs become enfeebled, and the greater becomes the liability to paralysis, to be followed by death. The Secretary has been, and still is, driving all the blood of the Union into the States and cities of the north and east, and with every step in that direction the circulation becomes more and more torpid and the paralysis more complete.

§ 2. Of the agricultural departments of France a very large proportion are steadily declining in population, the main reason therefor, as given in a highly interesting paper recently published,* being to be found in "a total absence of that power to supply themselves with circulating notes which elsewhere results from the presence of banks or other establishments of credit, or that of individuals whose signatures to such notes command the public confidence."

Agriculture, for this reason, fails in those districts to obtain the aid of capital, except on conditions so onerous as to be ruinous to the borrower. Just so has it always been throughout more than half the Union; the farmers of the Mississippi Valley, and the planters of the South and Southwest having been, even before the war, compelled to pay for the use of circulating notes twice, thrice, and often even five times the rate of interest paid by their brother agriculturists of New England and New York.

So did it continue to be until the needs of war compelled the Treasury to do that which it should long before have done, furnish a national machinery of circulation, by means of which the farmer might be enabled to buy and sell for cash, and to pay in cash his mason

---

* Journal des Economistes, Septembre, 1867.

and his carpenter; thereby, and for the first time in our history, enabling these latter in their turn to acquire that feeling of real independence which results from exercise of power to choose among contending shopkeepers that one which would most cheaply supply the cloth, the coffee, or the sugar required by their families and themselves. At once the whole position of affairs was changed; the needy farmer and laborer, begging for credit, disappearing from the stage, and the anxious trader, begging for their custom, taking their place. It was a revolution more prompt, more complete, and more beneficial than any other recorded in financial history; its effect having been that of supplying the inferior, the most useful, and the least dangerous currency—*the note*—to those portions of the country which, while abounding in labor and in natural wealth, were as yet too poor to command the services of that superior one —*the credit*—by which, in the course of time and in accordance with the Secretary's present teachings, it was to be replaced.

Of all the machinery of commerce there is none which renders so large amount of service as that which facilitates exchanges from hand to hand. The more it abounds the more rapid is the circulation, and, as in the physical body, the greater are the health, the strength, and the force. It is, however, the one that is always last obtained, and most difficult to be retained. In furnishing it gratuitously to the centre, south, and west, the Treasury rendered a larger amount of service to our whole people than it would have done had it given the gratuitous use of railroads whose *cost* would have been thrice as great as its own *amount*. That service was found in the increased demand for labor, to the great advantage of those who had it in its various forms for sale—the farmers, mechanics, and laborers of the Union. To some extent, however, it damaged those who made no profitable use of their own physical or mental faculties—annuitants, mortgagees, and other persons in the receipt of fixed incomes.

That, however, is the necessary result of beneficial changes of every kind, all such improvements manifesting themselves in an elevation of the labor of the present at the cost of accumulations of the past—the rate of interest always falling as labor becomes more productive. Instead, however, of so regarding it, those who suffered have, of course, insisted that it had been nothing but "a forced loan;" that, for that reason, it should, at the earliest possible moment, be repaid; and that the whole people should for their benefit, be deprived of all the vast advantage which, under pressure of the war, had been so promptly gained. By whom, however, had the loan been made? Had it not been by the whole body of the people? Assuredly it had, and that same body had been the recipient of its products.

It had been simply the one great corporation of the Union combining with its members for obtaining, free of charge, the use of machinery of inestimable value in default of which the societary circulation had previously been so much and so frequently arrested as to cause waste of labor to an annual amount twice greater than the circulation that had thus been furnished. It was that corporation combining with its members for their relief from the oppressive taxation of usurious capitalists, money-lenders on the one hand, and traders on the other. Of those who made the loan none complain. None suffer; there being not even a single one who cannot, on the instant, be reimbursed, obtaining from his neighbor property of value fully equal to that which he had given for his share of this, so-called "loan." What they do complain of is that, while willing to extend their loans, and to do so without charge of interest therefor, they are not permitted so to do; and here they complain with reason.

The Secretary insists, however, that this is only "paper money," of which there exists, in his opinion, so great a "plethora," that, at any sacrifice, this loan must be repaid. Seeking this "plethora," we look to the South and find plantations being almost given away, because of the almost entire absence of currency of any description whatsoever. Turning next to the Mississippi Valley we find currency so scarce that manufacturers and traders pay for its use twice and thrice the usual rate of interest; farmers, meanwhile, finding difficulty in obtaining it on any terms whatsoever.

Coming now to the centre, we find it to be so little superabundant as to compel the employment of bank certificates—a sort of bastard "paper money" that otherwise would not be used. Passing thence to the North and East, the centre of speculation, and therefore, perhaps, in both the past and the present, so largely favored by a finance minister who professes himself opposed to "speculation," we find an abundance, and perhaps even the "plethora" of which he has so much and so frequently complained. Taking, however, the whole Union, we find that of this "dishonored and dishonorable paper money" the quantity in actual circulation cannot be estimated at more than five hundred millions of dollars, or little more than a dozen dollars per head. With less than half the need of it, per head, France has a circulation more than one-half greater; and yet, with even this large supply, her agricultural districts are even now actually perishing for want of some representative of money to be employed in the effectuation of exchanges. Of all the countries of Europe there is none in which there exists in such complete abundance that superior currency which, as the Secretary assures us, and as we know to be the fact, tends to supplant the circulating note, as is the case in Britain. Yet even there do we find the circulating medium, per head, to be far greater in quantity than among ourselves. Nevertheless, with such facts before him, and in direct opposition to his own most recent teachings, the Secretary assures us that it is to the excess of "paper money" we are to look when desiring to find the "obstacle" which stands in the way of "a return to a stable currency!"

Scotland, as stated in the article above referred to, has for each 5000 of her population a place at which money operations may be transacted. Nevertheless, there is no country of Europe in which circulating notes are so generally used. This, according to the Secretary, should make of it a good place to sell in and a bad one in which to buy; there yet is none in Europe better in which both to sell and to buy.

Jersey, one of the little Channel islands, with a population of

55,000 gathered together in a space less than half that embraced within our city limits, has no less than seventy-three places at which monetary affairs may be transacted; and yet, with all this vast machinery for supplying the superior currency, her people use of notes, none of which are of less than $5 value, more than $400,000, or almost $8 per head. Add to this the gold and silver that must necessarily be used, and we obtain a larger proportion than is now in use by a people of little less than 40,000,000, scattered over half a continent, among by far the larger portion of whom there exist none of those appliances by means of which, in more advanced communities, the use of money, whether the precious metals or the circulating note, is so much economized. Excluding New York and New England, and allowing for the general absence here of those means, the circulation of Jersey is *ten times* greater per head than that of nearly forty of our States and Territories; and yet, not only does this little island enjoy the highest degree of prosperity, but there is not a spot in Europe in which excess of currency stands less in the way of both buying and selling with advantage. The facts and the Secretary's theory do not, therefore, harmonize with each other. So much the worse, he will probably reply, for the unfortunate facts.

Such as they are, my dear sir, they are now placed before you, and none can as I think hesitate to admit the general accuracy with which they have been presented. Should your leisure permit their careful examination, you will, as I confidently believe, arrive at the same conclusion with myself, to wit: That it is to the existence of a great monopoly, created under the present banking law, we are indebted for the existence of most of those obstacles which stand in the way of a restoration of financial peace; and, that if we would remedy the evils under which we suffer, we must commence with removal of the cause to which their existence is due.

How it may be removed with permanent benefit to all, I propose to show in another letter, and meanwhile remain,

Very respectfully, yours,

Gen. U. S. Grant.　　　　　　　　HENRY C. CAREY.
Philadelphia, December 31, 1868.

LETTER NINTH.

Dear Sir:—

Seven years since there still existed among the States in reference to one of the most important of all questions—the establishment of *institutions of credit*—a perfect equality of rights. Then, Illinois and Tennessee stood exactly on a par with New Hampshire and Vermont, and the little capitalists of Iowa found among the statutes of the Union none whose tendency was that of placing them in a position inferior to those of Maine in reference to any arrangements they might wish to make for facilitating among themselves exchanges of labor and labor's products. Among those statutes there could be found none whose direct effects had been, and must ever continue to be, that of placing the men of Missouri in the position of "hewers of wood and drawers of water" to the more favored people of New York and Massachusetts. If they still continued to barter corn for cloth, hogs for sugar, it was not because of interference of the Federal Government forbidding the adoption of measures tending towards enabling them to adopt the more civilized process of purchase and sale. If they continued to pay 20, 30, or 40 per cent. for the use of circulating notes furnished by Eastern banks, they had before them at least the hope that with time they might be enabled to establish institutions that would furnish such at more reasonable rates of interest. With the war, however, there came in this respect a total change, Congress having soon after its commencement enacted that before any association of capitalists, large or small, could be permitted to commence supplying their neighbors with machinery by means of which to make their various exchanges, they should lend to the government an amount one-ninth greater than that of the circulating notes to be supplied; and that the bonds they were thus required to buy should be placed in the Treasury, to be there held as security for payment of the notes.

That done, and the notes received, it was then further required that they should purchase a certain proportion of Treasury notes payable on demand, to be held by them as further security for payment on presentation of any portion of their own circulation. Further, in the event of failure of payment, their stockholders were made to a certain extent individually liable for any ultimate deficiency of assets, whether as regarded holders of notes, or owners of credits on their books.

Having thus defined the terms on which the several portions of the country might be allowed to obtain machinery of circulation, and *having provided such restrictions as rendered it most difficult so to do except in rich and populous districts*, it might have been supposed that then it would have been everywhere left to the people themselves to decide to what extent they would have institutions of credit empowered to supply circulating notes. Not so, however, the law providing that whensoever such circulation should have been issued to the extent of $300,000,000, all power for further issue should cease, and thus establishing a monopoly in the hands of those who first had taken possession of the little that had been allowed.

Compliance with these conditions was easy in those communities within which credit institutions already largely abounded, and in which, by the Secretary's own showing, circulating notes least were needed, to wit: New York and New England. Most difficult, however, must it prove in all of those in which such notes most were needed, to wit: the Centre, the West, and the South, those in which the superior currency of checks and drafts least existed. Most of all was it easy in those large cities in which, as the Secretary informs us, "not a fiftieth part of the business is transacted by the actual use of money;" and in which, as he further says, "except in dealings with the government, for the retail trade, for the payment of labor and taxes, for travelling expenses, the purchase of products at first hands, and for the banker's reserve, money is hardly a necessity." Such being the case, it was his duty, as Comptroller of the Currency, so to act as to secure to the States and Territories least provided with the superior currency the largest possible share of the limited quantity of the inferior one that had been thus allowed. Directly the reverse of this, however, we find him to have added $100,000,000 to the previously existing circulation of those States in which credits most existed, and $50,000,000 to that of the three cities in which circulating notes were least of all required; while actually diminishing by $10,000,000 the allowance to the whole country south and west of New England and New York.

By this course of action there was established a *monopoly of money power without a parallel in the world;* that monopoly, too, created by the Secretary himself in those very centres of speculation in which each additional million does more to produce "inflation" than could or would be done by a dozen millions scattered throughout the pockets of farmers and laborers of the east, the west, the south, or the southwest.

The counterbalance to this monopoly was found in the greenback—in machinery of circulation that had been created by the people themselves for the purpose of enabling each and all of them readily to exchange their services and products. The one tended toward giving capitalists of the cities power to compel the interior more and more to depend on them for performance of all their exchanges, and thus to give them more complete control over the farmer and the laborer. The other, on the contrary, tended toward enabling farmers and laborers to exchange among themselves freed from the control of city capitalists; and for that reason it has been that these latter, the journals in their pay, and the Treasury department, have been so unwearied in their efforts to drive it from the stage.

For accomplishment of that object they have done their utmost towards destroying the confidence of our people in each other, and in the country's future. From day to day has "contraction" been insisted on, accompanied by the assurance that prices must be made to fall; that property bought to-day must be almost valueless to-morrow; that mines opened, furnaces or houses built, this year, must prove in the next to be worth far less than cost. Raids have been made upon banks. Interest-bearing securities have been withdrawn from them for the express purpose of compelling them to heap up greenbacks in their vaults. Factories and mills have been closed that might and would have consumed hundreds of thousands of tons of coal and bales of cotton. Mines have been abandoned, and manufacturers have been ruined. Paralysis has been brought about through the whole extent of the Union, and all these things have been done to the ends that the people might be deprived of a circulating medium created by themselves and for themselves; that the monopoly of the extreme North and East might be perfected; and that the "speculator" might in this manner be driven from existence. To what extent this latter object has been attained, we may now inquire.

From the report of the Comptroller of the Currency we learn that on the first of January, 1867, the loans on private security by the banks of New England and New York were $404,000,000, and that in October following not only had there been *no contraction*, but there had been an actual *increase* of their amount.

At the first of those dates they held $297,000,000 of interest-bearing public securities. At the last, their amount had fallen $14,000,000, the whole effect of a nine months' vindictive warfare having been that of compelling them to disgorge *public* securities yielding them an annual interest of probably $800,000. Placing against this the higher interest that lenders had, by means of the Secretary's aggressive policy, been enabled to secure, the balance in favor of the banks would probably count by millions, for all of which they had been indebted to the policy announced in the celebrated but unfortunate Fort Wayne decree. The policy that carried us through the war favored those who had labor to sell and money to borrow. That of the Secretary, and of the money lenders of New York and New England, favors those who have money to lend and labor to buy; and hence it is that the societary circulation becomes daily more and more impeded, and that the Treasury daily loses power.

Throughout the North and East there was certainly a plethora of currency needing to be corrected. Has the Secretary, with all his efforts, succeeded in making this correction? On the contrary, he has not only proved himself utterly powerless in that direction, but has, by largely withdrawing that machinery on which, almost alone, were dependent the people of more than half the Union, made the centres of speculation relatively far more powerful than they had ever been before.

His policy has been wholly inoperative in all those centres of speculation in which "not a fiftieth part of the business is transacted by the actual use of money," the "plethora" still existing just where the Secretary had himself created it; monetary starvation being, meanwhile, the lot of two-thirds of the whole population of the Union, and their position, relatively to the highly speculative North and East, undergoing daily deterioration.

To what extent this course of action has tended towards facilitating resumption may be now examined.

2. The first step in that direction, whensoever it shall be made, will be the one that shall tend to replace in the Treasury the power that had been parted with at the moment when the existing monopoly had been created. As yet, every attempt in that direction has proved an entire failure, Congress having created a monster which, thus far, has proved far more powerful than its creator. Until it shall be dethroned—until it can be deprived of its present control over both people and State—there can be no financial peace, and it is with that alone that resumption can ever be brought about.

To the end that such peace may be established, we must commence by doing justice, re-establishing, under the National Banking Law, that equality of rights of which the Centre, the South, and the West so unjustly have been deprived, and thus placing the man of Missouri once again on a footing with his fellow-citizen of

Vermont. To do this must, however, as we are assured, tend to produce inflation, to raise prices, and thus to retard resumption. The answer to this is, that it is always expedient to do right; that we may not do evil that good may come of it; that universal experience teaches us that honesty is the best policy; and, that the road towards financial peace *cannot* lie in the direction of enabling the rich of the North and East to grow daily richer at the sacrifice of the rights of the poorer men, white and black, of Missouri and Minnesota, Georgia and Mississippi.

By whom, however, is it that such assertions are made? Is it not by the people of New England, who have, with their very limited population, secured to themselves a third of the whole money power of the Union? Is it not by men of New York, that other State which has secured to itself a fourth of the whole circulation allotted to more than forty States and Territories, extending over almost an entire continent? Is it not by those cities of the North Atlantic Coast, which have, by means of the present banking law, secured to themselves so nearly all the power to furnish circulation which, before the war, had been exercised by interior banks? Is it not, everywhere, by the men who desire to see a rise in the price of that great commodity, money, of which they have the command, and a decline in the prices of those they need to purchase— to wit, labor and labor's products? To all these questions there can be no answer other than this: that we are in the midst of a financial war whose object is the maintenance of a monopoly hostile to the best interests of the people; a monopoly pending whose existence there can be no resumption; and, *that the first step toward peace is to be found in such a re-establishment of governmental power as would result from dissolution of the present alliance with that portion of the community which desires that money may be dear and labor cheap.* Throughout the war the Treasury was in close alliance with those who desired that money might be cheap and labor dear, and if it desires now to bring about resumption it must commence by renewal of that understanding with the men who have labor to sell and money to buy which was brought to an untimely end at the moment when the Secretary, three years since, fulminated from Fort Wayne his declaration of war upon the credit of both the people and the State.

3. That the physical body may be sound in health, there must be steady and rapid circulation throughout the whole system, from the heart to the extremities, and thence back again to the heart. So, too, it is with the social body, societary health being entirely inconsistent with excessive circulation in the region of the heart, the extremities meanwhile becoming from time to time more entirely palsied, as is now the case throughout the Union. That this may be corrected, and that there may be established or re-established throughout the Centre, the South and the West, that rapidity of circulation without which there can be neither financial nor political health, we need an abolition of monopoly privileges. That we may then gradually calm the unnatural excitement existing in States and cities which now profit of that monopoly we need the adoption of measures tending to regulate the exercise of that

power over the currency which results from excess of loans and creation of credits on their books at one moment, and violent diminution of loans and suppression of credits at another, the two combining for the production of excitement at one moment and paralysis at another, and for prevention of anything like permanent financial peace. To that end we need a law declaring—.

First, that no bank shall hereafter so extend its investments as to hold in any form other than those of gold, silver, U. S. notes, or notes of national banks, more than twice its capital:

Second, that in the case of already existing banks whose investments are outside of the limits above described, any extension thereof beyond the amount at which they stood on the first of the present month shall be followed by instant forfeiture of its charter.

Having thus established a check upon further extension, the next step should be in the direction of bringing the operations of existing banks within proper limits. To that end, we need a provision imposing on all investment outside of the limits above described a tax for the present year of one per cent. In the second year let it be made $1\frac{1}{2}$ per cent.; in the third, 2; and in the fourth, 3. Thenceforth let the tax grow at the rate of a half per cent. per annum until, by degrees, all banks shall have so enlarged their capitals, or so reduced their loans, as to free themselves from its further payment.

Holding interest-paying securities to no more than double its capital, a bank would be always in a condition of perfect safety, and could give to its stockholders dividends of at least 10 per cent. Such stock would be preferable to almost any other securities in the market, and there would be no difficulty in so enlarging the foundation as to give to the whole structure the form of a true pyramid, instead of that inverted one which now presents itself to the eye of all observers.

Under the State bank system city banks furnished little or no circulation. Why? Because their deposits enabled them to do all the business required for making liberal dividends among their shareholders. The country banks then monopolized the circulation. Why? Because with deposits small in amount and without the profits of circulation they could not live. Let us have such a law as is above described and the city banks will at once find themselves forced to relinquish to their country competitors the whole business of furnishing circulating notes; and thus a second great step in the direction of ultimate resumption will have at once been made.

It may be said, however, that banks are now so heavily taxed by both State and Federal Governments as to make it difficult under such restrictions to continue the business in which they are now engaged, and that it is so is probably the case. That it may so cease to be, let the Treasury at once relinquish the few millions of revenue which result from bank taxation, at the same time providing against increase on the part of the States. In the whole list of taxes there are none so injurious, none which should be so carefully avoided, as those which tend to prevent the formation of institutions of credit; yet are State and National Governments vying with each other in the effort so to squeeze them as almost to drive them from existence! Were all bank taxes abolished; were the monopoly extinguished; and were governments to encourage rather than prevent the formation of such institutions; we should then be on the road towards raising the greenback to a level with the gold and silver coin. For every dollar so relinquished twenty would be added to the productive power of the nation as a consequence of the growth of faith in the future which would result from making that one step in the direction of financial peace.

4. The third step would be found in requiring banks to retain, in lieu of the greenbacks now required, all the gold received from the Treasury as interest on bonds therein deposited. Had this course been pursued for three years past they would this day hold sixty millions of gold, while the people would have in daily use an equal amount of circulating notes that now are hoarded. Let it be now adopted, the banking monopoly being simultaneously abolished, and the day will then be close at hand when the amount of interest payable to banks will reach $30,000,000 per annum; when the world at large will see that the day is fast approaching on which the greenback is to stand upon a par with gold and silver; and, that if their circulation be still continued it will be because our people will then have arrived at the conclusion that the way to insure steadiness of monetary action is to be found in the direction of maintaining the use of *a national medium of circulation not liable to be withdrawn on every occasion of disturbance in the relations of the always belligerent powers of Europe.*

5. The national banking law abounds in serious defects, all of which must be remedied before we can have perfect financial peace. Most important of all, however, are those above referred to, by the one of which there was created a Procrustean Bed measured for a body that has already, though yet in infancy, far outgrown it; while by the other there was placed in the hands of a limited number of persons, chiefly city bankers, a power so excessive that it has enabled them to set at defiance all the power of the government, and will, without action such as is above described, enable them so to do forever in the future.

By removal of the first we shall free ourselves from the absurd position in which we at this moment stand, that of having proposed to establish through the South a system under which money wages were to be paid, at the same time refusing to either South or West that power for creating the machinery in which such payments must be made, which is so freely exercised throughout the North and East.

By means of the second we shall not only greatly limit the power to produce financial disturbance, but also do very much towards limiting that extravagance of expenditure to which we stand now indebted for an adverse balance of trade in face of which resumption can never seriously be thought of, and can, certainly, never be brought about.

The three together furnish *the only terms* upon which financial peace can ever permanently be secured.

That we may have political peace, and that the Union may be

maintained, we *must* begin by recognizing the existence of perfect equality among the States in reference to the power of their people to determine for themselves what shall be the character of the machinery used in making exchanges from hand to hand, and to what extent it shall be used.

In another letter I shall ask your attention, my dear sir, to some facts connected with the national debt, and meantime remain, with great respect and regard,

Yours truly,

GEN. U. S. GRANT.   HENRY C. CAREY.

PHILADELPHIA, January 4, 1869.

LETTER TENTH.

DEAR SIR:—

THE surrender at Appomattox, though giving us, so far as regarded operations in the field, the peace that so anxiously had been desired, brought with it reason for apprehending the reverse of peace in the commercial and financial world. For several years the country had presented to view a scene of life and activity the like of which had never anywhere before been witnessed. All who had had labor or labor's products to sell had found a ready market, and among men, too, who could at once pay over the price upon which they had agreed. For the first time farmers and laborers throughout the whole country could go cash in hand seeking their supplies among those who could sell at the lowest rate. Demand had gone ahead of supply, the economy of labor thus produced exhibiting itself in the fact that, notwithstanding the absence of a million of men in the field, the nation had found itself enabled to contribute to the wants of government in a manner so remarkable as to have amazed the outside world, while almost as much astonishing ourselves. Never before had it so well been proved that in the social as in the physical body health, strength, and life are the inseparable accompaniments of rapid circulation.

Now, however, there was threatened a serious change in the power of production as well as in the machinery of circulation. For years we had had in the field hundreds of thousands of men busily engaged in the work of consumption while adding nothing to production. Thenceforth their services were to be given to increasing the supplies of food, clothing, and machinery placed at the command of our people, and there was danger lest, in the absence of governmental purchases, the machinery of circulation might prove wholly insufficient for making the exchanges work as smoothly as they till then had done. More labor would be seeking employment, and more commodities would be in market to be exchanged against labor, and any stoppage of such exchanges must not only affect the power of the whole people to provide satisfactorily for their own wants, but also greatly impair their power for aiding the various governments, local and general, amid the difficulties in which, for the moment, they were involved. The interests of all required, therefore, that rapid circulation should continue to be maintained.

Throughout the war individuals, cities, counties, States, had volunteered their aid in a manner wholly without precedent in the annals of the world. To so great an extent had this been done that it is certainly fair to estimate the voluntary donations at $600,000,000, the half of which, or $300,000,000, still remained a charge upon our people, involving payment of interest to the annual extent of little, if any, less than $20,000,000.

The interest on this local debt was probably a full seventh of that payable on the national debt. This would seem to have been but a small proportion, yet was it really an enormous one when we reflect that the local governments had been stripped of nearly every source of revenue except the lands and houses, mills, farms, and mines, that before had been so heavily taxed for maintenance of schools, roads, poor-houses, prisons, and for other matters with whose direction they stood charged. The effect of this now exhibits itself in the fact that local taxation has become so burthensome that cases could readily be cited in which the proceeding falls very little short of confiscation. The sums required for payment of interest on the various public debts being fixed quantities, it followed, of course, that every diminution in the prices of labor, or its products, tended to make the burthen more severe, while just as much ameliorating the condition of those who had interest to receive and labor or its products to purchase. In the natural course of things these latter—the men who had *lent* the government what it needed—were certain largely to profit; and the danger was great that those who had so freely *given* of their little means might largely suffer by the change. Of the two, these latter were most entitled to consideration, having given of their means and pledged their properties with no expectation whatsoever of remuneration. To them it was of the highest importance that the demands of the National Treasury should be limited to the smallest possible amount; that no present attempt should be made to pay the principal of the debt; that taxes should as rapidly as possible be abolished; and, generally, that the national power should be so exerted as to maintain that confidence in each other, and in the Union at large, by which the war had been so much distinguished, and to which we had been so much indebted for the success that had been obtained.

That all these things might be done; that the gap between war and peace might comfortably be bridged over; that the men who had labored and had given of their means might not be sacrificed for the benefit of those who had merely lent at heavy interest; and, that the power of the nation to contribute to the further support of government might remain unimpaired; it was essential that the Finance Minister should be capable of recognizing the truth of that proverb which teaches that *those who move gently move healthily, and those who move healthily have the best chance of life.* Directly the reverse of this, we have had for minister a man whose whole period of office has exhibited a series of convulsions brought about by himself and having for their effect that of making the rich richer and the poor poorer, most fully proving to the world how large is the amount of mischief that may be done by a man placed, as the present Secretary has been, in a position for the worthy filling of which he has not manifested possession of any single recommendation. Hardly had he been seated in his office before journalists known to be in his confidence gave to the world assurance that the price of gold was at once to be reduced, and that resumption was soon to be brought about. For the moment, however, public needs compelled retraction of such assertions. The Treasury was largely in debt to soldiers and contractors, all of whom would gladly have accepted notes payable on demand, and without interest, but the Secretary preferred competing with merchants and manufacturers by offering to take $600,000,000 at an extravagant rate of interest, coupled with a power to claim gold bonds at the end of three years' time. That sale accomplished, the country was next favored with a declaration of war against the circulating notes by means of which the government was then so greatly aiding the societary movement while saving nearly $30,000,000 per annum. Contraction was now to be the order of the day; prices were to be put down while taxes were to be maintained; the rich who held government bonds were to be made richer, while those who had *given* of their means to the support of government were to be made poorer; the banking monopoly was to be maintained, the national circulation being meantime withdrawn; and all these things were to be done that the Finance Minister might have placed at his disposal $200,000,000 a year to be applied to payment of principal and interest of the debt, which latter, as we were triumphantly assured, was to be speedily extinguished by means of a system whose obvious tendency was that of largely increasing the general rate of interest, thereby diminishing the power of our people profitably to employ their labor, or liberally to contribute to the support of government.

For the moment, Congress was led to give in its adhesion to the Secretary's measures of contraction. Very brief experience of its effects was, however, required for inducing it to limit its approval within $4,000,000 per month;

and but little more, happily, for causing it to be altogether withdrawn. So, too, has it been with regard to taxes, Congress having, in despite of his remonstrances, annihilated many of the most oppressive of them, and thus vetoed his schemes for burthening the present generation with actual payment of the entire debt.

That in the adoption of this course Congress has wisely acted will, as I think, be clear to all who shall carefully study the following facts : Taking the whole Union together, the average rate of interest paid by its taxpayers is not less than 15, if even less than 20 per cent. In New England, where institutions of credit and circulating notes abound, it is greatly less than this. In the Central States, where such institutions are more rare, and where circulating notes are much less freely supplied, it must exceed one per cent. per month. In the South, West, and Southwest, where such institutions have little or no existence, and where circulating notes are consequently scarce, it is greatly more than any of the figures I have named.* Those who pay these enormous rates of interest are the real parties liable, each in proportion to his means, for a debt of more than $2000,000,000, for which the Treasury stands indorser. So long as that indorsement shall be continued, they can have the loan at 5 or 6 per cent. ; but when the indorsement is withdrawn the share of each individual enters into the general category of his debts, paying the rate of interest at which he is accustomed to have his needs supplied—the average of all being not less than thrice the rate of the public debt. Such being the case, it becomes clearly obvious that the various schemes which have been propounded in reference to early extinction of the debt are merely contrivances by means of which the rich are to be made richer at the expense of their poorer neighbors.

Adding now to this, that simultaneously with this enormous withdrawal of capital from the real producers of the land, there was to be a withdrawal of nearly the whole medium of circulation, we have before us a scheme of spoliation of the poor for the benefit of the rich the parallel of which cannot be found in the history of any commercial nation of the world.

§ 2. The Secretary's theory in reference to the currency, as has been shown, is in direct conflict with his practice ; the former most earnestly teaching that the need for circulating notes everywhere exists in the *inverse* ratio of the use of checks, drafts, and other machinery for economizing money of every kind ; the latter, on the contrary, furnishing notes in the *direct* ratio of the existence of that superior currency which, as the Secretary himself informs us, everywhere tends to supersede the note. So too, as will now be shown, is it with reference to the public debt, his teachings being in the direction of maintaining inviolate the public faith, the tendency in the opposite direction of the public mind becoming, and that necessarily, more and more rapid as his policy is more fully carried out.

Seeing clearly that such *is* the present tendency, and correctly appreciating "the great interest and alarm excited by the doctrines recently promulgated," the Secretary has, in his Reports, devoted much space to lectures on the absolute necessity for paying the debt in gold, both principal and interest. Replying thereto, Congress might, my dear sir, with great propriety ask of him to show how far his own measures in the past had tended toward diminishing the amount of interest now to be paid ; toward lessening the present burthen of the debt ; toward increasing the general power to contribute to the revenue ; toward strengthening the hands of that loyal portion of our people to which we had been indebted for suppression of the rebellion, and to which alone the holders of our public securities can now, or in the future, look with any confidence for disposition to carry into full effect the contracts of the war. Admitting that this were done, let us now look to see what are the figures that must be given in the reply that would then be made.

---

* Even in Philadelphia an allowance of *one per cent. per month* fails to draw, within the first nine months of the year, more than two-thirds of the taxes on real estate. Failure throughout the year to profit of this large discount is followed by penalties, and yet the journals of the day show that more than 10,000 persons are at this moment in default. In estimating the average interest paid throughout the country, it is proper to take into consideration the great difference between the prices at which purchases of food and clothing may be made for cash, and those which must be paid by those who buy on credit.

In October, 1865, the total debt was $2,808,549,000, of which $1,162,000,000 were payable in gold. The total interest was $133,000,000, of which $67,000,000 were gold, and $66,006,000 currency. Admitting now that the character of the debt had remained unchanged, and taking the price of gold at 140, the quantity of lawful money to-day required for payment of interest on that amount of debt would not exceed $150,000,000.

In October last the debt stood at but $2,505,000,000, the gold portion of which had grown to $2,083,000,000. Three hundred millions less in quantity it now requires for interest nearly $130,000,000, being but $3,000,000 less than had been needed before reduction of the principal had been commenced. Of this the gold portion is $123,000,000, being, at 140, the equivalent of $173,000,-000 lawful money. Adding now to this the currency portion, say $7,000,000, we obtain as the total amount of lawful money this year required for satisfaction of claims for interest no less a sum than $180,000,000, being $30,000,000 more than had been needed when the debt, as stated by the Secretary himself, had been $300,000,000 greater. Adding further the interest on these $300,000,-000, we obtain $198,000,000 as the amount now payable by individuals or the State on the same amount of debt which had existed at the date of the decree which announced "contraction" as being the order of the day; and by means of which confidence, public and private, has been destroyed, and the societary movement so thoroughly paralyzed that the payment of even half of this enormous amount would be far more burthensome than would have been that of the whole on the day on which the Secretary entered on his most destructive career. In all other countries the public credit improves with diminution of the need for loans. Here, under our admirable system of finance, it seems, on the contrary, to deteriorate as the debt is more and more diminished.

The remarkable fact is thus presented, that precisely as the paralysis becomes more general—precisely as labor and all its products fall in price—precisely as lawful money becomes more valuable in the hands of those who hold it—precisely as it becomes less and less attainable by those who need to get it—precisely as taxation becomes more and more burthensome—precisely as these phenomena become more general throughout the land—the quantity of lawful money required for satisfaction of the claims of bondholders increases ; the poor being thus made poorer while the rich are being made richer, and banks, bankers, and treasury agents building palaces, while mills and mines are being closed, and working men and women deprived of power to obtain either the food or the clothing required by their families and themselves.

On an average the prices of labor and its products are at least a third less than had been the case at the date on which the Secretary announced to Congress and the people his determination to enforce "contraction." The $180,-000,000 lawful money of to-day would therefore purchase almost as much as could have then been bought with $300,000,000. As but half this latter sum, or $150,000,000, was then required, it is clear that the burthen of taxation for payment of interest has, except among the bondholders themselves, by means of the Secretary's policy been nearly doubled. Hence it is that the cry has become so general for discharge of the principal in lawful money! Hence it is that the word repudiation is now so freely used! That it shall soon become universal all that is needed is that the Secretary be allowed by Congress to proceed in the substitution of gold bonds for greenbacks, and for all other securities that make no demand for gold, whether for principal or interest.

Were it not for his profession of desire to maintain the public faith there would be good reason for believing that, determined upon bringing about repudiation, he had arrived at the conclusion that the shortest road thereto lay in the direction of making the debt from day to day more burdensome. Certain it is that had such been his wish, he could have chosen no better course of operation than that so consistently pursued almost from the hour that he was so unfortunately placed in the direction of the national finances.

How this tends to produce the present demand for gold and bonds for exportation will be shown in another and concluding letter, and meanwhile I remain,

Yours very respectfully,

HENRY C. CAREY.

Gen. U. S. Grant.
Philadelphia, January 13, 1868.

63

LETTER ELEVENTH.

Dear Sir:—

1. Thus far the Secretary's measures have all looked in the direction of diminishing the machinery of circulation, diminishing the productive powers of the nation, and destroying both individual and national credit; and therefore is it that now, after nearly four years of peace, the Treasury is paying interest at a rate more than twice greater than that paid by England or by France — a rate nowhere paralleled among nations with any real claims to rank as civilized. As a consequence of this our institutions of credit invest their means in Treasury bonds where before the war they would have been applied to meeting the demands of commerce. As a further consequence, thousands of individuals have withdrawn themselves from the active pursuits of life, finding it more profitable, and freer from risk, to accept in the form of interest returns almost as large as were before obtained by those engaged in manufactures or in trade. Maintenance of the bank monopoly enables stockholders to obtain dividends varying between 12 and 25 per cent.; and thus, look where we may, we find the whole Treasury power to have been, and now to be, exerted in the direction of enriching the already rich, while depleting those who need to labor, those to whom it had been almost entirely indebted for the means by aid of which there had been successful prosecution of the war. With every step in this direction luxury increases and importations from abroad tend more and more to make demand for all the gold we mine and all the bonds we fabricate. With each there is a growth of absenteeism making demand, for expenditure in foreign countries, of more of the proceeds of the few commodities we have for export. Such is the result at which we thus far have arrived, a single presidential period employed by the Treasury in producing financial convulsions having done more towards the production of a great moneyed aristocracy, having interests wholly opposed to those of the people at large, than could have been the case had all that time been employed in civil war.

So long as almost millions of men had been employed in consuming food, clothing, and other commodities, while producing nothing, farmers, mechanics, miners, and workingmen of all descriptions, could have the use of credits, circulating notes, and all other of the machinery of circulation, at moderate rates of interest. With return of those millions to production there should have been increase of individual and national credit, enabling those who laboured to obtain the use of circulating notes at constantly diminishing cost; and yet, so far is this from being the case that the average rate thereof is now rapidly obtaining the height at which it had stood before the war, with constantly increasing necessity for return to the practice of buying and selling on credit which had then so universally existed. Why is this? Let us see!

At the date of the creation of the existing bank monopoly eleven States were out of the Union, while others were in a state so disturbed that their people were wholly unable to avail themselves of its provisions, and thus to establish among themselves institutions of credit such as, under State laws, had previously existed. Since then peace has been restored; new States and Territories have been organized, and old States have been readmitted; Pacific railroads have carried population through a country of immense extent that before had been unoccupied; and thus the field throughout which there now exists demand for institutions of credit, and for machinery of circulation, has become at the least thrice, and probably four times, greater than it then had been. To a large extent this change had occurred before the Secretary's declaration of financial war issued from Fort Wayne in 1865—that declaration to which we stand indebted for nearly all the financial trouble that has since existed.

Common sense and common honesty at that moment demanded of the Federal Government removal of all restrictions by means of which the people of the States and Territories south and west of the Hudson had been to so great an extent deprived of power to create for themselves institutions of credit and machinery of circulation, and so almost entirely made dependent for this latter on the extreme North and East. Had their demands been acceded to, had justice been done, and had the monopoly then been terminated, there would have arisen throughout all that vast territory a demand for Treasury bonds to be deposited in the Treasury itself as security for circulation, to the extent of at least $300,000,000, *thereby so far diminishing the necessity for sending them abroad as would have made a difference of little less than that entire sum in the price received for those that needed to be exported.* The man who *must* go to market *must* pay the cost of getting there, whether his commodity be corn, cotton, or bonds, and there is no commodity that so much as these latter is affected by any increase in the quantity forced upon the market. Every step of our finance minister tended to produce such increase, and hence it is that the position in which, so far as regards rates of interest, we at this moment stand so nearly approaches that of the least civilized portion of the European world.

While thus by destroying the domestic market doing all in his power to increase the export of bonds, nothing has been omitted that could tend to diminish their money value in the eyes of foreigners. The greater the work to be accomplished, the less, as it seemed, must be the time allotted for having it done. Hundreds of millions of bonds were forced upon the market having but three years to run. Hundreds of other millions, bearing no interest and payable only at the pleasure of the government, were forthwith to be extinguished. Hundreds of millions of three year bonds were then to be replaced by others redeemable at the pleasure of the government at the end of five years' grace. With each and every step in these directions taxes became more and more onerous and discontent more universal, and so must they continue to do until at last we shall see the people arrive, despite all honest resolutions, at final repudiation of the debt.

2. Of all maxims the greatest is that brief one which teaches that to move gently is to move safely—*festina lente.* Had the Secretary properly appreciated its value he would have desired, as far as possible, to relieve the present generation from burthens created by the war—promoting the circulation of labor and its products while postponing to a distant period payment of the debt itself, and offering the best security in his power so as to enable him most largely to reduce the rate of interest for both the people and the State. Had he so appreciated it he would have seen the great States of Europe obtaining money at low rates of interest by means of creating securities running for the longest periods, and not liable to be disturbed, and must have then been led to imitate their example. Had he so appreciated it, he would have said to Congress, that a security not liable to be paid off without consent of the holders, bearing interest at the rate of five per cent., and subject to a tax of ten per cent., could be sold far more readily than another bearing the same interest, free from tax, but liable to be paid off at the end of even thirty years.

The question of payment, whether in gold or paper, would by this process have been at once placed out of view, no holder of a bond being required to surrender it except on terms agreeable to himself.

The question of taxation of bonds, now so freely used in political warfare, would likewise have been settled.

On such terms the amount required for annual interest might have been reduced to $110,000,000, one-tenth of which would have gone to a sinking-fund by aid of which the whole debt would, before the close of half a century, have been extinguished.

Such, and better even than this, might have been the arrangement with public creditors had the Secretary sought to do even justice to them and to taxpayers as in duty he was bound to do. Directly the reverse of this, the whole period of his administration has been characterized by a determination to benefit those who had money to lend, interest and commissions to receive, at the cost of those who had taxes and interest to pay, and labor to sell. With every step in this direction there has been such an increase in the power of public creditors that it is this day thrice greater than it was four years since when the Treasury was surrounded with hungry claimants for settlement of their accounts. Then, less that two-fifths of the public debt could make demand for gold. Now, with exception of the calumniated *greenback*, nearly the whole has been so changed in form that the Treasury can make no claim for reduc. tion of interest until it shall be prepared to offer payment in gold to all dis. sentients. Between bank monopolists on one hand, and bondholders on the other, it is, therefore, in a state of helplessness so pitiable as fully to account for the utter absence of faith in our financial future which now prevails, and which causes the present exorbitant demands for interest. Banks cannot be compelled to resume until the Treasury shall be prepared to furnish gold for every greenback that may be presented for redemption. Bondholders cannot be compelled to accept low interest until the Treasury shall be enabled to offer gold in payment for the bonds already matured. In this state of things we are assured that if we will only resume, *and thereby double the already large demand for gold*, we shall be enabled to sell our bonds at lower rates of interest!

The first step towards resumption is to be found in relieving the Treasury from the double thraldom which now exists. It must be enabled to dictate law to both banks and bondholders, doing equal and exact justice to all, creditors and debtors, borrowers of money and lenders of it. To that end, the bank monopoly should be abolished, thereby creating a domestic demand for bonds. Next, we need to see the creation of a security bearing lower interest, and of such character as would enable the Treasury to say to existing bondholders that they now must choose between accepting it, *or payment*.

Such a security would be found in a six per cent. bond subject to a tax of 10 per cent., and having forty or forty-five years to run, by the end of which time, *the proceeds of the tax would have paid the debt*. Bonds deposited by banks and bankers with the Treasury might be further taxed one per cent.; and this would soon yield a further sum of five or six millions that might be so applied. Bonds thus provided for could be sold at par for gold, and the Treasury would thus be enabled to relieve itself at once from that control of public creditors which now exists, while at the same time freeing itself from all need for collecting taxes beyond the moderate sum that, as we have reason to hope, will be required for meeting current demands upon it. Thenceforward there would be peace in the financial world.

To the one who might object to this as doing too much for the public creditors the answer would be, that the loss to our whole people resulting from the paralysis produced by the present hopeless Treasury dependence counts annually by hundreds of millions; that all arrangements thus far suggested have proved failures, and for the reason that they have involved violations of the public faith; and finally, that every dollar thus withdrawn from the Treasury in excess of the amount demanded by even the most favorable of them would be more than tenfold made up in the increased power of production resulting from the feeling of confidence that would be produced.

At the present moment the average *public* indebtedness, of our whole population, exceeds $60 per head. Twenty years hence, to all appearance, it will not, even if undiminished, exceed $30—the power per head, to pay it having meantime more than doubled. To hesitate, under such circumstances, about making with the public creditors such fair and liberal terms as at once to command their confidence and respect would be an act of folly so great that it would be difficult to find words in which to characterize it. The more thoroughly honest a man shows himself the smaller is always the cost at which he can command the service of the capital he needs to use.

3. The Sun and the Wind had once, as Æsop tells us, a dispute as to which of them could soonest compel the traveller to lay aside his cloak, and unable otherwise to decide the question they finally concluded to bring it to a practical determination. Mr. Wind taking precedence, he blew and blew, but the louder his roar the closer became the grasp of the traveller upon his outside garment. Despairing finally of accomplishing his object, he now gave place to Mr. Sun, under the influence of whose beams the hold upon the cloak was gradually relinquished, and at length abandoned altogether.

Studying now our operations for the past three years we find Mr. Wind to have been steadily at work, treasury threats of contraction having kept nearly even pace with popular threats of repudiation; editorial threats of forced resumption having gone hand in hand with an absenteeism which makes demand for all the gold we mine and all that we import ; increase of the public burthens travelling side by side with diminution of power for carrying the load imposed ; and the general result being that of causing every man who has anything to lose a desire to draw his cloak more closely round him, and to retire into some nook or corner of the commercial world in which he may safely stand until convinced that Mr. Wind and his companions, Clouds and Darkness, had finally abandoned the field, yielding place to the great source of light and heat, the Sun, to whom he might then look to see—

That justice be done to the people of all the States and Territories, placing them, so far as institutions of credit are concerned, and so far as law can accomplish that object, on a footing precisely the same as that now occupied by those of the Eastern States :

That justice be done to the commerce of the Union by bringing all such institutions under regulations tending to produce that regularity of action which so long has characterized the movements of those of the Eastern States :

That justice be done to such institutions wherever situated, by relieving them from taxes, and from absurd restrictions now existing, the direct effect of which is that of compelling them to overtrade and to incur risks the results of which are likely to result in ruin to their stockholders :

That justice be done to the working men who carried the country through the war, by abolishing as rapidly as possible the taxation under which so many of them now so severely suffer :

That justice be done to the public creditors, thereby securing the command of capital at the lowest rate of interest ; and finally,

That justice be done to the nation by proving to the world that in time of peace it is ready to carry into full effect the arrangements that during the war so well were understood.

With little exception the things thus proposed to be done are precisely the reverse of those which have been done since the peace, and to which we are indebted for the fact that the needs of the government for gold have been more than doubled, and, strangely enough, *as preliminary to resumption.* Let them be done, and it will soon be found that the needs, public or private, for gold will gradually decline until at length the greenback and the gold piece will stand on a level with each other, doing this as a consequence of an infusion of the superior currency of notes similar to that which now exists in Massachusetts, *the State which always pays gold, because none of her citizens need it.*

The course thus proposed would speedily extinguish the debt, doing this by means of a saving of interest consequent upon giving security of the highest order, as is always done by the great European States. Giving us peace it would inspire a confidence that would so stimulate production that taxation might soon cease to exist except in cases where its burthens are scarcely felt. Reducing the general rate of interest it would place our people more nearly on a level, in this respect, with those of Europe, and thus would largely contribute towards giving us that industrial independence without which there can be no political independence.

Sincerely hoping that such may prove to be the case, and begging you to excuse my repeated trespasses on your attention, I remain, with great regard and respect, Yours very truly,

HENRY C. CAREY.

Gen. U. S. Grant.
Philadelphia, January 13, 1869.

P. S. January 19.—The Senate Finance Committee has just now reported a bill nominally providing for resumption, but really for sacrificing all who have interest to pay, or labor to sell, at the shrine of those who have money to lend or labor to buy. Its true title would be—". An act providing for doubling the rate of interest throughout the country ; for making the rich richer and the poor poorer ; for bankrupting the people and the State ; for postponing indefinitely a return to use of the precious metals ; and for effectually securing repudiation of the national debt."

HOW PROTECTION, INCREASE OF PUBLIC AND PRIVATE
REVENUES, AND NATIONAL INDEPENDENCE,
MARCH HAND IN HAND TOGETHER.

REVIEW

OF THE

REPORT OF THE HON. D. A. WELLS,

SPECIAL COMMISSIONER OF THE REVENUE;

BY

H. C. CAREY.

PHILADELPHIA:

PROTECTION AND REVENUE, PUBLIC AND PRIVATE.

DEAR SIR:—

Your report just now published contains a passage to which I desire here to invite your attention, as follows:—

"As respects the relation of legislation by the national government to the results under consideration, if we except the adoption of a liberal policy in the disposition of the public lands, it is difficult, at least for the period which elapsed between 1840 and 1860, to affirm much that is positive, unless, in conformity with the maxim, that that government is best which governs least, absence of legislation is to be regarded in the light of a positive good. If important results followed the acquisition of California, such results were certainly neither foreseen nor anticipated; while as regards commercial legislation, a review of all the facts cannot fail to suggest a doubt whether the evils which have resulted from instability have not far more than counterbalanced any advantage that may have proceeded from the experience of a fluctuating policy.

"The Commissioner is well aware that this opinion will not be readily accepted by those who have been educated to believe that the industrial and commercial prosperity of the country was seriously affected by the legislation which took place during the years which elapsed from 1842 to 1846. But upon this point all investigation shows that the facts are entirely contrary to what may be regarded as the popular belief, which, indeed, in this particular, would appear to be based on little else than mere assertions, which, remaining for a long time unquestioned, have at last acquired historical truth. Thus, for example, it has been constantly asserted, both in Congress and out of Congress, that the production of pig iron was remarkably stimulated under the tariff of 1842—rising from 220,000 tons in 1842 to 800,000 tons in 1848—and that under the tariff of 1846 the same industry was remarkably depressed. Now, these assertions may be correct, but the most reliable statistics to which we have access, viz: those gathered by the American Iron Association, instruct us as follows:—

"Production of pig iron in 1830, 165,000 tons; in 1840, 347,000 tons. Increase in 10 years, 110 per cent.
"Production in 1845, 486,000 tons; increase in 5 years, 40 per cent.
"Production in 1850, 564,000 tons; increase in 10 years, 62 per cent.
"Production in 1855, 754,000 tons; increase in 5 years, 33 per cent.
"Production in 1860, 913,000 tons; increase in 10 years, 61 per cent.

"It thus appears that the great annual increase in the production of pig iron took place prior to the year 1840, and for 30 years was remarkably uniform at the rate of 10 to 11 per cent. per annum; and that since then, no matter what has been the character of the legislation, whether the tariff was low or high, whether the condition of the country was one of war or peace, the increase of the production has been at the average of about 8 per cent. per annum, or more than double the ratio of the increase of population.

"Again, as another curious illustration of an apparent misconception of the effects of past legislation upon the development of the country, take the following paragraph from the recent report of a Congressional committee:"

"No business man of mature age need be reminded of the revulsion which followed in consequence of the free-trade system of 1846—the decline of production, of immigration, of wages, of public or private revenue, until the culmination of the system in the tariff of 1857, with the memorable crises of that period; the general ruin of manufacturers and merchants, the suspended payments of the banks; the reduction of the Treasury to the verge of bankruptcy, and the unparalleled distress among the unemployed poor."

Here follows a series of statements constructed in a manner similar to that above given in reference to iron, the object of their production being that of proving that the views of the committee thus presented had had no foundation in fact; that they had allowed themselves to be deceived by "mere assertions" on the part of others; and, that the time had now come for setting the stamp of falsehood on all they had been accustomed to believe in reference to the tariff of 1846, and for obtaining such accurate views of the last twenty years of our commercial history as might be entitled to claim to have "the force of accepted historical truths."

To whom, however, are to be attributed the oft-repeated misstatements by which the committee had been deceived? No name is given, but you of course refer to me, the statements thus controverted having been first published over my own signature, so early as 1851, and since then many times republished; and the committee having been misled, if misled at all, by no other than myself. To me, therefore, it is that you have thus thrown down the glove, and I now take it up prepared on the one hand to prove the accuracy of the views you have thus called in question; or, on the other, to admit of having through a long series of years misled my fellow-citizens. Admit that such proof be furnished—that the "mere assertions" be now proved to be real "historical truths" fitted for even your own acceptance, where, I beg to ask, will you yourself then stand? Should it chance to be proved that it is not I that am required to impale myself on the horns of a dilemma which leaves but a choice between the admission of gross carelessness on the one hand, or grosser dishonesty on the other, does it not follow necessarily that you must be compelled to take the place you had prepared for me, and thus furnish yourself the proof required for establishing the fact that you are wholly disqualified for the office of public teacher? As it seems to me, such must be the case.

Leaving you, however, to reflect at leisure on the questions thus propounded, I propose now to analyze the "historical truths" of your report, first, however, giving a brief history of our tariff legislation for the last half-century, as follows:—

The revenue tariff period which followed the close, in 1815, of the great European war, was one of great distress both private and public. Severe financial crises bankrupted banks, merchants, and manufacturers; greatly contracted the market for labor and all its products; so far diminished the money value of property as to place the debtor everywhere in the power of his creditor; caused the transfer of a very large portion of it under the sheriff's hammer; and so far impaired the power of the people to contribute to the revenue that, trivial as were the public expenditures of that period, loans were required for enabling the Treasury to meet the demands upon it. With 1824, however, there came a partial attempt at remedy of the evils under which our whole people were then so severely suffering, a tariff having been then established under which pig iron and potatoes were abundantly protected, pipes and penknives being admitted at moderate ad-valorem duties. The rude products of agriculture were, in effect, prohibited from being imported in their original forms, but when they presented themselves in those of cotton and woollen cloths little difficulty was found. Slight was the benefit resulting from such a measure, yet benefit did result, and hence it was that it came so soon to be followed by the admirable tariff of 1828, the first really protective one ever established by Congress. Under it all was changed, and with a rapidity so great that but five years of its action were required for giving to the country a prosperity such as had never before been known; for so increasing the public revenue as to render necessary the emancipation from import duties of tea, coffee, and many other articles the like of which was not produced at home; for taking thus the first step in the direction of *real* freedom of external commerce; for finally annihilating the public debt; and for causing our people to forget the state of almost ruin from which they had been redeemed by the combined action of the tariffs of 1824 and 1828.

Northern submission to Carolinian threats of nullification next gave us the Compromise of 1833, by means of which the country was, within the next decade, to be brought under a strictly revenue tariff of 20 per cent. The South needed cheap food, and did not, therefore, desire that Western farmers should make a market at home which might tend to raise its price. Most generously, however, it permitted protection to remain almost untouched, until the first of January, 1836, and how gradual were the changes then and for several years thereafter to be made, will be seen from the following figures representing the duties to be paid on an article that had stood originally at 50 per cent.:

1829–33	1834–5	1836–7	1838–9	1840–41	1842 to June 30	thereafter
50	47	44	41	38	29	20

For the first two years general prosperity continued to be maintained. Thereafter, however, we find the whole period of its existence presenting a series of contractions and expansions ending in a state of weakness so extreme that bankruptcy was almost universal; that labor was everywhere seeking for employment; that the public credit was so entirely destroyed that the closing year of that unfortunate period exhibited the disgraceful fact of Commissioners, appointed by the Treasury, wandering throughout Europe and knocking at the doors of its principal banking houses without obtaining the loan of even a single dollar. Public and private distress now, August, 1842, compelling a return to the protective system we find almost at once a reproduction of the prosperous days of the period from 1829 to 1835, public and private credit having been restored, and the demand for labor and its products having become greater than at any former period.

Again, however, do we find our people forgetting that to the protective policy had been due the marvellous changes that were then being witnessed, and again, 1846, returning to that revenue tariff system to which they had been indebted for the scenes of ruin which had marked the periods from 1817 to 1828, and from 1835 to 1842. California gold now, however, came in aid of free trade theories, and for a brief period it was really believed that protection had become a dead issue and could never be again revived. With 1854, however, that delusion passed away, the years that followed, like those of the previous revenue tariff periods, having been marked by enormous expansions and contractions, financial crises, private ruin, and such destruction of the national credit that with the close of Mr. Buchanan's administration we find the treasury unable to obtain the trivial amount which was then required, except on payment of most enormous rates of interest.

Once again, 1861, do we find the country driven to protection, and the public credit by its means so well established as to enable the treasury with little difficulty to obtain the means of carrying on a war whose annual cost was more than had been the total public expenditures of half a century, including the war with Great Britain of 1812. Thrice thus, under the tariffs of 1828, 1842, and 1861, has protection redeemed the country from almost ruin. Thrice thus, under the revenue tariffs of 1817, 1833, and 1846, has it been sunk so low that none could be found "so poor to do it reverence." Such having been our experience throughout half a century it might have been supposed that the question would be regarded now as settled, yet do we find an officer of the government whose special duty it has been made to inquire into all the causes affecting the public revenue, and who has had before him all the evidence required in proof of the above "assertions," now venturing to assure Congress and the people that—

" There does not seem to be any reliable evidence which can be adduced to show that the change which took place in the legislative commercial policy of the country in 1846 had any permanent or marked effect whatever; while, on the other hand, the study of all the facts pertaining to national development from 1840 to 1860, and from 1865 to the present time, unmistakably teaches this lesson; that the progress of the country through what we may term the strength of its elements of vitality is independent of legislation and even of the impoverishment and waste of a great war. Like one of our own mighty rivers, its movement is beyond control. Successive years, like successive affluents, only add to and increase its volume; while legislative enactments and conflicting commercial policies, like the construction of piers and the deposit of sunken wrecks, simply deflect the current or constitute temporary obstructions. In fact, if the nation has not yet been lifted to the full comprehension of its own work, it builds determinately, as it were, by instinct."

How much of truth there is in all this, and what has been your warrant for making such "assertions" it is proposed now to examine, commencing with the iron manufacture.

Yours respectfully,
HENRY C. CAREY.

Hon. D. A. Wells.

January 23, 1869.

LETTER SECOND.

Dear Sir :—

In accordance with the promise in my last I now proceed to an examination of *the Iron Question*, basing the statements here to be made on facts collected by myself in 1849, and now adopted, so far as they were found available for your purposes, by yourself.

In 1810, prior to our second war with England, our furnaces numbered 153, with an average yield of 36 tons, giving a total produce of 54,000 tons. Protection afforded by the war caused a considerable increase, but there exist no reliable statistics in regard thereto. Peace in 1815 was followed by the, so called, revenue tariff of 1817, and that in turn as is so well known, by the closing of factories and furnaces; by the ruin of manufacturers and merchants; by the discharge of workmen everywhere; by the stoppage of banks; by the bankruptcy of States; by the transfer under the sheriff's hammer of a large portion of the real estate of the Union; and, by an impoverishment of our whole people general beyond all former precedent. The demand for iron had so far ceased that the manufacture was in a state of ruin so complete that not only had it lost all that it had gained in time of war, but had, as was then believed, greatly retrograded. In placing it, as I now shall do near the point to which b aid of non-intercourse and embargo acts it has been brought in 1810, I am, as I feel assured, doing it entire justice.

Such, with little change, continued to be the state of things until the passage of the semi-protective tariff of 1824, described in my former letter. By it full protection was granted to pig, bar, bolt, and other descriptions of iron, as well as to some of the coarser kinds of manufactured goods, the demand for iron being thus so far stimulated that the old furnaces were again brought into activity, others meanwhile being built; and the product being, by these means, carried up in 1828 to 130,000 tons, giving a duplication in the short period of four years, or 25 per cent. per annum. Two years later, under the tariff of 1828, it had grown to 165,000 tons, and by 1832 it had reached 200,000. if not even more, having thus trebled itself in the eight years which had followed the passage of the Act of 1824.

As nearly as may be the whole movement from 1817 to 1832 is presented in the following diagram, having examined which you may perhaps explain to what extent it furnishes material for the confirmation of your "assertion" that "the progress of the country through what we may term the strength of its elements of vitality is independent of legislation?" The history of the world presents no case of greater change as the result of sound legislation than will be found by those who study carefully the impoverished and unhappy condition of the country in the years that preceded 1824, and then compare with it the marvellous prosperity that marked the period of the thoroughly protective tariff of 1828.

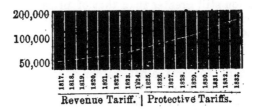

Revenue Tariff. | Protective Tariffs.

2. By the Act of 1832 tea, coffee, and many other articles, railroad iron included, were made free of duty, this last a serious blow to the then rapidly growing iron manufacture. As a consequence of this it was that England had, until after the passage of the tariff act of 1842, an entire monopoly of its supply, by aid of which she had then already imposed upon our people a taxation far greater than would, had it been so applied, given us furnaces and rolling mills capable of furnishing thrice more in quantity and value than Great Britain then produced of iron in all its varied forms. One year later, in 1833, came the Compromise tariff dictated by South Carolina, looking eventually to the establishment of a purely revenue system, but for the moment making changes so very gradual that its deleterious influence remained almost unfelt until after 1835. The production of iron continued, therefore, to increase in the three years which followed 1832, but it has been quite impossible to obtain any reliable statements in regard thereto; and for that reason it is, that in all tables hitherto furnished the whole of *that* growth has been credited to the revenue tariff policy, when it had properly belonged to the protective one.

For 1840 the product of iron is given at 347,000 tons, showing a gain of 147,000 in eight years from 1832, much of which, however, certainly resulted from the protection afforded from 1832 to 1836.

With 1841 there came, however, as already shown, the fifth reduction of duty under the Carolina nullification tariff of 1833, bringing with it, too, a close proximity of the horizontal twenty per cent. tariff that was to take effect in 1842–3. With each successive day, therefore, the societary movement became more completely paralyzed until there was produced a state of things wholly without parallel in the country's history, and even exceeding that of the revenue tariff period of 1817. The country swarmed with men, women and children reduced to beggary because of finding no employment, owners of mills and mines meantime reduced to bankruptcy because of finding little or no demand for any of their products. Banks stopped payment and seemed unlikely ever again to reach resumption. States made default in payment of their interest, the national treasury meanwhile begging at home and abroad, and begging, too, in vain, for loans at almost any rate of interest.

How all this affected the iron manufacture is clearly shown by the following facts. Smelting by aid of anthracite had been first introduced here in 1837, and as it was an improvement of vast importance it should have rapidly extended. Nevertheless, so depressed became soon after the condition of affairs that at the close of 1841 but six such furnaces, capable of yielding 21,000 tons, had been put in blast. The cause of this may be found in the fact that Carolinian "legislation" had reduced the price in 1841 to little more than half of that at which it had stood in 1837, and had so reduced the powers of our people as to cause a diminution of consumption still greater than that of price.

As a consequence of this ruinous condition of affairs, so many furnaces were closed as to make it highly doubtful if the production were even half of what it had been two years before. That it was under 200,000 tons there is the best reason for believing, yet have I always placed it at 220,000, preferring to err against, rather than for, myself. All the facts, as now presented, have already been before you, but you have selected those alone which suited, at the same time asserting that all that had been published in reference to years the first of which are now under consideration, had been "mere assertions," entitled to none of that consideration which should be given to "accepted historical truths."

3. Whatsoever the policy of a country, whether protective or anti-protective, peaceful or warlike, the longer it is continued the more thoroughly its powers for good or evil become developed. To *the latest* years in which such policy had been maintained it was that you, therefore, were required to look when desiring to enable yourself properly to exhibit its excellencies or its defects. Have you done this? Have you given *the latest* of the years of protection, and exhibited the growth of iron production to 200,000 tons in 1832? Have you given *the latest years* of the revenue tariff system, and thus brought to light the fact that from the close of protection under the tariff of 1828 to the close of free trade under the Compromise tariff, *notwithstanding an increase of population exceeding thirty per cent., there had been scarcely any increase whatsoever?* None of these things, as I regret to say, have you done. Directly the reverse, you have *suppressed* the last years of both, to the end that you might be enabled to assure the nation that "the great annual increase of production took place prior to the year 1840," production "in 1830 having been 165,000 tons; in 1840, 347,000; increase in ten years 110 per cent."

It has been said that " figures do not lie." That they may be made to speak the reverse of truth would seem to be here most clearly shown.

Desiring now to present clearly to your eye all that has above been said of the period now under consideration, I submit another diagram presenting—

First, A light line showing *the entire facts*, giving in all cases the *figures* you yourself have used; and

Second, A heavy line exhibiting *the facts selected by you for pre. sentation*, and exposing the process by means of which you have so carefully thrown out of view the rise, under protection, which occurred in the years subsequent to 1830, and the great fall, under the revenue tariff sytem, which occurred in the years that followed 1840.

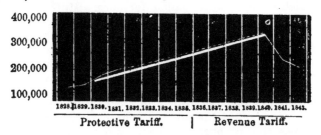

Protective Tariff. | Revenue Tariff.

Few, as I think, can study the picture thus presented without ad. mitting the ingenuity with which your selected facts had been ar. ranged. Whether or not they will as much admire the fairness of the presentation, it will be for time to tell.

In another letter I propose to review the movement under the protective act of 1842, and the revenue tariff act of 1846.

Yours, respectfully,
HENRY C. CAREY.

Hon. D. A. WELLS.
PHILADELPHIA, January 26, 1869.

LETTER THIRD.

DEAR SIR:—

The tariff of 1828 which was, as the country had been assured,. almost to destroy the revenue, had, on the contrary, proved so very productive as to make it necessary wholly to emancipate from duty most, if not even all, of the commodities not competing with our domestic products, and had thus furnished conclusive evidence that the road towards financial independence and *real* freedom of trade was to be found in the pursuit of a policy leading to industrial independence. Further proof of this was now being furnished, the customs revenue, under what had been claimed as the true revenue system, having declined to half the amount at which it had stood in 1833, and Congress finding itself compelled, in 1841, to retrace its steps by remanding to the list of duty-paying articles a large proportion of those commodities which had been freed by the Act of 1832. Still, however, the necessary work remained undone, each successive day bringing with it new evidence of a need for total abandonment of a policy nearly the whole period of whose existence had been passed amid financial convulsions of the severest kind—convulsions whose effect had been that of almost annihilating confidence, and thereby bringing about a state of things destructive alike of public and private revenues.

With August, 1842, therefore, we find the nation compelled to re-adoption of the protective and *real* revenue policy, followed at once by such restoration of confidence as enabled the Treasury to find all its wants promptly supplied at home. Thenceforth there was found no necessity for humbly knocking at the doors of foreign bankers, praying for relief. For the general restoration of confidence, however, much time was needed, ruin having been so widely spread as to make it indispensable that a bankrupt law should be enacted by means of which hosts of ruined merchants, miners, manufacturers, ship owners, land owners, might once again be enabled to get to work and seek the means by aid of which to repair their fallen fortunes. Mills and mines, too, needed to be repaired preparatory to setting laborers once again at work, and it was in such labors that the first year of the new policy was passed. Still another year was required for enabling the returning prosperity to make its way to the coal region, and it was not until the summer of 1844 that the men who had given their millions to its development became at length enabled to see reason for hope that they might at an early period be released from the burthen of debt imposed upon them in the revenue tariff period.* Thenceforth, however, all moved rapidly, new mines being opened, numerous furnaces being erected, and a rolling-mill for rails now for the first time making its appearance on the American soil. Throughout the long period of a dozen years British iron-masters had, by means of our own disastrous legislation, been secured in a monopoly of the control of supplies of rails, but the time had now come for obtaining that *real* freedom of trade which always results from the exercise of power to choose between buying at home or seeking supplies abroad.

The furnaces that in 1840, when pig had fallen to little more than half the price of 1837, had yielded but 347,000 tons, were now being driven to their utmost capacity, estimated at 450,000 tons, but, as there is good reason for believing, not less than 430 000

To this we have here to add—

First, the produce of 8 new anthracite furnaces blown in
  from 1841 to 1844 inclusive, with a capacity of . . 40 000
Second, that of 52 new charcoal furnaces capable of yielding 52 000†
Third, enlargements of old furnaces, estimated at . 35 000
                                                        ———————
  Total capacity at the close of 1844 . . . . . 557 000

The actual produce of 1845 is given by you at 486,000 tons, but there exists no certain evidence in reference thereto, and I feel assured that it must have exceeded half a million. So great was then the demand for iron of all descriptions that, notwithstanding the large increase of domestic product, the import of 1844 and 1845 rose to 212,000 tons, ex-

* NOTE.—Coal and iron are always last to feel the changes after a financial revulsion. In the present case, nearly two full years elapsed before there occurred any movement of property in the anthracite coal region. In proof of this it may be mentioned that in the early summer of 1844 it had been suggested to Boston capitalists that for the small sum of $3,000,000 they might be enabled to become owners of a full half of that region, together with improvements the cost of which had been probably five times that sum.

† The number of charcoal furnaces started in these years, in Pennsylvania alone,

ceeding by more than 25 per cent. that of the revenue tariff years 1842 and 1843.

To the quantity above obtained we have next to add as follows :—

Eighteen anthracite furnaces blown in in 1845 and 1846,
with a capacity of . . . . tons 84 000
Eighty two charcoal furnaces capable of yielding . . 82 000
Enlargements estimated at 35 000

Giving a total of 201 000

which added to the 557,000 already obtained makes a grand total of 758,000, or within seven thousand of the estimate then furnished by the Secretary of the Treasury, thus confirming the accuracy of the views that have heretofore been presented by myself.

Nominally, the tariff of 1846 became operative at the close of that year, but such was the general prosperity, greatly increased as it was by a demand for food created by the Irish famine—a demand that caused in that year an import from Europe of gold to the immense extent of $24,000,000—that its operation was almost entirely unfelt. In face of a large reduction of duty the price of pig-iron rose more than 10 per cent., and every existing furnace was tasked to its utmost to meet the wonderful demand that then existed. Increase of furnaces therefore went on, no less than 11 having been blown in, in the anthracite region, in 1847 and 1848, with a capacity of tons 54 000

Adding to this, for 18 charcoal furnaces in this State,
and only as many estimated for all the other States,
we obtain a further capacity of 36 000

90 000

by adding which to the 758,000 of previous years we obtain a grand total of 848,000 tons, admitting therein but 70,000 for enlargements in each and every year of works previously in operation.

By no correction of these figures that can even be attempted will it be possible to reduce the quantity to 750,000. Admitting, however, that such reduction be made, there still remains an increase in five years of more than 200 per cent., population meantime having grown less than 20 per cent.

Whence, you may ask, have the facts thus given been obtained? In answer I have to say, that they have been drawn from a source to which you yourself have had the readiest access, *the Statistics of the American Iron and Steel Association*, the difference between the results obtained by you on one side, and by me on the other, consisting only in this, that whereas, I have now, as always heretofore, given all the facts; you have given only those which seemed best fitted for enabling you to prove that " no matter what had been the character of the legislation, whether the condition of the country was one of war or peace, the increase of production had been at the average rate of about eight per cent. per annum, or more than double the ratio of the increase of population." How far there exists any warrant for this extraordinary assertion in reference to the years which followed the brilliant period above described, it is proposed now. to show, commencing with those of 1849 and 1850.

With the summer of 1848 commenced a paralysis resulting from deluge of our markets by British iron, the fiscal year 1848-9 exhibiting an import exceeding by nearly a quarter of a million tons that of 1846, and largely exceeding 300,000 tons. Then, for the first time did the warehousing system exhibit its power for mischief, British iron masters filling the public stores with their various merchandise, and borrowing on the certificates money at the lowest rates of interest, their American competitors meanwhile piling up products upon which, while remaining on their premises, they could not borrow a dollar at any rate of interest whatsoever. For them there existed no public stores the like of those so carefully provided for their rivals, that the latter might be enabled at once to borrow nearly the whole value of their merchandise, and then apply the proceeds to the fabrication of other hundreds of thousands of tons by means of which they might, and with the smallest measure of inconvenience, be enabled to overwhelm those Americans by whom had been created the great market the control of which they were now determined to secure for themselves.

Worse even than 1848–49 was the state of things exhibited in the fiscal year 1849–50, the import having exceeded 350,000 tons, and prices having been forced down to the half of those of 1838, and but two-thirds of those at which they had stood even in the destructive year of 1841. To sell at $20 was ruinous to all but the favored few who enjoyed advantages greatly exceeding those possessed by the mass of those engaged in the manufacture. As a consequence, furnaces were closed one after another, and as early as 1849 the product was supposed to have fallen to 650,000. So steadily, however, did the work of destruction proceed that in 1850 it was fully believed that production had been reduced much below 500,000, and might not prove greatly to exceed 400,000. The actual product, as given in your report, was 564,000, furnishing proof conclusive that the production of previous years must have reached, and probably exceeded, 800,000. No one familiar with the facts of that calamitous period can for a moment hesitate to admit that the production of 1850 had been less than two-thirds of that of 1847–8; or, that to obtain the true figures of these latter years it would be required to add at the least one-half to those furnished by the former. Doing this we obtain 846,000, and that that presents more nearly than any other figure the quantity of iron actually produced in the closing years of that prosperous protective period is my firm belief.

How the great facts compare with those small ones so carefully selected by you is shown in the annexed diagram, the heavy line giving, as before, the picture presented by yourself in the following words:—

"Increase in the production of pig iron: In 1840, 347,000 tons; in 1845, 486,000; in 1850, 564,775."

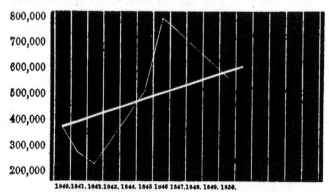

800,000
700,000
600,000
500,000
400,000
300,000
200,000

1840. 1841. 1842. 1843. 1844. 1845. 1846. 1847. 1848. 1849. 1850.

Having studied the above, and having seen how very carefully you had *suppressed* the calamitous revenue years 1841 and 1842; and then again *suppressed* the wonderfully prosperous period of protection from 1845 to 1848; I beg to ask that you then read again the following paragraph of your Report, and most particularly that portion of it here given in italics, as follows:—

" The Commissioner is well aware that this opinion will not be readily accepted by those who have been educated to believe that the industrial and commercial prosperity of the country was seriously affected by the legislation which took place during the years which elapsed from 1842 to 1846. But upon this point *all investigation shows that the facts are entirely contrary to what may be regarded as the popular belief, which, indeed, in this particular, would appear to be based on little else than mere assertions, which, remaining for a long time unquestioned, have at last acquired the force of accepted historical truth.* Thus, for example, it has been constantly asserted, both in Congress and out of Congress, that the production of pig iron was remarkably stimulated under the tariff of 1842—rising from 220,000 tons in 1842 to 800,000 tons in 1848 —and that under the tariff of 1846 the same industry was remarkably depressed. Now, these assertions may be correct, but," as you then proceed to prove by aid of carefully selected facts, there is really not, as you would have your readers believe, a single grain of truth to be found among them.

In my next, I propose to examine the remainder of the years that elapsed between the passage of the Act of 1846 and the breaking out of that rebellion of which latter it was the real cause.

Yours respectfully,
HENRY C. CAREY.

Hon. D. A. Wells.

Philadelphia, January 28, 1869.

NOTE.

Leaving wholly out of view numerous changes made from 1842 to 1848, in the construction of furnaces with a view to increase of their capacity, the new appliances of that period, including an extensive substitution of hot for cold blast, would alone, as it is believed, much more than account for the 70,000 tons claimed under the head of "enlargements."

LETTER FOURTH.

Dear Sir:—

In 1846, when the destructive tariff bill of that date was under discussion, Mr. Calhoun declared to persons who spoke with him on the iron question that if he could feel quite certain that rails would be supplied at *eighty dollars* per ton, he would promptly grant any amount of protection that could be asked for. At that moment the first rail mill, as has been shown, was less than two years old, and no man, or party of men, could yet feel warranted in giving any assurance to that effect. In the years that then immediately followed the progress of this branch of industry was so rapid that in 1850 the iron masters, as a body, proposed to Congress the establishment of a sliding scale by means of which the duty should be precisely that which might be needed for keeping rails steadily at *fifty dollars*—rising as the price fell below that sum, and falling as the price advanced beyond it. Advantageous, however, as would have been such an arrangement, it fell to the ground because it did not suit the views of British iron masters who were then deluging the American market with rails made of refuse materials, to be sold at forty dollars per ton, and even, as I think, less than that, with the intent and purpose of carrying into full effect the operation thus subsequently described in a Report to Parliament, to wit :—

" The laboring classes generally, in the manufacturing districts of the kingdom, and especially in the iron and coal districts, are very little aware of the extent to which they are often indebted for their being employed at all to the immense *losses* which their employers voluntarily incur in bad times, in order *to destroy foreign competition, and to gain and keep possession of foreign markets.* Authentic instances are well known of employers having in such times carried on their works at a loss amounting in the aggregate to three or four hundred thousand pounds in the course of three or four years. If the efforts of those who encourage the combinations to restrict the amount of labor and to produce strikes were to be successful for any length of time, the great accumulations of capital could no longer be made *which enable a few of the most wealthy capitalists to overwhelm all foreign competition in times of great depression,* and thus to clear the way for the *whole trade* to step in when prices revive, and to carry a great business before *foreign* capital can again accumulate to such an extent as to be able to establish a competition in prices with any chance of success. *The large capitals of this country are the great instruments of warfare against the competing capitals of foreign countries,* and are *the most essential* instruments now remaining by which our manufacturing supremacy can be maintained ; the other elements—cheap labor, abundance of raw materials, means of communication, and skilled labor—being rapidly in process of being equalized."

Such was the *warfare* then being carried out, and to what extent it proved successful it is my purpose now to show.

At the close of 1850 the receipts of gold from California had reached the then almost fabulous quantity of $68,000,000, stimulating into activity almost every branch of trade and manufacture; and yet, it was at that moment that the representatives of the most important of all manufactures were begging of Congress to give its assent to a bill providing *that full supplies of railroad bars should be forever secured to our people at prices less than they had paid for mere pigs but thirteen years before!*

The refusal of that body to give its assent to this most moderate proposition was of course equivalent to giving sanction to continuance of the war whose objects are above so well described, the result having been that while gold was coming in from the West at the rate of a million of dollars per week, iron flowed in from the East until, in all its various forms, the joint import of 1853 and 1854, had arrived at the extraordinary figure of *more than eleven hundred thousand tons, and at a price for pig iron but little less than that which three years before, when entering on the war, these warriors had been content to accept for railroad bars.** Their work had been done, the sacrifices had been made, conquest had been achieved, and they were now enjoying the fruits, taxing the people of the Union, in these two years alone, more than $20,000,000, and probably more even than $30,000,000; thereby enabling themselves to return to their own pockets, with immense interest, the money that had been expended in subsidizing journalists, in buying

---

* In those years pigs sold here at $36 to $37. In 1850 large quantities of rails were supplied at $40.

railroad presidents and others, in and out of Congress, and generally in carrying on the war.

The domestic product, as has been seen, had fallen from 800,000 tons in 1847-8 to 564,000 in 1850, and at or near that figure it probably remained during 1851 and 1852, as the import in those years, of iron and its manufactures, exceeded 700,000 tons, filling to repletion the public stores, and keeping down prices to little more than those of 1850.* Prices, however, running up with great rapidity, American furnaces are now again put in blast, and the product of 1854 is carried up to 716,000 tons, being *ten per cent. less* than it had been six years previously, the population being *twenty per cent. more.* From this time forward the figures are as follows :—

1855, 754,000;	1857, 874,000;	1859, 840,000;
1856, 874,000;	1858, 705,000;	1860, 913,000.

From 1848 to 1860 population had increased *forty per cent.,* the production of iron, taking the average of those years, having remained *almost stationary;* and yet it is of this period that you speak in the following words and figures :—

" Production in 1850, 564,000 tons; increase in five years, 40 per cent. In 1855, 754,000 tons; increase in five years, 33 per cent. In 1860, 913,000 tons; increase in ten years 61 per cent;" thereby proving to your own satisfaction, if not to that of those conversant with the real facts, " that no matter what had been the character of the legislation, whether the tariff was low or high, whether the condition of the country was one of war or peace, the increase of the production had been at the average of about 8 per cent. per annum, or more than double the ratio of the increase of population."

How you had been enabled to arrive at this beautiful production of " historical truth" is clearly shown in the following diagram, the heavy line, as before, following out your figures, and the others giving the *real* facts of the case as above recounted :—

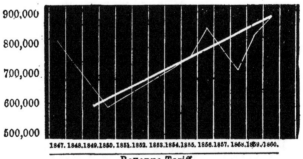

Revenue Tariff.

Professing to give a true picture of the working of the Compromise tariff, you *suppressed* its closing and most destructive years, 1841 and 1842. Professing now to furnish such a picture of the revenue tariff of 1846, you have *suppressed* the prosperous closing years of its predecessor of 1842, doing this, as it would seem, by way of enabling your fellow-citizens to determine on which side lies the " historical truth."

You have denied that " industrial and commercial prosperity," had

* Price of pigs in 1850, $20 82; in 1851, $21 35; in 1852, $22 63.

been " seriously affected by the legislation of the country in the years which elapsed between 1842 and 1846." You have denied that " the production of iron" had been " remarkably stimulated" under that tariff. You have denied that " under the tariff of 1846, that industry" had been " remarkably depressed." Allow me now to ask, not that you prove what you thus have said, but only that you furnish evidence that you had had before you any reliable evidence calculated to produce in your own mind a belief that there was in it even an approach to the real truth of the case.

2. How the national wealth was at this period being promoted will be seen on an examination of the following facts. The number of anthracite furnaces in 1854 was 77, of which 70 were in operation, and the capacity of the whole was 375,000 tons. The high prices of that and the previous year—the combined result of a re-establishment of British power, and a receipt of the precious metals averaging nearly a million per week—having stimulated our people to the erection of furnaces, we find their number to have arrived in 1856 at 92, of which 81 were then in blast and yielding 347,000 tons. Thenceforward, we find a downward movement as follows :—

	Total No.	Out of blast.	Capacity.	Product.
1857	94	28	504,000	307,000
1858	94	33	505,000	280,000
1859	95	31	580,000	364,000
1860	96	27	600,000	403,000

In the rapid growth of number we have here abundant proof of the promptitude with which our people have at all times been, as now they are, prepared to meet the demand, however created, that may exist. In the number out of blast we have evidence that millions of capital and therewith tens of thousands of working men, had been deprived of power to contribute toward the public revenue. It might, however, be supposed that import from abroad had made amends for large decrease in 1858 at home. On the contrary, decline of import had kept steady pace with that of production, the quantity then received having been less than a third of that of 1854, when domestic product had been greater.

The consumption of the three years 1846, '47, and '48, *the last* of the tariff of 1842, was, as nearly as can now be ascertained, of American 2,400,000, and of foreign 330,000, giving an annual average of 910,000. That of the three years 1858, '59, and '60, *the last* of the tariff of 1846, was, of American 2,460,000, of foreign 840,000, giving a total of 3,300,-000, and an annual average of 1,100,000, the increase of consumption being about 20 per cent.; population meanwhile having grown nearly 40 per cent. How those quantities were divided between transportation and production it is proposed now to show, as follows :—

The demand for railroads in the first of these periods was as follows :—

Increase of road 1200 miles, requiring at 80 tons per mile,	96,000
Iron for chairs, sidings, turn-outs, switches, bridges, locomotives, cars, depots, &c., &c., ...	48,000
Maintenance of 6000 miles of track, sidings, rolling stock, and other appurtenances, at 10 tons per mile, . .	60,000
Maintenance of 1000 miles of second track, . . .	10,000
Total, ...	214,000
Giving an annual average of, say, ...	71,000

Which deducted from 910,000 leaves for "boilers, tenpenny nails," and other instruments of production, an annual average of 830,000

For the second of these periods we have the following figures, to wit:—

Increase of road 5000 miles, as before, at 80 tons per mile, .	400,000
Sundries, as above, ...	200,000
Maintenance of 31,000 miles, as above, ...	310,000
" 6000 miles of second track, ...	60,000
Total, ...	970,000

Giving an annual average of 323,333 for railroad purposes alone.*

In the first of these the tonnage of our navigation somewhat exceeded 3,000,000. In the second it about as much exceeded 5,000,000, the *growth* exceeding that of the first by about 150,000. Of the increase in the quantity of canal boats, barges, &c., &c., we have no record, but it probably counted by hundreds of thousands of tons.

For all this *excess* new work, for the *excess* substitution of new for old, whether by the building of new boats and ships, or repair of old ones, the quantity of iron required must have been fully double that of the first period, and may be very moderately set down at 30,000 tons per annum, by adding which to the 323,000 required for railroad purposes, we obtain a joint consumption, for *transportation*, of 353,000 tons. Deducting this now from a total consumption of 1,100,000 tons, we have remaining for "tenpenny nails, boilers," and other machinery of *production* 747,000, being *eleven per cent. less* than in the former period, population having meantime become almost *forty per cent. greater.* How all this is to be made to accord with the assurance given by you to the nation, that "no matter what had been the character of the legislation, whether the tariff was low or high, whether the condition of the country was one of war or peace, the increase of the production had been at the average of about 8 per cent. per annum, or more than double the ratio of the increase of population," it is for you to show.

3. Of all the tests of advancing or receding civilization there is none so perfect as that which presents itself in the growing or declining consumption of iron. Such being the case an increase of 200 per cent. in *the popular consumption*, in the short period from 1842 to 1848, would seem to furnish explanation of the rapid advance in that prosperous period towards peace and harmony; the diminished *popular consumption* of the revenue tariff period which closed in 1860, in its turn, well accounting for that growing discord which led at length to a rebellion the cost of which in lives counts by hundreds of thousands, and in property by thousands of millions. Had the "legislation" of 1842 been maintained throughout the twenty years that followed, we should have had no civil war, and our total production of iron would this day exceed that of Britain. Having carefully studied the facts thus presented, it may perhaps be well that you read once again the following passage from your Report:—

* Outside of the quantity of road in operation, all the figures here given have been obtained from the best sources of railroad information, and are said to be below, rather than above, the truth. The railroad bars imported in these three years exceeded 260,000 tons. Our own rail mills had then a capacity of 70,000 tons, and may in the three years have yielded 100 or 120 thousand, giving a total of *rails alone* of 360,000 or 380,000. To this add the quantity of new iron required for combination with old rails re-rolled, and for all other railroad purposes, and it will be found nearly, if not even quite to confirm the estimate.

" As respects the relation of legislation by the national government to the results under consideration, if we except the adoption of a liberal policy in the disposition of the public lands, it is difficult, at least for the period which elapsed between 1840 and 1860, to affirm much that is positive, unless, in conformity with the maxim, that that government is best which governs least, absence of legislation is to be regarded in the light of a positive good. If important results followed the acquisition of California, such results were certainly neither foreseen nor anticipated; while as regards commercial legislation, a review of all the facts cannot fail to suggest a doubt whether the evils which have resulted from instability have not far more than counterbalanced any advantage that may have proceeded from the experience of a fluctuating policy."

What it is that may be *positively affirmed* in reference to that *fluctuation of policy* which struck down the great iron manufacture at the moment at which it had just begun to exhibit its power for good, would seem to be this; that in the British monopoly period which thereafter followed, we added somewhat less than *forty* per cent. to our population; *seventy* to our machinery for water transportation; and *five hundred* to that required for transportation by land; meantime materially *diminishing* the quantity of iron applied to works of production. When you shall have carefully studied all this, you may perhaps find yourself enabled to account for the facts, that in the closing year of the free trade period railroad property which had cost more than $1000,000,000 could not have been sold for $350,000 ; that ships had become ruinous to nearly all their owners; that factories, furnaces, mills, mines, and workshops had everywhere been deserted; that hundreds of thousands of working men had been everywhere seeking, and vainly seeking, to sell their labor; that immigration had heavily declined; that pauperism had existed to an extent wholly unknown since the great free-trade crisis of 1842 ; that bankruptcies had become general throughout the Union; that power to contribute to the public revenue had greatly diminished; and finally, that the slave power had felt itself to have become so greatly strengthened as to warrant it in entering on the great rebellion.

4. The movement since 1860, under protection, is presented in the following diagram, side by side with that of the latter years of the revenue tariff by which the former had been preceded, the heavy line, as before, representing the comparative figures given by yourself :—

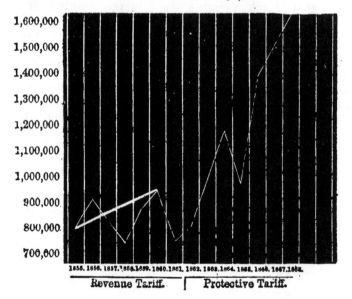

Revenue Tariff. | Protective Tariff.

Of the period from 1856 to 1860 here presented you say nothing in your general summary, given at page 9 of your Report, having preferred combining with it the previous years when California treasures were causing large increase of domestic product, and thereby enabling yourself to exhibit a decennial increase of sixty-one per cent. By so doing you have been also enabled to shut wholly out of view the calamitous free trade crisis of 1857, and the years that followed it, when the product, instead of showing "an annual increase of the production at the rate of about 8 per cent. per annum, or more than double the ratio of the increase of population," had exhibited the calamitous state of affairs above described.

Of the prosperous protective period that since has followed, your general summary, intended for widest circulation through the public journals, says *not even a single word*. Turning, however, to page 3, I find the following statement of the

Annual product of pig iron from 1863 *to* 1868.

					Tons.	Annual increase.
1863	•	•	•	•	• 947,604	
1864	•	•	•	•	.• 1,135,143	19.82 per cent.
1866	•	•	•	•	. 1,351,143	9.50 per. cent.
1867	•	•	•	•	. 1,447,771	7.16 per cent.
1868 (estimated)	.	.	•	•	. 1,550,000	7.06 per cent.

For the seven years from 1860 (when the production was 913,770 tons) to 1867, the average annual increase has been 8.35 per cent.

. The actual product of this last year has been, as I understand, more than 1,600,000 tons, showing *a duplication* as compared with the average of the closing years of the tariff of 1846. Those, however, who need to compare the present with the recent past, must do so for themselves, as you have been careful to avoid presenting *such* comparison. So, too, must they do if they would find any of the following "historical truths," to wit:—

That at the close of the Compromise Act of 1833 production had not increased *ten* per cent., whereas population had grown *thirty* per cent.

That in the final years of the protective Act of 1842 production had increased more than *two hundred* per cent., whereas population had grown but *twenty* per cent.

That in the final years of the revenue tariff Act of 1846 production had not advanced even *five* per cent., while our numbers had grown on the average of years, nearly *forty* per cent.

That, notwithstanding this large increase of numbers, the quantity applied *to production* had greatly diminished, while that applied to mere *transportation* had more than four times increased.

Leaving you now to reflect on the extraordinary *suppressions* thus exhibited, I shall now proceed to an examination of your chapter on "the taxation of pig iron."

Yours respectfully,

HENRY C. CAREY.

Hon. D. A. Wells.

Philadelphia, February 1, 1869

LETTER FIFTH.

DEAR SIR:—

Suppression of all facts adverse to further maintenance of foreign domination in reference to the greatest of all manufactures, and corresponding suppression of all tending to prove the advantage that had *invariably* resulted from every strike for independence, having enabled you with some appearance, though with none of the reality, of "historical truth," to make the extraordinary "assertion" that "no matter what had been the character of the legislation, whether the tariff was low or high, whether the condition of the country was one of war or peace, the increase of the production had been at the average of about 8 per cent. per annum, or more than double the ratio of the increase of population, you next proceed to speak of the present and the future, under the head of "Taxation on Pig Iron," as follows :—

"The article of pig iron affords a striking illustration of an instance where a duty originally levied for revenue and protection, or as an offset to internal taxes, has been continued long after its object has been fully attained, for the interest of the few, but to the detriment of the many.

"The existing duty on pig iron is $9, in gold; equivalent to over $12 currency. The average expenditure requisite to produce a ton of pig iron in the United States to-day may be fairly estimated as not in excess of $26 per ton, currency; and in the case of furnaces favorably situated as regards cheap coal and ore, and under good management, the actual cost, could it be truly ascertained, would not probably be found in excess of $24. Now, the selling price of Nos. 1 and 2 pig iron in the markets of the United States at present, and for the last year, has ranged from $37 to $42 per ton, with a demand continually tending to exceed supply.

"Under these circumstances the manufacturers of pig iron have, to the detriment of the rolling-mill interest, and to the expense of every consumer of iron from a rail to a ploughshare, and from a boiler plate to a tenpenny nail, realized continued profits which have hardly any parallel in the history of legitimate industry, the returns of one set of furnaces in one of the Middle States, communicated to the Commissioner, showing a yearly product of 35,000 tons, on a capital of $450,000, sold at a profit of from $10 to $13 per ton.

"The Commissioner, as he writes, (November, 1868,) has before him letters from the representatives of the bar and sheet-iron interests in nearly all sections of the country, to this effect: 'Our works are busy, but not remunerative. The profit of the iron manufacture is all absorbed by the manufacturers of pig metal. Our only hope is in equalization, and in a fair increase of protection by Congress at its next session.'

"Now, it would seem that if the manufacturers of pig iron had really at heart the great interests of American industry, they would of their own accord memorialize Congress to this effect: 'Our profits being far larger than is necessary for the prosperity and rapid extension of our business, we desire and can have no more efficient protection than what would of necessity be guaranteed to us by the prosperity and extension of the rolling-mill interest; and this protection can be readily attained, with benefit alike to producers and consumers, by affording under the existing tariff to the manufacturers of rolled iron cheaper raw material. We, therefore, request that the duty on pig iron, so far as it has heretofore been imposed or maintained for our benefit, may be relaxed or wholly abolished in. the interests of the associated branches of the iron industry, which are less prosperous.' The Commissioner has not, however, heard that any such movement has been contemplated, but on the contrary it is apparent from an inspection of House bill No. 1,211, now pending, that the manufacturers of pig iron propose to allow the representatives of the bar iron interest to ask from Congress at this session such further legislation as will, without reducing the present unduly enhanced cost of pig iron, guarantee to the latter at the expense of the consumers such additional profit as may render their business remunerative."

The answer to all this, and the extent of "detriment to the many," would both seem to be found in the facts, that the men who need "boiler plates and tenpenny nails," stoves, steam engines, and other machinery of comfort or production, are now enabled to consume *fifty per cent. more, per head*, of iron than they had done in the closing years of the revenue tariff of 1846; whereas, in these latter years they had consumed *forty per cent. less, per head*, than they had done in the corresponding years of the tariff of 1842. What is needed is, that this important commodity be placed within the reach of the largest portion of the community, and that such has invariably been the tendency of the protective policy is fully proved by—

First, The great increase of consumption from 1824 to 1835.

Second, Its extraordinary growth in the period from 1842 to 1848: and

Third, The great increase from 1861 to 1868.

Wholly overlooking the fact that there really *is* a perfect harmony in the real and permanent interests of society, your Report looks to stimulating discord by condoling with the mechanic for being required to aid in liberally rewarding the services of the farmer; then condoling with the latter for being required to contribute a small portion of his greatly increased receipts towards enabling the miner and the furnace man to obtain such wages as will enable his wife and children to live in comfort; then further condoling with the rolling miller in reference to the prosperity of the furnace man; and then, again, condoling with all for being, as you without the slightest reason assert they are, required to contribute a few cents per head, annually, towards that development of our great mineral resources to which alone can we look in the future for the establishment of either industrial or political independence, and to which at this moment we stand indebted for the facts thus given by yourself, to wit:—

"That within the last five years more cotton spindles have been put in operation, more iron furnaces erected, more iron smelted, more bars rolled, more steel made, more coal and copper mined, more lumber sawed and hewn, more houses and shops constructed, more manufactories of different kinds started, and more petroleum collected, refined, and exported, than during any equal period in the history of the country; and that this increase has been greater both as regards quality and quantity, and greater than the legitimate increase to be expected from the normal increase of wealth and population."

This is a remarkable state of things, but strangely enough, you do not, as I think, anywhere suggest to your readers that it occurs in a period when they are so heavily *taxed* by protection; or, that desiring to find the reverse thereof, they need only to turn to the closing years of the *untaxed* system of 1846 to find it. "Looking *now* around them," as you *might* well have said, "they would see the prosperity of the worker in iron keeping steady pace with that of railroad men; that in turn keeping pace with improvement in the condition of the farmer; the mechanic, the miner, and the laborer profiting again by the increased demand of the farmer for ploughs, harrows, and all other instruments used in the work of cultivation; and all combining to make such demand for iron as to cause consumption to advance *one-half more rapidly than population*. Let them then," as we may properly suppose you to have continued, "compare this with the paralysis from which they had been redeemed by the passage of the protective Act of 1861, and see that the consumption of iron, for purposes such as are above enumerated, had under the anti-protective policy, in the short period of a dozen years, *declined eleven per cent.*, *population meantime increasing forty per cent.;* and then, having carefully studied these facts of 'historical truth,' deliver judgment on the man who, placed in a situation of the highest responsibility, had deliberately ignored all these great facts, and so far trifled with them as to venture the assurance that—

"Study of all the facts pertaining to the national development from 1840 to 1860, and from 1865 to the present time, unmistakably teaches this lesson; that the progress of the country through what we may term the strength of its elements of vitality is independent of legislation and even of the impoverishment and waste of a great war. Like one of our own mighty rivers, its movement is beyond control. Successive years, like successive affluents, only add to and increase its volume; while legislative enactments and conflicting commercial policies, like the construction of piers and the deposit of sunken wrecks, simply deflect the current or constitute temporary obstructions. In fact, if the nation has not yet been lifted to the full comprehension of its own work, it builds determinately, as it were, by instinct."

2. Having told us what, as you think, the furnace man ought now to say, you may, perhaps, be disposed to read what, as it appears to me, you might with perfect truth and great propriety, yourself have said, as follows:—

"The iron manufacture, fellow-citizens, presents for consideration the most striking, as well as the most important chapter of our industrial history, exhibiting, as it certainly does, an energy, a determination of purpose, nowhere else, here or abroad, exceeded. Stricken down, and for the most part utterly ruined, in the closing years of the Compromise tariff, we find it, under the reviving influence of the protective tariff of 1842, starting at once into life and growing with a vigor that enabled it in the briefest period to treble the production, thereby making a great market for the country's labor, and for all the rude products of the farm and the plantation, as well as for those more finished yielded by the trained industries of the Northern and Eastern States; thereby, too, adding almost countless millions to the money value of the houses, lands, and mines of the country, and enabling their owners to contribute more largely to the public revenue.

"Again stricken down in the early years of the tariff of 1846, it is found once again, when large supplies of California gold had stimulated into activity the general movement of the country, starting into life, those engaged therein opening mines and building furnaces and rolling-mills, and thus preparing to profit of the opportunity thus supplied for enabling themselves to meet the demand that had been so produced.

"Again prostrated in the disastrous free trade period immediately preceding the rebellion, and that for the third time in less than twenty years, we find it rising, Antæus like, armed with an energy so great as, in the short period that has since elapsed, not only to have almost doubled the production, but to have exercised so large an influence on the iron trade of the world as to have checked the growth of British production in the manner here exhibited:—

"*Annual product of pig iron from 1863 to 1868.*

	AMERICAN.		BRITISH.	
	Tons.	Annual increase.	Tons.	Increase.
1863	947,604		4,510,040	
1864	1,136,497	19.82 per cent.	4,767,951	5.71 per cent.
1866	1,351,143	9.50 per cent.	4,819,254	1.08 per cent.
1867	1,447,771	7.16 per cent.		Decrease.
1868	1,600,000	10.60 per cent.	4,523,897	6.50 per cent.

" Such being the-facts," fellow-citizens, "it is clearly obvious that you may safely grant to this great industry all the protection for which those concerned in it may be led to ask, quite certain that the *thirty-five* furnaces now in various stages of preparation will be followed soon by as many more, and so on and on, each succeeding year diminishing the distance between ourselves and Britain, until at length the American Union shall become controller of the supply to more than half the world of this most useful of all commodities, and therewith controller of the commerce of the world. Hundreds of millions of acres abounding ir coal and ore are waiting that application of capital which will so surely come when its owners can feel assured that they are not fated to see repeated the scenes of ruin which had marked the closing years of the revenue tariffs of 1817, 1833, and 1846:"

Such, as it seems to me, would have been the American, the statesmanlike, the honest, presentation of this great question. In its place we are told that profits are too large, that " boiler plates and tenpenny nails" are too high, and that the way to lower them is to make such changes in our "legislation" as always in the past have produced, and must now produce, the effect of so diminishing faith in the future as to stop further building of furnaces, and so arrest increase of supply as to place British iron masters once again in the position in which they had stood in the calamitous years by which the rebellion had been preceded, and to which, more than to any other cause, the rebellion itself had been due.

3. Conquerors in the *warfare* waged in the early years of the revenue tariff of 1846, British iron masters, as has been shown, sold us a few years later pigs at a higher price than they had been then content to accept for railroad bars, thereby *taxing* the country, in two years alone, twenty, if not even forty millions of dollars. What, it may be proper here to ask, was the application of the proceeds of *that* taxation? Were they so applied as to add to the value of *our* land, *our* labor, or the produce of *our* farms? Were they so applied as to add to *our* public revenue? Did they not, on the contrary, go to adding to the value of lands, furnaces, houses, owned by men of whom we are now claiming that they shall render satisfaction for outrages perpetrated by the Shenandoah and the Alabama? That they did so you know as well as I.

Conquered in the strife, our own producers of iron had, in the unhappy closing years of that tariff, been nearly ruined. Protection having now largely increased the general power of consumption, they are found thence to profit in common with the farmer, the miner, the laborer, the tradesman, and the owner of houses and lots in our towns and cities. What, however, becomes of *their* profits? Do *they* go abroad to spend in Paris and in London the contributions of tenants left at home? Do *they* contribute to the resources of people and of governments that had gladly hailed the rebellion as precursor of final dissolution of the Union? *Do they not*, on the contrary, expend their profits in enlargement of their operations, thereby adding millions upon millions to the value of mineral lands that so much abound in nearly every quarter of the Union? *Do they not* thus make large additions to the demand for human labor? *Do they not* thus contribute largely to promotion of immigration? *Do they not* thus so add to the demand for farm products as greatly to promote improvement of cultivation? *Do they not* thus greatly aid in enabling all to purchase more freely of tea, coffee, sugar, and thus to contribute more largely to the public revenue? *Do they not*, in all these ways, contribute towards the growth of both individual and political independence?

Answering these questions, as you certainly must, in the affirmative, how are you to account for the *total suppression* of facts and ideas so important? Were you not, as Commissioner of the Public Revenue, bound to place the British and American *taxation*, and their effects, side by side, thereby enabling your constituents to see for themselves that whereas the whole proceeds of the former had been so applied as to promote the perpetuation of American *dependence*, those of the latter had gone, and must continue to go, in the direction of promoting the growth of American wealth and *independence?* Why has this not been done? Why is it that your Report has throughout been made so entirely in the interest of men who, as you know, are now flooding the country with money to be used in promoting such deception of our people as shall enable them to re-acquire the power that had been secured in the free trade years prior to the rebellion, and then so applied as almost to have made of that rebellion a revolution? To this important question I now invite your serious attention.

4. The general answer to your suggestions is, as it seems to me, to be found in the simple fact that *the power to consume iron is always greatest when the price is highest, and always smallest when the price is lowest.* Seeking evidence of this, you will do well to compare the prices and consumption of the protective year 1833 and the revenue tariff one of 1842; of this latter with the protective year 1846-7; of this again with the free trade year 1850; of this, in its turn, with the great California year 1854; of 1854 with the latter years of the free trade period which closed in 1860; and finally, those of the latter with those of the present hour, when consumption is advancing, despite of prices, so rapidly as to have excited in your mind fears that, with all our efforts, production cannot be made to meet it

The disease with which we are now, as you think, afflicted, is thus precisely the same with that with which we had been troubled in the closing years of the protective tariff of 1842. Such being the case, allow me to suggest that the remedy then adopted might now prove as effective as it then was found to be. Let us have again a strictly revenue tariff; let us have iron admitted at a low rate of duty; let us stop the building of furnaces; let the government in this manner give every aid in its power to British iron masters; and the day will then be near at hand when the disease will have changed its character, supply then going so far ahead of demand that the latter will then, as was the case in 1857, be reduced far below the point at which it had stood years before.

The road, and the only road, to freedom of external commerce leads through protection. The more thorough that protection the larger will be the public and private revenues, and the more rapid the advance. towards industrial and political independence.

Leaving you now to reflect on this suggestion, I propose to proceed to an examination of *the Lumber Question.*

Yours respectfully,
HENRY C. CAREY.

Hon. D. A. Wells.

Philadelphia, February 2, 1859.

LETTER SIXTH.

DEAR SIR:—

Coming now to *The Lumber Question*, I find you stating:—

"That the demand for the last few years has been fully equal to or has tended to exceed supply, which in turn has resulted in constantly augmented prices; the price, for example, of the cheapest varieties of lumber in the Albany, New York, market having advanced since 1861 about 100 per cent."

"The demand" having thus "exceeded the supply," "the price," as we see, has greatly "risen." The remedy for this would seem to be very simple. Let us return once again to the revenue tariff policy of the period from 1846 to 1860. Let us witness once again that condition of exhaustion which marked its closing years, and those of its free trade predecessor in 1842—years in which we built few houses; in which ships were ruinous to their owners; in which railroad stock failed to command in market even forty per cent. of its cost; in which farms were everywhere burthened with heavy mortgages; in which the little farmers of the West paid interest at any rate between 20 and 40 per cent. per annum; in which mills and furnaces were closed, and mines abandoned; in which laborers and mechanics by hundreds of thousands were wholly without employment; in which, as in 1842, agents were sent abroad to beg in Europe for loans; and, finally, in which the Treasury receipts exhibit more than $70,000,000, as the proceeds of "loans and treasury notes," thus bearing testimony to a constantly declining power to contribute to the public revenue; let us, as I say, return to the exhaustion of 1842, or to that of 1860, and we shall once again see the supply of lumber and of labor exceeding the demand, the prices of both becoming so reduced that while the lumberman shall find it difficult to obtain the food required by his family and himself, houses shall remain unoccupied and unproductive to their owners, because of the inability of miners, mechanics, and laborers to pay their little modicum of rents.

The great facts here presented, and that they are facts you know as well as I, find no place in your Report? Why? Because, like most of those presented in regard to iron, they did not suit your purpose. Had all been given you would have found yourself compelled to an exhibition of *harmony of interests*, resulting from protection, such as finds no parallel in any other portion of the earth. Giving the few you have selected, you have done your utmost towards persuading your fellow-citizens to believe that the protective system presents to view *universal discord*, high wages being injurious to the capitalist on the one hand, and increase of rents being ruinous to the laborer on the other.

The great demand for houses having caused increased demand for materials, "a supply of foreign lumber" is, as you tell us, "absolutely essential to meet the requirements of the country," and thence result "two things" which, as you assure them, "follow as a matter of necessity," to wit:—

"First, That whatever duty is imposed on the foreign product is paid wholly by the consumer, and is therefore equivalent to so much direct tax, and secondly, that the price of the imported article regulates and determines the selling price of the domestic product, at least for all that portion of the latter which is exposed to the competition of the foreign supply in the open and leading markets. Whatever, therefore, under these circumstances, enhances the price of foreign lumber, be it a tax or some other agency, will from necessity augment the price of the domestic product to the same extent. Or, in other words, a tax on the importation of foreign lumber becomes also a tax upon the consumers of the whole domestic product; with this essential difference, that in the one case the proceeds of the tax results to the benefit of the national treasury, and in the other to the benefit exclusively of private interests."

The answer to all this is found in the simple expression that the man who *must* go to market *must* pay the cost of getting there, be it in what form it may, whether that of waggonage, railroad charges, or customs duties. The farmer close to market obtains the full money value of his products; his competitor at a distance of 10, 20, 50, or 100 miles from market, selling at prices less by 20, 40, or 50 per cent., as the commodities they have raised need the application of more or less power to the work of transportation. Give to these latter turnpike roads, and diminution of "taxation" exhibits itself in the increased money value of both land and labor. Give them railroads, and the effect of further diminution of "taxation" makes itself manifest in a duplication of the price of land. Bring the market home by placing the consumer at their sides, and at once there arises such demand for the minor produce of the farm that land now sells readily for dollars, where before it could command but dimes.

Time and again, in that revenue tariff period in which were so thickly sown the seeds of the late rebellion, the farmer of Iowa had been required to make his election between using his corn as fuel or selling it at a dime per bushel. At Manchester, that bushel would command probably, *twenty yards* of cotton-cloth; and yet, when that cloth reached Iowa, a *single yard* of it would command in exchange another bushel—nineteen-twentieths of the farmer's power of purchase having perished somewhere on the road. Who, then, paid the "tax" of transportation? Was it not the farmer? Did he not, to his heavy cost, then learn to know that the man who *must* go to market *must* pay the cost of getting there? Assuredly he did. So, too, does the Canadian lumberman, sad experience having taught him that when our furnaces had been closed, and when houses had almost ceased to be built, the supply of his commodity had so far exceeded the demand as to free his neighbors across the line from all dependence on Canadian forests. Rejoicing now in the great demand resulting from protection of our iron, cotton, and other industries, and knowing well that abolition of duty would be followed by no reduction of price, he seeks to retain for himself his share of the millions that are now contributed to our public treasury; and to aid him in this effort it is, that you venture the assurance that prices here are fixed by those at which we obtain the trivial quantity which passes across our frontier.* Close the furnaces and mills, and stop the building of houses, and it will soon be found that prices are determined here, and *not* in the little markets of Toronto or of Montreal.

In confirmation of the views thus expressed, I now present for your

* *Exports from Canada of planks and boards for the fiscal years ending June 30, 1866, and 1867.*

					Total quantity. M feet.	Total value.	To the United States.
1866	.	.	.	.	465,812	$4,583,075	$4,508,554
1867	.	.	.	.	533,192	5,104,342	5,043,867

consideration the following passages from reports by the Collectors of Customs at two of the northern ports, as follows:—

"OGDENSBURG, August 3, 1868.

"The supply and demand in the United States is so much larger than in Canada, that importations from there affect our markets but little.

"The following articles are not, in my opinion, imported from Canada in sufficient quantities to affect our markets: Butter, cheese, eggs, wheat, rye, oats, barley and beef cattle. Our importations of these articles are so small, compared with our productions and with our exportations, that we can be affected but little by the supply from Canada."

"CLEVELAND, October 20, 1868.

"The chief articles of importation at this port are lumber and barley. The lumber market here is entirely controlled by the Saginaw market, and Canadian markets do not in the least influence us. The Canada market, to a great extent, is controlled by American markets, and the result is that the Canadian producer has to conform his prices to our market figures here; this virtually makes the Canadian pay the duties on foreign merchandise imported here, as he is compelled to sell his goods so as to enable the importer to pay the duties, and still not overshoot the American market. As the demand in Canada is not equal to the production, the producer is compelled to look to a foreign market for sale of his merchandise, and for this reason he must necessarily regulate his prices by that market to sell. The purchaser in buying always makes allowance for the duties, and the Canadian in his sale deducts the amount, and thus in reality pays the duty himself."

That each of Jupiter's satellites exercises over the movements of Jupiter himself some little influence is entirely undoubted, but it is so very slight that were the smaller body stricken from existence careful observation would be required for enabling astronomers to note the fact that change had really occurred. So, very nearly, is it here, Canada exercising scarcely more influence on the great internal movements of the Union than is exercised over the great planet by its insignificant dependant.

2. The builders of houses, and the constructors of bridges, required to choose between the perishable lumber and the imperishable iron, would certainly select the latter, but for the great difference of cost. That this may be diminished it is indispensable that there be competition *for its sale*, and the greater the competition the greater must be the tendency toward diminution in the quantity of labor to be given for a ton of iron, and toward substitution of the least destructible for the most destructible material. The more rapid the substitution the greater would be the tendency towards moving in the direction in which, as you here tell us, "the national interests are likely to be best subserved," to wit:—

"By restricting rather than stimulating the destruction of our forests, which, in consequence of the continually augmenting demand for lumber, are diminishing and receding with alarming rapidity. So certain, moreover," as you continue, "is the future advance in the price of lumber, owing to increased demand and diminished supply, that if it were possible to draw for the next ten years the whole domestic supply from foreign sources, the result would unquestionably be for the benefit rather than the detriment of the country; while in respect to private interests the increase in value of timber lands held in reserve during the same period would probably exceed any average interest that would be likely to accrue from a different employment of capital."

Clearly seeing, as it is here shown you do, that economy of lumber is greatly to be desired, you might, as it seems to me, have spoken to the people whose great interests you are required to guard, somewhat as follows, to wit:—

"Our lands, fellow-citizens, abound in the materials of iron to an extent unparalleled throughout the globe, and from them we can obtain to any extent, and through thousands and tens of thousands of years, the most imperishable of all the materials used for construction of houses, bridges, and all other of the various machinery required for the comfort and material advancement of our people. Our forests, on the contrary, are constantly diminishing in their extent, and now that, by aid of protection, our people are becoming daily more and more enabled to command the use of better dwellings, better roads, and better bridges, the "rapidity" of diminution becomes "alarming." Nevertheless, we still continue to use this destructible material to such extent that to estimate at $200,000,000 per annum the amount required for repairing the ravages of time and fire would, as I feel assured, be greatly within the mark. Desiring to see why it is that we still continue a practice so destructive, it may be well for you to study the facts, that under the protective tariff of 1828 great progress had been made in the work of so developing our resources as to warrant the hope that at no distant period iron might be largely substituted for the perishable lumber; that under the free trade period which followed, we retraced our steps, largely diminishing the proportion borne by population to iron production; that under the protective tariff of 1842 there was made a progress so wonderful as to make it certain that at no distant day iron would become so cheap as to insure its greatly increased application in the construction of edifices of every kind; that under its successor of 1846, we again retraced our steps, the closing years of that unhappy period exhibiting a large decrease in the use of iron for every purpose except that of roads, this, too, in face of a growth of numbers amounting to almost forty per cent.; that since the passage of Morrell tariff in 1861, production has gone so largely ahead of population that we are now daily substituting iron for the lumber that before had been so freely used; that the number of furnaces is at this moment being so largely increased as to give assurance of a production quadrupling in its growth that of population; that to cause that growth to become twice greater than the one now witnessed, we need only to give assurance to mine operators, land owners, furnace men, capitalists at home and abroad, that it is *our fixed determination* so to shape our policy as to relieve ourselves, and that at no distant day, from the necessity which now exists for laying waste our forests, as well as from an annual waste, by time and fire, of property *whose mere money value far exceeds that of all the iron and all the manufactures thereof*, now produced in Britain.

"Doing this, fellow-citizens, we shall make such demand for labor as will bring to the close neighborhood of our farmers tens of thousands of the iron workers of Europe; we shall relieve those farmers from a "tax" of transportation greater than would suffice to support the armies of the world; we shall add hundreds of millions to the money value of our lands; we shall so increase production as to enable each and all to contribute thrice more largely to the public revenue; we shall establish harmony among ourselves; we shall so closely knit together all the parts of the Union as to forbid the idea of future separation; we shall free ourselves from our present humiliating dependence upon men from whom we are now claiming satisfaction for depredations of the Alabama and the Shenandoah; we shall become the money lenders of the world instead of being, as now, the great money beggars; and, finally, we shall be enabled to say to the world, that the words of our president elect, "Let us have peace!" are meant by us to apply to the world at large, and that it is our fixed determination so to use the great resources placed at our command as to bring to a close the destructive warfare by which the world so long has been, and still is being, desolated."

Such, as I think, would have been the words of a statesman such as, in your Report, you claim to be. Such, however, are *not* the words of that Report, their place being occupied with others expressive of the troubles of consumers of "tenpenny nails," suffering at the hands of furnace men who, as you assure your fellow-citizens, are so secured by protective duties as to enable them to obtain twice or thrice the rate of profit that might properly be assigned them. Desiring to reduce that rate, you propose the adoption of such measures as shall at once annihilate that faith in the future to which we stand now indebted for a duplication of our iron product in the short period that has elapsed since the passage of the tariff Act of 1861; and yet, could you but be persuaded to study carefully the teachings here below given of your fellow-laborers of the *Evening Post*, you would, as I think, discover that it is to the fact that iron production is now profitable to those engaged therein we are to look for such reduction of prices as will secure largely increased application of that material, with constant diminution in the necessity for using lumber in our various works of construction as the only one that is within our reach.

" It is not unreasonable to expect that, just as ships from every part of the civilized world have flocked to the Chincha Islands in search of Peruvian guano, so will they before long crowd the wharves of Charleston in quest of that element of guano found there, which has the most lasting value. This long-hidden source of wealth cannot fail to draw to this now forsaken port the enterprise and capital necessary for its regeneration, and for the establishment of permanent prosperity. A company in Charleston, which is now engaged in the preparation of a fertilizer of which these phosphates are the chief constituent, finds a ready market at $60 per ton for this product. The cost of a ton of 2000 pounds, a they prepare it, is thus divided ; 1400 pounds crude phosphate, $5 60; 400 pounds sulphuric acid, $12 ; 200 pounds ground animal refuse, $1 50—total cost of material, $19 10. The cost of manipulation may carry the entire outlay to $25, which leaves a very wide margin for an increase in the cost of the phosphate. Either superphosphate of lime must become much cheaper, in consequence of this discovery, or the owners of the phosphate lands must become rapidly rich, FOR IT IS IMPOSSIBLE THAT SO LARGE A PROFIT AS $35 PER TON CAN LONG BE MADE IN A MANUFACTURE IN WHICH THERE IS NO MONOPOLY."—*Evening Post*

Of the perfect truth of the views thus presented no one can for a moment doubt. Liberal profits in the outset are the necessary preliminaries to cheap supplies of this valuable substance in all the future. Such being the case in regard to a commodity obtainable only from some few thousand acres, how infinitely more true must it be in reference to one that abounds in more than half the States of the Union, and so abounds as to make it certain that the day must come when we shall be the great iron producers of the world.

Leaving you to reflect on these suggestions, and to compare them with your own, I remain,

Yours respectfully,

HENRY C. CAREY.

HON. D. A. WELLS.

PHILADELPHIA, February 8, 1869.

LETTER SEVENTH.

DEAR SIR:—

Coming now to the *Cotton Trade*, we find the real facts to have been as follows:—

Consumption north of the Potomac, under the semi-protective tariff of 1824, 110,000 bales. Thenceforward, under the thoroughly protective tariff of 1828, we find it steadily rising until in the closing year of protection, 1835, it had reached 216,000, having nearly doubled in seven years, and its growth having been four times more rapid than that of population.

Seven years of the compromise and revenue tariff now follow, with an average consumption of 263,000, the closing year standing at 267,500, and showing an increase of 23 per cent., while population had grown 25 per cent. Of the crop of 1847–8, the closing years of protection under the tariff of 1842, the consumption was 531,000, having almost doubled in five years, and the growth having been nearly six times more rapid than that of population.

This, however, is by no means all, the growth south of the Potomac in this period having been great, and the prospect in the closing years above referred to having been such as to have led the editor of the *Charleston Mercury* to expression of a belief that before the lapse of another decade the South would have ceased to export raw cotton. Unhappily for him, and for his neighbors, Congress had then already cut the ground from under them, giving them a free trade tariff under which consumption was destined to go backward instead of forward.

Coming now to the closing years of that tariff we find it to have been as follows: of the crop of 1857–8, 452,000; 1858–9, 760,000; 1859–60, 792,000; total, 2,004,000; giving an average of 668,000, and exhibiting an increase of but 25 per cent., population meanwhile having grown nearly 40 per cent.

We see, thus, that while the power to purchase clothing increased with great rapidity in the two protective periods, it so declined under the anti-protective one as largely to increase the quantity that *must* be sent abroad in search of market. That such had been the case you have had full opportunity of knowing, all the facts having been time and again given to the world; and yet, most wonderfully, you have now staked your reputation on such a presentation of facts in regard to this great trade as is contained in the following words and figures, to wit:—

Increase in the domestic consumption of cotton, north of the Potomac: 1840, 297,000 bales; 1845, 422,000; 1849–50, 476,000; 1851–52, 588,000; 1855, 633,300; 1858–59, 760,000; 1859–60, 792,000.

For enabling you to obtain this regularity of growth, you had been required to *suppress* the progress upwards from 389,000 (not 422,000) in 1845, to 531,000 three years later; and then again to *suppress* one of the three closing years of the important revenue tariff period which commenced in 1848 and terminated with the rebellion, exhibiting throughout its whole existence a series of expansions and contractions, of wild speculation on one hand, and financial crises on the other, whose general result had been that of so depleting the country as to have brought public and private revenues back to nearly the condition in which they had stood in the years which had preceded the terrific crisis of 1842.

Further even than this, by confining yourself exclusively to the northern movement, you have been enabled to *suppress* entirely the great Southern one which had had its origin under the protective tariff of 1842, which had, in four years carried up the Southern consumption from almost nothing to 100,000 in 1847–8; and which had then given so great promise as almost to have warranted the prediction of the *Mercury* above referred to. Twelve years later, in 1860, it had receded to 87,500, giving a loss of more than *twelve* per cent.; population meanwhile having grown *forty* per cent. Having carefully studied these facts, and having seen to what extent "legislative enactments" had thus stimulated into activity the slumbering energies of the South, you may, as I think, with great advantage, review your own "assertions," with a view to satisfy yourself how far they are in accordance with "historical truth."

2. Of the movement since the re-establishment of protection your general summary, intended for widest circulation, says *not a single word*. Turning, however, to your second page we find the statement that here is reproduced, to wit:—

"The number of cotton spindles in the United States, according to the census of 1860, was 5,235,727. From 1860 to 1864 there was little or no increase of cotton machinery, but possibly a diminution—many mills, under the great demand for army clothing, having been converted into establishments for the manufacture of woolens. The number of spindles, however, at present in operation, is shown by the recent returns of the American Cotton Manufacturers' and Planters' Association, to be about 7,000,000, a gain of 31.78 per cent. in from four to five years, and mainly since the termination of the war in 1865. An estimate, based on less perfect data, given in the last annual report of the Commissioner, fixed this increase at only from 15 to 20 per cent."

Why, however, is it that you have not added to this the fact, that the consumption is now at the rate of a million bales per annum, and tends rapidly to increase?* Why have you not placed such figures side by side with those given above, and shown that whereas, the growth of eight years, under the tariff of 1846, had been but 204,000, that of the brief period since the peace, under protection, had been so rapid that the consumption was already one-half greater than had been that of the closing years of the free trade period? Had you, as in duty you were required to do, given these facts, and others that have above been furnished, would it have been possible for you seriously to make the "assertions" of the following paragraph here once again presented for your consideration?

"There does not seem to be any reliable evidence which can be adduced to show that the changes which took place in the legislative commercial policy of the country in 1846 had any permanent or marked effect whatever; while, on the other hand, the study of all the facts pertaining to national development from 1840 to 1860, and from 1865 to the present time, unmistakably teaches this lesson; that the progress of the country through what we may term the strength of its elements of vitality is independent of legislation and even of the impoverishment and waste of a great war. Like one of our own mighty rivers, its movement is beyond control. Successive years, like successive affluents, only add to and increase its volume; while legislative enactments and conflicting commercial policies, like the construction of piers,

* The ascertained consumption of the year ending at the close of August last was 881,000, and the real quantity probably more than 900,000.

and the deposit of sunken wrecks, simply deflect the current or constitute temporary obstructions. In fact, if the nation has not yet been lifted to the full comprehension of its own work, it builds determinately, as it were, by instinct."

3. The consumption of the closing years of the tariff of 1846 having been 668,000, we may now look to see how much of even that small quantity had been due to protection. The *growth* from 1829 to 1835 was, as has been shown, 116,000; that from 1843 to 1847-8, 264,000; total, 380,000. Adding now to this the original 110,000, we have a total of 490,000, leaving 178,000 as the total growth of the seven free trade years which ended in 1842, and the twelve such years which closed in 1860, giving an annual average of less than 10,000 bales, population meantime growing at the rate of millions annually, and the crop passing upwards from the 1,700,000 bales of the years 1839-42 to 4,700,000 of 1859-60. As a consequence of this the quantity forced on foreign markets grew with great rapidity, and with results to the cotton producing planters such as shall be now described.

The crop of 1814 was 70,000,000 pounds, the domestic consumption being nearly 30,000,000. The former increasing while the latter declined, there arose an increased necessity for pressing it on foreign markets, with the result here exhibited:—

Export 1815 and 1816,	. average 80,000,000	. product $20,500,000
" 1828 and 1822,	. " 134,000,000	. " 21,500,000
" 1827 to 1829,	. " 256,000,000	. " 26,000,000

The quantity had now more than trebled, while the receipt had increased little more than 25 per cent. The prices here given being those of the shipping ports, and the quantity to be transported having so greatly increased, and having required so great an extension of cultivation, it is reasonable to assume that the planter gave 256,000,000 of pounds for no more money than six years previously he had received for less than a third of that quantity.

1830 to 1832,	. average 280,000,000	. . .	$28,000,000
1840 to 1842	. . " 619,000,000	. . .	55,000,000
1843 to 1845	. . " 719,000,000	. . .	51,000,000
1849	. . " 1,026,000,000	. . .	66,000,000

We have here nearly 940,000,000 of pounds to be transported, additional to the quantity of 1815-16, and from an area that, because of an unceasing exhaustion of the soil, had been enormously extended. Such being the case, it may be doubted whether the price received on the plantations had been more than twice as great as that received for 80,000,000.

1850–1851	. . pounds 781,000,000	. . . $92,000,000

The great fact is here presented that the *less* cotton the planter sends to market, the *more* he obtains for it, while saving largely of the cost of internal transportation.

1852	. . . pounds 1,093,000,000	. . . $88,000,000

Here is an increase of 312,000,000 of pounds to be transported, accompanied with a diminution of gross receipt of $4,000,000; and of net receipt that cannot be estimated at less than $10,000,000. As compared with 1815-16, *the planter must have been giving five pounds for the price before received for one.*

The crop of that year had been 3,263,000 bales, and at that it remained, on an average of years until 1858-9 the Euro an demand steadil in-

creasing. So stationary a condition as regarded production, and continued for so long a period, should have brought a large increase of
price, and yet, in 1859-60, the closing year of the free trade period,
we find the planters giving 1,752,000,000 of pounds for $191,000,000,
being less than an average of 11 cents per pound for all, Sea Islands
included.

The reverse of this is what is now exhibited, the war having brought
with it diversification of pursuits, and the cotton grower raising his
his own food instead of going abroad to buy it. As a consequence, the
domestic demand now absorbs probably more than forty per cent. of the
total product, leaving but half as much to be exported as was sent
abroad in 1860; and the producer receiving *a hundred dollars* per bale,
where before he had been obliged to content himself with an average of
less than forty. *When the buyer finds himself compelled to seek the
seller the latter it is who fixes the price.* That he is now enabled
so to do would seem to be the effect of the "legislation" of 1861.

3. In the natural order of things the cultivator profits by improvements in manufacture; yet here, although each successive year had
brought with it increased facilities for the conversion of cotton, we find
the planter to have been, with great steadiness, giving more of it for less
money. The cause, as we then were told, was that too much cotton was
being produced, and the planters held meetings with a view to reduce
the quantity; yet the cultivation extended with decline of price. Struggle as they might, the case was still the same, more cotton being given
for less money, and that in spite of a great natural law in virtue of
which the planter should have had, annually, more iron, more gold,
more silver, more lead, and more of all the metals, for less cotton.

Adam Smith denounced the British system because it was based on
the idea of cheapening the raw materials of manufacture. Therefore
was it that it had been resisted by means of protective measures, by all
the civilized nations of the world—America alone excepted. In all of
them, consequently, raw produce had risen in price; while here alone,
had been exhibited a civilized community in which raw produce had during
half a century steadily declined in price—the farming and planting interests, strange to say, having been most consistent in the pursuit of a
policy tending to diminish the quantity of money to be received in exchange for a bale of cotton or a barrel of flour. Barbarism grows in the
ratio of the export of the rude products of the land, and consequent
exhaustion of the soil—the raising of such products for distant markets
being the proper work of the barbarian and the slave, and of those alone.

Protection looks to the prevention of such exhaustion, by bringing
consumers to the side of producers and thus promoting the growth
of wealth and civilization. That such has been its tendencies is clearly
shown in the brief history of the cotton trade given above; given, too,
in the belief that no one can study it without arriving at the conclusion,
that had the tariff of 1842 been maintained in existence the South
would soon have been filled with furnaces and factories, making that demand for labor which would have given freedom to the slave and enormous value to the land, and bringing with it that consciousness of the
existence of a general *harmony of interests* which would have knitted
North and South more closely together, and would have enabled us to
avoid the great sacrifice of life and fortune that has resulted from the
late rebellion.

Having studied carefully the facts here given, you may, as I think,

LETTER EIGHTH.

DEAR SIR :—

In your general summary our commerce with the exterior world is thus presented :—

"Exports and imports: In 1840, $238,000,000; 1845, $231,000,000 ; 1850, $300,000,000; 1855, $536,000,000 ; 1860, $762,000,000."

The increase here exhibited is certainly worthy of note, but far more worthy, as it seems to me, would have been a presentation of the cost at which it had been secured. Had you desired to make such presentation, and so to make it as to enable your constituents finally to decide as to the direction in which they might find "historical truth," your words would probably have been as follows :—

"From 1845 to 1860, fellow-citizens, the combined amount of our exports and imports had, as you see, more than trebled, the great change thus exhibited having occurred, however, not as a consequence of growing *power* for maintenance of foreign commerce, but because of an absolute *necessity* for seeking abroad a market for commodities that we had not permitted our people to use at home. At the first of these dates our cotton product but little exceeded 2,000,000 bales, and the domestic consumption, under the protective tariff of 1842, was then so rapidly growing as to warrant a belief that the day was fast approaching when it would call for more than half the crop, thereby relieving our planters from all necessity for forcing their product on foreign markets, and for submitting to the arbitrary will of men whose profits grew as they were more and more enabled to fix for themselves the prices at which they would consent to purchase. From 1842–3 to 1847–8 the home demand, *North and South*, had grown from 267,000 to 630,000 bales, but at the close of the dozen free trade years of the tariff of 1846, it had so slightly grown as to have required but 755,000, although our numbers had almost forty per cent. increased. As a consequence, we had been then required to seek abroad a market for a quantity twice greater than that of the *whole crop* of the period for 1842, the dependence of our planters on the foreigner becoming greater with each succeeding year. Under such circumstances our shipping grew, of course, with great rapidity, as did the *quantity* of commodities carried abroad to be changed in form and then returned to us for our own consumption, but our soil became from hour to hour more and more exhausted; the general result of this extraordinary course of operation having been, that while possessed of soil and climate unequalled for production of this great staple, the total contribution to the commerce of the world, *abroad and at home*, of States with a population of 8,000,000, a territory of hundreds of millions of acres adapted to the cotton culture, and so far as applied at all so applied, was less than that of single Northern States, and could scarcely be placed at a sum exceeding $800,000,000.

"Seeking now another item of the cost at which had been obtained this growth of foreign intercourse, we find the great iron manufacture to have been so stricken down that whereas, in the period from 1842 to 1848 it had so rapidly advanced as to warrant the belief that but few more years would be required for enabling it to stand fully side by side with that of Britain, the closing years of this period of growing foreign commerce had exhibited it as having remained entirely stationary, not-withstanding the great increase of population above described.

"Looking once again, fellow-citizens, you will find a fearful item of cost in this, that while our exports, gold excluded, scarcely exceeded $300,000,000, our farmers and planters were being 'taxed' for the main-tenance of *two and a half millions* of registered tonnage employed in carrying a really insignificant money value of rude products to for-eign markets. Add to the capital represented by this domestic shipping that represented by the vast quantity of foreign tonnage likewise so employed, and you will find, my friends, that *the total capital employed in the work of transportation must have closely approximated the annual value of the commodities carried.* Reflect then, I pray you, on the fact, that a single ship could bring from Europe cloths and silks sufficient to pay for the cargoes of a dozen carrying cotton, and that it must, there-fore, necessarily have followed, that the whole burthen of maintaining this machinery was being borne by *our own* farmers, *our own* planters, *our own* land holders, and you will then be disposed to agree with me in the belief that, as a part of the cost of this great foreign commerce we might here set down a 'tax' of transportation, within and without our own limits, greater than would have then sufficed for maintaining all the armies of Europe.*

"Turning your eyes now in another direction, you find our commerce with the outer world to have been swelled in the closing years of the *prosperous* free trade period by an export of $180,000,000 of gold, the withdrawal of which had been accompanied by paralysis so complete that mills and furnaces had been closed; that thousands and tens of thousands of working men had been reduced to a state of idleness; that immigration had tended almost to disappear; that small as had been the production of commodities for whose production either cotton or iron had been required, the supply had been greatly in excess of the demand; that power to contribute to the public revenue had become so much impaired as to render necessary the negotiation of large amounts of Treasury notes and bonds; and, that at the annual cost of *thou-sands of millions* of domestic commerce we had added *a couple of hun-dred millions* to the quantity of goods sent abroad, and as much to that which had been thence received.

"Throughout this unhappy period, fellow-citizens, railroads had largely increased in numbers and extent, its closing years presenting the extraordinary spectacle of a community possessed of more than thirty thousand miles of road, all of which it had been required to maintain in working order, its internal commerce meanwhile having so declined that shares in most important roads had been almost wholly

* At the moment here referred to France was exporting to the extent of $300,000,-000 of silks, cottons, and other finished articles, in so compressed a form that they could have been carried in fifty ships of 1000 tons each.

without price, while for the great majority the most that could have been obtained was from a fourth to a half of their original cost. That in the picture thus presented of the cost at which we had so much increased our dependence on foreign markets I do not at all exaggerate, proof is furnished in a paragraph written in 1848, accurately, as I think, presenting the facts of those British free trade years, as follows:—

"Looking, first, to our internal commerce, we find a mass of roads, most of which have been constructed by help of bonds bearing interest at the rate of 6, 8, or 10 per cent.—bonds that have been disposed of in the market at 60, 70, or 80 per cent. of their nominal value, and could not now, probably, be re-sold at more than half the price at which they were originally bought. Half- made, and little likely ever to be completed, these roads are worked at great expense, while requiring constant and great repairs. As a consequence of this it is, that the original proprietors have almost wholly disappeared, the stock being of little worth. The total amount applied to the creation of railroads having been about $1,000,000,000, and the average present money value scarcely exceeding 40, if even 30 per cent., it follows that $600,000,000 have been sunk, and with them all power to make new roads. Never, at any period of our history, have we been in this respect so utterly helpless as at present. Nevertheless, the policy of the central government looks steadily to the dispersion of our people, to the occupation of new territories, to the creation of new States, and to the production of a necessity for further roads. *That, Mr. President, is the road to physical and moral decline, and political death, as will soon be proved, unless we change our course.*"

"The more carefully, fellow-citizens, you shall study the picture here presented, the more, as I think, will you become satisfied of the perfect accuracy of the prediction with which it closes, and which since has come so near to being realized. With every hour that you shall give to its consideration the more you must become satisfied that the nation which sacrifices its internal commerce in the hope of creating a great foreign one, is building an inverted pyramid that must in time topple over and fall to utter ruin, as had so nearly proved to be the case with us at the close of the dreary British free trade period to which your attention has been now invited."

Having thus presented what, as it appears to me, you might with perfect regard to "historical truth," have said of the years preceding the rebellion, I propose in my next to review what you have said of those by which it has been since succeeded.

Yours respectfully,

HENRY C. CAREY.

Hon. D. A. Wells.

Philadelphia, February 11, 1869.

LETTER NINTH.

Dear Sir:—

Passing from amid the gloom and darkness of the closing years of the free trade period above described, we come now to the brilliant sun-light of recent protective years, so well exhibited by yourself in the passage of your Report which here is given, as follows :—

"An analysis of the railway system of the United States, which has been made for the first time during the past year, presents us with results which, were they not founded on incontrovertible data would seem fabulous. Thus the ratio of the gross earnings to the cost of the railroads of the whole country for the year 1867 was equal to about 21 per cent. ; for the northern States about 23 per cent. The railroads of the country, therefore, now receive their cost in a little more than four years, and this ratio of gross earnings to cost is steadily increasing with the increase of the railway system and traffic of the country.

* * * * * *

"The total amount of tonnage transported on all the roads of the country for the year 1851, is estimated by good authorities at not exceeding 10,000,000 tons. If from this we deduct 3,000,000 tons for coal and other cheap materials, and 1,000,000 tons for duplications, there will be left a merchandise tonnage of 6,000,000 tons in 1851, against 48,488,000 tons in 1867. The rate of increase in this period, therefore, has been equal to 100 per cent., and the actual increase 42,488,000 tons. At the estimated value of $150 per ton, the increase in the value of the railway merchandise of the country in 16 years has been 6,373,200,000, or at the rate of $400,000,000 per annum. And it should also be noted that one-half of this total increase has taken place in the seven years that have closed since 1860.

"The increased movement on the railways of the United States, which in the main represents increased product, also affords some indication of the progress of the development of the country. Thus, the earnings of the ten principal railway lines of the west exhibit for the first ten months of 1868 (with a decrease rather than an increase of freight rates) a gain of eight per cent. as compared with earnings of the corresponding months for the year 1861. Taking also the movements on the railways and canals of the State of New York, which are known to be accurate, and at the same time accessible, as a measure of comparison, for the whole country, we find that the total annual tonnage increased from 7,138,917 tons, in 1858, to 16,032,006, in 1868, an increase of 124 per cent. ; *while the annual value of the tonnage thus moved increased from $486,816,505, in 1858, to $1,723,330,207, in 1867, a gain of 254 per cent.*

"An examination of the railroad statistics of the whole country for the above period further indicates that during the ten years above referred to, or from 1858 to 1868, the increase of tonnage moved on the railways of the United States has been at a *rate sixteen times greater than the ratio of the increase of population.*"

The railroad corpse of 1860—the *Lazarus* of its day, a mass of offensive sores—has thus, as we see, been not only galvanized into life, but has been endowed with a life so vigorous as to be now generating children at a rate so rapid, that, as we learn from you—

"Since and including the year 1865, the year of the termination of the war, nearly 8,000 miles of railroad have been constructed in the United States, and the present ratio of increase is more than double the average of railroad history prior to 1860, (viz: 1,156 miles.)

"On the other hand," as you continue, "the average annual increase of railroads in Great Britain from 1860 to 1865 was only 571 miles, and in France during the same period 509 miles."

The change thus presented is the most marvellous of any elsewhere presented in the annals of the world. To what, it may now be asked, must these marvels be attributed? To any increase in the *quantity* of our exports of those raw products with which, and at constantly diminishing prices, whether measured in gold, lead, copper, or iron, we, before the war had been accustomed to deluge the little and contemptible market of Liverpool? Certainly not, *that* having, on the contrary, much diminished. Where else, then, shall the cause be sought? For answer to this question let me, if you please, again present another passage from your Report, being almost the only one, so far as I recollect, for the entire accuracy of which I should be disposed to make myself responsible before the world, as follows :—

"Within the last five years more cotton spindles have been put in operation, more iron furnaces erected, more iron smelted, more bars rolled, more steel made, more coal and copper mined, more lumber sawed and hewn, more houses and shops constructed, more manufactories of different kinds started, and more petroleum collected, refined, and exported, than during any equal period in the history of the country ; and this increase has been greater both as regards quality and quantity, and greater than the legitimate increase to be expected from the normal increase of wealth and population."

Compare this, I pray you, with the facts, that *the whole twelve years* of that British free trade period to which we stand indebted for the occurrence of the great rebellion, had presented an increase of cotton consumption of less than 10,000 bales per annum ; that the iron production of the closing years of that unhappy period gave an average scarcely, if at all, exceeding that of 1847–8 ; that the iron consumption, for purposes of production, in those years had been actually less in quantity than in the corresponding years of its protective predecessor ; that population had in the meantime increased nearly forty per cent. ; that the demand for labor had so much diminished that our streets were thronged with men who begged because not permitted to labor ; that immigration had, as a necessary consequence, almost died away ; that in those years of profound peace, because of the inability of our people to purchase sugar, coffee, tea, cloth, iron, and other commodities, the treasury had been obliged totally to exhaust its credit by borrowing no less than $70,000,000 ; that the export of gold in those closing years had amounted to no less than $180,000,000 ; compare, I say, these results of a policy looking to the building up of a little foreign commerce on the ruins of a domestic one that *should* before that time have become the grandest, the most magnificent, the world had ever known, and under the tariff of 1842 *would* so have done, and you will have little difficulty in understanding why it had been that at the close of that dreary period the great railroad interest of the country should have been in the state of utter ruin presented to your view in the closing extract given in my last.

2. Such having been, and such being now the *real* facts, you might, as it seems to me, with great propriety, have placed before the railroad owners and railroad makers of the country that remarkable parliamentary document an extract from which was given in a former letter, exhibiting the "immense losses" incurred by British iron masters "in order to destroy foreign competition, and to gain and keep possession of foreign markets," following it up by comments such as those that follow, to wit :—

The wealthy British "capitalists" my fellow-citizens, who are thus engaged in "taxing" the world for maintenance of a great monopoly have their agents everywhere, and always prepared for combination with every little private or local interest for the removal of fancied grievances of which *they know themselves to be the cause.* What *they* desire, as they know full well, is that food may be cheap and iron high in price. What *you* have reason to desire, and what by means of protection our farmers are seeking to obtain, is that these latter may be enabled to obtain more spades and ploughs, and better means of transportation, in exchange for less and less of food. When, however, the farmer complains of the price of corn, he finds the agent close at hand, Mephistophiles-like, to whisper in his ear that but for protection spades and ploughs would be cheaper, while food would command a higher price. When the railroad manager needs iron, he points to the low price at which foreign rails may be purchased, wholly omitting to call his attention to the facts that *British prices are always low when American people build furnaces, and when American railrodd companies make good dividends ; and always high when American furnaces have been blotted out of existence, when their owners have been made bankrupt, and when American railroad stocks are of little worth.* In proof of this, I now give you the following facts in reference to this important subject, as they present themselves in the several Reports on Commerce and Navigation, to wit:—

"At the close of the protective period, 1828–33—that one in which for the first time our iron manufacture made a great forward movement, and therefore the most prosperous one the country had ever known—the price at which British bar iron, rails included, was shipped to this country, was *forty dollars.*

"Eight years later, in 1841, when our mechanics were seeking alms; when our farmers could find no market; when furnaces and mills were everywhere closed, and their owners everywhere ruined; when States were repudiating, and the National Treasury was wholly unable to meet its small engagements; the *shipping price* of British bars had been advanced to *fifty dollars.*

"Eight years still later, in 1849, after protection had carried up our domestic product to 800,000 tons, and after the British free trade tariff of 1846 had once again placed our iron masters under the heel of the 'wealthy English capitalist,' we find the latter energetically using that potent 'instrument of warfare' by means of which he 'gains and keeps possession of foreign markets,' and shipping bars at THIRTY DOLLARS per ton. In what manner, however, was our railroad interest then paying for a reduction like this, by means of which they were being enabled to save on their repairs a tenth or a twentieth of one per cent, on their respective capitals? Seeking an answer to this question, I find, my friends, on comparison of prices in February 1848 and 1850, of thirteen important roads, that in that short period there had been a decline of *more than thirty per cent.!* This may seem to have been paying somewhat dearly for the whistle of cheap iron; and yet it is but trifling as compared with information contained in a paragraph of the same date now before me, in which are given the names of numerous important roads whose cost had been very many millions of dollars, but which, '*from prices quoted, and those nearly nominal, seem,*' as it says, '*to be of little or no value—not enough, nor one-fourth enough, to pay interest on the sums advanced for their creation.*'

"At the close of another term of similar length, say in 1857, we, find a scene of ruin more general than any that had been witnessed since the years of that British free trade period which terminated with the general crash of '42, when railroad stocks were almost worthless. What, however, was the price at which British iron masters were *then* willing, now that they had so effectually crushed out competition, to meet the demands of railroad managers? Were they still ready to accept $30 per ton as the shipping price? Did they *then* manifest any desire to help the friends who had so largely aided them in 'gaining and keeping possession' of this American market? Far from it! The more that railroad stocks went down, as a consequence of failure of the domestic commerce, the more determined did the British masters of our American stockholders show themselves, Shylock-like, to exact 'the pound of flesh.' In that unhappy period the shipping price of bars was $48, and that of railroad iron $42, the average having been FORTY-FOUR DOLLARS, or nearly fifty per cent. advance on the prices accepted in 1849, when our foreign lords and masters had been engaged in '*overwhelming all foreign competition in times of great depression,*' and thus '*clearing the way for the whole trade to step in when prices revived, and to carry on a great business before foreign capital could again accumulate so as to be able to establish a competition in prices with any chance of success.*'

" Twice thus, at intervals, had you had low British prices and great American prosperity as a consequence of that policy under which American competition for the *sale* of iron had largely grown. Twice, at similar intervals, had you had high British prices and universal American depression as a consequence of the re-adoption of that system under which you had been compelled to compete in a foreign market for the *purchase* of British iron. Twice, thus, had you been ' brayed' in the British free trade mortar, and twice had our transporters found prosperity by aid of those protective measures to which you have always shown yourselves so much opposed. Your British free trade experience would seem thus to have been a somewhat sad one.

" Looking now around, we see *railroad stocks selling for a thousand millions that would not, ten years since, have sold for four hundred millions.* What has caused this wonderful change? The re-creation, by means of a protective tariff, of a great internal commerce, *and nothing else.* Under that tariff mines have been opened; mills and furnaces have been built; demand has been created for labor and labor's products; commerce has grown; and road proprietors have participated with farmers in the advantages resulting from the creation of that great domestic market to which we stand now indebted for the extraordinary fact, that whereas in the closing years of the last free trade period, 1858–60, with 31,000 miles of railroad, the tonnage had been less than 8,000,000, that of the past year has exceeded 16,000,000, the annual value, meanwhile, having so increased that whereas the money value of the 8,000,000 of former years had been less than $500,000,000, that of the 16,000,000 of the later ones has been no less than 1,723,000,000!

" The more, my friends, that you shall study these great facts, the more must you become satisfied that your present prosperity has resulted from the pursuit in recent years of a policy tending to make a home demand for the country's labor and the country's products, and to bring about that full development of our wonderful mineral wealth to which we are, and that at no distant period, to be indebted for *a perfect control of the commerce of the world.* To that end there remains, however, much that is yet to be done. Large as is now our own production you are still dependent on foreigners for hundreds of thousands of tons of rails, and other hundreds of thousands of tons of iron that *should* be made at home, and that long since *would* have been so made, had men like you, interested in roads, fully appreciated the fact that *rail road shares grow in value precisely as the domestic commerce grows, and decline in value precisely as that commerce declines.* Had they done so in the past they would long since have so volunteered to say, as now they ought to say, that regard for their own private interests, as well as for those of the nation at large, required of them to go hand in hand with those engaged in the great iron manufacture, giving to it such complete protection as would have the effect of satisfying other capitalists, abroad and at home, that they might safely proceed to the building, *here,* of other furnaces and other rolling mills, and to the development of the millions upon millions of acres in which coal and iron so much abound. So doing, you would be preparing for a scene of prosperity among yourselves the like of which the world till then had never seen, and would have the satisfaction of knowing that your own large profits were then resulting from the adoption of measures whose effect had been that of doubling the productive powers of our people, while giving to the State that industrial and political independence, without which it can never attain to that commanding position which would enable it to say to the rest of the family of nations that peace, and not war, must in the future be allowed to prevail throughout the world."

To all this you may, perhaps, object, that there is not to be found in it a single word in relation to the fancied troubles of men who use "boiler plate and tenpenny nails;" or to other of the little facts which occupy so large a space in your voluminous Report. Such certainly is the case, and for the reason that the man who is here supposed to have made this little speech had arrived at the reasonable conclusion that when mills and engines, villages and cities, increase rapidly in number and in size, the men who make machinery generally profit thence *the harmony of all the real and permanent interests of the various portions of society being so perfect as to leave no room for the petty discords which you have sought to place in such bold relief.*

Yours respectfully,

HENRY C. CAREY.

Hon. D. A. Wells.

Philadelphia, February 14, 1868.

LETTER TENTH.

Dear Sir:—

The protective policy looks to bringing the consumer to the side of the producer and thus relieving the farmer and the planter from the burthensome "tax" of transportation—that "tax" which takes precedence of all claims either of the landowner or the State. The more thoroughly those great objects can be accomplished the greater is the increase in money value of labor, land, and the products of both; the more does the laborer in the field tend to take his place side by side, in point of freedom and of compensation, with the skilled artisan of the workshop; the more does agriculture tend to become a science; the more fruitful becomes the field; the larger becomes the domestic commerce; the greater becomes the power to maintain a profitable foreign commerce; the greater is the ability of all to contribute to the public revenues; and the more rapid is the tendency towards a real national independence.

That such have been the results obtained under the protective system which now exists would seem to be proved by facts which you yourself have furnished as here presented:—

The Continued Increase in the Agricultural Product of the United States, whether measured by Quantity or Value. — The aggregate crops of the Northern States for 1867 were believed to be greater than those of any previous year, while the crops for the past year are known to exceed in quantity and quality those of 1867.

In the State of Ohio the recent increase of sheep, hogs, and cereals is reported as follows:—

Number of sheep in 1865 . . . 6,305,796   Number of sheep in 1868 . . . 7,580,000

In the eight years last past the sheep of Ohio are reported as having more than doubled.

Number of hogs in 1865 1,400,000   Number of hogs in 1868 2,100,000

Cereal crops, including wheat, corn, and oats:—

1865 . . 107,414,278 bush.   1866 . . 118,061,911 bush.   1868 . . 141,000,000 bush.

The commercial return of the number of hogs packed at the West since the season of 1864-5 is as follows:—

1865-66 1,705,955   1866-67 2,490,791   1867-68 2,781,084

This latter number was, however, exceeded during the first three years of the war.

The present ratio of the increase of the crop of Indian corn for the whole country is put by the best authorities at an average of three and one-half per cent. per annum. The crop of 1859 was returned by the census at 830,451,707 bushels, and, adopting the above ratio of increase, the crop of 1868, acknowledged to be a full one, must be estimated at 1,100,000,000 bushels, and if sold at the assumed low average of 46 cents per bushel, would net over $500,000,000.

As respects the agricultural products of the Southern States, the returns collected by the association of cotton manufacturers and planters before referred to, show that the crop of 1867-8 was at least 2,500,000 bales, or about 65 per cent. of the average crop for the five years immediately preceding the war; while for the year 1868-9 the estimates are generally in favor of 2,700,000 bales. The results of the two crops upon the interests of the South will, however, be materially different. During the crop year 1867-8 the South did not raise food sufficient for its own subsistence, and a large part of the proceeds of the cotton of that year were used for the purchase of food, and also to repay advances for the previous purchase of stock and implements. This year, 1868-9, the South has raised food in excess of its necessities, and the proceeds of nearly the entire crop may be considered in the light of a surplus for future development.

The following are the estimated cotton crops of the South since the termination of the war: 1865-66, 2,154,476 bales; 1866-67, 1,954,988 bales; 1867-68, 2,498,895 bales; 1868-69, estimated 2,700,000 bales.

The culture of rice at the South, which at the termination of the war practically amounted to nothing, has also so far been restored that the product of the present year is estimated at 70,000 tierces; an amount probably sufficient for home consumption, and giving certain promise of a speedy renewal of the former extensive exports of this article.

The following is an estimate of the tobacco crops of the United States since 1850, prepared by a committee of the trade for the Committee of Ways and Means, at the first session of the 40th Congress:—

1850 . . . . . 201,350,663 lbs.	1865 . . . . . 183,316,953 lbs.
1853 . . . . . 267,353,082 "	1866 . . . . . 325,000,000 "
1854 . . . . . 177,460,229 "	1867 . . . . . 250,000,000 "

Further proof of the beneficial effects of a protective policy are furnished in your own remarkable statement, that while the *quantity* of commodities carried by our railroads had increased in 1868, as compared with 1858, in the proportion of 9 to 4, their *money value* had grown in the proportion of no less than 14 to 4—the *four hundred and eighty-six millions* of annual value of the unhappy closing years of that free trade period which ended in the clouds and darkness of 1861, having given place to the *seventeen hundred and twenty-three millions* which represent the brilliant sunlight of protection in the year which has just now closed.

That protection has thus greatly improved the condition of both farmer and planter is a fact that you yourself have thus placed beyond the reach of question. In what manner, however, has it affected that of the mechanic and the laborer? Have *they* gained or lost under a policy that has thus tended to raise the price of food? To this question the answer is, that the status of the whole class of workingmen is fixed by that of the laborer in the field. The greater *his* reward, the greater is the attraction towards agriculture, and the larger must be the *bonus* offered by the workshop, a fact with which you yourself are so well acquainted that you have, in conversation with myself, presented it as an obstacle standing in the way of our industrial development. So far, however, is this from constituting any real obstruction, that it is in that direction, and that alone, we have to look for further progress. Freedom of the body and the mind—development of the moral and the intellectual faculties—grow with the growth of *competition for the purchase of labor.* That such competition now exists is proved by your own presentation of agricultural progress here now placed side by side with the industrial phenomena which you yourself have furnished; the two most happily combining for establishment of the great fact that there really *is* a perfect harmony of all real and permanent interests, and that the discords you have presented have no existence except in your own imagination.

"Within the last five years"—years of protection, as you have omitted to advise your readers—

"more cotton spindles have been put in operation, more iron furnaces erected, more iron smelted, more bars rolled, more steel made, more coal and copper mined, more lumber sawed and hewn, more houses and shops constructed, more manufactories of different kinds started, and more petroleum collected, refined, and exported, than during any equal period in the history of the country; and this increase has been greater both as regards quality and quantity, and greater than the legitimate increase to be expected from the normal increase of wealth and population."

Competition for the purchase of labor having thus wonderfully increased, there *should* have been a great improvement in the condition of the whole body of the people who had that commodity to sell. The reverse of this, however, as you assure us, is the fact, the actual condition of workingmen at the moment when so many mills, houses, and factories are being built, so many roads are being made, and so many farms are being cleared, being really worse than it had been in the closing years of the last destructive free trade period, when mills and mines stood closed; when furnaces were out of blast; when machine-shops were idle; when houses everywhere stood untenanted; when laborers by tens and hundreds of thousands were wholly without employment; when manufacturers and merchants alike were being bankrupted; and when the sources of public revenue had so greatly failed that to meet the public expenditure, trivial as by comparison it then had been, there had existed a necessity for creating in three short years a public debt of $70,000,000.

Strange as such an "assertion" would seem to be, still more strange are the facts by means of which this great "historical truth" is sought to be established, tables being given by means of which it is now clearly proved, that whereas it costs weekly the large sum of $17 to maintain two parents and *one* child, the same parents and *six* children can be as well provided for at the much smaller cost of $13 50! When, however, a *seventh* child comes to be added, the cost of the family at once almost doubles, the $13 50 forthwith rising to $25! "Assertions" such as these can, excuse me for saying it, be no otherwise regarded than as supremely ridiculous, finding their parallel only in the efforts of British economists to prove that labor is always best paid at that period in the progress of society when population is small and employment, as we know, only occasional, presenting in proof thereof the *harvest* wages of the middle ages, and comparing *them* with the price of wheat, then a luxury that the laborer never tasted!

2. Turning now to another part of your Report, we find evidence counter to all this in the following passage, in which the italics are my own, to wit:—

"But whatever may be the force of specific examples, it is equally certain that a consideration of the whole subject will show that no material reduction of importations—certainly none proportionate to the means employed—can be effected through any practicable increase of the existing tariff. This will appear evident when we refleot, that the articles which constitute a very considerable part of the value of importations are not articles of strict luxury, which can be dispensed with at will, but *articles whose consumption the people will not relinquish except upon the pressure of extreme poverty or necessity;* or others which are absolutely essential to the continuance of great branches of domestic industry. Thus, for example, *the four articles of tea, coffee, sugar, and molasses, constituted nearly one-third of the net value of the imports for the fiscal year 1867–68,* exclusive of bullion and specie. Their consumption, moreover, is *not only constantly and rapidly increasing with every increase of wealth and population,* but the whole drift of popular sentiment is unmistakably inclined to favor a much larger importation through a reduction of the existing tariff. Another large class of articles, as the various dye-woods and dye materials, crude India-rubber, soda-ash, bleaching powders, guano, lumber, sulphur, hides and horns, hatters furs, ivory, raw silk, gums, rags, jute, saltpetre, tin, &c., are so essentially the raw materials of great branches of domestic industry, that while any interruption of their importation could only be attained at the expense of national decadence, an increased importation would infallibly indicate an increase of national prosperity. *On these two classes of articles alone, the increase in the value of imports growing out of perfectly legitimate and natural causes, will probably be sufficient during the next three years, to fully counterbalance any reduction in the value of imports which might be effected through any changes which it would be possible to make in the tariff in respect to all other articles of foreign growth and importation.* Thus, for example, the increase in the consumption of imported sugars for the year 1868 is reported as full *sixteen per cent.* above the consumption of the preceding year, while *for the year 1869 an increase of at least ten per cent. is anticipated.*"

To all this you might, as it seems to me, very properly have added, that our consumption of cotton which had grown in the free trade years 1835–42 and 1848–60, at the rate of but *ten thousand bales per annum,* has grown in the last four years at the rate of *eighty-five thousand,* and promises soon to exhibit *an annual increase equal to the whole hundred and seventy thousand of the* NINETEEN *years in which we were so busily engaged in the effort at building up a little foreign commerce on the ruins of a great domestic one.* Again, you might have told your constituents that for every yard of woolen cloth that had been used in the closing years of the last unhappy free trade period, we were now consuming two or more; that of iron applied to the production of stoves, ploughs, harrows, "tenpenny nails, boilers," or other machinery by means of which labor was to be lightened, or comfort increased, our consumption had already doubled and promised soon to be more than trebled; and so you might, as I think, have said in relation to all commodities required for promoting the convenience, comfort, or enjoyment of life.

Who, now, are the people whose consumption has so much increased? Are they to be found among the rich? Shall we look for them among the men of "fixed incomes," whose deteriorated condition you so much deplore? Do you, yourself, know any single man belonging to those classes of society who finds himself led to consuming more sugar, tea, coffee, cotton or woolen cloth, than he had done before? It is safe, as I think, to say that you could scarcely name even a single one. Where then shall they be sought? Is it not among farmers the prices of whose land and labor have been so much increased by reason of having the market brought nearer to the place at which the food is being produced? Is it not among laboring men who are building dwellings for themselves where before they had had no means with which to pay the mere rent of buildings owned by others? Is it not among the mechanics who now so largely increase their deposits in our saving-funds as preparatory to the purchase of houses; or, as the means of securing to their children and themselves support in case of accident? Is it not among thousands and tens of thousands of the gentler sex, the demand for whose services is now so great that, as you have yourself informed me, they find themselves enabled in the summer season to withdraw from work and seek a little mountain or sea-side recreation?

For answer to all this you tell us, that the farmer receives too much money for his corn and his pork; the woodchopper too much for his lumber; the miner too much for his coal; the furnace man too much for his iron; and that, as a necessary consequence, we are unable to send shoes, cars, and other finished commodities, abroad to be exchanged for wool, hides, and gutta percha. As a remedy we must, as you think, look to Canada for food and lumber; to Nova Scotia for coal; to Britain for coal and iron; thereby diminishing demand for the country's labor, and greatly diminishing its now, as you think, excessive money value.

Why, however, have you here *suppressed* the figures required for proving the truth of such "assertions"? Why is it, that you have failed to tell your constituents that, exclusive of flour, butter, cheese, lard, oils, metals, and other partially manufactured articles, those which now represent our export of manufactures are *nearly double* those of the *brilliant* closing years of the last free trade period, having risen from an average of $40,000,000, to over $78,000,000 for 1867 and 1868?

Why, I here repeat the question, have these important facts been so wholly suppressed? Is it for the reason that they alone furnish so complete a refutation of your free trade arguments?

Leaving you now to study these questions and to reflect how far the answers they must command can be made to harmonize with your "assertions," I propose to proceed now to an inquiry as to the influence exercised by protection on the one hand, British free trade on the other, on the important question of immigration.

Yours respectfully,
HENRY C. CAREY.

Hon. D. A. Wells.

Philadelphia, February 15, 1869.

LETTER ELEVENTH.

Dear Sir:—

All commodities tend to go *from* those places at which supply is in excess of demand and prices are low, *to* those at which, demand being in excess of supply, prices are high. None tend to leave these latter to go toward the former. So, too, is it with labor power, all men desiring to place themselves where compensation is high, and none desiring to leave such places to go to those in which wages are low. Such being the case, we may, perhaps, find in an examination of *the immigration question* means for determining as to how the condition of miners, mechanics, and working men generally, had been affected by "legislation:" whether it had improved under protection on one hand, or British free trade on the other. In making this inquiry it is needed to observe that it is not until the third year after a change of policy has been made that its effects, upward or downward, begin to make themselves seriously manifest in reference to this important question, increase or diminution of demand for labor going on gradually at home for a year or two, still another being then required for enabling knowledge of this change to make its way among those poor and uninstructed classes of Europe from among whom we have to look for supplies of men.

The protective tariff of 1829 had but fairly commenced to do its work in 1831, and it was not until 1832 that its effects exhibited themselves in the arrival of 45,000 persons, being fourfold the average of the decade through which the country just then had passed. Thenceforth the figures show an almost regular rise, as follows: 1833, 56,000; 1834, 65,000; 1835, 53,000; 1836, 62,000; 1837, 78,000; giving a total of 359,000 resulting from six years of protection, against 140,000 for the ten British free trade and semi-protective years by which that tariff had been preceded, and an average annual increase of nearly 46,000.

Of all machinery the most valuable is that of a well-grown man. To produce such a machine involves an average expenditure in food, clothing, and shelter, of not less than $1000. When made, it is capable of doubling, trebling, and quadrupling itself, not only in numbers, but in mental power, becoming thus more and more valuable from year to year; whereas, machines of wood or iron decay, become antiquated, and gradually pass from use. The *free gift* by Europe, annually, of these 46,000 human engines may therefore be regarded as having been of greater value to the country than would have been that of $46,000,000 of machinery of any other kind, and as showing a gain, in this direction alone, *resulting from protection*, of $276,000,000.

From and after 1837 the movement was irregular, but the general result, to and including 1844, showed a diminution, the average having been but 75,000.

Why was this? Simply, because British free trade had not only prevented increase of mills, furnaces, and other industrial establishments, but had to so great an extent closed those previously existing that our streets had become filled with men who asked for alms because they could not be allowed to work; and because thousands and tens of thousands, disappointed and disheartened, had returned to their early homes, prepared to teach their countrymen that starvation there was preferable to the starvation that here awaited them. One such man sufficed to stop the emigration of extensive neighborhoods.

Counter news arriving in 1844, and men learning everywhere how great, under the protective system of 1842, had here become the demand for labor, and how liberal its reward, we find the arrivals now running up from the 74,000 of 1844 to 102,000 in 1845; 147,000 in 1846; 240,000 in 1847; 229,000 in 1848; and 300,000 in 1849, giving a total of 1,018,000 in the five years which followed the commencement of the movement, against one of less than 400,000 in the five by which that movement had been preceded—giving a gain under protection of more than $600,000,000.

Had the tariff of 1828 been allowed to continue in existence, the tendency throughout the succeeding twenty years would certainly have been regularly upward, giving us, at the close of that period, at the smallest calculation, an immigration exceeding by millions that which actually did take place; and all these people would, from the moment of their arrival, have been customers to our farmers, making a market for food thrice greater than that afforded by the whole of Europe. Prosperity would then have reigned throughout the land, and we should have avoided the need for a general bankrupt law on one hand, while on the other, we should have escaped being compelled to send to Europe commissioners instructed to borrow, at almost any rate of interest, money for the public use, as the sole remaining means of avoiding public bankruptcy on the other.

Estimating at but $1000 per head the invaluable machinery of production thus shut out by the Carolinian tariff, we have here a *a loss that counts by thousands of millions*, to be added to those already exhibited as having resulted from failure to appreciate the fact that domestic commerce constitutes the basis on which a foreign commerce must rest, and that any attempt at building up this latter on the ruins of the former must end in utter failure.

The gain in this direction, under the tariff of 1842, having been $600,000,000, we have that amount of capital, in excess of previous years, added to our resources; that capital, too, multiplying itself so rapidly as at the close of another decade to have stood at twice the amount imported. Parents and children demanding food, while yet producing none, the market is thus brought home to the farmer, enabling him and his to treble, in this protective period, their consumption of cotton and of iron, while making such demand for tea, sugar, coffee, and other commodities as greatly to augment the public revenue.

2. California treasures being now brought to light and gold becoming most abundant, the new El Dorado attracts hosts of foreigners until in 1854 we find the immigration to have numbered more than 400,000. Thenceforth, however, a change is seen, gold going out by hundreds of millions to pay for labor employed abroad, and Europeans abstaining from emigration to a country in which mines were ceasing to be opened, furnaces ceasing to be built; and to which iron by hundreds of thousands of tons was being sent to be here exchanged for the precious metals. What was the double movement then performed is shown in the following figures :—

	Gold exported.	Immigration.	Diminution as compared with 1849.
1858	33,000,000	123,000	176,000
1859	57,000,000	119,000	181,000
1860	58,000,000	150,000	150,000
1861	30,000,000	89,000	211,000
1862	37,000,000	89,000	211,000
	215,000,000	570,000	929,000

The loss, as here exhibited, of the closing years of the British free trade period, as compared with the closing one of the brilliant period of the tariff of 1842, at $1000 a head, is $929,000,000, but were I here to add the great numbers who then re-emigrated, it would exceed $1,000,000,000.

No one, as I think, can study these facts without arriving at the conclusion that if the tariff of 1842 had been allowed to stand, we should in the decade preceding the rebellion have imported 2,000,000 more of people ; produced several millions more of children ; made millions upon millions more of iron; carried up our consumption of cotton to more than half the crop; quadrupled the money value of the land and labor of the country ; carried the slave rapidly onward towards freedom; and attained for the nation that political independence which has in all other countries grown with the growth of industrial independence. Abandoning that system and crippling our domestic commerce, a thousand millions were expended in the effort to obtain means of transportation from the valley of the Mississippi to the little and worthless markets of Liverpool and Havre, the result exhibiting itself in a diminution of productive power so great as to have necessitated large creation of both private and public debt; in a growth of slave power so great as to have led to the rebellion; and in a general weakness so extreme as to have caused the national existence to become dependent on the will of the governments of France and England.

Such had been the price at which we had acquired that great foreign commerce in which little short of $300,000,000 of capital, in the form of ships, had been required for carrying to the manufacturing nations of Europe that annual $300,000,000 of rude products to which, under the tariff of 1842, would have been given a value of *twice a thousand millions to be sent to all the various countries of the outside world, thereby giving us a commerce that would have been productive of strength and not of weakness.*

The larger the immigration the greater is the tendency to have the cost of transportation divided between the inward and outward cargoes, men being returned on the cotton ships. Under the tariff of 1842 the tendency was in the direction of substituting the import of men for that of iron, and thus throwing the "tax" of transportation upon other nations. Under those of 1846 and 1857 we substituted an import of cloth and iron for one of men, paying the "tax" ourselves, thereby impoverishing our people while enriching traders who have since rejoiced at our troubles, and who now regret the "Cause" that has been "lost," well knowing it to have been the British free trade one.

Having studied these facts, and that they *are* facts you know as well as I, you may, perhaps, be disposed to reconsider your "assertion" as to the influence on the past that has been exerted by "legislation."

3. Long continuance of the exhaustive process above described had been productive of almost universal discord, as a consequence of which we have now to enter upon a period of civil war, in the course of which hundreds of thousands of lives and thousands of millions of money are required as offerings on the altars of British free trade. Happily, the distress of the closing years of the anti-protective policy had, before the breaking out of the rebellion, compelled return to that system to which, in the few brief years from 1829 to 1835, and from 1842 to 1847, we had been indebted for *the whole* increase of our iron production; and for *nearly the whole* of that of cotton. Happily for us, mines had been opened, furnaces and mills had been constructed in the North. Happily for us, the South had persistently refused to avail itself of the wonderful mineral resources of Virginia, Tennessee, the Carolinas, and Alabama, as well as of its extraordinary advantages for the production of cotton cloth. Still more happily, British iron-masters and the British people generally, were led to hail the rebellion as a free trade revolution, and refused to give us credit, thereby throwing us on our own resources, and compelling us to do that which we should long before have done—LOOK AT HOME. Thenceforth, therefore, mines and mills were rapidly re-opened; houses and mills were built; and there was again created a demand for labor the like of that which had been seen in the years of the tariffs of 1828 and 1842, the result exhibiting itself in an immigration that in lieu of the 89,000 of the closing years of the British free trade period, has given the following figures, to wit, 1863, 174,000; 1864, 176,000; 1865, 248,000; 1866, 314,000; 1867, 312,000; 1868 (estimated), 300,000; total in six years, 1,524,000.

Large as is even this quantity, it presents by no means the increase that really has taken place. The arrivals from Canada, and through the St. Lawrence from Europe, have been so numerous that by their help annual average of 300,000, and exceeding by more than 200,000 that of the closing year of the British free trade period. The gain in this direction alone, compared with the same number of free trade years, is very moderately estimated at $1,200,000,000; or more than half that public debt which has resulted from blind pursuit of a British free trade policy, and with which we now are burthened.

This *excess* of $1,200,000,000 has been *presented to us in free gift*, and for the reason that we have now manifested some little determination to make at hóme the iron and the cloth required for domestic use. To that capital, and to that determination, we stand now indebted for the facts thus furnished by yourself, here once again presented for your careful consideration:—

"That within the last five years more cotton spindles have been put in operation, more iron furnaces erected, more iron smelted, more bars rolled, more steel made, more coal and copper mined, more lumber sawed and hewn, more houses and shops constructed, more manufactories of different kinds started, and more petroleum collected, refined, and exported, than during any equal period in the history of the country ; and that this increase has been greater both as regards quality and quantity, and greater than the legitimate increase to be expected from the normal increase of wealth and population."

4. The facts thus presented throw more light on the question you have ventured to discuss than any others that could be mentioned, and yet, your only reference to this most important subject, in the summary intended for general circulation, is in the words that follow, to wit:—

"Increase in immigration, 1840, 84,000; in 1845, 174,000; in 1850, 310,000, in 1854, 427,000."

You here *suppress* the facts, that taking the average of the free trade years of which 1840 had been a part, there had been a decrease and *not* an increase; that 1845 had been but the first year of recovery, in this direction, from the horrors of 1842; that thenceforward, under protection, the movement had been steadily upward, having already reached 240,000, so early as 1847 ; that the growth from 1850 to 1854 had been simply a result of the discovery of a new *El Dorado ;* that thenceforward there had been a decline until in the closing years of the free trade period it had fallen below a single hundred thousand ; and finally, that since the re-adoption of protection the growth had been so rapid as to warrant the idea that, but for the disturbing movements of the Treasury throughout the last three years, it would before this time have reached half a million, making an annual addition to our capital of more than $500,000,000.

Why is it that facts so important have been thus *suppressed ?* Why is it that you, a public officer, charged with most important duties, have so misrepresented the general movement? The answer to these questions is, as it appears to me, that if you had given all as they really had occurred, it would have been quite impossible for you to venture the "assertion" contained in the following paragraph of your Report here once more reproduced for your consideration:—

"There does not seem to be any reliable evidence which can be adduced to show that the change which took place in the legislative commercial policy of the country in 1846 had any permanent or marked effect whatever; while, on the other hand, the study of all the facts pertaining to national development from 1840 to 1860, and from 1865 to the present time, unmistakably teaches this lesson ; that the progress of the country through what we may term the strength of its elements of vitality is independent of legislation and even of the impoverishment and waste of a great war. Like one of our own mighty rivers, its movement is beyond control. Successive

years, like successive affluents, only add to and increase its volume while legislative enactments and conflicting commercial policies, like the construction of piers
and the deposit of sunken wrecks, simply deflect the current or constitute temporary
obstructions. In fact, if the nation has not yet been lifted to the full comprehension
of its own work, it builds determinately, as it were, by instinct."

Leaving you to reflect upon this suggestion, I shall proceed to an examination of the *Revenue Question.*

Yours, respectfully,
HENRY C. CAREY.

HON. D. A. WELLS.

PHILADELPHIA, February 18, 1869

LETTER TWELFTH.

DEAR SIR :—

The few facts in regard to the *Revenue Question* given in your Report
are in the few words that follow, to wit :—

"Increase in the public revenue: 1840, $19,000,000 ; 1845, $29,000,000 ; 1850,
$52,000,000 ; 1855, $74,000,000."

The regular advance that is here, by aid of selected facts, exhibited
is very beautiful, and would seem to furnish proof of your "assertion"
that "the progress of the country through what may be termed the
strength of its elements of vitality is independent of legislation." To
what extent the whole mass of facts tends in that direction it is proposed
now to examine, commencing with that first British free trade period
which so closely followed the conclusion of the peace of Ghent in 1815.

The war had stimulated the growth of manufactures, and to so great
extent as to have warranted a belief that the day of industrial independence was then already near at hand. But little later, however, there
came a "legislation" whose result was that of closing everywhere mills,
mines, and factories; destroying the domestic market for food, cotton,
wool, and all other of the rude products of agriculture; involving in
one common ruin farmers, manufacturers, and mechanics; and causing
a large portion of the real estate of the country to change owners under
the sheriff's hammer. Customs duties which in 1817 had yielded $26,-
000,000, gradually declined until, in 1821, their product had fallen to
but $13,000,000; the average of the three years that followed having been
but $18,000,000. As a natural consequence of this, "receipts from loans
and treasury notes," figured once again conspicuously in our finance
reports, $8,000,000 having been borrowed in 1820–21, and $10,000,000 in
the closing free trade years, 1824–25.

Under the semi-protective tariff of 1824 we find a change, labor coming once again into quick demand, and the increased power of our people
to contribute to the Treasury needs now carrying up the customs revenue
to $23,000,000, being nearly a third more than the amount then just
before yielded by its free trade predecessor. With 1828, however, came
real protection, and with it evidence of *a perfect harmony in the interests
of the people and the State,* customs receipts growing steadily until in
1832 they had reached the enormous amount of $28,000,000, bringing
therewith an absolute necessity for measures calculated to diminish

peting with our domestic products, were then released from duty,
proof thus being furnished of the perfect truth of the doctrine that
to efficient protection it is we are to look as the only road by which
to reach an entire freedom of external commerce.

Large as had been the reduction thus made the revenue still continued
to increase, the receipts from customs for 1833 having attained the figures of $29,000,000, bringing therewith a necessity for depleting the Trea-
sury by means of payment, at par, of that only portion of the public
debt which still remained, to wit, that held in Holland, amounting to
many millions, on which the interest had been only three per cent.

That protective "legislation" had thus proved itself capable of furnishing the road to financial independence for both the people and the
State, and that it had greatly benefited every portion of the community,
is shown in the following passage from a speech of Mr. Clay, of February, 1832, the perfect truth of every word of which must be admitted
by all now living who had had occasion to witness, as I myself did,
the marvellous change then accomplished by a few short pages of that
" legislation" which you now profess to regard as being of so very slight
importance :—

" Eight years ago, it was my painful duty to present to the other House of Congress
an unexaggerated picture of the general distress prevading the whole land. We
must all yet remember some of its frightful features. We all know that the people
were then oppressed and borne down by an enormous load of debt ; that the value
of property was at the lowest point of depression ; that ruinous sales and sacrifices
were everywhere made of real estate ; that stop-laws and relief laws, and paper
money, were adopted to save the people from impending destruction ; that a deficit
in the public revenue existed, which compelled Government to seize upon, and divert
from its legitimate object, the appropriations to the sinking fund to redeem the national debt ; and that our commerce and navigation were threatened with a complete
paralysis. *In short, sir, if I were to select any term of seven years since the adoption of
the present Constitution which exhibited a scene of the most wide-spread dismay and desolation, it would be exactly that term of seven years which immediately preceded the establishment of the tariff of* 1824.

" I have now to perform the more pleasing task of exhibiting an imperfect sketch
•of the existing state of the unparalleled prosperity of the country. On a general
survey, we behold cultivation extended, the arts flourishing, the face of the country
improved, our people fully and profitably employed, and the public countenance exhibiting tranquillity, contentment, and happiness. And if we descend into particulars, we have the agreeable contemplation of a people out of debt ; land rising slowly in value, but in a secure and salutary degree ; a ready though not extravagant
market for all the surplus productions of our industry ; innumerable flocks and herds
browsing and gamboling on ten thousand hills and plains covered with rich and
verdant grasses ; our cities expanded, and whole villages springing up, as it were, by
enchantment ; our tonnage, foreign and coastwise, swelling and fully occupied ; the
rivers of our interior animated by the perpetual thunder and lightning of countless
steamboats ; the currency sound and abundant ; the public debt of two wars nearly
redeemed ; and, to crown all, the public treasury overflowing, embarrassing Congress
not to find subjects of taxation, but to select the objects which shall be liberated
from the impost. *If the term of seven years were to be selected, of the greatest prosperi'y
which this people have enjoyed since the establishment of their present Constitution, it would
be exactly that period of seven years which immediately followed the passage of the tariff
of* 1824.

" This transformation of the condition of the country from gloom and distress to
brightness and prosperity, *has been mainly the work of American legislation fostering
American industry, instead of allowing it to be controlled by foreign legislation, cherishing
foreign industry.* The foes of the American system, in 1824, with great boldness and
confidence, predicted, first, the ruin of the public revenue, and the creation of a necessity to resort to direct taxation ; the gentleman from South Carolina (Gen. Hayne),
I believe, thought that the tariff of 1824 would operate a reduction of revenue to the
large amount of eight millions of dollars ; secondly, the destruction of our navigation ; thirdly, the desolation of commercial cities ; and fourthly, the augmentation

of the price of objects of consumption, and further decline in that of the articles of our exports. Every prediction which they made has failed, utterly failed. *Instead of the ruin of the public revenue with which they then sought to deter us from the adoption of the American system, we are now threatened with its subversion by the vast amount of the public revenue produced by that system.* As to the desolation of our cities, let us take as an example, the condition of the largest and most commercial of all of them, the great northern capital. I have, in my hands, the assessed value of real estate in the city of New York, from 1817 to 1831. This value is canvassed, contested, scrutinized, and adjudged, by the proper sworn authorities. It is, therefore, entitled to full credence. During the first term, commencing with 1817 and ending in the year of the passage of the tariff of 1824, the amount of the value of real estate was, the first year, $57,790,435, and after various fluctuations in the intermediate period, it settled down at $52,019,730, exhibiting a decrease in seven years of $5,779,705. During the first year of 1825, after the passage of the tariff, it rose, and gradually ascending throughout the whole of the latter period of seven years, it finally, in 1831, reached the astonishing height of $95,716,485! Now, if it be said that this rapid growth of the city of New York was the effect of foreign commerce, then it was not correctly predicted, in 1824, that the tariff would destroy foreign commerce and desolate our commercial cities. If, on the contrary, it be the effect of internal trade, then internal trade cannot be justly chargeable with the evil consequences imputed to it. The truth is, it is the joint effect of both principles, *the domestic industry nourishing the foreign trade, and the foreign commerce in turn nourishing the domestic industry.* Nowhere more than in New York is the combination of both principles so completely developed."

2. Passing now to the Carolinian compromise tariff of 1833, we enter on a scene of discord the precise parallel of that presented by the free trade period which had found its close in 1824. As on that occasion, the public revenue was for a brief period in excess of the expenditure, but passing onward we find receipts from customs gradually decreasing as the domestic commerce died away, until in 1840 they had fallen to the half of those of 1832, "receipts from loans and Treasury notes" meanwhile gradually making their appearance, until for 1841 they had reached the sum of $14,000,000. Adding this to similar receipts in the four previous years we obtain a total of $52,000,000 as the then amount of public debt; yet trifling as it was, the public credit had now so entirely disappeared as to make it necessary, as has before been stated, to send to Europe Messrs. Macalester and Robinson as Commissioners, empowered there to negotiate a loan to the paltry extent of ten or a dozen millions. Trifling as was the amount—less, as I think, than that of the three per cent. debt paid off some years before, and paid by means of efficient protective "legislation"—so entirely had prostration of our domestic commerce destroyed confidence abroad and at home that those gentlemen, after knocking at the doors of all the principal banking houses of Europe, returned without having obtained even a single dollar. General bankruptcy of the people and bankruptcy of the Treasury had thus resulted from but little more than half a dozen years pursuit of the policy now so strongly urged upon us by Manchester and Glasgow manufacturers; by those British iron-masters to whom we have in the past been so much indebted for that "warfare" by means of which "a few of the most wealthy capitalists" have been enabled to "destroy foreign competition and to gain and keep possession of foreign markets;" and by that whole British nation of which we are now claiming satisfaction for depredations committed on the ocean, a fair estimate of which would be twice greater than the annual amount, at the close of the last British free trade period, of that foreign trade at whose altar we had made a sacrifice of domestic commerce to such extent that it would even then have counted by thousands of millions.

The revenue having so far failed in 1841 Congress found itself compelled in that year to restore the list of duty-paying articles tea, coffee, and many other commodities that had been freed in 1832, thereby furnishing proof conclusive that the road to real freedom of trade was *not* to be found in the direction of importing cloth, iron, and other articles for whose production our soil and climate, and the genius of our people, had so well been suited. So entire, however, was the depression, so universal was then the waste of labor power, and so great the general poverty of our people, that even with this addition the customs yielded but $18,000,000 against the $29,000,000 of 1833, although population had fully a third increased. Such having been the case, Congress now found it necessary to give to the country that beneficent tariff of 1842 under which external commerce sprang once again into life, filling the Treasury, the great domestic commerce meanwhile making prompt demand for all that labor power of which the waste in the few preceding years had counted by thousands of millions of dollars.

How this great measure was received by your present friend, the *Evening Post*, and what were the predictions of its editors as to its effect upon the people and the public revenue, are shown in the fact that immediately upon its passage, they assured their readers that it would "annihilate all commerce;" that it would not be "allowed to subsist a single year;" that the wants of the revenue "would require its repeal;" that it was "a black tariff;" that it would "impoverish the laborer," "oppress the consumer," and "tax all classes" but those favored ones who, as you yourself now say of the lumber men, the pig-iron men, and others, were to profit by "restraining the importations and reducing the revenue."

How much of truth there was in all this is shown in the fact that the customs revenue of 1843, '44, and of the remaining protective years, proved to be nearly twice greater than had been that of the free trade of 1841, such having been the result of a protective policy by means of which our people had been enabled to use their own home-made cloth and iron, and to sell their own labor, thereby acquiring the means with which to pay for sugar, tea, coffee, and other products of distant countries. Search the history of the world and you can find no parallel, except perhaps in the one above so well described by Mr. Clay, to the marvellous change that had been then effected by a little "legislation."

3. The country was, however, for our British friends, entirely *too* prosperous. It was becoming industrially and politically independent, and that did not suit the views of the great "capitalists" who so long had been accustomed to "destroy foreign competition." Neither did it suit that great Slave Power which so long had been accustomed to look to the West for supplies of food. The greater the product of iron the less would become the need for sending corn, pork, and flour to the South, to be there, by means of slave labor, converted into cotton. Hence arose the fact that that great measure of independence, the admirable tariff of 1842, was, like its predecessor of 1828, and like it at the close of but four years of existence, superseded by that pro-slavery and British free trade measure of 1846 to which we stand to-day indebted for all the horrors of the late rebellion.

This, of course, was hailed as *a real revenue measure*. Protection had tended, as we were assured, to destroy the revenue, and therefore had protection been itself destroyed. For the moment, as before in 1836, the revenue *did really* increase, and in aid of such increase came now the great discovery of California treasures, making large demand for labor, and for the moment carrying up immigration to the extraordinary extent of 400,000. That point passed, however, we speedily arrive at a repetition of the ruin of all previous free-trade periods, 1857–60 giving the same decline of custom revenues, and same need for loans. that had been witnessed in 1840–42; as that before had given a second edition of the private and public bankruptcy of 1818–23.

The average customs revenue of these four years was $45,000,000, exceeding by little more than fifty per cent. that of the closing years of the tariff of 1828. That of the final year, when the paralysis had scarcely as yet commenced to do its work, was but $39,000,000, exceeding that of 1833 by but about *thirty-five per cent.*; population meanwhile having grown from less than fourteen to nearly thirty-three millions, giving an increase of *a hundred and twenty per cent.*

Protection being restored in 1861, the domestic commerce again, as in 1830–33, and as in 1843–48, revived, bringing with it great power for contribution to the customs revenue. As a consequence of this we find this latter to have grown *almost four hundred per cent.*, population meanwhile having increased but *twenty-five per cent.* Which now, I pray you, is THE REAL REVENUE TARIFF? That one which destroys the domestic commerce, or that which, by stimulating that commerce and with it the demand for labor, enables all to consume, or use, more largely of tea, coffee, sugar, cottons, woolens, " tenpenny nails, boilers," steam engines, houses, railroad cars, and all other things tending to promote the convenience and comfort of life?

4. Leaving you to reflect upon this important question, I now turn once again to the exhibit of public revenue presented in your Report, copied in the outset of this present letter. Turn to it yourself, I pray you, and then, if you can, give to your constituents answers to the questions that will be now propounded, as follows : —

Why is it that you have *suppressed* the fact that the customs of the, so-called, revenue tariff year 1840, had been *less* than those of the closing years of the protective period 1828–33, by more than thirty per cent., the population having meantime more than twenty-five per cent. *increased*?

Why have you *suppressed* the decline of customs revenue in the free trade years that had followed your *selected* year 1840 ?

Why have you *suppressed* the fact that the growth of 1855 resulted wholly from large receipts of California gold ?

Why have you totally *suppressed* the calamitous free trade years that followed 1855—saying not a word of that unhappy closing year 1860, elsewhere so frequently referred to ?

Why is it that you have said nothing of that poverty of the Treasury which had made it necessary to borrow more than $70,000,000 in the three years of profound peace which ended June 30, 1860, and therefore preceded all apprehension of civil war ?

Why is it that the closing years of *every* anti-protective tariff have exhibited scenes of public and private bankruptcy and ruin ?

Why is it that the closing years of all former protective tariffs have exhibited scenes of prosperity corresponding so precisely with those now furnished by yourself, the result of the protective policy now existing ?

Why was it—if, as you assert, " a tariff *is* a tax—that the protective tariff of 1828 so increased the revenue as to render necessary the absolute enfranchisement of tea, coffee, and many other articles, from payment of any " tax" whatsoever ?

Why was it that the anti-protective tariff of 1832 so decreased the revenue as to render necessary the re-imposition of all such taxes ?

Why is it that among the disagreeable bequests of the anti-protective tariffs of 1846 and 1857 is to be found a necessity for now raising annually hundreds of millions of revenue by means of "taxes" upon so many articles produced at home and needed for the convenience and comfort of life?

Why is it that your Report is in all respects so precisely in accordance with the views and wishes of those great British "capitalists" who are accustomed, "in their efforts to gain and keep foreign markets," to distribute money so very freely among those of our people who are supposed to be possessed of power to influence public opinion?

Leaving you to reflect on all these questions, I remain,

Yours respectfully,

HENRY C. CAREY.

Hon. D. A. Wells.

Philadelphia, February 18, 1869.

CONCLUSION.

Dear Sir:—

You have advised your constituents that—

"As respects the relation of legislation by the national government to the results under consideration, if we except the adoption of a liberal policy in the disposition of the public lands, it is difficult, at least for the period which elapsed between 1840 and 1860, to affirm much that is positive, unless, in conformity with the maxim, that that government is best which governs least, absence of legislation is to be regarded in the light of a positive good. If important results followed the acquisition of California, such results were certainly neither foreseen nor anticipated, while as regards commercial legislation, a review of all the facts cannot fail to suggest a doubt whether the evils which have resulted from instability have not far more than counterbalanced any advantage that may have proceeded from the experience of a fluctuating policy."

That fluctuations of policy are to be avoided is very certain, but what, I beg to ask, are those of which you have now been led to speak? Are they to be found in the changes forced upon us in 1824, '28, '42, and '61, by the almost universal ruin, public and private, of the closing years of those British free trade periods which commenced in 1817, in 1835, and in 1846? Are they not rather to be found in those several *abandonments of American policy* which led to the ruin of 1820, '23, of 1841, '42, of 1857, '61? To one of those systems of policy, the one American, the other British, you here object, but to which of them you are thus opposed you do not clearly state. Which is it? Are you in future to stand before the world as advocate of the great British capitalists who would compel our farmers to make all their exchanges in Liverpool; or of the farmer himself who seeks to have the market brought so near to home as to enable him to free his land and himself from that terrific "tax" of transportation by means of which he, in the past, has been so nearly ruined? We have here a very important question, and that you may be enabled to answer it with satisfaction to yourself, I propose now to furnish "a review of all the facts" that have thus far been developed, to wit:—

British free trade almost crushed out the great iron manufacture in the period from 1817 to '24; paralyzed it in that from 1835 to '42; and did the same in that from '48 to '60.

American freedom of commerce, resulting from protection against the "warfare" of British "capitalists," more than trebled the iron production from 1824 to '33; did the same from 1842 to '48; and has doubled it since 1861.

British free trade never permanently added a single ton to the iron production in the whole thirty years of its existence.

American freedom of commerce has added 1,500,000 tons in the less than twenty years that the country has been ruled by the tariffs of 1828, '42, and '61.

British free trade closed the cotton mills that had been brought into existence during the war for freedom of navigation, and for sailors' rights, which commenced in 1807 and found its close in 1815. It wholly arrested progress in the period which closed in 1842; and almost wholly in that which ended in '60; doing this in despite of that great discovery of California treasures by means of which the cotton manufacture should have trebled.

American freedom of commerce doubled the cotton consumption in the period ending in '33. It almost trebled it in that ending in 1847–8. It has added fifty per cent. thereto in the last four years, and promises soon to exhibit an increase so great as to make a home demand for half the crop.

British free trade prevented the growth of either the iron or cotton manufacture in the South, and thus prevented that diversification of employments which would peacefully and profitably have given freedom to the slave, while increasing tenfold the value of land.

American freedom of commerce gave to the South a cotton manufacture that in 1847 was of the highest promise. It now proposes to give to it every variety of manufacture, thereby greatly aiding the cause of freedom, while largely increasing the fortunes of those who own the land.

British free trade bankrupted merchants and manufacturers, and filled our cities with paupers in 1820, 1842, and 1860.

American freedom of commerce gave prosperity to merchants and manufacturers, and profitable employment to the laborer, in the periods which closed with 1835 and 1848; and is now doing the same under the protective tariff of 1861.

British free trade prevented immigration in the period preceding effective action of the tariff of 1828. It paralyzed it in that which closed in 1843–4. It had almost annihilated it in that which closed in 1861–2.

American freedom of commerce quadrupled immigration in the period controlled by the protective tariff of 1828. It quadrupled it again under that controlled by the tariff of '42; and it has now been more than trebled under the tariff of '61.

British free trade almost annihilated the railroad interest in the period which closed with 1842. It did the same in that which closed with 1861.

American freedom of commerce gave new life and vigor to the same interest in the period from 1842 to '48. To a far greater extent it has done the same under the tariff of 1861.

British free trade, throughout its several periods of existence, has looked to crushing out the domestic commerce; to increasing the necessity for seeking distant markets; and to throwing on our farmers all the "tax" of transportation.

American freedom of commerce has sought to bring the market to the farmer's door thereby freein him from all such "tax", while throwin on the foreign manufacturer all the expenses standing between his market and himself.

British free trade, throughout its whole existence, subjected our farmers to taxes so heavy that to a frightful extent their properties, in 1818–23, 1840–42, and 1857–60, changed hands under the sheriff's hammer.

American freedom of commerce, in all its several periods, has given prosperity to the farmer; and has already so far relieved him from the "tax" of transportation that, and for the first time in our history, he is now almost everywhere free from the burthen of mortgage and other debts.

British free trade gave us the financial revulsions of 1818–23, 1837–42, 1857–60; ruining merchants and manufacturers; almost annihilating public and private revenues; making the rich everywhere richer and the poor everywhere poorer; and forcing the Treasury to the creation of burthensome debts.

American freedom of commerce filled the Treasury to repletion in the period ending in 1835, and saved it from bankruptcy in 1842. It found the Treasury empty in 1861, and since then has supplied it with the means of making the most gigantic war recorded in the annals of the world.

British free trade, throughout, has looked to making Liverpool the hub of a great wheel of which American railroads were to be the spokes, as a necessary consequence of which there was no cohesion among the parts of which the Union had been composed. Of this discord, rebellion, civil war, were the unavoidable results.

American freedom of commerce looking, as it always *has* looked, to the creation of a great net-work of roads, tends toward bringing all the States into close communion each with every other, and thus establishing that complete *harmony of interests* to which alone can we look for perpetuation of the Union.

2. Such is the "review" for which, in the extract from your Report above given, you have seemed to call. Having studied it, and having satisfied yourself that it contains nothing that may not be "accepted as historical truth," you may, perhaps, be prepared to furnish answers to the following questions, to wit:—

Why is it that, if protection be really adverse to freedom and to the general prosperity of our people, immigration always grows with such rapidity when protection is most complete?

Why is it that, if British free trade be really favorable to freedom, men who previously had come among us with intent to stay, have always in free trade times so largely re-emigrated to Europe?

Why has it been that in the last few years hundreds of thousands of Canadians have abandoned their free trade country, and have preferred to settle in these benighted and protected States?

Why is it that of the emigrants who arrive at Quebec and Montreal, and who have the choice between free trade on the one hand and protection on the other, nearly all prefer to take the latter, selecting homes in our Western States?

Why is it that Nova Scotia and New Brunswick are almost in a state of rebellion, because of their feeling of the absolute necessity for closer connection with these protected States?

Why is it that nearly the whole population of Ireland would desire to fly from British freedom of trade and seek for homes in this now partially protected country?

Why is it that British emigration to Australia diminishes, and that to us increases, almost precisely as our protective policy is made more and more complete?

Why is it that Australia, after a most severe political contest, has just now elected a protectionist parliament?

Why is it that furnaces are built and mines opened in protective times, and abandoned in British free trade times?

Why is it that when we build furnaces and open mines railroads are always profitable to their owners, and capital is easily obtained for the construction of new lines of road?

Why is it that when mines and furnaces are abandoned railroad property so far declines that it becomes most difficult to obtain the means for building further roads?

Why is it that financial crises, resulting in the ruin of trade, are the *never failing* accompaniments of the British free trade policy?

Why is it that such crises never occur in periods of protection?

Why is it that the deposits in our saving funds so much increase in times of protection, and so much diminish in those of British free trade?

Why is it that Sheriff's sales are so numerous in British free trade times, and so few in number in those of protection?

Why is it that British free trade periods always end in almost total failure of public revenue and almost total bankruptcy of the treasury?

Why is it that protective tariffs are so favorable to increase of public revenue, and to reduction of the public debt?

Why is it that a protective tariff now produces annually nearly as much revenue as was obtained by aid of an anti-protective one in the whole period of Mr. Buchanan's administration?

Why is it that the Republican party—the party of liberty, of equal rights, of intelligence, and of sound morals—is so generally favorable to the protective policy?

Why is it that British free trade doctrines are so universally popular among men who believe in the divine origin of slavery—among sympathizers in the late rebellion—among foreign agents—among ignorant foreigners—and among the dangerous classes throughout the Union?

Why is it that, now that it diversifies its industry by raising its own food, the South obtains more for 2,000,000 bales of cotton than before it had received for 4,000,000?

Why is it that when the refining of our oil, thus fitting it for consumption, gives us now almost our only real free trade, the same results would not be obtained, and, on a much larger scale, by finishing our cotton and fitting it also for consumption?

Why is it that France, in making her last treaty with England, established a tariff more intelligently protective than our own?

Why is it that the maker of that treaty, Mons. Chevalier, had been led to tell his countrymen that—

"Every nation owes to itself to seek the establishment of diversification in the pursuits of its people, as Germany and England have already done in regard to cottons and woollens, and as France herself has done in reference to so many and so widely-different kinds of manufacturing industry. Within these limits," as he further says, "it is not an abuse of power on the part of the Government; on the contrary, *it is the accomplishment of a positive duty so to act at each epoch in the progress of a nation as to favor the taking possession of all the branches of industry whose acquisition is authorized by the nature of things.* Governments are, in effect, the personification of nations, and *it is required that they exercise their influence in the direction indicated by the general interest, properly studied, and fully appreciated.*"

Why is it that, small as are its natural advantages, France, the country *par excellence* of protection, has been enabled to establish a foreign commerce so vastly greater than our own ?*

Why is it that Germany, the country that has most persistently carried into effect the policy of protection, now stands in the lead of Europe, although so recently a mere collection of loose fragments, ready to be moved about in whatsoever direction might be most agreeable to France or England at one moment, Russia or Austria at another?

Why is it that our Union, at the close of a long course of policy directly the reverse, has recently with such difficulty escaped being broken into fragments?

Why is it that British policy, that policy whose imitation is urged upon us by all the advocates of that anti-protective system which has invariably resulted in destruction of the revenue, has so entirely crushed out of existence that whole race of small British proprietors "whose touch," according to Arthur Young, "turned sand into gold?"

Why is it that the British agricultural laborer has, by means of that policy, been reduced to a condition so nearly akin to slavery as to have before him no future but the poor house?

Why is it that all the countries of the earth which find themselves compelled to submit to the, so-called, free trade policy now urged upon the world by British traders, are this day in little better than a state of ruin?

Leaving you to furnish answers to these important questions, I here close this protracted review of your labors with the request that you read once again the following passage of your Report, and that you then determine with yourself how far its broad "assertions" are to be regarded as making any approach towards "historical truth;" how far, too, the Report itself is such an one as we had a right to expect from a man who, holding a most important office, had been fully informed of the fact that money was being unsparingly used by British manufacturers in the effort now being made for perpetuating our industrial dependence as the most efficient mode of preventing the growth of political independence.

"Study of all the facts pertaining to the national development from 1840 to 1860, and from 1865 to the present time, unmistakably teaches this lesson; that the progress of the country through what we may term the strength of its elements of vitality is independent of legislation and even of the impoverishment and waste of a great war. Like one of our own mighty rivers, its movement is beyond control. Successive years, like successive affluents, only add to and increase its volume; while legislative enactments and conflicting commercial policies, like the construction of piers and the deposit of sunken wrecks, simply deflect the current or constitute temporary obstructions. In fact, if the nation has not yet been lifted to the full comprehension of its own work, it builds determinately, as it were, by instinct."

Is there in all this a single word that you will now venture to reassert? I doubt it much.

Yours respectfully,

HENRY C. CAREY.

Hon. D. A. Wells.

Philadelphia, February 20, 1869.

---

* The average total of French foreign commerce for the last three years has been nearly $1,600,000,000, equivalent to more than $2,000,000,000 of our currency.

EXTRACT FROM A SPEECH OF THE HON. WILLIAM D. KELLEY, DELIVERED IN THE HOUSE OF REPRESENTATIVES, FEBRUARY 4TH, 1869.

" While recounting the manifold blessings that period brought to the working people of the country, the gentleman from Ohio reminded me that the working people were docile in that year (1860), and indulged in no strikes either for higher wages or against a reduction of their pay. He said:—

" ' It was a year of plenty, of great increase. I remember, moreover, that it was a year of light taxes. There was but one great people on the face of the globe so lightly taxed as the American people in 1860. Now we are the most heavily taxed people, except one, perhaps, on the face of the globe; and the weight of nearly all our taxes falls at last on the laboring man. This is an element which the gentleman seems to have omitted from his calculation altogether.

" ' The gentleman says that at the present time laborers are doing better than in 1860. I ask him how many strikes there were among laborers in 1860–61 ? Were there any at all ? And how many were there in 1868 ? Will the gentlemen deny that strikes exhibit the unsettled and unsatisfactory condition of labor in its relations to capital ? In our mines, in our mills and furnaces, in our manufacturing establishments, are not the laborers every day joining in strikes for higher wages, and saying that they need them on account of the high price of provisions, or that the capitalists get too large a share of the profits ?'

" The gentleman has my thanks for bringing this significant fact, so destructive of his own argument and that of Mr. Wells, to my attention. He knows that it was not until Jeshurun waxed fat that he kicked; and he ought to know that unemployed workmen, who had drawn the last dollar from the savings bank, and parted with furniture in exchange for food and fuel, were not in a condition to strike, and had no employers whose decrees they might resist. I need no more powerful illustration of the absurdity of the assertions of the Commissioner than the fact that the working-men of to-day, in contrast with their abject condition in 1860, find so wide a market for their labor, and are so comparatively easy in their condition, that when their rights or interests are assailed they are able to offer resistance to the assailant.

" Our positions are fairly taken, and as the condition of savings banks furnishes the truest and most general index to the condition of the laboring people, the facts I am about to present will overthrow him who is in error. Be the judgment of the general public what it may, I am confident that the memory of every American workingman who remembers the experience of 1860 will sustain me in this controversy. Having shown the loss of depositors and deposits in the only banks from which I could obtain information on those points in or about 1860, let me compare the condition in these respects of the same banks in 1867 and 1868:—

State or City.				Year.	Increase in number of depositors.	Increase of deposits.
New Hampshire	.	.	.	1867	4,967	$2,672,150 05
New Hampshire	.	.	.	1868	7,476	2,705,242 01
Massachusetts	.	.	.	1867	31,740	12,699,319 40
Massachusetts	.	.	.	1868	34,501	14,406,752 83
Rhode Island	.	.	.	1867	6,845	3,651,934 11
Rhode Island	.	.	.	1868	4,429	2,984,988 81
Philadelphia	.	.	.	1867	2,460	579,746 03
Philadelphia	.	.	.	1868	2,234	761,901 00
					94,682	$40,462,034 24

" The contrast these figures present to those of 1860 does not give the Commissioner's theory much support, and casts a shade of doubt over the accuracy of the position taken by the gentleman from Ohio. It may, however, be regarded as exceptional, and I therefore propose to present a broader range of facts, embracing the amount of deposits in the banks of Maine, New Hampshire, Massachusetts, Newark, New Jersey, and the only institution at Philadelphia from which I have been able to obtain this information for the years 1860-61 and 1867-68. I have sought for corresponding facts from all the other New England States and New York, but have not been able to obtain them. These tables are, therefore, as complete as industry and the broadest research possible in so limited a period could make them. As, however, they present so general a correspondence for both periods it is fair to presume that they indicate the condition of the savings banks and their depositors throughout the country. The total amount of deposits in these banks in 1860-61, 1867-68, was as follows :—

	1860.	1861	1867.	1868.
Maine . . .	$1,466,457 56	$1,620,270 26	$5,996,600 26	$8,132,246 71
New Hampshire	4,860,024 86	5,590,652 18	10,463,418 50	13,541,534 96
Massachusetts .	45,054,236 00	44,785,439 00	80,431,583 74	94,838,336 54
Rhode Island .	9,163,760 41	9,282,879 74	21,413,647 14	24,408,635 95
Philadelphia .	4,083,450 28	2,251,646 46	5,003,379 42	5,765,280 63
Newark .. .	{ 1,687,551 51 { 253,826 72	1,539,932 34 269,182 67	{ 4,405,726 46 { 1,116,762 26 { 325,920 57	5,430,874 60 1,338,596 94 468,160 74
	$66,569,307 34 65,330,002 65	$65,330,002 65	$128,759,038 32	153,823,667 07 128,759,038 32
Decrease . .	$1,239,804 69		Increase	$25,064,628 65

" This exhibit is as unfortunate for the Commissioner's facts and theories as that which preceded it, for they show that in spite of all his rhetoric about the crudities and oppressive character of the legislation of Congress the deposits in these banks, which fell off so largely in his season of prosperity, have increased $25,064,628 65 during the last year, and that the aggregate deposit at the close of 1868, his disastrous period, is largely more than double that of 1860, which he says was so prosperous. In the pursuit of a complete comparative table for these four years I have obtained an amount of information which, though it does not relate to the particular years alluded to, will not be without interest to the House and the country, and I will therefore proceed to present the figures with as much method as I can.

" Through the kind assistance of the honorable gentleman from the Troy district New York (Mr. Griswold), I have authentic statistics from the savings-banks of his State ; and though we were unable to obtain the figures for the years 1861 or 1868, I can present the number of depositors, the total amount of deposits, and the amount deposited during each year for the years 1860, 1866, and 1867. They were as follows :—

Year.	Total number of depositors.	Total amount of deposits.	Total deposited during the year.
1860	300,693	$67,440,397	$34,934,271
1866	488,501	131,769,074	84,765,054
1867	537,466	151,127,562	99,147,321

"From Vermont I have been able to obtain only the total amount of deposits for 1867 and 1868. They were as follows :—

Year.	Total amount of deposits.
1867	$1,898,107 58
1868	2,128,641 52

" From Connecticut I have only been able to obtain the total amount of deposits for 1860, 1861, and 1866. They are as follows :—

Year.	Total amount of deposits.
1860	$18,132,820 00
1861	19,377,670 00
1866	31,224,464 25

" Thus the figures derived from every quarter are consistent with each other, and the contrast between the condition of things that prevailed between 1857 and 1861— for the return to which the Commissioner sighs—and that from 1861 to the close of 1868, which he so deprecates, is in itself sufficient to show the grotesque absurdity of his theory, that the head of every family could save money and make deposits in 1860, and that none but unmarried people could do so in 1867 and 1868. Let me repeat his language on this point :—

"'Unmarried operatives, therefore, gain; while those who are obliged to support their own families in hired tenements lose. Hence deposits in savings-banks increase, while marriage is discouraged; and the forced employment of young children is made almost a necessity in order that the family may live.'

"The country will hardly believe that when every head of a family among the laboring people of New York could save money the whole number put at interest but $34,000,000 per annum, and that when their condition had been so sadly impaired by the unwise legislation of Congress that people feared to marry because their wages would not enable them to support families, they deposited $99,000,000 annually, or nearly three dollars for one, and that the number of depositors nearly doubled, and the total amount on deposit to their credit ran up one hundred and twenty-five per cent.

"Thus, in defiance of the Commissioner's facts, heartily as they are indorsed by the gentleman from Ohio, the returns from savings-banks prove that, with our labor protected and a cheap and expanded currency, our small farmers and workingmen have been able to lay up hundreds of millions of capital, upon which they receive interest and for their support in age or adversity. They are happily corroborated by other facts, which in a striking manner prove the superiority of the present condition of the classes of people to which I allude over that to which the Special Commissioner of the Revenue would lead them back. While accumulating capital in savings-banks they have felt themselves able to make still more ample provision for their families after they shall have been called away by the dread summoner, death."

After showing by equally exact figures the wonderful increase in life insurance, the honorable speaker thus proceeds :—

"When people in addition to laying up money at interest are insuring their lives, they are living well; but when, as in 1860, past accumulations in savings-banks are running down, and they are wasting their time in enforced idleness, they cannot live well and contribute freely to the support of the Government. Accept the recommendations of the Commissioner and you will paralyze industry, reduce wages, throw the producing classes upon their deposits for support, and deprive them of the power to keep up the insurance on their lives. Such facts as I have presented are sufficient to refute a thousand fine-spun theories. It may, with the ingenuity that fashioned this report, be said that the policies to which I have referred are on the lives of wealthy people. But such is not the case; two hundred and sixty-five out of each thousand of them are for $1000 or less; five hundred and forty out of each thousand are for $2000 or less; seven hundred out of each thousand for $3000 or less. Only three hundred out of each thousand are for amounts over $3000. These policies are the precautions taken by well-paid industry to provide for widowhood and orphanage after the head of the family shall have paid mortality's last debt.

"It is not improper, Mr. Chairman, that in concluding this branch of my subject I should say that I have presented no statement which is not warranted by official indorsement, and that I hesitate not to assert that could the business of the savings-banks and life insurance companies of the whole country be investigated, the results would conform to those I have produced. They are truly surprising, and should they through our widely diffused periodicals find their way across the waters, will prove an abundant antidote to the Commissioner's notice to those who have thought of emigrating to this country, but who desire to live in wedlock, that they may not hope to do so under the legislation of that Congress which has for several years been in such absolute government of the country as to render the veto power of the Executive nugatory. They are, in my judgment, important enough to produce some effect upon the credit of the country, for they show that our laboring people are saving and putting at interest hundreds of millions of dollars annually, and that the people at large are paying from their abundance more, largely more, than the interest on our national debt to life insurance companies, as a provision for their widows and orphans when they shall no longer be able to provide for and protect them."

THE UNDEVELOPED RESOURCES OF THE CENTRE AND THE SOUTH as exhibited, February 12, at a meeting of Northern and Southern gentlemen in Washington :—

CAPTAIN HOTCHKISS, OF VIRGINIA, stated that the rin i 1 object he wished to s eak been divided into several regions—the tide-water country, the middle section, of a somewhat sandy nature, comparatively level, and then at the foot of the Blue Ridge they cross into the great valley, the centre of agricultural wealth. Just upon the western border of that valley (the Shenandoah), they come in contact with a line of iron ore, which is very largely developed. There are a series of parallel valleys traversed by the Chesapeake and Ohio Railroad: and in the last of these valleys, upon the western slope of the North Mountain, there is a wonderful development of iron ore. This mineral region extends over fifty miles in length by some three or four in breadth, running northeast and southwest in almost a direct line, and between veins of sandstone and limestone the ore is obtained of the very finest quality, and in almost inexhaustible deposits. Several furnaces are in active and profitable operation. Captain Hotchkiss exhibited samples of ore and an analysis of the same, and stated that one establishment had refused two hundred and fifty thousand dollars for their works and privileges. Parties are now at work upon a railroad to connect with the great Kanawha coal fields, and expect to have it in running order within a period of eighteen months. This will bring the iron ore in immediate contact, as it were, with the coal field, and of course put it in a position to be readily manufactured. Several sites and furnaces have been purchased by Northern companies, awaiting completion of the railroads to the coal fields before commencing operations. The deposits of iron in many instances crop out, stand up and form portions of the mountain itself. They appear above the surface of the ground, and in many places thousands of tons stand up as the rocks that form the summit of the mountain, and they are worked simply by blasting, and in many instances are obtained by sledging. Several of the furnaces in this valley were destroyed when General Crook made his junction with Hunter during the war, and from this source much of the iron used by the Confederacy was obtained. While much has been developed, there still remains a great body of ore that has never been disturbed. The water power in the valley is not abundant. It is sufficient in some instances, but not enough generally for manufacturing purposes, or for conducting operations entirely by the use of water-power. Nearly all the property in that section could be consolidated or purchased together, with the exception of Elizabeth Furnace and the Millens property.

HON. WILLIAM D. KELLEY, OF PENNSYLVANIA, stated that during the last campaign, while travelling through Eastern Tennessee, he had witnessed the same wonderful deposits of iron ore along the line of railroad, and not only iron, but coal beds, lead, zinc, and nickel, which is said to be next to the precious metal. Already in Eastern Tennessee the development of one zinc establishment has built up a beautiful village. Through his Southern trip he found, to his surprise, the finest wheat fields he had ever seen in any region. He had seen in Louisiana fields of wheat that would yield to the acre twice as many bushels as the most fertile fields of the Northwest, and in localities where the expense of transportation to Liverpool or New York was comparatively nothing. On the farm of Hon. J. R. Robertson sixty bushels of Southern wheat to the acre has been raised, and it could be carried to the tropics in flour without danger of souring. Never before was such a thing known. These magnificent fields were visible from the railroad, and within sight of the steeples of New Orleans, while splendid patches of white clover could be seen in every direction; He had as soon expected to find gold growing on the trees as a natural crop of white clover within sight of New Orleans. The whole South abounds not only in natural agricultural wealth, but in iron regions, and in coal with which to smelt it. The South has also the richest copper region in our country, all within sight of a road soon to be constructed through the valleys of the mountain regions of Tennessee and Virginia, opening up vast fields for investment of Northern capital from the Northeast to the Gulf States—in which already handsome sums have been expended. Let us take an historical view of this country a hundred years hence, and we shall see that the material wealth of the South was transcendently in excess of the North, and that prior to the American war the greatest stores of the world were hidden from the sight of our people. Pennsylvania is abundantly rich, and yet East Tennessee, and some sections of other comparatively small States, are richer in diversified mineral wealth and great natural resources than our own boasted Commonwealth. He who wants to read the most wonderful work of nature should take "Owen's Geological Recognizance of Arkansas." The sculptors of the world will there find a marble composed of red sandstone converted by the process of time into a marble more beautiful than that of Carrara, and equally fine with any Italy has ever sent us. The vast deposits of coal, iron, marble, zinc, lead, copper, and nickel only await the labor and the capital of the North for their development. He would now state to his Southern friends that the laborers of the North were piling up their savings, amounting to nearly two hundred millions of dollars, which are ready to flow to the South as soon as the could be assured that a cordial welcome and a safe residence in that section awaited them. Mr. Kelley said he had recently ascertained some statistics in regard to savings banks and similar institutions, which showed that in one savings bank in the city of New York, in the year 1867, between ninety-nine and one hundred millions were deposited, to be returned with from four to five per cent. interest. In the States of Maine, New Hampshire, Massachusetts, and Rhode Island, they had these savings banks, one in Philadelphia, three in New York and New Jersey, and the resulting increase of deposits had raised in the year 1868 over 1867, more than twenty-five millions. In these States last year the depositors increased by ninety-four thousand, and the number of deposits over twenty odd millions. There is lying at rest, simply invested in Government bonds, a sufficient amount of money to quicken into active operations these fine mineral resources, and to send our commerce into the ports of all the nations of the world. The statistics brought before the commissioner of our revenue for this year show that while England has been losing in her copper production, we have been largely increasing, and while England has scarcely maintained her iron production, we have nearly doubled ours. As others have lost we have gained in the ratio indicated. Let us become as one family, insure us as sure a protection as we have at home, and we shall realize, or our immediate descendants will, a pecuniary condition of things for yourselves and for ourselves, brighter than the wildest visions of any age prior to the war.

COLONEL PRINTUP, OF GEORGIA, said he would briefly state that the iron region to which reference had been made extends into North and South Carolina, the northwestern portion of Georgia, into Alabama, and he presumed would reach to a portion of Mississippi also. In the mineral resources of the South no reference had yet been made to the gold mines of Georgia. They are situated along the northwestern portion of South Carolina. They were very extensively worked before the war, and great profits had been derived where operations were conducted in a scientific manner. But the iron regions of Alabama, of which he desired to speak particularly, are beyond description. There was hardly anything he could say to give his hearers an idea of the immense quantities of iron that existed in Alabama. Mountains of iron could be found in almost any portion of the State, which, by analysis, had been proven to yield from forty to seventy-five per cent. of pure iron. They have some of the finest ores in America, and the experiment of manufacturing steel from it is now being successfully prosecuted. Specimens of ore crop out at every step you take, and they seem to be quite as prominent as those in Tennessee. We cordially invite gentlemen from the North to come down among us and examine for themselves, and we will extend to them a very hearty welcome. The coal and iron beds of Alabama lie within a short distance of each other. There is a large iron mountain in Alabama, and within four miles of it you find plenty of coal, limestone, sandstone, and rich deposits of lead, all within a circumference of four miles. The mountain is almost a solid bed of iron. There is also an iron hill in Alabama which lies parallel to the Selma railroad, about sixty miles in length, composed almost entirely of iron. Superior sandstone, bituminous coal, and various other minerals, and splendid lead deposits are also here to be seen. The people of Alabama are a little behind in the way of cultivation, but they were in hopes the North would send them some good scientific farmers to improve their agricultural system, and they would profit by the example. Indeed, they had improved very much lately, from the fact that some Virginia farmers had gone down and introduced the system of Northern agriculture. This had benefited and enhanced their lands in value very materially. Clover had been successfully raised in small fields before the war, but he had no idea how long it would last. In the hills and valleys of Georgia they were enabled to raise all kinds of fruit. In the northern part of Georgia the peach is a spontaneous production, and all along the railroad you will see lines of peach trees; but this is not the case with apples, which only flourish with cultivation.

REVIEW

OF THE

FARMER'S QUESTION,

AS EXHIBITED IN THE RECENT REPORT OF THE
HON. D. A. WELLS, SPECIAL COMMISSIONER
OF THE REVENUE:

BY

H. C. CAREY.

" Then one of the twelve, called Judas Iscariot, went unto the chief priests,
and said unto them, 'What will ye give me, and I will deliver him
unto you?' And they covenanted with him for thirty pieces of silver.
And from that time he sought opportunity to betray him. * * *
And forthwith he came to Jesus and said 'Hail, Master,' and kissed
him."—St. Matthew, Chap. xxvi.

PHILADELPHIA:
COLLINS, PRINTER, 705 JAYNE STREET.
1870.

THE FARMERS' QUESTION.

At the opening of the present Congress, little more than a year since, the Special Commissioner of Revenue, Mr. Wells, made to that body a Report one of whose especial objects was that of proving to mechanics, laborers, and consumers generally, that their condition was being deteriorated by reason of the high prices of food and other necessaries of life. To enable his readers properly to understand the cause of this, if so it really was, it was needed that he should present to them the facts, that the three years prior to the date he had selected for presentation had been most unfavorable for both wheat and corn; that the total produce of the last of these had scarcely exceeded that of 1859; that the waste of war as to cows and cattle had not even yet been repaired; that their total number was still greatly less than it had been at the opening of the war; that high prices of both animal and vegetable food were necessary consequences of the facts thus exhibited; and, that time alone could be required for bringing about a state of things widely different from that which, as he alleged, then existed. For anything of this kind, however, we look in vain to his Report, the essential object of his labor having been that of proving that by means of *greenbacks* and protection "*the rich become richer and the poor poorer.*" To that end mere figures, unembarrassed by any such explanation, were greatly to be preferred; and therefore was it that the people of towns and cities were assured that not only had there been a duplication of the prices paid to the farmer for milk and butter, eggs and meat, potatoes and turnips, but that the—

"average increase in the price of a barrel of wheaten flour throughout the manufacturing States has been, from 1860 to July 1st, 1868, in excess of 90 per cent.; while the increase in the wages of laborers and operatives generally, skilled and unskilled, during the same period, has averaged about 58 per cent. Measured, therefore, by the flour standard, the workman is not as well off in 1867 as he was in 1860, by at least 20 per cent.; or, to state the case differently, the wages which in 1860 purchased one and a half barrel of flour now pay for about one and a quarter barrel."

Admitting, now, that all this had been true, and that laborers in the workshop had really suffered in the manner thus artfully described, is it not clear that laborers in the field must in a corresponding degree have profited? That they had so done had been made clearly obvious by the greatly improved condition of the agricultural interest throughout the Union—the mortgages by which farmers had before the war been so heavily burdened having almost entirely disappeared. Of all this, however, the report said not even a single word. Why was this? For the reason that better seasons were already giving better crops, those of 1867 and 1868 having been greater by fully 25 per cent. than the average of the three preceding years; the increase thus manifested bringing with it reason for hoping that the day might not be far distant when low prices for farm products might furnish the Commissioner opportunity for stimulating the men who followed the plough for a union with those who wielded the hammer to a war upon those *greenbacks* to which we had been so largely indebted for power to make the war, and upon that protective tariff to which we now owe our rapidly growing independence. That all this has since been done, and fully done, in the recent Report of this professed advocate of protection, but real British free-trader, shall now be shown.

II.

The hard conditions of mechanic life consequent upon high prices for food having been clearly exhibited in the Commissioner's report for 1868, much of that for 1869 is given to showing how severe are now our farmer's sufferings "under a system of currency which unsettles values," and "under a tariff which, without offering him sufficient compensation, unnecessarily increases the cost of his tools, his fuel, his fencing, and his shelter." In the first it was clearly shown that the people of villages, towns, and cities were being taxed for the benefit of men who cultivated the soil. Equally clearly has it just now been shown that the latter are at this moment being heavily taxed for maintenance of the former, the boot being thus adroitly fitted to the other leg. To the end of proving this, our Free Trade Commissioner, while professing to talk protectively, furnishes a table comparative of the prices of wheat and other commodities in 1859 and 1869, desiring thereby to demonstrate the fact that the quantity of iron, carpetings, salt, stoves, mackerel, and other commodities, obtainable in exchange for any given quantity of wheat in this latter year, under protection, is less by from 30 to 60 per cent. than it had been in the former Free Trade one. But a single year had elapsed since the great sufferers were thus to be found among *consumers of food;* but, the greatest of all are at present, as we are assured, to be found among that great *food-producing* interest which, now for the first time in our history, finds itself almost entirely discharged from that heavy load of debt by which it had in the past been burthened. To enable the reader fully to understand how our reliable Commissioner has been enabled to reach these remarkable results, I must begin by asking his attention to the following table of the export prices of wheat from 1859 to the present time, as furnished by the annual Commerce and Navigation Reports, as follows:—

Fiscal years.				Bushels.	Value.	Rate per bus.
1858–59	.	.	.	3,002,016	$2,849,192	94$\frac{9}{10}$ cts.
1859–60	.	.	.	4,155,153	4,076,704	98$\frac{1}{10}$ "
1860–61	.	.	.	31,238,057	38,313,624	1.22\frac{1}{2}$ "
1861–62	.	.	.	37,289,572	42,573,295	1.14$\frac{1}{8}$ "
1862–63	.	.	.	36,160,414	46,754,195	1.29$\frac{1}{3}$ "
1863–64	.	.	.	23,681,712	31,432,133	1. 2$\frac{1}{4}$ "
1864–65	.	.	.	9,937,152	19,397,197	1.95 "
1865–66	.	.	.	5,579,103	7,842,749	1.40$\frac{1}{2}$ "
1866–67	.	.	.	6,146,411	7,822,745	1.27$\frac{3}{4}$ "
1867–68	.	.	.	15,940,900	30,247,632	1.90 "
1868–69	.	.	.	17,539,193	24,349,638	1.38$\frac{1}{4}$ "

Average price under Tariff of 1857 . . . . 97 "
Average price under Tariffs of 1861 and '62 . . . $1.26 "
    "   "   1864 and subsequent . 1.58$\frac{1}{4}$ "

For 1866–67, and in 1868–9, the price is to a large extent made up from *California wheat exported at gold prices.* Allowing for this, the actual currency prices for this latter year must have reached $1.60.

Turning now to the Commissioner's Report, we find the price given by him in the table above referred to, to have been for 1859, $1.45, being *fifty-four per cent. above the real one;* that for 1869 being $1.35, or *fifteen per cent. less than the real one.* Further even than this, while the price of wheat in 1859 is thus falsely exaggerated the prices of commodities to be purchased with it are generally almost as falsely diminished, the reverse of all this being the case in regard to 1869; the wheat price being there cut down far below the truth, and the prices of other commodities as much exaggerated, as is shown in the following table every part of which I have reason to believe to be strictly accurate:—

Articles.	Prices in 1859.		Quantities which 100 bush. of wheat would purchase in 1859.		Prices in 1869.		Quantities which 100 bushels of wheat would purchase in 1869.		"Decrease per cent." [Increase, in fact.]	
	False prices.	True prices.	False Quantities.	True Quantities.	False prices.	True prices.	False Quantities.	True Quantities.	False rate decrease.	Real rate, increase.
Wheat	$1.45 p.bush.	95 cts.p.b'sh.	100 bush.	100 bush.	$1.35 p.bush.	$1.40 p.bush.	100 bush.	100 bush.		
English Bar Iron	$2\frac{1}{8}$ cts. p. lb.	3 cts. per lb.	6824 lbs.	3167 lbs.	$3\frac{1}{4}$ cts. p. lb.	$3\frac{1}{4}$ cts. p. lb.	4154 lbs.	4308 lbs.	39 p. ct.	35 p. ct. inc.
Collins' Axes . .	$9 per doz.	$9 per doz.	$16\frac{1}{9}$ doz.	$10\frac{1}{2}$ doz.	$12 per doz.	$12 per doz.	$11\frac{1}{4}$ doz.	$11\frac{2}{3}$ doz.	30 "	$10\frac{1}{3}$ " "
Lowell Carpets .	75 cts. p. yd.	75 cts. p. yd.	$193\frac{1}{3}$ yds.	$126\frac{2}{3}$ yds.	$1.30 per yd.	$1.20 per yd.	$103\frac{1}{13}$ yds.	$116\frac{2}{3}$ yds.	46 "	[8 " dec.]
Cut Nails . . .	3 cts. per lb.	$3\frac{3}{8}$ cts. p. lb.	4833 lbs.	2801 lbs.	5 cts. per lb.	$4\frac{3}{4}$ cts. p. lb.	2700 lbs.	2947 lbs.	43 "	5 " inc.
Blankets, 10–4 .	$\$3\frac{1}{2}$ per pair	$4 per pair	$41\frac{1}{2}$ pairs	$23\frac{3}{4}$ pairs	$5.50 p. pair	$4.75 p. pair	$24\frac{1}{2}$ pairs	$29\frac{1}{2}$ pairs	36 "	24 " "
Liverp'l Fine Salt	90 cts. p. bag	$1.50 per bag	$161\frac{1}{9}$ bags	$63\frac{1}{3}$ bags	$2.60 per bag	$2.60 per bag	$51\frac{12}{13}$ bags	54 bags	68 "	[$14\frac{1}{2}$ p.c.d.]
Boots	$4.50 p. pair	$4.50 p. pair	32 pairs	$21\frac{1}{9}$ pairs	$6.83 p. pair	$6.50 p. pair	$20\frac{1}{4}$ pairs	$21\frac{1}{2}$ pairs	37 "	2 " inc.
Sheffield C. Steel	14 cts. p. lb.	14 cts. p. lb.	$1035\frac{5}{7}$ lbs.	$678\frac{4}{7}$ lbs.	19 cts. p. lb.	19 cts. p. lb.	$710\frac{10}{19}$ lbs.	$736\frac{3}{4}$ lbs.	31 "	$8\frac{1}{2}$ " "
Stoves	$6 each	$6 each	$24\frac{1}{6}$ stoves	$15\frac{5}{6}$ stoves	$9.50 each	$7.50 each	$14\frac{1}{5}$ stoves	$18\frac{2}{3}$ stoves	41 "	21 " "
Mackerel, No. 1 .	$11 per bbl.	$15.50 p. bbl.	$13\frac{1}{5}$ bbls.	$6\frac{1}{8}$ bbls.	$27 per bbl.	$27 per bbl.	5 bbls.	$5\frac{5}{27}$ bbls.	62 "	15 " "
" No. 2 .	$10 per bbl.	$13.50 p. bbl.	$14\frac{1}{2}$ bbls.	7 bbls.	$16 per bbl.	$16 per bbl.	$8\frac{1}{2}$ bbls.	$8\frac{3}{4}$ bbls.	41 "	25 " "
Codfish . . .	4 cts. per lb.	4 cts. per lb.	3625 lbs.	2375 lbs.	$7\frac{1}{2}$ cts. p. lb.	6 cts. per lb.	1800 lbs.	$2333\frac{1}{3}$ lbs.	50 "	[2 " dec.]

The real facts thus presented show that instead of a decrease in the value of wheat, as measured by other commodities, ranging from 30 to 68 per cent., there has been an increase in respect to nearly all of them, while the decrease in any case has been entirely unimportant. That result, too, is obtained while taking the export price of wheat at but $1.40; whereas, by allowing for the fact that to a very large extent the returns to the Custom House were made in gold prices, it would have been carried up to $1.60. Had this latter price been taken there would have been no single instance of decrease, while the general ratio of increase would have been very far greater than is here exhibited.

The fiscal year closed on the 30th of June, and since then there has been a great glut in foreign markets, followed by large decline at home. Nevertheless, the shipping price from this port, even for November, was $1.40, or five cents more than the Commissioner then ventured to present as the ruling price of the year.

Were further proof required of the entire unreliability of the Commissioner, whether as regarded facts or figures, it would be found in the following comparative view just now furnished by highest free-trade authority, that of the *Journal of Commerce:*—[1]

	Fiscal Year 1859.	Fiscal Year 1869.
Wheat flour, State	$4.30	$6.80
Wheat flour, Western	4.60	6.60
Rye flour	3.75	7.00
Corn meal	3.40	5.50
Wheat, No. 1, spring	.83¼	1.70
Wheat, Michigan	1.25	2.12½
Rye	1.02	1.50
Oats	.55	.76
Corn, new Southern	.76	1.05

In face of these facts the Commissioner has ventured to assure the farmer that the prices of 1869, under a protective tariff, had been less than those of 1859 under a British free trade one! That he should so have done is, however, not at all extraordinary, it being in perfect keeping with the great majority of the statements of the *veracious* and voluminous documents he has given to the world.

How it is with "the other produce" that, according to the Commissioner, the farmer "raises under a tariff which without affording him any sufficient compensation unnecessarily increases the cost of his tools, his clothing, his fuel, his fencing, and his shelter," is shown in the following figures now likewise furnished to us by the *Journal of Commerce*, to wit:—

	Fiscal Year 1859.	Fiscal Year 1869.
Pork, mess, barrel	$17.00	$25.00
Pork, prime, barrel	13.00	28.00
Beef, plain Western, barrel	9.50	22.00
Beef, prime mess, tierce	9.00	28.00
Lard, pound	.11¼	.17¼
Butter, Western, pound	.18	.40
Butter, prime State, pound	.20	.48
Wool, Ohio fleece	.42	.57

[1] The prices given by the Journal are those of January 1, 1859 and 1869, and may properly be regarded as the average of those of the fiscal years 1858–59 and 1868–69.

The Commissioner was aware that such had been the real state of facts, or he was not. If he was, then has he now, as before in his Report for 1868, been guilty of misrepresentation so gross, and with such evil intent, as should exclude him from all respectable society. If he was not, then has he shown himself so utterly incompetent for the work he has undertaken as to warrant his prompt dismission from the public service.

That his philosophy is as false as are his facts, shall be shown in another article.

III.

The largest importers of food in the world are the people of these United States. Exporting it in the rude forms of wheat and corn, they re-import it when incorporated with wool, ore, and other crude materials, and made to take the forms of cloth, silks, and iron, in this manner importing a dozen bushels for each single one supplied to the manufacturing countries of Europe. Instead of making a market at home for their own products they thus make demand for those of Russian and German fields, thereby retaining themselves in a state of abject dependence upon a distant and worthless market, such as is well described by the Commissioner in the Report just now published, as follows, the italics being my own:—

"More wheat and other agricultural produce is and must be annually raised in the United States than is needed for home consumption, and the surplus, if disposed of at all, must find a market in foreign countries. But we can sell wheat in the markets of the world on the single condition of selling as cheap as others, inasmuch as, notwithstanding our magnificent natural advantages, the comparative nearness to the markets of Europe of the wheat-growing regions of the Baltic, the Danube, and the Crimea, reduces our superiority within very narrow limits. The American agriculturist does not, therefore, command his own price, but *the price commands him;* and what wheat is worth in Mark Lane, London, the central market of the world, is what the United States *must sell it for if it sells at all.* And about selling, or not, we have practically but very little discretion. *With an immense wheat-raising area we shall raise wheat, even if at the end of the year half the individual farmers find that they have not been able to pay their expenses.* * * * Where producers are numbered by hundreds of thousands, concert and discipline in such matters are absolutely hopeless; and with anything like a good season, it is morally certain that the United States will produce more of breadstuffs than the home demand, even when stimulated by the cheapness of food for men and for cattle, can absorb. *That balance will be sold abroad, whatever it may bring.*"

"An ordinary good crop, therefore, in the United States cannot be held at home. The surplus must find a market abroad, and *whatever it is worth for exportation measures the price of the whole crop,* inasmuch as there cannot be two prices for the same article, one for the home and another for the foreign market."

That the price of the whole crop *is* entirely dependent upon that which can be obtained in the British market for a surplus so trivial that its destruction, by fire or otherwise, would be a gain, and not a loss, to the general farming interest, is a fact well known to all who have given to the question even the slightest consideration.*

* Unquestionably, it would be better for the farming community, considered apart from the interests of the whole country, if that surplus could be *destroyed,* as the surplus coffee of Java was destroyed by the Dutch Company for the purpose of securing a higher price for the remainder; but such a disposition of the surplus wheat of this country is impossible. Remove the tail-board of a cart

Such being the case, it would seem to be of the highest importance that all our efforts should be directed towards maintaining prices in the regulating market, being directly the reverse of that which is desired by British manufacturers who seek to under-sell all others by means of cheap labor that is to be obtained only by cheapening everywhere the farmer's products. To that end they desire to compel the food producers of America and of Continental Europe to compete with each other for the possession of a market so insignificant that *to meet its whole demand upon the outside world requires scarcely more bushels of grain than are even now produced in the so recently settled State of Iowa, and not a fourth part of what, under proper cultivation, it can be made to yield.* So long as, happily for themselves, our crops continued short, our farmers contributed little towards reducing prices in the regulating market; but now that we have had three successive favorable seasons, creating a surplus for which an outlet must be sought abroad, we have the old result, Russian, German, and Hungarian wheat growers contending with us for the privilege of almost giving away their products in the poorest and most unreliable of all the markets of the world—one that has taken from us in the last dozen years, but 95,000,000 cwts. of wheat, or an average of but 14,000,000 of bushels per annum. Had those few millions been destroyed, British prices throughout most of that long period would have been higher by 10 or 15 per cent., and the annual money value of our general crop of food would have been greater by an average of, at the least, $100,000,000; that being the lowest estimate that can be made of the cost at which our farmers retain the *privilege* of "selling whole skins for sixpence and buying back tails for a shilling," a process that, with slight exception, has been in operation almost from the day when the country had become nominally independent.

Such being the present state of things, how is it to be with our farmers in the future? Continental Europe is alive with railroad operations looking to facilitation of communication between its fields and the manufacturing countries of Europe. Russia is rapidly preparing for railroad transportation of Asiatic as well as European wheat. We, ourselves, are making annually thousands of miles of roads nearly all of which look to the development of lands whose products are to come into competition with those already cultivated. The Lake Superior country calls aloud for immigration, offering to settlers lands capable of yielding to even very moderate cultivation forty bushels of wheat and eighty of oats to the acre. The Governor of Colorado does the same, assuring foreigners that the State possesses advantages for the production of food scarcely equalled elsewhere in the world. Southern farmers are now not only sup-

loaded with potatoes, to use a homely illustration, and it is of course true that if the potatoes nearest would not tumble out, the remainder need not; but, as the first potatoes have no choice whether they will obey the law of gravitation or not, the rest must take the chance all the same as if their falling did not depend on the action of others. In precisely the same way, with our own production of wheat, some must go abroad, and if the movement does not start at one point it will at another.— *Wells's Report*, p. xlvii.

plying that southern demand which before the war had made a market for western products, but are already largely supplying eastern markets with both animal and vegetable food. Preparation is thus being made for a deluge of food, to be forced upon the little British market, the like of which has never yet been known; one threatening our farmers with damage greater than any they ever yet have seen.

The extension of our railroad system within the last few protection years has been most extraordinary, and yet the lines now projected promise still more rapid extension in the future. Let them be made and let our farmers fail to provide for corresponding increase in the home demand for their products, and the result must inevitably exhibit itself in the form of a depression of the agricultural interests as great as, if not even greater than, has been ever known. *Let them, on the contrary, determine that all our cloths and all our iron shall be made at home, and the road making now in progress will be followed by increased prosperity to all, the old farmers and the new.*

The annual addition to our adult population from domestic and foreign sources can scarcely be estimated at less than a million of persons, male and female. Half a million of males are thus annually coming forward, seeking pursuits by means of which they may be enabled to provide subsistence for their families and themselves. Compel them all to become cultivators of the soil, and they become *competitors* with already existing farmers, with ruin to all. Enable them to apply themselves to the development of our wonderful mineral resources, to the building and working of furnaces and mills, and they become *customers* to already existing farmers, bringing the producer and consumer into close connection with each other, with profit to all. That they may be so enabled we must have a public policy that shall tend from year to year to diminish our surplus of food; to lessen our dependence on ever-varying foreign markets; to compel the foreign artisan who would supply us with finished goods to come and place himself here among the men who raise the wool and the food he so greatly needs. Such a policy we now, to a large extent, already have. Fully and faithfully carried out, it must result in the establishment of American independence, and therefore, probably, it is, that it has in *the last two years* become so offensive to the Special Commissioner of the Public Revenue. How sudden, and how complete has been the change in his opinions, will be appreciated by all who shall take the trouble to compare the propositions of his present Report *for annihilating the great steel manufacture of the Union*, with the following passage from his Report of 1867 :—

"On steel much higher rates of duty than those recommended upon iron are submitted. Although these rates seem much higher, and are protested against by not a few American consumers of steel, yet the evidence presented to the Commissioner tends to establish the fact, that if any less are granted, the development of a most important and desirable branch of domestic industry will, owing to the present currency derangement and the high price and scarcity of skilled labor, be arrested, if not entirely prostrated. This is claimed to be more especially true in regard to steel of the higher grades or qualities. It is also represented to the Commissioner that since the introduction of the manu-

facture of these grades of steel in the United States, or since 1859, the price of
foreign steel of similar qualities has been very considerably reduced through
the effect of the American competition, and that the whole country in this way
has gained more than sufficient to counterbalance the tax levied as a protection
for the American steel manufacture, which has grown up under its influence."

, Perfectly true as was then all this, it is even more so at the
present moment, when American competition has so forced down
the price of a commodity destined soon to become one of the most
important of all manufactures, that it is now offered in the British
market at £10 10s. per ton. Since the date of that Report, however, the Commissioner has, in some manner yet entirely unex-
plained, had his eyes fully opened to the great facts: that "a tariff
is a tax"; that the tendency of all tariffs is, "without offering him
any sufficient compensation," to increase the cost to the farmer "of
his tools, his clothes, his fuel, his fencing, and his shelter"; that
the domestic market, furnished by the millions of people employed
in the various manufactures of the Union, is really insignificant;
that "a surplus" of food exists and must, do what we may, continue
so to do; that to attempt to limit the dependence of our farmers
on Europe, is a pure absurdity; and, that we are bound, in all the
future, to continue the exportation of raw products, the proper
work of the barbarian and the slave, and of those alone. Such is
the result to which, after two years' careful meditation, here and
abroad, the Commissioner has arrived—doing this, too, in face of
the fact, that the British Provinces are being depopulated by reason
of the necessity experienced by their people for seeking elsewhere
the *protection* denied to them at home. Anxious to ameliorate the
condition of those unhappy cultivators of the soil who are being
so heavily "taxed" for the maintenance of our great consuming
population, he now proposes to collect, by means of duties imposed
on sugar, tea, coffee, chocolate, nuts, sardines, and other commodities that do *not* enter into competition with the farmer, the large
sum of $82,500,000; at the same time so reducing the duties on
foreign food that comes to us in the form of cloths, silks, iron, steel,
lead and tin, and that *does* compete with them, that they shall
yield only the sum of $53,000,000. Seeing this, they may well ex-
claim—"Save us from our friends"—such friends as Mr. Commissioner Wells—"and we will, ourselves, take care of those enemies
whose one great cry is, '*Cheap food and cheap labor!*' and who desire that there shall be but a single workshop for the world."

Quoting a foreign authority on the subject of wool, the Commissioner advises his readers, that "it is the last million pounds that
makes scarcity or abundance"—the last, as he well knows, that
determines the question as to whether the farmer shall, or shall
not, be compelled to sell his products abroad "for what they will
bring." Equally well does he know that, whereas, during the dozen
free trade years, from 1848 to 1860, the average domestic product
of iron had actually diminished, and had done so in the face of a
growth of population amounting to forty per cent., the last few
protective years have given us that increase of a million of tons
which had been required for causing abundance, while enabling us
to consume millions upon millions of food, that, had it been ex-

ported, would have so flooded the little foreign markets as to cause losses to the farmers of the world amounting to thousands of millions of dollars.* Clearly seeing all this, as he must, the Commissioner is, nevertheless, unceasing in his efforts at exciting distrust of the future in regard to this great fundamental manufacture, knowing, as he does, that the more it can be discouraged the greater must be the necessity for having "the last million" of food forced upon the British markets, to produce that "overstock," to which our farmers have so often in the past been indebted for the ruin by which they have been overwhelmed.

. Common sense teaches that the larger the domestic markets the less will be the need for exportation, and the greater the farmer's independence. Common honesty would, therefore, have led the Commissioner to unite with the President in urging upon our great agricultural population consideration of the fact, that " *The extension of railroads in Europe and the East is bringing into competition with our agricultural products like products of other countries,*" and, that "*self-interest, if not self-preservation, therefore, dictates caution against disturbing any industrial interest of the country. It teaches us, also, the necessity of looking* TO OTHER MARKETS FOR THE SALE OF OUR SURPLUS."

To look for honesty, however, to the man who has just now furnished tables professing to present a comparative view of the British free trade year 1859 with the protectionist 1869, and who has in their preparation added more than 50 per cent. to the wheat price of the former while largely deducting from that of the latter, would, as I fear, be quite as profitless as has in the past been the search for the philosopher's stone.

His whole Report, professedly prepared for the instruction of our farmers, has been written in the interest of British manufacturers— of the men who desire that food may be cheap and cloth and iron dear, and who are most liberal in their reward of those who aid in establishing their dominion over producers of raw materials throughout the world.   HENRY C. CAREY.

---

* How "the last million" of quarters of wheat is at this moment crushing down prices abroad is shown in the following paragraph giving the latest advices in relation to the English market :—

"Owing to the large stocks of grain at the outports, and to further large importations from abroad, there is no activity in the demand for wheat, and the tendency of prices is downward. The weather has, however, continued damp, and, consequently, the condition of the wheat exhibits no improvement. Fine dry samples of home grown produce have commanded, therefore, former prices. As regards foreign wheat, there is a fall of 1s. a quarter in Russian and American produce. The following statement of imports shows that, since the commencement of the season, our receipts of foreign wheat have been as much as 7,700,000 cwt. more than they were in 1868—9, while of flour there is an increase of 1,850,000 cwt. Of wheat and flour, therefore, there has been an increased importation of 8,850,000 cwt. Of Indian corn there has been an increase of 3,500,000 cwt.; oats, 1,750,000 cwt ; but in barley, beans, and peas, there is a considerable falling off."

Such being the case at a time when the British crop has been not only short but greatly injured, and when Russian and Hungarian roads remain unfinished, what must it be in near future, when British crops shall again be large, and when foreign roads shall be prepared to transport the produce of the great plains of Eastern Europe?

THE

INTERNATIONAL COPYRIGHT QUESTION CONSIDERED,

WITH SPECIAL REFERENCE TO THE INTERESTS

OF

AMERICAN AUTHORS, AMERICAN PRINTERS AND PUBLISHERS,
AND AMERICAN READERS:

BY
H. C. CAREY.

PHILADELPHIA:
HENRY CAREY BAIRD,
INDUSTRIAL PUBLISHER,
406 Walnut Street.
1872.

INTERNATIONAL COPYRIGHT.

AT the date, now many years since, of the writer's first inter-ference in the important case of authors *versus* readers—makers of books and venders of phrases *versus* consumers of facts and ideas—it had for several years been again on trial in the high court of the people. But few years previously the same plaintiffs had obtained a verdict giving large extension of *time* to the monopoly privileges they had so long enjoyed, the fourteen years secured to them at a time when our population was but 4,000,000 having been extended to twenty-eight years among 25,000,000, likely soon to become 100,-000,000.* Not content therewith they now claimed greater *space*, desiring to have those privileges so extended as to include within their domain the vast population of the British Empire, and ready in exchange for trivial advantages to themselves to grant to foreigners supreme control over a large portion of the supply of literary food required by our people. To that hour no one had appeared before the court, on the part of the defendants, prepared seriously to ques-tion the plaintiffs' assertion to the effect that literary property stood on the same precise footing, and as much demanded perpetual and universal recognition, as property in a house, a mine, a farm, or a ship. As a consequence of failure in this respect there prevailed, and most especially throughout the Eastern States, a general impres-sion that there was really but one side to the question; that the cause of the plaintiffs was that of truth; that in the past might had tri-umphed over right; that, however doubtful might be the expediency of making a decree to that effect, there could be little doubt that justice would thereby be done; and that, while rejecting as wholly *inexpedient* the idea of perpetuity, there could be but slight objection to so far recognizing that of universality as to grant to British authors the same privileges that thus far had been accorded to our own.

Throughout those years, nevertheless, the effort to obtain from the legislative authority a decree to that effect had proved an utter fail-ure. Time and again had the case been up for trial, but as often had the plaintiffs' counsel wholly failed to agree among themselves as to the consequences that might reasonably be expected to result

* Under both laws the right of renewal for fourteen years was secured to the author in the event of survivorship.

from recognition of their clients' so-called rights. Northern and Eastern advocates, representing districts in which schools and colleges abounded, insisted that perpetuity and universality of privilege must result in giving to the defendants cheaper books. Southern counsel, on the contrary, representing districts in which schools were rare and students few in number, insisted that extension of the monopoly privilege would have the effect of giving to planters handsome editions of the works they needed, while preventing the publication of "cheap and nasty" editions fitted for the "mudsills" of Northern States. Failing thus to agree among themselves they failed to convince the jury, mainly representing, as it did, the Centre and the West, as a consequence of which they had, on each and every occasion, fled the field without waiting for a verdict.

A thoroughly adverse popular will having thus been manifested, it was now determined to try the Senate, the chances for privilege here seeming to be better. With a population little greater than that of Pennsylvania, the New England States had six times the Senatorial representation. With readers not a third as numerous as were those of Ohio, the States of Carolina, Florida, and Georgia had thrice the number of Senators. By combining these heterogeneous elements the will of the people—so frequently and decidedly expressed—might, it was thought, be set aside. To that end, the Secretary of State, himself one of the plaintiffs, had negotiated the treaty then before the Senate, of the terms of which the defendants had been kept in utter ignorance, and by means of which the principle of taxation without representation was then proposed to be established.

Such was the state of affairs at the date at which, in compliance with the request of a Penusylvania Senator, the writer put on paper ideas that had already been expressed to him in conversation. By him and other Senators they were held to be conclusive, so conclusive that the plaintiffs were speedily brought to see that the path of safety, for the time at least, lay in the direction of abandoning the treaty and allowing it to be quietly laid in the grave in which it since has rested. That such should have been their course was at the time much regretted by the defendants, as they would greatly have preferred an earnest and thorough discussion of the question before the court. Had opportunity been afforded it *would* have been discussed by one, at least, of the master minds of the Senate ;* and so discussed as to have satisfied the whole body of our people, authors and editors perhaps excepted, that their course was that of truth and justice; and that if in the past there had been error it had been that of excess of liberality towards the plaintiffs in the suit.

The issue then evaded has now been again (1867) presented, eminent counsel having been employed, and the opening speech having then been made through the columns of a leading Massachusetts journal. Careful perusal of it, however, has resulted in obtaining evidence that there was in it nothing beyond a labored effort at reducing the

* Senator Clayton, of Delaware.

literary profession to a level with those of the grocer and the tallow-chandler. It was an elaborate reproduction of Oliver Twist's cry for "more! more!"—a new edition of the "Beggar's Petition," perusal of which must certainly have affected with profound disgust many, if not even most, of the eminent persons therein referred to. In it there was presented for consideration the sad case of one distinguished writer and admirable man who, by means of his pen alone, had been enabled to pass through a long life of most remarkable enjoyment, although his money receipts had, by reason of the alleged injustice of consumers of his products, but little exceeded $200,000; that of a lady writer who, by means of a sensational novel of great merit and admirably adapted to the modes of thought of the hour, had been enabled to earn in a single year the large sum of $40,000, though still deprived of very many other thousands she was there said fairly to have earned; of a historian whose labors, after deducting what had been applied to the creation of an extensive and costly library and most valuable antiquarian collection, had scarcely yielded fifty cents per day; of another who had had but $1000 per month; and, passing rapidly from the sublime to the ridiculous, of a school copy-book maker who had seen his improvements copied without compensation to himself, for the benefit of English children.

These might perhaps be regarded as very sad facts; but had not the picture a brighter side, and might it not have been well for the eminent counsel to have presented both? Might he not, for instance, have told his readers that, in addition to the $200,000 above referred to, and wholly as acknowledgment of his literary services, the eminent recipient had for many years enjoyed a diplomatic sinecure of the highest order, by means of which he had been enabled to give his time to the collection of materials for his most important works? Might he not have further told us how other of the distinguished men he had named, as well as many others whose names had not been given, had, in a manner precisely similar, been rewarded for their literary labors? Might he not have said something of the pecuniary and societary successes that had so closely followed the appearance of the novel to whose publication he had attributed so great an influence? Might he not, and with great propriety, have furnished an extract from the books of the "New York Ledger," exhibiting the tens and hundreds of thousands that had been paid for articles which few, if any, would care to read a second time? Might he not have told his readers of the thousands and tens of thousands paid for successive repetitions of single public lectures? Might he not, too, have told his readers that whereas half a century since, the inquiry had been made as to "who reads an American book," this country had already become the very paradise of literary men?* Would, how-

* The following paragraph, from a daily journal, furnishes a few facts illustrative of the views above presented: "The heirs of Noah Webster receive $25,000 annually from the sale of his Dictionary. Harper & Brothers pay Marcius Wilson an annual copyright of $16,000; and the same house has paid Anthon, Barnes, Robinson, Abbott, Motley, Prescott, or their heirs,

ever, such a course of proceeding have answered his present purpose ? Perhaps not ! His business was to pass around the hat, accompanying it with a strong appeal to the charity of the defendants, and this, so far as can be seen, is all that thus far has been done.

Might not, however, a similar, and yet stronger, appeal now be made in behalf of other of the public servants ? At the close of long lives devoted to the public service, Washington, Hamilton, Clay, Clayton, and many others of our most eminent men have found themselves largely losers, not gainers, by public service. The late Governor Andrew's services were surely worth as much, per hour, as those of the authoress of " Uncle Tom's Cabin ;" yet did he give five years of his life, and perhaps his life itself, for less than half of what she had received for the labors of a single one. Deducting the expenses incident to his official life, Mr. Lincoln would have been required to labor for five and twenty years before he could have received as much as was paid to the author of the " Sketch Book." The labors of the historian of Ferdinand and Isabella proved, to himself and family, ten times more productive than since have been those of Mr. Stanton, the great war minister of the age.—Turning next from civil to military life, we see among ourselves officers who have but recently rendered the largest service, but who are now quite coolly whistled down the wind to find where they can the means of support for wives and children. Studying the lists of honored dead we find therein the names of men of high renown whose widows and children are now starving on pensions, the annual amount of which is less than the monthly receipts of some of the authors above referred to.

Such being the facts, and that they are such cannot be denied, let us now suppose a proposition to be made that, with a view to increase the annual incomes of ex-presidents and legislators, and those of the widows and children of distinguished officers, there should be established a general pension system, involving an expenditure of the public moneys, and consequent taxation, to the extent of ten or fifteen millions a year, and then inquire by whom it might be supported. Would any single one of the editors who are now so earnest in their appeals for further grants of monopoly power venture so to do ? Would not the most earnest of them be among the first to visit on such a proposition the most withering denunciations ? Judging from what in the last few years has appeared in various editorial columns, it might safely be asserted that they would be so. Would, however, any member of either house of Congress venture to commit himself before the world by offering such a proposition ? Assuredly not !

upwards of $50,000 each, copyright on their works. Charles Scribner & Co. paid Headly $50,000 prior to 1859, and to Dr. Holland they have paid a larger amount. Hurd & Houghton still pay a copyright of $4000 on Cooper's works. We might mention Irving, Bancroft, Barton, and many others, which would make it apparent that the best authors derive as much or more from their books as sold in the trade, than if sold by subscription agents.'' To this it may be added, that one of the most active advocates of internal copyright is understood to have realized $120,000 as the profits of a single work.

Nevertheless, it is now coolly proposed to establish a system that would not only tax the present generation as many millions annually, but that would grow in amount at a rate far exceeding the growth of population, doing this in the hope that future essayists might be enabled to count their receipts by half instead of quarter millions, and future novelists to collect abroad and at home the hundreds of thousands that, as we are assured, are theirs of *right*, and are now, denied them. When we shall have determined to grant to the widows and children of the men who in the last decade have perished in the public service, some reasonable measure of justice, it may be time to consider that question, but until then it should most certainly be deferred.

The most active and earnest of all the advocates of literary *rights* was, some years since, if the writer's memory correctly serves him, the most thorough and determined of all our journalists in insisting on the prompt dismissal of thousands and tens of thousands of men who, at their country's call, had abandoned the pursuits and profits of civil life. Did he, however, ever propose that they should be allowed any extra pay on which to live, and by means of which to support their wives and children, in the interval between discharge from military service and re-establishment in their old pursuits? Nothing of the kind is now recollected. Would he now advocate the enactment of a law by means of which the widow and children of a major-general who had fallen on the field should, so far as pay was concerned, be placed on a level with an intelligent police reporter? He might, but that he would do so could not with any certainty be affirmed. She and they would, nevertheless, seem to have claims on the consideration of American men and women fully equal to those of the authoress of "Lady Audley's Secret," already, as she is understood to be, in the annual receipt from this country of more than thrice the amount of the widow's pension, in addition to tens of thousands at home.*

It is, however, as we are gravely told, but ten per cent. that she asks, and who could or should object to payment of such a pittance? Not many, perhaps, *if unaccompanied by monopoly privileges that would multiply the ten by ten and make it an hundred!* Alone, the cost to our readers might not now exceed an annual million. Let Congress then pass an act appropriating that sum to be distributed among foreign authors whose works had been, or might be, republished here. *That* should have the writer's vote, but he objects, and will continue to object, to any legislative action that shall tend towards giving to already "great and wealthy" publishing houses the *many* millions they certainly will charge for collecting the single *one* that will go abroad.†

* The London correspondent of Scribner & Co.'s "*Book Buyer*" says that Miss Braddon's first publisher, Mr. Tinsley (who died suddenly last year), called the elegant villa he built for himself at Putney "Audley House," in grateful remembrance of the "Lady" to whose "Secret" he was indebted for fortune; and Miss Braddon herself, through her man of business, has recently purchased a stately mansion of Queen Anne's time, "Litchfield House," at Richmond.

† New Jersey imposed a tax on travellers of ten cents per head, at the

"Great and wealthy" as they are here said to be, and as they certainly are, we are assured that even they have serious troubles against which they greatly need to be protected. In common with many heretofore competing railroad companies they have found that however competition among themselves benefits the public, it tends rather to their own injury, and therefore have they, by means of most stringent rules, established a "courtesy" copyright, the effect of which exhibits itself in the fact, that the prices of reprinted books are now rapidly approaching those of domestic productions. Further advances in that direction might, however, prove dangerous; "courtesy" rules, as we are assured by members of the Copyright Association, not being readily susceptible of enforcement. A salutary fear of interlopers still restrains those "great and wealthy houses," at heavy annual cost to themselves, and with great saving to consumers of their products. That this may all be changed; that they may build up fortunes with still increased rapidity; that they may, to a still greater extent, monopolize the business of publication; and, that the people may be taxed to that effect; all that is now needed is, that Congress pass a very simple law by means of which a few men in Eastern cities shall be enabled to monopolize the business of republication, secure from either Eastern or Western competition. That done, readers will be likely to see a state of things similar to that recently exhibited at Chicago, where railroad companies that had secured to themselves all the exits and entrances of the city were, as we were told, engaged in organizing a combination that should have the effect of dividing in fair proportion among the wolves the numerous flocks of sheep.

On all former occasions Northern advocates of literary monopolies assured us that it was in that direction, and in that alone, we were to look for the cheapening of books. Now, nothing of the sort is at all pretended. On the contrary, we are here lectured on the extreme impropriety of a system which makes it necessary for a New England essayist to accept a single dollar for a volume that under other circumstances would sell for half a guinea; on the wrong to such essayists that results from the issue of cheap "periodicals made up of selections from the reviews and magazines of Europe;" on the "abominable extravagance of buying a great and good novel in a perishable form for a few cents;" on the increased accessibility of books by the "masses of the people" that must result from increasing prices; and on the greatly increased facility with which circulating libraries may be formed whensoever the "great and wealthy houses" shall have been given power to claim from each and every reader of popular novels, as their share of the monopoly profits, more than he now pays for the book itself! This, however, is only history repeating itself with a little change of place, the argument of to-day, coming

same time granting to its collectors, the Camden & Amboy Railroad Co., a monopoly of transportation by means of which they were enabled to collect an extra dollar per head. This is precisely what the persistent advocates of international copyright seem determined that we shall do.

from the North, being an almost exact repetition of that which, twenty years since, came from the South—from the mouths of men who rejoiced in the fact that no newspapers were published in their districts, and who well *knew* that the way toward preventing the dissemination of knowledge lay in the direction of granting the monopoly privileges that had then been asked. The anti-slavery men of the present thus repeat the argument of the pro-slavery men of the past, extremes being thus brought close together.

The Counsel for the monopoly assures us that Russia, Sweden, and other countries are ready to unite with us in recognizing the "rights" now claimed. So, too, it may be well believed, would it be with China, Japan, Bokhara, and the Sandwich Islands. Of what use, however, would be such an union ? Would it increase the facilities for transplanting the ideas of American authors ? Are not the obstacles to such transplantation already sufficiently great, and is it desirable that they be at all increased ? Germany has already tried the experiment, but whether or not, when the time shall come, the existing treaties will be renewed, is very doubtful. Where she now pays dollars, she probably receives cents. Discussion of the question there has led to the translation and republication of the present writer's earlier papers, and the views therein expressed have received the public approbation of men whose opinions are entitled to high consideration. What has recently been done in that country in reference to domestic copyright, and what has been the effect, are well exhibited in an article from an English journal of the highest authority, a part of which, American moneys having been substituted for German ones, is here given as follows :—

"We have so long enjoyed the advantage of unrestricted competition in the production of the works of the best English writers of the past, that we can hardly realize what our position would have been had the right to produce Shakspeare, or Milton, or Goldsmith, or any of our great classic writers, been monopolized by any one publishing house—certainly we should never have seen a shilling Shakspeare, or a half-crown Milton ; and Shakspeare, instead of being, as he is, 'familiar in our mouths as household words,' would have been known but to the scholar and the student. We are far from condemning an enlightened system of copyright, and have not a word to say in favor of unreasoning competition ; but we do think that publishers and authors often lose sight of their own interest in adhering to a system of high prices and restricted sales. Tennyson's works supply us with a case in point—here, to possess a set of Tennyson's poems, a reader must pay something like 38*s.* or 40*s.* ; in Boston you may buy a magnificent edition of all his works in two volumes for something like 15*s.*, and a small edition for some four or five shillings. The result is the purchasers in England are numbered by hundreds, in America by thousands. In Germany we have almost a parallel case. There the works of the great German poets, of Schiller, of Goethe, of Jean Paul, of Wieland, and of Herder, are at the present time 'under the protecting privileges of the most illustrious German Confederation,' and, by special privilege, the exclusive property of the Stuttgart publishing firm of J. G. Cotta. On the forthcoming 9th of November this monopoly will cease, and all the works of the above-mentioned poets will be open to the speculation of German publishers generally. It may be interesting to our readers to learn the history of the peculiar legal restrictions which have so long prevailed in the German book-trade, and the results likely to follow from their removal.

"Until the beginning of this century literary piracy was not prohibited in the German States. As, however, protection of literary productions was, at last, emphatically urged, the Acts of the Confederation (on the reconstruction of Germany in the year 1815) contained a passage to the effect, that the Diet should, at its first meeting, consider the necessity of uniform laws for securing the rights of literary men and publishers. The Diet moved in the matter in the year 1818, appointing a commission to settle this question; and, thanks to that supreme profoundness which was ever applied to the affairs of the father-land by this illustrious body, after twenty-two years of deliberation, on the 9th of Nov. 1837, decreed the law, that the rights of authorship should be acknowledged and respected, at least, for the space of ten years; copyright for a longer period, however, being granted for voluminous and costly works, and for the works of the great German poets.

"In the course of time, however, a copyright for ten years proved insufficient even for the commonest works; it was therefore extended by a decree of the Diet, dated June 19, 1845, over the natural term of the author's life and for thirty years after his death. With respect to the works of all authors deceased before the 9th of November, 1837—including the works of the poets enumerated above—the Diet decided that they could all be protected until the 9th of November, 1867.

" It was to be expected that the firm of J. G. Cotta, favored until now with so valuable a monopoly, would make all possible exertions not to be surpassed in the coming battle of the Publishers, though it is a somewhat curious sight to see this haughty house, after having used its privileges to the last moment, descend now suddenly from its high monopolistic stand into the arena of competition, and compete for public favor with its plebeian rivals. Availing itself of the advantage which the monopoly hitherto attached to it naturally gives it, the house has just commenced issuing a cheap edition of the German classics, under the title 'Bibliothek fur Alle Meisterwerke deutscher Classiker,' in weekly parts, 6 cts. each; containing the selected works of Schiller, at the price of 75 cts., and the selected works of Goethe, at the price of $1.50. And now, just as the monopoly is gliding from their hands, the same firm offers, in a small 16mo. edition, Schiller's complete works, 12 vols., for 75 cts.

"Another publisher, A. H. Payne, of Leipzig, announces a complete edition of Schiller's works, including some unpublished pieces, for 75 cents.

"Again, the well-known firm of F. A. Brockhaus holds out a prospectus of a corrected critical edition of the German poets of the eighteenth and nineteenth century, which we have every reason to believe will merit success. A similar enterprise is announced, just now, by the Bibliographical Institution of Hildburghausen, under the title, 'Bibliothek der deutschen National-literatur,' edited by Heinr. Kurz, in weekly parts of 10 sheets, at the price of 12 cts. each. Even an illustrated edition of the Classics will be presented to the public, in consequence of the expiration of the copyright. The Grote'sche Buchhandlung, of Berlin, is issuing the 'Hausbibliothek deutscher Classiker,' with wood-cut illustrations by such eminent artists as Richter, Thumann, and others; and the first part, just published, containing Louise, by Voss, with truly artistic illustrations, has met with general approbation. But, above all, the popular edition of the poets, issued by G. Hempel, of Berlin, under the general title of 'National Bibliothek sammtlicher deutscher Classiker,' 8vo. in parts, 6 cts. each, seems destined to surpass all others in popularity, though not in merit. *Of the first part (already published), containing Burger's Poems, 300,000 copies have been sold, and 150,000 subscribers names have been registered for the complete series. This immense sale, unequalled in the annals of the German book-trade, will certainly induce many other publishers to embark in similar enterprises.*"—Trübner's *Literary Record,* Oct. 1867.

Judging from this, there must be soon little short of a million of families in possession of the works of Schiller, Burger, Goethe, Herder, and others, that till now had been compelled to dispense with their perusal. Sad to think, however, they will be of those cheap editions so much despised by American advocates of monopoly privileges! How much better for the German people would it not have been had their Parliament recognized the perpetuity of literary *rights*, thereby enabling the "great and wealthy house" of Cotta & Co. to carry into full effect the idea that their own editions should alone be published, thus adding other millions to the very many of which they already are the owners!

Mr. Bayard Taylor advises us that German circulating libraries impede the sale of books; that the circulation of even highly popular works is limited within 20,000; and that, as a necessary consequence, German authors are not paid so well as of right they should be. This, however, is precisely the state of things that, as we are now assured, should be brought about in this country, prices being raised and readers being driven to the circulating library by reason of deficiency of the means required for forming the private one. It is the one that *would* be brought about should our authors, unhappily for themselves, succeed in obtaining what is now demanded.

The day has passed, in this country, for recognition of either perpetuity or universality of literary *rights*. The wealthy Carolinian, anxious that books might be high in price, and knowing well that monopoly privileges were opposed to freedom, gladly co-operated with Eastern authors and publishers, anti-slavery as they professed to be. The enfranchised black, on the contrary, desires that books may be cheap, and to that end he and his representatives will be found in all the future co-operating with men of the Centre and the West in maintaining the doctrine that literary *privileges* exist in virtue of grants from the people who own the materials out of which books are made ; that those privileges have been perhaps already too far extended ; that there exists not even a shadow of reason for any further extension ; and, that to grant the universal monopoly which now is asked would be a positive wrong to the many millions of consumers, as well as a further obstacle to be placed in the road towards civilization.

The amount paid for public service under our various governments, local, state, and general, is more than, were it fairly distributed, would suffice for giving proper reward to all. Unfortunately the *distribution* is very bad, the largest compensation generally going to those who render the smallest service. So, too, is it with regard to literary employments ; and so is it likely to continue throughout the future. Grant all that now is asked, and the effect will be seen in the fact, that of the vastly increased taxation ninety per cent. will go to those who work for money alone, and are already overpaid, leaving but little to be added to the rewards of conscientious men with whom their work is a labor of love, as is the case with the distinguished author of the "History of the Netherlands."

Twenty years ago, Macaulay advised his literary friends to be content, believing, as he told them, that the existing "wholesome copyright" was likely to "share in the disgrace and danger" of the more extended one which they then so much desired to see created. Let our authors reflect on this advice! Success now, were it possible that it should be obtained, would be productive of great danger in the already not distant future. In the natural course of things, most of our authorship, for many years to come, will be found east of the Hudson, most of the buyers of books, meanwhile, being found south and west of that river. International copyright will give to the former limited territory an absolute monopoly of the business of republication, the then great cities of the West being almost as completely deprived of participation therein as are now the towns and cities of Canada and Australia. On the one side, there will be found a few thousand persons interested in maintaining the monopolies that had been granted to authors and publishers, foreign and domestic. On the other, sixty or eighty millions tired of taxation and determined that books shall be more cheaply furnished. War will then come, and the domestic author, sharing in the "disgrace and danger" attendant upon his alliance with foreign authors and domestic publishers, may perhaps find reason to rejoice if the people fail to arrive at the conclusion that the last extension of *his own privileges* had been inexpedient and should be at once recalled. Let him then study that well-known fable of Æsop entitled "The Dog and the Shadow," and take warning from it!

The present writer has no personal interest in the question herein discussed. Himself an author, he has gladly witnessed the translation and republication of his works in various countries of Europe, his sole reason for writing them having been found in a desire for strengthening the many against the few by whom the former have so long, to a greater or less extent, been enslaved. To that end it is that he now writes, fully believing that the *right* is on the side of the consumer of books, and not with their producers, whether authors or publishers. Between the two there is, however, a perfect harmony of all real and permanent interests, and greatly will he be rejoiced if he shall have succeeded in persuading even some few of his literary countrymen that such is the fact, and that the path of safety will be found in the direction of LETTING WELL ENOUGH ALONE.

The reward of literary service, and the estimation in which literary men are held, both grow with growth in that power of combination which results from diversification of employments; from bringing consumers and producers close together; and from thus stimulating the activity of the societary circulation. Both decline as producers and consumers become more widely separated, and as the circulation becomes more languid, as is the case in all the countries now subjected to the British free-trade influence. Let American authors then unite in asking of Congress the establishment of a fixed and steady policy which shall have the effect of giving us that industrial independence without which there can be neither political nor literary independence. That once secured, they would thereafter find no need for asking the establishment of a system of taxation which would prove so burdensome to our people as, in the end, to be ruinous to themselves.

PHILADELPHIA, Dec. 1867.

As shown by the figures, several years have now elapsed since the above pages were first furnished for perusal by those who might feel an interest in the question therein discussed. For inducement to their preparation and publication, their writer had only that resulting from an earnest desire to prevent what he knew must prove a most injurious course of action, whether considered with reference to the interests of our authors, our manufacturers, or those of the whole body of our people, consumers of their products. To that end he desired that our legislators, senators and representatives, should have placed before them the real facts of the case, becoming thus enabled, with some approach to accuracy, to determine for themselves the propriety of yielding to the clamor then existing for further privileges to be, at the cost of our many millions of readers, exercised by a few thousand men and women who wield the pen, and who already, under existing laws, have acquired the right to claim to constitute the best paid body of writers now existing in the world. Most glad has he since then learned that he had not labored in vain, the Secretary of the Association that had been formed for the purpose of engineering through Congress this scheme for compelling our people to pay double or triple prices for their supplies of intellectual food, having assured his constituents, and his readers at large, that to him must be mainly attributed their then recent disastrous failure.*

Together with the bill that had been thus so summarily sent to its grave unhonored and unmourned by any but those who had hoped to profit by its provisions, the House of Representatives had been favored with a Report, little study of which has since been needed for helping us to arrive at the conclusion that its author had been wholly destitute of the knowledge required for enabling him properly to appreciate the practical operation of his own bill, should it unfortunately become converted into law; and, that while almost entirely suppressing the views of those opposed to monopoly extension, he had allowed himself to be misled by interested parties into the presentation of a series of assertions directly opposed to all that daily experience shows us to be true, some of which are here given, as follows :—

I. That European copyright treaties had proved successes, having greatly promoted the transfer from nation to nation of works of the higher order ;† and that similar results might confidently be looked for here when we should have determined on the adoption of a similar course of action :

II. That the direct effects of monopoly extension were destined to exhibit themselves here in the form of a great increase in the consumption of books, products of both foreign and domestic minds, giving to their publishers both the power and the will to furnish them at greatly diminished prices :

III. That with this growing demand there must be an increasing tendency towards creation of a thoroughly independent literature :

IV. That simultaneously therewith, and as a consequence of prohibition of competition for the supply of intellectual food, its manufacturers, whether printers, paper-makers, or engravers, must find increased demand for their services, with constant increase in the reward of labor.

In all other departments of human employment it is insisted that

---

* Parton. "Topics of the Time," article *Log-Rolling at Washington.*

† This is nowhere positively asserted, but the whole tendency of the Report is that of impressing the idea on the reader's mind. After highly commending the European system, the Reporter proceeds as follows :—

"At present, our reading of foreign literature is confined chiefly to English books, some of them works of genius, some merely good, many of them either very stupid or utterly worthless. The last-named books are republished here, because they need no translation, and will serve to supply the demand for new books in a market where readers must take these or nothing. Establish international copyright laws, and we shall very soon see translations of the best French, German, Swedish, Danish, and other European books taking the place of these wretched English books. When it shall become necessary to buy the copyright of a worthless book published in Great Britain, publishers will prefer to secure instead translations of the best new books published in other countries. In this way books of a higher class will go into circulation, and the worthless English books, now so abundant in the market, will gradually disappear."

the more perfect the competition the lower must be prices, and the larger the consumption. The protectionist insists that domestic competition is needed for controlling the foreigner in his prices; the free trader, on the contrary, demanding that foreign competition be maintained as a means of controlling the domestic manufacturer. Here, in this great and most important branch of industry, we are, on the contrary, assured that all the facts teach the reverse, the true road towards reduction of prices and increased demand being found in the direction of creating monopolies that shall control, and in the most absolute manner, the supply of literary food, even to the total extinction of that source of supply which exhibits itself in those selections from foreign periodicals given in our daily, weekly, and monthly journals. How far all this may be regarded as true or false will be now examined under the various heads above described.

I. The grand obstacle to the transmission of written and published ideas from country to country is found in the cost of translation, this having proved so very serious as to have caused the movement to be sluggish to an extreme degree. To it has now been added a necessity for correspondence with, and payment to, the original author, Pelion being thus piled on Ossa with a view, as we are gravely told, to reduction of the obstacles that before had needed to be overcome. How far success has attended this extraordinary course of action we may now inquire.

By the British and French treaty, the type, or nearly so, of all that have since been made, copyright becomes absolute from the moment of publication, and so continues to the close of the second year; the right then ceasing to exist in the event of no republication having yet been made. By means of this restriction Victor Hugo has been enabled to obtain in England $5000 for his latest novel, Messrs. Erckmann-Chatrian, and possibly other novelists or dramatists, in some small degree following suit. When, however, we turn to the higher branches of literature or science, to industrial or professional works, we learn that it has become quite common to postpone translation and republication until expiration of the allotted period, and then to bring them before the public. So well is this now understood that even here there have occurred repeated cases in which the same process has been pursued in reference to works of the higher order, a sale for which it was hoped to find in Britain. Should evidence be desired that such is now a very common course of action, it will at any time be furnished, and of the highest order. That done, it will be for the advocates of monopoly privileges to show that the present system tends in any manner to the advantage of either country.

Turning now to Germany we find a state of things precisely similar—Carlyle, Hepworth Dixon, and a limited number of novelists, as shown in the note below,* receiving trivial payments for the right of

* The well-known Tauchnitz editions are protected by copyright, but it does not appear that the German publisher has made very liberal payments

reproducing their works in their original language. When, however, the cost of translation needs to be added to that of copyright so very little seems to be done as to render it very doubtful if, notwithstanding the large increase of population, the work of transference from foreign languages, and foreign countries, has even held its own.

That it cannot so have done would seem to be proved by the fact, that a catalogue of the new publications, domestic and foreign, 3000 in number, added to the great royal library connected with the Statistical Bureau at Berlin, in the quarter previous to the late war, embracing history, geography, and every department of industry and science, that of language alone excepted, exhibits but a single volume translated from the English; that one even being but little more than a rómance connected with Italian history. Others may possibly have escaped notice, but it seems quite safe to assert that a single half dozen would embrace nearly all the works contained therein translated from the French and English languages.

The *Magazin für die Literatur des Auslandes,* one of the oldest and most respectable of German literary journals, exhibits in its notices and advertisements for the last three months precisely seven translations from the English, as follows: two of Scott's "Lady of the Lake;" one each of Darwin, Lecky, and Ross Browne; and two others of no importance whatsoever. Comparing this with what appears to be done in England, we find a state of things very nearly similar, recent " general lists" of their own publications, twenty-five hundred in number, issued by five " great and wealthy houses," exhibiting but about a dozen translations from modern languages, half of even this small number being wholly unimportant.

Seeing thus how entire has been the failure of an attempt at obtaining increase of action by aid of accumulated burthens, might it not be well for the several governments now to retrace their steps ? Might it not be so for England, France, and Germany to substitute direct payment for grant of monopoly privileges, each appropriating an annual half million of dollars to be divided among foreign authors whose works should come to be either translated or republished in their original language ? By such an arrangement, while the self-imposed restriction on the circulation of ideas would be removed the amount distributed would probably be thrice increased—that increase going to producers of books of a higher order than those which now alone can bear the greatly heightened cost of reproduction.

Turning our eyes homeward, we find publishers engaged in dis-

---

to the English authors whom he reprints. Mr. Carlyle, for four volumes of his " Frederick the Great," received from Baron Tauchnitz only £225 ; Mr. Dickens, for his last novel " Our Mutual Friend," £150 ; Miss Mulloch, or her publishers, for a " Noble Life," £50 ; Mrs. Wood, for "Oswald Cray," £60 ; Miss Craik, for " Christian's Mistake," £50 ; Miss Kavanagh, for "Beatrice," £30 ; Mrs. Riddell, for "George Geith," £25 ; Miss Annie Thomas, for " On Guard," £25 ; Miss Edwards, for "Half a Million of Money," £40 ; Mr. Hepworth Dixon, for his " Holy Land," £40 ; Mrs. Oliphant, for " Agnes," £20 ; Florence Marryat, for "Love's Conflict," £25 ; and Mr. Charles Lever, for "Luttrell of Arran," £30.—*London Daily News.*

tributing the translated works of Madame Sand, Madame Mühlbach, and other novelists; doing this with a perfect confidence that their property therein is safe from interference. Occasionally there appears a work of somewhat higher order, but the total number of translations is so very small as to be wholly insignificant. Why is this? The field is open to all who see fit to give their time to the work of transferring the ideas of continental Europe to the towns and cities of this western continent. Why then is the work not done? For the simple reason that the number of books that will bear the cost of mere translation is so very small Pile upon this that of copyright, preceded by negotiations with foreign authors having exaggerated notions of the profits to be derived from reproduction here of works to which they themselves attach so high a value, and the business of translation will be then near to an untimely end.

Having studied the real facts of the case as here given, the reader may probably now unite with the present writer in an expression of regret that a gentleman, charged with examination of a question so important as is the one now under consideration, should have allowed himself to indulge in prophecies so wholly different from those he certainly would have made had he had any proper understanding of the subject.

II. "That the reader may fully understand the views, on the subject of prices, of the author of the Report, the passage referring thereto is here given, as follows :—

" 'The old objection, that such laws would increase the price of books, did not proceed from a careful study of the laws of trade, and, therefore, could not endure criticism. It will not now be urged by any person who has considered the matter in all its bearings. This objection assumed that the copyright would be a tax on the trade which the publishers must charge over to their customers—a grave mistake. It is the price paid for security in the market. To the publisher of a saleable book, as we have shown, this guarantee against injury from rival editions is an advantage for which he can afford to pay handsomely. The protected copyright of a foreign book would be worth to his business much more than it would cost. With this protection he would be able to sell the book cheaper, and readers would have books more beautifully manufactured in all respects, from the type to the last finish of the binding.' "

Simultaneously with the preparation of this paragraph publishers and journalists throughout the Union were vying with each other for precedence in the publication of a story of Mr. Dickens, little, if indeed any, short of a million of which must have been put into circulation at a cost so utterly insignificant that it would scarcely be possible here to estimate it. Had international copyright then existed a single house would have had a monopoly of its publication; the price would have been fifty cents; fifty thousand copies might have been printed; and thus, at a cost of $25,000 to the well-to-do portion of the community, millions of farmers, miners, artisans, their wives and children, would have been deprived of the pleasure derived from the perusal of "No Thoroughfare."—From week to week, for many months, the Messrs. Harper, by means of their "Weekly," have now been placing in the hands of 200,000 families portions of a new novel by Mr. Wilkie Collins, and at a merely nominal cost. Had international copyright existed throughout the present year the author would assuredly have told his American publishers that the price of the right for Britain and the Colonies had been $20,000; that the American market must certainly be worth at least half that sum; that they could readily indemnify themselves by the sale of 10,000 copies at $3.00; and that less than that he would not take. Whether or not he would have been contented with even so large a sum is very doubtful, more than half that having recently been offered, *and refused*, for the mere advance sheets of another novel by an author of little, if any, greater popularity. Under such circumstances, would not the 200,000 families who, as Messrs. Harper themselves assure their readers, are accustomed to look to their journal for supplies of literary food, have found themselves, so far at least as that novel was concerned, compelled to fast. Such, assuredly, would have been the case.

"The Living Age" furnishes weekly selections from the principal English journals, the quantity so supplied for eight dollars amounting annually to nearly 3400 heavy 8vo. pages, distributed among the working men of the country from the Atlantic to the Pacific, and from the Lakes to the Gulf of Mexico. How shall these people be supplied with literary food when copyright absolute, even without republication here, shall have been established for the three. months that follow publication?

Tennyson has just now favored the world with an "Idyll of the King," of which hundreds of thousands have already found their way into families like those above described. Had international copyright existed, from twenty to thirty thousand copies might perhaps have thus far been sent forth, printed on handsome paper and neatly put together, to be supplied to wealthy people at a cost of some eight or ten thousand dollars; but for that large class which needs to work there would have been none whatsoever.

Of Charles Reade's last novel the sale is said to have reached an hundred thousand, at an average cost to the purchaser of about forty cents. Under the system now proposed not a single one would have been issued at a less price than three dollars, there being no writer in Europe who has a more exaggerated notion of his really great abilities, or of his auctorial rights. At that price some ten or fifteen thousand copies would have been sold to wealthy purchasers, leaving the "mudsills" of society to wait until supplied by circulating libraries in the few towns and cities possessed of such institutions.

We are assured, nevertheless, that increase of the monopoly privilege will certainly be followed by so great an increase of sale that the hearts of authors and publishers must become so greatly softened as to induce them to supply the demand for intellectual food at prices even less than those now paid. How far past experience warrants expression of such a hope we may now inquire.

Of Tennyson's works there have at various times been published hundreds of thousands, and the whole, handsomely printed, may now be purchased for fifty cents. Of Longfellow's copyrighted works there has, until quite recently, been no edition that could be purchased at less than *six times that price.* If enlarged sale could in any case have had the softening effect above referred to, here it is that it would certainly have been found, the popularity of our great poet having been such that hundreds of thousands additional could have been sold had they been cheaply furnished.

Looking now across the Atlantic we find a state of things directly the reverse, the copyrighted works of the Laureate being there placed beyond the reach of any but the rich; his unprotected American competitors for public favor, on the contrary, exhibiting themselves on every railroad stall, and seeking purchasers at a shilling, or little more. (See page 9, *ante.*) Why now is it that neither the English publishers of the one, nor the American publishers of the other, can be persuaded to see with the eyes of our Reporter the great advantage to result from placing popular authors cheaply before the world?

Of Miss Alcott's charming little volume, entitled "Little Women," the sale here is said to have already reached 80,000 copies, the author's share of the profits having been no less than $12,000. No one more than the present writer rejoices at seeing that her reward has been so great, but he has looked in vain to find in the course of her publisher evidence that extensive circulation, under monopoly privilege, is likely to be attended with declining price. The companion work, "Little Men," is not sold more cheaply than its predecessor, nor will it be until the public shall cease to manifest a willingness to pay $3 for two small volumes containing probably fewer words than in the early days of copyright, with not a tenth of our present population, were given for a single dollar by the publisher of Brockden Brown's well known and then popular novel of "Ormond." When increased *time* was asked we were assured that to grant the demand would cheapen books, precisely as we are now told that all that is needed for attainment of this important object is increase of monopoly *space.*

Of Bret Harte's deservedly popular little volumes the sale has been exceedingly great, the public having paid $3 for two of them containing less than half the words that can now be purchased of Tennyson for 50 cents, if not even less.

Of Macaulay's England there have probably been sold 200,000 copies, costing the purchasers little, if any, more than as many dollars. Had international copyright existed, would he not have claimed that his book should be sold as high as were those of Bancroft and Prescott, $2.50 per volume? Assuredly he would, and both author and publisher would have largely profited by thus raising the price and cutting down the sale, thereby depriving probably 180,000 families of the privilege of reading his important work. If large sales are to be followed by reduction of prices why is it that the publishers of Bancroft, Prescott, and Longfellow show themselves so exceedingly indisposed to furnish evidence of the fact? Why is it that Bryant's Iliad cannot yet be purchased at less than $5, being ten times more than would purchase the Iliad of Pope? Why is it that now when sales are counted by tens of thousands the prices of American works are greatly higher than they had been when they counted by less than even single thousands? Why is it that authors and publishers are so nearly universally now united in the effort so to raise the prices of books produced abroad as to place them beyond the reach of the great mass of our reading public?

That great will be the effects of change such as is now proposed is very certain. How far it will be right for legislators so to act as to enable monopoly agitators to succeed in its accomplishment, they will decide after, and not as it is hoped before, careful study of the facts that have been here presented.

III. "International copyright laws would," says our Reporter, "very much increase the business of manufacturers, publishers, and sellers of books in the United States." In other words, a law whose especial object is that of raising the prices of republications to a level with those of the works of Harte, Longfellow, Miss Alcott, Prescott, and Bancroft, thus in large degree depriving of literary food nine-tenths of our whole people, is to cause greatly increased demand for the services of those engaged in the various processes required for preparation of such food! That the very reverse of this must be the result of abandonment of the system hitherto pursued will now be shown, as follows :—

By the bill reported three years since, and likely to be again brought before the House, copyright becomes absolute on the moment of publication, and so continues during the first three months that follow, to be still continued only in the event of republication here. Throughout that period the foreign publisher, secured in the entire control of the market, sends hundreds or thousands of copies to be sold to wealthy people at twice or thrice the price that would be now demanded for a reprint here, taking thus so entirely the cream of the market as to prevent all possibility of future interference. The ground having been thus occupied he declines republication, leaving the field open after having himself harvested all of the crop possessing any value. That the direct effect of measures such as are now proposed must be that of throwing into foreign hands the supply of works of a higher order that may hereafter be produced abroad, cannot be denied even by those now most actively engaged in preparing for the closing of our book-producing workshops.

In what manner, however, is it likely to operate with those popular novelists and poets who are now so largely paid abroad; whose appetite for money grows with what it feeds upon ; whose abuse of "piracy" has so long been showered on our devoted heads ;* and

* "Impudent robberies are committed every day ; but they would not have gone on so many weeks as years, had the case been reversed. America profits by the present state of things, England loses."
"The effrontery of the American publishers is perfectly amazing. They

who know so well that few except themselves can in any manner profit by the restriction on reproduction now so strongly urged. Let us see.

Secured for three months against interference, what is to prevent them from printing large editions for the American market, to be passed under our admirable *ad valorem* system at little more than the mere cost of manufacture; the author claiming, as of right, that as no copy money had been paid, no duty could be demanded upon that portion of the price of those which had been prepared for the British market. Desiring next to extend the time, all that by the bill now before us is required to be done is, that a week previous to its close "an arrangement shall be made in good faith with an American publisher for *its immediate* publication in the United States." Who, however, is to determine what is the meaning of the word "immediate"—the time necessarily required being in some cases ten, or even twenty, times greater than in others? Who will then be interested in seeing that such provision of the law be carried into practical effect? No one whatsoever! Let this bill become a law, and it will soon be as entirely nullified as our revenue laws daily are in regard to the large editions of Tennyson, Thackeray, and other popular and recent British authors, with which our markets are being flooded. Let those who doubt this now ascertain for themselves how large is the proportion of Bibles, Prayer-books, Shakspeares, Miltons, and other standard works, purchased by our people of foreign manufacture. That done, let them inquire of publishers what has been the cost of the stereotype plates that have now been rendered wholly useless. Doing this, they will learn that it counts by hundreds of thousands of dollars; that the manufacture of standard books has been, or is being, wholly transferred to Europe; and, that little beyond the establishment of international copyright is required for accomplishing as regards the literature of the day what has already so well been done in regard to that of the past. How all this is to result in giving increased employment to paper-makers and printers the Reporter may now, if he can, explain.

IV. "International copyright laws," says the Reporter, "would contribute promptly and successfully to develop our own literature, and to make it national."

Little more than half a century since, our sensibilities were greatly excited by the inquiry, "Who reads an American book?" The present copyright law came into action July 8, 1870, and in the year ending on the first of the following December, there were deposited in the Congressional Library 2734 volumes. In that ending the 1st

do not seem to have one atom of feeling or of decency; they all rob English authors of their rights, and then they likewise rob each other; for in spite of the twaddle about American publishers not reprinting English books against each other, any one has only to look at the American *Publishers' Circular*, and he will see that almost all the publishers have their own edition of popular English authors' works. We know of no other name for the American system of publishing than that of robbery."—*Tinsley's Magazine,* Dec. 1871.

of the present month the deposits rose to 5640 volumes, in addition to several thousand articles other than books. Were the inquiry repeated now it might be very satisfactorily answered, the inquirer being then requested to remark, that the wonderful change thus exhibited had been brought about under a system that had been for forty years denounced, and very foolishly denounced, by American authors as unfavorable to their interests. How those interests have been advanced; what is now their condition; and what are the prospects of gentlemen among us who are capable of producing books worthy to be read; are so well exhibited in the following paragraph from the pen of one of the most vigorous opponents of the existing system—one of the most determined of all the advocates of increased grants of monopoly privileges—that it is here submitted for the reader's consideration, as follows :—

"'The Life of Jesus, The Christ, by Henry Ward Beecher,' is not a theme for discussion on this page of The Tribune, nor is it ours to pronounce on its intrinsic merits ; but, happening yesterday to meet one of the publishers, we asked him how many copies of Vol. I. (first issued four weeks ago) had been sold and delivered; when he, after carefully scrutinizing his ledger, replied, 15,491 copies. This, for a richly illustrated, beautifully printed, and consequently dear book, strikes us as a remarkable sale, and a refutation of the current remark that nothing is read nowadays but newspapers and other periodicals. In fact, there were never before so many books read as in this year 1871 ; never before was decided, eminent, literary ability so well recompensed as it now is. Empty, trashy stories and jingle that its fabricators mistake for poetry do not sell—why should they ?—and not one book in a hundred by an unknown writer pays the cost of its publication, because not one in a hundred is so good as the cheaper works by famous authors which abound ; but even new books sell largely in our day whenever they deserve it. Such is the moral we deduce from the rapid sale of Dr. Beecher's great work.''

At seven dollars per copy, the price of the completed work, this gives more than $108,000 for the sales of a single month. Copyright enduring for 28 years, it may fairly be now anticipated that the yield of this work to its author will far transcend anything of the kind that thus far has been known.

Of all living writers the one here referred to, and his friend and neighbor of the " Tribune,"* are probably the two who have received the largest compensation for literary labor, yet are both dissatisfied with the system under which a state of things so gratifying as is that above described has been brought about.

Seeking now to learn the cause of the remarkable change here exhibited, our authors may, with advantage to themselves, here read a passage from a speech delivered by Mr. Cobden at or near the time when they were so anxiously laboring to bring about among ourselves, by treaty, a state of things closely resembling that to which England stands now indebted for the facts that free libraries have proved failures,† and that sittings in free churches remain to so great an extent unoccupied, as follows :—

* See note to p. 6, ante.
† "The free libraries of Birmingham, England, it is stated, are not appreci-

"You cannot point to an instance in America, where the people are more educated than they are here, of total cessation from labor by a whole community or town, given over, as it were, to desolation. When I came through Manchester the other day, I found many of the most influential of the manufacturing capitalists talking very carefully upon a report which had reached them from a gentleman who was selected by the government to go out to America, to report upon the great exhibition in New York. That gentleman was one of the most eminent mechanicians and machine makers in Manchester, a man known in the scientific world, and appreciated by men of science, from the astronomer royal downwards. He has been over to America, to report upon the progress of manufactures and the state of the mechanical arts in the United States, and he has returned. No report from him to the government has yet been published. But it has oozed out in Manchester that he found in America a degree of intelligence amongst the manufacturing operatives, a state of things in the mechanical arts, which has convinced him that if we are to hold our own, if we are not to fall back in the rear of the race of nations, we must educate our people to put them upon a level with the more educated artisans of the United States We shall all have the opportunity of judging when that report is delivered; but sufficient has already oozed out to excite a great interest, and I might almost say some alarm."

Having studied this, let them next ask themselves what have been the causes of the vast change now in progress in the relative positions before the world, of the two countries. Doing this, must they not find themselves forced to the conclusion that they are found in common schools, cheap school-books, cheap newspapers, and cheap literature? Has not each and every one of these aided in making authors, and in creating a market for their products? Having thus laid the foundation of a great edifice, are we likely to stop in the erection of the walls? Having in so brief a period created a great market for literature, is it not certain that it must continue to grow with increased rapidity? Assuredly it is; yet is it that vast market which our authors desire to barter for one in which hundreds of eminent men and women even now submit to the degradation of receiving the public charity to the extent of fifty or a hundred pounds a year! The law, as we now have it, invites foreign authors to come and live among us, participating in all the advantages we can offer them. As now proposed, it is to be an offer to tax ourselves for the purpose of giving them a bounty upon staying at home and increasing their competition with the well-paid literary labor of this country. Let the change

ated by the inhabitants, as from a recent report it appears that only three per cent. of them borrow books. In the brass-founding occupation six thousand men and boys and two thousand women and girls are employed, and only two hundred and ninety-two members of this trade took out books. In the button trade not one of the six thousand hands borrows a single volume. In the building trade, out of many thousand workmen, only fifty-five are returned as book-borrowers, and out of eight thousand gun-makers only one hundred and ninety-one. Of one hundred and thirty letter-carriers twelve only are borrowers, and out of four hundred policemen only nine. There are five free libraries in Birmingham, and this backwardness on the part of the working people to avail themselves of the opportunities offered to improve their minds has excited surprise and disappointment. It is, however, argued that the working people of Birmingham, after a long day's labor, are completely tired out, and are more disposed to amusement, or even sleep, than education."

be made; let the domestic market be thrown freely open; and publishers will not be slow to find among the thousands of educated and but half-employed men of England, means for freeing themselves from an exclusive dependence upon native authors. That this is the view now taken of our future under the system now proposed, the writer knows to be that of at least one eminent publisher. Were Belgrave Square to make a treaty with Grub Street providing that each should have a plate at the tables of the other, the population of the latter would probably grow as rapidly as the dinners of the former would decline in quality, and it might be well for our authors to reflect if such might not be the result of the measures now proposed.

Their adoption has been urged on some of our legislators, on the ground that consistency demands it of them. Being in favor of protection elsewhere, they are told that it would be inconsistent to refuse it here. Replying to this, it might fairly be retorted that nearly all the supporters of international copyright are advocates of the monopoly system to which in Britain they have attached the words Free Trade; and that it is not consistent in them to advocate protection here. To do this would however be as unnecessary as it would be unphilosophical. Both are perfectly consistent. Protection to the farmer and the planter in their efforts to draw the artisan to their side, looks to carrying out the doctrine of decentralization by means of annihilation of the monopoly of manufacture established in Britain; and our present copyright system looks to the decentralization of literature by offering to all who shall come and live among us the same perfect protection here granted to native authors. What is called free trade looks to the maintenance of the foreign monopoly for supplying us with cloth and iron; international copyright in like manner looking to continued maintenance of the monopoly which Britain has so long enjoyed of furnishing us with books; both tending towards centralization.

The rapid advance here made in both literature and science is a result of the *perfect protection* afforded by decentralization. Every neighborhood collects taxes to be expended for purposes of education, and it is from among those who would not otherwise be educated, and who are thus *protected* in their efforts to obtain instruction, that we derive our most thoughtful and intelligent men, and many of our best writers. The advocates of free trade and international copyright are, to a great extent, disciples in that school in which it is taught that it is an unjust interference with the rights of property to compel the wealthy to contribute to the education of the poor. Common schools, and a belief in the duty of protection, travel always hand in hand together. Decentralization, by the production of local interests, *protects* the poor printer in his efforts to establish a country newspaper, thus affording to young writers of the neighborhood the means of coming before the world. Decentralization next raises money for the establishment of colleges in every part of the Union, thereby *protecting* the poor but ambitious student in his efforts to obtain higher instruction than can be afforded by the common school. Decentralization, by creating a large market for the productions of his pen, next *protects* him in the manufacture of school-books, all the cost of this being paid for out of the product of taxes whose justice is now denied by those who advocate the British policy.   Rising to the dignity of author of books for the perusal of already instructed men and women he finds himself *protected* by an absolute monopoly having for its object that of enabling him 'to provide satisfactorily for his wife, his children, and himself.   Of all our people, none enjoy such perfect protection as do those connected with literature; yet do many of these oppose protection to all others, while actively engaged in enlarging and extending the monopoly by means of which they themselves have so greatly profited.   Such being the facts, it will scarcely answer for them to charge inconsistency on others.

Grievous as are the complaints of British authors, so far are they from suffering real injury under the protection above described that it is to the development of mind resulting from wide-spread education, and from an abundance of cheap literature, they stand to-day indebted for the fact that thrice more is now paid by American publishers for advance sheets, than is paid by all the publishers of Europe for actual copyright on the foreign books there reproduced; and that men like Tyndall, Huxley, Darwin, Spencer, and others, find here a market for their products far more profitable than is that of the whole European continent under that monopoly system with which its communities now are cursed.

V. The Reporter congratulates his countrymen on the fact that foreign authors and domestic publishers, having now arrived at a proper understanding, are fully disposed to co-operate for securing to the former all the privileges hitherto limited to native writers. As well, however, might he congratulate Western farmers on the fact that railroad managers had arrived at perception of the idea that it had been the public, and not themselves, who had thus far profited by railroad competition; that sad experience had taught them "that hawks should not pluck out hawks' e'en;" and that, by combination among themselves they might be enabled greatly to increase the rates of freight and transportation, exempt from danger of future interference.   In both cases the object is one and the same, taxation of the great body of the people for the benefit of the few engaged in writing or publishing books, or in the work of transporting corn or cotton.   Transporters and publishers are alike middlemen, admirable servants but hard and oppressive masters when vested with power to dictate terms to those they had been used to serve.   To a great extent combination among the latter has already been effected, affording reason for believing that peace has been now so thoroughly established as to forbid continuance of that competition to which readers, poor as well as rich, have recently stood indebted for power to command the works of several popular writers at less than the monopoly prices that previously had been maintained.   How such peace has operated in the past, and must operate in the future, is shown by the fact, that of the work of a popular author, price one dollar, issued within the last year by a house that had had no disputes to settle, the number sold is stated to have been 100,000; the actual cost of production, freed from demands for advance sheets, not having exceeded 22 cents. But for "courtesy copyright" there would have been more than one edition; the price would have been 50 cents; and the sale would probably have been trebled. Establish international copyright and the price will be thrice greater, enabling authors and publishers to divide among themselves out of·an edition of 20,000 more than has been now obtained out of 100,000; the dear people who are, as we are now assured, by aid of extended monopoly privileges to be supplied so cheaply, finding themselves then compelled to forego the advantage, hitherto enjoyed, of early perusal of new publications; and compelled, as now in England, to wait for cheaper editions until the aristocracy of book consumers had ceased to purchase.

The day has been when books were published in many towns and cities of the Union from which the printing press has now wholly disappeared, except so far as needed for the daily or weekly journal. From year to year centralization has advanced until some dozen or more houses now command nearly the whole publication business of the Union, and with the results above described. For strengthening and perpetuating the monopoly already so far established, all that is now needed is that "courtesy" *custom* be now made *law;* thereby depriving, in all the future, the great cities now rising in the West from in any manner participating in the advantages that elsewhere had resulted from bringing the producer of ideas in printed form to the neighborhood of their consumers. How, when but a few years hence the people of the great Mississippi Valley shall number 40 or 50 millions, that West will rest content under a system that makes it wholly dependent on Atlantic cities for intellectual food, it is for time to determine. How far our farmers, artisans, miners, and working men of all descriptions, will continue to remain content under a system that has already so far increased the cost of many reprints as to render them almost entirely unattainable by any but the rich, the reader may now determine for himself. It may be that he will arrive at the same conclusion with the present writer, to wit, that in grasping at the shadow, our writers have placed themselves in serious danger of losing the substance.

That such will be the result is as certain as it is that men who find themselves involved in darkness become discontented and seek a return to light. The millions now occupying the great Valley of the West, and the almost hundreds of millions destined yet to occupy it, neither can nor ought to submit to a system that is to place in the hands of a few authors and publishers, foreign and domestic, an entire control over the supply of that mental food to which they have hitherto been so much accustomed, and without which they cannot fit themselves for worthily occupying that place in the sphere of creation for which they had from the first been meant.

VI. With very many of the purveyors of scientific and literary food their work is a labor of love prosecuted often at heavy cost of both time and money, the men therein engaged finding their sole reward in the belief that they are rendering service to their fellow men, and rejoicing always when they see their ideas transferred to other countries, or translated into other languages. To such men it is that the world stands indebted for works that deserve to live, facts and ideas that merit reproduction. With another large class, the desire for profit stands first as stimulus to exertion, and here may be placed by far the larger portion who give their powers to the preparation of amusement for their fellow men and women, and are now by them so very largely paid. A third and very considerable class is composed of those who may be regarded as mere sellers of phrases, ready to give their time and talents, such as these latter may prove to be, to any description of work that can be made to pay, their sole incentive to exertion being found in the money that thus is earned.

At no time in the history of the world have the labors of both of these latter classes been so well rewarded, if not even so greatly over-paid. At none has the "sacred thirst for gold" increased with such rapidity—the appetite growing with what it feeds on, and the thrice-over-paid novelist failing fully to enjoy the thousands and tens of thousands now paid for the product of a few months of labor, because deprived of power to collect other thousands which he claims to be his of right; forgetting always, that his labor has been little more than that of co-ordinating facts and ideas that had been supplied to him by men of whom very many had died of actual want while engaged in their collection.

At no time, on the other hand, have there been so many men able and willing to give themselves to the work of collecting and arranging materials that may so be used, asking for themselves little more than that they be not allowed to perish while seeking thus to improve the condition, mental and moral, of their fellow men. Of these, few trouble themselves in any manner in regard to measures such as are now proposed, all experience teaching them that already existing obstacles are more than sufficient to prevent any rapid transference from country to country of the facts, or the ideas, to whose ollection or development their time is given. To these, the most deserving of literary laborers, international copyright cannot prove other than an unmitigated evil. To the others, mere butterflies of literature, it must give a power for taxation growing almost geometrically as population increases arithmetically; and hence it is that we have such an unceasing clamor on the part of interested men engaged in misleading legislators into the adoption of measures that cannot fail to prove injurious, and in a high degree, to their constituents and themselves.

As matters now stand, and as it is proposed that they be made to stand, all the advantage is on the side of the butterflies; toil and suffering being nearly all that is left for the working bees. To the end that this may be changed what is needed is that direct payment be substituted for that which is indirect, governments uniting in appropriating annual sums of money to be distributed, under proper regulations, among authors whose books may happen to be reproduced abroad, in their own or in any other language. Let this be done, and writers like Maine and Freeman will then be enabled to participate in the rewards of literary labor, now so almost entirely engrossed by men like Reade, Trollope, Tennyson, and Bulwer. Let it be done, and we shall then see reproduced among ourselves the "Village Communities," of the one, and the "Norman Conquest," of the other; their authors, and others like them, gladly surrendering, when needed for securing republication, their claims to state assistance; and finding in the fame thus earned, and in the good thus done, satisfactory reward for their most useful efforts. Byron rejoiced when he first saw an American edition of his works "coming," as it seemed to him; "from posterity;" and such would be now the feeling of the great mass of those who seek to instruct, and not merely to amuse, the existing generation.

To this it will be objected, that governments have no right to interfere in such matters, this objection being most strongly urged by those who are now most clamorous for such interference as would give us a taxation amounting to millions annually, while depriving farmers, artisans, miners, and working-men generally, their wives and children, of their accustomed supply of literary food. By the plan proposed, we should be enabled to continue to enjoy our present freedom, while doing justice to all around, and at a cost of a single million. By the other, we should be placing ourselves in the position of slaves to tyrannical masters, while contributing at the cost of millions to the maintenance and extension of a system injurious to the most useful and deserving of literary and scientific men, and destructive of those who would, with most advantage to themselves and to the community, become consumers of their products.

The question above discussed, and now before the nation for decision, is second in importance to none other that could here be named. Being so, we need feel small surprise at the persistent efforts of interested parties, home and foreign, at mystifying legislators into a belief that that is true which daily experience shows us to be false; at the persistent avoidance of free discussion on the floor of Congress; or at the desire that has more than once been manifested for surprising the House into action at a time when it abounded in new members who had given to the subject little of that attention its great importance so much demands. So far, happily, the conspirators have failed, as they have so well deserved to do. That their future may be as the past has been, nothing is now needed but that our legislators make themselves acquainted with the real facts of the case. The more thoroughly they shall do so, the more fully must they become convinced that the course hitherto pursued has been in accordance with truth and justice; and, that by continuing onward in the same direction we shall be doing that which most will tend towards improvement in the condition of our fellow men, both abroad and at home.

PHILADELPHIA, Dec. 30, 1871.

POSTSCRIPT.

As this sheet is passing through the press, the New York Tribune comes to hand bringing with it valuable information in reference to the course of literary affairs abroad, as follows:—

"The first part of George Eliot's 'Middlemarch' comes out in pea-green paper covers, a small 12mo. of 212 pages, well printed, and sold at $1.25. Its publication in numbers (of which there will be eight) is an attempt on the part of Messrs. Blackwood to break up the tradition which ordains that an English novel shall appear in three volumes at the price of $7.50. * * * If cheapness is an element of success with the public, the present issue of 'Middlemarch' is made with slight regard to it. As there will be eight parts, we shall have paid $10 for it when all are out; and as the ordinary price of a novel is $7.50, which nobody does pay, I don't see how the public are to gain. * * * Messrs. Blackwood are probably right in calculating that the public will much more readily buy 'Middlemarch' in eight parts at $1.25 each than in three or four volumes at once for $10. But still, it is not a very great advance toward cheap literature. * * * As for 'Middlemarch,' I hear that George Eliot retains the copyright, and that instead of receiving a percentage from Messrs. Blackwood, she pays a percentage to them by way of commission, and keeps the rest for herself. This was Dickens's plan during the greater part of his career. George Eliot is said to have received on a former occasion the largest sum ever agreed in advance to be paid by a publisher for a novel. She was given $30,000 for 'Romola,' which came out in 'The Cornhill Magazine,' then and now owned by Messrs. Smith & Elder."

Of all living novelists the authoress of "Adam Bede" stands in the lead as regards both circulation and compensation, and to her, therefore, it is we should look for that softening of authors' hearts by means of which "the masses of the people" are, as we are now assured, to be enabled to obtain perusal of popular books at steadily declining prices. What, however, are the facts as here presented? Not content with the $7.50 by means of which Sir Walter Scott, writing for a people less than half as numerous, was enabled, after dealing liberally with his publishers, to build up Abbotsford, this lady prints her own book, raises the price to $10, and then pays her publisher a commission on its sale—a case of greed that, as it is believed, finds in literary history no single parallel. Let her have copyright here, and we shall then learn how it is that our "masses" are to be made to pay for the enlargement of literary *privileges* now so clamorously demanded. *Tens* of thousands, printed for the author, will then be imported to be retailed at $5, if not even more, by her own agents; whereas, unless prevented by aid of *courtesy* copyright, *hundreds* of thousands will here be printed and sold for a dollar, if not even less. The lesson in reference to monopoly and its extension that this lady has just now furnished, is one that our legislators may study with advantage, and we may hope that they will profit of it. Let them answer to themselves the question, "If all this be done in the green wood, what will it be in the dry?"— at that date when English and American readers shall have thrice increased in number.

The time has come when the system of mystification and deception as to the real end in view should be abandoned. Of those whose knowledge of the subject gives to their opinions any value whatsoever, there are not five per cent. who do not, in their heart of hearts, know and feel that the object sought to be attained is that of giving us here a state of things closely resembling the British one above exhibited.

A MEMOIR

OF

STEPHEN COLWELL:

READ BEFORE THE

AMERICAN PHILOSOPHICAL SOCIETY,

FRIDAY, NOVEMBER 17, 1871:

BY

HENRY C. CAREY.

———

PHILADELPHIA:
HENRY CAREY BAIRD,
INDUSTRIAL PUBLISHER,
406 Walnut Street.
1871.

MEMOIR.

A life protracted considerably beyond the allotted threescore years and ten has brought me, in the course of nature, to the position of survivor to a host of personal friends whose lives had made them worthy of the remembrance in which they yet are held by those who had known them best. Of one of the worthiest of those whom I have familiarly known, and for their words and their works have most esteemed, it is that, in accordance with the request with which the Society has honored me, I have prepared the brief memoir that will now be read. For its preparation and for the proper performance of duty to the departed, to his surviving friends, and to the public which has a property in his memory, I claim to have little qualification beyond that resulting from long and familiar personal acquaintance; from a fellowship in the public labors to which were devoted so many of his life's best years; and from an earnest desire to aid in perpetuating the recollection thereof in the minds of those in whose service such labors had been performed.

An ardent pursuit of the same general course of study, in a yet unsettled department of inquiry, tends necessarily to the development of difference in modes of thought, even where, as has been the case with

Mr. Colwell and myself, the end in issue is substantially the same. Between us, however, there has never been any essential difference, and while it has been among the highest gratifications of my life, it has not been least of the assurances that have sustained me in my own course of speciality of labor, that his views of social and economic theory have so nearly coincided with those which I had been led to form.

This general coincidence of doctrine is here offered as a reason for avoiding that indulgence in eulogy of his literary labors which so justly is their due. A still stronger reason for preferring to allow the simplest and plainest history of his works to indicate his worth, is found in that modesty which constituted so striking a feature in his character, respect for which forbids that I should here say of him anything that would have been unacceptable if said in his bodily presence. That I can entirely restrain within these limits the expression of my apprehension of his character, and of his life's work, I do not say; but that I feel the repressive influence of this regard correspondent with the habitual deference which has throughout many years of intercourse governed my demeanor towards him, is very certain. Further than this, however, it will be enough for praise if I can succeed in making this memoir an adequate report of his active and energetic life.

Having thus explained the feelings by which I have been influenced, I shall now proceed to give such facts as have been attainable in regard to his unwritten history, and such indices of the works he has left behind him, as seem to claim a prominent place, and can be made to fall within the compass of the brief time allowed me for their presentation.

STEPHEN COLWELL was born in Brooke County, West Virginia, on the 25th of March, 1800. He died in Philadelphia on the 15th of January, 1871, having nearly completed his 71st year. He received his classical education at Jefferson College, Canonsburg, Washington County, Pa., where he graduated in 1819. He studied law under the direction of Judge Halleck in Steubenville, Ohio; was admitted to the Bar in 1821; practised the profession seven years in St. Clairsville, Ohio; and in 1828 removed to Pittsburgh where he continued so to do until the year 1836.

Indicative of that ability and industry which marked his whole subsequent life, and now so well accounts for the mass and quality of his attainments, are the facts that he graduated at the early age of nineteen, and entered upon his profession at twenty-one.

The practice of the law, however, was not the sphere of mental activity for which by tastes and talents he had been best by nature fitted. The study of this science was, nevertheless, a happy preparation for the inquiries in whose pursuit he afterwards became so much engrossed. Its exacter method, doubtless, corrected the mental habitude and the narrowing influence which an ardent mind is apt to catch from an exclusive devotion to the study of any single branch of literature or science. His writings everywhere bear witness in logic and in diction to the corrective influence of his legal acquirements. Social Science is that department of knowledge which especially receives its verification and practical adjustment in jurisprudence and civil government applied—the philosophy of Law being the crown and summary of sociology in all its branches.

Further, Mr. Colwell gave for a layman an unusual amount of study to the department of religious literature, and here also we find the guiding influence of his sociologic as well as of his legal training. A devoted religionist from earliest youth to the close of life, he gave himself to an ardent study of doctrine and of duty, meanwhile laboring as zealously and almost as constantly as if he had filled the office, of pastor in the church, in the propagation of such opinions as demanded conformity of life from professors of religion. His publications bear witness of his faithfulness, as his life in its every relation illustrated the morality and the charity which his faith enjoined.

It is not for us to sit in judgment upon religious doctrines, whether to applaud or to condemn them. His well known zeal, and his abundant labors in piety and charity, are here adduced for the simple reason that the portraiture of the man would be incomplete and most unworthy of its subject without distinct recognition of a feature so predominant in his character.

Were I here to venture an opinion, fully warranted perhaps by the subject, I should be disposed to say that the study of the theologian must be greatly influenced for safer direction and better uses when held in logical harmony with, and restrained of its speculative tendencies by, those rules of thought which must govern men in the actual duties and relations of life. To my mind it is clearly obvious that the religious writings 'of Mr. Colwell exhibit a healthy tone and a useful drift reflected from his economic studies; and in these latter a faithfulness of service and a dedication of spirit and endeavor, which happily illustrate the moral responsibility resulting from the sentiments of the former. To this I may perhaps be allowed to add, that if each and every man occupying an influential position could be induced with equal fidelity and ability to " show his faith by his works," the prevailing indifference to the claims of Christianity would speedily give place to a widely different spirit induced by the attractiveness of its illustration. Here, however, I am engaged mainly with the prominent traits of Mr. Colwell's own character and the influences that formed his life and gave direction to it. His education and effective development were not found alone in the studies by which he was so largely and so usefully occupied. Whatever of principle and policy resulted from the application of the student was induced and enriched and energized in another and even more exact training school than any that the speculations of science can afford. In the thirty-sixth year of his age, fresh and full of all that reading and reflection could supply, he entered upon the conduct of business affairs in an occupation that as much as any other, and probably even more, brought into service and severely tested both economic facts and principles. He became a manufacturer of iron first at Weymouth, Atlantic County, New Jersey, and afterwards at Conshohocken, on the Schuylkill. Throughout a quarter of a century of vicissitudes, inflicted upon that department of manufacture more mischievously than upon almost any other by an inconstant and often unfriendly governmental policy, opportunity was presented, as the necessity was imposed, for studying the interests of productive industry in the light of such actual and greatly varied experiences as might instruct even the dullest, and could not fail to teach one already so well qualified for promptly understanding all that actually concerned that and every other branch of industrial production. Before entering upon the arduous and trying experiences of this pursuit he had visited Europe, and there had studied the art and management of its advanced and varied industries.

The settlement of the large estate of his father-in-law, the late Samuel Richards, and the administration of those of several other members of his family, required and received as much attention during many years as would have constituted the entire business of many men who would have thought themselves fully occupied. In addition to private affairs, so considerable and so exacting, he was constantly engaged as a leading and working member of various public associations; industrial, mercantile, benevolent, and educational. The cha-·

racter, the extent, and the variety of these engagements, to which he was invariably attentive and punctual, may be inferred from a simple enumeration by their titles, as follows: he was a working member of the American Iron and Steel Association, from its origin to the close of his life; an active member of the African Colonization Society for more than a score of years; several years engaged in the management of our House of Refuge; nearly twenty years a Director of the Camden and Atlantic Railroad, whose Board of Directors, in a feeling notice of his death, say that, " having been an active member of the Board from its organization, and. having contributed very largely of his means, time, and labor in the prosecution and completion of this work; in many dark periods of this enterprise we could always look to Mr. Colwell for his matured judgment and able counsel."

He was a Director in the Reading and in the Pennsylvania Central Railroads, and for years held the office and performed the duties of a Trustee of the University of Pennsylvania; as also a similar position in the Princeton Theological Seminary. Simultaneously therewith, he was one of the Trustees of the Presbyterian General Assembly, and member of the Board of Education of the Presbyterian Church. After.the close of the Rebellion he gave large pecuniary assistance, and his usual energy of service, to the Freedman's Aid Society, as during the Rebellion he had contributed with like liberality to the work of both the Sanitary and Christian Commissions. Of his services in these great patriotic charities a gentleman well acquainted with their history says: "At the breaking out of the Rebellion he felt deeply for the distress in the camps and on the battlefield, and it was at his suggestion that the first man who left his home to assist the helpless and the wounded, took his way to the seat of war. He also contributed freely to supply comforts to those in the hospitals. To one of the acting stewards he said, 'Let nothing be wanting, and, if the Government funds are insufficient, I will see that the bills are paid.'" The same witness of his active benevolence to the suffering soldiers, and of his personal demeanor in its administration, further says: "Those who accompanied him on his visits to the Army of the Potomac, can never forget the kindness and respect with which he treated the humblest individuals."

In the patriotic services and sacrifices to which the country called its best citizens in the hour of its utmost need, he was, in every form of duty, one of the earliest, most constant, persistent, and efficient of the men in private life who gave themselves unreservedly to the salvation of the Union. The Union League of this city, in words which well might serve as a condensed memoir of his life and character, bears this testimony to his agency in the great work of their association: "With an intelligent and thoughtful mind, fully convinced of the necessity and usefulness of such an organization, and a heart warmly alive to its encouraging influences, it was peculiarly fitting that at the first formal meeting which led to the establishment of the Union League Mr. Colwell should be called upon, as he was, to preside. His name thus heads the list of signers of the constitution of the League; and he grew with its growth, ever in the forefront of whatever movement was planned for giving aid and comfort and support to his country and its government throughout the course of its struggle for existence, in resisting, by force of arms, a causeless and wicked armed Rebellion." Of his personal character and demeanor, they say: "We desire to bear testimony to those virtues which manifested themselves in all his intercourse with us; to the singleness and unselfishness of his purpose; to his courteousness and urbanity in our varied relations; to his firmness, cautiousness, and wisdom in the deliberations of our councils; to his patience, unwearying industry, and cheerful devotion of time, abilities, and means in aid of the cause so dear to all our hearts; to his constant, unwavering joy, and faith, and trust in the overruling providence of the God of our fathers amid the darkest hours of the country's peril, as well as in times of success and victory."

Such engagements as these, and numerous others kindred in their character and calling for similar labors, filled the middle and later periods of his life with occupation: his associates, and all with whom business intercourse and public enterprises connected him, testifying to the prompt, energetic, patient, and worthy performance of every duty thus assumed or imposed. Nearly half a century employed in public and private affairs making large demands for labor and care, and involving great responsibility, gave him that sound practical. experience which well and effectively woven into the studies of his life made him what he eminently became, a clear, safe, and thoroughly instructed economist. Concurrently with this practical training he was, in the best sense and fullest meaning of the word, a student. As early as his business life began, if not even earlier, he commenced the collection of a library of social science, political economy, finance, pauperism, organized charities, productive industries, and associate and cognate departments of science, now the largest and best to be found in the country. This grand collection has not been catalogued, or even classified, but it considerably exceeds five thousand volumes, and is estimated for the purpose of insurance at a value of twenty thousand dollars. To this library and to the books, pamphlets, periodical and newspaper articles of his own production, he devoted all his leisure. In several lists of cited authorities appended to his own publications and criticisms upon them, he furnishes evidence that he was, in the language of one of his familiar acquaintances, "one of the greediest of readers."

To the commonly accepted authorities on Political Economy, Finance, and Policy of Public Affairs, he, however, gave no more than that amount of faith and acceptance which they should command from a mind well stored with the facts and philosophy of their subjects. To a friend who expressed surprise at his vast collection of books and pamphlets on the single subject of Money, he replied, when asked if he had perused them all, "enough to know that there is really little or nothing in them of any value."

His library, besides its completeness in standard works, derives a special value from its collection of over twenty-five hundred pamphlets on topics usually embraced in what is called Political Economy; each separately bound and capable of classified arrangement. He regarded, and justly too, such smaller treatises as especially valuable for containing the best thoughts of the writers in the most condensed form, and likely thus to secure not only the greatest number but the most attentive of readers. For the most part he put his own publications on social and economic subjects into this unpretending form.

His judgment was too clear and too well poised to suffer the imposture of pretentious authorship. Knowing that book-makers are not always thinkers he gave his regards to those writers only who had something of their own to say, or knew how to give effective array to the valuable words of others. It would have been an excellent service to students, now abandoned to their own unformed judgment in the selection of works in this department, and thus condemned to promiscuous reading, if Mr. Colwell had in some effective way employed his eminent discernment in giving us an *index expurgatorius* of the books and treatises upon economic subjects which crowd our libraries, thus driving a stake through the worthless and the false among them, numerous as these latter are. In his Essay Preliminary to List's Political Economy, he has, indeed, shown his eminent capacity for estimating aright the economic authorities at their true value, confining himself, however, almost entirely to an analysis and commendation of those works which are worthy of reliance. It was more consonant with his taste and tendencies to select the good, than to annoy himself with the study and exposure of that which was calculated to be injurious. Often have I wondered at the patience, even more than at the diligence, great as it was, with which he conscientiously surrendered so large a portion of his months and his years to library labors. His toil, however, was made available for excellent uses, and the fruits of his literary industry exhibit themselves not only in the number but also in the value of his publications. Of that value but little can be traced to the thousands of volumes which had passed through his hands. Indeed, it is curiously significant that the best read man in economic literature stands now before us so little indebted to the books of his predecessors for the most valuable portions of his own productions. Never writing without having something worthy to be read, all that he did write was, as largely as can be affirmed of any other prolific author, in matter and manner his own. There was in him, however, nothing of arrogance, nothing of the scorner. In the whole course of his literary pursuits may be discovered a constant effort to promote and propagate important scientific truths bearing upon social welfare, under cover of such books as seemed to him to deserve extensive circulation. To the translation, annotation, and effective distribution of these he freely and devotedly gave his time, his labor, and his means. Among the leading instances of this kind, is the translation, by Mr. Matile, of List's National System of Political Economy, with his own invaluable Preliminary Essay, above referred to, and with copious marginal notes upon the text, from his own pen. In like manner he procured the translation (again by Mr. Matile) and the publication, for liberal distribution, of Chastel's "Charity of the Primitive Churches;" and also the republication of "The Race for Riches," by William Arnot, of Glasgow, with a corroborative preface and notes, by himself supplied.

This would be the place for giving special attention to that long and varied catalogue of his own contributions to the literature of political economy, finance, charity, and Christian ethics, in the form of pamphlets and essays, and other articles in the reviews, periodicals, and leading newspapers. With that detail, however, I will not here task myself nor use the passing hour of your time, preferring to append hereto a list of his works as full and complete as I have been able to make it. Mr. Colwell, as his family inform me, neither collected nor registered these productions, as a consequence of which my summary of them by their titles is necessarily incomplete, although not otherwise incorrect.

His labors of mind and pen, his endeavors, services, and subsidies in aid of the establishment and extension of collegiate education; his personal pressure upon all who were in the way of forwarding the great enterprise; his donations and legacies, all had this one grand leading aim—the propagation of sound doctrine in social duty, and its enforcement in the education not only of our scholars, but also of the reading people of our great community. To that object he dedicated his library in giving it to the University of Pennsylvania. Anxious to make the gift more effective, he coupled the grant, in his deed of trust, with a condition that required the endowment of a chair of social science; but his family, knowing his intention that the donation should in no event prove a failure, has waived the present performance of the condition, in the well warranted expectation that in good time it will be carried out.

With the like intent he labored long for the establishment of a professorship in the Theological Seminary of Princeton, an idea that, with the assistance of others in great measure brought to contribute by his own perseverance and his liberal advances, has now been carried into full effect. "His works do follow him"—the inauguration, on the 27th of September last, of a professorship of "Christian Ethics and Apologetics," in its promise fulfilling one of the dearest wishes of his heart.

What Mr. Colwell intended by the establishment of a chair of Christian Ethics, in Princeton, and what he regarded as the chief object of a chair of Social Science in the University of Pennsylvania, can scarcely be misunderstood if his own writings be studied for their ruling sentiment and leading purpose. Cultivating political economy as a theory of beneficence, he wrote his most elaborate and voluminous work upon the credit system, embracing therein all the agencies and instruments employed in foreign trade and domestic commerce, and gave a vast amount of time and thought to the literature of these several subjects in all their branches; but through all and over all the crowning aim and purpose of his endeavors stands out conspicuously, crystallized as it is in a definition of political economy in which, after reviewing the entire range of conflicting explications, he says: "When we meet a definition running thus—the science of *human welfare*, in its relations with the production and distribution of wealth, we shall begin to hope the doctrine of social, or political, or national economy, is beginning to assume its proper proportions." The sentiment of that definition directed all his studies, all his writings, and, as a passion, governed all his life. In religion, the faith that *works* by love; in economic theory, the best interests of humanity; in morals, the justice, mercy, and charity which practically exemplify the brotherhood of men; were the governing impulses of all the works of both his head and his hands.

In his "New Themes for the Protestant Clergy" we find such sentiments as these: "Creeds, but not without charity; Theology, but not without humanity; Protestantism, but not without Christianity." Again: "It is not enough for the Christian to be concerned only for the interests of men in the world to come, but for their best interests in this world." With some severity of rebuke, but far more earnestness of affection, he says: "We maintain that Christ himself should have the chief voice in defining Christianity, and that this has been denied him in most, if not all, the compends and summaries of Christian doctrine which are the bond of Protestant churches;" following this up by urging the fact that "the world now believes that the religion announced by the Author and Finisher of our faith embraces humanity as well as divinity in its range."

This remonstrance, and its implied censure, will be understood when we perceive that he went further, far further, in his apprehension of true Christian charity, than almsgiving extended to pressing cases of distress. The modern usage of devolving the relief of the poor upon the poorhouse system established by the civil law, he calls "the stigma of Protestantism;" and he demands from the professors of Christianity an earnest endeavor to give the poor *permanent* emancipation from the evils which they endure. He presses the charge against the Established Church of England, that it holds resources donated to its Catholic predecessors for relief of the poor, which now yield £50,000,000 per annum, while throwing the support of the suffering upon the charity of the State; at the same time quietly sustaining that system of industrial and commercial policy which takes from the labor of the realm two hundred and fifty millions of dollars for the use of the government, and five times more for the profit of capital. Nay further this gentlest of gentlemen, this most orthodox of churchmen, this most devout of worshippers, in the conviction that the failure of Christians to exemplify Christianity in their dealings with the world is the grand cause of the aversion and rejection it encounters, is led therein to find some justification for the socialism and the insurrectionary demonstrations now so rapidly and threateningly spreading throughout Europe and America, and exhibiting such a spirit of revolt among the masses of Christendom as is nowhere found in the pagan world.

In the battle-cry of the reformers now advancing upon the conservatism of our civilization, he hears the proclamation of "the fatherhood of God and the brotherhood of man"—a protest against "that notion of individual liberty which leaves every man to care for himself, and ruin to seize the hindmost."

To the almost universally prevalent doctrines of political economy he traces the apathy, indifference, and even hostility of the fortunate classes to the duties enjoined in the second table of the law, as it is summarized by the Great Teacher. Singling out the most distinguished and most popular of now existing disciples and advocates of the *laissez-faire* school of economists, he thus exhibits Herbert Spencer's "Social Statics": "The man of power and the man without; the man of wealth and the pauper, should each have the largest and most perfect liberty consistent with their not touching each other. * * * It forbids the thought of charity, or brotherhood, or sacrifice; it consecrates selfishness and individualism as the prime feature of society. * * * Its principle is the least possible restriction, the fewest possible enactments; the weak must be left to their weakness, the strong must be trusted with their strength, the unprotected man must not look for favor, and government must resolve itself into the lowest possible agent of non-intervention."

Than the view thus presented of the now-so-much lauded Spencerian social philosophy nothing could be more thoroughly accurate. The whole tendency of that modern economical school, to whose teachings our departed friend was so much opposed, has been, and is, in the direction of giving increased power to the rich and strong, while throwing responsibility on the shoulders of the poor and weak. "If the latter *will* marry, and *will* have children, why," say they, "should they not be allowed to pay the penalty of their crime, as so many millions of starving Irish have already done?" "Why," though in somewhat different words, now asks Mr. Spencer, "Why should not the poor remain in ignorance if unable to provide for educating their children and themselves?" "Why should the millionaire be required to aid in maintaining hospitals in which damage to poor laborers' limbs may promptly and properly be repaired?" "Is it not for every man to do as he will with that which is his own?" The new philosophy having answered this latter question in the affirmative, need we be surprised that the miserable selfishness thus given to the world as science should have excited the indignation of one who knew, and felt, that it must

be a mere pretence of science that could sanction
any course of conduct so wholly inconsistent with
the divine command, "that we do to others as,"
under similar circumstances, "we would that they
should do to ourselves?"   Assuredly not!

It would be difficult for me fully and completely
to express the strength of the humanitarian sym-
pathies exhibited in Mr. Colwell's plea for justice
to the victims of our reckless competition and our
voracity in the pursuit of material wealth.   To
prevent misconstruction of his severe animadver-
sions upon the existing agency of church and state
in the prevailing disorders of society, and to show
the bearing of his complaint I cite another passage from the " New Themes," as follows: "The
doctrine that property, real and personal, must
under all circumstances remain inviolate, always
under the ever-watchful vigilance of the law, and
its invaders subject to the severest penalties of dun-
geon and damages, may be very essential to the
maintenance of our present social system, but it
totally disregards the consideration that Labor, the
poor man's capital, his only property, should, as his
only means of securing a comfortable subsistence,
be also under the special care and safeguard of the
law.   The doctrine that trade should be entirely
free—that is, that merchants should be perfectly at
liberty, throughout the world, to manage their
business in that way which best promotes *their* interests—may suit very well for merchants, making
them masters of the industry of the world; but it
will be giving a small body of men a power over

the bones and sinews of their fellow men, which it would be contrary to all our knowledge of human nature if they do not fatally abuse, because they are interested to reduce the avails of labor to the lowest attainable point, as the best means of enlarging their business and increasing their gains. That philosophy," he continues, "which teaches that men should always be left to the care of themselves—that labor is a merely marketable commodity which should be left, like others, to find its own market value without reference to the welfare of the man, may appear plausible to those who forget the fatherhood of God and the brotherhood of men, but is utterly at variance with the precepts of Him who taught that those who stood idle in the market-place because no man had hired them, and were sent to work at the eleventh hour, should receive the same as those who had borne the burden and heat of the day."

It is not my business here and now either to commend or to impeach, but simply to state the attitude assumed by Mr. Colwell in reference to questions so much exposed to debate as these, and by him so sharply and earnestly treated. The great sensation produced in our religious world by their publication has given way to much more moderate feelings, and evidently enough to a better appreciation of their spirit and design. One of the representative papers of the church of which he was a life-long member, thus speaks of the controversy which his publications had aroused ten years since: "In one or two of his own books on this engrossing and all-important theme [Christian charity], he used language in regard to the apathy and criminality of modern professors of faith in Christ and his salvation, which was so severe as to arouse bitter hostility to his faithful and well-meant efforts. Would that now, when the mutual wounds have ceased to smart, in the case of most of those engaged in them, alas! by a departure from all the conflicts of the church militant, earnest men could be roused to examine their lessons and suggestions, forgetful of the occasional sharpness of the form in which they were conveyed." The most aggrieved having thus now come to acknowledge that "faithful are the wounds of a friend," they may also recollect that only once, and that in a strikingly pertinent instance, the founder of their faith is reported to have given way to indignation against a piety that subordinated humanity to theology. " When the rulers of the synagogue watched him whether he would heal the withered hand, in their church, on their Sabbath-day, he looked round about on them with *anger*, being *grieved* for the hardness, or, as the margin has it, the blindness, of their hearts." (Mark iii. 2–5.) That it was this sort of indignation, mixed with the same kind of grief, which induced the severity of remonstrance complained of at the time, is manifest in the whole tone, and yet more so in the special drift of his objurgations. The true construction of his aim, indeed, is found in his protest against the ruling doctrines of political and social economy which the churches, in common with the community, accept. A single sentence well represents him on this subject, as follows: "The social, political, and commercial institutions of the present day, founded upon, and sustained by, a selfishness heretofore unequalled, are the great barriers to the progress of Christianity." And again: "Political economy, strictly so called, is as much opposed to the spirit of Christianity as it is antagonistic to socialism; or, in other words, there is far more in common between socialism and Christianity than there is between the latter and political economy." The system of economic theory by himself adopted, is of course not the one intended here, but is that one which, referring to the North British Review, is thus described: "Followed out to the utmost, the spirit of political economy leads to the fatal conclusion—that the conduct of the social life should be left entirely to the spontaneous operation of laws which have their seat of action in the minds of individuals, without any attempt on the part of society, as such, to exert a controlling influence; in other words, without allowing the State or institutions for general government any higher function than that of protecting *individual* freedom."

It is, therefore, the *laissez-faire* theory of political economy which thus is charged with hostility at once to Christianity and humanity. The buy-cheap-and-sell-dear system elsewhere described by him as a policy " in trade and in society, which makes it not only the interest, but the natural course of every one to prey upon his fellow men to the full extent of his power and cunning, and is well fitted to carry selfishness to its highest limits, and to extinguish every spark of mutual kindness." His political economy was a system of philosophic benevolence, a doctrine of justice, mercy, and truth, with a resulting economic policy of protection to productive industry, leading to the highest human welfare. In the appendix and notes to his second edition of the " New Themes," he has given us a whole library of the literature of Charity.   In the hundreds of treatises there cited and briefly epitomized, he exhibits a breadth of survey and depth of inquiry that one would think must exhaust the subject.   It was the result of many years of labor, directed by a zeal that nothing could inspire and sustain but a heartfelt devotion to the work of social duty and remedial beneficence.   May I not here add, as a reflection that concerns the students of social science, that the system of economic doctrines which secured the assent of a mind so fully informed, so eminently endowed, and so long and zealously devoted to a search after truth, is entitled to all the confidence that authority can give, and justly claims most studious attention.

Having rendered his best personal services to the subject which he had so much at heart, he further evidenced his earnestness and solicitude for its still more formal and more adequate treatment by offering a prize of $500 for a treatise upon the law or doctrine of Christian charity, accompanying the offer with a general outline directory of the plan of the required work, indicating its essential points; among which are to be noted the organization of labor; international trade in its effects upon the rewards of domestic labor; the subject of public education; the law of charity as applying to the poor, the suffering, the imprisoned, the vicious, the insane, the intemperate, the dangerous, &c. &c.

I am not aware that any work of real merit was secured by the liberal reward offered. No such book having been published, it is presumable that no response was made.

There remains yet to be considered, in such manner as my limits allow, another and a highly important division of the service rendered to the public by Mr. Colwell, in an official position to which his high reputation called him in the 65th year of his age. In June, 1865, he was appointed upon the Commission, authorized by Act of Congress, "to inquire and report upon the subject of raising by taxation such revenue as may be necessary in order to supply the wants of the government, having regard to, and including the sources from which such revenue should be drawn, and the best and most efficient mode of raising the same." In the service imposed by this appointment he continued till the midsummer of 1866, when the work assigned was finished and fully reported. The labor thus undertaken and performed interrupted and even ended the active literary pursuits and practical work of his life. His family, whose tenderly affectionate watchfulness makes them the best and most competent witnesses, attribute to his exacting and exhausting toil in the duties of this position that failure of his health which soon afterwards obliged him to reliuquish, in great measure, his life-long pursuits both as student and as writer.

In the Report of the Revenue Commission, communicated to Congress in January, 1866, and published in a large octavo volume by authority of the House of Representatives, may be found the special reports of Mr. Colwell on " The Influence of Duplication of Taxes upon American Industry — upon the Relations of Foreign Trade to Domestic Industry and Internal Revenue — upon Iron and Steel—and on Wool and Woollens." Two other reports of his, one upon High Prices and their Relations with Currency and Taxation, and another, upon Over-importation and Relief, are not included in this volume. How he executed the work which fell to his share of the duties of the Commission, it is enough to say that *he* did it to assure us of finding therein' the fullest discussion of those vastly comprehensive subjects, based upon the most ample store of statistical facts, and arrayed with that force which the soundest theoretical principles, and the largest practical acquaintance with the details which enter into the several subjects of inquiry, alone could give.

The work done by him, outside of that which his own pen has reported, was of itself, and independently, worthy of permanent record. The Secretary of the Wool Manufacturers' Association, Mr. J. L. Hayes, an eminently capable witness, thus speaks of his agency and influence in harmonizing the conflicting interests of the agriculturists and manufacturers of this staple industry of the nation: "The conferences between the two committees (representing the respective parties) commenced in January, 1865, and were continued without much pause for six months. At the outset the two committees were widely apart in their views, and the traditional jealousies became at once apparent. Here the weight of character, disinterestedness, and moral power of Mr. Colwell came into play. He was personally present at many of these conferences, and I am convinced that the harmonious arrangement finally made was mainly due to his influence. This influence was perfectly unobtrusive, but both parties had absolute reliance upon Mr. Colwell's integrity and wisdom, and a mere hint from him was sufficient to give a right direction to our councils. Some of the suggestions which he made were of great practical value." Of one of these this gentleman says: " It has been in operation five years, and it is a constant surprise to manufacturers and growers that so brief an act, affecting so many really distinct branches of industry, should cover so much and operate so wisely." Again he says: " The bill, of which the chief features are due to Mr. Colwell's suggestions, is wonderfully sustained; its practical working is really remarkable for its success, * * * but the influence upon our own industry is by no means the chief object. The wool tariff is the key to the protective position in this country. It secures the agricultural interest and the West."

His treatment of this subject, and the reports upon trade, production, prices, and national finance, place him, in my judgment, highest among the authorities in our history in whatever combines knowledge of facts and soundness of economic principles. Quite sure am I that there is not so much of practical value and guiding principle to be learned even in that great storehouse of economic literature which he has given to the University. The earnest and intelligent student of the industrial and commercial policy of our country who may give to these reports the attention that is their due, will find himself prepared for a safe, clear, and satisfactory judgment upon all of the many questions therein embraced.

Incidentally, but necessarily, intermixed with the history and statistics of our national industries, an unusually effective examination of the theories of free trade and protection finds a deservedly prominent place in these reports; and the predominant claims of labor upon the care of government and the regard of the community is the pervading spirit and ruling impulse of all that he here has written. His heart was in this matter, and his philosophy most happily corroborated his philanthropy. The key to all his economic doctrines is in such simple self-proving propositions as these: "The highest condition of national welfare depends upon the highest condition of the masses of the people in point of morals, religion, intelligence, social ease, and comfort." "The industry of a nation is an interest so vital as to be equalled only by its internal liberties and its independence of foreign control. As the tendency of full employment is to exclude crime, the benefits of that high integrity which is the best cement of society, may be expected to reward a nation in which occupation is the most varied and labor best remunerated."

Last to be noticed, although not latest in its presentation to the world, is Mr. Colwell's highly valuable work on money and its substitutes, credit and its institutions, entitled, *"Ways and Means of Payment: a full analysis of the credit system, with its various modes of adjustment."* Its essential object is that of laying the axe to the root of that pestilent heresy which teaches that prices are wholly dependent on the supply of money; and that, to use the words of Hume, the only effect of an increase in the abundance of the precious metals is that of "obliging every one to pay a greater number of those little white or yellow pieces than they had been accustomed to do." The whole question of prices is here discussed with a care characteristic of its author; and his readers, however they may chance to differ from him in regard to details, can scarcely fail to agree with him in the belief he has here expressed, that "among the innumerable influences which go to determine the general range of prices, the quantity of money or currency is found to be one of the least effective." Truth, however, as is well known, travels but very slowly through the world, centuries having elapsed since demonstration of the fact that the earth revolved around the sun, and four-fifths of the human race yet remaining convinced that the sun it is that moves, and not the earth. So has it been, and so is it like to be, in the present case, the most eminent European economists still continuing to teach precisely what had been taught by Hume, and statesmen abroad and at home still constructing banking and currency laws under the belief that in the "quantity of money or currency" had been found one of the *most* effective causes of changes of price. Mr. Colwell's work was published in 1859, since which date so much light has been thrown on the subject as to make it serious cause for regret that his other engagements, and his failing health, should have prevented a re-examination of the case by aid of recent facts, all of which have tended to prove conclusively the accuracy of the views presented in the very instructive volume to which reference has now been made.

A word more and I shall have done. Of all the men with whom I have at any time been associated there has been none in whom the high-minded gentleman, the enlightened economist, the active and earnest friend to those who stood in need of friendship, and the sincere Christian, have been more happily blended than in the one whose loss we all so much regret, and of whose life and works I here have made so brief, and, as I fear, so inadequate a presentation.

APPENDIX.

LIST OF THE PUBLISHED WRITINGS OF STEPHEN COLWELL.

1. Letter to the Pennsylvania Legislature on the removal of the Deposits from the United States Bank. 8vo. pp. 45. 1834.
2. The Poor and Poor Laws of Great Britain. Princeton Review, January, 1841.
3. Review of McCulloch's British Empire. Princeton Review, January, 1841.
4. The Smithsonian Bequest. Princeton Review, 1842.
5. Sweden, its Poor Laws and their bearing on Society. Princeton Review, 1843.
6. In and Out of the County Prison. No date.
7. The Relative Position in our Industry of Foreign Commerce, Domestic Production, and Internal Trade. 8vo. pp. 50. 1850.
8. Memorial to Congress in relation to Tariff on Iron. 8vo. pp. 16. 1850.
9. New Themes for the Protestant Clergy, with Notes on the Literature of Charity. 12mo. pp. 384. 1851.
10. New Themes for the Protestant Clergy, with Notes on the Literature of Charity. Second Edition. 12mo. pp. 384. 1852.
11. Politics for American Christians. 8vo. 1852.
12. Money of Account. Merchants' Magazine. pp. 25. April, 1852.

13. Hints to a Layman. 12mo. 1853.
14. Position of Christianity in the United States, in its relations with Our Political System, and Religious Instruction in Public Schools. 8vo. pp. 175. No date.
15. Preface and Notes to The Race for Riches. 12mo. pp. 54. 1853.
16. The South: Effects of Disunion on Slavery. 8vo. pp. 46. 1856.
17. Preliminary Essay and Notes to The National Political Economy of Frederick List. 8vo. pp. 67. 1856.
18. Money of Account. Bankers' Magazine. pp. 25. July and August, 1857.
19. The Ways and Means of Payment. 8vo. pp. 644. 1859.
20. Money, the Credit System, and Payments. Merchants' Magazine. 1860.
21. The Five Cotton States and New York. 8vo. pp. 64. 1861.
22. Southern Wealth and Northern Profits. 8vo. pp. 31. 1861.
23. The Claims of Labor, and their precedence to the Claims of Free Trade. 8vo. pp. 52. 1861.
24. Gold, Banks, and Taxation. 8vo. pp. 68. 1864.
25. State and National System of Banks, the Expansion of the Currency, the Advance of Gold, and the Defects of the Internal Revenue Bill of June, 1864. 8vo. pp. —. 1864.

Reports made from the Revenue Commission:—Those marked with an asterisk published in the Reports of the Committee.

26. Upon High Prices and their relations with Currency and Taxation. 1866.
27* Influence of the duplication of Taxes on American Industry. 1866.

of Foreign Trade to Domestic Industry
ternal Revenue.   1866.
ortation and Relief.   1866.
Steel.   1866.
  Manufactures of Wool.   1866.
  Suggestions and Remarks.   8vo. pp. 19.

CPSIA information can be obtained
at www.ICGtesting.com
Printed in the USA
BVHW04*1211210918
528171BV00010B/209/P

9 780484 584241